The World Legal Review

Volume 5

Fostering Development through Opportunity, Inclusion, and Equity

The World Bank Legal Review
Volume 5
Fostering Development through Opportunity, Inclusion, and Equity

The World Bank Legal Review is a publication for policy makers and their advisers, judges, attorneys, and other professionals engaged in the field of international development with a particular focus on law, justice, and development. It offers a combination of legal scholarship, lessons from experience, legal developments, and recent research on the many ways in which the application of the law and the improvement of justice systems promote poverty reduction, economic development, and the rule of law.

The World Bank Legal Review is part of the World Bank Law, Justice and Development Series managed by the Research and Editorial Board of the Bank's Legal Vice Presidency. Publication of *The World Bank Legal Review, Volume 5* was made possible with support from the OPEC Fund for International Development.

The World Bank Legal Review

Volume 5

Fostering Development through Opportunity, Inclusion, and Equity

Hassane Cissé

N. R. Madhava Menon

Marie-Claire Cordonier Segger

Vincent O. Nmehielle

Editors

THE WORLD BANK
Washington, D.C.

The World Bank Legal Review

Volume 5

Fostering Development through Opportunity, Inclusion, and Equity

EDITORS

Hassane Cissé
Deputy General Counsel, Knowledge and Research, World Bank

N. R. Madhava Menon
*Hon. Professor & IBA Chair in Continuing Legal
Education, National Law School of India, Bangalore*

Marie-Claire Cordonier Segger
*DPhil (Oxon), MEM (Yale), BCL & LLB (McGill)
Senior Legal Expert, Sustainable Development,
International Development Law Organization (IDLO)*

Vincent O. Nmehielle
*Professor of Law and Head of the Wits Programme on
Law, Justice and Development in Africa School of Law,
University of the Witwatersrand, Johannesburg, South Africa*

PRODUCTION EDITOR

Elizabeth Hassan
Associate Counsel, World Bank

Contents

Foreword

JAN ELIASSON
DEPUTY SECRETARY-GENERAL OF THE UNITED NATIONS

We are at a crucial moment for shaping the world we want. The Report of the High-Level Panel of Eminent Persons on the Post-2015 Development Agenda sets out an ambitious yet practical vision for tackling poverty and sustainable development. It reflects a growing realization that the rule of law is fundamental for responsive institutions and is a driving force for development.

This understanding was confirmed when the United Nations General Assembly held its first High-level Meeting on the rule of law in September 2012. The resulting Declaration recognizes that rule of law and development are strongly interrelated and mutually reinforcing and should be reflected in the post-2015 international development agenda. The Declaration also reaffirmed that the rule of law is indispensable for upholding peace and security, as well as respect for human rights.

The World Bank Legal Review highlights the breadth of reach of the rule of law and, most critically, its centrality to development. The theme, *Fostering Development through Opportunity, Inclusion, and Equity*, speaks to the holistic nature of development and its relationship to the rule of law.

Reflecting the World Bank's work to mainstream law and justice into the development process, the authors explore innovative ways in which the rule of law can be used to help achieve opportunity, inclusion, and equity. The United Nations Secretary-General has also made it a priority to mainstream the rule of law across the work of the United Nations system.

The rule of law is a concept at the very heart of development and people's daily life across the world. It is the land deed in the hands of the farmer, the entrepreneur's legitimate contract, the badge of a trusted police officer, and the birth certificate that lets a child be counted.

But the rule of law also ranges well beyond these particular matters. The World Bank rightfully applies a justice lens to the protection of the environment, anticorruption, the economy, and the empowerment of marginalized groups and communities.

This edition of *The World Bank Legal Review* is a significant contribution to scholarship on the rule of law and comes at a critical time. Our shared challenge—and obligation—is to build a future guided by the rule of law as a vehicle for people's security, rights, and economic well-being.

Preface

ANNE-MARIE LEROY
SENIOR VICE PRESIDENT AND GROUP GENERAL COUNSEL
THE WORLD BANK

The world is confronted by a wide array of complex challenges that demand attention. They range from fragile and conflict situations to the alarming progression of climate change, from the worrisome state of food security to the persistent inequities and societal imbalances that limit people's access to and enjoyment of public goods. In some countries, political instability is threatening the sustainability of development outcomes that have taken years of painstaking effort to achieve. Addressing these challenges is a top priority for development institutions today.

The World Bank is striving to meet the increasing needs of its member countries not only through its lending instruments but also by providing technical assistance, knowledge sharing, and advisory services. Institutionally, the change process is strategically designed to reposition the Bank to carry out its mandate more efficiently while evolving with the times. The twin goals of eradicating extreme poverty and boosting shared prosperity have also set the Bank on a path to not only secure positive outcomes in its operations, but also ensure that such outcomes translate to better lives for all, especially the poor.

The Legal Vice Presidency is actively supporting the Bank as it works to meet its obligations. With the help and expertise of its team of lawyers, legal analysts, and global partners, the Legal Vice Presidency is devising creative, viable, and sustainable legal solutions that will help transform development aspirations into reality. *The World Bank Legal Review* is one such effort. This year's volume, subtitled *Fostering Development through Opportunity, Inclusion, and Equity*, explores critical issues affecting development, emphasizing that we stand a better chance of achieving more meaningful impact when development processes are inclusive and equitable, and provide adequate opportunities for all.

Now is a time not only for action but also for reflection, as the international community strives to set the post-2015 development agenda. The peoples of the world are clamoring for a louder voice and greater participation in the process of reform at the national, regional, and international levels; and recent actions by the international community indicate a willingness to engage more actively in that process. At the same time, lessons learned over the years equip us with the tools we need to create more targeted, proactive, and, consequently, successful engagement. To realize our ambitions, law and justice must play an enhanced and overarching role, as demonstrated by the chapters in this volume.

This, the fifth volume of *The World Bank Legal Review,* has greatly benefited from the input of seasoned development experts under the guidance of our distinguished editors: Deputy General Counsel for Knowledge and Research, Hassane Cissé; Professor N. R. Madhava Menon of the National Law School of India University (NLSIU); Dr. Marie-Claire Cordonier Segger of the International Development Law Organization (IDLO), Rome; and Professor Vincent O. Nmehielle of the University of Witwatersrand, South Africa.

I sincerely thank Jan Eliasson, the Deputy Secretary-General of the United Nations, and Irene Khan, the Director-General of IDLO, who graciously wrote this volume's foreword and afterword, respectively. Now more than ever, overcoming global challenges requires enhanced commitment and multi-stakeholder partnerships among development institutions. Jan Eliasson's and Irene Khan's valuable insights have greatly enriched this volume. I also thank all the contributors for their impressive and well-researched contributions. Their thoughts, perspectives, and recommendations are as important as they are timely. My sincere appreciation also goes to Dr. Nigel Quinney for his stellar and invaluable editorial assistance.

This volume's chapters have been organized under five main headings: law and the economy, justice and rule of law reform, environmental and natural resources law, governance and anticorruption, and empowerment and equity for diverse communities. Each of these five parts contains interesting and insightful discussions on the role of law and justice in development, offering innovative and dynamic recommendations on how a synergy among law, justice, and development can inspire and facilitate more viable and sustainable solutions to development challenges.

Contributors

Hdeel Abdelhady is Founder and Principal of MassPoint Legal and Strategy Advisory PLLC, a boutique law and strategy firm in Washington, D.C., representing banks, companies, and organizations in market entry, finance and corporate transactions, investment disputes, and regulatory compliance. Ms. Abdelhady has practiced law in Washington and in Dubai with international law firms and as in-house (secondment) counsel to financial institutions. Her legal experience spans industries, cultures, and legal environments; she has worked on matters involving the United States, Africa, Asia, Europe, Latin America, and the Middle East. Before law school, Ms. Abdelhady worked with an award-winning Washington political media strategy firm, where she was responsible for research and analysis of congressional, gubernatorial, and mayoral campaigns and elections; ballot referenda; and corporate issues media. Ms. Abdelhady holds a J.D. from The George Washington University Law School, where she is a Professorial Lecturer in law, and a B.A. (political science and history) from the University of Pittsburgh.

Rachelle Alterman is the Founding President (2006–2010) of the International Academic Association on Planning, Law and Property Rights. Holding degrees in planning and in law from Canadian and Israeli universities, Professor Alterman specializes in cross-national comparative analysis of planning laws, land use regulations, and property rights. Her most recent book is *Takings International: A Comparative Perspective on Land Use Regulations and Compensation Rights* (American Bar Association Press, 2010). Professor Alterman is based at the Technion–Israel Institute of Technology, where she holds the Azrieli Chair in Town Planning. She serves on the editorial boards of leading academic journals. As visiting professor, she has taught at major American and Dutch universities. The Association of European Schools of Planning named her Honorary Member (the fifth person so honored). Professor Alterman has also served as a consultant for the United Nations, the Organisation for Economic Co-operation and Development, the World Bank, and a variety of other public bodies. See http://alterman.technio.ac.il.

Fabiano de Andrade Correa is a Brazilian lawyer and holds a Ph.D. in international law from the European University Institute in Florence, Italy. Currently, he serves as Legal Specialist at the International Development Law Organization (IDLO), in Rome, providing expertise for program development and implementation on issues related to trade and sustainable economic development. Mr. de Andrade Correa is a qualified lawyer with the Brazilian Bar Association, and before joining IDLO he practiced law with a leading Brazilian law firm and clerked with the Court of Justice of the state of Rio Grande do Sul, in Porto Alegre, Brazil. He is also a member of the Brazilian Branch of the International Law Association, serving as alternate representative to the Committee on International Law and Sustainable Natural Resources Management, and an Associate Fellow with the Centre for International Sustainable Development Law (CISDL). He holds a law degree (LL.B., UFRGS, Brazil) and a master's degree in international relations (Escuela Diplomatica/Universidad Complutense de Madrid, Spain).

Pulapre Balakrishnan is Professor of Economics at the Centre for Development Studies, Thiruvananthapuram, of which he is currently the director. He has written in the professional journals and is the author of the books *Pricing and Inflation in India* (Oxford University Press, 1991) and *Economic Growth in India: History and Prospect* (Oxford University Press, 2010). Mr. Balakrishnan has held appointments at the University of Oxford, the Indian Statistical Institute at Delhi, and the Indian Institute of Management at Kozhikode and has served as Country Economist for Ukraine at the World Bank. See http:// pulaprebalakrishnan.in.

Giovanni Bo is an Associate Counsel with the Operations Policy Practice Group of the World Bank's Legal Vice Presidency. He joined the Bank's Legal Department in 2010 and worked, as an advisory lawyer, in the Environmental and International Law Practice Group and, as an operational lawyer, in the Latin America and the Caribbean Practice Group. Prior to joining the Bank, he was legal researcher at Human Rights Watch and worked for the European Commission, in Brussels. He has also practiced European Union law in the Brussels office of Pavia & Ansaldo. A foreign-trained attorney admitted to practice law in the state of New York, he holds an LL.M. in international and comparative law from The George Washington University Law School (2009), an advanced degree in European Union law from the University of Bologna (2007), a Certificate in legal studies from University College London (2004), and an LL.B. from the University of Genoa (2004). His recent publications include "The US Challenge to the Inclusion of Aviation Activities within the EU Emissions Trading Scheme: A US-EU Dispute with Global Repercussions" (World Bank, 2011) and "Activities in the Seabed and Ocean Floor beyond the Limits of National Jurisdiction: The Responsibilities and Obligations of States and International Organizations" (World Bank, 2011).

André Boraine is the Dean of the Faculty of Law at the University of Pretoria. Over the years he has taught a variety of law subjects at both undergraduate and postgraduate levels, and he supervises doctoral students on a continuous basis. He is on the roll of practicing attorneys and is involved in practical legal training programs of candidate attorneys as well as insolvency practitioners. He was the INSOL Scholar for 2008 and has been recognized as an exceptional achiever at the University of Pretoria. He is also a National Research Federation–rated researcher. His current research interests include insolvency law, the law of civil procedure, and aspects of property law and consumer protection. He has published widely and regularly presents papers at local and international conferences. During 2011, he served as a consultant to the World Bank in relation to an ROSC analysis of the South African insolvency law system. Mr. Boraine is a coauthor of a leading book on insolvency in South Africa: *Meskin: Insolvency Law* (LexisNexis).

Charles Boudry served as an Associate Counsel in the Environmental and International Law Unit in the Legal Vice Presidency of the World Bank. Before joining the Bank, Mr. Boudry worked for the Swiss law firm of Bär & Karrer in the litigation and international arbitration practice group. He holds an LL.M. from Duke Law School (Duke-Geneva Scholar, 2011) and a master's in economic law from the University of Geneva.

Naomi Burke-Shyne is an Australian lawyer with 10 years' experience in law and human rights. She joined the International Development Law Organization's HIV and Health Law Initiative in 2009. Under this program, Ms. Burke-Shyne worked extensively across Asia and the Pacific, managing technical assistance initiatives in Bangladesh, India, Indonesia, Nepal, Pakistan, Papua New Guinea, the Philippines, Sri Lanka, and Timor-Leste. She has a strong background in the rights of marginalized populations and has worked closely with people living with HIV, men who have sex with men, transgender people, and sex workers on discrimination and the right to health. Ms. Burke-Shyne practiced as a lawyer in Australia prior to joining IDLO and holds a master's degree in international and community development from Deakin University, Australia, and an LL.B. from the University of Queensland.

Cyril Chern, the Secretary of the Dispute Board Federation (DBF), Geneva, is also a Barrister at Crown Office Chambers, London, and a Chartered Architect, Chartered Arbitrator, Accredited Mediator, and Adjudicator and holds the degrees of B.Arch. in architecture and engineering and J.D. He is a Fellow of both the Chartered Institute of Arbitrators and the Dispute Board Federation and is on both the FIDIC President's List of Adjudicators and its Assessment Panel and is a dispute board trainer for FIDIC, the DBF, and the International Chamber of Commerce. Dr. Chern is the author of *Chern on Dispute Boards* (1st and 2nd editions, Wiley-Blackwell), *International Commercial Mediation* (Informa), and *The Law of Construction Disputes* (Informa). He is also the coauthor of *Emden's Construction Law* and its "ADR and Dispute Boards" section (LexisNexis). His newest books, *The Commercial Mediator's Handbook* and *Construction Delay and Damage,* will be published in early 2014.

Hassane Cissé joined the World Bank in 1997 after serving for seven years as Counsel at the International Monetary Fund. He has been Deputy General Counsel, Knowledge and Research, of the Bank since 2009. In this capacity, he provides intellectual leadership on strategic legal issues facing the Bank, oversees advisory services on law and justice reforms, and leads the Bank's knowledge agenda on law, justice, and development. He is the editor-in-chief of the World Bank's Law, Justice and Development Series; has authored several papers on international economic law and law, justice, and development; and coedited the 2012 and 2013 volumes of *The World Bank Legal Review.* Prior to his current position, Mr. Cissé served for several years as Chief Counsel for Operations Policy of the World Bank. In this capacity, he contributed to the modernization and simplification of the Bank's legal and policy framework, and as legal adviser on governance and anticorruption, he led the exercise that resulted in the adoption by the Bank in 2006 of an expanded policy framework for sanctions. He was appointed in 2007 to serve as a member of the World Bank's newly established Sanctions Board. Mr. Cissé obtained his LL.B. from Dakar University in Senegal, where he graduated at the top of his class; he also holds an LL.M. degree from Harvard Law School as well as graduate law degrees from the Universities of Paris I Panthéon-Sorbonne and Paris II Panthéon-Assas and a graduate degree in history from Paris I University. Mr. Cissé is a member of the World Economic Forum Global Agenda Council on the Rule of Law.

Marie-Claire Cordonier Segger, D.Phil. (Oxon), M.E.M. (Yale), B.C.L. and LL.B. (McGill), is Senior Legal Expert, Sustainable Development, for the International Development Law Organization. She has 20 years of global treaty negotiations and programming experience that spans 79 countries of the Americas, Africa, and Asia Pacific, and she has published over 80 papers and 18 books in five languages, including *Sustainable Development Law* (Oxford University Press), *Sustainable Justice* (Martinus Nijhoff), and *Legal Aspects of Implementing the Cartagena Protocol on Biosafety* (Cambridge University Press). She coleads the World Bank Global Forum on Law, Justice and Development Thematic Working Group on Environment and Natural Resources Law and serves on the Editorial Board of *The World Bank Legal Review*. In an academic capacity, Dr. Cordonier Segger also coedits the Cambridge University Press series Implementing Treaties on Sustainable Development and serves as Senior Director for the Centre for International Sustainable Development Law (CISDL). She is an Affiliated Fellow of the Cambridge University Lauter-pacht Centre for International Law (LCIL); Visiting Professor of the University of Chile Faculty of Law; Rapporteur of the International Law Association (ILA) Experts Committee on International Law and Sustainable Development of Natural Resources; and Councilor of the World Future Council. Dr. Cordonier Segger also is on the boards of ILA Canada, Nigeria's *Journal of Sustainable Development Law and Policy*, and the *Cambridge Journal of International and Comparative Law*. Previously, Dr. Cordonier Segger has served as Senior Director of Research for Sustainable Prosperity, A/Director of International Affairs for Canada's Ministry of Natural Resources, Americas Portfolio Director for the International Institute for Sustainable Development and UN Environment Programme, and Associate Fellow of the Royal Institute for International Affairs.

Robert Delonis is a Senior Litigation Specialist in the World Bank Group Integrity Vice Presidency (INT). He advises INT investigators regarding their inquiries into allegations of fraud, corruption, collusion, and coercion affecting World Bank–supported activities; argues resulting sanctions cases in the World Bank Group's administrative sanctions system; and leads the negotiation of settlements in cases for which an amicable resolution is pursued. Prior to the formation of INT's Special Litigation Unit, he was a core team member on INT's Detailed Implementation Review of the India Health Sector and a team member (and, briefly, acting head) of INT's Voluntary Disclosure Program. Before joining INT in 2006, he practiced law in the Washington, D.C., office of a multinational law firm, focusing on civil litigation. He is a graduate of Georgetown University and New York University School of Law.

Anupama Dokeniya is a Governance Specialist in the Governance and Public Sector Group at the World Bank. She works on the implementation and monitoring of the Bank's Governance and Anticorruption Strategy; leads analytical work on transparency, accountability, and open governance issues; and advises country teams in these areas. She has developed and delivered several learning programs on governance and transparency issues in developing countries, consulted on the use of information and communication technology for development, and worked as a journalist. She holds a Ph.D. in communications and international development from Cornell University.

Frank Fariello is a Lead Counsel with the Operations Policy Practice Group of the World Bank's Legal Vice Presidency. He is the Bank's primary legal focal point for its Governance and Anticorruption Strategy and sanctions system. Since joining the Bank in 2005, he has also worked on a range of other legal policy issues, including the Legal Harmonization Initiative, Bank engagement in the criminal justice sector, and the legal aspects of the Bank's Middle-Income Countries strategy. He is Vice Chair of the American Bar Association's International Anticorruption Committee. His recent publications include "Coordinating the Fight against Fraud and Corruption" and "Transforming through Transparency: Opening Up the World Bank's Sanctions System" (*The World Bank Legal Review*, volumes 3 and 4, respectively). He has lectured at the Joint Vienna Institute, George Mason University, and the New York University School of Law. Prior to joining the Bank, he was Special Adviser to the Vice President of the International Fund for Agricultural Development (IFAD) and Senior Counsel in IFAD's Office of the General Counsel. Prior to IFAD, he practiced corporate law in a number of New York–based law firms, including Skadden, Arps, Slate, Meagher & Flom. He holds a B.A. in history (magna cum laude) from Brown University (1980) and a J.D. from New York University Law School (1983). He is admitted to practice law in the state of New York.

Edesio Fernandes (LL.M., Ph.D.) is a Brazilian legal scholar based in the United Kingdom, specializing in the legal dimensions of land, urban, housing, and environmental processes and public policies. He is a member of DPU Associates and of the teaching faculty of the Lincoln Institute of Land Policy (LILP). He has worked as both a lecturer and a consultant in several countries and has published widely in English, Portuguese, and Spanish. He is the author, among other publications, of the Policy Focus Report on land regularization programs in Latin America (LILP, 2011). In 2003, he was Director of Land Affairs at Brazil's Ministry of Cities, and in that capacity he coordinated the formulation of the National Program to Support the Sustainable Regularization of Consolidated Informal Settlements in Urban Areas.

Sean Fraser is an associate with the Canadian law firm Blake, Cassels & Graydon, working in the Litigation and International Dispute Resolution practice groups. He also serves as an Associate Research Fellow with the Human Rights and Poverty Eradication Division of the Centre for International

Sustainable Development Law. Mr. Fraser previously spent time working for the South African History Archives' Freedom of Information Programme in Johannesburg, South Africa, where he was involved with various public education and advocacy campaigns that focused on improving the content and implementation of access to information laws in that country. He holds an LL.M. in public international law from Leiden University's Advanced Studies program, where he specialized in peace, justice, and development, as well as a J.D. with a specialization in business law from Dalhousie University, and a B.Sc. (with distinction) from St. Francis Xavier University.

Kalidou Gadio, a Mauritanian national, is the General Counsel of the African Development Bank. Prior to this position, he served within the Bank as Country Director for North Africa Region I and as the Manager of the Operations Affairs Division in the Legal Department. Before joining the Bank, Mr. Gadio worked with Coudert Brothers in New York as an Associate Attorney and with Jeantet et Associés, an international law firm in Paris. He holds an LL.M. from Harvard Law School (1987), an advanced degree in international law from the Sorbonne, University of Paris II, and a *license en droit* from the University of Mohamed V in Morocco. Mr. Gadio is a member of the New York and Connecticut Bars and a former member of the Paris Bar.

José M. Garrido is Senior Counsel at the Legal Vice Presidency of the World Bank in the Finance, Private Sector Development and Infrastructure Unit, specializing in the areas of insolvency and creditor/debtor regimes. A prominent international lawyer and academic in Spain, he has held the chair in commercial and corporate law at the University of Castilla–La Mancha since 2001. Professor Garrido was also the General Counsel of the Spanish Securities Commission and was appointed a High Level Company Law Expert for the European Commission. He coordinated the work of the World Bank Insolvency Task Force on the treatment of personal insolvency and has published extensively on matters of access to credit, particularly in the area of secured transactions. Professor Garrido holds a Ph.D. in insolvency law (University of Bologna), an LL.M. in corporate and commercial law (University of London), and a J.D. (University of Alcala).

Markus W. Gehring, LL.M. (Yale University), J.D. (University of Hamburg), M.A. (University of Cambridge), is Deputy Director of the Centre for European Legal Studies (CELS) and University Lecturer at the Faculty of Law, University of Cambridge. He is Director of Studies in Law and a Fellow at Hughes Hall and serves as Lead Counsel for Trade, Investment and Finance Law with the Centre of International Sustainable Development Law (CISDL). Dr. Gehring has been a Visiting Professor at several universities around the world and is *ad personam* Jean Monnet Chair in Sustainable Development Law in the Faculty of Law, Civil Law Section, at the University of Ottawa. He is a member of the Frankfurt Bar. Selected publications include *Sustainable Development in World Trade Law* (Kluwer Law International, 2005) and *Sustainable Development in World Investment Law* (Kluwer Law International, 2010). Dr. Gehring also coedits the Cambridge University Press series Implementing Treaties on Sustainable Development.

Matthew Glasser recently joined the World Bank's Legal Vice Presidency. His legal career began in 1977 as a Municipal Bond Counsel and then a City Attorney in Colorado, and he has also worked as a registered professional lobbyist in Washington, D.C., for Colorado cities. Just before joining the Bank's urban sector team in 2003, Mr. Glasser worked as an adviser in the South African National Treasury, where he helped develop regulatory frameworks for municipal borrowing and financial emergencies. For more than 20 years he has worked with national and local governments in Africa, Asia, and Europe on policy and legislation regarding urban issues. Mr. Glasser is currently working on a book exploring the legal, regulatory, and institutional framework within which the world's cities operate. He obtained his J.D. from Cornell University Law School, Ithaca, and B.A. (cum laude) and MBA from the University of Colorado.

Beth Anne Hoffman is currently an Operations Analyst in the Environmental and International Law Unit in the Legal Vice Presidency of the World Bank. Over her 18 years in the World Bank, Ms. Hoffman has held positions in the Judicial Reform Unit of the Legal Vice Presidency and as a Public Sector Specialist in the Poverty Reduction and Economic Management Unit in the Latin America and the Caribbean Region. She has worked on projects related to privatization and decentralization in Argentina, Brazil, and Chile as well as justice reform initiatives in all of the Bank's five regions. She contributed to the justice, governance, and land law sections of "Beating the Odds: Sustaining Inclusion in a Growing Economy—A Mozambique Poverty, Gender and Social Assessment," which won the Africa Region's 2009 Chief Economist's Best Practice Award for Economic and Sector Work. Ms. Hoffman holds a master's degree from Georgetown University's School of Foreign Service and a dual bachelor's degree in politics and Spanish from Lake Forest College.

John-Mark Iyi, LL.B. (Honors), B.L., LL.M., was the 2010 Webber Wentzel Scholar in the School of Law, University of the Witwatersrand, Johannesburg, South Africa, where he is completing a Ph.D. He is also currently a Programme Associate at the Wits Programme on Law, Justice and Development in Africa. Mr. Iyi has also served as a Research/Teaching Associate in the school. His research focuses on public international law and international peace and security from an African perspective. Mr. Iyi's most recent publications include "The Duty of an Intervention Force to Protect Civilians: A Critical Analysis of NATO's Intervention in Libya" (*Conflict Trends*, 2012); "The Legal Framework for Sub-regional Humanitarian Intervention in Africa: A Comparative Analysis of ECOWAS and SADC Regimes" (*SADC Law Journal*, 2012); "Democracy and the Development Crisis in Sub-Saharan Africa: Revisiting Some Preconditions for a Developmental State Alternative," in *International Economic Law: Voices of Africa* (Siber Ink, 2012); "The AU/ECOWAS Unilateral Humanitarian Intervention Legal Regimes and the UN Charter" (*African Journal of International & Comparative Law*, forthcoming); and "The Role of the African Union

Continental Early Warning System in Preventing Mass Atrocities," in *Africa and the Responsibility to Protect: Article 4(h) of the African Union Constitutive Act* (Routledge, 2013).

Nicholas Joseph is Somalia Project Officer at the International Development Law Organization (IDLO), where he undertakes a range of programming, research, and legal advisory tasks relating to constitution building and justice reform in support of national partners in Somalia. He coauthored a report on the implementation of the judiciary chapter of the Provisional Constitution of Somalia and supported national efforts in planning for the development of the justice sector in Somalia. Prior to his appointment as project officer, Mr. Joseph was Legal Associate at IDLO, where he authored briefings for national partners in South Sudan on the design of the constitutional process and the appropriate design of governance mechanisms within the constitutional commission and wrote a report outlining the options and ramifications for extending the constitution-building process beyond the constitutionally mandated timelines. He received his law degree from the University of Sheffield.

Robert Kibugi is a Lecturer in law at the University of Nairobi's Centre for Advanced Studies in Environmental Law (CASELAP) and School of Law. He previously taught at the Faculty of Law, University of Ottawa, in Canada. His legal and policy research agenda focuses on, among other subjects, public participation in natural resource governance; land use law for sustainable development; climate change, including the role of law and policy in the adaptation and mitigation of climate change; energy law; water resources management and rights; and water and sanitation. He holds an LL.B. and an LL.M. from the School of Law, University of Nairobi, and an LL.D. from the Faculty of Law, University of Ottawa. He is an advocate of the High Court of Kenya. Mr. Kibugi has published various chapters and articles in peer-reviewed books and journals.

Jeni Klugman is the Director of Gender and Development at the World Bank Group, where she serves as lead spokesperson on gender equality issues and is responsible for developing strategic directions to support the institution's gender and development priorities. She also serves on several advisory boards, including the World Economic Forum's Advisory Board on Sustainability and Competitiveness and those related to the work of the Council on Foreign Relations. Prior to taking up her position at the Bank in August 2011, Ms. Klugman was the director and lead author of three global Human Development Reports published by the United Nations Development Programme: *Overcoming Barriers: Human Mobility and Development* (2009), *The Real Wealth of Nations: Pathways to Human Development* (2010), and *Sustainability and Equity: A Better Future for All* (2011). From 1992 to 2008 she held various positions at the Bank, focusing on poverty, inequality, and human development in low-income countries in Africa, Asia, and Europe. Ms. Klugman has published widely on topics ranging from poverty-reduction strategies and labor markets to conflict, health reform, education, and decentralization. She holds a Ph.D. in economics from the Australian National University, as well as postgraduate degrees in law and development economics from Oxford University, where she was a Rhodes Scholar.

William T. Loris is Senior Lecturer and Director of the Loyola University Chicago LL.M. Program on Rule of Law for Development. His degrees include a J.D. from the University of Santa Clara and a master's in international and comparative law from the Vrije Universiteit Brussel. After 10 years of service as a Legal Adviser to USAID in West and Central Africa and in Egypt, he co-founded the International Development Law Organization (IDLO). Mr. Loris served IDLO as General Counsel and as Director of Programs. He was appointed as IDLO Director General for two terms, during which he became known as a leading advocate for the rule of law throughout developing countries and countries in economic transition. He has served on the World Economic Forum's Global Agenda Council on Corruption and has been recognized by Santa Clara University for his service to his profession and to humanity and by Lithuania for his assistance during its transition.

Siobhán McInerney-Lankford is Senior Counsel at the World Bank Legal Vice Presidency (Africa Practice Group) and former Senior Policy Officer, Institutions, Law and Partnerships for Human Rights, Nordic Trust Fund, Operations Policy and Country Services Vice Presidency. She is an expert in international human rights law, advising the World Bank in this area since 2002 and regularly representing the World Bank in international human rights fora, including the United Nations, European Union, and Organisation for Economic Co-operation and Development (OECD). From 2006 to 2008, she served as chair of the OECD's Development Assistance Committee Human Rights Task Team, and she was the World Bank representative to the UN High-Level Task Force on the Right to Development from 2007 to 2009 and at the UN OHCHR Vienna+20 meeting in 2013. Before joining the World Bank, she worked in private practice in Washington, D.C. She has published widely on human rights law and teaches occasionally. Dr. McInerney-Lankford holds an LL.B. from Trinity College, Dublin, an LL.M. from Harvard Law School, and a B.C.L. and D.Phil. in EU human rights law from the Law Faculty at Oxford University.

N. R. Madhava Menon holds degrees from Kerala University (B.Sc. and B.L.), Aligarh Muslim University (LL.M. and Ph.D.), and Punjab University (M.A.). He was enrolled as an Advocate in the Kerala High Court in 1956 at the early age of 20. Dr. Menon left active legal practice and in 1960 joined the faculty of Aligarh Muslim University, where he continued his teaching and research until 1965, when he joined Delhi University and rose to become Professor and Head of the Campus Law Centre. During this period, he was deputed to serve as Principal of Government Law College, Pondicherry, and Secretary of the Bar Council of India Trust. In 1986, at the invitation of the Bar Council of India, Dr. Menon moved to Bangalore to set up the National Law School of India University (NLSIU) and to initiate a new model of legal education, the five-year integrated LL.B. program. He served NLSIU as its Founding Vice Chancellor for 12 years. The success of the Bangalore model led to the establishment of 15 similar law schools elsewhere in India. From 1998 to

2003, he served as the Founding Vice Chancellor of the National University of Juridical Sciences, from where the Supreme Court sought his services to set up the National Judicial Academy (NJA) at Bhopal. Dr. Menon was the Founding Director of NJA until 2006, when he retired from active employment. On his retirement, the government of India appointed him as a member of the Commission on Centre-State Relations (2006–2010) and decorated him with several awards, among other honors. Dr. Menon now holds the International Bar Association Chair on Continuing Legal Education at the National Law School, Bangalore. He also is the Chairman of the Menon Institute of Legal Advocacy Training, an educational charity based in Trivandrum, where he lives. Dr. Menon is the author of more than a dozen books on legal education, the legal profession, judicial training, and the administration of justice.

Mihaylo Milovanovitch is Senior Policy and Systems Development Specialist at the European Training Foundation (ETF) of the European Union, and an Edmond J. Safra Network Fellow at Harvard University. Prior to joining the ETF, he was responsible for peer reviews and thematic analyses of education policies in Central Asia, Eastern Europe, Latin America, and the Middle East–North Africa region for the Organisation for Economic Co-operation and Development (OECD). A major area of his work is the governance and integrity of education systems, and the development of sector-specific approaches to corruption prevention, such as the OECD integrity of education systems methodology for assessing education sector integrity. Past responsibilities of Mr. Milovanovitch have included the planning and coordination of educational cooperation with East Europe for the federal government of Austria and the education and youth agenda of the Stability Pact for Southeast Europe. He holds a master's degree in advanced international studies from the Vienna Diplomatic Academy and a master's degree from the Munich School of Philosophy.

Matthew Morton is a Young Professional in the World Bank's Gender and Development team, where he works on gender-based violence and women's economic opportunities. Before joining the Bank, Mr. Morton served as Special Adviser to the Commissioner of the U.S. Administration on Children, Youth, and Families. There he led efforts to integrate evidence-based policy making with a focus on child trauma and youth homelessness. As a researcher, Mr. Morton served as a lecturer and investigator at the University of Oxford's Centre for Evidence-Based Intervention, consulted for the European Commission on impact evaluation, and conducted research on youth empowerment programming. He received a B.A. in political science at Stetson University and an M.Sc. and D.Phil. in evidence-based social intervention at the University of Oxford.

Moses Mulumba currently heads the Center for Health, Human Rights and Development. He has previously worked in the areas of disability law and policy, environmental law and policy, and the development dimensions of intellectual property law. Mr. Mulumba's current areas of interest include health law and policy, international human rights law, health regulation, development dimensions of intellectual property rights, access to medicines, and maternal health rights. He has been an African Adviser to the HIV and the Law Commission and coordinates the health equity work within EQUI-NET in 16 East and South African Countries. His current projects include developing a model for community participation in health systems, formulating goals for global health and for governance for global health post-2015, developing a model law on regulatory aspects of satellite-enhanced telemedicine and eHealth for Sub-Saharan Africa (eHSA), and litigating the right to health in Uganda. He has an LL.B., a postgraduate Bar Course Diploma, an M.Phil., and an LL.M.

Vincent O. Nmehielle, a Barrister and Solicitor of the Supreme Court of Nigeria, has over 22 years of professional and academic experience. He is currently a Professor of Law and Head of the Wits Programme on Law, Justice and Development in Africa at the University of the Witwatersrand (Wits) School of Law in Johannesburg, South Africa, where he has taught since February 2002 and where he held the Bram Fischer Chair in Human Rights Law from 2002 to 2004. He was a Professorial Lecturer in law at the Oxford University and George Washington University Human Rights Program in 2003 and 2004. From 2005 to 2008, Professor Nmehielle served as the Principal Defender of the UN-backed Special Court for Sierra Leone in Freetown, Sierra Leone. He holds an LL.B. from the Rivers State University of Science and Technology, Port Harcourt, Nigeria; an LL.M. in international law from the University of Notre Dame; and an SJ.D. in international and comparative law from The George Washington University, Washington, D.C. Professor Nmehielle specializes in international and comparative law, and his professional, academic, and research interests lie within the areas of law, governance, justice, and development in Africa. He has written and consulted on constitutional issues, human rights, international justice, and governance in Africa. His recent works include *Africa and the Future of International Criminal Justice* (Eleven International, 2012).

Sriram Panchu is a Senior Advocate in India. In 1985, he founded a citizens' group, Citizen, Consumer and Civic Action Group, which has become involved in a number of public causes. He has appeared in a wide range of public interest cases, often relating to corruption and good governance, environmental protection, and consumer rights. His articles on these issues have been published in leading journals and newspapers. Mr. Panchu serves on the boards of several charitable and public institutions. He is also a mediator and has worked to make the mediation process a part of India's legal system. He was appointed the first Honorary Organizing Secretary of the Madras High Court Mediation and Conciliation Centre, the first such center in India. Mr. Panchu has published two books on mediation.

David Patterson is head of social development programs at the International Development Law Organization (IDLO), based in Rome, Italy. He was a founding member of the Canadian HIV/AIDS Legal Network in 1993, and from 1994 to 2008, he worked with the UN system (UNAIDS and UNDP) and national and international NGOs on law, HIV, health, and development. Since

2009, Mr. Patterson has managed IDLO's health law program, which has supported initiatives on HIV-related law and policy in 23 countries. In 2011, he addressed the UN General Assembly on IDLO's support for legal services for people living with HIV and key affected populations. Recent work explores legal frameworks for responding to noncommunicable diseases, intellectual property law, access to medicines, and litigation as a tool to advance the right to food. Mr. Patterson holds master's degrees in law (McGill), and science (SOAS, London), and postgraduate qualifications in community health (Montreal) and development program evaluation (Carleton, World Bank).

Annette Pearson is a lawyer who has conducted postgraduate studies in criminology. She is an international consultant in the fields of criminal justice, alternative legal services, access to justice, sociolegal research, victimology, and victims' assistance and restorative justice. Recently, she has focused on access to justice projects aimed at decentralizing, integrating, and diversifying justice services, as well as projects involving alternative conflict resolution mechanisms for marginal communities in large cities and populations in small war-stricken towns. She has been resident in Colombia since 1975, and since 1994 she has worked closely with the Colombian Justice House Program as designer and promoter, first national coordinator, staff trainer, and an evaluator and coordinator of the U.S. Agency for International Development Agency's project on international cooperation for community justice houses. She is a vice president of the World Society of Victimology.

Paul Prettitore is a Senior Public Sector Specialist in the Public Sector Reform Unit of the Middle East and North Africa Region. He holds a J.D. from the Catholic University of America and is a member of the District of Columbia Bar Association. His work within the World Bank focuses on the justice sector and poverty, as well as on broader issues of public sector reform, accountability, and governance. During his Bank career, he has worked on programs in Djibouti, Egypt, Iraq, Lebanon, Mongolia, Morocco, Palestine, Syria, and Yemen. Prior to joining the Bank, Mr. Prettitore was the Property Law Coordinator at the Office of the High Representative in Sarajevo, Bosnia and Herzegovina, where he coordinated issues related to postconflict land restitution and human rights issues.

Avni Rastogi graduated from National Law School of India University, Bangalore, in 2010. She worked in the Corporate Affairs Department of an oil and gas public sector company in New Delhi for two years. She now works with Sriram Panchu in his mediation practice and as a researcher on mediation and governance issues. She also works as a project coordinator and researcher with Transparent Chennai, an action research group based in Chennai that creates, curates, and disseminates data on civic issues to enable better planning.

Melanie Roestoff is Professor in the Department of Mercantile Law, University of Pretoria. She holds the degrees B.L.C., LL.B., LL.M. (cum laude), and LL.D. (2002). The title of her thesis is "A Critical Evaluation of Debt Relief Measures for Individuals in the South African Insolvency Law." Since her appointment at the University of Pretoria in 1990, Professor Roestoff has taught a variety of law subjects at both undergraduate and postgraduate levels. In 2010, she was admitted as an attorney of the High Court. She is also author or coauthor of numerous publications in a wide variety of peer-reviewed journals and has presented papers at numerous national and international conferences. Ms. Roestoff is coauthor of one of the leading textbooks on insolvency law in South Africa: *Mars: The Law of Insolvency* (9th edition; Juta).

Yolanda Saito, LL.B. (cum laude; University of Ottawa), B.A.Sc. (University of British Columbia), is a member of New York State Bar, a Legal Specialist, Green Economy and Biodiversity, at the International Development Law Organization, and leads the global initiative on Legal Preparedness for Achieving the Aichi Biodiversity Targets. She also serves as the pro bono Program Coordinator and as an Associate Fellow with the Human Rights and Poverty Eradication program at the Centre for International Sustainable Development Law and is a Senior Fellow with the One Justice Project. She has previously worked in litigation and administrative law with Ecojustice Canada, ECOLEX Ecuador, Canada's Air India Inquiry, and McCarthy Tétrault LLP. She has authored briefs and publications on sustainable development law issues, and is currently working on a manuscript on the incorporation of the principles of sustainable development into the jurisprudence of international and regional courts from 1992 to 2012.

Elisa Slattery has a decade of experience working in health, law, and human rights. In September 2012, she joined the International Development Law Organization (IDLO) Social Development Unit, where she has been working on disability, access to safe medicines, and health and gender issues. Prior to joining IDLO, she was the Regional Director of the Africa Program at the Center for Reproductive Rights, a nongovernmental legal organization. Her fact-finding projects in the region focused on abuses of women in health care facilities, discrimination against women living with HIV, and maternal mortality. She has extensive experience working with accountability and human rights mechanisms at the national, regional, and international levels. Ms. Slattery holds a J.D. from Columbia Law School and an M.A. from Duke University.

Bart Stevens is a Senior Communications Officer in the World Bank Group Integrity Vice Presidency, where he coordinates integrity training programs. In 2005, he was responsible for the development and implementation of the communications strategy for the launch of the Bank's Voluntary Disclosure Program. Prior to joining the World Bank in 1999, Mr. Stevens was a Senior Communications Manager at the European Bank for Reconstruction and Development, in London, where he set up the Bank's internal communications function. Previously, he worked for more than eight years at the Exxon Chemical International headquarters in Brussels, where he focused on public affairs as well as internal and crisis communications issues. Mr. Stevens holds an M.A. in international affairs and economics from the Johns Hopkins University School of Advanced International Studies and a law degree from the Katholieke Universiteit Leuven, Belgium.

Patricia O. Sulser is a Chief Counsel at International Finance Corporation (IFC), based in Washington, D.C. She is the Global Lead Lawyer for IFC InfraVentures, a $150 million internally managed fund established by IFC in 2008 to fund and proactively develop private and public-private partnership (PPP) infrastructure projects in the poorest emerging-market countries. Ms. Sulser has been involved in the financing of complex, multiparty infrastructure projects for her entire career at IFC and, before, in private practice in the New York; London; and Hong Kong SAR, China offices of Shearman & Sterling. She leads the IFC Legal Department Public-Private Partnership practice group and coordinates with colleagues from the World Bank Group and other development financial institutions on the G20 and World Bank Group PPP agenda. Ms. Sulser is also a certified mediator and has provided legal support for IFC's establishment of mediation centers around the world. In addition, she actively promotes the use of alternative dispute resolution (including dispute adjudication boards) in PPP and infrastructure projects worldwide as the best means of keeping these important projects on track. She has recently been appointed to the Dispute Board Federation Advisory Panel and is a member of the Chartered Institute of Arbitrators.

David F. Varela is Special Adviser to the Minister of Government of the Republic of Colombia and the first Policy and Strategy Director of the National Agency for State Legal Defense of Colombia, which was established in 2011 to direct the legal defense activities of more than 300 public sector agencies at the federal level. Mr. Varela worked in the Public Sector Management Unit of the Latin America and the Caribbean Region of the World Bank Group from its Washington, D.C., headquarters between 2007 and 2012. He was responsible for the design and supervision of more than 20 large justice-reform projects supporting judicial authorities in numerous Latin American countries and Morocco. From 1999 to 2002, Mr. Varela worked in the Latin America and the Caribbean Division of the Legal Vice Presidency of the World Bank in Washington, D.C. He received his LL.M. in international business law from the Institute of Comparative Law of McGill University (1989), and both a graduate degree in economics and social sciences and a J.D. from Universidad Javeriana (1984). He has written extensively on legal subjects and published two books on justice reform: *Improving the Performance of Justice Institutions: Lessons from OECD Countries Relevant for Latin America* (2011) and *The Itagüí Courts: A Case Study in Leadership and Management* (2002).

Emilio C. Viano has an LL.B. and three master's degrees in law, an M.A. in sociology and anthropology, and a Ph.D. (summa cum laude) in the sociology of law (New York University). Recently, he has taught and undertaken research chiefly at American University's School of Public Affairs and Washington College of Law, but he has also been a professor at the University of Paris, University of Cordoba (Argentina), Panteion University (Athens), University of Bologna, China University of Political Science and Law (Beijing), and Shanghai International Studies University, among other institutions. His work in law, criminal justice issues, and governance has been recognized by his election as President of the Scientific Commission and as a Voting Member of the Board of Directors of the International Society of Criminology (Paris). He is member of the Task Force for the Creation of the UN World Security University. He also chairs the committee organizing the World Congress of Criminology to be held in Mexico in August 2014. Dr. Viano has consulted worldwide, especially in the developing world and particularly on security issues. He has published extensively, often speaks at international conferences and universities, and often appears as a political analyst on television and radio stations worldwide.

The World Bank Legal Review

Volume 5

Fostering Development through Opportunity, Inclusion, and Equity

Opportunity, Inclusion, and Equity as Imperatives for Meaningful Law and Justice-Guided Development

VINCENT O. NMEHIELLE AND N. R. MADHAVA MENON

In our globalized world, it is commonplace to throw around the concept "development" in a manner that assumes that, somehow, we all share the same understanding of what it means. In reality, there is no universally accepted definition of the concept. As has been observed,[1] a broad reading of development, such as that offered by the report of the Independent Commission on International Development Issues, situates development within the context of economic growth as "desirable social and economic progress,"[2] based on the idea that "without [economic] growth and social change one cannot speak of development."[3] Scholars such as Walter Rodney put people at the center of the development process. From this perspective, at the individual level, development implies "increased skill and capacity, greater freedom, creativity, self-discipline, responsibility and material well-being."[4] Despite the subjective nature of those categories, Rodney maintains that "it is indisputable that the achievement of any of those aspects of personal development is very much tied in with the state of the society as a whole."[5] The emphasis on people in the development process also received the scholarly approval of Julius Nyerere, a respected African statesman and the first president of Tanzania.[6] According to Nyerere, "roads, buildings and increased crop output are not development but tools of development";[7] for these to be development, they must help to "develop the minds and understanding of people" or be used "for other

---

1   Yolanda T. Chekera & Vincent O. Nmehielle, *The International Law Principle of Permanent Sovereignty over Natural Resources as an Instrument for Development: The Case of Zimbabwean Diamonds*, 6 African J. Leg. Stud. 18 (2013) (hereinafter, Chekera & Nmehielle).

2   Independent Commission on International Development Issues, *North–South: A Programme for Survival* 48 (Pan Books 1980), cited in Chekera & Nmehielle, *supra* note 1, at 18.

3   *Id.*

4   Walter Rodney, *How Europe Underdeveloped Africa* 9 (Tanzania Publg. H.; Bogle-L'Ouverture 1972), cited in Chekera & Nmehielle, *supra* note 1, at 18–19.

5   *Id.*

6   Julius Nyerere, *Freedom and Development (Uhuru na Maendeleo): A Selection from the Writings and Speeches, 1968–1973* 59 (Oxford U. Press 1974), cited in Chekera & Nmehielle, *supra* note 1, at 19.

7   *Id.*

things that improve the health and comfort of the people."[8] In short, the defining feature of development is that it "serves the people."[9]

One cannot interrogate an understanding of the concept of development without highlighting the widely acclaimed views of Amartya Sen. Sen argues that economic growth is merely one aspect of development.[10] Traditional notions of development that conceptualize development as purely a matter of economic growth fail to appreciate that "economic growth [is] no more than a means to some other objectives."[11] Development must concern itself with "entitlements of people and capabilities these entitlements generate."[12] Those individuals, organizations, and governments that champion development must commit themselves to reducing that which deprives people and to broadening the choices available to people.[13]

Sen's views are echoed by Nayaran et al., who point out that "deprivation represents a multidimensional view of poverty that includes hunger, illiteracy, illness and poor health, powerlessness, voicelessness, insecurity, humiliation, and a lack of access to basic infrastructure."[14] Sen himself sees development in the light of whether people are empowered or disempowered: "whether they can live long, escape avoidable morbidity, be well nourished, be able to read and write and communicate, [and] take part in literary and scientific pursuits," among other human endeavors.[15]

Despite the normative and ideological disagreements that exist regarding the notion of a human right to development, the 1986 United Nations Declaration on the Right to Development[16] adopts a decidedly balanced perspective and cements the people-centered nature of the development process. As recognized in Preamble 2 to the declaration, development must be understood as "a comprehensive economic, social, cultural and political process which aims at the constant improvement of the well-being of the entire population and of the individual on the basis of their active, free and meaningful participation in the development and in the fair distribution of benefits resulting therefrom."[17]

---

8   *Id.*

9   *Id.,* at 60.

10   Amartya Sen, *Development: Which Way Now?*, 93 Econ. J. 745, 748 (1983), cited in Chekera & Nmehielle, *supra* note 1, at 20.

11   *Id.,* at 753.

12   *Id.,* at 754.

13   E. Wayne Nafziger, *From Seers to Sen: The Meaning of Economic Development* 1 (paper presented at the UN U./World Inst. Dev. Economics Research Jubilee Conference, June 17–18, 2005), cited in Chekera & Nmehielle, *supra* note 1, at 20.

14   Deepa Narayan et al., *Voices of the Poor: Can Anyone Hear Us?* 4–5 (Oxford U. Press 2000), cited in Chekera & Nmehielle, *supra* note 1, at 20.

15   Sen, *supra* note 10, at 754.

16   *Declaration on the Right to Development*, Res/41/128 (adopted by the U.N. General Assembly, Dec. 4, 1986), cited in Chekera & Nmehielle, *supra* note 1, at 21.

17   *Declaration on the Right to Development*, Preamble 2.

In a further step toward giving content to the meaning of development, the eight Millennium Development Goals (MDGs),[18] as articulated in 2000 under the auspices of the United Nations and other development agencies, exemplify global aspirations to improve the well-being of the world's poor and reflect the general agreement of the majority of the world's countries and development institutions regarding the tangible attributes of development (with particular resonance in developing countries). The MDGs do not, however, define what development is or is not.

Yet, while the definition of development remains protean, a clear consensus exists that development must serve people and society, and must prioritize how the development process affects people, particularly the poor and the most vulnerable in society. As Peet and Hartwick argue, "human emancipation and human welfare"[19] must be central to development. The title of this volume drives the message home. *Fostering Development through Opportunity, Inclusion, and Equity* speaks to the holistic nature of the development process, a process that should not only encourage all stakeholders to participate in the process but also directly engage them. This volume generally and this introductory chapter in particular posit that such participation must be guided by the law and accord with the broader notion of justice for development as a concept to be meaningfully appreciated today. A process that takes place without giving stakeholders an opportunity to participate, or that excludes stakeholders, is not only an unfair and inequitable process but also one that is likely to fall foul of the notion of justice in a society that is governed by the rule of law. Thus, equitable participation necessitates a careful inquiry into the conceptual underpinnings of *opportunity, inclusion,* and *equity* as law and justice tools that can be used to secure elements of meaningful development.

Opportunity as Key for Development: Inclusion and Equity as Strategies for Achieving Development

"Opportunity" is an important dimension of the equality guarantee enshrined in most constitutional documents. Denial of equal opportunity in terms of access to basic needs such as health, education, work, leisure, and housing, particularly in societies with a long history of discrimination and exploitation based on race, caste, gender, and religion, results in skewed development inimical to the rule of law and equal justice under law. Arguments based on equity and inclusion can be advanced to equalize development opportunities

---

18   These goals as articulated include the eradication of "extreme poverty and hunger"; the achievement of "universal primary education"; the promotion of "gender equality" and the empowerment of women; the reduction of "child mortality"; the improvement of "maternal health"; the need to "combat HIV/AIDS, malaria and other diseases"; and ensuring "environmental sustainability" and the development of "a global partnership for development." *See We Can End Poverty 2015: Millennium Development Goals—A Gateway to the UN System's Work on the MDGs,* available at http://www.un.org/millenniumgoals/.

19   Richard Peet & Elaine Hartwick, *Theories of Development: Contentions, Arguments, Alternatives,* 2d ed., 1 (Guilford 2009), cited in Chekera & Nmehielle, *supra* note 1, at 21.

through the introduction of appropriate policies and regulations of the governments concerned. These policies relate not only to the prohibition of discrimination but also, and more importantly, to the creation of conditions in which equality of outcomes or substantive equality will appear in communities previously long excluded from development. To a certain extent, affirmative action measures such as reserving a certain number of places for excluded groups in schools and universities can help to meet demands for equal opportunity for those groups. In the progressive realization of the conditions that tend to ensure equality of opportunity for all, development may have to take certain forms that may not make economic sense in the short term. However, the wisdom of designing and implementing locally owned policies, laws, and institutions becomes apparent once the needs of future generations (of whose heritage we are stewards) are taken sustainably into account, especially if those local measures and actors address failures of management over global public goods, such as biodiversity and climate change. This notion of sustainable development can be achieved through the assertion of many important principles, including through legal and institutional reform that ensures the integration of environmental and social considerations into economic decision making that affects many sectors of policy and law related to poverty reduction and broader sustainable development goals.[20] In essence, legal systems consciously make choices, intervening in economic planning and social reconstruction to help create conditions of equal opportunity for all. In balancing such choices with the freedom and liberty of individuals, the judiciary also plays a critical role. Inclusive growth or growth with social justice is advocated in many societies as a conceptual foundation on which to build sustainable development under the rule of law. In India and South Africa, for example, the legal system has embraced this model of law and development.

When he was U.S. president during the civil rights movement, Lyndon B. Johnson spoke of the significance of "opportunity" in individual and social development:

> Freedom is not enough. You do not wipe away the scars of centuries by saying, "Now you are free to go where you want and do as you desire, and choose the leaders you please." You do not take a person who, for years, has been hobbled by chains and liberate him, bring him up to the starting line of a race and then say, "you are free to compete with others" and still justly believe that you have been completely fair. Thus, it is not enough just to open the gates of opportunity. All our citizens must have the ability to walk through those gates. This is the next and more profound stage of the battle for civil rights. We seek not just freedom but opportunity. We seek not just legal equity but human ability, not just equality as a right and a

---

20   Marie-Claire Cordonier Segger & Ashfaq Khalfan, *Sustainable Development Law: Principles, Practices and Prospects* (Oxford U. Press 2004); Marie-Claire Cordonier & C. G. Weeramantry eds., *Sustainable Justice: Integrating Social, Economic and Environmental Law* (Martinus Nijhoff 2004).

theory but equality as a fact and equality as a result. . . . To this end equal opportunity is essential, but not enough.[21]

Fifteen years earlier, the Indian social reformer and constitutional expert B. R. Ambedkar had pinpointed a contradiction between political equality, on the one hand, and social and economic equality, on the other hand. Addressing the Constituent Assembly while presenting the draft of the republican constitution, Ambedkar said:

> On the 26th January, 1950 we are going to enter a life of contradictions. In politics we have equality and in social and economic life, we will have inequality. In politics we will be recognizing the principle of one man one vote and one vote one value. In our social and economic life, we shall, by reason of our social and economic structure, continue to deny the principle of one man one value. How long shall we continue to live this life of contradictions? How long shall we continue to deny equality in our social and economic life? If we continue to deny it for long, we will do so only by putting our political democracy in peril.[22]

These statements, from two very different continents, highlight the challenges that legal systems in liberal democracies have faced in guiding development without losing civil rights or political democracy. The roads traveled by such legal systems are different and the distance covered has varied. Yet, their destination is the same, namely equal opportunity for all and equality before law. The strategy they have employed has been to adhere to the rule of law while balancing rights to equality, freedom, and liberty. In the process, different jurisdictions have evolved systems of equality, jurisprudence, and access to justice that have helped to make development sustainable and inclusive.

In terms of development, equity entails the manner in which "resources and opportunities are distributed in society"[23]—a fair manner that takes all groups and individuals into account so as to level the "playing field to achieve

---

21   Lyndon B. Johnson (1965), as quoted in the *Report on the Equal Opportunity Commission* (Ministry of Minority Affairs, Government of India 2008). One is also reminded of the statement of British suffragist Harriot Stanton Blatch (1856–1940) on the lack of voting opportunity for marginalized groups, as quoted by Susan B. Anthony & Ida Husted Harper in *History of Woman Suffrage*, vol. 4, ch. 18 (1902):

> I have seen in my time two enormous extensions of the suffrage to men—one in America and one in England. But neither the negroes in the South nor the agricultural laborers in Great Britain had shown before they got the ballot any capacity of government; for they had never had the *opportunity* to take the first steps of political action. Very different has been the history of the march of women toward a recognized position in the State. We have had to prove our ability at each stage of progress, and have gained nothing without having satisfied a test of capacity. (emphasis added)

Available at http://quotes.dictionary.com/i_have_seen_in_my_time_two_enormous#zms-hfAhipiiLzWA.99.

22   *Constituent Assembly Debates* (vol. 11) 944–945 (1943).

23   Josephine Tucker & Eva Ludi, *Empowerment and Equity*, in *Poverty Reduction and Pro-poor Growth: The Role of Empowerment* 227 (OECD 2012). Available at http://doi.org/10.1787/9789264168350-en.

equality of opportunity."[24] The emphasis on equity is particularly important in the context of global commitments to more sustainable development, including the commitment to establish regimes and regulatory instruments necessary to secure sound stewardship of natural resources in a way that is intergenerationally equitable, demonstrating respect for the needs of both present and future generations, as is increasingly recognized in international courts and tribunals.[25] When opportunity, inclusion, and equity are present in a society, an enabling environment can be facilitated, which in turn can promote economic empowerment, "political voice," access to justice, the delivery of and "access to public services," the reduction or extermination of "discrimination and social exclusion," and more just and sustainable development outcomes.[26] Conversely, the absence of opportunity, inclusion, and equity leads to exclusion, which lays the foundations for a heated polity of "conflict and insecurity," with risks of ethnic war in societies in Sub-Saharan Africa (and other regions of the world) "where one or more ethnic groups face active discrimination."[27] The "Occupy" movements that followed the global economic meltdown in many developed countries, like the Arab Spring revolutions that started in Tunisia and blew across Libya and Egypt and into Syria, provide a glimpse into how societies can respond to various forms of lack of opportunity, exclusion, and inequity in governance.

Law by its very nature is an instrument of social order, and as such it is well positioned to respond to the societal yearning for development by mainstreaming opportunity, inclusion, and equity—all elements of justice in sustainable development. Effective, strong, and functional legal and judicial institutions are essential in the global quest to accelerate development around the world. In other words, there cannot be effective development without the rule of law, which, as characterized by the World Justice Project in the *Rule of Law Index*, hinges on "four universal principles":

I. The government and its officials and agents are accountable under the law.

II. The laws are clear, publicized, stable, and fair, and protect fundamental rights, including the security of persons and property.

III. The process by which the laws are enacted, administered and enforced is accessible, fair and efficient.

IV. Justice is delivered by competent, ethical and independent representatives and neutrals who are of sufficient number, have

---

24 *Id.*

25 Marie-Claire Cordonier Segger & Yolanda Saito eds., *Sustainable Development in International Courts and Tribunals* (Routledge forthcoming).

26 Tucker & Ludi, *supra* note 23, at 227–232.

27 *Id.*, at 232.

adequate resources, and reflect the makeup of the communities they serve.[28]

This quartet of principles reinforces the contemporary view of development as people centered, because a society based on the rule of law as articulated by the World Justice Project will clearly serve the interest of the society at large. To these four principles, we can add a fifth, underscored and explained in the assembled works of this volume: regulatory and institutional reforms are coherent and participatory across sectors, integrating social, economic, and environmental considerations to meet the sustainable development needs of present and future generations.

While such principles are typically embodied in legislation, they are equally represented in subsidiary legislation, such as regulations, as well as administrative directives and policies for the implementation of various legislative endeavors, and administrative actions that eventually touch on development plans and initiatives. Deploying these principles in the development process is bound to promote equal opportunity, inclusion, and equity—all pivotal elements of justice. We cannot create a better world, one that caters to the diverse needs of our global society, without entrenching the theme of this volume in the development process. Opportunity, inclusion, and equity in global development are clearly the foundation stones of the MDGs, and their importance is growing yet greater in the context of a new post-2015 sustainable development agenda that builds on the gains of implementing the eight Millennium Development Goals while identifying new development challenges.

Thematic and Specific Issues Covered in This Volume

This volume is made up of 32 chapters organized into 5 thematic parts. Part I, "Law and the Economy," includes chapters 1–7; part II, "Justice and Rule of Law Reform," is made up of chapters 8–13; part III, "Environmental and Natural Resources Law," spans chapters 14–18; part IV, "Governance and Anticorruption," comprises chapters 19–24; and part V, "Empowerment and Equity for Diverse Communities," includes chapters 25–30. The volume ends with a concluding chapter and an afterword.

Law and the Economy

Chapter 1, by Patricia O. Sulser and Cyril Chern, is titled "Keeping Public-Private Partnership Infrastructure Projects on Track: The Power of Multistakeholder Partnering Committees and Dispute Boards in Emerging-Market Infrastructure Projects." The authors posit that unlike traditional public infrastructure projects, public-private partnership (PPP) projects have not generally specified the use of contemporary dispute resolution methods, including facilitative mediation, dispute boards, and conciliation. They propose that stakeholders in complex, multistakeholder infrastructure projects structured

---

28   Mark David Agrast et al., *Rule of Law Index 2012–2013 Report* 3 (World Justice Project 2012).

as PPPs or fully private sector projects in emerging markets adopt a culture and routine mechanism to anticipate, evaluate, and resolve disputes on a real-time basis through the use of "multistakeholder committees," called "partnering committees," that include the appointment of a subset group, called a "standing dispute board," empowered to identify and ultimately to resolve disputes on a real-time basis and expeditiously.

Chapter 2, by Beth Anne Hoffman and Charles Boudry, is titled "Protecting Traditional Practices and Country of Origin in Developing Countries through Fair Trade and Intellectual Property Rights." The authors interrogate ways to protect traditional and local producers of commodities such as coffee. Specifically, the authors explore Ethiopia's legal and policy measures to bolster coffee exports through branding and trademarking coffees on the international market that began in mid-2000.

In chapter 3, "Tools for More Sustainable Trade Treaties with Developing Countries," Markus W. Gehring explains that impact assessments can be applied not only to transboundary development projects but also to development policies and plans such as trade agreements. This leading expert discusses how new forms of impact assessments, mandated by law or policy, can be expanded to take into account not just physical environmental issues but also questions of equity, inclusion, and opportunity. He argues that by doing so, the processes can identify and encourage more sustainable trade treaties with developing countries. With a focus on the European Union's Sustainability Impact Assessment, the author highlights the connection between law, policy, and development.

André Boraine and Melanie Roestoff's chapter, "The Treatment of Insolvency of Natural Persons in South African Law: An Appeal for a Balanced and Integrated Approach," addresses South Africa's statutory and nonstatutory procedures pertaining to the insolvency of natural persons as well as aspects of the legal position regarding the regulation of insolvency practitioners and the insolvency reform initiatives currently on the table. They argue that with regard to natural persons, although the system provides for both liquidation and repayment plans for overindebted consumer debtors, presently there is no principled view and approach regarding the treatment of the insolvency of consumer debtors in South African law.

José M. Garrido's chapter, "The Role of Personal Insolvency Law in Economic Development: An Introduction to the World Bank *Report on the Treatment of the Insolvency of Natural Persons*," puts the World Bank report in context. The chapter describes the approach taken by the report and the main issues that a personal insolvency regime needs to address in order to contribute to development and to counteract the negative side effects of increased access to finance. The author posits that the concept of discharge occupies a central role, because it provides the possibility for insolvent debtors to return to a productive life for their own benefit and for the benefit of society as a whole.

In chapter 6, "Specialized Insolvency Regimes for Islamic Banks: Regulatory Prerogative and Process Design," Hdeel Abdelhady proposes the adoption of specialized, administratively managed resolution regimes for Islamic banks. The author argues that the proposed resolution model is substantively appropriate and multipurpose in that it addresses, in a practical way, current deficits in relevant legal and regulatory environments, advances the sharia policy of effective market regulation, incorporates banking and capital market provisions that fit the cross-market nature of Islamic banking, and advances the convergence of Islamic and conventional insolvency regimes.

Part I closes with Fabiano de Andrade Correa's chapter, "The Role of Law in the Green Economy: Challenges and Opportunities for the Liberalization of Environmental Goods and Services." The chapter explores how law can support the green economy by analyzing the challenges and opportunities related to the liberalization of trade on environmental goods and services (EGS). The author contends that trade can be a driver in the transition to a green economy by, among other relevant objectives, helping to create and strengthen markets for goods and services that respond to sustainable development considerations. He further argues that while the inclusion of EGS liberalization in a regional context can help propel regulation and incentivize the transition to a green economy, the point remains that regional measures cannot by themselves create an effective global regulatory framework.

Justice and Rule of Law Reform

Part II opens with chapter 8, "Institutional Responses to Social Demands: Enhancing Access to Justice in Colombia," in which David F. Varela and Annette Pearson propose a policy of rationalization for the new options for access to justice, especially by vulnerable social groups, made possible by the 1991 Constitution of Colombia.

In chapter 9, "The Role of Access to Information in Promoting Development," Sean Fraser examines the status of the right to development in international law and the role that access to information plays in promoting tangible human development. The author argues that although the right to development has gained acceptance among states and scholars, its practical implementation has been underwhelming in light of its vast potential. He posits that the failure to maximize the benefits of the right is due, at least in part, to the inaccessibility of information that groups and individuals can use to promote and protect their human rights.

In chapter 10, "The Search for Opportunity and Inclusion: Insecurity and Migration," Emilio Viano explores the impact of the lack of rule of law on migration and the security of the migrant. The author argues that migrants are often caught in the middle of "the push and pull" in this regard and become very vulnerable to exploitation and victimization at all stages of the migration journey. The chapter examines measures and policies designed to alleviate the situation that leads to the trafficking, exploitation, enslavement, and servitude of migrants. The author stresses the importance of respecting the rule of law, especially international refugee law, in the countries of destination in order to ameliorate the current situation and prevent victimization.

N. R. Madhava Menon's contribution, chapter 11, is titled "Toward a National Framework Law on Water for India" and inquires into how to meet the water demands of India's 1.3 billion people in terms of both quantity and quality, given the constraints of geography and the country's rainfall pattern. Almost half the rainfall that the country receives happens during a period of only two to three weeks, and about 90 percent of river flows occur in just four months in a year. In the same vein, 70 percent of surface water is contaminated by biological, toxic, organic, and inorganic pollutants. The author argues that the scheme for the distribution of powers for water management between the three levels of government has not worked well, hence the adoption of a National Water Policy and an attempt to legislate a framework law on water management that is binding on all three levels. The chapter examines the elements of the framework law and the prospects of its adoption in view of the emerging crisis in water availability and governance.

In chapter 12, "Targeting Justice Sector Services to Promote Equity and Inclusion for the Poor in Jordan," Paul Prettitore examines the state of service delivery for the poor in the justice sector of Jordan. Drawing on data from a novel household survey devoted solely to justice sector issues that was conducted by the Jordanian Department of Statistics in 2011, the author discusses the reforms introduced to benefit poor users of court services. He assesses the current state of the delivery of justice sector services to the poor and explores policy development; the demand side of services; gaps in service delivery; new services under development; and gender aspects of service delivery. The chapter also highlights a number of areas in which reforms might gain traction.

To end part II, Nicholas Joseph's chapter, "Serving the Justice Needs of the People: Adopting an Access to Justice Approach in Somalia's Rule of Law Reform," examines the potential of "bottom-up and pro-poor approaches" in the development of access to justice in Somalia as a postconflict country. In this regard, the author discusses how the Somali government as well as interveners in the country can focus on equity, inclusion, and opportunity in developing rule of law cultures, rather than strengthening and often solidifying the elite status of justice and legal institutions.

Environmental and Natural Resources Law

Part III begins with Edesio Fernandes's chapter, "The Challenges of Reforming the Urban Legal Framework: A Critical Assessment of Brazil's City Statute 10 Years Later." The author explores the topic against the background that in development discourses, management of natural resources occupies a significant place and several principles have evolved and found universal acceptance. Law on urban development is part of this package of principles. However, there are serious shortcomings with the implementation mechanisms in place. These shortcomings are generally the result of pressure groups and of sociopolitical processes. The author points out that Brazil's urban policy law of 2001 is a case study on the subject that highlights the pitfalls in the legal regulation of urbanization and its effect on development policies.

In chapter 15, "Innovative Legal Measures for Climate Change Response in the Green Economy: Integrating Opportunity, Inclusion, and Equity," Marie-Claire Cordonier Segger and Yolanda Saito argue that for a greener economy to truly take root, participatory legal and institutional reforms are needed, as are new economic opportunities for all. The authors point out that innovative legal instruments are currently being pioneered to address climate change in many countries. However, they argue, in order for these reforms to be just and implementable, they must also resolve important challenges of inclusion and equity, ensuring that the poorest and most vulnerable can access the benefits of climate finance and the new global green economy. The authors underline that, as recognized in "The Future We Want," the declaration of the 2012 United Nations Commission on Sustainable Development, there is a need for countries to move away from old economic practices that externalize environmental and social costs, widening disparities in human security and wasting scarce resources, and to start implementing a new green economy that responds to pressing priorities of climate change, poverty reduction, and sustainable development.

In chapter 16, "The Constitutional Basis of Public Participation in Environmental Governance: Framing Equitable Opportunities at National and County Government Levels in Kenya," Robert Kibugi examines the 2010 Constitution of Kenya as an interesting example of how governance is envisaged by the general society to maximize public participation and sustainable development. The constitution provides choices and opportunities to the administration to follow universally accepted principles in environmental decision making. The author argues that in the context of this constitutional provision, informed decisions can be made at all levels of government for equitable and sustainable development in Kenya.

"Do planning regulations contribute to social justice or exacerbate social disputes?" is the question examined in chapter 17 by Rachelle Alterman. "Planning Laws, Development Controls, and Social Equity: Lessons for Developing Countries" finds that planning regulations do exacerbate social disparities, more so in developing countries because regulations are vulnerable to greater misuse in the developing world. Focusing on development control instruments, the author advises decision makers in developing countries, including representatives of aid organizations, to be careful in allowing the transplantation of planning laws from advanced economies to developing ones, because those laws may not take local circumstances into account.

In a similar vein, Matthew Glasser in chapter 18, "Land Use Law and the City: Toward Inclusive Planning," draws out the relationship between urban law and development outcomes. The author posits that when the laws are inappropriate or impractical for the majority of the city population, an informal sector vulnerable to eviction develops that raises problems of human rights protection. The contention is often about affordable access to the city, jobs, and other opportunities that very often get protection from the courts even if the settlements are informal and therefore outside the law. He concludes that good urban law must consider affordability and access to the city.

Governance and Anticorruption

Corruption subverts governance, undermines the rule of law, and wreaks havoc on the lives and livelihoods of people, particularly the poor. Although anti-corruption laws are in place in most jurisdictions, their impact is generally limited. This issue is perceived in terms of access to justice and denial of basic rights and has led to organized movements seeking accountability in governance. In chapter 19, "Fighting Corruption in Education: A Call for Sector Integrity Standards," which begins part IV, Mihaylo Milovanovitch argues in favor of sectorwide standards of integrity and a sector-specific prevention approach to fighting corruption. The author recommends cross-border agreements against malpractices as an effective way to combat corruption.

In chapter 20, "The Battle between Corruption and Governance in India: Strategies for Tipping the Scale," Sriram Panchu and Avni Rastogi focus on big-ticket corruption, given the limited resources available for the fight against corruption and the possible impact of exposing and punishing corruption at the highest level of government on the lower rungs of officialdom. The authors recommend the establishment of a strong, high-profile, independent authority to oversee and discipline the leadership of the government and state bureaucracy.

In chapter 21, "Leveling the Playing Field: A Race to the Top," Bart Stevens and Robert Delonis submit that any strategy to fight corruption needs to ensure that the operating field is level and allows the private sector to operate in an environment of fair competition and equal treatment under the rule of law. They recommend a model of partnership between development agencies and private firms based on voluntary disclosure, negotiated resolution agreements, and an integrity compliance system as the best way to level the field. The authors point out that this model was evolved by the World Bank Group, which created a sanctions system that excludes firms and individuals that undermine fair competition from bidding in World Bank–supported development project contracts.

It is, however, interesting to note that Frank Fariello and Giovanni Bo, in chapter 22, "The World Bank Group Sanctions System and Access to Justice for Small and Medium-Size Enterprises," find the World Bank's sanctions system not to be as effective vis-à-vis small and medium-size enterprises, which, unlike larger enterprises, simply refuse to engage with it, possibly because of an "access to justice" issue for such small and medium-size enterprises. The authors suggest modifications to make the system fairer and to more adequately address the lower capacities of small and medium-size players in accessing justice under the system.

As a way of dealing with corruption in governance, William T. Loris, in chapter 23, "Private Civil Actions: A Tool for a Citizen-Led Battle against Corruption," recommends encouraging and facilitating civil actions by citizens. This could be accomplished by providing for specific remedial and recovery measures and empowering victims of corruption with support from media and civil society to fight corruption. He contends that the threat of criminal prosecution will succeed in fighting corruption only if political will and commitment are present along with an independent, noncorrupt judiciary. Even so, private civil actions duly sanctioned by the legal system can become an additional weapon in a citizen-led battle against corruption.

Chapter 24, "Fostering Opportunity through Development Finance in Africa: Legal Perspectives from the African Development Bank," looks at international economic governance and development. Kalidou Gadio proposes a purposive rather than literal construction of the mandate of the African Development Bank in order to promote innovative economic interventions for sustainable development in African countries. This approach would take into account the circumstances of the various countries, some of which have been affected by conflicts and thus require innovative service delivery.

Empowerment and Equity for Diverse Communities

Against the background of mainstreaming the marginalized in development by providing for equal opportunities, part V begins with Vincent O. Nmehielle and John-Mark Iyi's chapter, "Nation Building, State Reconstruction, and Inclusiveness: Issues on South Sudan as a New State and Somalia as a Failed but Reemerging State." The authors opine that South Sudan and Somalia share some significant characteristics: both have been conflict zones in decades of civil wars; and the ethnic groups and clans of both states have a common history of political exclusion, social injustice, and economic inequality. Both have also recently started out on the path of nation building and state reconstruction. The chapter examines the prospects of nation building and reconstruction in both states and uses a cause-and-effect analysis to argue for a development approach that is based on the rule of law, social justice, and equality. The authors contend that some core values of governance, when entrenched in constitutive instruments of the state, function as indispensable drivers of social cohesion, political stability, and socioeconomic development; they also argue that nation building and reconstruction efforts in these countries must be anchored on these norms. For meaningful development to occur, both states must design policies that emphasize uniting factors while addressing grievances and other structural issues that, if left to fester, heighten group differences.

In chapter 26, "Enabling Equal Opportunities for Women in the World of Work: The Intersections of Formal and Informal Constraints," Jeni Klugman and Matthew Morton argue that multiple constraints in culture, markets, and institutions inhibit women from accessing equal opportunities. They maintain that law reform in this regard can easily be thwarted by implementation challenges, including information gaps, institutional biases, and adverse social norms. The authors contend that law reform that is supplemented by policy efforts can, to a certain extent, redress gender gaps, particularly in the world of work.

David Patterson, Elisa Slattery, and Naomi Burke-Shyne's chapter, "The Role of Law in Promoting the Right to Health for Diverse Communities," finds discrimination and stigma in the delivery of health services to be a serious problem in realizing the right to health in diverse communities. They argue that unless proactive policies supported by legal sanctions are adopted, vulnerable groups in diverse communities will be denied the right to health.

Along the same lines, Siobhán McInerney-Lankford and Moses Mulumba in chapter 28, "The Right to Health and Development: The Case of Uganda," highlight the centrality of the right to health in shaping health policy and delivery of health services. The authors draw out the content of that right in relation to development goals, pointing out how human rights can add value to development policies and programs.

In a conceptual analysis of India's experience in development, Pulapre Balakrishnan argues in chapter 29, "Mainstreaming the Marginalized in Development: Conceptualizing the Challenges in India," that "capability" lies at the core of freedom, opportunity, and development. The author contends that it is the marginalized sections of Indian society that lack capability. Although the Indian Constitution has some impressive provisions regarding building capability, they are inadequate when it comes to capacitating the marginalized. The author concludes that the "future of development in India lies squarely in the space of politics," with concrete political action needed to implement the provisions of the constitution.

The final element in part V is Anupama Dokeniya's chapter, "The Right to Information as a Tool for Community Empowerment." It posits that the right to information is universally acclaimed as an effective instrument to fight corruption by exposing it in the public. Referencing examples from India and Mexico, the author explains how the right to information has been used as a tool to expose the corrupt practices of administrative officials and thereby mobilize people to demand corrective action. She concludes that the full potential of this tool is not yet realized in many communities because of low awareness, weak civil society groups, and the unwillingness of officials to release information.

In the concluding chapter of the volume, Hassane Cissé and Marie-Claire Cordonier Segger emphasize that, now more than ever, there is an urgent need to mainstream law and justice into development, given the critical development challenges the world faces, such as state fragility and conflict, climate change, food insecurity, bad governance, and persistent gender inequality. They argue that viewing these issues through a justice lens would more effectively promote the rule of law, eradicate extreme poverty, and ultimately achieve broader development goals. This approach should also guide and inform global actions in mapping out a robust post-2015 development agenda.

Indeed, the issues covered in this volume highlight the fact that law is an instrument able to foster inclusion and equal opportunity in the development process. Indeed, inclusion and equal opportunity are at the root of governance, whether economic or political governance. Sustainable global development can be achieved only if the law is deployed to help develop and implement policies and programs that ensure opportunity and minimize marginalization.

PART I

LAW AND THE ECONOMY

Keeping Public-Private Partnership Infrastructure Projects on Track

The Power of Multistakeholder Partnering Committees and Dispute Boards in Emerging-Market Infrastructure Projects

Patricia O. Sulser and Cyril Chern

Efforts to expand and improve traditional and social infrastructure and public services (such as water and sanitation; electricity generation, transmission, and distribution; roads, railways, ports, and airports; hospitals and clinics; schools; and prisons) are intrinsic to sustainable economic growth and poverty alleviation, especially in fragile and conflict-affected states and rural areas, where the poorest communities can lack the broad and inclusive access required to enjoy a dignified existence and to graduate from extreme poverty.[1] When successfully implemented, these infrastructure projects and public services can directly address issues of opportunity, inclusion, and equity, as explained in more detail below.[2] It is therefore important to develop tools that enhance the successful implementation of these projects and the delivery of public services. This chapter addresses one such tool.

The direct cost of building and maintaining this infrastructure is indisputably very high. Due to the size and complexity of these projects and the varied interests of the parties involved, disputes inevitably arise during the course of public-private partnership (PPP) and private sector infrastructure development projects. Unlike traditional public infrastructure projects, PPP projects have to date not generally specified the use of contemporary dispute resolution methods, such as facilitative mediation, dispute boards, and conciliation. Left unresolved, disputes can result in enormous unplanned costs and delays,

---

1   The International Finance Corporation (IFC) uses the term "traditional" infrastructure to mean water; sanitation; electricity generation, transmission, and distribution; roads, railways, ports, and airports; and some logistics, etc. It uses the term "social" to refer to hospitals, clinics and health services; educational facilities; and prisons, etc. IFC invests in and mobilizes resources for all of these kinds of projects and also provides advisory services in both the traditional and social infrastructure areas, primarily to governments but also to corporations, covering structuring of public-private partnerships and investment-climate work, among other things.

2   *See* World Bank, *Infrastructure, Strategy*, available at http://web.worldbank.org/WBSITE /EXTERNAL/TOPICS/EXTINFRA/0,,contentMDK:23117980~menuPK:8497224~pagePK:641 68445~piPK:64168309~theSitePK:8430730,00.html; and 7(1) Jobs 14–15 (2013), an IFC private sector development-solutions publication.

and in unnecessary damage to reputations and relationships—this in a sector that can ill afford any of these consequences.

This chapter proposes that stakeholders in complex multistakeholder infrastructure projects structured as PPPs and fully private sector projects in emerging markets adopt a culture and routine mechanism to anticipate, evaluate, and resolve disputes on a real-time basis. This chapter further proposes that this be achieved through the use of multistakeholder committees called "partnering committees,"[3] which include the appointment of a subset group, called a "standing dispute board," which is empowered to identify and ultimately to resolve disputes contemporaneously and expeditiously. Finally, this chapter shows how to incorporate the necessary processes into the project structure, how to select and empower the boards, how to justify the cost, and how to maximize effectiveness, all with a view to keeping projects on budget and on track, to ensuring optimal results, and to preserving the business environment for future projects.

Context: Public Infrastructure and Traditional Dispute Resolution

Poor infrastructure development can cost economies billions of dollars a year in missed opportunities and negative drag on economic growth.[4] In fact, the International Bank for Reconstruction and Development was established to help rebuild the infrastructure of Europe after World War II because of the importance of infrastructure to the region's renewed economic growth. Stated in the positive, successful implementation of infrastructure projects and delivery of public services are the engine of growth. Importantly, they also contribute directly to the promotion of opportunity, inclusion, and equity. They are typically designed to provide affordable access to all segments of the population, including indigenous populations, rural communities, and the poorest and marginalized. For instance, opportunities are created through job creation as a result of the investments themselves and through increased economic development as a result of improvements to a country's infrastructure; there is more equity when people can receive the infrastructure service involved. Generally, tools that encourage and facilitate PPP and private sector investments

---

3   In some large and complex projects, a "steering committee" is appointed and meets regularly to take stock of the project's progress. Such a committee is not typically empowered to resolve disputes and frequently does not meet physically, including at the site or even in the country.

4   See *IFC Support to Infrastructure, Transactions in Power, Transport and Water* (Intl. Fin. Corp. 2009), available at http://www1.ifc.org/wps/wcm/connect/62aa5680498390a982c4d2336b93 d75f/InfrastructureBooklet_FINALweb.pdf?MOD=AJPERES&CACHEID=62aa5680498390a 982c4d2336b93d75f; see also *Africa's Infrastructure: A Time for Transformation* (Agence Française de Développement, World Bank 2010), available at http://siteresources.worldbank.org /INTAFRICA/Resources/aicd_overview_english_no-embargo.pdf. There are myriad scholarly articles written by economists on the relationship between infrastructure and economic growth, easily found by searching any of the more common Web-based search engines, such as Google, or relevant institutional and academic databases.

in infrastructure would certainly increase access to basic resources and create more equity between segments of the population.

Major projects for the delivery and operation of infrastructure and public services in developed countries are notoriously difficult to prioritize, plan, approve, implement, and operate. They are a natural context for conflict given their high profile and the high stakes for governments, users of the services, and the public at large, the latter of which is often taxed or charged, directly or indirectly, to pay for the millions (often, billions) required for the construction and operation of these projects over the long term. Two limited examples of major infrastructure projects gone wrong are the Big Dig in Boston[5] and the Channel Tunnel in England,[6] each of which suffered significant delays and enormous cost overruns for various reasons, including legitimate reasons not due to any party's fault.

Implementing projects for the delivery and operation of basic infrastructure and public services in emerging markets can be even more challenging given the constraints on public budgets[7] and government's technical or human capacity, including the capacity to monitor and supervise works by third parties. Projects in fragile and conflict-affected states and in rural areas designed to provide broad and inclusive access to the poorest communities present another layer of challenges, even if projects are smaller and smaller sums are involved. Such projects have been an area of intense strategic focus for the G20, the World Bank Group, and other international-development financial institutions dedicated to the alleviation of poverty around the world.[8]

Given the constraints on emerging-market governments, there is consensus around the need to mobilize the private sector to provide financial and

---

5   The Central Artery/Tunnel (CA/T) project, known informally as the Big Dig, was a massive project begun in 1982 in Boston that rerouted the city's central highway into a 3.5-mile tunnel. The project also included the construction of a tunnel, a bridge, and an elevated highway. The Big Dig was the most expensive highway project in the United States and was plagued by, among other things, rising costs, delays, design flaws, and allegations of poor execution and use of substandard materials, not to mention criminal charges. The project was originally scheduled to be completed in 1998 at an estimated cost of $2.8 billion (in historical dollar values). The project was completed nearly ten years late at a cost overrun of more than $10 billion (nearly 190 percent over planned costs).

6   The Channel Tunnel from Dover/Folkestone, England to Calais, France, is a 50-kilometer undersea rail tunnel running beneath the English Channel. "From the word go, construction of the channel tunnel was blighted by delays which caused a rapid escalation of costs. By the time Eurotunnel opened in May 1994, it was one year behind schedule and £2bn ($3.6bn) over budget. Before the first passenger car had boarded Le Shuttle for the short trip from Folkestone to Calais, the original business plan was in tatters." *See* Jeff Randall, *How Eurotunnel Went So Wrong*, BBC News (June 13, 2005), available at http://news.bbc.co.uk/2 /hi/business/4088868.stm.

7   Developing countries, especially the poorest countries and those with limited natural resources, have limited ability to raise funds through taxation or to charge for public services, and end users are often unable to afford tariffs charged for such services.

8   *See* World Bank, *Infrastructure*, available at http://web.worldbank.org/WBSITE/EXTERNAL /NEWS/0,,contentMDK:20127296~menuPK:34480~pagePK:34370~theSitePK:4607,00.html.

technical support to governments for the delivery of public services, with a special emphasis on the poorest countries (especially fragile and conflict-affected states) and frontier regions and sectors in middle-income countries.[9] Infrastructure projects can be publicly financed and operated (with private contractors building and delivering the works to the government, often under a fixed-price arrangement). Alternatively, a government may transfer the financial, commercial, construction, and operational risk wholly or partially to the private sector. The partial but significant transfer of these risks to the private sector in partnership with the government is the essence of a PPP. There is a copious amount of literature on the history and current practice involved in public procurement and PPPs, but this is not within the scope of this chapter.[10] Successful implementation of the first few PPPs or privately financed infrastructure projects in a country can be critical to that country's ongoing ability to garner public support and attract to its infrastructure program the scarce foreign and domestic resources that are necessary to ensure its economic growth. This means assuring that the projects are structured in a balanced way, with capable partners meeting their respective obligations so as to maintain on-time, on-budget delivery and consistent and reliable operations of the infrastructure in question.

In reality, misunderstandings, differences of opinion, and disagreements inevitably arise among two or more stakeholders during the life of even the best-planned infrastructure projects, regardless of size. Disputes can arise at the project level, among the direct stakeholders (such as between the private construction contractor or operator and the government or the purchasers of the goods or services), or at the financing level, between investors/lenders and the private company implementing the project, or among any of those parties and the government because of political or economic events in the country. Rapid resolution of any such disputes is critical to keeping fundamentally good projects on track and also to building and maintaining confidence among the many stakeholders in these complex projects—private sector players, as well as governments and the local community—so that they will be inclined to make follow-on investments in the country.

The most common forms of dispute resolution, especially in countries without a track record of private sector investment in infrastructure projects and public services, are litigation in courts and, to a somewhat lesser extent, arbitration (and variations thereof).[11] In these situations, a third party (a judge

---

9   See World Bank, *Fragility, Conflict and Violence,* available at http://web.worldbank.org /WBSITE/EXTERNAL/PROJECTS/STRATEGIES/EXTLICUS/0,,menuPK:511784~pagePK:64 171540~piPK:64171528~theSitePK:511778,00.html.

10   See World Bank, *PPP Infrastructure Resource Center,* available at http://ppp.worldbank.org /public-private-partnership/; *see* also International Finance Corporation, *Advisory Services,* available at http://www1.ifc.org/wps/wcm/connect/AS_EXT_Content/What+We+Do/Advi sory+Services/About+Us/Public-Private+Partnerships.

11   Arbitration is often a preferred dispute resolution mechanism for construction projects because of the ability to select arbitrators with expertise on the complex issues that are inherent in the infrastructure construction industry, and because the time and expense of arbitra-

or arbitrator), who may have no expertise in the matter at hand, evaluates past events and evidence (including the terms of the contracts), decides which party is "right" or "wrong," and imposes a decision on the stakeholders. Projects may be delayed for months or even years during the formal legal proceedings.[12] In many developing countries, even if there is a functioning and reputable judiciary, courts may have enormous backlogs, adding to the potential delays.[13] Appointing experienced arbitrators, who often have full schedules, and agreeing on hearing dates can add to the delay. In addition to the effect of the actual delays on the project timetable, delays can often lead to significant cost overruns (time is, after all, money), in some cases making the project no longer financially and economically feasible.[14] Adding the polarization of the parties and the deterioration of relationships to these delays and cost overruns can produce a nice recipe for scuttling an emerging economy's prospects for achieving development outcomes.

In public sector projects expected to cost more than $10 million and to be financed directly or indirectly by the World Bank, the parties are required to establish dispute boards[15] to expedite the settlement of disputes.[16] These dispute boards are to be formed at the beginning of the contract for the proposed works, although in practice they are often not established until a dispute arises. They are empowered to make recommendations and, in some cases, depending on which type of board they are, to provide interim decisions in

---

tion compared to litigation are usually less. Nevertheless, not every developing country has implemented legislation for the enforcement of foreign arbitral awards. Also, arbitration can still be extremely expensive and nearly as time-consuming as litigation. Moreover, local arbitral procedural rules apply even to international arbitration, and these local procedural rules can often be subjective and unpredictable.

12   Construction disputes can take five to six years to resolve, even in a fast-track court system, and the project is often stopped during that period. This is the reason, in fact, that dispute boards were started after arbitration itself became stalled in the process. The Dispute Board Federation, in its Annual Board Report, June 2009, determined that the average delay, worldwide, on construction projects without an ADR or Dispute Board process averaged seven years, and in some countries, such as India, went as long as 20 years.

13   Many international investors require in their investment documentation that the parties submit to the jurisdiction of the courts of New York or England for the resolution of disputes, although it is not uncommon for rights against sponsors to need to be enforced in the jurisdiction of the sponsor if the sponsor has assets only in its country. Investor-state disputes often are required to be resolved in local courts.

14   Most PPPs and private sector infrastructure projects, which are often structured as limited-recourse financings (as opposed to corporate financings), are heavily dependent on timely completion and the commencement of revenue generation. Delays usually mean higher interest on construction loans and possibly escalation of construction costs. In addition, delays in generating revenues can mean that the ability to pay for operating and maintenance costs (including loan principal and daily costs) can be jeopardized. In some cases, governments impose an obligation on concessionaires and operators to pay liquidated damages for delays for which they are responsible to compensate the government for the cost of "cover" and lost opportunity.

15   These can be either a dispute review board that gives advisory opinions only or a dispute adjudication board that gives binding and immediately enforceable decisions.

16   See full discussion below.

respect to disputed matters. In PPPs and private sector projects (including ones in which the World Bank may be involved), there is often no comparable mechanism required to be built into the project for early and ongoing identification and resolution of disputes. The political and economic costs to countries of projects being delayed or fully derailed as a result of conflicts that end up in formal legal proceedings are enormous.

Building on the idea of dispute boards as employed in publicly procured projects financed by the World Bank and as contemplated in certain standard bidding and construction contracts of other institutions (see below), two proposals are made. First, the parties to PPPs and private sector projects should establish a similar approach to responsive and proactive dispute resolution. This would involve a partnering committee being instituted at the inception of the project and remaining fully involved through the life of the project as a means of keeping stakeholders routinely and frequently apprised of progress and any unexpected challenges in meeting their respective expectations. Second, for large infrastructure projects, the partnering committee should include a dispute board from the inception of the project. In practice, on smaller projects, the dispute board can and does substitute entirely for the partnering committee, with each party choosing a member, and those members choosing a collective chair. In either case, the dispute board should have the power to help facilitate resolution of any dispute among the parties by encouraging the appointment of an impartial mediator (if the parties have not already pursued mediation) or to impose a decision on the parties when a negotiated settlement is not possible, ensuring that the parties have the greatest opportunity to resolve disputes promptly and to keep the project on track. The decision can be binding or nonbinding, depending on the parties' agreement, as described below.

The Challenge to Deliver

The World Bank Group[17] is at the forefront of the international-development financial institutions supporting PPPs in the traditional and social infrastruc-

---

17 The World Bank Group consists of five organizations: the International Bank for Reconstruction and Development lends to governments of middle-income and creditworthy low-income countries. The International Development Association provides interest-free loans—called credits—and grants to governments of the poorest countries. The International Finance Corporation is the largest global development institution focused exclusively on the private sector. It helps developing countries achieve sustainable growth by financing investment, mobilizing capital and loans in international financial markets, and providing advisory services to businesses and governments. The Multilateral Investment Guarantee Agency (MIGA) promotes foreign direct investment into developing countries to support economic growth, reduce poverty, and improve people's lives. MIGA fulfills this mandate by offering political risk insurance (guarantees) to investors and lenders. The International Centre for Settlement of Investment Disputes provides international facilities for conciliation and arbitration of investment disputes. See World Bank, *About Us*, available at http://web.worldbank.org/WBSITE/EXTERNAL/EXTABOUTUS/0,,pagePK:50004410~piPK:36602~theSitePK:29708,00.html.

ture sectors in emerging markets.[18] Increasingly, the World Bank Group is involved in cutting-edge, first-of-a-kind infrastructure projects with transformational potential and the ability to be repeated and scaled up across the emerging world. The World Bank Group's ability to support the successful financing and sustained implementation and operation of a sound private sector or PPP project is central to enhancing investor confidence more generally in the country and thereby to boosting development outcomes. The demands and expectations to produce development results in these most challenging environments and to reach the broadest base of the population—including rural and urban environments—are high. There are even greater challenges for a developing country with limited government, judicial, financial, or technical capacity, little or no history of private investment, a nascent legal system, or a limited track record of interpreting and enforcing contracts, as can be the case in new countries or countries that have just entered a postconflict phase. Particularly because of these challenging circumstances, it is critical that the parties have an effective and efficient way to expedite resolution of the disputes that will inevitably arise in these high-profile, high-stakes infrastructure projects. It is also important to find an effective way to monitor the progress of the job itself, and to act as a control, such as by providing on-site monitoring, and to aid in the prevention of fraud.

PPPs and Disputes That Arise

Public-private partnerships in the infrastructure sector typically involve multiple stakeholders. The typical "public" stakeholders might include, for example, government and/or state-owned and/or municipal enterprises as (1) grantor of a concession or license, (2) regulator, (3) purchaser or off-taker of the public services or products being generated by the private operator for distribution to consumers, and, sometimes, (4) investor. On the private sector side, such a project might involve (1) a private company (the borrower or investee company that is licensed by the government to evaluate the feasibility of the project and to design, construct, and operate the project on a certain timetable and at an agreed-on, often regulated, tariff); (2) private construction contractors and other service providers hired by the private operator to enable the private operator to meet its obligations to the government under its concession, license, or off-take agreement; (3) lenders and political risk providers; and (4) investors—traditional shareholders as well as private equity investors and others who have invested in, and who are therefore interested in, the financial success of, the private operator. Finally, such a project will include the ultimate beneficiaries of the public services (including potentially private, commercial, and industrial consumers or users) as well as the local community. All of these stakeholders have distinct interests in pursuing projects, including anticipated "rewards" commensurate with the risks taken in the project in the case of private sector stakeholders, and "value for money"

---

18 *See* World Bank, *Annual Report 2012,* available at http://siteresources.worldbank.org /EXTANNREP2012/Resources/8784408-1346247445238/AnnualReport2012_En.pdf.

in the case of government stakeholders and end users. In some cases, one or more parties may have an interest in delaying resolution of the dispute and any payment or other obligations they may have as a result of the resolution of the dispute. Most large, multiparty infrastructure projects involve not only extensive construction phases but also operations over a long period, sometimes up to 50 years.

Disputes might arise as a result of poor or untimely performance by the private operator; unexpected increases in costs of certain components or services that disproportionately disadvantage a particular party;[19] a natural *force majeure* event that physically delays or impedes the project development, construction, delivery of equipment, or operation; disputes among shareholders of the private operator (e.g., over funding obligations); breaches by the government or its agencies; macroeconomic changes or changes in the political or regulatory environment; or laws that make the original terms of the concession or license disadvantageous for one or more of the parties.[20] In some cases, the local community can be negatively affected by the proposed project; for example, community members may need to be resettled or compensated, or they may not understand how their needs will be met. In either case, if disputes are left unaddressed or unresolved, relationships among the stakeholders can deteriorate and, ultimately, the project can falter. PPPs are additionally surrounded by intense public scrutiny, and when something goes wrong in the project (e.g., a unilateral renegotiation of a concession's terms by the government,[21] or a breach or unexcused deficient performance by the private operator), it often results in political fallout in the country. Lengthy and expensive litigation or investor-state or other arbitration to resolve these disputes can jeopardize the viability of the project or derail its implementation or operation, and will at a minimum be frustrating to the private operator and its contractors, investors, and lenders, as well as to the local government, end users, and local community. In addition, certainty of outcome in formal proceedings (in litigation and also in arbitral proceedings) is not assured even in seemingly strong cases, particularly in local arbitral fora or courts, which may not have a long history of interpreting private commercial contracts or may seem biased. Ultimately, these frustrating and often unpredictable formal dispute resolution processes can seriously undermine both investor confidence and potential contractor interest in investing in the country or in a project involving the same government or local parties.

---

19   According to a recent World Bank study, roughly 70 percent of hydropower projects were completed with cost overruns exceeding 30 percent, and a majority of projects were finished with 50 percent overruns. One or more parties must pay for or bear these cost overruns.

20   *See Renewables, Retro-active FiT Cuts in Bulgaria Cause Sector Fury,* See News (Sept. 17, 2012), available at http://renewables.seenews.com/news/retro-active-fit-cuts-in-bulgaria-cause-sector-fury-303005.

21   *See Toolkit for PPPs in Roads and Highways, Contract Renegotiation and Adaptation* (Public-Private Infrastructure Advisory Facility 2009), available at http://www.ppiaf.org/sites/ppiaf.org/files/documents/toolkits/highwaytoolkit/6/pdf-version/4-37.pdf.

The Need for Communication and Effective Dispute Resolution

It is vital in complex infrastructure projects that the parties keep as open a dialogue as possible in order to address contentious issues and changes in circumstances or perspectives as they arise and, ideally, even before they turn into full-fledged disputes. While it is important that the original commercial deal among the stakeholders be respected, particularly when unforeseen "neutral" changes have arisen, a forward-looking creative solution that involves adjustment to the originally negotiated terms of a contract may be a reasonable, and perhaps the most favorable and sustainable, outcome. However, representatives of parties may become anxious about the possible fallout within their constituencies because they have suggested a solution that departs from the negotiated contract, or because they are not empowered to consider alternatives to the negotiated contract terms. In addition, the parties may be reluctant to appear "weak" in negotiations by suggesting a compromise solution, or they may be concerned about the risk of compromising their legal rights and remedies by agreeing to an "alternative" means of dispute resolution, such as mediation or a dispute board mechanism. Yet, without a pre-agreed-on and routine mechanism for airing and ideally resolving concerns before they turn into disputes, the disputes that result may be difficult or impossible to anticipate or to resolve through direct negotiations among the parties—at least not in a time frame that is reasonable given the time and resources involved (including staff and management time, external legal counsel time, etc.)—and may lead to the deterioration of the project, relationships, and trust among the parties, as described below.

Dispute Resolution Proposal for PPPs

Partnering Committees: Composition and Role

It is therefore proposed that, as a matter of best practice in the construction and operation of traditional and social PPPs and privately financed infrastructure projects around the world, each significant stakeholder be represented on a partnering committee[22] that conducts periodic meetings (occasionally on-site and/or in country) from the inception of the project (for example, monthly during development and construction and less frequently during operations). Thus, the partnering committee for a power generation project might consist of a member from each of the private developer/operators; each of the major material supply, construction, or services providers; the government (usually a representative from the lead ministry and/or their external advisers) and any government entity purchasing services from the private operator or having

---

22   Sometimes, these committees are called "steering committees" or "project development committees" and are included in a country's standardized PPP contracts, together with extensive reporting obligations about the project's progress. This mechanism is critically important, too, if the government or a government agency has an obligation to perform certain functions to enable the private operator to deliver its works or services on time; e.g., a private power plant operator's ability to connect to the government-owned transmission line or grid.

an ownership interest in the project; possibly the regulator, the lenders, and investors; and, depending on the size, profile, and dynamics of the project, a representative from the local community. However, the membership of the partnering committee can vary according to the project and the desires of the stakeholders. The size and composition of the partnering committee needs to be sufficiently streamlined and managed to be and to remain productive and not become sidetracked on minor issues or used as a forum for complaints or delays. The specific mandate of the partnering committee would be (1) to keep stakeholders apprised of project progress and any obstacles that have arisen that could affect the expectations of any of the parties or the scope, price, or timing of the project; (2) to provide an early-alert mechanism to any concerns of one or more stakeholders; (3) to provide a frequent and routine forum for the parties to directly negotiate resolution of any disputes, where possible; and (4) to commit to engage a mediator to facilitate the resolution of disputes if the parties are unable to do so on their own through direct discussions and negotiations.[23] PPP projects can and should affect the bottom-line issues of opportunity, inclusion, and equity when they allow for local-level input from those who will be using the project, those who will benefit from it, and those who will be impacted negatively by it; hearing all those voices and providing for their inclusion in the early stages of the project through a partnering committee will satisfy those vital needs. If used conscientiously as a means of engaging the local community, a partnering committee can also be an effective means of avoiding official complaints by the local community to the World Bank's Inspection Panel and to the IFC's and MIGA's Office of the Compliance Adviser/Ombudsman, both independent recourse mechanisms whose mission is to address complaints by people affected by World Bank Group projects and to enhance the social and environmental accountability of the World Bank Group institutions.

Active Commitment to Mediate

The power of mediation is essentially accepted in the construction industry. Many financial institutions and companies involved in complex international construction and infrastructure projects routinely provide in their contracts for, and routinely use, alternative dispute resolution (ADR), and specifically mediation, as a mechanism of "first resort" when there is an incipient conflict brewing among the parties or when direct negotiations over a ripe conflict break down or are overly prolonged.[24] (In this chapter, arbitration is consid-

---

23   Agreements to mediate can be tailored to ensure that the only disputes required to be mediated are those that (1) are good candidates for mediation and (2) do not jeopardize the parties' legal rights and remedies. A balance must be struck, however, between reassuring parties that they do not give up too much by agreeing to mediate and creating a situation in which the parties use the exclusions from the agreement to mediate as an excuse not to mediate. In situations in which the parties are reluctant or refuse to mediate, the dispute board (discussed in the next section) can play an important role in urging the parties to try, at least for an agreed-on period, to mediate disputes toward a negotiated settlement.

24   Construction industry contracts standardized by the International Federation of Consulting Engineers (FIDIC) include provisions for "amicable settlement" of disputes among parties,

ered a formal means of dispute resolution, much like litigation.) The International Institute for Conflict Prevention and Resolution (CPR) reports that over 4,000 companies and 1,500 law firms have established policy and signed a formal pledge committing themselves to explore ADR options before pursuing litigation.[25] These ADR mechanisms can fall along a wide-ranging continuum, between mediation on the one end and arbitration and litigation on the other. For example, such ADR mechanisms might include expert determination. In 1996, General Electric Company (GE) began the process of systematic use of mediation, and in 1998, GE initiated a company-wide Early Dispute Resolution (EDR) program tied to GE's Six Sigma Quality initiative to eliminate "defects" in the company's processes and products. As of 2011, GE routinely used mediation globally to resolve disputes of all sizes and complexity. EDR is considered by GE to address the demands of its clients through (1) minimal waste of executive and managerial time; (2) preservation of important business relationships; (3) maximization of outcome; and (4) predictability of results. GE's policy of preferring mediation in the first instance for the resolution of disputes is based on a hardheaded, commercial analysis of the costs of formal litigation or arbitration versus ADR mechanisms.[26]

Critical features of any voluntary mediation are its consensual and confidential nature, its flexibility in structure and process, and its adaptability to the needs and desires of the parties, including the need to control the outcome. To further expedite resolution of disputes among the parties and keep projects on track, it is therefore recommended that the parties select a few mediators on a standby basis, up front, to be available to facilitate the resolution of disputes among the parties as and when disputes arise that cannot be negotiated directly toward resolution. Indeed, in large infrastructure projects, the dispute board often includes pre-agreed-on mediators, to avoid a dispute over the selection of mediators just at the time when the parties could benefit from trying mediation toward a settlement.

Including a provision for mediation before or during the dispute board process—as proposed here, especially in PPP and related contracts—can be an important legal and "political" basis for parties to try mediation and thereby to avoid criticism for acting beyond their authority and outside the contract

---

and the FIDIC generally endorses the use of ADR mechanisms to reach such an amicable settlement. However, there is no specific requirement to attempt an amicable settlement prior to a decision by the dispute board. In practice, if a dispute is "brewing," the parties either ask the dispute board for its opinion on the situation or hire a mediator. If a dispute hardens and the dispute board renders a decision, there is a 56-day cooling-off period during which the parties are urged to resolve the dispute amicably (by whatever means they choose, it being taken for granted that this means mediation). Then, if there is no settlement, the party in whose favor the decision was made can go to arbitration for enforcement of the decision. *See infra,* note 30, on subclauses 20.4 and 20.5 of FIDIC contracts.

25 *See* http://www.cpradr.org. CPR's Banking and Financial Services Committee is actively involved in the development of best practices for use of ADR among banks and other financial institutions.

26 CPR has an excellent tool kit, available online, for early case assessment.

terms. This may be especially true for government contract counterparties. To avoid further criticism, the language could also explicitly preserve the right of any party to pursue formal legal proceedings in parallel with the mediation or at any time (in case of abuse of the mediation process by any party or threat to any party's rights or remedies of forestalling formal legal proceedings).

The continued operation of the partnering committee and the commitment to mediate disputes during the life of the project are important to ensure that there is an early warning of any changes in circumstances or challenges during the operations, or any deterioration in the assets or services. In this way, the parties can more consistently preempt the development of any disputes or "bad blood" among the parties during perhaps the most vulnerable period of the project and resolve such disputes informally, when possible.[27]

The Establishment and Role of the Embedded Dispute Board

It is also proposed that a standing subgroup of the partnering committee be established as a dispute board (DB) for the specific PPP project. The DB should be empowered to refer disputes to mediation and ultimately to adjudicate the dispute if a negotiated settlement among the parties is not possible. The DB should be able to refer a dispute to mediation either before it adjudicates the dispute or during the adjudication step, described below. The mediation and adjudication steps could run in parallel with each other, and the contract could allow mediation to continue as long as needed, even into further adjudicative processes.

The DB can be a dispute resolution board giving opinions or, in the opinion of the authors, it should be a dispute adjudication board with the power to effectively resolve a dispute in the event the disputing parties are unable to do so on their own. The proposed adjudicative mechanism would be structured as a hybrid of the "dispute review boards" contemplated for sizable publicly procured projects financed by the World Bank[28] and the "dispute adjudica-

---

27 Some argue that a project is most vulnerable to interference by a government after the sponsor has poured all its money into and completed construction of the project. Given the long life-span of some infrastructure projects, there could be a tendency for the periodic meetings to be postponed or canceled, or for stakeholder representatives to change or not participate. These factors should be taken into account in the structuring and organization of partnering committees and in setting realistic expectations based on the requirements of the project. If the project is operating smoothly, there may not be a need for a partnering committee for the full life of the project.

28 The World Bank's standard form contract for procurement of works financed by the World Bank is broadly based on the FIDIC documents. Under international competitive bidding, the World Bank's Procurement Guidelines (para. 2.43) require that the conditions of contract for goods, works, and nonconsulting services include dispute settlement provisions, and, essentially as the preferred approach, further require that contracts provide for international commercial arbitration in a neutral venue "unless the Bank has specifically agreed to waive this requirement for justified reasons such as equivalent national regulations and arbitration provisions, or [because] the contract has been awarded to a bidder from the Borrower's country." In the case of works, supply and installation, and single responsibility (including turnkey) contracts, the dispute settlement provisions shall also include "mechanisms such as dispute review boards or adjudicators, which are designed to permit a speedier dispute

tion boards" that are used extensively in the private construction industry all over the world[29] and that are enshrined in various model construction contracts, such as the widely used international procurement contracts of the International Federation of Consulting Engineers (FIDIC) for major construction works.[30]

Dispute adjudication boards were introduced into the FIDIC model documents (there are several versions) over a decade ago and are now included in harmonized contract conditions that have been adopted by most multilateral and bilateral development financial institutions, including the World Bank, for works to be financed and procured in accordance with the rules of such institutions and using the FIDIC contracts.[31] While there are slightly different structures in the different forms of FIDIC contracts, essentially the FIDIC form of dispute adjudication board includes appointment of the board at the inception of the project with powers to impose interim binding decisions on the parties pending resolution through a negotiated settlement among the parties or through a final arbitral award.[32] The World Bank's comparable provision, included in its standardized contract for publicly procured works in projects costing over $10 million to be financed by the World Bank, states that "[i]n the case of works, supply and installation, and single responsibility (including turnkey) contracts, the dispute settlement provisions shall also include mechanisms such as dispute review boards or adjudicators, which are designed

---

settlement." The World Bank's Standard Bidding Documents for Works describe the details of these boards. The World Bank's procurement guidance and template contracts are available at http://web.worldbank.org/WBSITE/EXTERNAL/PROJECTS/PROCUREMENT/0,,pagePK:84271~theSitePK:84266,00.html.

29   Various forms of DBs have been used in the U.S. construction industry since the 1960s in connection with underground construction (such as tunneling) and water management projects. Most credit the 1975 building of the Eisenhower Tunnel project in Colorado as the first such use of a DB, in the current form. *See* Shaun Beaton, *Dispute Resolution Boards in Power Project Development*, Infrastructure J. (2002), http://www.ijonline.com/pdf/pdf/review2002 review2002_power_dispute_resolution.pdf; and Cyril Chern, *Chern on Dispute Boards* 8–9 (2d ed., Wiley 2011). They are now used in other industries, as well, such as the insurance, telecoms, financial services, and maritime industries.

30   Dispute adjudication boards were introduced into the FIDIC model documents (there are several versions) over a decade ago. Subclause 20 of the FIDIC Conditions—"Red Book" (1999) and the 1999 editions of the other FIDIC contracts for major works, namely, the Conditions of Contract for Plant and Design-Build (the "Yellow Book") and Conditions of Contract for EPC/Turnkey Projects (the "Silver Book") (the three Books together being the "1999 FIDIC Books"), as updated and added to Design, Build and Operate (the "Gold Book").

31   As of 2013, the FIDIC harmonized contract conditions had been adopted by the World Bank, European Bank for Reconstruction and Development, Asian Development Bank, African Development Bank, Black Sea Trade and Development Bank, Caribbean Development Bank, Council of Europe Development Bank, and Inter-American Development Bank, among other institutions. *See* http://fidic.org/node/321.

32   *See* http://FIDIC.org; and Chern, *supra* note 29, at 8–10. Note that this mechanism permits the parties to refer the dispute to formal resolution in the courts or arbitration, as the case may be. The "interim" nature of the decision of the DB is reassuring to parties who may be worried about compromising their formal legal rights and remedies.

to permit a speedier dispute settlement."[33] The World Bank's 2011 Standard Bidding Documents for Works provide a mechanism for the establishment of a similar dispute adjudication board for public works.

There is a good deal of literature to explain the advantages of dispute adjudication boards, including that the parties consider the input and decisions of their dispute board to be at least as fair and informed as those of any court or arbitral tribunal, and that they take a fraction of the time and cost of going to arbitration. In addition, the dispute board typically helps in keeping the parties "talking" and helps to "separate the people from the problem," to use popular conflict resolution vernacular. As a result, sometimes the mere existence of the dispute adjudication board is enough to preempt a dispute from escalating into an entrenched battle among the parties. The Dispute Board Federation in Geneva has indicated, based on anecdotal research, that something approaching 98 percent of all disputes referred to a dispute board have been successfully resolved. Moreover, of the dispute board decisions that have been appealed to a court or arbitral tribunal, only a small fraction have been overturned. For example, the US$2 billion Ertan Hydroelectric Dam project in China had 40 disputes referred to its dispute review board, none of which continued to arbitration. At the US$2.5 billion Katse Dam project in South Africa, 12 disputes were referred to the dispute board, and, of these, only 1 went on to arbitration, where the DB decision was upheld. When dispute adjudication boards are not effective, it is often a result of delay in the DB's appointment because of concerns over the costs of having a standing dispute board.[34]

The dispute adjudication board mechanism required for public procurements financed by the World Bank is not specifically required for PPP contracts to be financed by the World Bank and is not routinely established up front, but rather is delayed to the time when a dispute has arisen.[35] As a matter of best practice, therefore, and in contrast to alternative dispute resolution

---

33   See Section VII, General Conditions, Clause 20, Claims, Disputes and Arbitration, which introduces a dispute board that may comprise one or three members, as may be determined by the employer and specified in the contract data (Part A of Section VIII, Particular Conditions) without regard to the estimated cost of the contract.

34   Chern, *supra* note 29, at 20–24.

35   Depending on the project and financing structure and the World Bank's involvement (e.g., a Bank loan or guaranty), PPP contracts can sometimes be procured under "open competitive bidding procedures" determined acceptable to the World Bank. In these types of PPP projects, the World Bank has flexibility with respect to requiring (or not requiring) compliance with the detailed procedures of international competitive bidding, including the provision for a dispute review board or similar mechanism contained in its standard contracts. However, a Guidance Note and Information Note on Procurement in Public-Private Partnerships do seem to suggest (specifically in the Information Note) that the contract include some mechanism for settling disputes:

     Dispute Resolution

     • The Contract must specify a procedure for handling disputes under the terms of the Contract…. [A] common form of dispute resolution involves a three stage process as follows:

mechanisms that may provide primarily for a facilitated means of reaching a negotiated settlement among the parties,[36] the proposed DB for complex, multiparty PPP and private sector infrastructure projects (whether or not they use contracts or financing from institutions that require it) would involve appointment—*at the inception of the project*—of a standing DB consisting of impartial and independent experts who monitor the progress of the works and address—*in real time*—contentious issues as they arise and before they turn into true disputes. The role of the DB should be: (1) in the first instance, to refer unresolved disputes that may have arisen to mediation for an attempt at a negotiated settlement among the parties;[37] (2) to recommend a proposed solution or problem-solving method, if the negotiated-settlement approach (e.g., mediation) is proving to be ineffective; and (3) when necessary, to impose a decision on the parties (typically after an informal opportunity for parties to present their positions through written papers, interviews with personnel, and, in some cases, an informal hearing). It is proposed that decisions of the DB should ideally be *binding* on the parties, pending final resolution of

---

- the Grantor and Concessionaire consult with each other for a fixed time period (possibly involving different levels of internal consultation) in an attempt to come to a mutually satisfactory agreement;

- if consultation fails, the parties may then (except in the case of certain types of dispute) put their case before an expert to decide. The expert is appointed from a panel (e.g. of construction or operation experts) whose appointment is regulated by the Contract. It may be appropriate in certain circumstances to substitute other forms of Alternative Dispute Resolution ("ADR") for this type of expert determination. Disputes relating to the mechanics of price variations may go to a financial expert agreed between the parties at the time, and

- if either party is dissatisfied with the expert's decision, it may refer the matter either to arbitration (itself a form of ADR) or to the courts for a final and binding decision. The method of appointing the arbitrator should be set out in the Contract.

http://intranet.worldbank.org/WBSITE/INTRANET/OPERATIONS/INTPROCUREMENT/0 „contentMDK:23051237~menuPK:60000186~pagePK:60000209~piPK:60000211~theSitePK:27 8020~isCURL:Y,00.html. Note that many parties elect to skip the internal consultation requirement as they assume that it would have taken place before the dispute had escalated. Some clients elect to forgo expert determinations or make such determinations nonbinding, preferring instead to rely on arbitration for binding resolution. With respect to partial risk guarantees of the World Bank, commercial lenders often drive the issue. Generally, the World Bank's rules require a procurement process that meets the "economy and efficiency" standard, which is largely undefined and leaves some flexibility for the World Bank to determine what makes sense within the context of the particular project.

36   *See* Chern, *supra* note 29, at 6–8. While there is a continuum of ADR techniques, ADR usually has as its objective a negotiated settlement among the parties, often reached through the facilitation of a neutral third party. There is often no agreed-on mechanism for the neutral third party (mediator) to impose a decision (especially one that is binding) on the parties.

37   Judges are increasingly ordering parties to try to reach a settlement through mediation before resorting to the court for resolution of the dispute. Indeed, in some jurisdictions, the law requires parties to try to resolve their disputes through mediation before pursuing a remedy in court. Not every dispute is a good candidate for ADR or mediation—especially as a sole mechanism for resolution of the dispute at hand, and there are often excellent reasons for pursuing formal legal remedies in court or in arbitration instead of, or in parallel with, ADR. There is ample literature on the advantages and disadvantages of the many mechanisms of ADR and the features that make a project a good candidate for ADR in the circumstances. It is also critical to find a quality mediator.

the matter in accordance with a negotiated settlement among the parties or through a final judgment or arbitral award.[38] A binding decision ensures that the partnering committee and DB process are not used as a stalling tactic.

It is worth emphasizing that, with the interim binding-decision structure, once the DB has given its decision, the decision must be adhered to. As a result, the project is not stalled or the timeline delayed while the unhappy party takes the dispute further to arbitration or review. In other words, delays are banished in this system.

Given the expertise and independence of DB members, DB decisions are usually considered efficient, rational, and extremely well tailored to the dispute and project. An experienced DB can actually prevent disputes from arising, by giving informal advice to the contracting parties and by encouraging parties to consider, in advance of any formal dispute, points of potential friction. A DB may also be creative and not necessarily tied to the letter of the underlying contract if there is some inherent deficiency or unfairness in the contract or if circumstances have fundamentally changed. As a result, DB members are often considered trusted members of the project administration and are frequently asked to give advisory opinions to the parties on some point, even before any dispute arises. Notwithstanding their flexibility in resolving disputes, DBs may not be suitable for resolving/adjudicating all the disputes that can arise in PPP transactions; in particular, they may not be able to deal with highly charged political issues and similar problems, including attempts by any party (public or private) to use the DB to renegotiate fundamentally sound terms on which parties based their decisions to enter into the project contracts. In a formal or informal project administration role, a DB can also influence the willingness and ability of the parties to perform their respective obligations. In some cases, DBs have been helpful in preventing corruption by supervising disbursements of moneys for agreed-on purposes throughout the life of the project and at the time of the final accounting among the parties. Use of a DB also has an important role to play in promoting the inclusion agenda, as during hearings; the DB is not limited to hearing evidence from the contractual parties themselves. Indeed, the DB is under a duty to find out the truth from whatever source is necessary; for example, this occasionally can include hearing members of local tribes or other affected community members on the issues.

An important feature of a DB's ability to impose a decision on the parties (whether or not the decision is binding) is the speed of the dispute reso-

---

38　There is great debate over the advantages and disadvantages of binding vs. nonbinding decisions of DBs. *See* Chern, *supra* note 29, at 4–5. Decisions of DBs as used in the United States have usually been nonbinding recommendations, whereas dispute adjudication boards used in many other parts of the world are usually empowered to render a binding decision, which can be appealed in a formal arbitration but which is binding pending a final resolution through a negotiated settlement of the parties or a final arbitral award. In its standardized documents, the International Chamber of Commerce offers parties three kinds of DBs under its Dispute Board Rules from which to select. *See* http://www.iccwbo.org/Products-and -Services/Arbitration-and-ADR/Dispute-Boards/Standard-ICC-Dispute-Boards-Clauses/.

lution. While litigation and arbitration can often take years, a standing DB can impose a decision extremely promptly in view of the members' ongoing familiarity with the project. DBs may be able to deliver such a recommended settlement or decision within as little as one month of the full exchange of information about the dispute or hearing, with a normal time limit being 84 days from the inception of the dispute and notification to the DB. The time savings can often be critical to the project's viability as well as to maintaining the parties' relationships.[39]

It is both customary and essential that the DB include members with real-world experience, including engineering, construction, commercial, and, often, legal expertise. In larger projects, it is common for there to be three members; in smaller projects, a single member with the right skill set can be adequate. Thus, a DB might consist of one person selected by the owner, one selected by the contractor, and the third (often the chair) selected by the first two, each subject to the approval of the parties to the contract.[40] The chairperson's role is critical to the fairness, credibility, and efficiency of the DB in resolving disputes. He or she must continually take all the facts and circumstances, and the parties' legitimate interests and bargaining positions, into account. This can be especially important if the DB is asked to assist in the resolution of a matter involving the affected local community.

Frequency of Dispute Board Meetings

During construction, the DB should meet frequently (e.g., every month or every other month), and make occasional visits to the site. Although a project is arguably more vulnerable to disputes during the construction phase, during operations, problems can also arise that threaten revenues and, potentially, the viability of the project. The operations phase is also the phase during which many stakeholders have a declining interest in the project; for example, if they have already secured their returns or, in the case of the government, if it has less capacity to continue to focus on the project. It is therefore recommended that the DB portion of the partnering committee remain actively involved and meet, if less frequently, at least semiannually or annually, depending on the complexity and dynamics of the project. This continuing role for the DB is important to maintaining an open environment in which to identify problems

---

39   For a good discussion about the complexities surrounding the enforceability of DB decisions, *see* Christopher R. Seppälä, *An Engineer's Dispute Adjudication Board's Decision Is Enforceable By An Arbitral Award* (White & Case Dec. 2009), available at http://www.whitecase.com/files/Publication/5787c9a1-5ebb-4858-aa74-b0543f0b5fec/Presentation/PublicationAttachment/72 45da26-5ade-4380-b638-b361a26ac8f7/article_FIDIC_conditions_Dec09.PDF.

40   Some professionals believe that permitting the appointment of a DB representative by each party can create a situation in which there is a "representative" of each party and only one true neutral in the DB. It is interesting to note that the Supreme Court of Colombia declared this process unconstitutional a number of years ago. Thus, a better practice may be to have the main stakeholders agree on the names of the three DB members. Note, too, that in some eastern European countries, in long-term concessions, DBs can have varying membership for the project depending on the nature of the dispute. *See* Chern, *supra* note 29, at 11.

and attempt to resolve them before they morph into rigid disputes and ultimately threaten to derail or destroy the viability of the project.

Dispute Board Costs

DB costs should be shared equally by the contract parties. The total cost of
establishing and operating a DB has been estimated to range from as little
as 0.015 percent to 0.05 percent of total project costs. Parties often consider
this a reasonable price to pay to avoid not only significant project delays or
cost overruns but also the delays and direct costs associated with formal legal proceedings. Indeed, some contractors bidding on contracts that include
a dispute adjudication board process have developed a practice of adjusting
downward the premium they would otherwise include in a contract tender
that includes only formal dispute resolution. The cost of a DB can often be
justified solely in terms of its contribution toward cementing and preserving
relationships among the parties, which has a particular value for parties that
may wish to do repeat business.[41]

Incorporating Partnering Committees and Dispute Boards into the Project

It is impossible for construction and other project contracts for a PPP or private infrastructure project to anticipate all events that will arise during the
project's construction and operation. Nor can these contracts fully provide for
all remedies that might be appropriate in the circumstances, even if there is a
general agreement on allocation of project risks among the parties. Many project contracts provide for dispute resolution but only briefly explain a process
that might be used by the parties leading up to formal legal proceedings. It is
critical for the parties to incorporate partnering committees, mediation, and
the DB structure into their project contracts to provide a road map for how the
parties can anticipate and resolve disputes on a real-time basis, all within the
objective of respecting the parties' original commercial understanding and
keeping the project on track.

Summary

Whether infrastructure projects for the delivery of public services are government owned and operated, PPPs, or privately financed and operated, disputes will inevitably arise. There is growing confidence in and use of dispute
adjudication boards in large infrastructure and construction projects around
the world, and these structures are often already built into publicly procured
projects. To preserve the expectations of the parties regarding the timing and
costs of PPPs and privately financed infrastructure projects, and to keep these
projects on track, it is proposed that, consistent with best practice, a partnering committee with an embedded dispute board be established and become

---

41   *See* Chern, *supra* note 29, at 19; and Beaton, *supra* note 29.

active at the inception of each project. If structured to provide a meaningful flow of information among the stakeholders, including affected local community members, a partnering committee can, together with a dispute board, be instrumental in early identification and resolution of any disputes that arise before the parties and affected local communities become entrenched in their positions. In addition, a DB can play an important role in supporting a mediated settlement agreement among the parties. When necessary, a DB can also impose an interim binding decision on the contracting parties, pending resolution of the matter through a negotiated settlement or a final arbitral award. The costs associated with such a mechanism are more than outweighed by the confidence that project stakeholders and investors will have in infrastructure investments generally in the country.

Protecting Traditional Practices and Country of Origin in Developing Countries through Fair Trade and Intellectual Property Rights

Beth Anne Hoffman and Charles Boudry

Ethiopia is widely regarded as the birthplace of coffee. With more than 30 native types of coffee plants, coffee is an integral part of Ethiopia's cultural heritage. The Ethiopian coffees Sidamo, Yirgacheffe, and Harrar are known as some of the finest coffees in the world. Coffee makes up a large portion of Ethiopia's economy, accounting for more than 30 percent of the country's total export revenues. Moreover, nearly 20 percent of Ethiopia's population earns its living through coffee. Despite coffee's importance—both on the international market and to the domestic economy—coffee farmers in Ethiopia make approximately US$1–$2 per day.

Ethiopia is a textbook example of how countries or producers can extract higher export prices on the international market through the production of specialty commodities. Since the collapse of the state-controlled coffee sector, Ethiopian coffee growers have pursued different methods to gain greater profits. There is considerable experience in country in producing certified organic and/or shade-grown coffees, as well as Fair Trade–certified coffees. Most recently, the same producers have also used registered trademarks for specific Ethiopian coffee exports.

In the mid-2000s, with considerable experience with the Fair Trade certification process, the Government of the Federal Republic of Ethiopia (Government of Ethiopia; GoE) chose to exercise its intellectual property rights (IPRs) on certain varieties of coffee beans. Early work on defining coffee within the framework of IPRs was done through a value chain analysis financed by the United Kingdom's Department for International Development (DfID) and in partnership with the Ethiopian Intellectual Property Office (EIPO). It was under the DfID project that the Ethiopian coffee trademarks were registered internationally for Harrar (and Harar), Sidamo, and Yirgacheffe coffees. During this time, much of the domestic legal framework was enacted to support the intellectual property claims. The World Bank financed a follow-up to the DfID project. Both of these projects were aimed at improving the livelihoods (and ultimately the revenues) of coffee producers in Ethiopia through Fair Trade certification and coffee name trademarking. These projects and their outcomes are described in this chapter.

The case of Ethiopian specialty coffees highlights the fact that accessing high-value or specialty markets through legal means can bring international recognition for traditional knowledge. IPRs can protect products on the international market when trademarked. The level at which interventions of this type can achieve financial success is ultimately affected by the overall openness of markets, the capacity of the legal system to assert these rights in international markets, and the overall sustainability of the intervention. Other market externalities, such as land ownership, access to credit, and the participation of women and children in the production process, were also factors in Ethiopian coffee production.

Commodities and High-Value Markets

IPRs are one way that farmers and other producers may seek to distinguish their products on the international market and earn higher profits for their products. Methods for the decommodification of coffee include Fair Trade certification, and organic, shade-grown, or sustainably grown products. Fair Trade certification is governed by standards established by private international organizations. Fair Trade standards are meant to be applied to production regardless of existing domestic legal and regulatory laws.[1]

Fair Trade began as a social movement in the 1960s. Its aim was to bring fair prices to producers in developing countries. Coffee was one of the first products that received the Fair Trade brand, and it remains the single most important Fair Trade product.[2] Produced in developing countries by smallholders, coffee is well suited for this movement.[3] Fair Trade promises fair prices for products by sidestepping certain perceived market failures or anomalies. Furthermore, Fair Trade has the promise of bringing the producer closer to the consumer. Fair Trade–certified products are largely marketed as providing ethical value-added for the consumer.

Fair Trade is not a process governed by national laws; it is a voluntary process whereby producers adhere to 10 specific international standards that can be applied to nearly any production system as long as the Fair Trade social standards are met.[4] Producers pay a Fair Trade organization to certify their product's adherence to certain criteria.[5] Certification includes site visits to producer organizations to inspect production methods. In many cases, Fair Trade standards are more stringent than domestic norms, and the onus is on

---

1   *World Development Report 2008: Agriculture for Development* 132 (World Bank 2008).

2   Loraine Ronchi, *Fair Trade and Market Failures in Agricultural Commodity Markets* (World Bank Policy Research Working Paper No. 4011, 2006).

3   Peter Leigh Taylor, *In the Market but Not of It: Fair Trade Coffee and Forest Stewardship Council Certification as Market-Based Social Change*, 33(1) World Dev. 136 (2005).

4   Kristina Sorby, *Production Costs and Income from Sustainable Coffee* 4 (World Bank Report No. 29598, 2002).

5   The Fair Trade Labeling Organization (FLO) regulates all organizations that provide Fair Trade certifications.

the producer organization(s) to meet the Fair Trade standards in order to be certified. The costs for the certification process are borne by the producers themselves and can be substantial relative to an individual farmer's or small-holder's income.

Fair Trade standards are applied independently of local laws and standards. Often, Fair Trade standards require a level of organization and regulation that may not exist in many developing countries. These standards center around 10 main issues: creating opportunities for economically disadvantaged producers; transparency and accountability; fair trading practices; payment of a fair price; ensuring no child labor and no forced labor; commitment to nondiscrimination, gender equity, and women's economic empowerment and freedom of association; ensuring good working conditions; providing capacity building; promoting Fair Trade; and respect for the environment.[6]

Without a local organization or cooperative to manage the many Fair Trade standards, a smallholder or subsistence farmer may not understand their importance or how they will be evaluated during the certification or re-certification process. Implementing these standards on an isolated or individual basis would be an onerous and expensive process. As a result, Fair Trade producers are generally organized in cooperatives to better manage the risks, to deal with the resulting bureaucracy from the application of Fair Trade standards, and to ensure quality.

Within the Fair Trade standards, some are more easily implemented than others; this was particularly the case with Ethiopian coffees. For example, relatively few smallholders or subsistence farmers use commercial inputs—such as fertilizers—when farming, which makes managing Fair Trade's environmental concerns relatively easy compared to meeting other standards. In the case of Ethiopian coffee farmers, it has been reported that approximately 90 percent do not use any inputs in growing their coffees, making them virtually organic.[7] Fair Trade studies have long posited that by adhering to Fair Trade ecological and environmental practices, growers may reap larger yields, and therefore bigger profits.[8]

Issues related to transparency and accountability, capacity building, fair pay and prompt payments, and the promotion of Fair Trade mainly apply to the management of a farmers collective. As such, their impact on a small-holder would be minimal, though it is conceivable that the collective would ask a premium or contribution to manage these risks.

---

6   See the FLO World Fair Trade Organization (WFTO) website for a complete set of the standards, available at http://www.wfto.com/?option=com_content&task=view&id=2&Itemid=14 (accessed July 31, 2013).

7   Overseas Development Institute, *Ethiopia Trademarking and Licensing Initiative: Supporting a Better Deal for Coffee Producers through Aid for Trade* (2009), available at http://r4d.dfid.gov.uk/PDF/Outputs/TradePolicy/aidfortrade.pdf.

8   Sorby, *supra* note 4, at 1.

The Fair Trade standards more difficult to implement and sustain are those related to labor. In the Ethiopian coffee sector, the majority of smallholders use informal labor practices. Subsistence farming is often characterized by a structure in which the entire family participates. This means that (pregnant) women and children are often involved in production. In many cases, domestic law permits their participation, or the law is not enforced due to the rural nature of agricultural production. Cultural norms and practices may dictate that these practices are acceptable; some of these norms and practices may directly contravene prevailing law.

The Fair Trade certification process, however, views gender and child labor standards largely in black and white. By allowing children or pregnant women to work on Fair Trade–certified farms, the local producer risks losing certification and the market premiums afforded by the Fair Trade label.[9] Similarly, many coffee farmers depend on migrant labor when harvesting. The highly transient nature of migrant labor may make it difficult for smallholders to monitor the labor supply and, ultimately, to fully adhere to Fair Trade standards.[10]

The issues of access to land and credit underlie the Fair Trade model but are not explicitly addressed by the Fair Trade standards. Access to land and land rights have a direct bearing on what crops are produced and how they are produced. Though Fair Trade welcomes and promotes the participation of women producers in its networks through its gender standard, it falls short of advocating for women's land rights. Similar to the issue of labor discussed above, cultural norms and practices may contravene national laws regarding women's inheritance of land. Without directly addressing issues of inheritance or a woman's right to hold property, the Fair Trade standard on gender may miss an opportunity to build equity and capacity within producer communities and organizations.

Linked to the issue of landholdings, access to credit can be a pressing issue for smallholders engaged in Fair Trade production. Access to credit allows farmers to buy new seeds or seedlings and fertilizers. Credit may also help a family ensure that a child receives health care or education. Credit for smallholders may be particularly difficult to obtain due to their geographic location and industry.[11] Microcredit may be better suited to subsistence farming, as the cooperatives themselves may be more able to provide for their members' needs than regular commercial banks can. Given this, and the comparatively high cost of certification, it is somewhat surprising that Fair Trade organiza-

---

9   For an interesting discussion on child labor and adherence to the Fair Trade standards, *see* Leonardo Becchetti & Marco Constantino, *The Effects of Fair Trade on Affiliated Producers: An Impact Analysis on Kenyan Farmers,* 36(5) World Development 823–842 (2008).

10   *See,* generally, Cathy Farnworth & Michael Goodman, *Growing Ethical Network: The Fair Trade Market for Raw and Processed Agricultural Products* (background paper for the *World Development Report 2008*).

11   *World Development Report 2008, supra* note 1, at 143.

tions have not taken a more proactive approach to provide a more enabling financial environment for their producers.

Credit could ultimately remove one of the biggest barriers to market entry and increase production. It could also provide a form of insurance for producing families to weather market declines. Surveys of Ethiopian coffee farmers have shown that a lack of credit greatly affects their willingness to buy agricultural inputs to boost production. In some cases, farmers have reported not wanting to take credit at all.[12]

Finally, with regard to both organically grown and shade-grown products, the majority of smallholder coffee production in Ethiopia is done through subsistence farming. The certification process for these kinds of agricultural products is fairly streamlined. Ethiopian coffees are largely—if not entirely—produced without commercial fertilizers, GMO seeds, or other means that would degrade the environment. If coffee production were to shift from smallholders to larger farms, care would need to be taken to ensure that a commitment to organic or shade-grown farming would continue to ensure certification and, ultimately, market premiums.

Intellectual Property Rights and Agricultural Products

There is a range of IPRs that can be used to seek protection for an agricultural product: trademarks, geographical indications (GIs), and traditional knowledge (TK). Each country has its own intellectual property (IP) system, but some general rules can be delineated. As with the Fair Trade standards described above, adherence to any of the methods below will create value-added commodities for export to other markets. All are relevant legal instruments for the Ethiopian coffee case: trademarks and GIs are recognized in key export markets, such as the European Union and the United States, Ethiopia's main export markets for coffee, and TK is receiving increasing attention from the international community.

Trademarks

A trademark serves to distinguish a product or service from similar goods, products, or services. It prevents confusion among consumers about the product origin and protects the owner's goodwill.[13] A trademark does not refer to the quality of the processes used to elaborate the service or manufacture the good. It attaches to a good or services regardless of either the manufacturing

---

12   Samuel Gebreselassie & Eva Ludi, *Agricultural Commercialisation in Coffee Growing Areas of Ethiopia* (research paper prepared for the Future Agricultures Consortium, Mar. 2008), available at http://r4d.dfid.gov.uk/PDF/Outputs/Futureagriculture/coffee_paper.pdf.

13   Maria Brownell, *Coffee Trademark Licensing for Farmers: Brewing a Farmer-Owned Brand*, 14 Drake J. Agric. L. 299 (2009).

process or the location of the manufacturing process. The value of a trademark depends on the intrinsic quality of the product or service itself.[14]

Under U.S. trademark law, a party can file an application with the United States Patent and Trademark Office (USPTO) to register a word, a logo, a device, a slogan, a package design, a scent, a color, or a shape. If the application is accepted, the registered trademark becomes the private property of the registering party and can be used or licensed only by that party on the goods or services identified in the application.[15]

A trademark owner has a right to permit nonowners to use the owner's mark, in which case the parties will enter into a license agreement. A trademark owner can also prevent others from using the same or a similar mark on otherwise similar products. In the United States, trademark owners must protect their trademark by policing for its unauthorized use and can actively enforce their right by excluding every other entity from using their trademark, in order to prevent it from becoming diluted or generic.[16]

A trademark for a geographic region raises some issues because it gives the owner the exclusive right to use the trademarked name commercially. Generally, a geographically descriptive term cannot be granted a trademark because it is only descriptive, the reason being that all place-names should remain available for use by all competitors. However, this rule has an exception, and to overcome the descriptive nature of a geographic term, the term must have acquired a "secondary meaning." A term has a secondary meaning when the product is considered significant beyond the physical location of the goods.[17] Thus, when a geographic term is associated with qualities independent of its physical location, the secondary meaning test is proven, and the product can be registered. This test of secondary meaning was applied to the Ethiopian case.

Geographical Indications

A GI is a name or sign used on certain products that indicates the region of origin of a specific good or service and relates to some standard of quality associated with the good or service. There is no universal definition for what constitutes a GI. It can include certification marks, designated GIs, protected designations of origin, protected GIs, and appellations of origin.[18]

---

14   Mary O'Kicki, *Lessons Learned from Ethiopia's Trademarking and Licensing Initiative: Is the European Union's Position on Geographical Indication Really Beneficial for Developing Nations?*, 6 Loy. U. Chi. Intl. L. Rev. 324–325 (2008–2009), at 319.

15   *See U.S. Trademark Law: Rules of Practices and Federal Statutes* (U.S. Pat. & Trademark Off., Aug. 2012), available at http://www.uspto.gov/trademarks/law/tmlaw.pdf.

16   Brownell, *supra* note 13, at 300.

17   *Id.*, at 296.

18   O'Kicki, *supra* note 14, at 321.

The United States and the European Union have different approaches regarding GIs. Under U.S. trademark law, GIs are registered and protected with the USPTO as a certification mark and must meet the secondary meaning requirement to be registered. A certification mark indicates that the good or service bearing the mark possesses certain qualities or is made according to traditional methods, as determined by a party, such as a trade group or a government entity, including state agricultural agencies, but not by a manufacturer itself. The mark indicates that the manufacturer adhered to third-party standards when producing the product. Certification marks tend to be owned by a collective group that establishes the standard or criteria that a product must meet to bear the organization's certification mark.[19]

There are several differences between a trademark and a certification mark in the U.S. IPR system. First, a certification mark is used by a third party, not by the original manufacturer itself, to indicate some attribute or quality of the goods. Second, while trademark owners are required to prevent every other entity from using their trademark, a U.S. certification mark owner cannot exclude other manufacturers that meet the standards and criteria as defined by the registered certification mark. In this respect, the U.S. system of certification marks creates opportunities for new producers and enables them to be associated with a particular certification mark, which can be a very valuable asset. A study found that consumers would be willing to pay 60 percent more for a wine labeled "Napa Valley" than for a wine labeled "California."[20]

In the European Union, GIs are given a registration and protection system independently of trademarks. This is a core element of the EU trade and agriculture policy, and the European Union established a single system for the registry of GIs for some products intended for human consumption and certain foodstuffs, but not all. This system provides protection for two categories of GIs: protected designation of origin and protected GIs. The EU system also offers protection for traditional specialty guaranteed.[21]

A protected designation of origin covers agricultural products and foodstuffs that are produced, processed, and prepared in a given geographical area using recognized know-how. Thus, a protected designation of origin product is tied both to the land through production and to the people who process and prepare the good. It is important to note that the European Union places a high value on the human skill associated with the preparation of a good.[22] In order to qualify for GI protection, at least one of the stages of production, processing, or preparation must take place in the geographical area. Because only

---

19   *Id.*

20   *Id.*, at 321 & note 78.

21   *See,* generally, the European Commission's definitions of geographical indicators and traditional specialties for definitions and lists of specific products, and so on, *Geographical Indications and Traditional Specialties,* available at http://ec.europa.eu/agriculture/quality/schemes/ (accessed Apr. 23, 2013).

22   O'Kicki, *supra* note 14, at 323.

one of the three stages needs to occur within the designated region, protected GIs are not as closely tied to the land as protected designation of origins. As for the traditional specialty guaranteed protection, it highlights the traditional character, either in the composition or in means of production, and it is not directly connected to the land.[23]

The TRIPS Agreement and Geographical Indications

Geographic origin has been cited in trade for over a century, and in their current form, GIs are governed by the 1995 WTO Agreement on Trade-Related Aspects of Intellectual Property Rights (TRIPS Agreement). Article 22.1 of the TRIPS Agreement defines GIs as "indications which identify a good as originating in the territory of a Member, or a region or locality in that territory, where a given quality, reputation or other characteristic of the good is essentially attributable to its geographic origin." This broad definition encompasses many of the different permutations of GIs that are legally recognized by WTO member countries.[24] Moreover, the TRIPS Agreement (Articles 41 ss.) requires that all WTO members provide a certain level of protection for IPRs, including the legal means for a member country to assert and enforce its IPRs.

The TRIPS Agreement provides two levels of protection for GIs, depending on the product considered. For products other than wines and spirits (Article 22), a GI is protected to the extent it does not cause consumer confusion or mislead the public as to the origin of the product. The protection of a GI is therefore not absolute. An appellation such as "Camembert-like cheese made in Canada" is permitted, since the origin is clearly mentioned. Wines and spirits benefit from an additional protection under Article 23: GIs can be used only for products that originated in the place indicated by the GI in question. Thus, only producers of Champagne from the Champagne region of France can use the term "Champagne" to identify their products. "Champagne-like" and "produced by the Champagne method" are prohibited product designations under the TRIPS Agreement.[25] The European Union advocates that the protection granted to wines and spirits be extended to all registered GIs.[26] This means that product designations such as "Camembert-like cheese made in Canada" would no longer be authorized if the European Union succeeds in its efforts.

The strong legal protection granted to wine and spirit GIs under Article 23 of the TRIPS Agreement is similar to the legal protection provided by the trademark system. For example, the GoE has registered the word "Harar" as a trademark for its coffee in several countries (see below for a description of the

---

23   *See Geographical Indications and Traditional Specialties, supra* note 21.

24   O'Kicki, *supra* note 14.

25   *Id.*, at 324.

26   The Special Session of the TRIPS Council in WTO discussed at length the issue of applying GI for wine. This discussion can be found at Communication from the European Communities, *Geographical Indications*, TN/C/W/26, TN/IP/W/11 (June 14, 2005), available at http://www.wto.org/english/tratop_e/trips_e/gi1_docs_e.htm (accessed Apr. 23, 2013).

Ethiopian case), so only the GoE has the legal right to use and to license the word "Harar" for coffees. "Harar-like" and "in the style of Harar" are unacceptable uses of the word. In the same vein, only producers from the Champagne region, meeting the criteria described in the GI registration, can use the word "Champagne" in their label.[27]

Traditional Knowledge

Traditional knowledge (TK) is not protected under the TRIPS Agreement. Currently, countries seeking IP protection for TK in the international market must fit it into one of the IP categories that is protected under the TRIPS Agreement. In principle, because GIs are not "intended to reward innovation, but rather to reward members of an established group or community adhering to traditional practices belonging to the culture of that community or group," it is understandable that some developing nations would embrace the GI system as a means to protect their TK.[28] In other cases, communities have sought to establish trademarks.

TK has received increasing attention in a range of recent international policy discussions. There have been considerable efforts to enshrine TK protection in the law—most notably with the World Intellectual Property Organization (WIPO's) establishment of the Intergovernmental Committee on Intellectual Property and Genetic Resources, Traditional Knowledge, and Folklore (the IGC).[29] The IGC's mission is to draft and reach an agreement on an international legal instrument (or instruments) that will ensure the effective protection of TK, traditional cultural expressions, and genetic resources.[30] The IGC suggests the following definition(s) for TK: "[refers to]/[includes]/[means] know-how, skills, innovations, practices, teachings and learnings of [indigenous [peoples] and [local communities]]/[or a state or states] that are dynamic and evolving, and that are intergenerational/and that are passed on from generation to generation, and which may subsist in codified, oral or other forms."[31]

Efforts to protect TK by a new system of IPRs focus almost exclusively on the knowledge of indigenous people. The proponents of a new legal regime invoke concepts of property to enhance the protection of TK. A 2009 WIPO report states that "holders of TK should be entitled to fair and equitable sharing

---

27   O'Kicki, *supra* note 14, at 325.

28   *Id.*

29   Stephen R. Munzer & Kal Raustiala, *The Uneasy Case for Intellectual Property Rights in Traditional Knowledge*, 27 Cardozo Arts & Ent. L.J. 37, 38 (2009).

30   WIPO uses the term *traditional knowledge* to encompass traditional knowledge, genetic resources, and traditional cultural expressions. For more on how all three subtopics fit under WIPO's TK classification, *see* http://www.wipo.int/tk/en/igc/index.html (accessed Apr. 23, 2013).

31   *Protection of Traditional Knowledge: Draft Articles Rev. 2* (Apr. 26, 2013), available at http://www.wipo.int/edocs/mdocs/tk/en/wipo_grtkf_ic_24/wipo_grtkf_ic_24_facilitators_document_rev_2.pdf (accessed Aug. 5, 2013).

of benefits arising from the use of their knowledge."[32] The objectives of the TK legal protection would be to promote respect for TK; deter the misappropriation of TK; empower TK holders, who are typically marginalized indigenous communities; and protect tradition-based innovation.[33] Proponents advocate the creation of sui generis rights via international treaties and the establishment of global databases of TK. There are those who oppose an establishment of a legal instrument to protect TK, voicing concern that this type of IP protection would be "contrary to how many indigenous communities conceive of their cultural heritage."[34] The concept of TK will continue to evolve with the continued work of the IGC and the overall efforts of WIPO.

The Case for Ethiopian Fine Coffees

By the mid-2000s, the GoE already had enacted a considerable legal framework to protect Ethiopia's cultural and agricultural heritage. This included, inter alia, Trademark Registration & Protection Proclamation No. 501/2006; Access to Genetic Resources and Community Knowledge and Community Rights No. 482/2006; the Plant Breeders' Right Proclamation; Copyright and Neighboring Rights Protection Proclamation No. 410/2000; and Research and Conservation of Cultural Heritage Proclamation No. 209/2000.

In the international sphere, Ethiopia has been a member of WIPO since 1998. The GoE is also a signatory to the Convention on Biological Diversity. It signed the Nagoya Protocol on Access to Genetic Resources and the Fair and Equitable Sharing of Benefits and the Cartagena Protocol on Biosafety to the Convention of Biological Diversity, as well as the International Treaty on Plant and Genetic Resources for Food and Agriculture.

Coffee historically has been a major export for Ethiopia. The collapse of the International Coffee Agreements in the late 1980s and the almost simultaneous collapse of the state-run coffee trade that occurred with the overthrow of the Derg led to disarray and a precipitous drop in coffee earnings for the country. State-run coffee cooperatives collapsed, leaving many to rebuild after losing their records and premises due to looting. Over time, and with the reestablishment of coffee cooperatives and export agencies, the coffee sector began to rebuild. With market liberalization, prices paid to producers began to rise by the 1990s, and the government allowed some gourmet coffees and organics to be sold directly on the international market.

Private land ownership, which had been abolished by the Derg, remained state controlled in the post-Derg (post-1991) period. This fact is important because all of the country's land belongs to the GoE and the government claims

---

32   WIPO, *Intellectual Property and Traditional Knowledge* 11 (Booklet No. 2), available at http://www.wipo.int/freepublications/en/tk/920/wipo_pub920.pdf; cited in Munzer & Raustiala, *supra* note 29, at note 3.

33   Munzer & Raustiala, *supra* note 29, at 39.

34   *Id.*

the right to direct all economic initiatives. Recognizing that coffee would re-
main one of the country's chief exports, the GoE's first Poverty Reduction
Strategy paper—*A Plan for Accelerated and Sustained Development to End Poverty
(PASDEP) (2005–2009/10)* noted that

> due consideration will also be given to the production of high value/
> cash crops like fruit and vegetables, coffee, tea and spices which
> could play a significant role in improving the living standards of
> smallholder farmers and strengthening the foreign currency earning
> capacity of the country.[35]

The PASDEP gave the GoE a strong role in supporting the coffee production. This included targeted assistance to coffee preparation industries and the
provision of adequate warehouses and storage facilities both in the *woredas*
and centrally. Moreover, maintaining the quality of the coffee exports was a
priority for the GoE. In this regard, the PASDEP called for, inter alia,

- Improving the quality and agricultural products to supply export markets, improving existing standards and produce new
  ones, and ensure the introduction and control of proper observation of standards;

- Establishment of coffee and tea inspection and auction centers
  in major coffee growing *woredas*.[36]

It was against this backdrop that the GoE began to work with DfID to
develop its ability to enforce and manage its IPRs internationally in the early
2000s. As part of DfID's efforts, and in order to build capacity within the GoE
to support these claims, the project provided technical assistance to the Ethiopia Intellectual Property Office, established in 2003.

The overall aim of DfID's support was to afford coffee producers a means to
negotiate coffee prices through the operation of a transparent market. The project was based on a value chain analysis and a value capture strategy that entailed the use of trademarks, branding and licensing, and brand management.

DfID brought together the biggest actors in the national coffee market
with the creation of the Ethiopian Fine Coffee Stakeholder Committee. This
committee included local coffee farmers cooperatives, the relevant line ministries, EIPO, and the Ethiopian Coffee Exports Association Board. Through
the creation of this committee, as well from as the direct support to EIPO, the
DfID project assisted in crafting trademark strategies and policies to maintain
and protect the value of four high-value Ethiopian coffees—Harrar, Harar (another trademarked name for Harrar), Sidamo, and Yirgacheffe—on the international market.

---

35 Government of Ethiopia, Ministry of Finance and Economic Development (MoFED), *Ethiopia:
    Building on Progress, A Plan for Accelerated and Sustained Development to End Poverty (PASDEP)
    (2005/06-2009/10)*, vol. 1: *Main Text* (MoFED, Sept. 2006), available at http://siteresources
    .worldbank.org/INTETHIOPIA/Resources/PASDEP_Final_English.pdf.

36 *Id.*, at 106.

The DfID project undertook a value chain analysis for these Ethiopian coffees. The objective of the value chain analysis was to ensure that value was accrued at the production end of the coffee value chain. The DfID project also worked with a law firm on a pro bono basis to register the four coffees in 33 international markets, including the United States, the European Union, Japan, Canada, Australia, and Saudi Arabia. Early indications from this trademarking effort showed an increase in export prices on the order of 50–100 percent.[37] Trademarks may be more lucrative for producers to use, because they require less up front as compared to Fair Trade. This is important for a farmer making only a slight margin on products and is a different approach from Fair Trade certification, which requires compliance with a number of standards and relatively costly site inspections before crops are certified.

The DfID effort also sought to establish more transparent mechanisms for exporting. The collapse of the Derg regime and the resulting liberalization of the coffee sector resulted in the corresponding collapse of the old systems and agencies supporting Ethiopia's coffee exports. The Ethiopian Coffee Purchase and Sales Enterprise and the Ethiopian Coffee Export Enterprise emerged as government-controlled agencies in the early post-Derg period. By the 2000s, even these state-run companies were being phased out and replaced by private entities. Work was under way in Ethiopia to create a nationwide commodity exchange linked to various warehouses to handle coffee auctions.

Maintaining the brands established with DfID assistance, however, meant that coffee farmers needed to understand and apply the brand and ensure that quality was preserved. This would be a long-term process, as historically there had been little emphasis on coffee quality in Ethiopia. The World Bank would help finance, *inter alia*, a government-sponsored campaign to raise awareness among coffee farmers.

Trademark Dispute with Starbucks

In March 2005, the GoE filed trademark applications with USPTO for three of Ethiopia's specialty coffees: Harrar, Sidamo, and Yirgacheffe. This application took some companies, including U.S.-based Starbucks, by surprise. In 2004, Starbucks had applied for trademark registration of a limited-edition coffee. Shirkina Sun-Dried Sidamo. Ethiopia, working with Oxfam and a U.S.-based pro bono law firm, requested that Starbucks withdraw its trademark application to allow its own trademark application to move forward. Starbucks' initial response to Ethiopia was that a certification mark or a GI was a more appropriate designation for Ethiopia's heritage coffees.[38] Eventually, Starbucks withdrew its application for Shirkina Sun-Dried Sidamo, stating it was a limited-edition coffee, but the dispute did not end there.

---

37   Overseas Development Institute, *supra* note 7, at 10.

38   O'Kicki, *supra* note 14, at 329–330.

The National Coffee Association (NCA), representing U.S. coffee roasters, importers, retailers, and distributors, including Starbucks, objected to Ethiopia's applications for trademarking Harrar and Sidamo by filing notices of opposition with USPTO. The NCA contended that Sidamo and Harrar historically have been used in the United States. Furthermore, the NCA posted that these were generic terms for coffee from geographical regions of Ethiopia and therefore did not meet the legal criteria to qualify for trademark registration. This point of view was adopted by USPTO, which did not register these trademarks.[39]

Ethiopia appealed this decision, arguing that the names had acquired secondary meaning to consumers (that is, consumers recognized the words as a source of quality and for characteristics of the coffee) and were not generic words for coffee. Ethiopia eventually succeeded, and, in February 2008, the USPTO recognized Ethiopia's qualification under the secondary-meaning test and granted Ethiopia a trademark for the coffee-producing regions.[40] Ultimately, Starbucks signed a licensing agreement with Ethiopia recognizing Ethiopia's ownership of the names.

The World Bank Intellectual Property Rights Project

The World Bank coffee project came about at a time when the Bank was actively looking into Fair Trade as a way to raise profits for farmers and induce development. In the lead-up to the 2008 World Development Report, *Agriculture for Development* (WDR), considerable research was done by the Bank on the impacts of Fair Trade. *Agriculture for Development* recognized the growing trend of producing high-value or niche agricultural products for export. The WDR called this trend "decommodification," as producers sought alternative markets for these products.[41] Yet, the report offered no specific policy recommendations on Fair Trade as a result of this research. On the contrary, the WDR cited a number of concerns about Fair Trade, related to rationing of Fair Trade products in the export markets due to saturation, and the high cost for farmers to do business with the Fair Trade organizations themselves.[42] The report made recommendations for governments to establish enabling environments for agriculture and agricultural exports, with specific support to smallholders through strong producer organizations and more transparent market mechanisms.

IPRs fit squarely within the World Bank's operational policies. Specifically, the Bank's Indigenous Peoples Policy (Operational Policy 4.10) of the same period endorses the use of IPRs as one of nine initiatives to support

---

39   *See* http://tsdr.uspto.gov (case no. 78589307) for the proceedings documents; cited in O'Kicki, *supra* note 14, note 133.

40   An Ethiopian trademark for Yirgacheffe was awarded by the USPTO in August 2006.

41   *World Development Report 2008, supra* note 1, at 132.

42   *Id.*, at 133.

development and poverty reduction.[43] The policy further recognizes cultural ties to lands, as well as the species and fauna of indigenous peoples.[44] The World Bank's support for Ethiopian coffee fits well within this framework.

The GoE first approached the World Bank for technical assistance with EIPO and for the protection and enforcement of the country's IPRs. The request came in as EIPO's involvement with DfID was drawing to a close. At the time the World Bank grant was developed, the Ethiopian government claimed that Ethiopian coffee names had been misappropriated in both local and foreign markets, the most visible example of which was the U.S. trademark dispute with Starbucks. The GoE asserted that the country's unique cultural, biotech, and agricultural assets held considerable promise as IP assets on the international market. With the proper branding and enforcement of the country's IPRs, these products could be appropriately valued and could generate the export income anticipated by the government. The promotion and enforcement of IPRs was seen as an effective policy tool to promote social and economic development in the country.

The World Bank project, Managing and Enforcing Intellectual Property Rights: Creating a Driver of Growth—an Institutional Development Fund (IDF) grant—was approved in June 2006 for US$496,000.[45] The project closed in October 2010. The project objective was to strengthen the capacity of EIPO to manage, brand, and protect IPRs in Western markets. Although the country had considerable potential for branding other IPRs for other products, such as leather, flowers, spices, and traditional medicine knowledge, the IDF grant focused solely on coffee. The main beneficiaries of the project activities were EIPO, Ethiopian coffee growers' organizations, and coffee growers more generally.

The grant had three main activities: to assess IP assets within the country, building local capacity to undertake these types of assessments; to build the capacity of Ethiopian administrative and justice sector teams to enforce IPRs; and to empower local IPR owners.

Due to delays in project approval, the IP asset valuation exercise was ultimately done with the assistance of DfID prior to that project's closing. The Starbucks case helped transform EIPO's role, further transforming the

---

43　The 2005 Indigenous Peoples Policy was important in that this version of the policy contained nine specific product lines for which Bank-financed projects could actively provide assistance to indigenous communities. One of these product lines dealt specifically with intellectual property rights. OP 4.10, para. 22(h).

44　For purposes of the World Bank–financed Ethiopian coffee project, however, the policy framework was adapted to the circumstances but not applied because the GoE does not recognize indigenous peoples.

45　This type of grant is given to build just-in-time capacity for a discrete need within the government. Prior to 2011, the IDF gave priority to grant proposals that focused on one of five areas: public expenditure management and financial accountability; procurement; results-oriented monitoring and evaluation systems; systemic legal and judicial reforms; or nonfocus or other. The Ethiopia IDF grant focused on systemic legal and judicial reforms.

agency's responsibilities and changing the scope of many of the planned IPR activities. In mid-2007, EIPO embarked on a process of reorganization with World Bank support. It sought to broaden its responsibilities from serving as a conventional IP registry to more broadly engaging in advocacy activities on a national, regional, and international scale. EIPO placed the country's innovations and products at the fore with this restructuring. As part of the reorganization and expansion of its activities, EIPO proposed to undertake greater outreach to small and median enterprises within Ethiopia, as well as build greater awareness of IPRs in local universities and industries.

A large portion of the grant activities involved the creation of a licensing and branding program within EIPO. Originally, the World Bank project envisioned the creation of specialized capacities within EIPO to manage trademark registration, foreign supply chain licensing, brand management, and stakeholder engagement. Recognizing that there was low recognition and knowledge of IPRs within various government agencies, the World Bank project scaled back its original aim to create a licensing program within EIPO. Rather, a comprehensive training program was designed and implemented using a train-the-trainers approach. Under this initiative, four EIPO staff members were trained on issues relevant to certification.

The project sought to expand the number of coffees trademarked in international markets. EIPO chose to pursue the licensing of Limu and Nekemte coffees internationally, first by developing a value capture analysis for these two coffees. Brand guidelines were also drafted for these two coffees, based largely on the precedent set by the guidelines developed for Harar, Harrar, Sidamo, and Yirgacheffe coffees. The project engaged the same U.S.-based law firm that had worked on the Starbucks case and the trademark claims for the four trademarked coffees on a pro bono basis.[46] At the project's conclusion, it was estimated that the legal services provided for the trademarking of these two coffees cost close to US$1.0 million, more than twice the total amount of the grant. This figure is relatively conservative; a considerable amount of legal work was done drafting model licensing contracts and creating an umbrella brand standard and trademark.

As part of EIPO's new advocacy and outreach efforts, an Intellectual Property Rights Center was established in Addis Ababa to house information regarding IPRs. The center is open to the public. EIPO launched a website in Aramaic to describe EIPO's role and responsibilities. In addition, the grant financed a number of outreach activities to empower local producers, including television and radio programs, as well as leaflets regarding the role of intellectual property in their own personal lives and on the role that EIPO has played in the enjoyment and enforcement of those rights.

---

46   Ultimately, this activity led to the registration of only one coffee in one international market. This was due to a dispute between EIPO and the pro bono law firm over minor, nonlegal fees paid by the firm in the course of licensing. EIPO disputed the firm's claim that the government needed to pay the charges. At the end of the project, EIPO and the firm were in a stalemate over the payment of the fees and additional licensing.

The grant's more successful activities involved the outreach activities related to IP and coffee growers themselves. A number of radio and television programs were produced and aired on local stations to empower local IPR owners on IPR protection. These activities were targeted specifically at small producers, cooperatives, local business owners, and IP lawyers.

The grant was active in creating and disseminating local knowledge regarding IPRs. EIPO delivered specific training to the coffee farmers cooperatives and other stakeholders regarding the importance of maintaining the respective brands. Through their own experiences with producing other decommoditized coffees—such as organics, shade-grown, and Fair Trade coffees—various Ethiopian coffee farmers unions[47] were aware of the importance of quality and began to ensure quality in their own production. Furthermore, the licensing agreements to use the trademarked brand names of coffee were royalty free for the coffee farmers, meaning that any additional profit accrued to the coffees at the point of sale accrued to the coffee farmer.

The grant had the least success in building the capacity of local Ethiopian administrative and justice sector teams. This was due in large part to the general outward/export orientation of the project. Local judges, lawyers, investigators, and other government officials were less involved in the enforcement of IPRs. There was little buy-in for the project's activities by the customs and other enforcement officials.

Project Outcomes

The World Bank project built on a number of crucial building blocks already in place in Ethiopia. The fact that the project implementation was not dependent on the passage of new laws or structures—most of which were created under the DfID project—meant that the time frames for implementation were short. Furthermore, when the project was designed, it was conceivable that the project outcomes could be met by the end of the project's original three-year term. It was also conceivable that certain targets for capacity building within EIPO and among the coffee growers could be met during the original implementation period.

The World Bank project largely succeeded due to the presence of an enabling framework for trade within the country. On a much larger scale, and as measured by the website produced by Doing Business, it is more costly, time-consuming, and bureaucratic to export out of Sub-Saharan Africa than it is to export out of Latin America.[48] Africa-specific studies, notably a World Bank

---

47   A number of coffee cooperatives emerged in the post-Derg era. These include the Oromia Coffee Farmers Cooperative Union, the Yirgacheffe Coffee Farmers Cooperative Union, the Sidama Coffee Farmers Cooperative Union, and the Kaffa Forest Coffee Farmers Cooperative Union.

48   Cf. data in *Trading across Borders*. Published by the Doing Business Project, World Bank Group, available at http://www.doingbusiness.org/data/exploretopics/trading-across -borders (accessed Apr. 1, 2013).

report on mango production in Mali, cite the need to leverage economies of scale though the creation and support of producer organizations in country.[49] The DfID and World Bank projects tapped into well-organized, existing coffee farmers cooperatives to boost exports and ensure export quality. The considerable experience in country with Fair Trade branding as well as organic branding on the international market helped to create a culture of quality coffee.

A Success Story: The Oromia Coffee Farmers Cooperative Union

The Oromia Coffee Farmers Cooperative Union (OCFCU) was established in 1999 in Addis Ababa to facilitate the direct export of coffee produced by small farmers organized in cooperatives throughout the state. It is the oldest of the existing coffee farmers unions; it was one of the most active coffee farmers cooperative unions under the World Bank project. The OCFCU operates in Oromia regional state, where 65 percent of the country's coffee is grown. It is responsible for processing, marketing, and commercializing coffee for its members. OCFCU comprises 197 primary cooperatives, representing some 200,000 farming families. The OCFCU oversees quality control and a processing plant and has established a bank for cooperative members.

The World Bank project also benefitted from the Ethiopian Commodities Exchange (ECX), established in 2008. The ECX was initially supported by the GoE. The ECX provided a transparent, real-time platform for trading coffee and other commodities. It also served as an independent verification body for the qualities and types of coffees delivered. Compared to the Derg era, when the state controlled coffee trade through the creation of cooperatives, set prices, and mandated only two auctions per year, the ECX provides coffee farmers greater transparency, timeliness, and assurance that their coffee will be marketed correctly, reducing transaction costs for farmers and traders.

A long-standing history of coffee exports in country, an existing culture of agricultural cooperatives, and a growing appreciation for quality within the coffee farmers cooperative unions were the main factors that were already present. Furthermore, the government's own policies to promote specialty coffees through special pricing mechanisms, and later EIPO's support of IPRs in international markets, helped boost exports and profits.

On the whole, the use of trademarks did bring better prices to producers and farmers in Ethiopia. Farmers saw the greatest increases in profits when producing a combination of Fair Trade, organic, and trademarked coffees. WIPO estimates that prior to the enforcement of IPRs, Ethiopian smallholders received approximately US\$1 per kilo of coffee; the final market price ranged from US\$20 to US\$28 per kilo. WIPO also reported that Yirgacheffe farmers' income doubled in 2007 with the use and enforcement of IPRs.[50] This rise in

---

49   Morgane Danielou, Patrick Labaste, & Jean-Michel Voisard, *Linking Farmers to Markets: Exporting Malian Mangoes to Europe* (World Bank Africa Region Working Paper No. 60, 2003).

50   *See* communications of WIPO: *The Coffee War: Ethiopia and the Starbucks Story*, available at http://www.wipo.int/ipadvantage/en/details.jsp?id=2621 (accessed Apr. 4, 2013).

prices had a direct impact on local coffee-farming communities and individuals. The coffee unions have self-reported an increase in investments in coffee-producing communities through the provision of physical infrastructure for schools, the creation of health posts, and the development of freshwater supplies, among other developments.[51]

The project had mixed success when it came to promoting IP issues internally. By the end of the project, there was considerable awareness among local coffee producers regarding their ability to use IP to extract a higher price on the market for their coffees. The project had more limited traction in discussing these issues with government officials, such as judges and customs officials. For a majority of these officials, IP will remain a theoretical issue until clear domestic cases of IP infringement arise. Some observers have hinted at the fact that kickbacks may be at play with regard to inspectors and those involved in the export trade. Maintaining clear governance structures and transparency, with direct oversight by concerned stakeholders, will be the only way to ensure that such problems are minimized.

By the end of the World Bank project, EIPO had let a number of trademark licenses lapse on the international market. Trademarks in the United States require constant policing and research to enforce. Keeping licenses and trademarks current requires a level of internal organization, planning, and financial resources that fell outside the scope of this project. This leads to questions regarding the overall viability and sustainability of IPR interventions such as this.

A Possible Way Forward

Fair Trade and trademarking (through the enforcement of IPRs) can help promote development within countries that pursue export-led growth. Both Fair Trade and IPRs have their strengths and their weaknesses. A combination of the two may provide the best way to promote equitable development while helping coffee farmers mitigate prevailing market risks.

World Bank research has shown that Fair Trade can deliver higher prices to producers and access to high-value markets.[52] The *World Development Report 2008: Agriculture for Development* recognized that by linking agribusiness and smallholders, there could be reductions in rural poverty.[53] As illustrated by the Ethiopian case, Fair Trade certification and IPRs can complement existing trade regimes. There is evidence that Fair Trade creates real impacts at the local level through the creation of a more level playing field for coffee farmers. There is also evidence of concrete improvements in Ethiopian Fair Trade pro-

---

51   See the table *Life Improving*, published by the Oromia Coffee Farmers Cooperative Union, available at http://www.oromiacoffeeunion.org/LifeImproving.php (accessed Apr. 4, 2013).

52   Ronchi, *supra* note 2, at 1.

53   *World Development Report 2008*, *supra* note 1, at 135.

ducer communities through the building of health posts, schools, and clean drinking wells.

At the same time, the same research shows that Fair Trade does not supplant international trade mechanisms. As a single cash crop, coffee faces a number of externalities on the international market that are difficult to overcome. Regardless of special trademarks or brands, coffee prices remain volatile on the international market. Like conventional coffee, Fair Trade coffee exports can face market saturation. Ethiopian smallholders, cognizant of the risk of solely producing coffee, often raise other crops as well as produce to feed their own families.

Furthermore, Fair Trade mechanisms cannot wholly protect Fair Trade products from market failures. This was certainly the case for Ethiopian coffee in the fall of 2012, as local prices for coffee were higher than international prices. Many coffee farmers turned to the production of local consumable products to weather the drop in international prices. Without support to further diversify exports—both on a general level and with respect to the protection of the country's TK through IPRs—Ethiopia will lose market share and development potential.

However noble Fair Trade's objectives are, it can create unintended incongruences within markets. A community risks considerable harm by losing Fair Trade certification but may feel disempowered to apply the standard for cultural or financial reasons. Indeed, the decertification process would inflict considerable financial harm on a community or producer organization, as the fees paid to the Fair Trade certifying organization are substantial. These opportunity costs—and the level of risk involved to the producer itself—may discourage current and new entrants into the Fair Trade market.

With respect to Fair Trade's child labor standards, producers can quickly fall into trouble and lose Fair Trade certification if children perform tasks during (re)certification site visits. Some research has indicated that while labeling (such as Fair Trade) may be a deterrent for using child labor in the production of the Fair Trade goods, this labor pool may be shifted into domestic production where child labor is not an issue.[54] One study of organic and Fair Trade producers in Kenya showed that they employed virtually the same (high) levels of child labor as conventional means of production.[55]

Building greater outreach on this standard, in particular by international Fair Trade groups to local producers, may go a long way toward changing attitudes regarding these practices. Furthermore, there may be real and pressing economic needs for children to be involved in production. If Fair Trade organizations would adopt a more graded or phased application of this standard,

---

54   Jean-Marie Baland & Cédric Duprez, *Are Fair Trade Labels Effective against Child Labour?*, 12 (Discussion Paper No. 6259, Ctr. Econ. Policy Research, 2007), available at http://www.cepr .org/pubs/dps/DP6259.asp.

55   Leonardo Becchetti & Marco Constantino, *The Effects of Fair Trade on Affiliated Producers: An Impact Analysis on Kenyan Farmers*, 36(5) World Dev. 823–842 (2008).

one where children would attend school but could also work for a prescriptive amount or period of time, communities could reap the double benefits of Fair Trade and increased human capital.

In the case of the Fair Trade gender standard, its promotion of women's rights within the production of Fair Trade–labeled goods is commendable. Yet, the standard is silent regarding the support of a woman's right to hold land. Women, particularly in Africa, can face tremendous obstacles to owning and working their own farms. Although much has been written about large-scale land grabs in Africa, smaller land grabs within communities over inheritance tend to impact women the most.

Female land ownership in Ethiopia—for example, of land received by women through post-Derg land distribution or through the death of their husbands—does not automatically give the women a right to cultivate their own fields. Labor restrictions do not allow women to use oxen to plow fields. Many women keep their fields in coffee production because they are able to hire migrants and temporary labor to work during the harvests more easily than if they are growing other crops.[56] Continued restrictions on women working their own land, and dwindling pools of migrant workers, will have a negative, long-term impact on women heads of household if the economy continues to diversify and offers more skilled, higher-paid jobs.

The IPR approach to trademarking of coffees, as noted above, has an external focus and therefore does not have the same level of impact on social development within the coffee-producing communities. Unlike with Fair Trade certification, a farmer does not face (substantial) up-front costs to the trademark or brand using IPRs, as the Ethiopian licensing agreements are royalty free. The trademark approach is less interventionist for the individual coffee farmers, although coffee farmers associations may pass some of their overhead costs on to the producers through fees. The quality of the coffees is ensured through the coffee farmers associations as well as the ECX.

Maintaining market share and quality have been constant problems for all producers in Ethiopia. If the country continues to pursue export-led growth through exports such as specialty coffees, the local coffee farmers cooperative associations must continue their outreach and capacity-building activities within communities around these issues. Additional policy supports from the GoE or capacity-building activities from international Fair Trade associations can be extremely beneficial in creating a strong culture of quality and brand adherence.

To date, few cases of World Bank–financed projects have involved the enforcement of IPRs. One reason may be the reluctance to use such a legal-based and (inherently) costly activity in pursuit of development. Unfortunately, an impact evaluation of the World Bank project's activities fell outside the purview of the IDF grant. An evaluation of the cost-effectiveness of the IPR

---

56   Gebreselassie & Ludi, *supra* note 12, at 14.

intervention would be useful, as the World Bank has provided a specific policy recommendation to undertake protection of traditional knowledge through IPRs in its Indigenous Peoples' Policy.

From the data gathered in the World Bank project, it is apparent that some of the profits made through decommoditization have been reinvested into the community. It is difficult to measure the quantitative impact of the Bank-financed IPR intervention, either on a cost basis (cost to farmer) or a benefits basis. Furthermore, it is difficult to separate a purely Fair Trade coffee from a trademarked coffee because production is so intertwined in Ethiopia. Some anecdotal evidence points to certain economic and social gains made at the cooperative level. In the future, impact evaluations would be useful to gauge the overall effectiveness of enforcing IPRs on the international market.

What is apparent from the World Bank–financed project is that IPRs require specialized legal knowledge. This knowledge and capacity are often beyond the scope of a domestic IP agency such as EIPO. It is highly unlikely that EIPO (or any national government) would be the main actor in drafting future licensing agreements. A greater appreciation by local agencies of the content of an agreement and the steps taken to file and fulfill such an agreement would go a long way toward ensuring greater sustainability of IP assets over the long term. Future twinning arrangements with (pro bono) law firms and local IP agencies would ensure greater understanding and appreciation of how these agreements and rights work on the international level. Building capacity within local legal communities—through specialized training provided by local bar associations, Fair Trade training and legal advisory services provided by international Fair Trade organizations, and specific courses in law schools—could help build the technical capacity to run domestic IP programs and reduce the involvement of other international actors. This approach will take considerable time to consolidate. As noted above, some of the teaching will remain theoretical in developing countries until there is a landmark IPR case.

The World Bank project brought an understanding to Ethiopian coffee growers and exporters alike that trademarks could bring value above and beyond that of merely Fair Trade–certified coffee. As a single cash crop, coffee exports face a number of market externalities that are difficult to overcome. Without greater diversification of crops or products for export, Ethiopian coffee farmers will continue to weather cycles of boom and bust. Further diversification of Ethiopia's export base, including the pursuit of protecting other TK assets on the international market through trademarks, and continued adherence to Fair Trade standards by producer organizations in country, can bring considerable equitable development to Ethiopia while growing the economy. The gains made through Fair Trade certification and the use of trademarks positively affected those involved in the Ethiopian coffee sector. The larger question remains whether or not these gains can be sustained financially and institutionally.

Tools for More Sustainable Trade Treaties with Developing Countries

Markus W. Gehring

The European Union has long struggled to find the right tools to integrate social, economic, and environmental priorities into its trade policies and treaties and to foster opportunity, inclusion, and equity. This has become more important since the Lisbon Treaty entered into force on December 1, 2009. One element of the Lisbon Treaty, the Treaty on European Union, is to "foster the sustainable economic, social and environmental development of developing countries with the primary aim of eradicating poverty" (Article 25). This general objective is also binding for the EU's international trade policy or, to be more precise, for the EU's "common commercial policy," per Article 205 of the Treaty on the Functioning of the European Union.

One of the most important tools that the EU has implemented to achieve this objective is a detailed process of the assessment of the impact of trade treaties.[1] Impact assessments are an integral part of environmental policy making and increasingly address social concerns such as health impacts.[2] An earlier generation of environmental impact assessment (EIA) methodologies focused almost exclusively on the risks for the natural, biophysical environment that were engendered by specific development projects.[3]

The prototypical EIA procedure involves a preliminary scientific or information-gathering phase and a report, which is then followed by a decision to proceed with the activity (a finding of "no significant impact") or to undertake a more in-depth assessment. An initial screening is performed to determine if a project triggers the EIA requirement.[4] If an EIA is necessary, a scoping phase follows, whereby the party in charge of the EIA determines which impact should be considered as well as which alternatives should be assessed.[5] Following this phase, a full assessment may be required, which

---

1   G. Duran & M. E. Marin, *Environmental Integration in the EU's External Relations: Beyond Multilateral Dimensions* 234 (Hart Publg. 2012).

2   For more information on the evolution from environmental to sustainable development assessment, *see* M. C. Cordonier Segger & A. Khalfan, *Sustainable Development Law* 175 (Oxford U. Press 2004).

3   *See* M. Gehring & M. C. Cordonier Segger, *Sustainable Development through Process in World Trade Law*, in *Sustainable Development in World Trade Law* 191, 192 (M. Gehring & M. C. Cordonier Segger eds., Kluwer L. Intl. 2005).

4   *United States National Environmental Policy Act (NEPA) and Agency Planning*, 40 C.F.R. secs. 1501.3, 1501.4, 1507.3, 1508.9 (2002).

5   There are varying approaches to and varying emphases in the different stages. For example, the EIA process in the United States under NEPA is a detailed two-tier process in which

includes more comprehensive investigations and studies, public meetings or consultations, and the publication of more-in-depth studies supplemented with recommended measures to mitigate risks and enhance benefits (a management plan).[6]

At national levels, the United States National Environmental Policy Act of 1969 (NEPA) is generally considered to have introduced the concept of the EIA.[7] NEPA requires a report that includes an "assessment of the likely or potential environmental impacts of [a] proposed activity."[8] In the 1970s, many nations adopted NEPA-style EIA processes, including Canada (1973), Australia (1974), New Zealand (1974), Colombia (1974), Thailand (1975), France (1976), and the Netherlands (1979).[9] The 1987 publication of the Brundtland Report, *Our Common Future*, which called for improved environmental impact assessments, also contributed to the evolution of national laws on the issue.[10] By 1999, half of the 48 Sub-Saharan African countries had adopted EIA legislation.[11] Even though political regimes, regional priorities, and cultural values are different in various countries, EIA processes tend to be consistent.[12] As with other emerging themes in contemporary international law, the contours of national EIA policy and law have gained increasing normative resonance in the international arena.[13] As a consequence, EIAs have been included in both

---

an environmental assessment is conducted to determine the necessity of pursuing a full environmental impact statement. An environmental impact statement is not required if there is a finding of no significant impact (FONSI) at the end of the environmental assessment. To some extent, then, the environmental assessment combines the scoping phase and the baseline study. *See* 40 C.F.R. secs. 1501.3, 1501.4, 1506.6. Other jurisdictions take a more streamlined (or less rigorous, depending on one's perspective) approach to the scoping process that may or may not involve public participation. *See*, for example, Dennis Te-Chung Tang, *New Developments in Environmental Law and Policy in Taiwan*, 6 P. Rim L. & Policy J. 245, 257–263, 304 (1997); European Commission, *Guidance on EIA Scoping* pt. A (2001), available at http://ec.europa.eu/environment/eia/eia-guidelines/g-scoping-full-text.pdf.

6   European Commission, *supra* note 5, at 194.

7   NEPA, sec. 102, 42 U.S.C. sec. 4332 (2000). *See* Kevin R. Gray, *International Environmental Impact Assessment: Potential for a Multilateral Environmental Agreement*, 11 Colo. J. Intl. Envtl. L. & Policy 83, 89 (2000); Christopher Wood, *Environmental Impact Assessment: A Comparative Review* 1 (2d ed., Prentice Hall 2002).

8   United Nations Environment Programme (UNEP), *Governing Council Decision: Goals and Principles of Environmental Impact Assessment*, princ. 4, UNEP/GC.14/17 Annex III, UNEP/GC/DEC/14/25 (June 17, 1987) (hereinafter, UNEP EIA Principles), reprinted in UNEP, *Principles of Environmental Impact Assessment*, 17 Envtl. Policy & L. 36 (1987).

9   Wood, *supra* note 7.

10   World Commission on Environment and Development, *Our Common Future: Brundtland Report* (Oxford U. Press 1987).

11   Mohammed Bekhechi & Jean-Roger Mercier, *The Legal and Regulatory Framework for Environmental Impact Assessments: A Study of Selected Countries in Sub-Saharan Africa* 13 (World Bank 2002).

12   Erika L. Preiss, *The International Obligation to Conduct an Environmental Impact Assessment: The ICJ Case Concerning the Gabcikovo-Nagymaros Project*, 7 N.Y.U. Envtl. L. J. 307, 310 (1999); Alexandre S. Timoshenko, *The Problem of Preventing Damage to the Environment in National and International Law: Impact Assessment and International Consultations*, 5 Pace Envtl. L. Rev. 475, 481–482 (1988).

13   After a certain amount of international consensus (*see* the growing literature on international

multilateral environmental agreements at the international level and in trade agreements at the global and regional levels.

The requirement to conduct an impact assessment has become common in international law. The Convention on Environmental Impact Assessment in a Transboundary Context (Espoo Convention) specifically contains such obligations for the parties to the treaty. The obligation to undertake EIAs has, in international law, become applicable beyond the limits of national jurisdiction, when activities are proposed to take place in areas of "common concern" or "common heritage" of humanity. In this vein, duties to conduct a variety of EIA procedures are found in the 1991 Protocol to the Antarctic Treaty on Environmental Protection[14] and under the 1982 UN Convention on the Law of the Sea (UNCLOS).[15] For example, the International Tribunal on the Law of the Seas concluded in 2001 that the United Kingdom had breached its obligations under UNCLOS in relation to the authorization of the MOX (mixed oxide fuel) plant, inter alia, by refusing to carry out a proper environmental assessment of the impacts on the marine environment of a MOX plant.[16] In an ITLOS case involving a proposed development in a disputed area between Singapore and Malaysia, the judges imposed provisional measures that included an impact assessment.

The International Court of Justice (ICJ) has found a duty to conduct EIAs before proceeding with serious transboundary projects under customary international law as well as treaty law, in the case concerning the Danube Dam[17]

---

environmental law, e.g. Philippe Sands, *Principles of International Environmental Law*, 3d ed. (Cambridge U. Press 2012), on the necessities of EIAs, norms associated with the assessment policy have "filtered back" from international to national and regional laws in three manners: through the influence of soft law; under state obligations to implement specific international obligations; and under obligations in customary international law. *See* M. Gehring & M. C. Cordonier Segger eds., *Sustainable Development in World Trade Law* 194 (Kluwer L. Intl. 2005).

14   *See Antarctic Environmental Protocol*, 30 I.L.M. 1461 (1991), art. 23(1). Nine parties have ratified the protocol to date, but all 26 Antarctic Treaty consultative parties are required to bring it into force. *See* also *Convention on the Conservation of Antarctic Marine Living Resources* (May 20, 1980), T.I.A.S. No. 10240, 1329 U.N.T.S. 48.

15   *United Nations Convention on the Law of the Sea* (UNCLOS), vol. 1833 U.N.T.S. 3; 21 I.L.M. 1261 (1982 preamble, arts. 192, 194). *See* also *Agreement for the Implementation of the Provisions of the UN Convention on the Law of the Sea* (Dec. 10, 1982), relating to the conservation and management of straddling fish stocks and highly migratory fish stocks, U.N. Doc. A/CONF.164/38 (1995), 34 I.L.M. 1542 (1995). Straddling Stocks Agreement, preamble and arts. 2, 5, address issues such as the inadequate management of high-seas fisheries, the overutilization of fishing resources, and the inadequate regulation of fishing vessels. UNCLOS states, at art. 206: "When States have reasonable grounds for believing that planned activities under their jurisdiction or control may cause substantial pollution of or significant and harmful changes to the marine environment, they shall, as far as practicable, assess the potential effects of such activities on the marine environment and shall communicate reports of the results of such assessments in the manner provided in article 205."

16   ITLOS, *The MOX Plant Case (Ireland v. United Kingdom), Provisional Measures*, [2001] ITLOS 10 (Order of Dec. 3, 2001).

17   For an expression of the customary principle, see Preiss, *supra* note 12, at 206. Judge Schwebel, speaking for the majority, took judicial notice of the vulnerability of the environment and the

as well as more recently and more explicitly in the Pulp Mill and Costa Rica/ Nicaragua cases. One can now persuasively argue that there are customary obligations to consult on and cooperate in the implementation of projects that might affect other states' interests. The weight of evidence has led many legal scholars and the ICJ to find that there is a customary international law requirement to do an EIA when transboundary impacts could result from a proposed course of action.[18] Transboundary EIA obligations are particularly well established with regard to international waterways. Given that 261 major river basins are shared by two or more sovereign nations, waterways constitute a significant class of transboundary environment requiring improved planning, regulation, and management.[19]

Questions remain as to whether and how impact assessment might be applied to broader development policies and plans, such as trade agreements, rather than simply transboundary development projects, and how new forms of impact assessments mandated by law or policy might be expanded to take into account not just physical, environmental issues but also questions of equity, inclusion, and opportunity.

The application of impact review and assessment tools to trade agreements has, from the start, been inextricably linked to questions of law, policy, and development. One of the main reasons for engaging in impact assessments is to increase the information base in order to avoid trade decisions that might be harmful for the environment; however, impact assessments are increasingly being performed in the context of broader development issues. The explicit sustainable development objective of virtually all assessment

---

importance of having risks assessed on a continuous basis. These provisions were construed by Judge Weeramantry in a minority opinion as "building in" the principle of EIA. He added that a duty of EIA is to be read into treaties whose subject can reasonably be considered to have a significant impact on the environment. The Experts Group on Environmental Law of the World Commission on Environment and Development in 1984 identified EIA as an emerging principle of international law. For examples of treaty obligations in this respect, see *Convention on the Law of the Non-navigational Uses of International Watercourses* (Watercourses Convention) (36 I.L.M. 700 (1997), G.A. Res. 51/229, U.N. GAOR, 51st Sess., 99th mtg., U.N. Doc. A/RES/51/229 (1997): ILC, 1997); *Convention on the Protection and Use of Transboundary Watercourses and International Lakes* (Helsinki Water Convention) (1936 U.N.T.S.) 269; 31 I.L.M. 1312 (1992): United Nations Economic Commission for Europe (UNECE), 1992, at art. 3(1)(h), where states are required to develop, adopt, implement, and, as much as possible, render compatible relevant measures to ensure that an EIA is applied. *See* also International Law Commission (ILC), *Draft Articles on the Non-navigational Uses of International Watercourses*, U.N. Doc. A/46/10 (1991), at 161, and U.N. Doc. A/CN.4/L492 & Add. 1 (1994).

18   In the 2010 Pulp Mill on the River Uruguay ICJ case between Argentina and Uruguay, the court considered and stated that it is a requirement under "general international law" to undertake an EIA when there is a risk that the proposed industrial activity may have a significant adverse impact in a transboundary context, in particular, on a shared resource. *See* also *Dispute Regarding Navigational and Related Rights* (*Costa Rica v. Nicaragua*), Judgment of 13 July 2009, para. 64. In the literature, *see* Patricia Birnie, Alan Boyle, & Catherine Redgwell, *International Law and the Environment*, 3d ed. (Oxford U. Press 2009); Sands, *supra* note 13; Gehring & Cordonier Segger, *supra* note 13.

19   Aaron T. Wolf et al., *International River Basins of the World*, 15 Water Resources Dev. 387, 391 (1999).

tools applied to trade agreements underlines this trend. Trading partners now view sustainable development as a global concept that applies to their international relations. This impression is most pronounced in the European Union, where the foreign policy objective that applies to trading relations also concerns sustainable development at home and abroad. One of the first international organizations to consider such assessments was the Organisation for Economic Co-operation and Development (OECD), through its 1993 *Procedural Guidelines on Trade and Environment,* which pinpointed "reviews" as a tool for legal and policy coherence.[20] In 1994, the OECD proposed a complete methodology,[21] which has had a substantive influence on the development of impact assessment tools in many countries.[22] Since these early attempts, the scope and procedures of these instruments have evolved considerably.[23]

Several impact assessment instruments are now being applied to evaluate proposals for trade liberalization and new trade law. Trade impact assessments have distinct scope, requirements, attributes, and legal foundations in different national, regional, and international contexts. The earliest types of impact assessment, typically found at the national level, were concerned with reviewing the environmental effects of trade. As a result, assessments often considered only environmental issues, making little reference to social issues (i.e., indigenous peoples, gender, health, poverty, social development). Examples of such tools include Canadian environmental assessments and U.S. environmental reviews of new trade agreements.

More recent impact assessment instruments for sustainable development seek to integrate elements of economic, environmental, and social concerns. The sustainability impact assessment methodology that is employed by the EU is one example of this approach. These distinctions are important—certain states, regions, and international organizations are simply evaluating the national or international environmental effects of their potential trade policies without focusing on social equity and inclusion elements, while others are undertaking broader sustainability assessments of trade policies. These differences are, at least in part, a reflection of the diversity of contexts and origins of existing assessment methods and mandates. In this chapter, when distinctions between the environmental and sustainable types of impact assessment are not relevant, the generic term "impact assessment" is used.

This chapter considers current practices in impact assessments related to trade treaties, especially how these instruments place greater emphasis on

---

20   OECD, *Procedural Guidelines on Trade and Environment* (1994) (hereinafter, OECD, *Procedural Guidelines*).

21   OECD, *Methodologies for Environmental and Trade Reviews,* OCDE/GD(94)103 (hereinafter, OECD, *Methodologies*).

22   C. Tebar Less, *The OECD Methodology for the Environmental Assessment of Trade Policies and Agreements: Types of Effects to Evaluate,* in *The International Experts' Meeting on Sustainability Assessments of Trade Liberalisation—Quito, Ecuador, 6–8 March 2000, Full Meeting Report* 82 (WWF 2000).

23   Gehring & Cordonier Segger, *supra* note 13.

opportunity, inclusion, and equity, and how, through this refinement, impact assessments can assist trade agreements better reflect law, justice, and development concerns. The first section elaborates the rules concerning the basic structure and methodologies of impact assessments as they are being used across jurisdictions. The second section considers existing impact assessment mechanisms with relevance to trade in specific jurisdictions, such as the NAFTA environmental reviews, the U.S. and Canadian processes, the EU's instruments, and those used by certain international organizations, discussing the opportunities presented by these processes. The third section analyzes the existing mechanisms and their rules, considering how they might better reflect the sustainable development principle of equity through measures to ensure greater attention to inclusion and offering recommendations.

Rules Governing Impact Assessments of Trade Agreements across Jurisdictions

All impact assessment mechanisms for trade treaties share certain elements. However, differing time frames and degrees of integration between environmental, economic, and social considerations exist. This section explains the general analytical framework and methodology of environmental assessments of trade negotiations and treaty texts.

Impact assessment normally follows four main steps: conduct a scoping exercise; perform an initial review; publish the preliminary assessment (which informs negotiators of the party that uses an impact assessment); and prepare a final assessment. Ongoing reviews may be mandated as follow-up.

Most impact assessments are structured to examine the economic effects of trade liberalization scenarios that are likely to result from a new treaty, to ascertain the potential environmental effects of this liberalization, and to analyze the potential significance of projected environmental impacts to provide a basis from which to identify options to enhance positive benefits while mitigating negative effects. Impact assessments that are oriented toward sustainable development objectives, such as those undertaken by the EU, investigate economic and environmental as well as social development implications of trade negotiations. Each trading relationship is distinct, and trade agreements have the potential to affect few or many sectors of the parties' economies. A trade agreement may be as simple as a single tariff reduction or business negotiation with few environmental consequences, or it may provide the legal underpinnings of a full-blown economic partnership and cooperation process in which goods, services, public procurement, intellectual property, investment, competition, and other provisions are expected to be agreed to and where several potentially serious environmental and social impacts may be identified. In the case of the U.S. environmental reviews, only negotiations that reach a certain magnitude of economic relevance are subject to the next phase of the assessment, which involves increased consultation and analysis of the potential environmental impact in the United States. In most other countries, assessment might end at the initial review phase if no significant environmental impacts are foreseen, a finding of no significant impact (FONSI).

The definition of "significant" is by no means settled. As noted by legal scholars,

> Agreements such as the Espoo Convention, the North American draft TEIAA264, the East African MOU, and others specifically require a transboundary environmental impact assessment (TEIA) to be conducted for activities that are likely to have a "significant" impact on the environment. The definition of "significant" in these instruments varies, or is frequently vague or as-yet undetermined.[24]

To minimize uncertainty, international instruments or national laws often prescribe a nonexhaustive list of specific activities that require a transboundary or other environmental impact assessment.[25]

The objective of an initial review is to identify the potential impacts of the trade negotiations on the environment. The level of analysis is variegated and depends on the mandate of the impact assessment. Some environmental assessments merely examine the effects wrought on a domestic level (Canada), whereas others investigate transboundary impacts once a certain threshold is crossed (United States). Still other processes, such as sustainability impact assessments, take a global perspective in analyzing the impacts (EU). Definition of the key issues that are relevant and identification of areas in which further investigation is necessary are achieved through a broad consultation process that engages authorities from various interested government departments, as well as expert groups and academics; public stakeholders and civil society organizations, including representatives of vulnerable groups; and the private sector. In the scoping or initial review phases, experts and consultants assess the range of potential issues. Information-gathering and scientific studies typify the process at this point.[26] In some countries, including the United States, the public is invited to participate in the scoping stage to help identify impacts, alternatives, and data sources.[27] The environmental impact assessment can provide an important mechanism for advancing the transparency, participation, and accountability advocated by Principle 10 of the Rio Declaration,[28] and may provide an opportunity for vulnerable citizens to advocate for greater inclusion of their interests and needs at the initial stages of trade negotiations. Due to this participatory element, impact assessment processes could be a

---

24   Angela Z. Cassar & Carl E. Bruch, *Transboundary Environmental Impact Assessment in International Watercourse Management,* 12 N.Y.U. Envtl. L. J. 222 (2004).

25   *Id.* This article gives many examples, including appendix I of the Espoo Convention and the bilateral agreement between Estonia and Latvia.

26   *See* Gehring & Cordonier Segger, *supra* note 13, at 194.

27   Julie Teel, *International Environmental Impact Assessment: A Case Study in Implementation,* 31 Envtl. L. Rep. (Envtl. L. Inst.) 10,291, 10,294–10,306 (2001).

28   *United Nations Conference on Environment and Development: Rio Declaration on Environment and Development* (adopted June 14, 1992), U.N. Doc. A/CONF.151/5/Rev.1, 31 I.L.M. 874, 878.

tool for diverse sectors of societies to use as they seek greater economic and social inclusion. When taken seriously and effectively implemented, public participation measures can provide local and underrepresented interests an opportunity to be heard and to participate in decision making that affects their environment and livelihoods.[29]

In terms of further steps, in most cases, the preliminary assessment document is discussed formally, informing the negotiators as to projected economic and environmental impacts of trade liberalization in certain areas and in certain processes, and in some cases requiring a formal internal or externally released reply from the responsible authority. For some countries, the report, even at this initial phase, may contain mention of mitigation proposals, particularly if potential impacts are familiar from previous trade agreements. For example, if the preliminary scoping or review identifies that an importing party might be vulnerable to pressure to lower its environmental standards in order to attract investment, the preliminary report might note that this impact could be addressed by the inclusion of provisions committing all parties not to lower standards to attract investment. Some instruments also consider a "zero-line approach" when appropriate—the preliminary assessment may suggest ceasing negotiations on trade liberalization in a specific product area. For example, if a preliminary scoping exercise notes that the liberalization of wood and wood products holds the potential to increase rates of illegal extraction of timber from protected areas, the preliminary report might recommend that the parties not increase market access by liberalizing trade in this sector without first assuring themselves that forest governance has been strengthened.

To give a more specific example, the preliminary appraisal of measures for inclusion in the proposed WTO Millennium Round Agenda[30] led to the initial EU sustainability impact assessment findings presented in table 1.

After publication of a preliminary assessment that informs negotiators, a final and more detailed assessment report is prepared that addresses the issues raised in the scoping and initial review. Often, the responsible authority will need to commission in-depth studies that will result in reports on key projected impacts (positive or negative) that might be important for the negotiations and encompass the consultation of relevant authorities in other departments, including scientific and economic commissions. To continue with the earlier example, following the initial findings of the EU sustainability impact assessment of the World Trade Organization (WTO) Millennium round of trade negotiations, the most important measures that were found to hold potential for adverse or other impacts were subjected to a review and

---

29   Nicholas A. Robinson, *International Trends in Environmental Impact Assessment*, 19 B.C. Envtl. Aff. L. Rev. 591, 594 (1992).

30   Colin Kirkpatrick, Norman Lee, & O. Morrissey, *WTO New Round: Sustainability Impact Assessment Study (Phase Two Report)* S.14 (Mar. 2004).

Table 1. Significant Sustainability Impacts of the WTO New Round According to Colin Kirkpatrick et al.

Impact on	Significant impacts								
	Scenario 1 (business as usual)			Scenario 2 (liberalization)			Scenario 3 (moderate liberalization)		
	A	B	C	A	B	C	A	B	C
EU countries	0(-1)	0	0(-1)	±1	±1	±1	-1/+1	-1/+1	-1
Developing countries	0	0	0	±1	±1	±1	-1/+1	-2/+1	-1
Least-developed countries	0	0	0	±1	±1	±1	-1/+1	-2/+1	-1
Global	0	0	0	±1	±1	±1	-1/+1	-1/+1	-1

Note: This table summarizes the outcomes of a scoping exercise. In the column headings, "A" represents economic impacts (changes in the level of average real income; net fixed capital formation; and employment); "B" represents projected social impacts (changes in level of equity and poverty, health, and education; and gender inequality); and "C" represents environmental impacts (changes in air, water, and land quality; biological diversity; and air resource stocks). In the table, "0" is a nonsignificant impact compared with the base condition; "1" denotes areas where a lesser significant impact is projected, and "2" is where a greater significant impact can be projected. The symbol "+" is used to represent a potential positive impact, whereas "-" is used to represent a negative impact, and "±" raises the potential for positive and negative impacts, meaning that the net effect is uncertain and/or varies according to context. Parentheses indicate situations in which the impact in the base situation can be compared with the existing situation. The use of -/+ notes a range indicating variation over time.

presented in a general summarized report with proposed measures to enhance positive outcomes and to reduce or mitigate potential negative outcomes for the societies, environments, and economies affected. These later phases of the sustainability impact assessment took into account the outcomes of public participation processes, including consultations with nongovernmental organizations (NGOs). Numerous workshops were held both in Europe and in the developing country trading partner in every phase of the assessment, with a dedicated and accessible website used to publish reports and other documents.[31] The site was promoted on social media to allow for exchanges of opinions in less formal settings. Although, due to other factors, the WTO

---

31 *Id.*

Ministerial Conference in Seattle was ultimately unsuccessful,[32] the sustainability impact assessment process provided opportunities for the inclusion of otherwise unheard voices, defusing certain elements of public concern and reducing the potential for conflict, as well as influencing the European Community negotiation position.

Most impact assessments also contain an *ex post* final assessment, prepared after the negotiations have been concluded and the final text has been approved. The closing report illustrates how some negotiation positions may have changed due to the contents of the preliminary assessment. The final report might illuminate the trade-offs and balance between economic liberalization and environmental protection,[33] thereby explaining motives behind decisions that potentially have adverse environmental effects but were accepted in order to secure other benefits deemed important by the mandated decision makers.

Rules Governing Impact Assessments of Trade Agreements by Jurisdiction

The section above presents the main components shared by most trade agreement impact assessments, drawing on examples of actual environmental assessments and sustainability impact assessments. This section provides an illustrative overview of the methodologies and practical applications of impact assessments for trade agreements at national and regional levels and discusses several examples of practical applications that highlight the opportunities for law and sustainable development provided by these instruments.[34]

The OECD was the first international organization to address the field of environmental assessments, following studies undertaken in some of its member states.[35] As early as 1994, a methodology for such assessments was proposed,[36] and *OECD Methodologies for Environmental and Trade Reviews* was

---

32   *See* Gary Sampson, *Trade, Environment and the WTO: The Post-Seattle Agenda* (Overseas Dev. Council 2000). *See* also, P. Grady & K. Macmillan, *Seattle and Beyond: The WTO Millennium Round* (Global Economics Ltd 1999); Edith Brown Weiss, *The Rise or the Fall of International Law*, 69 Fordham L. Rev. S.345 ff. (2000).

33   Bernard Hoekman, Aaditya Mattoo, & André Sapir, *The Political Economy of Services Trade Liberalization: A Case for International Regulatory Cooperation?*, 23(3) Oxford Rev. Eco. Policy 367–391 (2007).

34   The fields and areas of applications are many. See Katarina Granah, *Study to Inform a Subsequent Impact Assessment on the Commission Proposal on Jurisdiction and Applicable Law in Divorce Matters* (European Policy Evaluation Consortium 2006), or Siripen Supakankunti & Wattana S. Janjaroen, *Impact of the World Trade Organization TRIPS Agreement on the Pharmaceutical Industry in Thailand*, 79(5) Bull. of the World Health Org. (2001).

35   Cristina Tebar Less, *The OECD Methodology for the Environmental Assessment of Trade Policies and Agreements: Types of Effects to Evaluate*, in *The International Experts' Meeting on Sustainability Assessments of Trade Liberalisation* (Mar. 6–8, 2000, full meeting report, Gland 2000), S.82ff.

36   OECD, *Methodologies, supra* note 21.

adopted at a joint session of trade and environment experts.[37] Before this, in 1993, the OECD ministers had adopted procedural guidelines on trade and the environment suggesting the examination and review of economic and environmental policies.[38] The guidelines endorse the use of reviews as a tool for legal and policy coherence:

> Governments should examine or review trade and environmental policies and agreements with potentially significant effects on the other policy area and identify alternative policy options for addressing concerns. Governments may co-operate in undertaking such examinations and reviews. Governments should follow-up as appropriate: to implement policy options to re-examine the policy agreements and any measure in place, and to address any concerns identified in the conclusion of such re-examinations.[39]

Since these guidelines were drafted, there have been significant advances in thinking regarding environmental assessments that show that the OECD guidelines are flawed. The OECD's recommendations were founded on an alternative-based approach, favoring cooperation between states on a bilateral or even multilateral level. This was not adopted in subsequent state initiatives but remains a valid suggestion. The OECD also recommended retrospective assessments following the main assessment but, again, none of the OECD member states adopted this approach. All discussed impact assessment instruments fall short of these OECD recommendations. From another perspective, the guidelines did not recommend public participation in the assessment process, which has proven to be an essential part of these assessments. During early discussions, reviews and assessments were conceptualized as pure expert exercises rather than as opportunities for public participation and the inclusion of different sectors. The methodology adopted by the OECD builds on this approach. Without reference to public participation, these approaches constitute a violation of the principle of precaution through process.

It took years to develop methodologies for environmental assessments of trade measures. Although no formal conclusions were adopted at a workshop on assessing the environmental effects of trade liberalization held in 1999, the record of discussions reveals that the 1994 *OECD Methodologies for Environmental and Trade Reviews* were still seen as a valid approach, in particular with regard to the different types of impacts that an assessment of a trade measure should address.[40] The methodology has not been significantly amended since. There have been discussions in the WTO to develop a common approach, but these were overshadowed by the Doha Round discussions. So when assessments at the national level were first recommended in the Doha Declaration,

---

37   Originally founded as the OECD Joint Session of Trade and Environment Experts, now meeting as the Joint Working Party on Trade and Environment.

38   OECD, *Procedural Guidelines, supra* note 20.

39   *Id.*

40   OECD, *Assessing the Environmental Effects of Trade Liberalisation Agreements: Methodologies—Proceedings of the Paris Workshop* 11 (OECD 2000).

there was little to suggest further efforts at the multilateral level.[41] Gaps in methodologies were revealed in the WTO Committee on Trade and Environment discussions. The absence of a specific methodology for assessing impacts in trade, services, and investment was subject to criticism by WTO member states. Furthermore, the need for intensified research concerning the integration of social aspects into environmental assessments was identified.[42]

In current practice, several methodologies are being tested in parallel. This section introduces the principal instruments, providing analysis of the legal foundations of each trade impact assessment (IA) tool, including its political context; the evolution of the IA tool's scope and methodological content; a brief step-by-step outline of how the IA tool functions in practice; an explanation of the IA tool's modes of public participation and consultation; and a concrete example in which the IA tool was applied to assess the impacts of a particular trade negotiation.

The European Union's Sustainability Impact Assessments on Trade

The European Union, in accordance with Agenda 21 and the 1992 Rio Declaration, established the sustainability impact assessment, a mechanism crafted to include environmental and social concerns in economic policies to promote sustainable development.[43] Since the 1990s, the commission has developed processes implementing the "precautionary principle" with the goal of "better understand[ing] the benefits and costs of its policies and to manage risk, including ex-ante assessment of policies (i.e. assessment in advance of implementation)."[44] Sustainability impact assessments seek to identify potential social, economic, and environmental impacts using indicators from all three pillars of sustainable development. In the quest for a fully developed and rigorously defined methodology, indicators and measurements have both quantitative and qualitative attributes.[45] Today, the sustainability impact assessment is at the vanguard of holistic impact assessment tools, showing evi-

---

41   Doha WTO Ministerial Declaration (4th Ministerial Conference, Doha, Qatar: WT/MIN(01)/DEC/1; 41 I.L.M. 746 (2002), 2001), para. 6.

42   *See* Richard Tarasofsky, *Report on the Workshop "Methodologies for Environmental Assessment of Trade Liberalisation Agreements"* (WTO-Document WT/CTE/W/133, Feb. 18, 2000).

43   European Commission, Directorate-General of Trade, *Draft Handbook for Sustainability Impact Assessment* 1 (European Commn. 2005) (hereinafter, *SIA Handbook*), available at http://trade-info.cec.eu.int/doclib/docs/2005/april/tradoc_122363.doc,

44   The precautionary principle is at the intersection of three areas of law (economic, social, and environmental) within the broad rubric of international sustainable development law. The precautionary approach to risk management commits states, international organizations, and civil society, particularly the scientific and business communities, to avoid activity that may cause significant harm to human health, natural resources, or ecosystems, including in the face of scientific uncertainty. *See* Cordonier Segger & Khalfan, *supra* note 2, at 100.

45   Although the commission currently proposes to determine the methodology for each sustainability impact assessment, it considers the incorporation of a mix of qualitative and quantitative methods, such as case studies, modeling, statistical estimations, and expert opinion, to be beneficial.

dence of being a fully integrated instrument and including recommendations for enhancement and mitigation.

Member-state and NGO demands leading up to the WTO Ministerial Conference in Seattle prompted the Directorate General for Trade of the EC (the DG Trade) to commission a study conducted by a research team affiliated with the University of Manchester. This team was tasked with developing a methodology for an *ex ante* sustainability impact assessment. After the methodology was formalized (with degrees of context-specific flexibility), the DG Trade inaugurated several studies using the framework for assessing the impact of trade policy on sustainable development. After refining, the sustainability impact assessment consisted of four main phases:

- *Screening:* to determine which measures require SIA because they are likely to have significant impacts

- *Scoping:* to establish the appropriate coverage of each SIA

- *Preliminary sustainability assessment:* to identify potentially significant effects, positive and negative, on sustainable development

- *Mitigation and enhancement analysis:* to suggest types of improvements that may enhance the overall impact on sustainable development of new trade agreements/measures[46]

These phases are infused with avenues of public participation and consultation with civil society organizations. Numerous workshops and consultations, both formal and informal, are held at each phase of the process. A website provides public access to reports and timely publications.

One of the more unconventional and controversial features of the sustainability impact assessment methodology is the investigation of the impacts on the (often developing country) trading partner(s) in trade negotiations, rather than simply the impacts on the commissioning EU state. Unfortunately, research collaboration with trading partners is not always reciprocal. For instance, although strong collaborative links between researchers were possible for the sustainability impact assessment of EU-Mercosur trade negotiations and the SIA of the EU-Mediterranean trade negotiations,[47] the sustainability impact assessment of the EC–Cooperation Council for the Arab States of the Gulf trade negotiations did not unfold as smoothly.[48] The means of mobilizing public participation in the studies varied, from extensive debates and consultations to merely an administered website. As the private consultancy noted, "The NGO world did not show a big interest in the topic, nevertheless engagement

---

46   See Gehring & Cordonier Segger, *supra* note 13, at 211.

47   *See Final Report EU-Mercosur SIA* (Mar. 2009), available at http://trade.ec.europa.eu/doclib /docs/2009/april/tradoc_142921.pdf.

48   *See* PriceWaterhouseCoopers, *Sustainability Impact Assessment (SIA) of the Negotiations of the Trade Agreement between the European Community and the Countries of the Cooperation Council for the Arab States of the Gulf (GCC)* (PWC 2004), available at http://trade-info.cec.eu.int /doclib/docs/2005/january/tradoc_121208.pdf.

was done at several moments. NGO from the Gulf Cooperation Council (GCC) have not even replied to our requests to get their view, input (sic)."[49] In a recent sustainability impact assessment of the EU-Canada Comprehensive Economic and Trade Agreement (CETA), consultants obtained positive responses from the public in the EU, but comparatively little input from Canadians. As noted in the study, possible reasons included "that domestic issues, including climate and transportation policies take most importance; that CETA represents a small portion of Canada's trade; and that Europe is generally perceived as an environmental leader. For these reasons, CETA appears to generate little interest or worries in the environmental community."[50] If similar reasoning were transposed to a developing country context, where the possibility for consultation might be much more limited than in Canada, this would raise serious concerns as to participation and the potential value for inclusion of diverse groups and especially the most vulnerable elements of society that could be affected by the degradation of resources or other impacts of trade liberalization.

The EU-Andean trade sustainability impact assessment provides a useful example of the methodology and its outcomes.[51] In 2006, the EU and Andean countries began negotiations for a regional trade agreement; and in 2008, pursuant to the *Draft Handbook for Sustainability Impact Assessment* (*SIA Handbook*),[52] the EC commissioned a sustainability impact assessment of these negotiations. The sustainability impact assessment investigators, during the initial assessment, focused on increasing outreach, including by establishing a dedicated website that attracted more than 3,000 unique visitors. One-day consultations were conducted in Lima and other cities, and inputs were actively solicited from a variety of stakeholders, ranging from local grassroots NGOs to government departments.[53]

The study concluded that the impact on trade for the EU was predicted to be insignificant; as for the Andean countries, an increase in trade and investment flows between 3 to 10 percent was predicted. Although the methodology takes a broad-brush approach, this report nevertheless provides an example of how a sustainability impact assessment can highlight both potential impacts and opportunities for development. The analysis started with a modeling of the expected economic impact. It used two scenarios, a modest scenario of 50 percent liberalization of services and an ambitious scenario with 75 percent liberalization of services. As concluded in the sustainability impact assessment, the economic impact of the trade accord was positive:

---

49 *Id.*, at 36.

50 *Final Report for the EU-Canada Sustainability Impact Assessment (SIA) on the EU-Canada Comprehensive Economic and Trade Agreement*, footnote 11, available at http://trade.ec.europa.eu/doclib/docs/2011/september/tradoc_148201.pdf.

51 *EU-Andean Trade Sustainability Impact Assessment* (hereinafter, *EU-Andean Trade SIA*), available at http://trade.ec.europa.eu/doclib/docs/2010/april/tradoc_146014.pdf.

52 *SIA Handbook, supra* note 43.

53 *EU-Andean Trade SIA, supra* note 51, at 136.

> The modeling analysis shows modest income gains for all econo-
> mies in all settings and scenarios, with the biggest absolute gains
> occurring in the EU and Colombia, where real incomes are projected
> to increase by up to €4 billion and €2.8 billion respectively. In rela-
> tive terms, the expected income gains are estimated to be highest
> for Bolivia and Ecuador, where real income is expected to increase
> by between 0.5 and 2 percent of GDP. The impact in the EU is only
> marginal, at less than 0.1 percent of GDP. On an aggregate level, real
> income across all Andean countries will increase by €5 billion under
> the ambitious scenario.[54]

In other words, economic modeling predicted large overall gains for the
developed country partner and significant relative gains for the developing
country partners. As the report noted, however, the trade agreement could
also generate important social and environmental impacts. These might include unmanaged expansion of the agricultural frontier, with the potential to
exacerbate biodiversity loss and exponentially increase illegal logging, and
expansion of mining and petroleum extraction, with related environmental
impacts and social conflict in rural areas. The assessment identified several
sustainable development opportunities, including increased monitoring and
reporting on EU companies and their compliance with corporate social responsibility (CSR) standards in mining, oil, and gas, as well as cooperation
to strengthen education, to make forestry activity more sustainable, and to
improve financial, public utilities, and environmental service sectors, among
others. The assessment identified important development opportunities if
the liberalization is accompanied by careful services regulation. The report
stressed that, "with effective domestic regulatory control, market opening in
the basic utilities sector improves access for the poor to affordable and reliable
services in water, energy, communications and transportation. Liberalization
of distribution may result in some reduction in prices for consumers."[55] Unfortunately, the response by the commission after the negotiations were concluded was somewhat lackluster with regard to regulatory assistance:

> In this respect, the Commission services recall that the findings of
> this SIA are available to the governments of Andean countries which
> have the prime responsibility for the strengthening of their national
> and regional legislations in this area. In addition, the Commission
> services point out that the Commission has already been playing a
> substantial role in promoting this regulatory capacity building via
> its actions in the region.[56]

It is unclear if the simple fact that the sustainability impact assessment itself
is available to government regulators will open new sustainable development

---

54   *Id.*, at 9.

55   *Id.*, at 108.

56   *Commission Services Position Paper on the Trade Sustainability Impact Assessment (SIA) of the
     Multiparty Trade Agreement with Andean Countries* (Nov. 2010), available at http://trade
     .ec.europa.eu/doclib/docs/2010/november/tradoc_146987.pdf.

opportunities for the developing country trading partners or support participatory processes for inclusion of vulnerable or excluded groups.

The recommendations of the EU-Andean sustainability impact assessment report do highlight specific development opportunities in the area of
biofuels, noting the expected expansion of biofuel production in the region
due to the economic treaty with the EU.[57] Development opportunities such as
increased market access for the export of biodiesel and bioethanol along with
measures to address challenges such as the pressure to increase landholding
to the detriment of social cohesion, are discussed. Environmental impacts are
not neglected, and the sustainability impact assessment signals potential challenges generated by conversion of tropical forest to farmlands for biofuels.
The sustainability impact assessment reported that biofuels produced with
tailored and appropriate technologies, sourced from existing agricultural
lands without replacing food crops, could benefit the Andean countries and
highlighted specific regions where this might occur. This balanced assessment
seems to have benefited from significant background research and stakeholder
input. Careful analysis can maximize trade and economic opportunities for
the developing country partner, if accompanied by appropriate policy measures, regulations, and enforcement capacity.

The sustainability impact assessment gives special attention to the needs
of vulnerable groups. In the Andean countries, the focus is on the needs of
indigenous populations. The sustainability impact assessment highlights
the vulnerability of indigenous groups as one of the main social concerns in
the region, alongside rural poverty. It establishes clear linkages between increased deforestation and conglomeration in the agricultural sector and the
vulnerability of indigenous populations. Thus, the sustainability impact assessment highlights that

> in so far as poverty is deeper in rural areas, particularly in more re-
> mote areas, indigenous peoples are adversely affected by insufficient
> access to basic goods and services. Although little information exists
> about non-contacted indigenous peoples, there is evidence that the
> way of life of those who inhabit the Peruvian Amazon and the tropi-
> cal forest of Bolivia are under constant threat, as modernization and
> commercial economic activity continues to penetrate these areas.[58]

The European Commission, in its response, took this concern into consideration, highlighting further cooperation initiatives and enhanced support to
Andean governments to address poverty, education, and health concerns.[59]
This focus, coupled with new cooperation measures to promote opportunities,
inclusion, and equity, is one of the most important benefits of the sustainability impact assessment process for these countries. The European Commission
white paper demonstrates that despite the lack of explicit legal frameworks,

---

57   *Id.*, at 74–81.
58   *Id.*, at 32.
59   *Id.*, at 8.

the de facto requirement that the commission take sustainability impact assessment outcomes into account can help this tool serve the interests of inclusion and equity. For several sustainability impact assessments, as is clear from the responses of the commission to the studies, the inputs were carefully considered and influenced the negotiating position of the EU, particularly with regard to mitigation or flanking measures.

The U.S. and Canadian Environmental Assessments/Reviews

In 1991, the United States conducted pilot assessments on certain aspects of negotiations for the North American Free Trade Agreement (NAFTA).[60] At first, U.S. NGOs litigated to apply general EIA laws to trade negotiations, arguing that the office of the United States Trade Representative (USTR) should conduct an environmental impact statement of its negotiation positions for NAFTA under the U.S. National Environmental Policy Act (NEPA).[61] However, because the final decision as to whether or not to sign a trade agreement rests with the U.S. president, the U.S. Court of Appeals found that a trade agreement could not be considered an "action of an agency" and dismissed the request.[62] Several years later, on November 16, 1999,[63] President Bill Clinton signed Executive Order (EO) 13.141, which codifies environmental reviews as an internally binding assessment obligation for trade negotiations, using terminology to avoid confusion with an environmental impact statement and to prevent litigants from using environmental review results in future litigation.[64] The political context was significant in this instance. In preparation for the Seattle WTO Ministerial Conference, the U.S. sought to strengthen inclusion of civil society into trade negotiations. EO 13.141 contained essentially the same phases as required under the NEPA, belonging to the same family of legal instruments as the environmental impact statement. The environmental review — an *ex ante* procedure laden with public participation requirements — is tripartite in character and avoids imposing any conditions on the trade negotiation process. The first phase is initiated by a notice in the *Federal Register* describing the proposed trade agreement and soliciting public comments and statements about the scope of the environmental review. In the second phase, the environmental review is to be published where practicable and further comments are encouraged. The final phase constitutes the final environmental review, the content of which contains a compendium of public concerns that were considered by the drafting body.

---

60 U.S. Trade Representative (USTR), *Draft Review of U.S.-Mexico Environmental Issues* (USTR 1991). For a full account of the history, *see* J. Salzmann, *Executive Order 13.141 and the Environmental Review of Trade Agreements*, 95 Am. J. Intl. L. 368 (2001).

61 *Public Citizen v. Office U.S. Trade Representative*, 822 F. Supp. 21 (D.D.C. 1993).

62 *Public Citizen v. Office U.S. Trade Representative*, 5 F.3d 549 (D.C. Cir. 1993).

63 *U.S. Federal Registry* 64(.222) of 18.11.1999, 63.169.

64 Executive Order 13.141, sec. 7, contains the usual disclaimer for executive orders: "This order is intended only to improve the internal management of the executive branch and does not create any right, benefit, trust, or responsibility, substantive or procedural, enforceable at law or equity by a party against the United States, its agencies, its officers, or any person."

Several features of the instrument are noteworthy for the purposes of this chapter. First, environmental reviews are primarily an instrument used to assess environmental, rather than social or other, impacts:

> The United States is committed to a policy of careful assessment and consideration of the environmental impacts of trade agreements. The United States will factor environmental considerations into the development of its trade negotiating objectives. Responsible agencies will accomplish these goals through a process of ongoing assessment and evaluation, and, in certain instances, written environmental reviews.[65]

If the environmental effects (positive and negative) are determined to be transboundary in nature and have ramifications for the United States, the assessment may take on a more global character.[66] Edicts within the environmental review procedures provide for cooperation to build the capacity of trading partners for environmental protection in order to ensure "the promotion of sustainable development."[67] Governmental actions that may impede sustainable development are prohibited. Coordination between the administration and Congress, as well as encouragement toward participating in international environmental agreements, is included in the Trade Act of 2002.

By 2013, six U.S. environmental reviews had taken place. The environmental review for the Central American Free Trade Agreement (CAFTA), which considered the impact of including the Dominican Republic in the trade agreement, was published in February 2005.[68] The disclosure reiterated an interim review in 2003[69] and pronounced that the modified membership

> may have relatively greater effects on the economies of Central America and the Dominican Republic. In the near term, however, net changes in production and trade are expected to be relatively small because exports to the United States from these countries already face low or zero tariffs. Longer term effects, through invest-

---

65   Executive Order 13.141, sec. 1.

66   USTR, *Guidelines for Implementation of EO 13.141* (USTR 2001), app. C.G: "Transboundary and global impacts may include those on: Places not subject to national jurisdiction or subject to shared jurisdiction, such as Antarctica, the atmosphere (including ozone and climate change features), outer space, and the high seas; Migratory species, including straddling and highly migratory fish stocks and migratory mammals; Impacts relating to environmental issues identified by the international community as having a global dimension and warranting a global response; Transboundary impacts involving the boundaries of the United States; Environmental resources and issues otherwise of concern to the United States." Available at http://www.ustr.gov/sites/default/files/guidelines%20for%2013141.pdf.

67   Trade Act of 2002, sec. 2102(b)(11)(d).

68   USTR, *Final Environmental Review of the Dominican Republic–Central America–United States Free Trade Agreement* (USTR 2005), available at http://www.ustr.gov/assets/Trade_Agreements /Bilateral/CAFTA/asset_upload_file953_7901.pdf.

69   USTR, *Interim Environmental Review of the U.S.–Central America Free Trade Agreement (CAFTA)* (Aug. 22, 2003), available at http://www.ustr.gov/assets/Trade_Agreements/Bilateral/CAFTA /asset_upload_file946_3356.pdf.

ment and economic development, are expected to be greater but cannot currently be predicted in terms of timing, type and environmental implications.[70]

Canadian environmental assessments of trade agreements are also founded on phased analytical reviews, intergovernmental discussion procedures, and public comment periods, although the Canadian environmental assessments appear to have less scope regarding international issues than the U.S. environmental reviews do. Canada's environmental assessments of trade agreements were also adopted in a particular political and historical context. In 1994, Canada carried out a brief *ex post* environmental review of the Uruguay Round WTO Agreements, perhaps in part to reassure the Canadian public and stakeholders as to what had been agreed on.[71] In 1999, the newly consolidated Department of Foreign Affairs and International Trade (DFAIT) undertook to assess the outcomes of the Uruguay Round agreements anew, after their first four years of operation, to prepare for the expected WTO Millennium Round negotiations (later postponed by the WTO Ministerial Conference in Seattle in 2000). The *Retrospective Analysis of the 1994 Canadian Environmental Review of the Uruguay Round of Multilateral Trade Negotiations* was published in November 1999.[72]

Increasing domestic pressure from agencies, civil society groups, and others led the Canadian government to introduce the internally binding Cabinet Directive on Strategic Environmental Assessment of Plans and Policies in 1999.[73] After the positive experience of introducing an informal environmental impact statement framework in the 1980s prior to formally adopting the Canadian Environmental Assessment Act (CEAA) in 1992 and its entry into force in 1995, the Canadian government may have anticipated a similar approach for environmental assessments of trade agreements.[74] The 1999 cabinet directive mandates that every governmental policy be assessed as to its environmental impact.[75] Trade policy was included in Annex 1 of the cabinet directive, because the CEAA is not applicable to trade policy.[76] Binding guidelines were also adopted, detailing all necessary assessments and regulated public

---

70   *Id.*, at para. 4.

71   Department of Foreign Affairs and International Trade (DFAIT), *1994 Canadian Environmental Review of the Uruguay Round of Multilateral Trade Negotiations*, available at http://www.dfait-maeci.gc.ca/sustain/EnvironA/strategic/urugay-en.asp.

72   *See* DFAIT, http://www.dfait-maeci.gc.ca/tna-nac/documents/retrospective-e.pdf.

73   See Gehring & Cordonier Segger, *supra* note 13, at 206.

74   *Id.*

75   Canadian Environmental Assessment Agency (CEAA), *Strategic Environmental Assessment: The 1999 Cabinet Directive on the Environmental Assessment of Policy, Plan and Program Proposals; Guidelines for Implementing the Cabinet Directive* (CEAA 1999) (hereinafter, *Guidelines for Implementing the Cabinet Directive*).

76   For its history, *see* Canadian Environmental Assessment Agency, *The Canadian Environmental Assessment Act: Introduction* 2d ed. (2011), available at http://www.ceaa-acee.gc.ca/default.asp?lang=En&n=0DF82AA5-1; the complete text is available at http://laws-lois.justice.gc.ca/eng/acts/C-15.21/page-1.html.

participation.[77] Later, in addition to consultations with provinces and territories, representatives from the first nations (i.e., indigenous nations), and other civil society representatives, this framework was expanded to bilateral, regional, and multilateral trade negotiations. The *Framework for Conducting Environmental Assessment of Trade Negotiations* was adopted through a decision of the cabinet in February 2001.[78] Implementation of the cabinet directive on strategic environmental assessments in the area of trade policy was allocated to DFAIT.

The Canadian environmental assessment of trade agreements consists of three primary phases. In the initial environmental assessment, a DFAIT-led interagency committee analyzes the scope of the negotiations and the range of potential negative or positive environmental impacts within Canada from the economic effects of the potential treaty. If these are found to be minimal, the formal assessment halts at this stage.[79] If a second phase is mandated, it involves the elaboration of a draft study, with a third phase resulting in a final report. The draft environmental assessment is intended to assist Canadian trade negotiators. The final report describes the result of the trade negotiations and speculates on the role the assessment played in reaching the conclusion. All stages are guided by public participation requirements, including the publication of drafts; a website designed for interested stakeholders to comment on the assessment; interdepartmental and multilevel government consultation; and an explicit feedback loop in which concerns that have arisen are factored into the investigation. *Ex post* monitoring and *ex post* assessment might be recommended but are not mandatory.[80]

Several features are noteworthy. First, the Canadian environmental assessments focus almost exclusively on environmental issues, rather than social and development issues. Despite this narrow scope, the Canadian government refers to the assessment instrument as an indispensable decision-making tool for promoting sustainable development. Environmental assessments contribute to the enhanced transparency and good governance principles of sustainable development by encouraging "more open decision making within the federal government by engaging representatives from other levels of government, the public, the private sector and non-governmental organizations in this process."[81] The environmental assessment guidelines succinctly summarize these objectives: "to assist Canadian negotiators integrate environmental considerations into the negotiating process by providing information on the environmental impacts of the proposed trade agreement; and to address pub-

---

77   CEAA, *Guidelines for Implementing the* Cabinet Directive on the Environmental Assessment of Policy, Plan and Program Proposals (Privy Council Off. & CEAA 2010).

78   DFAIT, *Framework for Conducting Environmental Assessments of Trade Negotiations* (DFAIT Feb. 2001), available at   http://www.international.gc.ca/trade-agreements-accords-commerciaux /env/framework-cadre.aspx.

79   *See* Gehring & Cordonier Segger, *supra* note 13, at 208.

80   *Id.*

81   DFAIT, *supra* note 78.

lic concerns by documenting how environmental factors are being considered in the course of trade negotiations."[82]

The Canadian assessment process seeks a balance between public participation and new ideas and direct impact on the negotiation, that is, the question as to how the assessment results influence the negotiations. It does not assess social and developmental concerns explicitly and is restricted to environmental impacts within Canada (even though certain health issues are considered). The procedure eschews any investigation of environmental impacts on the trading partner or potential implications on a global level.

The environmental impact assessments of the United States and Canada are similar in their outcomes. For instance, the 2003 *Initial Strategic Environmental Assessment Report of the Canada–Central America Four Free Trade Negotiations* (El Salvador, Guatemala, Honduras, and Nicaragua) concluded that the small quantity of trade flows overall would have negligible economic effects, and therefore, the environmental consequences were insignificant for Canada.[83] Even in areas where increased exports such as high-value paper and plastics were likely, the Central America negotiations were deemed to preclude adverse environmental effects. The assessment did not consider effects of the negotiations on the C4 countries (El Salvador, Guatemala, Honduras, and Nicaragua), nor was a more regional approach to an environmental assessment considered. Given the limited scope of Canada's environmental assessment process, this missed opportunity is regrettable but understandable. Basic support for further studies in the C4, coupled with international coordination of assessment efforts, might have enabled Canada to address impacts with regard to the trading partners.

As another example, Canada's initial environmental assessment of the proposed free trade agreement (FTA) with Andean countries concluded:

> While FTAs with the Andean Community are expected to provide increased market access into Canada, it is unlikely that there will be a substantial increase in trade in services as a result of these negotiations. Canada is already quite open in most services sectors and no domestic regulatory changes are expected as a result of FTAs with the Andean Community. There may be some increased services exports to Andean countries, but it is difficult to segregate the effects of the Canada-Andean Community trade negotiations from those resulting from Canada's other trade negotiations or implementation of existing regional or bilateral trade agreements or from unilateral liberalization. Generally speaking, while the environmental impacts are not expected to be significant, we will need to consider indirect

---

82   *Id.*, at 4.

83   DFAIT, *Initial Strategic Environmental Assessment Report of the Canada–Central America Four Free Trade Negotiations (El Salvador, Guatemala, Honduras and Nicaragua)* (DFAIT 2003), available at http://www.international.gc.ca/trade-agreements-accords-commerciaux/env /EAlist-listeEE.aspx.

or cumulative impacts and the synergies between environmental goods and services which may increase the impact.[84]

In other words, these types of assessment are less helpful to developing country partners and have less potential to identify development opportunities than they are to Canada. In spite of vigorous public participation provisions, the restricted scope of the assessments, together with their focus on environmental impacts of economic changes alone, appears to limit their ability to signal opportunities for sustainable development cooperation, inclusion, or equity in developing countries.

Securing Greater Equity through Trade Impact Assessments

Some observations can be made about the role that impact assessments might play in securing more equitable trade agreements.

Economic Considerations Continue to Dominate Trade-Related Impact Assessment Instruments

Impact assessments require economic analysis to assess the likely impact of proposed economic development in the parties to a trade negotiation or financial arrangement. An impact assessment is based on relative consensus on simple cases (for example, tariffs) that use commonly acknowledged econometric calculations. The influence of impact assessments extends beyond initial flows of trade in goods to shape infrastructure projects (harbors, roads, airports) and facilities for trade in services such as transport, health, education, and other vulnerable social sectors. Therefore, careful consideration of equity issues, including the potential for a trade agreement to widen or narrow existing income and other disparities, is important.

The European Union: Sui Generis in Its Application of Developmental and Social Concerns in Trade-Related Environmental Impact Assessments

The United Nations Environment Programme (UNEP) gave special recognition to the EU for its fully integrated impact assessment instrument.[85] Although most environmental impact assessment tools fail to explicitly consider social and developmental issues, the EU's sustainability impact assessments model amalgamates economic, social, and environmental issues using a mix of measures and indicators constantly undergoing refinement. The *SIA Handbook* enunciates the virtues of a flexible, context-specific methodological approach to sustainability impact assessment. In keeping with its cutting-edge status in impact assessment innovation, the EU is considering proposals to extend

---

84   *Canada–Andean Community Free Trade Negotiations—Initial Environmental Assessment Report* (Jan. 2008), available at http://www.international.gc.ca/trade-agreements-accords -commerciaux/agr-acc/andean-andin/ea-andean-andine.aspx?lang=en.

85   UNEP, *Reference Manual for the Integrated Assessment of Trade-Related Policies* (UNEP 2001).

sustainability impact assessments to human rights. This development, from the perspective of securing increased law, justice, and development through opportunity, inclusion, and equity, is a step in the right direction.

Public Participation Has Become Central, Although Successful Engagement Is Inconsistent at Best

Most impact assessment mechanisms and practices rely on domestic public inputs to direct the extensiveness of the study and to identify potential environmental or social impacts of trade liberalization. Expert groups work with the public and with civil society organizations but are expected to investigate the validity of concerns raised through consultation feedback cycles. At a minimum, initial impact assessment reports are published or available on government websites, and solicitation of comments occurs. Final drafts of impact assessments seek to incorporate issues deemed material, often addressing concerns that have arisen through public participation. Impact assessment procedures such as the EU's sustainability impact assessment procedure integrate sustainable development concerns, taking potential social impacts into consideration. These impact assessments depend on strong public participation and often have a broad range of participation mechanisms instilled in their methodologies. Numerous workshops and consultations, at both formal and informal levels, are held at each phase of the assessment. Sustainability impact assessments hold the potential to facilitate cross-boundary consultations through a coordinated structure of transfrontier public discussions.[86] As an essential tool for signaling concerns related to equity and potential disparities in the effects of a potential trade negotiation, public participation and engagement procedures offer an excellent starting point. However, inconsistencies remain, in part due to lack of support, in terms of capacity and resources. The DG Trade is considering the formalization of such processes, as discussed in the *Draft Handbook for Sustainability Impact Assessment (SIA Handbook)*, and this is one area in which further development of impact assessment instruments holds the potential for equity and inclusion.[87]

Regulatory Reviews, a Fundamental Aspect of Environmental Impact Assessments, Seem Less Applicable in Sustainability Impact Assessments

Chiefly in the case of the Canadian environmental assessments and the U.S. environmental reviews of trade negotiations, regulatory reviews are an integral part of the assessment process. In contrast, the *SIA Handbook* has no provisions mandating the analysis of regulations. Indeed, EU consultants rarely give regulatory analysis a central role in the studies undertaken. Assessing the

---

86 Transboundary consultations, however, are not easy to organize. For example, the allocation of responsibilities for facilitating these international discussions raises important questions that could require clarification. In addition, discrepancies related to substantive and temporal issues that may exist in the scoping process need to be assuaged.

87 *SIA Handbook, supra* note 43.

regulatory impact of trade liberalization is interesting to lawyers specifically because of the need to harmonize international commitments with the national legal framework. Not surprisingly, the majority of studies undertaken merely reiterate that trade positions requiring negative modifications to national environmental regulatory configurations are untenable. However, this trend may be diminishing; due to increased public awareness concerning investment arbitration, recent U.S. environmental reviews have attempted to rebuff the argument that investor-state arbitration processes could be used to negatively influence U.S. environmental laws.[88]

Conclusions

Differing methodologies and applications of impact assessment tools and several deficiencies inhibit the evolution of impact assessments of trade agreements into a universally utilized instrument that integrates principles of sustainable development, serving as a tool for opportunity, equity, and inclusion.

The focus of the current instruments—principally national—has a limiting effect on their applicability.[89] This defect is clearest in the case of Canada, where global environmental impacts of trade negotiations enter analysis only if they affect Canada. The national nature, even though endorsed by the WTO Doha Ministerial Declaration, could lead to imbalances in scenarios in which bilateral trade negotiations take place among trading partners with disparate resources and stringency of regulation. This situation may be exacerbated if parties to an existing regional trade agreement enter into a trade agreement with a third country, which then assesses the impact in a necessarily narrow way (for example, the case of the U.S.-Andean trade agreement).

One potential solution to the paucity of impact assessments with a global perspective is embodied in the framework of the EU sustainability impact assessment, which mandates a reciprocal impact assessment on trading partners. Although some critics have argued that the overall effect of the sustainability impact assessment is limited, there is growing evidence that the EU Commission's reports have legal value and can be referred to as administrative practice. On several occasions, negotiation teams amended their positions based on a sustainability impact assessment finding. Employing regional

---

88   The case in question was the environmental review assessing the Australia-U.S. Free Trade Agreement. The USTR took the position that regulatory alterations were not intrinsically detrimental to U.S. interests in the case of an "open economic environment and the shared legal traditions and the confidence of investors in the fairness and integrity of their respective legal systems." For further discussion, see M. Kerr, *Sustainable Development in the Australia-US Free Trade Agreement,* in Gehring & Cordonier Segger, *supra* note 13, at 499, 510. *See* lengthy discussion in USTR, *Final Environmental Review of the Dominican Republic–Central America–United States Free Trade Agreement* (USTR 2005); USTR, *Final Environmental Review of the United States–Morocco Free Trade Agreement* (July 2004), available at http://www.ustr.gov /assets/Trade_Agreements/Bilateral/Morocco_FTA/asset_upload_file569_5831.pdf.

89   Nicholas Low, *Global Ethics and Environment* (Routledge 1999).

impact assessments to overcome a lack of parity among trading partners involves methodological and structural innovation as well as increased information exchange. However, attempts by NAFTA trading partners to initiate an integrated assessment process at the regional level have not progressed beyond discussions about abstract methodology issues. In fact, the EU is the sole region to produce a self-reflective environmental assessment. The multilateral forum of the WTO provides another potential solution to the inadequacies of national and bilateral impact assessments.

Moving beyond the narrow focus of common impact assessments of trade, there is greater potential for applying strategic environmental assessments to negotiations. When environmental impact assessments are applied to projects, target-related indicators (performance based, specific timeline) limit the reach of enhancement and mitigation recommendations. Conversely, strategic-level assessments incorporate process-related indicators such as the soundness of institutional planning, management processes, and mechanisms. Indeed, strategic environmental assessments have already been formulated and implemented in most states for the analysis of land use plans or policies. Broadly defined in Article 2.6 of the 2003 Protocol on Strategic Environmental Assessment (the Kiev Protocol), strategic environmental assessments are

> the evaluation of the likely environmental, including health, effects, which comprises the determination of the scope of an environmental report and its preparation, the carrying out of public participation and consultations, and the taking into account of the environmental report and the results of the public participation and consultations in a plan or programme.[90]

Thus, the Kiev Protocol explicitly regulates the impact assessment of plans and programs but is not binding at the policy level. This protocol is an international treaty designed to mitigate the tension between internationally delimited impact assessment procedures and state freedom to govern the exploitation of the environment. Trade policy and negotiations are not covered under the protocol, which mentions the importance of assessing the environmental and developmental (particularly health) impact of plans and programs. The Kiev Protocol limits the assessment of plans and programs to the following areas: agriculture; forestry; fisheries; energy;[91] industry, including mining; transport; regional development; waste management; water management; telecommunications; tourism; and town and country planning or land use.

Other international cooperation has been based on the foundations laid out in the Kiev Protocol. UNEP adopted a more inclusive approach to impact

---

90   The Kiev Protocol was entered into force on July 11, 2010. By June 2013, 25 countries had ratified the protocol. It was negotiated in the context of the 1991 Espoo Convention (30 I.L.M. 800). For more information, see UNECE Components of Strategic Assessment, available at http://www.unece.org/env/eia/sea_protocol.html.

91   Jochen Lamp, *The Baltic Sea Gas Pipeline: A Transnational Infrastructure Project as Touchstone for International Environmental Standards*, 58(4–5) Osteuropa 383–391 (2008).

assessments, fabricating an expanded definition that considers "the economic, environmental and social effects of trade measures, the linkages between these effects, and aims to build upon this analysis by identifying ways in which the negative consequences can be avoided or mitigated, and ways in which positive effects can be enhanced."[92]

UNEP avoided proposing a single methodology, suggesting instead that countries carefully tailor their assessments to the specific sector of trade and potential impacts at hand. After testing and refining integrated assessment methods through various country studies,[93] UNEP developed a considerable amount of analytical data that can be used by developing countries and others seeking to undertake specific studies, but it has not developed any rules.[94] The scope of these studies has been national in character.

As this chapter has indicated, the inconsistencies and patchiness of the current international impact assessment regime leave plenty of room for improvement to galvanize environmental protection and to graft sustainable development issues firmly onto trade negotiation proceedings. In this sense, the evolution of the sustainability impact assessment in the European Union can serve as an example. Given that the current scale and scope of the described assessments are restricted, a genuinely collective review mechanism is advisable. Broader participation is possible and necessary. Multilateral—or at least multilaterally coordinated—assessment could provide superior results because the impact on all participating members would be explored simultaneously. Akin to the case of transnational projects, broader information and participation can drive legal innovations as ameliorative results feed more easily into the negotiation process.

An expanded commitment to equity, informed by the precautionary principle, might be met procedurally by some form of impact assessment adopted at the institutional level of the WTO.[95] The obligation to perform an impact assessment can be called "precaution through process."[96] Conducting simultaneous assessments at the WTO level can help overcome resource and regulatory imbalances. Perhaps the most egalitarian of the international financial institutions, the WTO operates on a *do ut des* basis, precluding any

---

92   UNEP, *Reference Manual for the Integrated Assessment of Trade-Related Policies* (UNEP 2001), available at http://www.unep.ch/etb/publications/intAssessment/refmaniaFinal.pdf.

93   UNEP Economics and Trade Programme, *Country Projects on Trade Liberalisation and the Environment and on the Design and Implementation of Economic Instruments*, available at http://www.unep.ch/etu/etp/acts/capbld/cp.htm.

94   *See* UNEP, *Annual Report* 68 (UNEP 2006).

95   *See* Gehring & Cordonier Segger, *supra* note 13, at 191, 192.

96   *See* M. Gehring, *Nachhaltigkeit durch Verfahren im Welthandel* (diss., U. Hamburg 2005). *See* also C. Weeramantry's separate opinion in *New Zealand v. France;* he saw the obligation to perform an environmental impact assessment as ancillary to the precautionary principle, ICJ Decision (Sep. 22, 1995), ICJ Request for an Examination of the Situation in Accordance with Paragraph 63 of the Court's Judgment of Dec. 20, 1974 in the Nuclear Tests (*New Zealand v. France*) Case, ICJ Reports (1995), 344.

single country from swaying the outcome of negotiations. Even though a full WTO review, comprising all the negotiations and impact assessments on the 148 member states, would probably be untenable, subsets of the membership might be able to undertake such a task. However, the dearth of commitment on devising a coherent methodological framework has obstructed fruitful progress on this front. Arguably, the best place for coordinating assessment efforts within the WTO is the Trade Policy Review Mechanism (TPRM). The rationale for embedding multilateral impact assessments in the TPRM is tripartite: congruencies in the objectives and outcomes of the tools,[97] adherence to comparable principles, and feasibility within the established institutional arrangement.[98] Furthermore, discussion on such an innovation may not be politically charged; information provided in a trade policy review is barred from applicability in dispute settlements. An incipient WTO strategic impact assessment body would be more likely to receive acclaim if it were molded from existing institutional structures.[99]

There are myriad parallels between impact assessments and current trade policy review mechanisms. Both instruments are designed to exchange and obtain information but are not teleological toward results rendered.[100] Moreover, both trade policy reviews and impact assessments adhere to analogous principles: trade policy reviews scrutinize the degree to which WTO members fulfill their WTO commitments; impact assessments analyze the extent to which states ponder the multifarious implications of new areas of trade. Thus, impact assessments could be considered part of the WTO pledge to support sustainable development initiatives and policies of its members. Furthermore, the transparency attribute of trade policy reviews is shared by impact assessments, making impact assessments relevant in different stages of the trade policy review process. One offshoot of such coherence would be to enable members to include their latest national trade impact assessments in their mandatory country reports. As the trade policy reviews are currently configured, national impact assessments are considered extraneous: Switzerland included sections on trade and the environment in its 2000 trade policy review country report, but the WTO secretariat was unable to review those aspects.[101]

Another point of connection resulting in improved complementarity between nationally derived impact assessments and trade policy reviews could

---

97 Bernard M. Hoekman & Will Martin, *Developing Countries and the WTO: A Pro-active Agenda* (Blackwell 2001).

98 Kym Anderson & Bernard M. Hoekman, *The WTO's Core Rules and Disciplines* 2 (Edward Elgar, 2006).

99 Tilman Santarius et al., *Balancing Trade and Environment — An Ecological Reform of the WTO as a Challenge in Sustainable Global Governance* 46 (Wuppertal Paper No. 133, Wuppertal Inst. for Climate, Env., Energy, Feb. 2004).

100 *Id.*, at 45.

101 *See* Trade Policy Review Body, *Joint Trade Policy Review Switzerland and Liechtenstein*, (Minutes of Meeting, Dec. 4 & 6, 2000, WTO-Dokument WT/TPR/M/77/Add.1 vol. 24, Jan. 2001).

be the augmented range of information gathering executed by the WTO secretariat. The secretariat could extend its focus on other international financial institutions to embrace environmental or developmental (including human rights—an integral aspect of sustainable development) organizations. Finally, the publication requirements of the TPRM are in line with common impact assessment tools. Concerns arising from the impact assessment consultation process could be brought to the table at the multilateral level to abet coordination. Participation in these debates should be extended to NGOs, similar to the multifaceted consultation requirements of extant impact assessments.[102]

At a fundamental level, a truly multilateral impact assessment regime would have to ensure broad developing country participation to countervail perceptions that the innovation is yet another way to move forward with disguised protectionism. Some observers fear that impact assessments could become a precondition for trade agreements[103] or could consume the diminutive resources of strained environmental ministries. Substantive inclusion of other international stakeholders and transferring elements of the process to competent international organizations such as UNEP and UNDP are alternatives worthy of examination.[104]

There are many lessons to be learned from national and regional assessment measures in order to facilitate greater equity and inclusion within the WTO. The framework encompassing current national impact assessments is conducive to public participation, although useful enhancement and mitigation recommendations are limited by the national scope of the mechanism. Moreover, integrated impact assessments are indicative of substantive advances but have uneven sway on the outcomes of national negotiation positions. This chapter has highlighted the need for participation and coordination efforts at the regional level for regional trade agreements, as well as the potential for progress at the multilateral level for the WTO. Inherent difficulties exist in efforts to innovate existing multilateral organizations and to open up proceedings and decision making to heretofore excluded participants. Attempts by the WTO to replicate impact assessment strategies tested by other international organizations (such as the World Bank) have led to critiques from developing countries. Any innovation in institutional mandate and avenues of participation within the fledgling impact assessment regime need to be broad based and conducted in a manner that facilitates ownership of the process for developing countries. The long-term premises of sustainable development, founded on both intragenerational and intergenerational equity, necessitate a high threshold of consensus and proactive commitment.

---

102 OECD, *Trading Up: Economic Perspectives on Development Issues in the Multilateral Trading System* (OECD 2006).

103 USAID provided funding for the Jordanian side of the impact assessment process for the U.S.-Jordan Free Trade Agreement.

104 Frank Biermann, *A World Environment Organization: Solution or Threat for Effective International Environmental Governance?* (Ashgate 2005).

The Treatment of Insolvency of Natural Persons in South African Law

An Appeal for a Balanced and Integrated Approach

ANDRÉ BORAINE AND MELANIE ROESTOFF

The increased availability of credit around the world and the recent global financial crisis have emphasized the need for modern and effective regimes for the insolvency of natural persons.[1] An effective and efficient personal insolvency regime, and hence its ability to assist in counteracting poverty, economic exclusion, and inequality, can play an important role in the economic development of a country, especially in South Africa.[2]

To better understand the availability and operation of personal insolvency and debt relief measures in South Africa, one must have an understanding of the socioeconomic conditions in South Africa and the levels of overindebtedness of natural person debtors in that society.[3]

South Africa can largely be classified as a developing economy, although it contains elements of a highly developed economy and elements of an extremely underdeveloped economy. The differences between these two extremes are stark, and there are few bridges between these two landscapes.[4]

As of the latest national census, South Africa had 50 million inhabitants, of whom around 25 percent were formally classified as unemployed and around

---

1   See Working Group on the Treatment of the Insolvency of Natural Persons, *Report on the Treatment of the Insolvency of Natural Persons* 2 (Insolvency and Creditor/Debtor Regimes Task Force, World Bank 2012), available at http://www-wds.worldbank.org/external/default /WDSContentServer/WDSP/IB/2013/05/02/000333037_20130502131241/Rendered/PDF/771 700WP0WB0In00Box377289B00PUBLIC0.pdf.

2   See Michael R. Rochelle, *Lowering the Penalties for Failure: Using the Insolvency Law as a Tool for Spurring Economic Growth; The American Experience, and Possible Uses for South Africa*, 2 J. South African L. 315 (1996). With regard to financial inclusion in South Africa, see World Bank, *South Africa Economic Update: Focus on Financial Inclusion* (May 2013). As indicated in this report (at v), this topic is especially important for South Africa because it could help reduce poverty and inequality and stimulate job creation.

3   See Hermie Coetzee & Melanie Roestoff, *Consumer Debt Relief in South Africa: Should the Insolvency System Provide for NINA Debtors? Lessons from New Zealand* (forthcoming).

4   For a general discussion of the socioeconomic context and social policy needs in South Africa, see Marius P. Olivier, Nicola Smit, & Evance R. Kalula, *Social Security: A Legal Analysis* (LexisNexis Butterworths 2003).

23 percent lived below the national poverty line.[5] Although white South Africans are generally perceived to be rich and black South Africans are generally perceived to be poor, the "new" society that has taken shape since the advent of the current democratic order in 1994 is not so clear-cut. To be sure, the former apartheid laws did exclude the majority of South Africans from many opportunities in the economy, including the credit markets. Despite this—and despite the fact that great inequalities still exist—the financial position of many black South Africans has improved over the past 20 years.[6] Although the average white-headed household still earns more than 5.5 times the income of the average black-headed household, there has been a significant rise in the number of black-headed households that can be described as middle-class.[7] Overindebtedness can affect—and is affecting—all communities.

Of the estimated 50 million South Africans, nearly 16 million (almost a third) receive government social grants, such as children's grants, disability grants, or old-age grants.[8] However, the number of South Africans liable for personal income tax is significantly less than this figure.[9]

When it comes to granting credit, there was a major increase in the microloan market during the 1990s, when South Africa embraced a democratic constitution. This also gave rise to a significant problem of overindebtedness, especially among black South Africans.[10] Since June 2007, there has been an ongoing deterioration in the number of consumers in "good standing." At the end of December 2012, credit bureaus had recorded 19.97 million active credit consumers, of whom 9.34 million had impaired credit records. Thus, only

---

5   World Bank, *Poverty Headcount Ratio at National Poverty Line (% of Population)*, available at http://search.worldbank.org/data?qterm=national+poverty+rate&language=EN&format (accessed Apr. 10, 2013); *See Quarterly Labour Force Survey* (Statistical Release P0211, Statistics South Africa, July 31, 2012), available at http://www.statssa.gov.za/publications/P0211 /P02114thQuarter2012.pdf (accessed Apr. 10, 2013).

6   The income-expenditure survey conducted by Statistics South Africa indicates that the annual household income of white-headed South African households increased by 0.4 percent between 2005–2006 and 2010–2011, while the corresponding figure for other population groups ranged between 28 and 37 percent. *See Income and Expenditure of Households* (Statistical Release P0100, Statistics South Africa, 2012).

7   Murray Leibbrandt et al., *Trends in South African Income Distribution and Poverty since the Fall of Apartheid* (Social, Employment and Migration Working Paper No. 101, Organisation for Economic Co-operation and Development, May 28, 2010).

8   *See* Pravin Gordhan, *2012 Budget Speech* (Feb. 22, 2012), available at http://www.treasury.gov .za/documents/national%20budget/2012/speech/speech.pdf. (accessed Apr. 10, 2013).

9   Oupa Magashula, *Address by the Commissioner of SARS to the Standing Committee on Finance on the 2011 Tax Statistics* (May 23, 2012), available at http://www.sars.gov.za/home .asp?pid=63144 (accessed Apr. 12, 2013). The South African Revenue Services (SARS) reported a growth in the individual tax register from 1.7 million in 1994 to 6 million in 2010. A further growth to more than 12 million was reported in 2011 following a policy change to register all individuals in formal employment. However, this figure does not reflect the number of individuals actually liable for income tax because all salary earners, irrespective of whether they are liable, must now be registered with SARS. *See* Coetzee & Roestoff, *supra* note 3.

10   André Boraine, *Some Thoughts on the Reform of Administration Orders and Related Issues*, 36 De Jure 217, 230 (2003).

53.2 percent of active credit consumers were in good standing.[11] Many of these overstretched or debt-stressed, if not insolvent, consumers will be subject to some kind of debt collection procedure.

Certain individual debt collection procedures, including wage garnishee orders, have become notorious due to abuses in the South African system. Garnishee orders have even been blamed for labor unrest, because these orders are not limited to a prescribed percentage of the debtor's income, giving rise to a zero paycheck situation for some debtors.[12] Debtors subject to garnishee orders are technically insolvent but are usually not able to file for sequestration with the view of ultimately obtaining a statutory discharge following rehabilitation because they do not meet the requirements set by the Insolvency Act 24 of 1936.

The Insolvency Act provides for sequestration, which entails a liquidation of assets; other statutes provide for debt-restructuring procedures, namely, the Magistrates' Courts Act 32 of 1944 (MCA) and the National Credit Act 34 of 2005 (NCA).[13] In addition, voluntary debt restructuring is possible for some debtors.

This chapter discusses and evaluates the statutory and nonstatutory procedures pertaining to the insolvency of natural persons, the regulation of insolvency practitioners, and the insolvency reform initiatives on the table in South Africa. The chapter demonstrates that the current South African system does not follow a balanced approach and it does not provide adequate debt relief to all insolvent or debt-stressed individuals. There is no principled view or approach regarding the treatment of the insolvency of natural persons in South African law. This chapter is therefore an appeal to South African lawmakers to address this weakness; in this regard, it proposes suggestions for insolvency law reform.

---

11 National Credit Regulator, *Credit Bureau Monitor Fourth Quarter* (Dec. 2012), available at http://www.ncr.org.za/publications/CBM%20Dec%202012.pdf (accessed Apr. 10, 2013).

12 "In incidents, entire pay checks have been absorbed for the repayment of debt through garnishee orders, while in other cases miners have been forced to repay in excess of ten times their outstanding debt." *See* Malcolm Rees, *Mines to Investigate Garnishes*, Moneyweb (Apr. 3, 2013), available at http://www.moneyweb.co.za/moneyweb-economic-trends/mines-to investigate-garnishees. For proposals to improve the position, *see* Working Document on Magistrates' Courts Amendment Bill (Feb. 21, 2013), available at http://www.northernlaw.co.za/Documents/magistrate_court/Working%20document%20Magistrates'%20Courts%20Amendment%20Bill%2021Feb13.pdf.

13 For a detailed discussion of the South African statutory measures, *see* Melanie Roestoff & Hermie Coetzee, *Consumer Debt Relief in South Africa: Lessons from America and England; and Suggestions for the Way Forward*, 24 South African Mercantile L.J. 53 (2012); Lienne Steyn, *Statutory Regulation of Forced Sale of the Home in South Africa* 349 (L.L.D. thesis, U. of Pretoria, 2012); André Boraine, Corlia van Heerden, & Melanie Roestoff, *A Comparison between Formal Debt Administration and Debt Review: The Pros and Cons of These Measures and Suggestions for Law Reform*, part 1, 45(1) De Jure 80 (2012), part 2, 45(2) De Jure 254 (2012).

Sequestration under the Insolvency Act

The insolvency of natural persons is primarily regulated by the Insolvency Act,[14] which provides that a sequestration order can be obtained upon application to the South African High Court[15] by a creditor for compulsory sequestration of the debtor's estate[16] or upon application for voluntary surrender of his or her estate by the debtor.[17] After a sequestration order is granted, the debtor is formally referred to as an "insolvent."

The granting of a sequestration order is based on a number of statutory requirements, but the "advantage for creditors" requirement is the decisive factor regarding whose estate will be sequestrated and whose will not.[18] One of the most important questions used to determine compliance with this requirement is if the creditors will receive a pecuniary benefit.[19] In practice, this relates to the question of whether unsecured concurrent creditors will receive at least a dividend based on the pari passu principle. The size of the dividend is not prescribed in the Insolvency Act, but some courts require an indication in the case of voluntary surrender that the dividend will be at least 20 cents to the rand.[20] The court will consider other factors within the realm of the advantage principle, such as whether the trustee will be able to unearth other assets, and also alternative repayment measures, such as an administration order under the MCA or debt review under the NCA.[21] The court hearing the matter has discretion to grant the sequestration order.[22] The requirement of the advantage of creditors plays a significant role in the exercise of this dis-

---

14   *See*, in general, Jennifer M. Kunst et al., *Meskin: Insolvency Law*, chs. 2–3 (LexisNexis 2012), Eberhard Bertelsmann et al., *Mars: The Law of Insolvency in South Africa*, chs. 3–5 (Juta 2008).

15   The sequestration procedure is therefore expensive. *See* Melanie Roestoff & Stéfan Renke, *Debt Relief for Consumers: Insolvency and Consumer Protection Legislation* pt. 2, 27 Obiter 98, 99 (2006).

16   Insolvency Act of 1936, secs. 8–12 (hereinafter Insolvency Act).

17   *Id.*, at secs. 3–7.

18   *Id.*, at secs. 6, 10, 12.

19   *See Meskin & Co. v. Friedman* (1948) 2 SA (W) 555, 559; *Lynn & Main Inc. v. Naidoo* (2006) 1 SA (N) 59, 68; *Ex parte Bouwer & Similar Applications* (2009) 6 SA (GNP) 382, 386.

20   In the past, the South African courts have set the minimum dividend at 10 cents on the rand for each concurrent creditor (*Nieuwenhuizen & Another v. Nedcor Bank Ltd.* [2001] 2 All SA 364 (O) 367; *Ex parte Kelly* [2008] 4 SA 615 (T) 617). In recent times, however, a dividend of 20 cents on the rand is generally regarded as the minimum benefit that has to be established before a sequestration application will be granted (*Ex parte Ogunlaja & Others* [2011] JOL 27029 (GNP) para. 9).

21   *See* C. H. Smith, *The Recurrent Motive of the Insolvency Act: Advantage of Creditors* 7 Modern Bus. L. 27 (1985). *See* also *Jhatam v. Jhatam* (1958) 4 SA 36 (N); *Behrman v. Sideris* (1950) 2 SA 366 (T); *London Estates (Pty) Ltd. v. Nair* (1957) 3 SA 591 (D); *Ex parte Ford & Two Similar Cases* (2009) 3 SA 376 (C). *See*, further, C. Van Heerden & A. Boraine, *The Interaction between the Debt Relief Measures in the National Credit Act 34 of 2005 and Aspects of Insolvency Law*, 12 Potchefstroom Electronic L.J. 22 (2009).

22   *Julie Whyte Dresses (Pty) Ltd. v. Whitehead* (1970) 3 SA 218 (D) 219.

cretion, and the court will not grant an order if it deems the application to be an abuse of the sequestration process.[23]

After sequestration, an insolvent debtor may be rehabilitated, which in principle gives the debtor a discharge of presequestration debt.[24] Sequestration coupled with rehabilitation under the Insolvency Act is the only formal statutory procedure that provides for a discharge of debt of overburdened debtors. In some instances, unsecured creditors either will receive no payment or will receive only a trifling dividend in lieu of the original debt. Still, as a rule, the debtor will enjoy the advantage of the discharge that follows rehabilitation. The advantage to creditors is decisive in this regard. If the court cannot be convinced of such advantage, the estate will not be sequestrated and the debtor will not receive the statutory discharge. This situation causes a differentiation between debtors whose estates can be sequestrated and those who are overburdened but who cannot obtain a sequestration order due to the absence of an advantage to creditors. Such differentiation may be irrational in some instances.[25]

This situation is illustrated by *Van Rooyen v. Van Rooyen (Automutual Investments (EC) (Pty) Ltd., Intervening Creditor).*[26] In this instance, two former members of a close corporation, S and V, bound themselves as sureties for the due performance of certain contractual payments in favor of a creditor of the close corporation. The estate of S was subsequently sequestrated, but no dividend was paid out to the creditors. In view of the sequestration of S's estate, V became liable for the total remaining debt of the close corporation. Because

---

23 *See Craggs v. Dedekind; Baartman v. Baartman & Another; Van Aardt v. Borrett* (1996) 1 SA (C) 935, 937; *Ex parte Steenkamp & Related Cases* (1996) 3 SA (C) 822, 825; *Van Eck v. Kirkwood* (1997) 1 SA (SE) 289, 290; *Van Rooyen v. Van Rooyen (Automutual Investements (EC) (Pty) Ltd., Intervening Creditor)* (2000) 2 All SA (SE) 485, 490; *Beinash & Co. v. Nathan* (1998) 3 SA (W) 540, 542; *Lemley v. Lemley* (2009) JDR 0445 (SE) 4. Because sequestration can eventually afford a debtor a discharge of his or her debts, the process of compulsory sequestration has in the past been used—or, according to some, abused—by debtors in the form of an application for a so-called friendly sequestration to obtain debt relief. *See* Roger G. Evans, *Friendly Sequestrations, the Abuse of the Process of Court, and Possible Solutions for Overburdened Debtors,* 13 South African Mercantile L.J. 485 (2001). *See* also *Esterhuizen v. Swanepoel & Sixteen Other Cases* (2004) 4 SA (W) 89, 92. This phenomenon developed because proving advantage in a compulsory sequestration application is less onerous than proving advantage in a voluntary sequestration application. Unlike voluntary surrender, which requires positive proof of advantage for creditors, compulsory sequestration requires only a "reasonable prospect" that it will be to the advantage of creditors—compare the wording of the Insolvency Act, secs. 10(c) and 12(1)(c). Furthermore, no formal requirements are prescribed with regard to compulsory sequestration; Catherine Smith, *Friendly and Not So Friendly Sequestrations,* 3 Modern Bus. L. 58, 59 (1981). However, regarding applications for voluntary surrender, the South African courts have tightened their approach to thwart abuse of the process. *See,* for example, *Ex parte Bouwer & Similar Applications, supra* note 19, at 386, and, further, Bertelsmann et al., *supra* note 14, at 63.

24 *See* Insolvency Act, sec. 129.

25 *See* André Boraine & Roger Evans, *The Law of Insolvency and the Bill of Rights,* in *The Bill of Rights Compendium* para. 4A8 (LexisNexis 2009 update); Lee Steyn, *Human Rights Issues in South African Law,* 13 Intl. Insolvency Rev. 1, 11 (2004).

26 *See Van Rooyen v. Van Rooyen, supra* note 23. *See* also Boraine & Evans, *supra* note 25, at para 4A8; Evans, *supra* note 23, at 503.

V could not repay this debt, her mother brought an application for compulsory sequestration of her estate, but the application was denied due to the fact that the court did not accept that there would be an advantage for creditors. Because her debt amounted to more than R 50,000, she could not apply for administration under Section 74 of the MCA. Debt review under the NCA, which was not an option at the stage when the *Van Rooyen* case was decided, would offer relief only if the debt qualified as a credit agreement as provided for by this act. As is discussed below, the alternative procedures of administration and debt review do not provide discharge for overburdened debtors. Moreover, South African insolvency legislation does not provide for a procedure for dealing with assetless estates or no-income-no-asset (NINA) debtors.[27]

Rehabilitation and Discharge of Debt under the Insolvency Act

The only statutory discharge offered to natural person debtors in South African law is provided for by Section 129 of the Insolvency Act. Sequestration followed by rehabilitation of the insolvent affords the debtor a discharge of all presequestration debts.[28]

An insolvent will automatically be rehabilitated after 10 years from the date of sequestration. However, any interested party is entitled to apply to the court within that 10-year period to prevent automatic rehabilitation.[29] An insolvent may also be rehabilitated by means of a court order.[30] The Insolvency Act provides various conditions and different time limits before the debtor may apply for rehabilitation, but he or she usually has to wait four years from the commencement date of sequestration.[31]

An insolvent may apply for rehabilitation to the same court that granted the sequestration order.[32] The application must be supported by an affidavit in which the insolvent declares that he or she has made a complete surrender of his or her estate and has not granted or promised any person any benefit or entered into any secret agreement with the intent to induce the trustee or any creditor not to oppose the application. The affidavit must contain information relating to the dividend paid out to the creditors and the current income, expenditures, and assets of the insolvent.[33] Anyone with an interest in the estate may object to the insolvent's rehabilitation.[34] The insolvent

---

27 *See* Roestoff & Coetzee, *supra* note 13; Coetzee & Roestoff, *supra* note 3.

28 Insolvency Act, sec. 129(1)(b).

29 *Id.*, at sec. 127A.

30 *Id.*, at sec. 124.

31 *See* the proviso to the Insolvency Act, sec. 124(2).

32 *See*, with regard to formal defects in aplications for rehabilitation, *Ex parte Mason* (1981) 4 SA 648 (D); *Ex parte Anderson* (1995) 1 SA 40 (SE); *Ex parte Minnie et Uxor* (1996) 3 SA 97 (SE); *Ex parte Elliot* (1997) 4 SA 292 (W); *Ex parte Van Zyl* (1997) 2 SA 438 (EC).

33 Insolvency Act, sec. 126.

34 *Id.*, at sec. 127(1).

must furnish security with the registrar of the high court in the value of at least R 500 for any costs incurred due to the opposition of the application for rehabilitation.[35] The insolvent must usually also give notice to the master of the high court and/or his or her trustee, as well as in the *Government Gazette*, depending on the specific statutory ground he or she relies on, prior to bringing the application.[36] The statutory grounds for rehabilitation by court order are as follows:

- The insolvent may apply for rehabilitation after 12 months have elapsed since the date of confirmation of the first trustee's account. The insolvent must publish a notice of the intended application in the *Government Gazette* at least six weeks prior to the application.[37]

- When the insolvent had been sequestrated previously, he or she may apply for rehabilitation three years after date of confirmation of the trustee's first account. Also, six weeks prior, notice must be given to the master and creditors with the publication of a notice to that effect in the *Government Gazette*.[38]

- When the insolvent has been convicted of any fraudulent act in relation to his or her existing or previous insolvency, or any other offense under Sections 132, 133, and 134 of the Insolvency Act, the insolvent may apply for rehabilitation after five years have elapsed from the date of conviction. Six weeks' prior notice must be given.[39]

- When no claims were proved by any creditor, the insolvent has not been convicted of an offense mentioned in Section 124(2)(c), and this is the first time that his or her estate has been sequestrated, the insolvent may apply for rehabilitation six months after the application for his or her sequestration. Six weeks' prior notice must be given.[40]

- When a composition is agreed to as indicated in Section 119(7) of the Insolvency Act, and where the master of the high court certifies that at least 50 cents on the rand was paid in respect to all claims proved against the estate, or when security was given for such payment, the insolvent may apply for rehabilitation. The insolvent must give three weeks' notice of the application in the *Government Gazette*, and a copy of the notice must also be handed to the trustee.[41]

---

35   *Id.*, at sec. 125.

36   *Id.*, at sec. 124.

37   *Id.*, at sec. 124(2)(a).

38   *Id.*, at sec. 124(2)(b).

39   *Id.*, at sec. 124(2)(c). In none of the cases mentioned in sec. 124(2) will the court order rehabilitation within four years after sequestration without the master's recommendation—proviso to sec. 124(2). *See* also *Ex parte Porrit* (1991) 3 SA 866 (N); *Ex parte Anderson* (1995) 1 SA 40 (SE); *Greub v. The Master* (1999) 1 SA 746 (C).

40   Insolvency Act, sec. 124(3).

41   *Id.*, at sec. 124(1).

- When all claims have been paid in full together with interest, the insolvent may, at any time after confirmation of the distribution account, apply for rehabilitation. Three weeks' prior notice must be given to the master and the trustee.[42]

The court hearing the application may refuse, postpone, or grant the requested order for rehabilitation and may also impose conditions for rehabilitation.[43] Before granting the order, the court must be convinced that the statutory requirements referred to above have been met and that the rehabilitation of the debtor is indeed desirable. It is thus accepted in South African law that an insolvent does not have a right to rehabilitation but that rehabilitation is a discretionary matter in the hands of the courts.[44] Such discretion must be exercised judicially and not arbitrarily.[45] It is normally expected that both the trustee and the master will provide a report as to the desirability of rehabilitation in a particular instance. Apart from the facts stated in the application of the insolvent, the court will also consider these reports and objections to rehabilitation raised by creditors, if any.[46] When exercising its discretion, the court will consider the desirability of rehabilitation in the sense of whether the insolvent deserves to be rehabilitated. In this regard, the question is if the insolvent is a person who ought to be allowed to trade with the public on the same basis as any other honest person.[47]

Subject to any conditions imposed by the court, rehabilitation ends sequestration; discharges all the insolvent's presequestration debts, except those arising out of any fraud on his or her part; and relieves the insolvent of every disability resulting from sequestration.[48] A claim for maintenance (alimony) is an ongoing obligation, and even a rehabilitated insolvent will remain obliged to pay maintenance out of future income. The court hearing the matter may also impose conditions for rehabilitation, including an order that certain debts will not be discharged upon rehabilitation.[49]

---

42   *Id.*, at sec. 124(5).

43   *Id.*, at sec. 127(2) and (3). *See*, further, *Kruger v. The Master* (1982) 1 SA 754 (W); *Ex parte Le Roux* (1996) 2 SA 419 (C); *Ex parte Theron; Ex parte Smit; Ex parte Webster* (1999) 4 SA 136 (O); *Ex parte Fourie* (2008) 4 All SA 340 (D).

44   *Ex parte Hittersay* (1974) 4 SA 326 (SWA).

45   *Ex parte Phillips* (1938) CPD 381.

46   *Ex parte Goshalia* (1957) 2 SA 182 (N); *Ex parte Isaacs* (1962) 4 SA 767 (W).

47   *Ex parte Heydenreich* (1917) TPD 657, 658; *Greub v. The Master* (1999) 1 SA 746 (C).

48   Insolvency Act, sec. 129(1).

49   *Id.*, at sec. 129, read with sec. 127(3) and (4).

Alternative Statutory Procedures

South African law provides two statutory debt-restructuring models for natural person debtors: administration order under the MCA[50] and debt review under the NCA.[51]

Administration Orders under the MCA

Natural person debtors who are unable to pay the amount of any judgment against them or to meet their financial obligations and who do not have sufficient assets capable of attachment to satisfy such judgment or obligations may apply to a magistrate's court for an administration order that would, if successful, compel the creditors to accept a rearrangement or restructuring of the debt.[52]

Although this procedure does provide debt relief for natural person debtors, its application is limited in that it applies only when the debts amount to not more than R 50,000.[53] The procedure offers no discharge,[54] and debtors may thus remain under debt almost indefinitely. Debts that are claimable only in the future, that is, after the granting of a particular administration order, are not included in the order.[55]

In terms of an administration order, a court will assist the debtor by appointing an administrator to take control of the debtor's financial affairs and to manage the payment of debts due to creditors.[56] In terms of the order, the debtor has an obligation to make monthly or weekly payments to the administrator. The administrator, after deducting necessary expenses and a specified remuneration determined by a prescribed tariff, must in turn make a regular distribution out of such payments to all proven creditors.[57] The procedure has an element of a collective judicial procedure and is therefore sometimes described as a modified form of insolvency proceedings.[58]

---

50 Administration orders are regulated by the Magistrates' Courts Act (MCA), sec. 74. *See*, in general, L. T. C. Harms et al., *Civil Procedure in the Magistrates' Courts* paras. 37.1–37.10 (Butterworths 1997); Torquil J. M. Paterson, *Eckards' Principles of Civil Procedure in the Magistrates' Courts* 218 (Juta 2005).

51 *See* National Credit Act (NCA), sec. 86. *See*, also, in general, C. Van Heerden, *Over-indebtedness and Reckless Credit* (ch. 11) & *A Practical Discussion of the Debt Counselling Process* (ch. 14), in *Guide to the National Credit Act* (J. W. Scholtz ed., LexisNexis 2008); J. M. Otto & R.-L. Otto, *The National Credit Act Explained* 64 (LexisNexis 2013).

52 MCA, sec. 74(1).

53 Government Notice R1411, in *Government Gazette* 19435 (Oct. 30, 1998).

54 *See* MCA, sec. 74U.

55 *Cape Town Municipality v. Dunne* (1964) 1 SA (C) 741, 744. *See*, further, *Carletonville Huishoudelike Voorsieners (Edms) Bpk v. Van Vuuren en 'n Ander* (1962) 2 SA (T) 296, and M. A. Greig, *Administration Orders as Shark Nets*, 117 S.A.L.J. 622, 624 (2000), for a discussion of *in futuro* debts as well as criticism of the exclusion thereof.

56 MCA, sec. 74E.

57 *Id.*, at sec. 74I–J.

58 H. J. Erasmus & D. E. Van Loggerenberg, *Jones and Buckle: The Civil Practice of the Magistrates'*

A restructuring sanctioned by court order thus basically entails a repayment plan that will provide for an extension of the repayment period. It is implicit in the procedure that the debtor must have a regular income, because he or she must make weekly or monthly payments to the administrator to be distributed among the creditors. The amount that the debtor must pay to the administrator is based on an approximation of the difference between the debtor's future income and the sum of a reasonable amount required for the maintenance of the debtor and his or her dependents, periodic payments to be made under credit agreements per the NCA, payments to be made under an existing maintenance order, periodic payments to be made under a mortgage bond, and certain other future debts.[59] Secured debt, insofar as it qualifies as *in futuro* debt, is thus excluded from an administration order, and an order for the rescheduling of such debt is therefore not possible. However, the court will usually and may at its discretion, when calculating the amount to be paid to the administrator in terms of the order, make provision for the periodic payment that a debtor is obliged to make under a credit agreement under the NCA as well as for the periodic payments under a mortgage bond.[60]

Administration under Section 74 of the MCA first and foremost provides for a debt-restructuring plan in the form of a repayment plan However, Section 74C(1)(b) and Section 74K allow in principle for property to be realized (by selling) by the administrator if a court authorizes such sale. However, this provision is seldom used in practice. Furthermore, if the property to be sold is subject to a credit agreement under the NCA, the written consent of the credit provider must first be obtained.[61]

Administration has become subject to severe criticism due to, among other reasons, the following:[62]

- Various abuses are manifest in the system.
- There are many practical difficulties, especially the lack of capacity of some courts to deal with all the applications.
- There is no proper regulation of administrators.
- No maximum time period for repayment or discharge is provided for.
- Because no discharge or maximum period for repayment is provided for, the added administration costs and interest cause the amount of debt to escalate to such an extent that many debtors never get out of debt.

Courts in South Africa 305 (Juta 1996); *Weiner NO v. Broekhuysen* (2003) 4 SA 301 (SCA) 305. *See,* further, for a diverging opinion, C. P. Joubert, *Artikel 74: Magistraatshowewet 32 van 1944 Soos Gewysig,* 19 Tydskrif vir Hedendaagse Romeins-Hollandse Reg 135, 138 (1956).

59   MCA, sec. 74C(2).

60   *Id.*

61   NCA, sec. 74C(1)(b)(i).

62   *See* Boraine, *supra* note 10, at 230.

- Because the procedure is limited to those instances in which the debt is not more than R 50,000, many debtors are excluded from this procedure.

- It is not clear to what extent this procedure and debt review under the NCA should or could coexist.[63]

Debt Review under the NCA

Section 86 of the NCA covers debt review.[64] The NCA regulates various aspects relating to "credit agreements." Not all types of debt are regulated by this act.[65] The purpose of NCA Section 3(g) is to address and prevent overindebtedness of consumer debtors and to provide mechanisms for resolving overindebtedness based on the principle of satisfaction by the consumer of all responsible financial obligations. The cornerstone of debt relief under the NCA is thus full satisfaction, and not to provide a discharge of any kind.[66]

In order to assist overindebted consumers, the NCA created the office of debt counselors, persons designated to offer and conduct the services of debt counseling and debt review that may lead to the restructuring of credit agreements regulated by the NCA.[67]

The process of debt review commences with a consumer applying to a debt counselor to be declared overindebted and to be placed under debt review.[68] During the initial debt review process, the debt counselor is obliged to review the debtor's credit agreements in order to determine whether the debtor is overindebted and whether reckless credit was extended.[69] A consumer is overindebted if the preponderance of available information at the time of the determination indicates that the consumer is or will be unable to satisfy in a timely manner all the obligations under all the credit agreements to which he or she is party. This is determined with regard to the person's financial means, prospects, and obligations and probable propensity to satisfy all the obligations of all his or her credit agreements in a timely manner.[70] The NCA

---

63   *See* Boraine, van Heerden, & Roestoff, *supra* note 13, at 267.

64   NCA, sec. 86, should be read with the National Credit Regulations, reg. 24. For a detailed discussion of the debt review process, *see* M. Roestoff et al., *The Debt Counselling Process: Closing the Loopholes in the National Credit Act 34 of 2005*, 23 Potchefstroom Electronic L.J. 247, 255 (2009).

65   The NCA applies only to "credit agreements" as defined in sec. 8. These are a credit facility, a credit transaction, a credit guarantee, or a combination thereof. Usually, two elements can be identified in credit agreements, namely, a deferral of payment and a charge, interest, or fee. *See* sec. 1 for the definitions of the different credit agreements; Otto & Otto, *supra* note 51, at 20.

66   *See*, further, NCA, sec. 3(i); *Collett v. FirstRand Bank Ltd.* (2011) 4 SA 508 (SCA), at 514.

67   NCA, secs. 86–87.

68   *Id.*, at sec. 86(1), read with the National Credit Regulations, reg. 24(1). Debt review may also be initiated by any court hearing any matter in which a credit agreement is being considered and it is alleged that the debtor is overindebted; NCA, sec. 85.

69   NCA, sec. 86(6).

70   *Id.*, read with NCA, sec. 79.

furthermore prescribes certain penalties for the credit provider in the case of reckless credit granting under Sections 83 and 84.

An assessment by a debt counselor regarding the overindebtedness of a consumer will determine the way forward. In this regard, NCA Section 86(7) provides that if, as a result of an assessment conducted under Section 86(6), a debt counselor reasonably concludes that a consumer is not overindebted, the debt counselor must reject the application, even if he or she has concluded that a particular credit agreement was reckless at the time it was entered into.[71] However, if the debt counselor concludes that the consumer is not overindebted but is nevertheless experiencing, or likely to experience, difficulty satisfying all the consumer's obligations under credit agreements in a timely manner, the debt counselor may recommend that the consumer and the respective credit providers voluntarily consider and agree on a plan of debt re-arrangement. If such a plan is accepted by (all) the credit provider(s), the debt counselor may obtain a consent order from a magistrate's court under Section 86(8)(a) to effect the restructuring as provided for by the NCA in Section 86(7)(c)(ii). Should the debt counselor conclude that the consumer is indeed overindebted, the debt counselor may issue a proposal recommending that the magistrate's court make either or both of the following orders as provided for in the subsections of Section 86(7)(c) of the NCA:

- That one or more of the consumer's credit agreements be declared to be reckless credit, if the debt counselor has concluded that those agreements appear to be reckless
- That one or more of the consumer's obligations be rearranged by:
  - Extending the period of the agreement and reducing the amount of each payment due accordingly
  - Postponing during a specified period the dates on which payments are due under the agreement
  - Extending the period of the agreement and postponing during a specified period the dates on which payments are due under the agreement
  - Recalculating the consumer's obligations because of contraventions of NCA Part A[72] or B[73] of Chapter 5 or Part A[74] of Chapter 6

When a debt rearrangement is ordered, the effect is usually that the amount of the installment is reduced and the payment term is extended. In practice, the debt counselor does not receive and distribute payments on be-

---

71   In such an instance, the debtor may, with the approval of the magistrate's court, apply directly to the court for an order covered by NCA, sec. 86(7)(c).

72   Dealing with unlawful agreements and provisions.

73   Dealing with disclosure, form, and effect of credit agreements.

74   Dealing with collection and repayment practices.

half of the debtor; this function is assigned to independent payment distribution agents.[75]

Although the court has limited restructuring powers, it is empowered to force, or "cram down," a rescheduling of debt upon creditors. The court is also empowered to order such rescheduling with regard to secured debt, which includes, inter alia, obligations with regard to home mortgages. Compared to foreign systems, such as Chapter 13 repayment plans in the U.S. Bankruptcy Code, this is revolutionary.

No provision is made in the NCA for a debt counselor to realize a debtor's assets or to make such a recommendation to a court. In practice and in view of the determination of overindebtedness under Section 79,[76] assets available for realization may be taken into consideration for the purposes of debt restructuring. In *Standard Bank of South Africa Ltd. v. Panayiotts,* it was held that "financial means" under Section 79 also include assets and liabilities and that "prospects" under Section 79 include prospects of improving the consumer's financial position, such as increases in and liquidation of assets.[77] In the case of credit agreements that involve goods as the subject matter of the agreement, the consumer's financial means and prospects must therefore include the prospect of selling the goods in order to reduce the consumer's indebtedness.[78] It therefore appears that South African courts are not willing to allow consumers to include a credit agreement in the eventual rearrangement order or to retain the subject matter of the agreement if they believe that such goods are luxurious and unnecessary for the maintenance of the consumer and his or her dependents.[79]

Debt review followed by debt restructuring under the NCA is in high demand among South African natural person debtors due to economic woes and because the majority of their debts amount to credit agreements as regulated by the NCA. However, the process is not without difficulties. Following are the most significant:[80]

- Debt restructuring under the NCA does not offer a discharge. The NCA envisages full repayment of the debt, and no time limit is prescribed regarding the rescheduling of the debt repayment period.

---

75 *See,* with regard to payment distribution agents, E. Van Zyl, *Registration and the Consequences of Non-registration,* in *Guide to the National Credit Act* para. 525 (J. W. Scholtz ed., LexisNexis 2008).

76 Sec. 79(1)(a) provides that the debt counselor must take into consideration the debtor's "financial means, prospects and obligations."

77 *Standard Bank of South Africa Ltd. v. Panayiotts* (2009) 3 SA 363 (W) para. 47.

78 *Id.,* para. 77.

79 *See* Boraine, van Heerden, & Roestoff, *supra* note 13, at 94.

80 *See* Roestoff & Coetzee, *supra* note 13, at 68–70; Boraine, van Heerden, & Roestoff, *supra* note 13, at 93–103.

- A particular credit agreement that has already commenced will be excluded from the debt review application.[81] In this regard, the Supreme Court of Appeal held that the provisions of Section 86(2) would bar the consumer from including that specific agreement in the debt review procedure as soon as a Section 129(1)(a) notice has been delivered in respect to that specific agreement.[82]

- The fact that the procedure does not provide for a discharge causes debtors to remain in debt almost indefinitely and causes an escalation in the amount of the debt, due to the cost and interest factor.

- As in the case of administration orders under the MCA, there seems to be a lack of capacity in some magistrates' courts to deal with the many applications, and this causes delays in the matters being heard within a reasonable time.

- The NCA does not specifically prescribe the procedure to be followed or the information to be disclosed when a debt review application is brought to court. It is not clear what the hearing entails. The procedure may be regarded as cumbersome, costly, and slow.

- The NCA provides that a credit provider may give notice to terminate the debt review process 60 business days after the date on which the consumer applied for the debt review.[83] In this regard, the Supreme Court of Appeal held that a referral of a debt review matter to the court does not bar the credit provider from terminating the debt review.[84] A credit provider may therefore terminate the process in respect to a specific agreement as soon as 60 business days have elapsed, irrespective of whether the matter is pending in court. Such termination is not necessarily a dead end for the consumer, because the NCA provides that a court may order that the debt review resume in regard to a credit agreement that is being enforced by litigation.[85] However, courts are reluctant to order a resumption of debt review, and it seems that an order will be granted only if a court is convinced that the consumer will eventually succeed in the application for debt review.[86]

- Although nearly the majority of consumer debts amount to credit agreements under the NCA, this debt-restructuring procedure is applicable to only credit agreement debt, not to other types of debt that a consumer may have. This aspect restricts the applicability of the procedure. In practice,

---

81   NCA, sec. 86(2).

82   *See Nedbank Ltd. v. National Credit Regulator* (2011) 3 SA (SCA) 581, 590. A Section 129(1)(a) notice is a letter that a credit provider must send to a defaulting consumer before the credit provider may commence legal proceedings to enforce the agreement.

83   NCA, sec. 86(10).

84   *Collett v. FirstRand Bank Ltd., supra* note 66.

85   NCA, sec. 86(11).

86   *Collett v. FirstRand Bank Ltd, supra* note 66, at para. 19; *Wesbank v. Schroder* (2012) JOL 28767 (EL) paras. 16, 17.

debt counselors sometimes use the voluntary distribution procedure in conjunction with the statutory procedure in order to deal with noncredit agreement debt as well.[87] It is possible to restructure some debt under the NCA and other debt in terms of an administration procedure, but these procedures are not well aligned.[88]

- As a result of the decision in *Investec Bank Ltd. v. Mutemeri and Another*,[89] a debtor who opts for debt review as a form of debt relief may be barred from continuing with this process when a creditor decides to apply for the compulsory sequestration of the debtor's estate. In that case, the court held that an application for compulsory sequestration did not amount to debt enforcement under the NCA,[90] and therefore did not preclude the applicant creditor from proceeding with an application for sequestration.[91] The debtor is therefore given no choice as to how to deal with his or her financial dilemma and will be forced to lose his or her assets and be subjected to the social stigma of being insolvent.[92]

Nonstatutory Procedures

Natural person debtors may, with the cooperation of creditors, use an informal creditor agreement that may amount to a voluntary debt restructuring or voluntary composition. This method is based on the contractual principle of consent, but some creditors are not prepared to participate in such a voluntary system. When the creditors accept a rescheduling of payment, it is also referred to as a voluntary distribution.

Insolvency Practitioners

Although South African insolvency law in the broadest sense does not provide for regulated insolvency professionals, there are attorneys, accountants, and auditors who act as such. There are also other persons without formal qualifications who take appointments as insolvency practitioners. In general, only the trustee appointed per the Insolvency Act is viewed as an insolvency

---

87 *See* Boraine, van Heerden, & Roestoff, *supra* note 13, at 267.

88 *Id.*

89 *Investec Bank Ltd. v. Mutemeri and Another* (2010) 1 SA 265 (GSJ). *See*, further, *FirstRand Bank Ltd. v. Evans* (2011) 4 SA 597 (KZD), and *Naidoo v. Absa Bank Ltd.* (2010) 4 SA 597 (SCA), confirming the decision in *Mutemeri*. *See* the discussion of *Naidoo* by N. Maghembe, *The Appellate Division Has Spoken: Sequestration Proceedings Do Not Qualify as Proceedings to Enforce a Credit Agreement under the National Credit Act 34 of 2005,* 14 Potchefstroom Electronic L.J. 171 (2011).

90 *See* NCA, sec. 130(1).

91 NCA, sec. 88(3); *Investec Bank v. Mutemeri, supra* note 89, at 274–277. *See*, for a detailed discussion of the *Mutemeri* case, A. Boraine & C. Van Heerden, *To Sequestrate or Not to Sequestrate in View of the National Credit Act 34 of 2005: A Tale of Two Judgments* (2010), 13 Potchefstroom Electronic L.J. 84 (2010).

92 *See* Roestoff & Coetzee, *supra* note 13, at 62–63; Maghembe, *supra* note 89, at 177–178.

practitioner; the insolvency fraternity in South Africa does not generally view debtors who apply for alternative debt relief measures such as administration orders or debt review to make use of formal bankruptcy procedures. Although insolvency practitioners appointed to deal with the liquidation of assets per the Insolvency Act are not compelled by law to belong to a professional body, there are statutory bars against the appointment of certain persons to act as trustees under the Insolvency Act.[93] With regard to the administration of a sequestrated estate, the master of the high court fulfills a supervisory role and can thus be seen as a type of regulator.[94] The master has discretion to appoint a person to act as a trustee in the case of sequestration, but will in practice appoint only persons with some expertise in the field who are not barred from such appointments.

The NCA created the office of the debt counselor, a person designated to offer and conduct the service of debt review. Debt counselors are regulated by the national credit regulator (NCR), a regulatory body, and must comply with certain statutory requirements, undergo training, and register as such under the NCA before they may act as such.[95]

In the case of administration orders, there is no regulatory body except when the administrator is, for example, also an attorney or an accountant who might be disciplined by his or her respective professional body in the event of misconduct. However, a court has certain statutory powers[96] to deal with an administrator who fails to meet his or her statutory duties.[97] There are no formal requirements or disqualifications set for administrators appointed by the court under Section 74 of the MCA.

All the categories of "insolvency practitioners"—namely, trustees, debt counselors, and administrators—are in principle subject to systems of prescribed fees, which are borne by the debtor or his or her insolvent estate in the case of sequestration.[98] At present, there is no state funding available to meet these fees when the debtor or the debtor's estate cannot meet them.

If an estate is sequestrated under the Insolvency Act and there is a shortfall to meet the costs of administering such an estate, certain creditors may

---

93   That is, a system of negative licensing. *See* Insolvency Act, sec. 55.

94   The master does not supervise the debt review and administration procedures.

95   *See* National Credit Regulations, reg. 10.

96   *See* MCA sec. 74E(2). *See*, further, *Stander v. Erasmus* (2011) 2 SA 320 (GNP) 324.

97   *See*, for example, MCA, sec. 74J.

98   The trustee is entitled to have the remuneration be taxed by the master according to tariff B in the second schedule to the Insolvency Act; *see* Insolvency Act, sec. 63(1). The debt counselor's remuneration consists of an initial application fee of R 50; *see* NCA, sec. 86(3)(a), read with sch. 2 of the regulations. A debt counselor may also claim the fees prescribed by the Debt Counselling Association of South Africa (DCASA). Currently, debt counselors are bound to this fee structure as a condition of their registration as debt counselors; Boraine, van Heerden, & Roestoff, *supra* note 13, at 259. In general, the remuneration of an administrator is capped at 12.5 percent of the regular payments received from the debtor for the purposes of distribution among creditors; MCA, sec. 74L(2).

become liable toward the estate to settle these costs by means of a system of contributions.[99] In the case of debt review under the NCA, debtors must in principle pay the fees of debt counselors, but those who earn less than R 2,500 per month may apply for assistance from the NCR.[100]

Insolvency Law Reform Initiatives

The South African Law Reform Commission has been working on new insolvency legislation since 1987; it published a report and a draft Insolvency Bill in 2000.[101] One of the aims of the reform project is to have one piece of insolvency legislation that deals with the insolvency of both individuals and other entities, such as companies. In March 2003, the cabinet accepted the concept of a new unified Insolvency Act, but this initiative has stalled. Likely due to the Companies Act of 2008, a further working document containing the Draft Insolvency and Business Recovery Bill in the format of a working document was completed by the Department of Justice in 2010. It is unclear when the government will take this new piece of legislation forward.

The 2010 Draft Insolvency Bill uses the term "liquidation" when referring to both the liquidation of juristic persons and the sequestration of natural persons. The advantage for creditors requirement is, however, retained in the 2012 draft bill.[102] However, little changed from the Insolvency Act 24 of 1936 in principle, and the draft bill as the latest document dealing with insolvency reform in South Africa does not introduce a revolutionary new insolvency system. For all intents and purposes, the Insolvency Act 24 of 1936 is still the main piece of legislation that deals with personal insolvency insofar as it relates to the liquidation of assets of insolvent debtors, and at present it is still unclear when the reform initiatives as mentioned above and further discussed below will be taken forward

The 2010 Insolvency Bill proposes an alternative debt relief measure to sequestration in the form of a preliquidation composition.[103] The composition is supervised by the court, and provision is made for an investigation into

---

99   *See* Insolvency Act, sec. 106. *See,* with regard to contribution in general, David Burdette, *Kontribusiepligtigheid van Skuldeisers in Insolvente Boedels,* Nov. De Rebus 1004 (1993); David Burdette, *New Problems Relating to Contribution in Insolvent Estates,* 63 T.H.R.H.R 458 (2000).

100   NCR press release (July 2008).

101   South African Law Commission, *Report on the Review of the Law of Insolvency* (Project 63) vol. 1 (explanatory memorandum) and vol. 2 (draft bill) (Feb. 2000) (hereinafter 2000 Explanatory Memorandum and 2000 Insolvency bill, respectively).

102   *See* 2000 Insolvency Bill, cls. 7(1)(b) and 8(1)(c), and the concomitant 2000 Explanatory Memorandum, at 15. From the 2010 Insolvency Bill, it appears that the commission has not changed its mind in regard to retaining the advantage for creditors principle; *see* cls. 3(8)(a)(ii), 10(1)(c)(i), 11(1)(c).

103   *See* 2010 Insolvency Bill, cl. 118.

the affairs of the debtor.[104] Although the proposed composition is in essence a debt-restructuring device, a prescribed majority of creditors can bind the minority.[105] If the majority do not accept the composition and the debtor is unable to pay substantially more than what is offered in the composition, the court must declare that the proceedings have ceased and that the debtor is in the position in which he or she was prior to the commencement thereof. Alternatively, the court must determine if Section 74 of the MCA can be applied to the debtor; if it can be, the court must apply the provisions accordingly and within the discretion of the presiding officer.[106]

Administration orders became extremely popular after 1994, to such an extent that they were referred to as "an industry." Many observers feel that the unregulated nature of this industry gave rise to serious abuse. It was widely believed that unscrupulous administrators were holding unsuspecting consumer-debtors at ransom—and that these debtors would never escape their financial problems. There were indications that many individuals who had to rely on so-called microlenders ended up under the administration regime, which has aggravated their debt situation rather than affording relief. In spite of the fact that a Micro Finance Regulatory Council was established in 1999 to accredit lenders and monitor their behavior, problems in this area persisted.

These and other complaints prompted the Department of Justice to implement a reform project in 2001.[107] The Centre for Advanced Corporate and Insolvency Law, based at the University of Pretoria, conducted this project with the view of advising on reform. As a result of this preliminary investigation, which culminated in the *Interim Report on the Review of Administration Orders in Terms of Section 74 of the Magistrates' Courts Act 32 of 1944*, the Department of Justice requested the South African Law Reform Commission to appoint a project committee to make formal proposals regarding the reform of administration orders. The project committee was appointed in 2003, and the project registered as Project 127, Review of Administration Orders.[108] This project was eventually suspended, pending the promulgation of the NCA, but, contrary to expectations, the NCA did not deal with administration orders.

---

104   *Id.*, at cl. 118(10)(e).

105   That is, a majority in number and two-thirds in value of the concurrent creditors who vote on the composition; 2010 Insolvency Bill, cl. 118(17).

106   *See* 2010 Insolvency Bill, subcls. 118(22)(a) and (b). The commission's proposal in the 2000 Insolvency Bill afforded the debtor the option to convert to liquidation and rehabilitation under the proposed Insolvency Act in instances in which the composition was not accepted by the required majority; *see* the discussion of this proposal by M. Roestoff & L. Jacobs, *Statutêre Akkoord voor Likwidasie: 'n Toereikende Skuldenaarremedie*, 30 De Jure 189, 207 (1997).

107   See Boraine, *supra* note 10, at 218; Roestoff & Coetzee, *supra* note 13, at 66.

108   See Boraine, *supra* note 10, at 219.

Conclusion

The main point of criticism against the South African insolvency system for individuals is that it is largely creditor oriented despite the worldwide trend to accommodate debtors seeking relief. The South African system does not provide adequate debt relief to insolvent or debt-stressed individuals, and the proposals of the South African Law Reform Commission do not address this situation. Moreover, there is no principled view or approach regarding the treatment of the insolvency of natural persons in South African law. Even when the insolvency reform initiatives discussed above are considered, there is no sense of integrating the various procedures in order to establish an over-arching framework. For example, it is not clear if and how administration and debt review could operate in the same case. It is also not clear why provision should be made for two coexisting procedures serving the same purpose, namely, to provide for debt reorganization. The legislature, when introducing the NCA in 2007, missed a golden opportunity for comprehensive reform.

South African law needs a complete overhaul of its debt relief measures. Existing statutory procedures should be streamlined by eliminating the overlap between the different procedures and the unnecessary duplication of regulators and "insolvency practitioners." A principled approach should be adopted to deal with the liquidation of assets, debt restructuring, and asset-less estates in a coherent way. With regard to debt-restructuring measures, lawmakers should devise one single measure providing for all debt reorganization cases. Lawmakers should build on the existing and well-established system of debt counseling that is regulated by the NCR as the regulatory body under the NCA.

The South African personal insolvency system must abandon its creditor-oriented approach. The system should provide adequate debt relief and equal treatment to all insolvent or overindebted individuals. The *Van Rooyen* case illustrates the plight and dilemma of many overburdened debtors in South Africa. Because many creditors do not receive significant benefit from the sequestration of the estate of their debtors, in spite of the advantage of creditors' principle, debtors are treated inequitably, in that many are left without relief in the form of a statutory discharge.[109] This exclusion infringes the basic constitutional right of equality under the South African Constitution[110] and upholds the dualism in the South African economy.[111]

As Rochelle suggests, a discharge of debt and a fresh-start policy in personal insolvency could be an effective tool for spurring economic growth and development. In his words:

---

109   *See* Boraine & Evans *supra* note 25, at para. 4A8.

110   *See* South African Constitution (1996), sec. 9(1); Boraine & Evans, *supra* note 25, at para. 4AB; Steyn, *supra* note 25, at 11.

111   *See* Coetzee & Roestoff, *supra* note 3.

Improving the citizen's economic lot is a central priority for most national governments. Insolvency laws can have a significant role to play in this work. Were the penalties for failure lowered from their current levels in South Africa, citizens and companies would take more economic risks to succeed. More businesses would start, more jobs would be created, and society as a whole would benefit. Those who fail would not become modern lepers, but instead would receive another chance to be productive for themselves and society.[112]

---

112 *Supra* note 2, at 315.

The Role of Personal Insolvency Law in Economic Development

An Introduction to the World Bank *Report on the Treatment of the Insolvency of Natural Persons*

José M. Garrido

The association between insolvency law and economic development is frequently overlooked. The idea of insolvency evokes failure and poverty, which is indicative of a lack of economic development. However, the role of insolvency law is broad, and insolvency law serves several important functions in an economy. It is a useful instrument to reallocate assets to more productive uses, and an appropriate reorganization or debt-restructuring framework provides instruments to preserve valuable businesses under distress. Traditional business insolvency regimes, however, tend to lack the appropriate treatment of the indebtedness of natural persons. An effective personal insolvency regime provides solutions for indebted persons while attaining broader goals for inclusive economic development.

A couple examples illustrate the connection between personal insolvency law and economic development. In India, the indebtedness of farmers has resulted in severe social problems, with an alarming number of farmers committing suicide.[1] In Hungary, the crisis created by the expansion of mortgage credit denominated in foreign currencies, especially in Swiss francs, resulted in the default of one-quarter of all mortgage loans in the country, creating an enormous social conflict.[2] Both examples show that the connections between financial stability and personal indebtedness have become stronger and that the issue of personal insolvency is at the forefront of an agenda for inclusive economic development and shared prosperity in both developed and developing nations.

This chapter provides an introduction to the work undertaken by the Working Group of the World Bank's Insolvency Task Force. The first section

---

[1] *See* K. Nagaraj, *Farmers' Suicides in India: Magnitudes, Trends and Spatial Patterns* (2008), available at http://www.macroscan.org/anl/mar08/pdf/farmers_suicides.pdf, reporting 190,753 suicides from 1995 to 2006, and considering the figure an underestimation; *see* also A. R. Vasavi, *Shadow Space: Suicides and the Predicament of Rural India* (Three Essays Collective 2012), referring to 199,132 suicides in the period 1997–2008, according to official records, which tend to underestimate the real number of suicides. Although there is a constellation of causes for this suicide epidemic, personal indebtedness is considered to be one of the major factors.

[2] *See* Tamas Egedy, *The Effects of Global Economic Crisis in Hungary,* 61(2) Hungarian Geographical Bull., 155, 162–163 (2012).

provides background on the project. The second section describes the issues covered in the World Bank's *Report on the Treatment of the Insolvency of Natural Persons* (hereinafter World Bank report) and the contribution of the report to a better understanding of the essential issues in the treatment of the insolvency of natural persons.[3] A short conclusion examines possible future developments in this area.

Background to the World Bank's Involvement in Personal Insolvency Law

The World Bank developed its insolvency and creditor rights (ICR) initiative as part of the standards and codes initiative of the international financial architecture. Per the mandate of the Financial Stability Forum, the World Bank developed a standard for the assessment of ICR regimes, known as the ICR standard.[4] This standard comprises the World Bank Principles for Effective Insolvency and Creditor Rights Systems[5] and the recommendations from the United Nations Commission for International Trade Law (UNCITRAL) Legislative Guide on Insolvency Law.[6] The World Bank is responsible for the development of the standard and for the assessment of the legal, regulatory, and institutional frameworks in business insolvency. Those assessments are conducted under the program of reports on the observation of standards and codes (ROSC), which has covered more than 60 countries. The experiences of the ROSC program have been positive, and the program has contributed to numerous reforms in various legal systems, which have resulted in more efficient insolvency systems responsive to the needs of developing economies and contributed to the solution of crises in the corporate and financial sectors.

The original focus of the ICR initiative was exclusively on business insolvency systems. There is a clear justification for this: at the time the insolvency initiative was launched and the first version of the World Bank Principles was passed, the main concern was to deal with the aftermath of the Asian and Latin American corporate and financial crises of the late 1990s. These crises affected the corporate sectors first, and the contagion then spread to the financial sector. Efficient mechanisms to restructure loans and to reorganize businesses were identified as a main element missing in the countries that suf-

---

3   World Bank, *Report on the Treatment of the Insolvency of Natural Persons*, para. 7 (hereinafter, World Bank report), available at http://www-wds.worldbank.org/external/default/WDSContentServer/WDSP/IB/2013/05/02/000333037_20130502131241/Rendered/PDF/771700WP0WB0In00Box377289B00PUBLIC0.pdf.

4   *See Creditor Rights and Insolvency Standard* (2005), http://siteresources.worldbank.org/GILD/ConferenceMaterial/20774191/ICR_Standard_21_Dec_2005_Eng.pdf.

5   *See* World Bank, *Principles for Effective Insolvency and Creditor/Debtor Regimes*, available at http://siteresources.worldbank.org/INTGILD/Resources/ICRPrinciples_Jan2011.pdf. The principles were originally formulated in 2001 and revised in 2005 and 2011.

6   United Nations Commission for International Trade Law, *Legislative Guide on Insolvency Law*, parts 1–2 (United Nations 2004), available at www.uncitral.org/pdf/english/texts/insolven/05-80722_Ebook.pdf.

fered the consequences of the crises most intensely. Some scholars have commented that financial stability is the first precondition for economic growth,[7] and therefore the focus on business insolvency and on restructuring mechanisms for distressed companies is entirely justified. As a result of the efforts of the international community in dealing with insolvency and restructuring frameworks in systemic crises, a comprehensive and flexible standard is now available for all countries and there is a growing body of knowledge and experience about the effectiveness of institutions and rules dealing with business insolvency.

However, the global financial crisis in 2008 showed a very different picture: in many of the countries where the crisis had the worst impact, the crisis originated in the financial sector and subsequently affected both businesses and individuals. The crisis also showed, for the first time, the connections between personal indebtedness and a systemic crisis: the origination of the financial crisis in the subprime lending practices in the U.S. market demonstrated clear links between unlimited credit expansion to businesses and individuals and macroeconomic financial stability.[8] This was particularly apparent in certain countries, such as the Baltic states.[9] Analyses of the global financial crises have concluded that the indebtedness of natural persons and the lack of proper mechanisms to deal with it may have serious social and economic repercussions.[10]

There are further considerations on the importance of personal insolvency law.[11] Insolvency is a phenomenon that occurs only in societies in which credit is widespread. Without credit, there is no insolvency and there is no need for an insolvency regime. Yet, the need for an insolvency framework manifests itself in all societies in which access to credit becomes the foundation for the development of economic activities. This is the explanation for the development of the first insolvency regimes in the Middle Ages.[12] But in medieval societies, access to credit was restricted to merchants and the aristocratic class. In modern society, access to credit is a fundamental tool for every individual. It is the basis for the acquisition of housing, for the development of professional

---

7   *See,* for example, William C. Dudley, president and chief executive officer, Federal Reserve Bank of New York, Speech, *Financial Stability and Economic Growth* (Bretton Woods Comm., Intl. Council Meeting 2011, Washington, DC, Sept. 23, 2011), available at http://www.bis.org/review/r110927c.pdf. In the words of Dudley, "A stable financial system is a prerequisite for sustainable economic growth."

8   *See* Stijn Claessens et al., *Cross-Country Experiences and Policy Implications from the Global Financial Crisis,* 25 Econ. Policy 267 (2010).

9   On the crisis in the Baltic states, *see,* generally, Gediminas Macys, *The Crisis and Economic Recovery in Baltic Countries,* 2 Intl. J. Humanities & Soc. Sci. 202 (2012).

10   *See* Nick Huls, *Consumer Bankruptcy: A Third Way between Autonomy and Paternalism in Private Law,* 3 Erasmus L. Rev. 7 (2010).

11   Throughout this chapter, and in the World Bank report, the expressions "personal insolvency" and "insolvency of natural persons" are used interchangeably.

12   *See* Louis E. Levinthal, *The Early History of Bankruptcy Law,* 66 U. Pa. L. Rev. 223 (1918).

and economic activities, for education, and for the satisfaction of consumption needs. Access to credit and entrepreneurial skills are motors of economic development.[13] A modern economy is based on credit, with many positive effects for development; but a credit-based economy means that individuals sustain considerable levels of debt,[14] and this results in higher rates of personal insolvency.[15] In essence, the rise in consumer bankruptcies is a by-product of the rise of consumer credit.[16]

Strategies for economic growth and poverty reduction are frequently based on the expansion of available credit, especially for small and medium-size enterprises and households. The increase of the importance of access to finance and the development of financial intermediation have created the need for an insolvency regime. Greater access to credit brings about more economic opportunities while allowing more possibilities for individuals to incur debts and to default on payments. Constructive solutions to the negative consequences of indebtedness are useful tools for sustainable and inclusive economic development. The regulation of personal insolvency has an influence on how individuals perceive and deal with risks in their economic activity, and determines whether and how individuals suffering from an excessive debt burden can return to a productive economic life.

The increasingly recognized importance of personal insolvency law has attracted the attention of academic researchers[17] and several regional organizations and international associations.[18] It is in this context that the World

---

13   *See* Huw Lloyd-Ellis & Dan Bernhardt, *Enterprise, Inequality and Economic Development,* 67 Rev. Econ. Stud. 147 (2000).

14   *See* International Monetary Fund (IMF), *Dealing with Household Debt,* chap. 3 in *World Economic Outlook: Growth Resuming, Dangers Remain,* vol. 1 (IMF 2012). *See* also Yan Liu & Christopher Rosenberg, *Dealing with Private Debt Distress in the Wake of the European Financial Crisis: A Review of the Economics and Legal Toolbox* (IMF Working Paper WP/13/44, 2013).

15   *See* House of Commons, Public Accounts Committee, *Helping Over-Indebted Consumers* (UK Parliament, 2010). According to the report, UK consumers had some £1,459 billion of outstanding debt as of November 2009, and personal borrowing represented 160 percent of household annual pretax income.

16   *See* the pioneering work of Teresa Sullivan, Elizabeth Warren, & Jay Lawrence Westbrook, *As We Forgive Our Debtors* (Oxford U. Press 1989); David A. Moss & Gibbs A. Johnson, *The Rise of Consumer Bankruptcy: Evolution, Revolution, or Both,* 73 Am. Bankr. L. J. 311 (1999).

17   *See* Jacob Ziegel, *Comparative Consumer Insolvency Regimes: A Canadian Perspective* (Hart 2003); Johanna Niemi, Iain Ramsay, & William Whitford eds., *Consumer Bankruptcy in Global Perspective* (Hart 2003); Kent Anderson, *The Explosive Growth of Personal Insolvency and the Concomitant Birth of the Study of Comparative Consumer Bankruptcy,* 42 Osgoode Hall L.J. 661 (2004); Jason Kilborn, *Comparative Consumer Bankruptcy* (Carolina Academic Press 2007).

18   *See* Johanna Niemi-Kiesiläinen & Ann-Sofie Henrikson, *Report on Legal Solutions to Debt Problems in Credit Societies* (report prepared for the Bureau of the European Committee on Legal Co-operation, 2005), available at http://www.coe.int/t/e/legal_affairs/legal_co-operation /steering_committees/cdcj/cj_s_debt/CDCJ-BU_2005_11e%20rev.pdf; Udo Reifner et al., *Consumer Overindebtedness and Consumer Law in the European Union: Final Report* (report presented to the Commn. of the European Communities, Health and Consumer Protec. Directorate-General, Sept. 2003), available at http://news.iff-hh.de/media.php?id=1886; INSOL International, *Consumer Debt Report: Report of Findings and Recommendations* (2001), available at http://www.insol.org/pdf/consdebt.pdf (a second version of the INSOL report was

Bank Insolvency Task Force, in sessions held in Washington, D.C., in January 2011, considered the topic of the insolvency of natural persons. The task force reviewed a survey covering 59 countries that highlighted, among other aspects, the lack of personal insolvency systems in the low- and middle-income countries included in the survey.[19] The data, together with an analysis of the global financial crisis and its connections with the indebtedness of individuals, prompted the task force to create a working group to study the treatment of the insolvency of natural persons.[20]

The working group comprised academics, judges, practitioners, and policy makers from many countries. The working group was formed to "study the issue of the insolvency of natural persons and produce a reflective report on this matter, suggesting guidance for the treatment of the different issues involved, taking into account different policy options and the diverse sensitivities around the world."[21] Within the working group, a drafting committee was established, comprising specialists in comparative approaches to personal insolvency regimes.[22] The drafting committee produced successive versions of the report that were submitted to the working group. The working group commented on those drafts and debated them in meetings held in Washington, D.C., in November 2011 and December 2012, when the substantive work of the working group was concluded.

The World Bank *Report on the Treatment of the Insolvency of Natural Persons*

The objective of the working group was to produce a document that could serve as guidance for policy makers considering reforms in the area of personal insolvency law. However, the issue of personal insolvency presents

---

published in 2011). *See* also Nick Huls, *Toward a European Approach to Overindebtedness of Consumers* 16 J. Consumer Policy 215 (1993); European Commission, Enterprise Directorate General, *Best Project on Restructuring, Bankruptcy and a Fresh Start, Final Report of the Expert Group* (2003), available at http://ec.europa.eu/enterprise/policies/sme/files/sme2chance/doc /failure_final_en.pdf; European Commission, *Towards a Common Operational European Definition of Over-Indebtedness* (2008), available at http://ec.europa.eu/social/BlobServlet?docId =5093&langId=en.

19 The survey was directed by Adolfo Rouillon at the World Bank. The results of the survey are available at http://siteresources.worldbank.org/EXTGILD/Resources/Jan11-CI-Rouillon.pdf. The full name of the task force is World Bank Insolvency and Debtor/Creditor Regimes Task Force.

20 *See* the concluding remarks of the task force meeting by Vijay S. Tata (chief counsel, LEGPS, World Bank), available at http://siteresources.worldbank.org/EXTGILD/Resources/WB_TF _2011_Consumer_Insolvency.pdf. *See* also Susan Block-Lieb, *Best Practices in the Insolvency of Natural Persons*, available at http://siteresources.worldbank.org/EXTGILD/Resources /WB_TF_2011_Consumer_Insolvency.pdf.

21 *See* World Bank report, *supra* note 3, para. 7.

22 The drafting committee included Jason Kilborn, from the John Marshall Law School of Chicago (chairman); Jose M. Garrido, senior counsel at the World Bank (secretariat); Charles D. Booth, from the University of Hawaii; Johanna Niemi, from the University of Helsinki; and Iain Ramsay, from the University of Kent.

challenges and does not lend itself easily to a unified or uniform treatment. Attitudes to personal insolvency law are embedded in the society, the culture, and the history of a particular country. Whereas business insolvency law responds to a set of common problems in modern economies, albeit using different legal techniques, the social implications of the policy options in business insolvency are less intense than those of personal insolvency law.[23] Therefore, although the problems of personal indebtedness are virtually universal, there are substantial differences in the way those problems are treated.[24]

The working group recognized the difficulties of creating a standard in the area of personal insolvency law. Even a standard such as the one used for business insolvency (the ICR standard), which is eminently functional and allows for important variations, would be too rigid for the development of solutions to the problem of personal indebtedness in different parts of the world. It was clear from the start, therefore, that the result of the working group would not be a model, a template, or a standard for the regulation of personal insolvency. Instead, the approach favored was nonprescriptive, based on the idea that an organized report could arrange all the important topics that a personal insolvency system needs to address and show the advantages and disadvantages of different, tested approaches to the problems that typically arise in the development of such systems. In this way, the report acknowledges that a list of best practices in personal insolvency law may be premature, but it offers a catalogue of problems and solutions. Policy makers can use the report as a checklist for the topics to address in a reform or as an analytical tool for an already-existing system.

Another task for the working group was to determine the relation between a report on the treatment of the insolvency of natural persons and the ICR standard, which applies to business insolvency regimes. The difficulty lies in the fact that the ICR standard applies not only to companies and other legal persons but also to natural persons engaged in business activities. The insolvency law was initiated with the insolvency of merchants, long before companies became the main vehicle for organized economic activity. Traditional insolvency systems are not designed to deal with the problems of indebtedness of natural persons in a modern society. There are important differences between systems developed to address the insolvency of traders and

---

23   There is an exception to this general observation: the treatment of workers in the insolvency of businesses tends to be a topic in which opposing policies and traditions clash. In practice, the international standard offers only very general guidance on how to solve the issues of worker protection in the insolvency of businesses.

24   This is demonstrated by the existence of a rich comparative legal literature on the subject: *See*, for a variety of countries and methodological approaches, Jason Kilborn, *The Innovative German Approach to Consumer Debt Relief: Revolutionary Changes in German Law, and Surprising Lessons for the United States,* 24 Nw. J. Intl. L. & Bus. 257 (2004); Jason Kilborn, *Out with the New, In with the Old: As Sweden Aggressively Streamlines Its Consumer Bankruptcy System, Have U.S. Reformers Fallen Off the Learning Curve?,* 80 Am. Bankr. L.J. 435 (2007); Junichi Matsushita, *Japan's Personal Insolvency Law,* 42 Texas Intl. L.J. 765 (2007); Rafael Efrat, *Global Trends in Personal Bankruptcy,* 76 Am. Bankruptcy L.J. 81 (2002); Iain Ramsay, *Comparative Consumer Bankruptcy,* U. Ill. L. Rev. 241 (2007).

merchants, on one hand, and systems designed to treat the insolvency of natural persons, on the other hand.

In some states, a distinction has been drawn between the insolvency of merchants and the insolvency of consumers.[25] This distinction may be feasible—and effective—in a number of legal systems, but the line between consumers and entrepreneurs is increasingly blurred in both developed and developing economies. In fact, a common pattern in developing economies is the existence of a high percentage of self-employed persons.[26] Taking into account that the distinction between entrepreneurs and consumers is not useful in most economies, the question is how to draw a relevant distinction between a standard designed for business insolvency and the issues raised by the insolvency of natural persons. No clear dividing line categorizes persons according to the degree of sophistication or complexity of their economic activities, and the definitions of traders, typical of the commercial codes in 19th-century Europe, are an unsuitable basis for different regimes. The distinction lies, instead, in the different approaches that the law takes toward insolvency. Defined as such, the function of the World Bank report is not to create a different standard for the insolvency of natural persons as opposed to a standard for business insolvency, but to analyze the questions that refer to insolvent debtors as persons, rather than paying attention to other considerations.

What distinguishes a system for the regulation of personal insolvency, as opposed to business insolvency, is that the personal element occupies the central position in such a system. Of course, personal insolvency systems have implications for the economy of a country, as the most recent financial crises have shown, but the main considerations in the design of a personal insolvency system exceed the purely economic aspects and must focus, first and foremost, on the human element present in these insolvencies. This concept colors the World Bank report and distinguishes clearly the subject matter and the approach followed from the documents in which the business insolvency standard is based.[27] In essence, the World Bank report recognizes that there are overlapping areas in the regime of business insolvency and in a personal insolvency regime: both regimes aim for "increasing and more fairly distributing payment to creditors, streamlining procedures, and enhancing economic performance for the ultimate benefit of society,"[28] but the difference is that business insolvency focuses on credit protection and the preservation of enterprise

---

25   For example, in the United States, the words "consumer bankruptcy" are most frequently used to refer to the insolvency of natural persons. Paradoxically, there are many procedures in the U.S. Bankruptcy Code that apply to both consumers and business actors.

26   *See* Carlo Pietrobelli, Roberta Rabellotti, & Matteo Aquilina, *An Empirical Study of the Determinants of Self-Employment in Developing Countries*, 16 J. Intl. Dev. 803 (2004).

27   The World Bank report states clearly that it does not conflict with the business insolvency standard. In fact, the report takes a different look at the issues that the insolvency of individuals creates, and it explicitly refers to the standard in all cases in which the insolvency of a natural person does not present peculiarities and can be adequately treated in accordance with the approaches recommended in the standard.

28   *See* World Bank report, *supra* note 3, at para. 51.

value, whereas an insolvency regime for natural persons places the human elements of indebtedness problems at the center of the system, with the main goal of alleviating those problems for the benefit of debtors and society as a whole.

The Benefits of an Effective Personal Insolvency System

The World Bank report raises awareness about the importance of a personal insolvency system by examining the benefits produced by a well-designed regime for the treatment of personal insolvency.[29] There are substantial differences as compared with business insolvency systems, where the protection of credit is the overriding concern. A personal insolvency system represents a balanced solution to the problems of indebtedness of individuals, taking into account not only the interests of creditors but, more important, the interests of debtors and the interests of society as a whole. A personal insolvency regime provides relief to "honest but unfortunate" debtors and their families, and it benefits society as a whole by addressing wider social issues.[30]

The World Bank report cites numerous benefits flowing from the existence of an efficient insolvency system. These benefits can be grouped under common themes, showing how personal insolvency can benefit creditors, debtors, and society as a whole.

A sound financial sector benefits from an effective personal insolvency system. A well-functioning personal insolvency system encourages proper valuation of accounts, because it forces creditors—especially financial institutions—to recognize the loss of value of their claims and to take remedial action. A personal insolvency system reduces wasteful collection costs and efforts, and it can also reduce the destruction of value that results from fire sales, especially in systemic crises. The existence of a personal insolvency system encourages responsible lending. Such a system reduces negative externalities produced by inaccurate risk assessment[31] and helps concentrate losses on those who are prepared to deal with losses in an efficient and effective way.

Even more important, an effective system for the treatment of the insolvency of natural persons directly benefits the debtors and their families, providing them with incentives to continue being productive and to solve their indebtedness problems. These benefits flow to society as a whole in a number of ways: by reducing social costs of illness, crime, and unemployment;[32] by

---

29   *Id.*, at para. 58ff.

30   On the challenges faced by personal insolvency systems from a social point of view, *see* Teresa Sullivan, Elizabeth Warren, & Jay Lawrence Westbrook, *The Fragile Middle Class: Americans in Debt* (Yale U. Press 2000).

31   *See* Jason J. Kilborn, *Twenty-Five Years of Consumer Bankruptcy in Continental Europe: Internalizing Negative Externalities and Humanizing Justice in Denmark*, 18 Intl. Insolv. Rev. 155 (2009).

32   *See* INSOL report (2001), *supra* note 18, at 4: "Solving consumer debt problems can be very complex. Unfortunately, these problems are frequently caused by or in relation to socio-psychological factors, such as divorce, redundancy, job loss, addiction, disability etc. These situations interfere with the quality of life and in many respects may have serious conse-

increasing the production of taxable income; by maximizing economic activity and encouraging entrepreneurship; and by enhancing stability and predictability in the financial system and the economy.

An effective and efficient personal insolvency regime, therefore, both avoids waste and increases productivity, and it contributes to a healthier and more stable economy. These benefits deserve careful consideration by policy makers and provide a justification for the importance of developing adequate regimes for the treatment of the insolvency of natural persons. The World Bank report considers the impediments in achieving the objectives of a personal insolvency system. Those impediments are identified as fraud, stigma, and moral hazard. These factors may operate at different levels of intensity, reducing the benefits of a personal insolvency system.[33] Cultural and historical peculiarities of each society may require different responses to these issues,[34] but the experience of a number of systems shows that these concerns may be overcome.

Core Legal Attributes of an Insolvency Regime for Natural Persons

The World Bank report describes the main attributes of a personal insolvency regime.[35] In including such a description, the report makes no attempt to promote any particular system as the "ideal" regime for the treatment of the insolvency of natural persons. The report includes the essential elements of a system, with different possibilities and options and their corresponding advantages and disadvantages, as experienced in numerous legal systems of both developed and developing countries. The report acknowledges that the design of a personal insolvency regime needs to take into account the peculiar traits of a nation—social, economic, and cultural—in a more marked fashion than a business insolvency system does. A one-size-fits-all approach is expressly discarded. Another important concept is that personal insolvency law does not exist in a vacuum: it is essential to consider connections with the general insolvency regime and connections with the regulation of consumer and commercial credit.

The World Bank report concentrates on the legal attributes that are germane to personal insolvency regimes. There are numerous issues—for instance, the regulation of avoidance actions or the regulation of insolvency professionals—for which the solutions provided by general insolvency regimes require practically no additional consideration. The report focuses on aspects that may require special treatment in a regime for the treatment of the insolvency of natural persons: the general design of the regime; the relationship

---

quences for the health of the debtor and his or her family and the way they live. They may become socially isolated or retreat from life altogether."

33 *See* Rafael Efrat, *Personal Bankruptcy in the 21st Century: Emerging Trends and New Challenges; The Evolution of Bankruptcy Stigma,* 7 Theoretical Inq. L. 365 (2006).

34 *See* Iain Ramsay, *Between Neo-liberalism and the Social Market: Approaches to Debt Adjustment and Consumer Insolvency in the EU,* 35 J. Consumer Policy, 421 (2012).

35 *See* World Bank report, *supra* note 3, at para. 126ff.

of the formal insolvency regime with alternative informal solutions; the role of courts, agencies, and intermediaries; the conditions for access to the insolvency process; and the solutions to the insolvency process and the discharge of the debtor.

General Regime Design: Procedural Options and the Relation with Informal Workouts

There are many options for the design of a personal insolvency regime: in some countries, a special statute for the treatment of consumer indebtedness represents the way in which a separate insolvency regime is introduced. In other countries, there is a closer integration with the general insolvency regime, and the general insolvency statute includes a regime that either is flexible enough to accommodate the needs of natural persons or incorporates special rules and procedures for natural persons.[36] The decision regarding which options to use depends mostly on the characteristics of the national legal system and the political implications of enacting a special statute for consumers or individual debtors.

In any case, a formal insolvency regime can serve as the backdrop for informal negotiations, as creditors and debtors "bargain in the shadow of insolvency law."[37] It is important that an insolvency regime provide for the possibility of resolving insolvency through informal negotiations, often called *workouts*, with subsequent savings in costs, fees, and administrative and judicial resources. There are important advantages to negotiated solutions: apart from lower costs, the most noticeable ones are the avoidance of stigma and a less adverse impact on debtors' scores in credit information systems. There are also advantages in the fact that informal negotiations tend to yield better outcomes for creditors and can provide for greater flexibility to accommodate the needs of both the debtor and the creditor, taking into account, additionally, that financial institutions generally prefer to renegotiate loans than to resort to formal enforcement or insolvency proceedings.

There are obstacles to voluntary negotiations, however. Some creditors refuse to negotiate and, in so doing, boycott a negotiated solution to the insolvency of the debtor. Other creditors do not engage actively in negotiations, exhibiting considerable apathy.[38] As with creditor apathy in business insolvency, the law can provide mechanisms to deal with holdout and inactive creditors by imposing the binding force of agreements on those creditors.

The experience in the few systems in which informal alternatives to insolvency have been successful suggests that several elements perform a useful

---

36   *Id.*, at para. 139ff.

37   Following the classic expression of Robert H. Mnookin & Lewis Kornhauser, *Bargaining in the Shadow of the Law: The Case of Divorce*, 88 Yale L.J. 950 (1979).

38   The phenomenon is similar in some of its traits to that of rational apathy of shareholders in corporate law: *see* Robert C. Clark, *Vote Buying and Corporate Law*, 29 Case W. Res. L. Rev. 776 (1978–1979).

role in promoting negotiations, such as professional assistance in negotiations at a very low cost, or without cost, and a standstill agreement so that there is no immediate threat of the enforcement of claims.

The Institutional Framework

An essential part of a personal insolvency system is a well-functioning institutional framework.[39] Ideally, the institutional framework reduces the overall costs of the system by minimizing errors in the treatment of insolvent debtors and by providing for timely resolution of cases, with predictable results for all parties. The design of an institutional structure for a personal insolvency system must take into account the context of existing institutions and the availability of professional intermediaries in any particular country.

A factor in personal insolvency systems is the large number of cases.[40] The high number of individual insolvents, together with the relative homogeneity of many of these cases, allows for standardized systems of treatment and requires a reconsideration of the costs and resources necessary to resolve cases in which the legal controversies tend to be less complex than those that arise in corporate or business insolvencies.

The institutional framework to be adopted depends on the capability of the state. In some institutional frameworks, an administrative agency is in charge of the insolvency procedures; others are characterized by hybrid public-private systems in which public insolvency procedures coexist with private restructuring alternatives; and still others are court-based systems. Although the majority of countries have court-based systems, some countries have adopted administrative approaches, with courts taking a role only in disputed cases.

Intermediaries are very important in most systems. In several countries, public agencies play a significant role in the insolvency of natural persons. Hybrid public-private models exist in which the primary actors are insolvency practitioners who perform several functions in the personal insolvency process under the supervision of a public regulator.[41]

Access to the Formal Insolvency Regime

A main challenge in implementing a personal insolvency regime is the creation of enough incentives for honest and unfortunate debtors so that they are

---

39 *See* World Bank report, *supra* note 3, at para. 152ff.

40 *See*, for example, Edward J. Janger, *Crystals and Mud in Bankruptcy Law: Judicial Competence and Statutory Design*, 43 Ariz. L. Rev. 559, 615 (2001), which highlights the well-known fact that every year there are more than one million consumer bankruptcy cases in the United States.

41 In this regard, the English individual voluntary arrangement, which consists of a payment plan agreed to outside the court with the assistance of an insolvency practitioner, provides a good example; *see* Adrian Walters, *Individual Voluntary Arrangements: A "Fresh Start" for Salaried Consumer Debtors in England and Wales?*, 18 Intl. Insolv. Rev. 5 (2009).

able to use the insolvency process without being deterred by stigma or by the costs of the procedure itself.[42]

The World Bank report lists the main approaches used to finance personal insolvency processes. Those approaches include state funding; cross-subsidization of low-value insolvencies by higher-value estates; state subsidies to professionals involved in the process and write-off of court costs when there is an inability to repay; levies on creditors, such as taxation of distressed debt to fund cases for which individuals have no ability to pay; and no state support beyond general public funding of the court system.

On the issue of standards for access to individual insolvency, the World Bank report emphasizes that standards should be transparent and certain and should ensure against improper use by creditors or debtors. There are different philosophies on this issue. On the one hand, open access represents an approach whereby any individual who meets an insolvency test gains access to an insolvency procedure that allows an ultimate discharge of debts. On the other hand, numerous systems include additional requirements, with the purpose of addressing the problems of moral hazard and debtor fraud. When high barriers to access are used, the risk is that they can result in a large number of individuals being driven out of the formal economy, with negative consequences for themselves, for creditors, and for society. It is possible to address the problems of abuse of process, or of questionable conduct within the process itself, by imposing sanctions or denying some or all of the benefits of the insolvency process.

Payment through Liquidation or through a Payment Plan

Personal insolvency law comprises many of the features of traditional business insolvency law: it is a collective process in which creditors participate to protect their interests, and one of main goals of the process is the satisfaction of claims. However, in personal insolvencies, creditor participation is reduced due to a lack of incentives for creditors to take part in procedures in which the absence of valuable assets is the rule. This lack of resources does not justify a complex structure of creditor participation through creditors' meetings or creditor committees.

Regarding payment to creditors, there are important qualifications in personal insolvency law. There are two fundamental approaches to payment, as in business insolvency: creditors may receive a payment through the liquidation of the debtor's assets, or they may receive a payment through a plan funded with the debtor's future income.

Payment presents one of the most intense conflicts in personal insolvency law. If personal insolvency aims at the preservation of the person, allowing the debtor to resume a productive life, then a liquidation cannot include all

---

42   *See* World Bank report, *supra* note 3, at para. 186ff.

the assets of the debtor nor can a payment plan absorb all the future income of the debtor.

In most legal systems, natural persons are allowed to keep some of their essential assets. Exemptions, therefore, represent a relevant aspect of the personal insolvency regime and of the debt enforcement regime in general.[43] Typically exempt assets are automobiles, household furnishings, postcommencement salaries, retirement plans, and professional equipment. Differences in the treatment of exemptions can create incentives and disincentives for debtors, although the effects of those incentives and disincentives on the conduct of actual debtors have often been overstated.[44] The family home is an exemption in some legal systems, but this exemption can be alleged by the debtor against unsecured creditors and does not affect the rights of mortgage creditors to enforce their security. The social problem caused by the loss of housing as a result of mortgage foreclosures may require extraordinary measures, especially in the context of a systemic crisis.[45]

Exemptions are clearly connected to the notion of a fresh start. When debtors exit from insolvency, discharge their debts, and obtain a fresh start, they should own sufficient property to meet their basic needs. In some systems, exemptions have provided the only relief to debtors, in the absence of a discharge, but experience shows that exemptions alone, without the extinction of debt, are insufficient to provide debtors with the opportunity of resuming a normal, productive life.

Because available assets of natural person debtors often have little or no value, personal insolvency regimes increasingly incorporate payment plans based on the future income of debtors. In some cases, a payment plan is an alternative to traditional liquidation, but in other cases, the most valuable assets of debtors are liquidated and the payment plan is a subsequent phase of the procedure.

The requirement of a payment plan based on future income in exchange for the discharge of debt has given rise to the notion of earned start, rather than a simple fresh start.[46] However, including future income in the insolvency of natural persons raises a number of other issues. For example, a personal insolvency system cannot achieve its basic goals if debtors do not preserve a sufficient portion of their income to cover their basic needs. In this regard,

---

43   *Id.*, at para. 223ff.

44   *See* William J. Woodward Jr. & Richard S. Woodward, *Exemptions as an Incentive to Voluntary Bankruptcy: An Empirical Study*, 57 Am. Bankr. L.J. 53 (1983); *see* also Susan Block-Lieb & Edward J. Janger, *The Myth of the Rational Borrower: Rationality, Behavioralism, and the Misguided "Reform" of Bankruptcy Law*, 84 Texas L. Rev. 1481 (2006).

45   *See* Michelle J. White, *Bankruptcy: Past Puzzles, Recent Reforms, and the Mortgage Crisis* (NBER Working Paper No. 14549, Dec. 2008), available at http://www.nber.org/papers/w14549; Adam J. Levitin & Joshua Goodman, *Mortgage Market Sensitivity to Bankruptcy Modification* (paper presented at the 2008 Am. L. & Economics Assn. Conference), available at http://law.bepress.com/cgi/viewcontent.cgi?article=2485&context=alea.

46   *See* World Bank report, *supra* note 3, at para. 262ff.

the discussion mirrors the debate on property exemptions. But additional issues need to be considered in the design of a personal insolvency system, and perhaps the most important one is the duration of payment plans. There are substantial differences in the duration of plans that can be linked to social and cultural issues. Although from a purely logical perspective, longer payment plans should result in higher payments to creditors, the experience in several systems suggests that payment plans extending over periods of many years create disincentives for debtors and do not result in significantly higher rates of repayment to creditors. Debtors who have no valuable assets and cannot generate significant disposable income are known as NINAs (no income, no assets). These debtors may have no access to the formal insolvency system, and, if they are granted access, they may be unable to comply with the requirements of a payment plan. In those cases, the main goals of the insolvency system may not be achieved if these persons cannot receive relief. This observation illustrates the broader issue of the crisis of payment plans. Payment plans can be regarded not primarily as an instrument to extract a higher payment from debtors, but rather as a mechanism that prevents moral hazard and abuse of the insolvency system and that inculcates the notions of payment responsibility and financial discipline.

Some systems have introduced incentives for the productivity of debtors in payment plans. This is an interesting approach, because persons who are producing virtually all excess income for third parties—the creditors—can easily devote their efforts to covering only their basic needs, rendering the payment plan ineffective. Combining incentives with penalties can create a positive dynamic in payment plans.

A payment plan requires monitoring tools, and it may need to provide for the necessity of revising the circumstances of the debtor and modifying the plan, especially when the insolvency regime establishes a long rehabilitation period for debtors.

Discharge

Discharge is the essential feature and one of the most salient characteristics of modern systems for the regulation of the insolvency of natural persons.[47] One of the principal purposes of an insolvency system for natural persons is to reestablish the debtor's economic capability, in other words, economic rehabilitation,[48] and discharge is the most effective way in which the debtor can resume productive activity for society. It is also the most effective incentive for the use of a personal insolvency regime.[49]

---

47   See Thomas H. Jackson, *The Fresh-Start Policy in Bankruptcy*, 98 Harv. L. Rev. 1393 (1985); Margaret Howard, *A Theory of Discharge in Consumer Bankruptcy*, 48 Ohio St. L.J. 1047 (1987); John C. McCoid II, *Discharge: The Most Important Development in Bankruptcy History*, 70 Am. Bankr. L.J. 163 (1996).

48   *See*, for instance, Richard M. Hynes, *Why (Consumer) Bankruptcy?*, 56 Ala. L. Rev. 121 (2004).

49   See Emily Kadens, *The Last Bankrupt Hanged: Balancing Incentives in the Development of Bankruptcy Law*, 59 Duke L.J. 1229 (2010).

The World Bank report analyzes the three main elements in a rehabilitation policy.[50] Discharge of debts is the most important one, but two additional elements are connected to the treatment of indebtedness: debtors should not be discriminated against after having been subject to an insolvency process (principle of nondiscrimination); and debtors should be in a position to avoid excessive indebtedness in the future, which may require the adoption of measures to change debtors' attitudes concerning the use of credit, depending on the circumstances of each case.[51] In some systems, debtors are not allowed into the insolvency system again until the passage of a period of time.

The discharge of debt provides a fresh start for the debtor by extinguishing unpaid debts. This notion is contrary to traditional principles of the law of obligations, however, and many legal systems reject the notion of a straight discharge. Most systems try to favor "honest but unfortunate" debtors over persons responsible for fraudulent or reckless behavior, but these distinctions are not always easy to draw. A requirement of good faith of the debtor is important to justify the loss of creditor rights caused by the discharge. Additionally, debtors need to "earn" a discharge by surrendering their nonexempt assets to creditors and/or by complying with a payment plan for a specified period of time.

To be effective, a discharge should include as many debts as possible. Certain debts may be excluded from the discharge due to social or economic considerations, including child and spousal support, fines and other sanctions, and taxes; the examples differ depending on the country. A more problematic issue that affects the effectiveness of discharge is the sureties given by members of the debtor's family. Because discharge generally affects only individual debtors, family members who have guaranteed debts may find themselves in a difficult situation. There is a trend toward greater flexibility in the treatment of guarantees, although the issue presents numerous challenges.

Conclusion

Insolvency is an inevitable consequence of credit. As economies grow and access to credit becomes widespread, the need for an effective personal insolvency law will become more apparent. Developing an effective insolvency regime that provides solutions to the complex and sensitive problems of the indebtedness of natural persons and assists in returning debtors to a productive life requires a deep knowledge of legal techniques and considerable experience in their implementation. The World Bank report condenses knowledge

---

50   *See* World Bank report, *supra* note 3, at para. 354ff.

51   Prevention of overindebtedness requires policies that are broader than the regulation of insolvency. *See* Claudia Lima Marques, *Fundamentos Científicos da Prevenção e Tratamento do Superendividamento*, in *Prevenção e Tratamento do Superendividamento* 15 (Claudia Lima Marques, Clarissa Costa Lima, & Káren Bertoncello eds., Departamento de Proteção e Defesa do Consumidor & Sistema Nacional de Defesa do Consumidor 2010).

and experience in this area and is an extremely useful instrument for research-ers and policy makers.

The World Bank report is not prescriptive, and it does not purport to offer solutions that are applicable to all countries. Instead, the purpose of the report is to provide a comprehensive list of issues to consider in the design of a per-sonal insolvency system and an analysis of the positive and negative effects of the different policy choices available in the configuration of the legal regime. In this regard, the report represents an approach that is very different from that of international standards. The report acknowledges the impact of cul-tural, legal, and social differences; policy makers can assess the consequences of their policy choices, and the implicit message that emerges favors a more humane and equitable treatment of debtors. Indeed, the history of bankruptcy law evidences a clear trend toward a more humane treatment of debtors. There has been a long evolution from the extreme treatment of debtors un-der primitive Roman law, which included the (possibly figurative) killing and dismemberment of debtors.[52] The contrast with modern insolvency systems is striking: debtors are provided an opportunity to restart a productive activity and are assisted by social and educational programs. A personal insolvency system has become an important element for the promotion of equity and inclusion in modern societies.

Recently, Colombia became the first Latin American country to introduce a personal insolvency regime with the notion of the discharge of debts as a core element.[53] The Colombian regime provides for discharge through liqui-dation or through the completion of a payment plan. The drafters of the new law have declared that the World Bank report was a valuable element in their analysis of the reform and a useful tool to guide choices among different policy options with the ultimate goal of designing an effective system. It is hoped that policy makers in other countries will rely on the World Bank report, and that the treatment of personal indebtedness and personal insolvency becomes an essential element in policies that seek to achieve inclusive and sustainable economic development.

---

52   See Geoffrey MacCormack, *Partes Secanto*, 36 Tijdschrift voor Rechtsgescheidenis 509 (1968); *see also* S. Laurence Shaiman, *The History of Imprisonment for Debt and Insolvency Laws in Pennsylvania as They Evolved from the Common Law*, 4 Am. J. Leg. Hist. 205 (1960). Although the killing and dismemberment of the debtor seems to be fictional, the alternative of selling the debtor as a slave was used, not to mention the practice of imprisonment for debts, which was common in European countries for many centuries.

53   *See* Ley 1564 (2012) (Colombian General Code of Procedure), secs. 531ff.

Specialized Insolvency Regimes for Islamic Banks

Regulatory Prerogative and Process Design

Hdeel Abdelhady

The failures of large financial institutions in 2007 and 2008 revealed the inadequacy of existing insolvency regimes to resolve failed firms while limiting the impact to the financial system, public funds, and market confidence.[1] In response, governments have studied and adopted measures to better manage the insolvency of financial institutions, with a focus on systemically important financial institutions (SIFIs) and attention to smaller firms. In the United States, the Dodd-Frank Wall Street Reform and Consumer Protection Act created a special framework for the resolution of systemically important financial companies.[2] In the United Kingdom, the Banking Act 2009 established a Special Resolution Regime to facilitate the swift and orderly resolution of failed firms.[3] Multilaterally, the G20 Financial Stability Board has moved to strengthen and standardize resolution frameworks.[4] These measures share common policy objectives; namely, the timely detection of risk, early regulatory intervention, the avoidance of government bailouts and related moral hazard, and enhanced market discipline.

---

[1]   In this chapter, Arabic terms such as *mudaraba*, *mudarib*, and *Shari'ah* appear with alternative phonetic spellings, due to differences in spelling between the author and some quoted sources. Because the differences are minor and the meanings remain clear, source spellings are intact. The terms *Shari'ah* and *Islamic law* are used interchangeably.

[2]   Orderly Liquidation Authority (OLA) under Title II of the Dodd-Frank Wall Street Reform and Consumer Protection Act, Pub. L. No. 111-203, 124 Stat. 1376 (2010) (codified as amended in scattered sections of 12 U.S.C. and 15 U.S.C.) (hereinafter Dodd-Frank). In this chapter, OLA, a substantively harmonized and administratively managed resolution regime, is discussed as a framework of reference for the design of insolvency regimes for Islamic banks, which, like some financial companies subject to OLA, straddle banking and capital markets and are well-suited for insolvency frameworks that combine banking and capital market rules and administratively managed insolvency processes

[3]   Banking Act 2009, 2009, ch. 1, secs. 90–122 (Eng.). *See* also, for a brief overview, Her Majesty's Treasury, *Banking Act 2009 and the Establishment of the Special Resolution Regime*, available at http://www.hm-treasury.gov.uk/fin_stability_bankingact_srr.htm (accessed May 2, 2013). Notably, the Special Resolution Regime includes resolution mechanisms used in the United States for decades, such as bridge banks and regulator-brokered transfers of failed bank assets and liabilities to healthy firms.

[4]   *See*, for example, Financial Stability Board, *Key Attributes of Effective Resolution Regimes for Financial Institutions* (Oct. 2011), enumerating the "core elements . . . necessary for an effective resolution regime."

Notably, Islamic banks and other Islamic financial institutions have been absent from recent discussions on the resolution of failed banks.[5] This is not unexpected. Islamic financial institutions are not—individually or collectively—sufficiently large or interconnected to qualify for SIFI status.[6] But there is no reason to wait for Islamic banks to become systemically important to adopt regimes for their resolution. Islamic banks are not yet "too big to fail," but they are too young to risk failure.[7] Many governments, in Muslim-majority and other jurisdictions, have embraced Islamic banks, but only half-heartedly: they have taken steps to attract funds through Islamic finance, but have yet to construct the legal and regulatory infrastructure needed to support its sustainable growth within their borders. This approach has proved passable, but it is neither legally sustainable nor economically optimal. Particularly in Muslim-majority jurisdictions, Islamic banking has the potential to boost economic and finance sector development and financial inclusion. To realize this potential, enabling legal and regulatory environments are required to facilitate the sustainable growth of Islamic banking. Such environments must include insolvency regimes for Islamic banks that, like other well-crafted regimes promote market confidence, allow for early detection of risk and regulatory intervention, and impose market discipline on Islamic banks and their counterparties, including by necessitating, if not mandating, improved disclosure and contracting practices.

---

5   Although the World Bank and the Islamic Financial Services Board (IFSB), an Islamic financial services standard-setting body, have explored "[e]ffective insolvency regimes for Islamic financial institutions," with a focus on framing some of the issues.

6   Information about the systemic importance of Islamic banks has been, and is, relatively scant. For example, the authors of a 2008 International Monetary Fund (IMF) publication believed their paper was "the first to provide a cross-country empirical analysis of the role of Islamic banks in financial stability." Martin Čihák & Heiko Hesse, *Islamic Banks and Financial Stability: An Empirical Analysis* 3 (International Monetary Fund Working Paper No. WP/08/16, 2008). Available literature on Islamic banks and financial stability is based on theoretical models, rather than on "formal empirical analysis." (*Id.*, at 5.)

7   Uncertainty as to the nature of Islamic financial instruments and investor rights at default has had a chilling effect. For example, the *sukuk* market was adversely affected by a leading Shari'ah scholar's 2007 opinion raising doubts about the legality of some *sukuk* (commonly described as "Islamic bonds") then on the market. *See*, for example, Robin Wigglesworth, *Sharia Boards: Scholars Hold Sway over the Success of Products*, Financial Times (May 5, 2009), available at http://www.ft.com/cms/s/0/91c1636e-3836-11de-9211-00144feabdc0 .html#axzz2UMouSeaW (accessed May 5, 2013). Dubai World's November 2009 request to halt debt repayments, including payments to holders of a $3.5 billion *sukuk* issued by the property developer Nakheel, exposed uncertainty as to the legal rights and obligations of *sukuk* holders in default or other distress. *See*, for example, Heiko Hesse & Andreas Jobst, *Debriefing Nakheel: Wider Implications for the Sukuk Market*, Roubini Global Economics, Economonitor (Apr. 29, 2010), available at http://www.economonitor.com/blog/2010/04/debriefing -nakheel-wider-implications-for-the-sukuk-market/ (accessed May 5, 2013). In banking, some Egyptian consumers and regulators remain skeptical of Islamic banking as a result of decades-old fraud cases involving Islamic institutions. *See*, for example, *Flirting with Islamic Finance, infra* note 21 ("For many years, Egyptians have had reservations against Islamic finance, after firms like Al-Rayan and Al-Saad stripped thousands of Egyptians of millions of pounds in Ponzi schemes in the mid-1980s").

This chapter advocates the adoption of specialized, administratively managed (nonjudicial) resolution regimes for Islamic banks, for the following reasons:[8]

- Insolvency regimes must mirror the unique features of Islamic banking; profit-sharing investment accounts are discussed as an example of those unique features.

- Early intervention and expeditious resolution at failure are necessary to protect consumers, maintain confidence in banks, and preserve the assets of failing or failed banks. These objectives would be best met through nimble, administratively managed processes rather than through the courts and subject to generic bankruptcy laws, particularly in jurisdictions in which the courts and/or insolvency laws are not suited for bank failures or where existing procedures might lead to ad hoc outcomes.[9]

- Islamic banking is, where Shari'ah compliance is concerned, effectively self-regulating, at both the firm and industry levels. Self-enforced Shari'ah compliance is appropriate given the relative youth of Islamic banking and the potential innovation benefits of laissez-faire approaches. But because Shari'ah shapes all aspects of Islamic banking, self-regulation must be tempered by robust process-based and outcome-driven regimes that disallow the monopolization of information to an extent that regulators are limited in their ability to obtain, process, validate, and act on information pertinent to the health of Islamic banks.

Importantly, the positions advanced in this chapter are premised on the view that defining legal outcomes through specialized insolvency regimes for Islamic banks will propel—as a matter of necessity—Islamic banks, standard-setting bodies, and regulators to improve existing Islamic banking regulation, with much needed policy direction and urgency.

Islamic Banking

Islamic banking has grown rapidly in the past 35 years,[10] reaching an estimated value of $1.1 trillion in 2012.[11] Since 2008, growth has accelerated even

---

8   This chapter is concerned only with Islamic banks, and not with Islamic windows of conventional banks.

9   In some jurisdictions, bank resolution can be ad hoc, even where the law provides for the regulation of banks by a single authority. For example, in the United Arab Emirates, "onshore" banks are supervised by the Central Bank. The Central Bank may appoint a liquidator and not itself liquidate insolvent banks (which are also subject to generally applicable insolvency laws). Such a framework does not ensure uniformity of outcomes. *See* United Arab Emirates Union Law No. 10 of 1980, *Concerning the Central Bank, the Monetary System, and Organization of Banking.*

10 Since shortly after the establishment of Dubai Islamic Bank in 1975. The first modern Islamic bank was Mit Ghamr, established in 1963 in Egypt. The establishment of Dubai Islamic Bank is used as a time marker here given the bank's comparatively large size, wider commercial banking mandate, and greater visibility.

11 Camilla Hall, *Islamic Banking: Impressive Growth Underscores Success*, Financial Times (Mar. 27, 2012), available at http://www.ft.com/cms/s/0/09a99422-7291-11e1-9be9-00144

faster. By some estimates, Islamic banking broke $1 trillion in 2009, from $947 billion in 2008.[12] "One potential scenario" predicts that "global Islamic banking assets with commercial banks . . . [will] reach $1.8 trillion in 2013 . . . representing average annual growth of 17%."[13] In the Middle East and North Africa, Islamic banking assets are projected to more than double to $990 billion by 2015, from $416 billion in 2010.[14] In Gulf Cooperation Council states, Islamic banks have "crossed the . . . important 25% [market share] threshold which means . . . [they] are competing in the conventional market as well."[15] At the firm level, it is expected that Islamic banks will take near-term steps to achieve scale through mergers and expansion.[16]

The growth of Islamic banks should be welcome. They have the potential to facilitate financial inclusion, including by meeting the needs of financially marginalized individuals and small and medium-size enterprises (SMEs) and capturing assets traditionally beyond the reach of formal economies. According to the World Bank, approximately "2.5 billion adults lack access to formal financial services, limiting their ability to benefit from economic opportunities, improve their health and education, and raise their income levels."[17] In the Middle East and North Africa, a natural market for Islamic banks, "only 18% of adults have a bank account."[18] In Egypt, the most populous Arab state, fewer than 10 percent of Egyptians have bank accounts, according to some estimates.[19] In Indonesia, the largest Muslim country by population, SMEs "are facing a credit crunch," notwithstanding the relative liquidity of Indonesia's commercial banks.[20] In other majority-Muslim jurisdictions, the market poten-

---

feab49a.html#axzz2UKZvZVYt (accessed May 5, 2013). This is a conservative estimate. Ernst & Young, for example, estimates the 2011 value of global Islamic banking assets at $1.334 trillion. Ernst & Young, *World Islamic Banking Competitiveness Report 2013: Growing beyond DNA of Successful Transformation*, 6 (Dec. 2012), available at http://www.mifc.com/index.php?ch =151&pg=735&ac=818&bb=file1 (accessed May 3, 2013).

12   Pejman Abedfar, Philip Molyneux, & Amine Tarazi, *Risk in Islamic Banking* 2 (LAPE working paper, May 3, 2012). Cumulative estimates include both wholly Islamic banks and Islamic windows of conventional banks.

13   Ernst & Young, *supra* note 11, at 6.

14   Ernst & Young, *The World Islamic Banking Competitiveness Report: A Brave New World of Sustainable Growth 2011–2012* 8 available at http://www.ey.com/Publication/vwLUAssets/IBCR _Report/$FILE/IBCRReport2011(LR)%20Final.pdf (accessed May 3, 2013).

15   *Id.*, at 19.

16   *Id.*, at 66, 70.

17   World Bank, *Financial Inclusion: Helping Countries Meet the Needs of the Under-Banked and Under-Served*, available at http://www.worldbank.org/en/results/2013/04/02/financial -inclusion-helping-countries-meet-the-needs-of-the-underbanked-and-underserved (accessed May 3, 2013).

18   *Id.*

19   Business Today Egypt, *Payroll Potential*, available at http://www.businesstodayegypt.com /index.php?url=news/display/article/artId:39/payroll-potential/secId:3 (Jan. 1, 2011) (accessed May 3, 2013).

20   Jay K. Rosengard, *If the Banks Are Doing So Well, Why Can't I Get a Loan? Regulatory Constraints to Financial Inclusion in Indonesia* 1 (Kennedy Sch. of Govt., Mossavar-Rahmani Ctr. for Bus.

tial for Islamic banking is strong due to religion-based demand.[21] In minority-Muslim jurisdictions, regulators are keen to develop Islamic banking and finance to cater to small Muslim populations and to attract foreign funds.[22]

With the growth of Islamic banking and its potential comes the need for substantively appropriate regulation and effective enforcement. An International Monetary Fund (IMF) study on Islamic banks and financial stability found that "Islamic banks pose risks to the financial system that . . . differ from those posed by conventional banks . . . [due to] the specific features of Islamic contracts, and the overall legal, governance, and liquidity infrastructure of Islamic finance."[23] The same study concluded that large Islamic banks, compared to small Islamic and small and large conventional banks, were the least stable of the group.[24] "[L]arge Islamic banks . . . [had] significantly lower z-scores [a stability measure] than small Islamic banks," while large conventional banks were found to have "significantly higher z-scores than small commercial banks."[25] The growth of Islamic banks in number and size necessitates and underscores the importance of tailored regulation and insolvency frameworks.

& Govt. Working Paper No. 2011-15, Harv. U. 2011).

21 Some research has shown a preference among Muslim consumers for Islamic banking when it is available and perceived to be truly Shari'ah compliant. This sentiment was illustrated in an article about an Egyptian consumer who planned to transfer her savings to Islamic banks "after spending the last 15 years unwillingly investing her money in interest-bearing investment certificates . . . [and feeling that her profits were] never blessed." Sherine Abdel-Razek, *Flirting with Islamic Finance*, 1092, Al-Ahram Weekly (Apr. 5–11, 2012), available at http://weekly.ahram.org.eg/2012/1092/ec1.htm (hereinafter *Flirting with Islamic Finance*). The article reflects the preference of some Muslim consumers for Islamic banking, as well as their skepticism, noting the view of some Egyptians that "even Islamic banks in Egypt did not apply Sharia law completely."

22 For example, in South Africa, where 2 percent or less of the population is Muslim, authorities are working to position the country as an Islamic finance hub. Xola Potelwa, *S. Africa's FNB Hires New Sharia Committee, Faces Regulation Challenges*, Reuters (Apr. 30, 2013), available at http://www.reuters.com/article/2012/08/28/safrica-fnb-sharia-idAFL5E8JQ3OM20120828 (accessed May 3, 2013). Similarly, in Zambia, where approximately 12 percent (or less) of the population is Muslim, the country's central bank governor explained that Zambia's relatively small Muslim population includes "'high value businessmen who control a very significant share of the Zambian economy,' making their exclusion from the banking sector hurtful to the economy." Other Muslim-minority jurisdictions, such as the United Kingdom; Hong Kong SAR, China; and Singapore, have pursued Islamic finance with varying degrees of ambition.

23 Čihák & Hesse, *supra* note 6, at 4–5, countering the minority view that Islamic banking, as practiced, for example, in Malaysia, "is not very different from conventional banking . . . [and thus] for purposes of financial section analysis, Islamic banks should be treated similarly to their commercial [conventional] counterparts."

24 *Id.*, at 13–16 and generally. Finding also that Islamic banks — small and large — "appeared to be more stable than commercial banks . . . [a] result [that] seem[ed] driven by small Islamic banks that have higher z-scores than small commercial banks (indicating higher stability), while large Islamic banks have lower z-scores than large commercial banks." (*Id.*, at 13–14.)

25 *Id.*, at 14 & note 12, noting that these findings were at 1 percent. The authors indicate a positive correlation between "greater income diversity" (i.e., nonlending-based income) and increases in z-scores in large Islamic banks, "suggesting that a move from lending-based operation to other sources of income might improve stability in those banks." (*Id.*, at 17.)

Islamic Banks in Practice

Four of the bedrock principles of Shari'ah that shape Islamic banking are

- The prohibition of *riba*, a term commonly described as interest but that more broadly connotes the predetermination of fixed and guaranteed returns with elements of excessive risk asymmetry[26]
- Profit and loss sharing (PLS)
- The avoidance of *gharar*; that is, uncertainty to a degree that would obfuscate or frustrate economic or contractual purpose[27]
- The avoidance of speculation

As to the prohibition of interest, the Accounting and Auditing Organisation for Islamic Financial Institutions (AAOIFI) has a standard on the conversion of banks from conventional to Islamic that is emphatic. That standard requires as a prerequisite of conversion that "[a]ll traces of conventional transactions whereby the bank originated monetary assets and is liable to pay interest for them must be liquidated."[28] The prohibition of interest—the primary measure of profit and marker for managing assets and liabilities in conventional banking—in principle distinguishes Islamic banks in all aspects of their operations.

Islamic Banking: Commercial Landscape

To compete with conventional counterparts, Islamic banks often benchmark profit margins to prevailing interest rates (e.g., Libor), both in extending credit and in sourcing funding through deposits. For example, *ijarah* (lease finance) and *murabaha* (cost-plus-profit sale-based financing) transactions (on the asset side of the banks' balance sheets) are typically benchmarked to interest rates. On the liability side of the balance sheet, Islamic banks raise funds through

---

26   The concept of *riba* is well elucidated, as follows:

> [R]iba—a term literally meaning "an excess" and interpreted as "any justifiable increase of capital whether in loans or sales"—is the central tenet of the [Islamic] system . . . *riba* covers not only usury but also the charging of "interest" as widely practiced. This prohibition is based on arguments of social justice, equality, and property rights. Islamic law encourages the earning of profits but forbids the charging of interest because profits, determined ex post, symbolize successful entrepreneurship and creation of additional wealth, whereas interest, determined ex ante, is a cost that is accrued irrespective of the outcome of business operations. . . . Social justice demands that borrowers and lenders share rewards as well as losses . . . and that the process of accumulating and distributing wealth in the economy be fair and representative of true productivity.

Hennie Van Greuning & Zamir Iqbal, *Risk Analysis for Islamic Banks* 7 (International Bank for Reconstruction and Development/World Bank 2008).

27   AAOIFI, a key standard-setting body, defines *gharar* as "a state of uncertainty that exists when the process of concluding a transaction involves an unknown aspect . . . gharar refers to the status of results that may or may not materialize." AAOIFI, *Shari'a Standards for Islamic Financial Institutions*, Shari'a Standard No. (31), *Controls on Gharar in Financial Transactions*, para. 2/1 (Accounting and Auditing Organisation for Islamic Financial Institutions 1432H-2010) (entire compilation, hereinafter *AAOIFI Shari'a Standards*).

28   *AAOIFI Shari'a Standards*, *supra* note 27, Shari'a Standard No. (6), *Conversion of a Conventional Bank to an Islamic Bank*, para. 6/1.

PLS-based investment accounts (discussed below), which often are managed to achieve competitiveness with conventional interest-bearing deposit accounts.[29] Such practices have not gone without criticism. Both from within and outside the Islamic finance industry, Islamic banks have been accused of mimicking conventional products, rather than providing truly Shari'ah -compliant offerings. Critics often cite the practice of benchmarking profits to interest rates as proof. Some Muslim consumers are skeptical as to the authenticity of Islamic banking products and refrain from Islamic banking for that reason.

Legal Landscape: Gaps and Gray Zones

Most of the jurisdictions in which Islamic banks operate, including those in which Shari'ah is a source of law, have yet to adopt comprehensive legal frameworks tailored to Islamic banking. Where Islamic banking contracts have been litigated under civil law, results have been confusing and unhelpful to the extent that litigation has not yielded Shari'ah precedent.[30] Although standard-setting bodies such as AAOIFI and the Islamic Financial Services Board produce helpful frameworks, these frameworks are generally nonbinding and are not always timely.[31] As noted above, Islamic banks are largely self-regulating where Shari'ah compliance is concerned: substantive decisions as to the Shari'ah soundness of products and governance are made by Shari'ah supervisory boards that comprise Shari'ah scholars who are recruited and remunerated by the banks they supervise and whose decisions are often proprietary.

---

29 *See*, for example, V. Sundararajan, *Profit Sharing Investment Accounts—Measurement and Control of Displaced Commercial Risk (DCR) in Islamic Finance*, 19(1) Islamic Econ. Studies, 42 (2011) (hereinafter Sundararajan 2011) noting commercial pressures on Islamic banks to provide "market related returns that might deviate from the underlying asset returns to which IAH are contractually entitled." In marketing *mudaraba*-based accounts, some Islamic banks indicate, but do not commit to, expected returns comparable to prevailing interest-based returns on functionally similar conventional products. Other observations on the likeness of Islamic and conventional banking are at, for example, Abedfar et al., *supra* note 12, at 10–11, discussing findings from Malaysia that "only 0.5% of Islamic bank finance is based on PLS principles"; from Pakistan, that *mudaraba* companies that "are supposed to operate in the form of PLS mainly follow non-PLS modes of finance"; from Indonesia, where "PLS modes of finance accounted for 35.7% in the financing of Islamic banks . . . by the end of 2008"; and, noting one interesting finding that "while Islamic banks appear to refrain from practicing PLS modes of finance they face possible greater withdrawal risks than conventional banks."

30 *See*, for example, Hdeel Abdelhady, *Islamic Law in Secular Courts (Again): Teachable Moments from the Journey*, 18 Intl. L. News (Fall 2009), discussing *Shamil Bank of Bahrain EC v. Beximco Pharmaceuticals Ltd.* (2004) All E.R. 1072; *Shamil Bank of Bahrain v. Beximco Pharmaceuticals Ltd.* (2003) All E.R. (Comm.) 849; Hdeel Abdelhady, *The Front Office Generates Revenue, the Back Office Creates Value: Operational Excellence Is the Key to Unlocking Lasting Value in Islamic Finance* (ABA & Hawkamah, the Inst. of Corp. Governance [DIFC] white paper). Both publications are available at http://www.masspointpllc.com/#!masspointnews-and-publications /c17jc (accessed May 3, 2013).

31 For example, AAOIFI's standard on the important subject of distribution of profit from PSIAs was issued in 2009, more than six years after AAOIFI's Shari'ah Board decided, in 2003, to issue a standard on the subject. *AAOIFI Shar'ia Standards*, Shari'a Standard No. (40), *Distribution of Profit in Mudarabah-Based Investment Accounts*, App. A: Historical Note on Preparation of Standard (hereinafter AAOIFI 40).

Such deficient and sometimes incongruous legal environments breed ambiguity as to the rights and obligations of Islamic banks and their counterparties, generally and at insolvency. The profit-sharing investment account (PSIA), a deposit product that yields no interest but is often managed to compete with interest-based deposits, is discussed here as an example of the issues that exist and can arise in jurisdictions lacking clear Islamic banking regulation and insolvency regimes.

PSIAs: A Unique "Liability" of Islamic Banks

Like their conventional counterparts, Islamic banks rely on customer deposits as a source of core funding. However, Islamic banks do not offer interest or other fixed, guaranteed returns on deposits (demand deposits[32] and others), but rather provide nonfinancial incentives to current account holders, such as bill payment, checkbooks, and debit cards.[33] Of interest here are PSIAs, which, from the consumer perspective, are functionally similar to, for example, conventional savings or certificate of deposit accounts.[34] Based on *mudaraba*,[35] PSIAs are of two kinds: "restricted" and "unrestricted."[36] They constitute a

---

32   Current (or checking) accounts are known as *amanah* accounts. *Amanah*, an Arabic term, means, inter alia, "trust," and its definition includes "deposited in trust" and "a deposit." *The Hans Wehr Dictionary of Modern Written Arabic* 35, 36 (J. Milton Cowan ed., 4th ed., Spoken Language Services, Inc. 1994) (hereinafter *Wehr Dictionary*). From the Shari'ah perspective, Islamic banks are custodians of funds held in such accounts. Appropriately, an absolute reserve requirement attaches to *amanah* accounts.

33   *See*, for example, Rodney Wilson, *Legal, Regulatory and Governance Issues in Islamic Finance* 41 (Edinburgh U. Press 2012), discussing current account services offered by Dubai Islamic Bank.

34   *Mudaraba*-based Islamic banking accounts are referred to by some key regulators as PSIAs, a term that is used herein to refer only to *mudaraba*-based accounts. *See*, for example, Dubai Financial Services Authority (DFSA), *The DFSA's Islamic Finance Regulatory Regime*, available at http://www.dfsa.ae/Pages/DoingBusinesswithDFSA/IslamicFinance/IFRR.aspx (accessed May 2, 2012); and Bank Negara Malaysia, *Guidelines on Musharakah and Mudharabah Contracts for Islamic Banking Institutions*, available at http://www.bnm.gov.my/guidelines/01_banking /04_prudential_stds/15_mnm.pdf (accessed May 2, 2012). The DFSA is the regulator of financial (conventional and Islamic) and related activities in the Dubai International Financial Centre. Bank Negara Malaysia is Malaysia's central bank.

35   *Mudaraba* is a form of Islamic partnership between one or more providers of capital (*rab al-maal*, pl. *arbab al-maal*) and one or more parties providing labor or other services, such as investment management (the *mudarib*). *Mudaraba* generally and *mudaraba*-based bank products are discussed in *AAOIFI Shari'a Standards*, *supra* note 27, Shari'a Standard No. (13), *Mudaraba* (hereinafter AAOIFI 13), and AAOIFI 40, *supra* note 31. *Mudaraba*-based investments also appear on the asset side of Islamic banks' balance sheets (with the Islamic bank as capital provider and a third party as *mudarib*). Like PSIA holders, Islamic banks risk the loss of their capital in such arrangements, which raises separate but related regulatory and insolvency risk issues that are not discussed in this chapter.

36   Restricted *mudaraba* accounts typically are held by more sophisticated customers (e.g., in the High Net Worth bracket). Unlike unrestricted accounts, restricted *mudaraba* transactions are limited to certain investments (e.g., specific projects, industries) per the instruction of or agreement with the capital provider; thus bank discretion is limited. Importantly, restricted *mudaraba* accounts are not balance sheet liabilities for Islamic banks.

significant portion of Islamic banks' liabilities. By one estimate, more than 60 percent of Islamic banks' funding derives from PSIAs.[37]

PSIAs are generally available to all classes of customers, regardless of sophistication, and often with relatively small opening or minimum balance requirements.[38] Funds deposited are pooled with bank funds and invested by the bank at its discretion. Profits, if any, are distributed between the bank and PSIA depositors, according to pre-agreed-on percentages. Risk between the bank and PSIA depositors must be shared coextensively. According to AAO-IFI:

> It is not permissible for the capital provider to give the *mudarib* two amounts of capital on condition that the profit earned on one of the two amounts would be taken by the *mudarib* while the capital provider would take the profit earned on the other amount. It is not also permissible for the capital provider to state that the profit of one financial period would be taken by the *mudarib* and the capital provider would take the profit of the following financial period.[39] Similarly, it is not permissible to assign the profit from a particular transaction to the *mudarib* and the profit from another transaction to the capital provider.[40]

---

37   Sundararajan 2011, *supra* note 29, at 42. "A survey of [a]nnual [r]eports of Islamic banks in different countries showed that about 62% of total assets of those banks were funded, on average, by profit sharing investment accounts." (*Id.*, at note 1.) *See* also V. Sundararajan, *Risk Measurement and Disclosure in Islamic Finance and the Implications of Profit Sharing Investment Accounts, Proceedings of 6th International Conference on Islamic Economics and Finance* 118 (Munawar Iqbal et al. eds., Islamic Development Bank 2007) (unrestricted *mudaraba* accounts represented "nearly zero to 80%" of the total deposits of some Islamic banks).

38   For example, Mashreq al Islami, the Islamic banking arm of Mashreq Bank, according to its website, requires an initial minimum deposit amount of AED 3,000 (roughly $816 per May 2013 exchange rates) to open a *mudaraba*-based "savings account," the mechanics of which are described on the website as follows:

> Under the Mudarabah (Fund management) arrangement, depositor (Rab Al-Mal) authorizes the bank (Mudareb) to invest the deposit according to the unrestricted Mudarabah. Funds of the term investment and Savings accounts are invested according to unrestricted Mudarabah basis in the joint investing pool between the depositors and the shareholders and the realized profits from the joint investment pool are distributed between the depositors according to their respective shares in investment.

Mashreq al Islami, *Personal Banking, Savings Accounts*, available at http://www.mashreqalislami .com/english/personal/accounts/savings-account/#faq-47573 (accessed May 4, 2013).

39   Interestingly, however, AAOIFI provides that "when loss is incurred in one *mudarabah* operation, it can be covered from the profits of other operations, and if it exceeds the profits it should be covered from capital. What should really matter is the final result of the liquidation at the end of the financial period specified by the institution." AAOIFI 40, *supra* note 31, at para. 3/2/1. *Shari'ah* merits aside, this allowance should come with explicit requirements for disclosures to PSIA depositors and regulators and policies for management and accounting.

40   AAOIFI 13, *supra* note 35, at para. 8/6. The Shari'ah requirement of coextensive risk is elemental. For example, in agricultural investment and sharecropping, the "Prophet [Muhammad (PBUH)] . . . prohibited speculative sharecropping arrangements, such as agreements giving parties rights to yields from specific tracts of agricultural land or specific produce from sharecropped land . . . [and] required that parties agree to apportion the total agricultural produce, whether in percentages or by other measures." Hdeel Abdelhady, *Islamic*

Owing to their nature and objectives, PSIAs have been likened to open-ended mutual funds and other collective investment schemes. But because they are offered by deposit-taking banks, regulatory classification of PSIAs varies. In the Dubai International Financial Centre, PSIAs are classified specially for regulatory purposes. In the United Kingdom, bank-offered PSIAs are treated as "deposits," a classification necessitated by the deposit-taking function of the offering bank but incompatible with the nature of the product.[41] AAOIFI describes PSIAs as "demand deposits" in one standard,[42] and likens the role of *mudarib* to an asset or fund manager in another standard.[43]

In theory, PSIA depositors bear the risk of loss of principal, except in cases of bank negligence, misconduct, or breach of contract. Therefore, no reserve requirement attaches to PSIAs.[44] In reality, however, Islamic banks engage in "return smoothing" to avoid depositor withdrawals in response to losses and to achieve parity with returns offered by conventional banks. They do this by various means, including

- Maintaining profit equalization reserve (PER) accounts and investment risk return (IRR) accounts, essentially rainy-day funds in which excess periodic profits are held to cover periodic profit shortfalls and capital losses[45]

- Forgoing, in favor of PSIA depositors, a portion of the bank's pre-agreed-on percentage of profits (as *mudarib*)

Finance as a Mechanism for Bolstering Food Security in the Middle East: Food Security Waqf, 13(1) Sustainable Dev. L. & Policy 29, 33 (2012), available at http://digitalcommons.wcl.american .edu/cgi/viewcontent.cgi?article=1524&context=sdlp (accessed June 11, 2013).

41   The Islamic Bank of Britain, for example, was required by the now-defunct Financial Services Authority to offer capital certainty to PSIA depositors as a condition of offering PSIA "deposit" accounts. To bridge the gap between Shari'ah and banking regulations, the Financial Services Authority and the Islamic Bank of Britain agreed to a two-step process whereby PSIA depositors were entitled, as a matter of law, to capital certainty at the time of account opening and thereafter could, by agreement with the Islamic Bank of Britain, forgo capital certainty. Andrew Henderson, *Islamic Financial Institutions,* in *Islamic Finance: Law and Practice* 54, 69 (Craig R. Nethercott & David M. Eisenberg eds., Oxford U. Press 2012). This two-step process, expedient on the front end, could lead to uncertainty in the absence of explicit, effective disclosure. For example, would depositors' waivers of capital certainty have been acceptable and effective only upon their having verifiably received and agreed to express disclosures as to the nature and consequences of such waivers? Would the waivers, particularly those given by retail customers, be enforceable against customers in the event of bank insolvency (thus foreclosing any claims to deposit insurance)? Even if yes, would or should public policy tolerate, or allow a repeat of, such an outcome, to the detriment of consumer confidence?

42   AAOIFI 40, *supra* note 31, at para. 2.

43   AAOIFI 13, *supra* note 35, at para. 9/4. This original Shari'ah standard on *mudaraba*, under the heading "Duties and Powers of the Mudarib," states that "the mudarib must carry out all the work that any similar asset or fund manager would be liable."

44   *See* Greuning & Iqbal, *supra* note 26, at 19–20.

45   PER and IRR accounts are employed to further a common objective, but their mechanics differ. Excess profits are reserved in PER accounts to cover future shortfalls in profit. Funds are reserved in IRR accounts to compensate for losses of principal.

- Deducting from profits owed to shareholders to bolster returns to PSIA depositors[46]

The transfer of profits from shareholders to PSIA depositors is known as *displaced commercial risk*, because the risk of loss is "displaced" to shareholders to maintain a competitive position.[47]

PSIAs raise a number of issues for Islamic bank insolvency and supervision, not only because of the risk of loss borne by depositors, but also because of the way these accounts are managed. The Dubai Financial Services Authority (DFSA) highlighted some of these issues in its comments to the G20 Financial Stability Board on effective insolvency regimes for SIFIs:

> The structures used in Islamic finance raise substantial questions [in insolvency] about depositor preference and deposit insurance. A common structure in Islamic banking is the . . . (PSIA), which in market terms plays a similar role to a conventional deposit account. It is in principle an investment product, in which both return and principal are at risk, but in practice, banks use various smoothing mechanisms to provide a return very similar to a conventional deposit and often mirroring conventional interest rates in the same market. Some regulators therefore follow the underlying principle, and treat PSIAs as investments; others treat them as deposits. Views in this area tend to be strongly held, and the situation is further complicated by the fact that there has been no legal test of this position in an insolvency.[48]

In addition to the classification of PSIA accounts, determinations of depositor preference, and rights to deposit insurance (where available), important questions about PSIA depositor treatment vis-à-vis Islamic banks, nondepositor creditors, and other PSIA depositors must be addressed.[49] For example, should less sophisticated PSIA depositors be treated more favorably than their more sophisticated counterparts? Retail consumer protection would require this result.[50] Should all PSIA holders be given low or no priority

---

46 *See*, for example, Sundararajan 2011, *supra* note 29, at 48–49. In an extreme case, "the International Islamic Bank for Investment and Development in Egypt . . . distributed all of its profits to investment account holders and nothing to shareholders from the middle to late 1980s." Greuning & Iqbal, *supra* note 26, at 176–177.

47 Sundararajan 2011, *supra* note 29, at 48.

48 G20 Financial Stability Board, Press Release, *Comments Received on the FSB Consultative Document on Effective Resolutions of SIFIs, DFSA Draft Comment Letter to the FSB* (hereinafter *DFSA Comments*), available at http://www.financialstabilityboard.org/press/c_110909t.pdf (accessed May 3, 2013).

49 A rudimentary question is whether PSIA depositors are creditors at all, particularly in the absence of bank negligence, misconduct, or breach of contract (events that would trigger different kinds of claims and perhaps render them judgment creditors).

50 Consumer protection and the maintenance of market confidence would justify strict disclosure requirements and depositor priority preferences tied to the relative sophistication of PSIA holders, using, for example, proxy measures of "sophistication," such as the net worth or annual income criteria, applied to determine accredited investor status in the

because they assumed risk of loss? If so, are prevailing standards of disclosure sufficient to justify this outcome?[51] If yes, would the policy objectives of consumer protection and market confidence outweigh a contract-based assignment of responsibility at insolvency? In addition, there are insolvency-related issues relevant to return smoothing practices. For example, are PER and IRR accounts the property of the bank, or do PSIA holders have some claim to those funds in insolvency? If the latter is the case, how and in what percentages should PSIA depositor claims to PER and IRR accounts be fixed? More important, do regulators understand return smoothing and related accounting and distribution practices sufficiently to isolate claims to them in insolvency? At what point should the Islamic bank's profit for managing PSIAs be considered realized, and how does this factor into insolvency?[52] And do regulators have the information needed to determine if an insolvency is attributable to negligence or misconduct, which would trigger clear PSIA depositor claims? These are just some of the questions surrounding PSIAs in insolvency. Questions about the nature of Islamic banking and the classification and preference of claims in insolvency are numerous and have yet to be clearly answered or comprehensively identified.[53]

United States for purposes of allowing exemptions from registration requirements. See, for example, United States Securities & Exchange Commission, *Accredited Investors*, available at http://www.sec.gov/answers/accred.htm (accessed May 3, 2013).

51 Typically, parties that contract for the least risk (e.g., secured creditors) are accorded higher priority in bankruptcy. Shareholders, commensurate with their risk and presumed exertion of control, have low priority. In such creditor hierarchies, PSIA depositors occupy a legal no-man's-land because they share risk like shareholders but have no control and are treated as depositors but have no capital certainty.

52 Related to these questions are AAOIFI standards on the realization of distributable profits, including that "realization of profit in investment accounts does not take place before protecting the capital" (AAOIFI 40, *supra* note 31, at para. 3/1/1); "[r]ealization of profit in investment accounts does not take place before . . . [inter alia] [l]iquidation of *mudarabah* assets, which can be either actual liquidation . . . or legal liquidation" (*id.*, at para. 3/1/2/1); "[i]t is permissible to pay advance amounts to the holders of accounts before actual or legal liquidations so that final settlement can be made later on [and] [a]fter actual or legal liquidation the institution is committed to make necessary additions to, or deductions from, the advanced amounts so that each holder of an investment account receives his exact share of the profit" (*id.*, at para. 5/3). As these and other *mudaraba* standards make clear, attribution of entitlement to profit requires meticulous and transparent accounting and reporting that is very specific as to, inter alia, time and finality.

53 With respect to return smoothing, neither the size of PER and IRR accounts nor the internal policies governing their management are sufficiently clear. What checks are in place to ensure that PER and IRR accounts are properly used and accurately represented in regulatory disclosures, annual reports, and customer documentation? Publicly available information does not facilitate ready verification that PER and IRR funds are consistently managed and distributed in strict accordance with PSIA account documentation, articulated policies, and applicable standards. Could PER and IRR funds be appropriated for other purposes, such as to raise firm value or shareholder returns? One study of Islamic banks showed that "Islamic banks [generally] yield lower stock returns for their investors . . . but [yielded higher returns] during the crisis [period of Q4-2007 and Q4-2008]." Thorsten Beck, Asli Deirguc-Kunt, & Ouarda Merrouche, *Islamic vs. Conventional Banking: Business Model, Efficiency and Stability* 21 (World Bank Policy Research Working Paper No. 5446, World Bank 2010). These authors state that the "higher liquidity reserves and better capitalization [of Islamic banks] can explain the higher stock returns." But it is reasonable to question what, if any, role funds

Specialized Insolvency Regimes for Islamic Banks

Insolvency regimes for Islamic banks should reflect the nature of Islamic banking,[54] comport with Shari'ah insolvency rules, and further Shari'ah-based objectives for market regulation. In dual jurisdictions in which Islamic and conventional banks operate side by side, considerations of judicial economy are particularly relevant.[55] The design of resolution regimes should compensate for any general weaknesses of legal and regulatory infrastructure, such as the inexperience or inadequacy of courts or regulators to expeditiously manage bank insolvencies in the absence of specialized frameworks.

In designing insolvency regimes for Islamic banks, it is not sufficient to focus only on achieving convergence of Shari'ah and conventional insolvency rules. Shari'ah insolvency rules developed and applied in the context of single debtors, bilateral relationships, or relatively small groups are not, by themselves, sufficient to inform resolution regimes for Islamic banks. Rather, Shari'ah insolvency rules must be interpreted in accordance with, and further the objectives of, Islamic legal and historical views of market regulation, which require that regulators be empowered to ensure lawful market conduct, impose market discipline, promote transparency, and protect consumers. Similarly, it is insufficient to examine conventional insolvency regimes applicable only to banks, because Islamic banking encompasses banking and capital market activities. The remainder of this chapter focuses on some fundamental Shari'ah insolvency rules, the nature and objectives of Shari'ah market regulation, and an example from the United States of a substantively harmonized, administratively managed insolvency regime.

---

reserved in PER and IRR accounts could play in such an atypical performance, particularly at times in which PSIA depositor expectations for returns might be low (such as during a financial crisis). Although it is accepted that Islamic banks were not directly exposed to losses incurred by conventional banks in the 2007–2008 period (an obvious explanation for the atypically better return to shareholders), it is also accepted that Islamic banks typically yield lower returns to shareholders. Such issues underscore the need for robust, uniform accounting rules and practices, meaningful reporting requirements, and effective disclosure. Without verifiable information, the conclusiveness of some empirical analyses of Islamic banks' performance (however measured) is open to doubt.

54   Regulators need to decide whether to tailor insolvency frameworks to Islamic banking as understood in theory or as practiced, where there is divergence. As indicated above, Islamic banking theory and practice are not always or reliably the same. Presumably, regulators prefer that Islamic banking be truly Islamic, to justify and promote competition with and to secure the benefits of Islamic banking. But regulations must be practical. This is yet another policy question that is crystallized by insolvency considerations.

55   The author is aware of only two wholly Islamic banking systems, one in Sudan and one in Iran.

Shari'ah View: Insolvency (*Taflīs*) and Regulatory Prerogative (*Hisba*)

Insolvency regimes for Islamic banks must conform to, or be compatible with, Shari'ah rules on bankruptcy (*taflīs*)[56] and Shari'ah generally. But the extraction of rules from one area of Shari'ah (bankruptcy) without consideration of other relevant areas (market conduct and regulation) is an approach that lacks policy direction. This section discusses some of the basic elements of Shari'ah insolvency and market regulation, which together should inform policy choices on matters such as depositor and other creditor priority in bankruptcy.

Shari'ah Foundational Principles on Insolvency

Shari'ah bankruptcy rules share common principles with what are regarded as modern insolvency rules. The rules of *taflīs* and varying opinions of classical Shari'ah scholars were articulated not long after the advent of Islam.[57] Islamic law recognizes insolvency as a legal status that triggers both creditor standing to bring claims and judicial authority to intervene in the financial affairs of debtors.[58] Classical Shari'ah jurists recognized both balance sheet and cash flow insolvency, and courts (judges) were authorized to "interdict" debtors (declaring the debtor insolvent as a matter of law) and prohibit the sale or other disposition of assets during the pendency of insolvency proceedings.[59] Shari'ah deals also with creditors' rights and respective priorities, but there are questions as to how those priorities would play out in contemporary practice. The DFSA has highlighted some of the issues:

> [W]e note that thinking about insolvency in the context of Shari'a law is at a relatively rudimentary level. . . . To give just one example, traditionally creditors are only those with matured debt, which clearly limits the ability of many who would normally be deemed creditors to take part in insolvency proceedings. One important feature of traditional Shari'a thinking is that all unsecured creditors rank *pari passu*, which clearly limits the ability to establish a hierarchy of claims. More work will therefore need to be done to consider

---

56   The Arabic *taflīs* means bankruptcy or insolvency, or the "declaration of bankruptcy." *Wehr Dictionary, supra* note 32, at 850.

57   As evidenced by Ibn Rushd's writing discussed here, *infra* note 58.

58   Ibn Rushd, *The Distinguished Jurist's Primer*, vol. 2 (*Bidāyat al-Mujtahid wa Nihāyat al-Muqtahid*), *The Book of Taflīs (Insolvency; Bankruptcy)*, 341–352 (Imran Ahsan Khan Nyazee trans., Garnet 2000) (hereinafter Ibn Rushd). Ibn Rushd, full name Abū al-Walīd Muhammad ibn Ahmad ibn Rushd, or Averöes, as he is referred to in Western literature, was a distinguished jurist and a judge (*qādī*) in Cordova. This work is a book on *khilāf* (Arabic term that, in this context, means different views or disagreement), that is, a "discipline that records and analyzes the differences among Muslim jurists." (*Id.,* at 33.) It is the equivalent of a modern treatise or restatement of law that catalogs majority and minority views on points of Islamic law. The purpose of the book was, in Ibn Rushd's words, "for guidance of the (would-be) *mujtahid* [jurist] in whatever he may encounter of the [legal] issues of this book." (*Id.*)

59   *Id.,* at 342–344. "The term *iflās* [bankruptcy], in the law . . . [has] two meanings. First, when the debts completely cover the assets of the debtor, and his wealth does not suffice to pay his debts. Second, when he does not have any known wealth at all." (*Id.,* at 341.)

how effective resolution regimes can be implemented in countries where Shari'a law is a significant element of the legal system. There may also be instances in Islamic finance where Shari'a may be held to apply to particular transactions even within a common or civil law system.[60]

The DFSA is correct, except that more work is needed to do more than just "consider how effective resolution regimes can be implemented in countries where Shari'a law is a significant element of the legal system." More fundamentally, work is needed to fashion Shari'ah-compliant insolvency rules that reflect the reality that Islamic banks deal with the public and intermediate on a large scale. Shari'ah-based market regulation is instructive in this respect.

Shari'ah-Based Market Regulation: Hisba[61]

Islamic law and historical practice favor a strong role for regulators in setting binding standards of market conduct and carrying out market supervision. The Islamic framework of government includes the office of the market supervisor (al Muhtasib), the mandate of which is, broadly, "to promote good . . . and prohibit evil."[62] Bound by law and possessing delegated authority, the Muhtasib's function, like that of the modern regulator, is decidedly executive in nature.[63] The Muhtasib's powers are greatest in the areas of commerce and trade.[64] In the markets, the Muhtasib is duty-bound to promote transparency

---

60　*DFSA Comments, supra* note 48. As to creditor priority, this interpretation is not entirely representative (and neglects Shari'ah views on market regulation, which should influence interpretations as to creditor priority and other matters). For example, Shari'ah accords higher priority, assuming certain conditions exist, to parties that have sold or financed property to a debtor but have yet to be paid in full at the time of the debtor's insolvency. For example, "If the corpus of the thing [the property] itself, because of which the creditor has a claim against the insolvent, has expired, the debt exists as a liability of the insolvent. If, however, the thing exists and has not expired, but the creditor did not take possession of the price (*thaman*) . . . [*some* jurists held that] the owner . . . has a prior right to it, unless he relinquishes it and participates in the liquidation." (*Id.*, at 341.)

61　*Hisba* derives from the Arabic root *hasb*, meaning, inter alia, "reckoning or opinion." Similarly, the terms *hisāb* (meaning, inter alia, "accounting") and *muhtasib* (meaning "accountant, bookkeeper, comptroller, auditor") share the same lineage. *Wehr Dictionary, supra* note 32, at 205–207.

62　Abū al-Hasan Al-Māwardi, *The Ordinances of Government (Al-Ahkām al-Sulhāniyya w' al-Wilāyāt al-Dīniyya)*, 260–280, 260 (Wafaa H. Wahba trans., Garnet 2000) (hereinafter, Al-Māwardi). "The market supervision, or public morals office . . . is an injunction to promote good if obviously forsaken, and prohibit evil if manifestly done. As God, exalt Him, says: 'Let there be among you a nation who invite the good, enjoin kindliness, and forbid indecency' " (citing the Qur'an 3:104).

63　*Id.*, at 260–280, discussing the role of the *Muhtasib* as an official office of the state in respect to both public morals and the regulation and supervision of commerce in the marketplace. *See* also Karen Stilt, *Islamic Law in Action: Authority, Discretion, and Everyday Experiences in Mamluk Egypt* (Oxford U. Press 2011), discussing historical accounts of the *Muhtasib* in Mamluk Egypt (hereinafter, Stilt). The role of the *Muhtasib* encompasses both the oversight and regulation of commercial activities and the oversight and regulation of public morals (related to such matters as public prayer). This chapter is concerned only with market regulation.

64　Al-Māwardi, *supra* note 62, at 262.

and market discipline, ensure lawful market conduct, maintain market confidence, and protect consumers[65] against unlawful and deceptive practices.[66] To achieve these ends, the *Muhtasib* is required to formulate rules based on practical knowledge of the marketplace.[67] According to one historical account of the *Muhtasib's* rule-making role during the Mamluk period in Egypt (1215–1517):

> For all of their detailed rules . . . the *fiqh* [i.e., law or jurisprudence] books did not offer much guidance on how the *muhtasib* should identify infractions and punish them. . . . A *muhtasib* needed to know the tricks [of the market] and how to identify them, and the [*Muhtasib's*] manuals gave very practical advice on how to detect fraud in the various trades. On a daily basis, the *muhtasib* himself added another layer of discretion in deciding how to approach the regulation of the markets."[68]

At the same time, the *Muhtasib*, consistent with the principle of freedom of contract in Islamic law, respected market participants' contracts, so long as their transactions were understood by them and not harmful to others (in contemporary practice, this position would support, for example, strict disclosure and the restriction of some products to sophisticated consumers).

This brief description of the *Muhtasib* indicates that the role of the regulator, from the Shari'ah perspective, is clear, requiring practical regulation, consumer protection, responsiveness to market realities, and respect for the rights of qualified parties to contract as they see fit. The approaches and objectives of Shari'ah market regulation should be reflected in insolvency regimes for Islamic banks.

Specialized Insolvency Regimes for Islamic Banks: Administrative Management and Substantive Hybridization

Because Islamic bank operations are complex in the sense that they encompass traditional banking and capital market activities, and because they offer sophisticated products to both sophisticated and unsophisticated customers, specialized regimes for their resolution should be multifaceted, with banking and capital market components and strong consumer protection objectives.[69]

---

65   "Consumer protection was a core part of the *muhtasib's* job." Stilt, *supra* note 63, at 127, explaining that in Mamluk Egypt, "the [*muhtasib's*] appointment decree from the sultan focuses almost exclusively on market-related behavior, indicating a strong interest in commercial transactions. From the sultan's perspective, ensuring that the markets were running smoothly was more than a concern for the average person's welfare."

66   Al-Māwardi, *supra* note 62, at 261–262.

67   *Id.,* at 279–280. "The market supervisor does not avoid reasoning based on customary practice, although he refrains from reasoning in jurisprudence." (*Id.,* at 279.)

68   Stilt, *supra* note 63, at 127.

69   Indeed, the post–financial crisis adoption of OLA is testament to the need for timely adoption of insolvency regimes that fit the realities of the market and financial firm operations. Arguably, revisions to U.S. bankruptcy laws and processes should have been made in tandem with or not long after the enactment of the Gramm Leach Bliley Act in 1999, a law that,

An instructive example of such a specialized, substantively harmonized, and administratively managed framework is the Orderly Liquidation Authority (OLA) regime under Dodd-Frank.[70] The multiparty and multidisciplinary process by which OLA was formulated is also instructive because the process of designing Islamic bank insolvency regimes should include Shari'ah experts, regulators, standard setters, and Islamic banks.[71] The remainder of this chapter discusses aspects of the OLA framework, with a focus on some of the powers of the FDIC as receiver (separately of deposit-taking banks and OLA-eligible financial companies) and the treatment of insolvent broker-dealers (also a part of the OLA framework).

---

inter alia, repealed the "affiliation" sections of the Banking Act of 1933 (commonly known as the Glass-Steagall Act), and thereby removed the statutory wall separating banks, securities firms, and insurance companies in the United States and opening the door for their affiliation and competition. See Gramm-Leach-Blilely Act, Pub. L. No. 106-102, sec. 101, 113 Stat. 1338, 1341 (1999).

70   This chapter does not suggest that Islamic banks and OLA-eligible entities have the same operations or are exposed to or pose the same risks. It is important to note that orderly liquidation is a last resort option available only when it is determined that, inter alia, orderly liquidation is necessary to avoid damage to the financial system and protect public funds from bailout scenarios. Furthermore, OLA-eligible financial entities, particularly bank holding companies, conduct different business lines through subsidiaries. Islamic banks conduct traditional banking and capital market operations via a single entity, and such organizational differences have implications at resolution. Finally, it is worth noting that the OLA framework has not been unanimously embraced; for example, doubts have been raised about the FDIC's ability to orderly liquidate financial behemoths subject to OLA and the constitutionality of OLA itself. See, for example, Stephen J. Lubben, The Flaws in the New Liquidation Authority, N.Y. Times (April 18, 2012), available at http://dealbook.nytimes.com/2012/04/18/the-flaws-in-the-new-liquidation-authority (accessed May 5, 2013); United States House of Representatives Committee on Financial Services, July 9, 2013, Subcommittee on Oversight and Investigations Hearing titled "Examining Constitutional Deficiencies and Legal Uncertainties in the Dodd Frank Act," available at http://financialservices.house.gov/uploadedfiles/070913_oi_memo.pdf (accessed July 9, 2013). Views on the merits of OLA in the U.S. context aside, the framework is instructive for Islamic bank insolvency design as a substantively harmonized, administratively managed resolution regime. And, in any case, the components of OLA discussed herein, for example, SIPA liquidation and FDIC resolution mechanisms, are instructive as stand-alone features of U.S. bankruptcy and resolution regimes.

71   See, for example, Board of Governors of the Federal Reserve System, Study on the Resolution of Financial Companies under the Bankruptcy Code, 1 (July 2011), explaining that Dodd-Frank required the board of governors of the Federal Reserve System, in consultation with the Administrative Office of the United States Courts, to conduct a study of various options for a resolution framework. Multiple federal agencies, such as the Securities and Exchange Commission and the Commodities Futures Trading Commission, which have exclusive or shared subject-matter authority over OLA-eligible entities, have a role in the rule-making and orderly liquidation process.

FDIC Resolution of Deposit-Taking Banks

The FDIC-administered resolution regime[72] provides for a number of mechanisms that aid in furthering three primary policy objectives:

- To maintain public confidence in banks and the financial system

- To preserve and, where practicable, maximize failed bank assets and liabilities by, for example, the transfer of liabilities and assets to a healthy institution (purchase and assumption) or by establishing a bridge bank

- To minimize the cost of resolution to deposit insurance funds[73]

In addition, in FDIC resolution, the FDIC has the power to repudiate contracts, disallow claims, and recover assets fraudulently transferred up to five years before or after its appointment as receiver.[74] Importantly, some of the FDIC's resolution powers (applicable in bank resolutions) are available, in modified form, in orderly liquidation.[75] These and other aspects of the FDIC resolution process are attractive for the relative flexibility they provide.[76]

In the case of Islamic banks, receivership powers similar to those of the FDIC, particularly the ability to repudiate contracts, transfer assets to healthy institutions, and establish bridge banks (or bridge frameworks), are important, particularly in cases in which Shari'ah bankruptcy rules might limit a failed or failing bank's ability to accelerate and recover against counterparties that are in default at or around the time of the bank's distress or insolvency.[77] The ability to transfer assets and liabilities to a healthy Islamic bank or to create a bridge bank is also important given the absence of (demand) deposit insur-

---

72   The FDIC's role as receiver, and not as deposit insurer, is discussed in this chapter.

73   *See* Federal Deposit Insurance Corporation, *FDIC Resolutions Handbook* 81–88, available at http://www.fdic.gov/bank/historical/reshandbook/ (accessed May 3, 2013) (hereinafter *FDIC Resolutions Handbook*). Transfer by purchase and assumption (P&A) is the most used resolution method. *Id.*, at 82.

74   The FDIC's powers in some regards here are broader than those of a bankruptcy trustee under the Bankruptcy Code (judicially managed); for example, the FDIC may repudiate contracts without regard to type, but a bankruptcy trustee may repudiate only executory contracts. (*Id.*, at 67–83.)

75   In the OLA context, for example, the FDIC has the power to organize a "bridge financial company," the functional equivalent of a bridge bank. Dodd-Frank, Pub. L. No. 111-203, sec. 210(a)(1)(F) (codified at 12 U.S.C. sec. 5390(a)(1)(D)) (Lexis 2013).

76   Generally, a study of the U.S. experience in supervising and resolving banks is worth review, as it reveals lessons learned (even if not always heeded). As the FDIC has stated: "The . . . FDIC learned many lessons about resolving failing financial institutions as it managed the banking crisis of the 1980s and 1990s. The number of failing institutions, their varied businesses, and asset sizes afforded the FDIC a wide range of resolution experiences. Because the crisis lasted a long time, the FDIC had to conduct resolutions at all phases of various economic cycles." *FDIC Resolutions Handbook, supra* note 73, at 81.

77   In addition, prevailing Shari'ah interpretations prohibit the assessment and retention of monetary penalties for delinquency in payment (penalties may be assessed to impose discipline but may not be retained by Islamic banks, and thus must be allocated to charity or disgorged if reflected as income to a bank). Some Islamic banks use positive incentives, such as rebates, to encourage counterparty discipline. *See,* for example, Abedfar et al., *supra* note 12, at 11 & note 9.

ance in most relevant jurisdictions and to facilitate the transfer of restricted *mudaraba* accounts to other institutions.[78]

In addition to the affirmative powers of the FDIC in resolving deposit-taking institutions (and its similar powers in the OLA context), the FDIC, as a matter of case law and statute, has the authority to deem "improperly documented agreements" nonbinding on failed banks, an important tool for preserving assets ánd imposing market discipline.[79] In the Islamic banking context, imposition of market discipline through such authority would be particularly helpful in light of some of the suboptimal contracting practices that have become known.[80]

OLA and SIPA Broker-Dealer Insolvency

The orderly liquidation framework encompasses insolvency rules and procedures for failed broker-dealers, a relevant element because Islamic banks engage in intermediation functions similar to those of broker-dealers that provide full (trade and advisory) and limited (trade and incidental services only) brokerage services. Some Islamic banks provide investment advisory, placement, and incidental services in various jurisdictions, including in the capacity of a *mudarib* and *wakeel* (agent under a *wakala* [agency] agreement). To the extent that Islamic banks place client funds and provide advisory services, the treatment and disposition of some customer accounts (particularly unrestricted *mudaraba* and *wakala*) will be an issue in insolvency. In connection with this, the United States Securities Investor Protection Act (SIPA) is relevant to the extent that it provides for an insurance program that protects the customers of certain insolvent broker-dealers and a specialized bankruptcy procedure for broker-dealers.[81] In bankruptcy (only Chapter 7 liquidation is available to broker-dealers), the Securities Investor Protection Corporation (SIPC) is

---

78   The insurability of PSIA deposits is questionable (risk is borne in principle by PSIA depositors), but some observers have advocated for insuring PSIA depositors in some fashion. As noted below, the SIPC's (privately funded) insurance fund for broker-dealers is an interesting model that might have relevance for Islamic banking where nondemand liabilities (i.e., PSIAs) are concerned. As to the ability of regulators to transfer liabilities and/or assets to healthy firms, regulators must have access to verifiable information about other firms in the market—this is yet another instance in which insolvency considerations highlight pre-insolvency regulatory matters that need attention.

79   This is a special defense of the FDIC to claims on a failed bank's assets. As the FDIC explains: "Like a bank regulator, the receiver must be able to rely upon the books and records of the failed financial institution to evaluate its assets and liabilities accurately . . . unless an agreement is properly documented in the institution's records, it cannot be enforced either in making a claim or defending against a claim by the receiver." *FDIC Resolutions Handbook*, *supra* note 73, at 74.

80   For a discussion of some representative cases, *see*, for example, Abdelhady, *Islamic Law in Secular Courts (Again)*, supra note 30; and Abdelhady, *The Front Office Generates Revenue, the Back Office Creates Value, supra* note 30.

81   The insurance fund, mandated by federal statute and maintained by the Securities Investor Protection Corporation (SIPC) (the SIPC fund) is available only to customers of insolvent SIPC members, who are required to contribute to the SIPC fund. 15 U.S.C.S. sec. 78ddd (2013).

authorized to intervene and initiate (with court approval) a SIPA liquidation.[82] In a SIPA liquidation, the trustee (SIPC or a court-appointed trustee) is required to deliver securities (name securities) to customers of the failed broker-dealer, to the extent practicable.[83] This feature of SIPA-based insolvency reflects two relevant objectives of the SIPA process: to promote continuity in market activity and to protect consumers. Both the SIPA and the SIPA-specific insolvency procedures for broker-dealers are worthy of consideration in the development of insolvency regimes for Islamic banks as a component of a harmonized resolution regime relevant to their capital market functions.

Conclusion

The story of the growth of Islamic finance and banking has been recounted many times, with good reason. In a relatively short period, Islamic banking has become an international industry, estimated to control more than $1 trillion in assets and with stellar growth projections. The potential of Islamic banks to contribute to economic and financial sector development and financial inclusion is well understood. But the full potential of Islamic banking will not be realized without adequate legal and regulatory support.

As Islamic banks continue to expand across borders and in size, the risks associated with Islamic banking will increase as a practicality of doing business. Islamic banking is too young to absorb the shocks of poorly managed bank failures. But it is sufficiently mature to be understood and effectively regulated, including in insolvency. Owing to the nature of Islamic banking and the need for streamlined, expeditious resolution of failed banks, an administratively managed insolvency regime that combines laws appropriate to Islamic banks' various lines of business is desirable. One model for such a substantively harmonized, administratively managed regime is the orderly liquidation framework in the United States. Regulators, Islamic banks, standard-setting bodies, and other interested parties are well advised to undertake a collaborative process to develop and implement an insolvency regime for Islamic banks now, rather than to bear the reputational and economic costs of poorly managed bank failures in the future.

---

82   11 U.S.C. sec. 742 (2013).
83   11 U.S.C. sec. 78fff(1)(b)(1) (2013).

The Role of Law in the Green Economy

Challenges and Opportunities for the Liberalization of Environmental Goods and Services

Fabiano de Andrade Correa

The green economy is a concept developed by the United Nations Environment Programme (UNEP) aimed at fostering a transition to a new kind of economic growth for both developed and developing countries. It involves the *greening* of eleven key sectors of the economy toward a less carbon-intensive and more resource-efficient development model. It is thus considered one of the most important economic vehicles for sustainable development and a new paradigm that can drive growth of income and jobs with less stress put on the environment.

There are two important legal points related to the promotion of the green economy. First, the lack of a binding definition of this concept raises criticism regarding its scope and objectives. Second, law and regulation have an important role in promoting the implementation of these objectives, at both the national and international levels. The liberalization of trade in environmental goods and services (EGS), for example, is important to the greening of the economy and to the expansion of cleaner technologies worldwide. However, the lack of a legal definition of EGS, and of a binding timetable for their liberalization, hinders progress in this area.

This chapter provides a brief discussion of these issues, first commenting on the definition of the green economy and the role that trade plays in promoting it, then examining the legal challenges facing liberalization of EGS. Considering the lack of progress of liberalization of EGS at the multilateral level, the chapter presents examples of forward-moving regional initiatives, such as among the Asia-Pacific Economic Cooperation (APEC) agreement parties and in trade agreements signed by the European Union (EU).

Any statements of fact, opinion, or analysis expressed herein are entirely those of the author and are not attributable to the International Development Law Organization.

Information contained in this chapter draws partly upon work included in Fabiano de Andrade Correa, "The Implementation of Sustainable Development in Regional Trade Agreements: A Case Study on the European Union and MERCOSUR," Ph.D. thesis defended at the European University Institute, Florence, Italy, in June 2013.

The Concept of the Green Economy

The green economy was conceived by UNEP as an economic model that would improve human well-being and social equity while also significantly reducing environmental risks and ecological scarcities:

> In its simplest expression, a green economy is low carbon, resource efficient, and socially inclusive. In a green economy, growth in income and employment should be driven by public and private investments that reduce carbon emissions and pollution, enhance energy and resource efficiency, and prevent the loss of biodiversity and ecosystem services. . . . The key aim for a transition to a green economy is to eliminate the trade-offs between economic growth and investment and gains in environmental quality and social inclusiveness. The main hypothesis . . . is that the environmental and social goals of a green economy can also generate increases in income, growth, and enhanced well-being.[1]

The green economy agenda implies a departure from many accepted practices in key sectors of the economy, recognizing that "business as usual" economic practices cannot respond to global challenges such as climate change, loss of biodiversity, and the remaining worldwide inequality. The UNEP green economy report thus proposes the greening of eleven key sectors of the economy: agriculture, fisheries, water, forests, energy, manufacturing, waste, buildings and construction, transportation, tourism, and cities. It also proposes innovative solutions to challenges that are fundamentally linked to the manner in which economic development is framed and guided by policy makers. The basic premise is that economic development combined with improved human well-being and environmental protection will result in stable economic growth. Numerous actors, especially within the private sector, have important roles in this process of change. Governments and policy makers can play a key role in "kick-starting" financing for the green economy, as well as in creating and implementing laws and policies that will guide and support the transition in each sector.[2]

The concept of the green economy is both ambitious and promising in its aim to promote sustainable development through a new economic model based on environmental sustainability while still providing livelihood opportunities. In this regard, a green economy can provide a better alternative for international cooperation in the pursuit of sustainable development than development aid, because the aim of a green economy is to build an economic system that will work for the sustainable development of all nations. At the same time, the idea of a green economy is controversial for three main rea-

---

1   United Nations Environment Programme (UNEP), *Towards a Green Economy: Pathways to Sustainable Development and Poverty Eradication—A Synthesis for Policy Makers* (2011), available at http://www.unep.org/greeneconomy.

2   International Development Law Organization (IDLO) & Centre for International Sustainable Development Law (CISDL), *Green Economy for Sustainable Development: Compendium of Legal Best Practices* (2012).

sons: there is no clear definition of what it means, its scope being very broad; its relationship to sustainable development is unclear, and it consequently provokes fears that the international community will return to focusing solely on the economic sphere as opposed to the three-pillar model of the former; and it engenders concern that it might lead to "green protectionism" and new conditionalities in official development assistance trade and investment patterns.[3]

Despite the criticism to which it is susceptible, the green economy is a powerful concept that was cited by the United Nations during the Rio+20 summit meeting in 2012 as one of the most important tools in the pursuit of sustainable development. Rio+20 renewed the commitment of the international community to the promotion of an "economically, socially and environmentally sustainable future for our planet and for present and future generations," acknowledging the need to further mainstream sustainable development at all levels.[4] The green economy in the context of sustainable development was one of the two overarching themes of the conference, and the outcome document of Rio+20, *The Future We Want*, dedicates a section to it. Although the provisions of the document do little to clarify the contours of the concept of the green economy, they address the two main concerns of most stakeholders: the conceptual ambiguity related to sustainable development, especially regarding how it is to be a promotional tool and not a replacement of the former; and the economic and commercial implications of the adoption of the green economy as a main policy goal, especially regarding the fear of green protectionism and new green conditionalities. The language used is vague, affirming that "we consider green economy in the context of sustainable development and poverty eradication as one of the important tools available for achieving sustainable development and that it could provide options for policymaking but should not be a rigid set of rules." Nevertheless, it expressly states that green economy policies should be consistent with international law, should effectively avoid unwarranted conditionalities and unilateral actions outside national jurisdiction, and should not constitute a means of arbitrary or unjustifiable discrimination or disguised restriction on international trade (paras. 56–58).

Despite these critical issues, the outcome document supports a less imposing and more cooperative approach in implementing green economy policies, which are fundamental for dealing with key issues such as the modification of production and consumption patterns, the transition to a more sustainable lifestyle, and the participation of all relevant stakeholders from the public, private, and civil society sectors. The main challenge is to put into practice policies and instruments that will facilitate concrete progress toward the goals of the green economy.

---

3   Holger Bär, Klaus Jacob, & Stefan Werland, *Green Economy Discourses in the Run-Up to Rio 2012* (FFU Report 07-2011, Envtl. Policy Res. Ctr., Freie Universität Berlin 2011).

4   *The Future We Want*, UN Document A/66/L.56, UNGA 66th Session, July 24 2012. (UNCSD outcome document), available at http://www.uncsd2012.org/thefuturewewant.html.

Trade and the Green Economy

Trade is considered one of the main drivers of the world economy.[5] According to a recent UNEP report examining various trends worldwide, the sum of world exports of goods and commercial services amounted to US$22.3 trillion at the end of 2010, growing at an average annual rate of 5 percent between 2000 and 2011. Merchandise and commercial services exports rose from 14 percent in 1970 to 29.3 percent in 2011. In developing countries, the rate had reached 45 percent before the financial and economic crisis of 2008. Trade between developing countries was the most dynamic segment of global trade in the first decade of the 21st century, increasing from 39.2 percent of total exports in 2002 to 50 percent in 2010. However, despite creating economic growth, increasing volumes of trade put additional stress on natural resources and increased greenhouse gas emissions. Increased demands for natural resources by emerging economies coupled with the already unsustainable levels of resource consumption in more developed countries led to an unprecedented surge in resource consumption and trade in the period 1995–2010.[6]

The UNEP report makes clear that to nurture sustainable development, trade must be accompanied by regulations that can facilitate the transition to a green economy, thereby fostering the exchange of environmentally friendly goods and services (including environmentally sound technologies), increasing resource efficiency, and generating economic opportunities and employment. The transition to a green economy, in turn, will have the potential to create enhanced trade opportunities: opening new export markets for EGS, increasing trade in products certified for sustainability, promoting certification-related services, and greening international supply chains. The adoption of more resource- and energy-efficient production methods as part of the green economy is important in securing access to and building long-term competitiveness in international markets. Consequently, a green economy will increasingly be seen as a gateway to new opportunities for trade, growth, and sustainable development.[7]

Yet, while a shift to more sustainable trade practices may advance economic and social development, a number of important obstacles remain, such as the lack of or weak regulatory frameworks and enforcement mechanisms. Thus there is a role for law and regulation to play in the implementation of these policies, to be addressed through concerted efforts at the international, national, regional, and local levels.

---

5   *See,* for example, Joseph Stiglitz, *Fair Trade for All: How Trade Can Promote Development* (Oxford U. Press 2005).

6   UNEP, *Green Economy and Trade: Trends, Challenges and Opportunities* (report prepared by the Trade, Policy and Planning Unit of UNEP, 2013), available at: http://www.unep.org/greeneconomy/GreenEconomyandTrade.

7   *Id.*

The Green Economy and the Law

The promotion of a green economy requires enabling conditions. International law, the international community's main tool for achieving consensus, determining common paths of action, and establishing national laws and regulatory instruments, is the key component that enables the promotion of a green economy. This chapter focuses on both the international and the regional frameworks related to this issue.

The rationale of international law as a body of rules and norms that governs the interaction between states and other international actors has undergone change.[8] This rationale can be explained in three different ways: First, international law works as the law of nations, given their interest in following similar rules or applying like standards in their domestic legal orders, including, for example, commercial transactions. Second, it is justified due to states' interest in reciprocally limiting liberties so as to respect sovereignty and justify noninterference in internal matters; third, and more important, states have found international law instrumental as a means of achieving common international goals.[9]

This three-fold justification for the existence of international law parallels the transformations that have occurred in international relations and to which this system of rules attempts to respond. First, international law has changed in regard to the actors to which it attributes legal personality and which affect its functioning. International law is still made chiefly by states and focuses on states, but it has also evolved from a system that merely safeguards the peaceful coexistence of states to a system that tries to guide states and other relevant actors toward the different objectives that emerge at the international level. Second, international law has seen a considerable evolution in scope, which has expanded from the safeguarding of coexistence and sovereignty to the regulation of common objectives such as peace, human rights, security, and environmental protection. Third, international law currently not only aims at producing legal rules that create obligations through the traditional form of treaty making with binding power and led by states but also works increasingly through "soft law" to codify the conduct or opinion of different actors regarding desirable paths to follow. In such ways, these norms contribute to solidifying the international legal order.[10]

These observations serve to show that international law is more than ever a vital instrument for the international community in its attempt to regulate the globalized, interdependent international relations that characterize the current international scene. International conferences such as Rio+20, with its soft-law documents and policy concepts such as the green economy, should be seen as part of this process. However, lack of concrete progress on relevant

---

8   Christopher Joyner, *International Law in the 21st Century: Rules for Global Governance* (Rowman and Littlefield 2005).

9   Mark Janis, *International Law* (Wolters Kluwer, 2008).

10   Joyner, *supra* note 8, at 24.

regimes for the implementation of agreed-on policy goals, including those for the green economy, might hinder the advancement of those goals. One example is the finalization of negotiations on relevant trade law and green economy issues.

The Green Economy and International Trade Law

The development of new multilateral rules under the World Trade Organization (WTO) can provide opportunities for effective collective actions to solve global problems. For example, the rules-based multilateral trading system can provide transparency, predictability, and the necessary legal framework for promoting the trade-related aspects of a green economy. However, the lack of progress in the creation of new rules on important sectors within the WTO, such as the stalled Doha negotiations, is creating a barrier for the effective contribution of trade to the green economy. One example is the liberalization of trade in EGS.

Liberalizing trade in EGS can create new markets and export opportunities and provide access to "green" goods and technologies at lower costs and with greater efficiency. Increased deployment of cheaper and better-quality environmental goods helps countries pursue their national environmental policy objectives and counter environmental degradation and climate change, facilitating the transition to a green economy. Moreover, EGS represents a significant opportunity for development: in 2006, the global market for the environmental sector was valued at $690 billion. This figure could rise to $1.9 trillion by 2020, with the greatest market potential in developing countries.[11]

Negotiations on EGS liberalization were part of the WTO Doha Round mandate, and the Doha Declaration, in paragraph 31(iii), called for the "reduction or, as appropriate, elimination of tariff and non-tariff barriers to environmental goods and services." The mandate, however, defined neither EGS nor the speed or depth of liberalization to be achieved, making progress difficult, as no international agreement exists on the definition of EGS. A number of organizations have proposed unilateral definitions; the Organisation for Economic Co-operation and Development (OECD) defined EGS as "activities which produce goods and services to measure, prevent, limit, minimize or correct environmental damage to water, air and soil as well as problems related to waste, noise and ecosystems." However, the lack of agreement on how to define and categorize EGS at the multilateral level has been one of the main barriers to progress in negotiations on liberalization of trade in such products at the WTO, and much of the debate within the WTO negotiations has centered on the identification of specific environmental goods for liberalization. Further, despite the Doha mandate to reduce or eliminate tariff and nontariff barriers to EGS, substantial obstacles remain; it is estimated that the

---

11   UNEP, International Trade Centre, and International Centre for Trade and Sustainable Development (ICTSD), *Trade and Environment Briefings: Environmental Goods and Services* (ICTSD Programme on Global Econ. Policy and Institutions, Policy Brief No. 6, ICTSD).

average world tariffs on EGS are bound at a level of 8.7 percent, almost three times higher than the average applied rate for all goods, considering full use of preferences, at 3 percent.[12]

Regional Initiatives for the Liberalization of EGS

Regional trade agreements, if properly designed, can offer significant opportunities to promote sustainable practices and be a driver of policy reforms, increased capacity development, strengthened environmental regulation, and better cooperation among relevant ministries. In light of the challenges highlighted above, and given the relevance of liberalizing EGS trade for the achievement of green economy and climate change objectives in the context of sustainable development, liberalization of certain EGS through other frameworks, such as regional or bilateral trade agreements, can be an option.

Asia-Pacific Economic Cooperation

One recent example is the decision to begin liberalizing trade in environmental goods in the Asia-Pacific Economic Cooperation (APEC) agreement. In 2010, APEC members[13] adopted the Honolulu Declaration, in which they outlined plans to develop a list of environmental goods that "directly and positively contribute to our green growth and sustainable development objectives." On September 9, 2012, APEC members meeting in Vladivostok, Russia, agreed to voluntarily liberalize tariffs on 54 environmental goods. The Vladivostok Declaration signatories welcomed and endorsed the APEC list and committed to reducing applied tariff rates on the listed goods to 5 percent or less by the end of 2015. The deal has been considered a political breakthrough in that it represents the first international agreement to liberalize trade on EGS. The 54 subheadings identified in the APEC list are subject to further refinement as so-called ex-outs (products that can be further subdivided because they serve two or more functions), based on national tariff classifications. The products will now need to be interpreted in the individual national tariff schedules of member countries because different APEC members may use different tariff codes and different product descriptions for the ex-outs.[14]

The APEC outcome could also have an important and positive "signaling" effect on the WTO as well as on other regional trade blocs that want to undertake similar initiatives. While some observers have been critical of the lack of enforceability of the APEC outcome, the voluntary, nonbinding nature of APEC decisions could have been a factor in ensuring a successful environmental goods agreement and likely encouraged members to be bolder than

---

12   *Id.*

13   APEC comprises 21 members: Australia; Brunei; Canada; Chile; China; Hong Kong SAR, China; Indonesia; Japan; Malaysia; Mexico; New Zealand; Papua New Guinea; Peru; the Philippines; Russia; Singapore; Republic of Korea; Chinese Taipei; Thailand; the United States; and Vietnam.

14   Mahesh Sugathan & Thomas L. Brewer, *APEC's Environmental Goods Initiative: How Climate-Friendly Is It?* 6(4) Bridges Trade BioRes Rev. (Nov. 2012).

they would have been at the WTO. Furthermore, given the political weight behind any APEC ministerial decision, it seems unlikely that members would attempt to raise tariffs once they had been lowered.[15]

Regional Trade Agreements of the European Union

Sustainable development is an important principle in the European Union's legal framework, and its guiding treaties and policies determine the pursuit of this objective at all levels of activity.[16] Based on this framework, the European Union has increasingly sought to integrate sustainable development concerns into its trade policy and has been including the liberalization of EGS in its recent trade agreements, which represent an important incentive for these issues to move forward.

The European Union currently has a wide array of trade agreements:[17] 28 in force, 9 completed but not yet in force (5 of which are economic partnership agreements, or EPAs, with African and Pacific countries), and several others under negotiation (with partners such as MERCOSUR, Canada, India, Malaysia, and the Gulf Cooperation Council; furthermore, future negotiations are said to be starting soon with the United States, Japan, the Association of Southeast Asian Nations (ASEAN), and Morocco.[18] EU trade agreements have

---

15   *Id.*

16   The Lisbon Treaty reaffirmed this commitment, and in one of the provisions that it shares with the Treaty on European Union, art. 3(3), states: "The Union shall establish an internal market. It shall work for the sustainable development of Europe." In addition, regarding the external dimension, art. 3(5) states that

> *in its relations with the wider world, the Union shall* uphold and promote its values and interests and contribute to the protection of its citizens. It shall *contribute to peace, security, the sustainable development of the Earth,* solidarity and mutual respect among peoples, free and fair trade, eradication of poverty and the protection of human rights, in particular the rights of the child, as well as to the strict observance and the development of international law, including respect for the principles of the United Nations Charter. (Emphasis added.)

Moreover, under Title V, covering the general provisions on external actions, art. 21.2 determines that

> the Union shall define and pursue common policies and actions, and shall work for a high degree of cooperation in all fields of international relations, in order to: (d) *foster the sustainable economic, social and environmental development of developing countries, with the primary aim of eradicating poverty;* . . . (f) help develop international measures to preserve and improve the quality of the environment and the sustainable management of global natural resources, in order to ensure sustainable development; . . . and (h) promote an international system based on stronger multilateral cooperation and good global governance. (Emphasis added.)

These provisions show that sustainable development became a guiding principle of EU policies in general, being granted a place in the *constitutional* treaties. Further, a "sustainable development strategy" complements the legal framework, establishing priorities for actions and work plans.

17   Agreements that would require notification under either art. XXIV, GATT, or art. V, GATS.

18   European Commission, *The EU's Free Trade Agreements—Where Are We?* (Mar. 25, 2013), available at http://ec.europa.eu/trade/creating-opportunities/bilateral-relations/agreements/#_europe.

become not only significant in number but also among the most sophisticated instruments used in advancing trade liberalization, market access, and other policy objectives. This expansion of agreements—in terms of number, depth (i.e., the way in which the European Union seeks to deepen economic integration, to extend beyond the traditional removal of tariff barriers and quotas to regulatory policy, and beyond trade in goods to services and investment), and breadth (i.e., the embedding of economic integration into the wider relationship with the partner country or region)—is related to the many goals pursued by the bloc through its trade policy.

These agreements can be seen as part of the framework within which countries can move toward accession to the European Union. They provide the core of relations between the European Union and its neighbors who are not candidates or potential candidates; they have become a basic means for pursuing EU development policy goals; and they are used for accessing markets.[19] This last aspect has been emphasized in *Global Europe: Competing in the World*, a communication by the European Commission's Directorate General—Trade, which discusses the external aspects of EU competitiveness in the context of the European Union's broader competitiveness agenda, presented in the Lisbon strategy for growth and jobs.[20] The commission, while claiming that "there will be no European retreat from multilateralism," argued the value of trade agreements in furthering the European Union's market-opening objectives, pointing out that while the WTO provides the basic ground rules for trade relations as well as a framework for ongoing negotiation, free trade agreements (FTAs) can include issues not yet covered by the WTO, including investment, public procurement, competition, and other regulatory issues. In addition, the commission referred to the stalled Doha Round, and while it recognized the problems that FTA proliferation can cause for the multilateral system, it defended the idea that under the right conditions FTAs could "build on" the WTO and "prepare the ground" for multilateral liberalization, acting as a stepping-stone rather than a stumbling block. Furthermore, as sustainable development has become one of the main overarching objectives of EU policy in general, trade agreements have progressively integrated the promotion of this goal, including green economy–related issues such as liberalization of EGS.

The analysis in this section focuses on four EU agreements that provide an overview of how the above issues have been integrated: (1) the EPA concluded with the Caribbean Forum (CARIFORUM) in 2008, the first such agreement to include a "trade and sustainable development" chapter; (2) the FTA signed with the Republic of Korea, considered the European Union's flagship agreement given its deep level of integration and broad coverage; (3) the association agreement (AA) signed with the Central American countries, the first and

---

19   Marise Cremona, *The European Union and Regional Trade Agreements*, in *European Yearbook of International Economic Law*, vol. 1, part 2, 245–268 (Christoph Herrmann & Jorg Philippe Terhechte eds., Springer 2010).

20   *Global Europe: Competing in the World: A Contribution to the EU's Growth and Job Strategy* (communication, European Commission, Directorate General—Trade, Oct. 4, 2006).

only biregional association agreement concluded thus far and among the most advanced agreements in terms of references to sustainable development; and (4) the FTA concluded with the Andean countries, the latest one to include a "trade and sustainable development" chapter, with innovative references to climate change and biodiversity. These agreements represent an innovative form of integration of sustainable development objectives within a trade instrument, progressively including positive integration measures, in the sense of using trade to promote important goals of sustainable development such as the transition to a green economy and the fight against climate change. These measures include liberalization of trade in important sectors such as EGS, renewable energy, transfer of green technologies, support for certification, and labeling schemes aimed at making the supply chain more sustainable, such as "fair trade" certified timber and fishing schemes, among others. The fact that these issues can be included in measures aimed at liberalization within the trade relations of parties represents an important building block for the establishment of a multilateral framework regulating these issues, which is currently lacking.

The Economic Partnership Agreement with CARIFORUM. The EU-CARIFORUM EPA[21] was signed on October 15, 2008, and was the first to be concluded among the African, Caribbean and Pacific (ACP) Group of States negotiations. One of the main changes introduced by the agreement was the reciprocal granting of preferences by the two sides, instead of the nonreciprocal, preferential (duty-free) market access for ACP states, which encompasses trade in goods, services, trade-related issues, and development cooperation, with strong emphasis on sustainable development and regional integration. The preamble of the EPA contains several references to sustainable development, including "the need to promote economic and social progress for their people in a manner consistent with sustainable development."

These preamble references are reinforced in Part II of the agreement, "Trade-Related Issues," and chapters 4 and 5 deal with environmental and social issues, respectively. Among the measures included is a commitment to facilitate trade in socioenvironmentally friendly goods. Article 183 provides for the promotion of international trade in such a way as to ensure sustainable and sound management of the environment, in accordance with other undertakings in this area, including the international conventions to which they are party and with due regard to other respective levels of development. In this regard, the parties undertake "to facilitate" trade in goods and services considered to be beneficial to the environment, such as environmental technologies, renewable and energy-efficient goods and services, and eco-labeled goods. Article 191 recognizes the benefits and importance of facilitating commerce in "fair and ethical trade" products.

---

21 Economic Partnership Agreement between the CARIFORUM States and the European Community and Its Member States, OJ L 289/I/3, 30/10/2008.

The Free Trade Agreement with South Korea. The 2006 "Global Europe" strategy mandated the negotiation of a new generation of FTAs focusing on countries with high potential for the EU economy. These FTAs would be ambitious in eliminating tariffs as well as far-reaching in the liberalization of services and investment, and in finding novel ways of effectively tackling nontariff barriers. In this context, the negotiations with Korea, the European Union's fourth-largest trading partner outside Europe, were launched in 2007 and concluded in 2009. The European Union–Korea FTA[22] is considered the most comprehensive agreement ever to have been negotiated by the European Union in terms of trade issues, with import duties eliminated on nearly all products; far-reaching liberalization of trade in services, including provisions on investments in both services and industrial sectors; and strong discipline applied to the enforcement of regulations pertaining to intellectual property (including geographical indications), public procurement, competition rules, transparency of regulation, and sustainable development.

This FTA also includes several provisions on sustainable development. In Article 1, the parties "commit, in the recognition that sustainable development *is an overarching objective,* to the development of international trade in such a way as to contribute to the objective of sustainable development and strive to ensure that this objective is integrated and reflected at every level of the Parties' trade relationship" (emphasis added). In this regard, a chapter on "trade and sustainable development" was inserted, featuring, among other provisions, a determination that the parties "shall strive to facilitate and promote trade and foreign direct investment in environmental goods and services, including environmental technologies, sustainable renewable energy, energy efficient products and services and eco-labelled goods, including through addressing related non-tariff barriers." The nature of the sustainable development–related provisions in this agreement were thus very similar to those of the CARIFORUM EPA. The difference here, however, was that all of those measures were condensed into a "trade and sustainable development" chapter, which was more specific in listing socioenvironmental goods whose liberalization was to be facilitated by the parties.

The Association Agreement with Central America. The AA between the European Union and Central America (CA) is a particularly relevant agreement for EU external relations because it is the first biregional AA to be finalized within the interregional approach to international relations, which was adopted by the European Union in the 1990s.[23] The EU-CA AA[24] follows a three-pillar format that includes chapters on political dialogue, cooperation, and trade. The AA also has very comprehensive coverage of sustainable-development issues.

---

22   *Free Trade Agreement between the European Union and Its Member States, of the One Part, and the Republic of Korea, of the Other Part,* Off. J. of the European Union (L 127/6, May 14, 2011).

23   See, in this regard, Fredrik Söderbaum & Luk Van Langenhove eds., *The EU as a Global Player: The Politics of Interregionalism* (Routledge 2006).

24   *Agreement Establishing an Association between the European Union and Its Member States, on the One Hand, and Central America, on the Other,* Off. J. of the European Union (May 30, 2010).

Among other provisions is the "trade chapter," featuring "trade and sustainable development" (Title IV), in which the parties explicitly express their stance on the "benefit of considering trade related social and environmental issues as part of a global approach to trade and sustainable development."

The trade chapter also contains trade-related provisions that go beyond the facilitation of trade in environmental goods and services and "fair trade" and other labeled goods, as in the Korea FTA. Article 288, "Trade Favoring Sustainable Development," contains recognition by the parties of the value of international cooperation in support of trade schemes and trade practices favoring sustainable development, and determination that the parties "shall endeavor to" (a) facilitate and promote trade and foreign direct investment in environmental technologies and services and renewable-energy and energy-efficient products and services, including through addressing related nontariff barriers; (b) facilitate and promote trade in products that respond to sustainability considerations, including products that are the subject of schemes such as fair and ethical trade schemes, eco-labeling, organic production, and those involving corporate social responsibility (CSR) and accountability; (c) facilitate and promote the development of practices and programs aiming to foster appropriate economic returns from the conservation and sustainable use of the environment, such as ecotourism. Article 289 contains specific provisions on trade in forest products, including a commitment "to work together to improve" forest law enforcement and governance and "to promote trade in" legal and sustainable forest products through instruments such as the use of the Convention on International Trade on Endangered Species (CITES) with regard to endangered timber species; and certification schemes for sustainably harvested forest products; regional or bilateral Forest Law Enforcement Governance and Trade (FLEGT) voluntary partnership agreements. Article 290 deals with trade in fish products, addressing particular issues and making reference to multilateral conventions that the parties undertake to adhere to and effectively implement, such as the agreement for the implementation of the provisions of the UN Convention on the Law of the Sea relating to the conservation and management of straddling fish stocks and highly migratory fish stocks; cooperation to prevent illegal, unreported, and unregulated (IUU) fishing, to exchange scientific and nonconfidential trade data, experiences, and best practices in the field of sustainable fisheries, and, more generally, to promote a sustainable approach to fisheries. Thus, this chapter contains not only the liberalization of EGS but also windows of opportunity to encourage trade in key areas such as fisheries and forestry products, which are of great relevance for the sustainability agenda. This approach has been reproduced and enhanced in the next agreement analyzed.

The FTA with Colombia and Peru. The Colombia-Peru agreement is an FTA signed in 2012,[25] similar in structure to the Korea FTA, but including deeper sustainability provisions, like those in the Central America AA. A "trade and

---

25   *Trade Agreement between the European Union and Its Member States, of the One Part, and Colombia and Peru, of the Other Part*, Off. J. of the European Union (Dec. 21, 2012).

sustainable development" chapter has also been inserted, featuring trade-related provisions that go beyond even those of the Central America AA. Article 271, "Trade Favoring Sustainable Development," contains recognition by the parties of the value of international cooperation in support of trade schemes and trade practices favoring sustainable development, and a determination that the parties "shall strive to facilitate and promote" (a) trade and foreign direct investment in environmental goods and services; (b) business practices related to CSR; and (c) the development of flexible, incentive-based and voluntary schemes.

Articles 272–275 contain specific provisions on (a) trade in biodiversity products (Article 272), with commitments to: endeavor to jointly promote the development of practices and programs aiming to foster economic returns from the conservation and sustainable use of biological diversity; endeavor to create conditions to facilitate access to genetic resources for environmentally sound uses and not to impose restrictions that run counter to the objectives of the United Nations Convention on Biological Diversity (CBD); confirm that access to genetic resources shall be subject to the prior informed consent of any party providing such resources, unless otherwise determined, and to take appropriate measures, in accordance with the CBD, to share the results of research and development and the benefits arising from the commercial and other utilization of genetic resources with the party providing such resources; strengthen the capacity of national institutions in relation to the conservation and sustainable use of biological diversity; (b) trade in forest products (Article 273), including a commitment to work together to improve forest law enforcement and governance and to promote trade in legal and sustainable forest products through instruments such as CITES, with regard to endangered timber species; the development of systems and mechanisms for verification of the legal origin of timber products throughout the market chain and voluntary mechanisms for forest certification; (c) trade in fish products (Article 274), addressing particular issues and cooperation in the context of regional fisheries management organizations of which they are parties, to revise and adjust the fishing capacity for fishery resources, adopt tools for monitoring and control, to ensure full compliance with applicable conservation measures, and adopt actions to combat IUU fishing; (d) trade and climate change issues (Article 275). The measures would include facilitating the removal of trade and investment barriers to access to innovation, development, and deployment of goods, services, and technologies that can contribute to mitigation or adaptation, taking into account the circumstances of developing countries; and promoting measures for energy efficiency and renewable energy that respond to environmental and economic needs and minimize technical obstacles to trade.

The provisions contained in these trade and sustainable development chapters have been made as a quasi-soft-law obligation, without a precise definition of modalities or timelines. Thus, while these provisions represent a starting point that can be used to move forward with these novel and important issues, how they will be implemented with this very diverse set of partners remains to be seen.

Conclusion

The analysis undertaken in this chapter allows us to conclude that law has a relevant role in the promotion of the green economy. International law represents the instrument for the international community to agree on common goals and paths of action, while regional and national law remain fundamental in the implementation of such goals in a more specific context. One important area, in this regard, is trade law, given the key role played by trade in the promotion of the green economy. However, considering the stalled negotiations at the multilateral level in the WTO, the regional sphere constitutes a valuable means to move forward with the implementation of trade and green economy issues.

The liberalization of EGS, for instance, despite being featured as an important point within the Doha negotiations, has not progressed at the multilateral level. Thus, any progress achieved in this area in the context of regional trade agreements will represent an important building block for this issue to move forward. The two regional initiatives discussed in this chapter show different aspects of this matter.

The APEC list of environmental goods represents a first initiative to establish a timeline for liberalization of EGS. Services, however, are not included, and will apply only to APEC's member-state markets. Furthermore, it is hard to assess how significant the eventual tariff reductions will be, as it is uncertain how individual APEC countries will implement the commitment and how they will define the ex-outs for which they decide to reduce applied tariffs in terms of their own tariff schedules. The APEC decision, in any case, remains of high political significance, and lessons learned from this approach can be useful in designing similar initiatives in other regional groupings, and also at the WTO.[26]

The other initiative analyzed, the EU trade agreements, represent the other side of this issue. The commitments in these agreements are broader and would apply to the markets of both the European Union and the partner, thus fostering the liberalization of EGS in a wider context. However, the measures in the EU agreements are drafted as soft obligations without precise definitions of modalities or timelines to "facilitate," "strive to," and "incentivize" the liberalization of trade in goods and services that might have a beneficial social and environmental impact, such as EGS, fair trade products, trade in certified timber, and sustainable fisheries.

These provisions represent a starting point that can be used to move forward with these issues, which are fundamental to the transition to a green economy and sustainable development but are also still left outside a multilateral framework. At the same time, most of these measures are drafted in

---

26 For more information, *see* Renee Vossenaar, *The APEC List of Environmental Goods: An Analysis of the Outcome and Expected Impact* (Issue Paper No. 18, Intl. Ctr. Trade & Sustainable Dev., 2013).

"soft" language and open-ended obligations. In this regard, a multilateral framework would still be important to ensure coherence and effectiveness in relation to the wider sphere, and national measures would have an important role to play in assuring the implementation of these provisions in an effective and appropriate way.

PART II

JUSTICE AND RULE OF LAW REFORM

Institutional Responses to Social Demands

Enhancing Access to Justice in Colombia

DAVID F. VARELA AND ANNETTE PEARSON

Over the past 40 years, Colombia has made great strides in addressing issues related to access to justice. The impetus for change has been multifaceted: Colombian nongovernmental groups have demanded new social priorities; regional social movements have pushed for improvements in the areas of human rights, land policy, and ethnic issues; international legal and political theories regarding access to justice have come into greater focus. The strongest institutional response has come from progressive constitutional developments in the administration of justice. Since the Constituent Assembly approved a new constitution in 1991, Colombia has witnessed groundbreaking progress in jurisprudence and pronounced institutional development in many branches of the justice sector.

Long-term strategies for the justice sector, and access to justice in particular, were recently articulated in the government's *Visión Colombia Segundo Centenario: 2019.*[1] A Commission of Experts subsequently explored these strategies to augment plans for justice reform and issued its final report in June 2010.[2] Both of these policy documents focus on reducing the barriers that hinder access to justice, rationalizing the use of justice services, and promoting wider use of alternative (nonjudicial) justice mechanisms.

---

1   Departamento Nacional de Planeación, *Visión Colombia Segundo Centenario: 2019; Garantizar una justicia eficiente* (2008). This document contains the ground rules, the aspirations, and the guiding principles of the Colombian political system, economic model, and social developments. However, all these achievements are just the base that will enable the country to make a qualitative and competitive leap toward the new economic, political, and social scenarios of the 21st century. To do this, it is necessary that both the state and society take responsibility for undertaking a great, collective planning exercise, both medium- and long-term, that goes beyond four-year development plans.

2   The Commission of Experts for the Reform of Justice (Comisión de Expertos de Reforma a la Justicia), was created by Presidential Decree No. 4932 in December 2009. The commission issued its *Final Report* in Bogotá in June 2010 (hereinafter, Commission of Experts). The strategic areas for review included structural issues concerning the judiciary; the relationship of the judiciary to the other branches of government and civil society; the functions of the Ministry of Justice and the Office of the Attorney General; the national coverage of judicial services; *tutela*, or constitutional protection order, and other constitutional mechanisms; responsibility and judicial ethics; judicial delays; and the role of jurisprudence, disciplinary regimes, and alternative justice. *See* http://www.cej.org.co.

165

This chapter looks at the policy of rationalization from the perspective of access, especially for vulnerable social groups. In the Colombian context, the term *rationalization* refers to the distribution of public demand for justice services among a wide range of traditional and alternative conflict resolution mechanisms that have been developed since the constitutional reforms of 1991. Following this introductory section, the next two sections of the chapter provide background information on how the concept of access to justice has changed in Colombia since 1991. Changes in the way access to justice was defined led to the creation of wide-ranging programs to combat a number of barriers that reduced access, especially for poor and vulnerable groups. The fourth section introduces the concept of rationalization, underscoring the fact that it must go beyond the simple diversification of formal, informal, and administrative options for resolving legal disputes and social conflicts. A pyramid model of dispute resolution alternatives is presented as a conceptual framework for examining the challenges that this proposal poses for the articulation of the justice sector in Colombia.

National institutions and legislative developments have progressively charged municipalities with tasks that the justice sector previously considered national responsibilities. The fifth and sixth sections identify a number of issues related to the delegation of justice services that are not adequately considered in rationalization policies, as currently proposed by the Commission of Experts. For that matter, these services are not fully discussed in government proposals that seek to expand access to justice in general.

In short, rationalization of justice services from an institutional point of view fails to consider access barriers from a citizen's point of view, ignores the very limited national coverage of several significant justice operators, and does not differentiate between those problems that can be addressed fairly by local, informal, or administrative justice alternatives and those problems in which rights are not yet well recognized and for which fast-track access to judicial forums is vital.[3]

Changes in the Concept of Access to Justice

The Right of Access to Justice

The Constitution of 1991 represents a critical milestone in Colombia's transformation toward a more just, peaceful, and democratic state—a social state based on the rule of law (*estado social de derecho*). The constitution not only introduced substantial reforms to overhaul the justice system but also trans-

---

3   This chapter focuses its discussion of rationalization and access to justice on poor households and vulnerable groups, and in particular on women. In no way is this meant to take away from the significant barriers faced by other vulnerable groups, such as ethnic communities, children and adolescents, people with disabilities, victims of the internal conflict, and the elderly.

formed the concept of access to justice dramatically. Features of jurisprudence under the constitution and subsequent Constitutional Court include

- Access to justice as a fundamental right
- Legal justification for differential treatment and affirmative action to promote equality for historically deprived population groups
- Special jurisdictions providing for community and ethnic-community justice systems
- Promotion of alternative dispute resolution mechanisms as options for access to justice

This conceptual modification made it unacceptable to define access to justice merely as access to the courts or to legal representation via public defenders and legal aid clinics. Simplified and more user-friendly judicial mechanisms were introduced to safeguard people's rights and interests: a writ to order administrative officials to fulfill their obligations (*acción de cumplimiento*); a procedure to protect collective rights (*acción popular*); another to protect the rights of specific social groups (*acción de grupo*); and a fast-track, citizen-initiated action to protect fundamental rights (*acción de tutela*). From the public perspective, the most important of these measures has been the *acción de tutela*, which can be availed through less formal proceedings, with minimal legal requirements (e.g., the presence of a lawyer is not necessary), and for which a fast judicial decision is required by law. For instance, in 2001 Decision 1195, the Constitutional Court ruled that the right of access to justice consisted of

> appropriate and effective procedures to determine legal rights and obligations; timely resolution of controversies without unjustified delays; respect for due process; availability of a broad and sufficient range of mechanisms to resolve conflicts; specific mechanisms to facilitate access for the poor; and national coverage of justice services.

New Institutional Actors

The Constitution of 1991 broadened the range of institutional and civilian actors involved in the administration of justice and the protection of human rights. New entities and institutions were created, including the Constitutional Court, the Public Prosecutor's Office (Fiscalía General de la Nación; FGN), and the Ombudsman's Office (Defensoría del Pueblo), which includes the public defenders system. At the community level, equity-based justice services were created, comprising special jurisdictions for justices of the peace (*jueces de paz*) and the office of the equity conciliator. Under the Colombian constitution, Special Jurisdictions for Indigenous Communities allowed authorities in indigenous communities to have jurisdiction within their territories, in accordance with their "uses and customs." In addition, executive and local government agencies, in cooperation with some private actors, were charged with justice-sector duties to ensure access to national government-provided alternative and complementary services to the court system.

The Constitutional Court and National Agendas

Since the passage of the constitution, the Constitutional Court has become a key proponent of ensuring access to justice. Since its inception, the court has taken groundbreaking and progressive steps in making jurisprudence more accessible for the protection of individual and social rights. It has protected the rights of women, forcibly displaced populations, indigenous and Afro-Colombian communities, children, prisoners, religious minorities, the elderly, and the handicapped. It has upheld such social rights as the right to health and the right to a dignified dwelling. Despite some criticism, the court has assumed a role that goes beyond the judicial decision itself, extending to the supervision of compliance, such that "effective enjoyment of rights" is realized.

Access to justice has also been included in national public policy and sector-specific development agendas. For example, it has been mainstreamed in the National Program to Promote Non-violent Family Relations, known as Haz Paz, which addresses domestic violence issues, and has been incorporated into the objectives of Red Unidos, a social protection network created to reduce extreme poverty in Colombia.[4] As a product of the 14th Ibero-American Judicial Summit Meeting in March 2008, Colombia signed the Brasilia 100 Regulations Regarding Access to Justice for Vulnerable Groups. Through these actions, the state has recognized the importance of access to justice as a tenet of social inclusion and citizenship.

Programs and Services to Address Access Barriers

During the past two decades, increased attention has been placed on reducing the barriers that citizens face, especially the poor, in securing access to justice and pursuing legal recourse and remedies in a variety of settings. In addition to streamlined instruments to defend fundamental rights (e.g., *tutela*),[5] a sig-

---

4   Previously known as Red Juntos, this program aims to address the multidimensional nature of poverty and has 45 strategic objectives, 2 of which deal directly with access to justice: (1) household members should know their rights and duties as citizens and be able to identify their legal needs and the appropriate justice institution for resolving disputes (i.e., access to alternative methods of conflict resolution are favored over the court system); and (2) household legal matters should receive prompt attention from justice operators and be considered relevant for alternative conflict resolution mechanisms. The World Bank–financed Justice Services Strengthening Project is financing the first national survey of unmet basic justice needs. *See* World Bank, Report No: 47338-Co, Project Appraisal Document on a Proposed Adaptable Program Loan in the amount of US$20 million to the Republic of Colombia for a Justice Services Strengthening Project—Phase I (APL1) in support of the First Phase of the Justice Services Strengthening Program, November 6, 2009, Poverty Reduction and Economic Management Sector Management Unit, Colombia and Mexico Country Management Unit, Latin Americans and the Caribbean Region.

5   While *tutela* was never intended to be a grand-scale solution to the larger access to justice problem, its widespread popularity demonstrates that reducing barriers created by judicial procedures, judicial culture, and rules of legal representation can improve access to justice. It may also generate externalities for regular cases that are crowded out by the priority allocated to *tutelas*. The Commission of Experts for Justice Reform recognized the contribution made by *tutelas* to access goals and recommended maintaining them, but proposed modi-

nificant number of programs and projects have been developed at the national, departmental, and municipal levels, sometimes in combination with other justice objectives or national goals. These programs address barriers such as costs and delays associated with litigation, excessive procedural formalities, difficulties due to language and cultural differences, lack of information on legal rights, and the need for legal advice and representation.

Substantial reforms have been made to civil and criminal justice systems. A public prosecutor's agency and a public defense system have been established, and the number of public prosecutors and public defenders has been increased. New administrative and community justice agencies have been set up; the number of conciliation centers has grown; and innovative "one-stop"

Box 1. Small Claims Courts

Upon the request of the Colombian Judicial Superior Council, the World Bank has been entrusted with the design of a management model for a proposed "small claims court system" with jurisdiction over civil, commercial, and family matters. This initiative, a follow-up on previous attempts to address concerns over the inability of the current system to serve low-income users adequately, hopes to fill a vacuum that the justices of the peace and other alternative dispute resolution mechanisms have been unable to fill.

This initiative is still at the inception stage, making the feasibility of the final proposals unpredictable, but it is worth mentioning that an ambitious participatory methodology has been accepted by both the council and the Bank. This methodology will allow substantial fieldwork to be conducted to create a blueprint of a proposal that subsequently will be validated by other justice-sector participants.

The two main challenges of the design process identified so far are (1) differentiating these "small claims courts" from the traditional municipal courts while minimizing or eliminating any overlap or duplication; and (2) developing a particular workflow that could provide a "firewall" for these courts, protecting them against the litigious practices common in the rest of the Colombian court system, which can potentially transform even the simplest judicial process into a protracted set of motions and countermotions.

The international experience reviewed by the Bank team indicates that one of the most relevant features of "small claims courts" is mandatory pro se representation (i.e., no attorneys should be allowed to represent either party), which would be fully consistent with the small amounts involved, the low complexity of the issues, the low-income profile of most users, and the zero-cost approach required by these users. The optional pro se representation risks converting small claims courts into another municipal court, as seen in the experience of São Paulo State in Brazil, where lawyers seek to benefit from the addition of a new layer of the court system and perpetuate traditional practices.

---

fications when they were used against decisions made by the highest courts in the judicial structure.

programs—community justice houses and victim assistance centers, for example—have been created, mainly at the municipal level. New types of judges to deal specifically with small claims, land, agrarian, and other rural matters, or who can deal with issues in multiple areas of law, were on the statute books for years before recent developments regarding land restitution and small claims courts with multiple jurisdiction have opened the way to innovation within the judicial branch (see, for example, box 1).

Among the various alternative dispute resolution (ADR) methods, conciliation has become the most popular in Colombia because it provides prompt and effective means for dispute settlement at a relatively low cost. For instance, conciliation can contribute to rapid contract enforcement and help solve minor family and neighborhood conflicts. The private sector considers conciliation a substitute for a slow court apparatus; however, because contract enforcement through the judiciary is not predictable, some companies prefer to use conciliation even if it involves higher costs in the short term. About three hundred formal conciliation centers operate in Colombia, and independent mediators (most but not all of whom are lawyers) are very active. Conciliation services in Colombia are provided via *conciliación en derecho* (with lawyers as conciliators operating within the applicable legal framework; see box 2) and *conciliación en equidad* (with nonlawyer conciliators deciding in equity). In marginal areas, *conciliación en equidad* may be the most suitable conciliation mechanism

---

Box 2. *Conciliación de Derecho*

"Conciliation based on law" is increasing in importance in Colombia. Conciliators work in centers approved and supervised by the Ministry of Justice and Law (Ministerio de Justicia y Derecho) and can be located at universities, chambers of commerce, and centers created by private and public agencies. The number of centers has grown from 11 in 2001 to 345 in March 2011. Between 2002 and 2009, a total of 523,232 conciliations were undertaken in these centers.

The distribution of the 25,899 conciliators associated with the centers still privileges larger cities.

Area	Number of cases	Percent of total
Civil and commercial	39,711	73.77
Criminal	386	0.71
Family	12,061	22.4
Other special cases	1,672	3.1

Source: Ministerio del Interior y Justicia (MIJ), "Conciliation Based on Law" (2007).

Information on the socioeconomic status of the clients of the centers is not available; however, based on the fees charged, it appears that low-income groups and vulnerable sectors of the population do not use this type of mechanism. Each center is responsible for submitting routine reports to the MIJ on the number of requests, hearings, and cases resolved. Based on the data observed, gender-differentiated data are not collected.

for many disputes. These claims include, for example, noncompliance with payment of debts, rental agreements and other types of contracts, disputes between neighbors, and matters related to property boundaries. These reforms and new developments have given rise to a considerable increase in the number of justice operators, both formal and informal (see table 1).[6] According to national statistics, the total number of justice-sector operators doubled from 16,073 in 2003 to 32,935 in 2008.

Table 1. Increase in the number of formal and informal justice operators*

	2003	2004	2005	2006	2007	2008
Judges	3,970	4,073	4,073	4,285		4,479
Public defenders	1,015	1,138	1,369	1,795	2,011	2,257
Public prosecutors	3,638	3,640	3,640	3,640		4,051
Family defenders	513	495	513	497		527
Notary publics	613	613	613	613		856
Labor inspectors	179	179	179	179		328
Municipal *personeros*	1,098	1,098	1,098	1,098		1,098
Law-based conciliation centers	185	216	236	259	286	310
Potential law-based conciliators (Public officers with conciliation powers)	4,786	5,636	6,486	7,334		14,820
Equity conciliators	823	1,862	2,424	3,365		5,203
Elected *jueces de paz*	. . .	834	1,401	1,418		1,054

* Figures for potential law-based conciliator include municipal *comisarías de familia* and *inspectores de policía*.

Source: Departamento Nacional de Planeación, *Visión Colombia Segundo Centenario: 2019; Garantizar una justicia eficiente* (2008), p. 7, based on figures from the Ministry of the Interior and Justice, the Public Prosecutor's Office, and the Judicial Superior Council.

Understanding the Legal Needs of the Population: Initial Findings

Empirical studies of (unsatisfied) legal/justice needs of the population can significantly improve the design of public policies and the delivery of justice services.[7] Legal experts and proponents of access to justice contend that examining the complexity of justice needs helps in determining the level of intervention necessary and contributes to the development of sound policies. A full-fledged national study on the unsatisfied legal/justice needs of the

---

6   "Formal justice" is the impartial and coherent application of laws and institutional regulations; "informal justice" is applied by a variety of voluntary persons who seek to strengthen peaceful coexistence and who have been trained and authorized to assist with the handling of certain types of citizens' disputes.

7   This section draws on the text of *Colombia—Justice Sector: Social Assessment* (World Bank Dec. 4, 2008).

population has yet to be conducted in Colombia.[8] In the past five years, however, empirical work has taken place in cities and small municipalities that shed light on these issues.

The Corporación Excelencia en la Justicia (CEJ) Study

CEJ released the first study in Colombia on unsatisfied legal needs of Colombian households (June 2008).[9] The purpose of the study was to learn about the legal needs of poor households (low to medium-low income groups) in the cities of Armenia and Chía, what they did about those needs, and how satisfied they were with the outcomes.[10] Underpinning the rationale of the study is the notion that justice reforms should benefit the poor, and that their needs and preferences should inform the design of interventions. Specifically, the study argues that equal and effective access to justice has the potential to empower disadvantaged groups and reduce their vulnerability.

The study's findings reaffirm the common belief that the court system is profoundly disconnected from the lives of many Colombians. Some of the study's major findings:

- *There is a high level of unsatisfied legal needs among poor households.* A significant proportion of poor households facing a situation with a legal dimension did not turn to any part of the justice sector for help.

The study asserts that lack of access deepens the vulnerability of poor households. Although the principle of access to justice is reflected in the legal system, in reality, the average citizen faces significant economic, cultural, and institutional obstacles that constrain access. Of the households surveyed in the cities of Armenia and Chía, 84 percent stated that they did not turn to the formal court system for help to resolve a legally oriented conflict.[11]

---

8   This activity is being supported under the ongoing World Bank–financed Justice Services Strengthening Project (Loan No. 7824-CO) and should be finalized by the end of 2013.

9   Corporación Excelencia en la Justicia (CEJ), *Estudio de necesidades jurídicas insatisfechas en las ciudades de Armenia y Chía* (CEJ 2008). The study did not assess the (unmet) legal/justice needs of the rural population, for which poverty levels are higher, or how the presence of armed conflict at the municipal level significantly affects access.

10   The study examined legal/justice needs in 13 areas: labor, family, neighborhood disputes, housing, public services, health, education, criminal matters, discrimination, debt, identity matters, consumer rights, and civil responsibility.

11   These findings are consistent with justice-sector data. Based on a 1997 justice survey, the CEJ estimated that 63 percent of crimes go unreported and that 40 percent of all reported crimes go unpunished. The 1997 survey indicated that people do not seek judicial relief because of lack of trust in the transparency and effectiveness of the system. The same survey reported that chronic congestion, excessive delays, a complex and cumbersome procedural framework, and difficulties in execution of judicial orders contributed significantly to this lack of trust (cited in DPK Consulting, *Reforma de la justicia colombiana: Informe final* 10, 15 (project report for Judicial Conflict Resolution Improvement Project, World Bank, Aug. 2004) (available in the World Bank project file for closed Loan No. 7081-CO, Judicial Conflict Resolution Improvement Project) (hereinafter, DPK Consulting).

- *The reasons people gave to stay away from the court system can be grouped as follows: pervasive distrust in the system, lack of legal empowerment to demand justice remedies, high opportunity costs, insufficient knowledge of the justice system, and a sense that the problem was best resolved outside the system.*

In 2008, a second study of unsatisfied conflict resolution needs among poor and nonpoor households[12] found that the types of conflicts that most affect poor households are related to housing, health, family, and criminal victimization. Nearly 51 percent of households sampled in Bucaramanga, Buenaventura, and Cienaga did not turn to the justice sector to resolve their conflicts. Of those that did, 27 percent turned to the formal agencies (i.e., the judiciary, the FGN, and the police) and 13 percent to the informal mechanisms (e.g., conciliation centers, elected *jueces de paz*, equity conciliators, and *casas de justicia*).[13]

The majority of family-related and health-related disputes were taken to *casas de justicia*. Only about 8 percent of the disputants sought judicial remedies, of which 50 percent of claims were made through *tutelas* claims (of which 75 percent were related to health rights); 19 percent of the claims were made through *acciones populares*, and 6 percent through class action suits.

The study compared the conflict resolution needs of poor households with those of nonpoor households, as well as the steps taken to resolve such conflicts. Of those households sampled, the study found that poor households were most likely to suffer from an unsatisfied need, and at the same time the most likely to turn to the formal or informal justice sector, in spite of their lack of confidence in sector authorities. In addition, poor households reported a higher level of vulnerability in terms of crime and victimization than nonpoor households.[14]

A major source of confusion for users is the classification of particular operators or programs as "formal" or "informal," because several cross a commonly held but poorly conceived divider line and thereby play an important bridging or complementary role. Furthermore, such titles imply a separation involving a capacity or quality judgment, which is confusing for the public and counterproductive for the justice system.

A second matter of concern as one considers the growing dimension of the conciliation field is the persistent lack of precision in the number and distribution of active equity conciliators and *jueces de paz*. The difficulties inherent in sustaining voluntary community justice services and subsidiary responsibilities assigned to busy public servants belie what appears to be a very strong

---

12 Fedesarrollo, *desarrollo de una metodología para la identificación de necesidades insatisfechas de resolución de conflictos* (2008).

13 For a description of each such informal justice mechanism, *see Colombia–Justice Sector: Social Assessment, supra* note 8.

14 The findings of the two studies coincide with national-level studies conducted by the National Planning Department that revealed high levels of victimization but low levels of resort to the courts for redress. *See* DPK Consulting, *supra* note 11.

presence throughout the country. Indeed, a complete list of justice and conflict resolution instances and operators is not available.[15]

While there has been a significant increase in the number and the types of justice operators, there has also been significant concentration, principally in the main towns and cities of Colombia. The constitution and legislation guarantee the presence of basic judicial authorities (judges, public prosecutors, and public defenders) in every municipality; however, budget deficits; numerous, spatially dispersed, smaller towns, with meager populations (which implies a very low cost/benefit ratio); and poor security conditions (due to ongoing armed conflict and organized crime) have led to less than full compliance.

To help remedy these problems, the Consejo Superior de la Judicatura has set up Judicial Units for Municipalities, which provide criminal justice services by sharing justice personnel among several towns. Eighty-one such units were operating and were providing services to 251 municipalities in 2008. Other national justice institutions have distributed their human resources based on similar criteria, but these were not necessarily in strict alignment with the judicial capacity. However, entities such as the Forensic Medicine Institute and family defenders are so few in number that there is no alternative but to reassign their tasks to other local officials. This creates enormous challenges at the municipal and community levels.

Besides the lack of personnel in many parts of the country and the uncertainty of the justice services available in any particular place, the absence of an articulated justice-system model hinders effective access to justice. Such a model would identify, connect, and activate the potential of multiple justice operators and programs in any particular location and seek to ensure their interaction in a coherent and collaborative system.

Local Justice Services Provision: Two Mechanisms in Need of Rationalization

As a result of the constitutional provisions for strengthening local governments, responsibility for the delivery of several types of justice services has increasingly been delegated to municipalities. For example, the Ministry of Justice calls on mayors to promote community conciliator programs, set up municipal conciliation centers, and elect *jueces de paz* using municipal budgets. Also coming under the responsibility of local governments have been entities that facilitate the initial response (at least) to conflict resolution and peaceful coexistence requirements in family matters, disputes between neighbors, the use of public grounds and facilities, and protection against human rights abuses and environmental problems. These entities include the *casas de justicia, centros de convivencia, comisarías de familia, inspectores de policía–personerías.* The

---

15   The World Bank–financed Justice Services Strengthening Project for Colombia (Loan No. 7824-CO) is also financing regular updates to the Justice Ministry's "justice map," which is meant to reflect the full range of providers of justice services.

Box 3. *Casas de Justicia*

The *casas de justicia* are multiagency venues that provide information on rights, legal advice, and conflict resolution services. A variety of conciliation options are offered, together with administrative and some formal justice services (Decree 1447 of 2000). Since 1995, the Ministry of the Interior and Justice, with support from USAID, has constructed a system of *casas de justicia* comprising some 81 houses. Originally designed for cities with populations in excess of 100,000, *casas de justicia* provide rapid solutions to everyday interpersonal disputes and neighborhood conflicts. Other issues they address include personal identity verification, domestic and sexual violence, and criminal cases of lesser gravity. Services for displaced populations are also provided, and matters of institutional abuse are considered.

Since 2005, a regional model—consisting of a main justice house in a medium-sized municipality and satellite houses in neighboring, much-smaller towns— has been developed to reach municipalities in zones severely affected by armed conflict. As many as 20 of the new justice houses have adopted this model, seeking to cooperate with government efforts to reestablish a state presence in such territories. Many of the new facilities will serve Afro-Colombian and indigenous communities in rural-conflict and post conflict situations, a critical step for achieving peace in Colombia.

The purpose of the *casas de justicia* is to facilitate "one-stop" access to legal help for poor people in marginalized or conflictive neighborhoods, and to promote peaceful-dispute resolution and social cohesion. Although they vary in design, *casas de justicia* incorporate local prosecutors, public defenders, municipal human rights officers, municipal neighborhood affairs units, *comisarías de familia*, legal aid specialists, social workers, and psychologists in a variety of conciliation services. Many justice houses also include other entities such as nongovernmental women's organizations, youth mediation services, children's playrooms, and university law clinics, and personnel such as forensic doctors, community police officers, and representatives for ethnic-communities.

Casas de justicia eliminate or reduce common access barriers and bring justice closer to the people, both physically and culturally. Procedures are free of charge, easy to arrange, and informal. Legal representation (having a lawyer present) is not required. Disputes are resolved in a timely manner. However, the sustainability of the houses is dependent on the continued participation of various institutions from the justice sector, some of which have insufficient staff to assign to small town projects; municipal political will to assume justice and conflict resolution commitments;, and municipal budgets for justice services. Unfortunately, all of these factors are compounded when justice houses are located in small, war-torn areas.

Children and Adolescent Code of 2006, for example, requires municipal operators to play a subsidiary role in towns where there is no family defender.[16] Similar legislation also calls on municipal operators when forensic medical staff and judicial police are not on hand in small municipalities.

These municipal-based programs provide access to justice for many people, but simply calling for an increase in their use, or for an expansion of the programs countrywide, is not a sound measure for improving access. Policy makers must develop a better understanding of the benefits and current challenges from the perspectives both of the users of these systems and of the local governments in charge of service delivery. By way of example, this section provides an overview of the opportunities and challenges of the national justice houses (*casas de justicia*) program and equity, or community, conciliators (*conciliadores en equidad*) (see boxes 3 and 4).

Decentralized delivery of justice services can be an important mechanism to expand access, especially in terms of extending national coverage to smaller municipalities and towns located in rural conflict areas. It also can help eliminate or reduce barriers to justice by providing services that are culturally and physically accessible and responsive to the needs of the community. However, these benefits are compromised by structural problems that limit impact, such as unclear roles or overlapping jurisdictional responsibilities, insufficient or ineffective institutional coordination, reduced number of professionals prepared to live and work in many municipalities, lack of training and operational capacity, absence of quality controls, and undue political influence in appointments, all coupled with severe municipal and departmental budget limitations.[17]

Can the Use of Justice Services Be Rationalized? The Proposed Strategy to Address Access Issues

The Commission of Experts for Justice Reform promoted rationalization as part of a policy approach to deal with the crisis of judicial congestion and case backlogs, which has worsened in the face of increasing demand for court services. Congestion in the system contributes to delays in the settlement of disputes, sluggish response times, higher transaction costs, and widespread dissatisfaction with the delivery of justice services. To deal with this problem, the commission proposed an interlinked strategy that included the development of a strategic modernization plan, new procedural codes with an urgent

---

16   Article 98 of the code assigns municipal operators these responsibilities, which normally belong to family defenders.

17   There are exceptions that should be noted, such as the undertakings of the Antioquia state government, 2008–2011, which has trained community conciliators, supported the creation of municipal family disputes officers (*comisarías de familia*), and built nine *casas de justicia*. Efforts made by larger cities such as Bogotá and Medellín are also noteworthy.

Box 4. Equity (Community) Conciliators

Conciliación en equidad (equity conciliation) is a community justice mechanism whereby an impartial third party, called the equity conciliator, helps his or her fellow community members solve their everyday types of conflicts. Agreements reached are recorded in a document called the *Acta de conciliación en equidad*, which has the same effect as a judicial ruling. Both law-based and equity-conciliation options are legally regulated and are recognized as an alternative form of conflict resolution by Law 23 of 1991 and Law 446 of 1998. A network of community mediators and equity conciliators has been established that receives support from civil society organizations such as Red de Justicia Comunitaria (Community Justice Network).

Equity conciliation was first created as a tool to reduce the caseload of the judicial sector but has since been appreciated as having an important role in conflict transformation and community development, especially in remote geographical areas. In Decision C-893 2001, the Constitutional Court stated, "equity conciliation enhances democracy because it prevents conflict, strengthens the justice system, and allows people to actively participate in the solution of their own conflicts."[18] In certain contexts, the legitimacy of equity conciliators comes from the legal framework, and in other places, from the community itself and community-based conflict resolution practices that are based on community knowledge and traditions.

Although more than 5,800 equity conciliators have been trained, an undetermined, lower number of those remain active.[19] According to a USAID evaluation, the reasons given for these desertions include "displacement by the armed conflict, absence of technical assistance by the Ministry of the Interior and Justice, lack of support by municipal governments, abandonment by NGOs and other supporting institutions, low motivation due to the lack of institutional incentives, and poor promotion of the practice in the host communities."[20] In some areas, an additional obstacle to the successful development of a conciliation program is the insufficient integration of conciliation practices with community traditions and practices.[21] The community and voluntary nature of the function makes it difficult to adequately monitor and evaluate their work. To address this issue, some observers have proposed the use of local coordination points. Such points could include *casas de justicia, centros de convivencia,* community councils, municipal offices, or any other central point within the community. A different initiative in this same direction is a national call center in Bogotá that provides advice and information to conciliators and endeavors to obtain copies of the agreements (*actas*) that result from the conciliators' activities.

---

18   For a grassroots analysis of the impact of equity conciliation and challenges faced, *see* Maria Lucia Zapata, *Peacebuilding from the Grassroots: Equity Conciliation and Conflict Transformation in Colombia* (Mar. 2008), available at http://www.beyondintractability.org/casestudy/zapata-peacebuilding.

19   While community conciliators are trained and certified under the supervision of the Ministry of Justice, it is nearly impossible to know at any given point how many of those trained remain active. In its 2009 report to Congress, the ministry reported that 5,700 community conciliators were present in more than 230 municipalities. *See* Ministry of Justice, *Annual Report to Congress* (2009).

20   Checchi and Company Consulting, Inc., *Colombia Administration of Justice Program, Final Report* 16 (Sept. 2006).

21   *See* Zapata, *supra* note 18.

focus on the civil procedural code, use of new technologies, rationalization of the use of a wide range of justice services, and a short-term emergency plan to reduce the case backlog.[22]

The assumption is that rationalization would enable the judicial system to better respond to demand by, first, filtering certain types of cases to out-of-court forums based on the principle that not all disputes require the intervention of a judge and not all clients are best served by judicial procedures, and, second, promoting greater use of alternative justice mechanisms.[23] In its report, the commission identified two main benefits (outcomes) of such a policy approach: less litigation and consequently a reduction in the number of cases filed; and better outcomes and access for users because of less delay, cost, and procedural formalities associated with ADR.[24]

The key aspect of rationalization is greater use of out-of-court ADR facilities. For the commission, this means greater promotion of the benefits of ADR in general, and greater use of conciliation centers; administrative mechanisms for dispute resolution, including those available at the Defensoría del Pueblo, the Procuraduría General de la Nación (PGN), the Instituto de Bienestar Familiar (Law 640, 1991); community-level equity conciliation processes (Law 23, 1991); arbitration; and an expanded use of the notary publics when the matter at hand is not a dispute or when no legal rights are at stake. In essence, the commission envisions an extreme effect of rationalization via ADR with the court system as the last resort for conflict resolution.[25] However, while the National Planning Department's *Visión Colombia Segundo Centenario: 2019* supports rationalization, it places greater weight on other issues that should be factored into rationalization policies, namely, the need to promote social harmony and peaceful coexistence.

Filtering the demand for judicial services can potentially have important efficiency gains, improve access to justice, and support long-term peace building. Rationalization policies, however, must go beyond the simple diversification and growing national coverage of formal, informal, and administrative options for legal decisions and conflict resolution services. If this is to serve access to justice goals, it must also focus on the conflict resolution needs of people in large cities, small towns, rural areas, and socially disadvantaged groups.

The studies by Corporación Excelencia en la Justicia and Fedesarrollo identified five characteristics related to unsatisfied conflict resolution and legal needs in Colombian municipalities. First, poorer social classes need information and advice, offered freely, by local institutions to help understand their rights and decide how best to deal with their legal needs and conflicts.

---

22   Commission of Experts, *supra* note 2, at 64–66.

23   L. 446, 1998, art. 65, and L. 640, 2001, art. 19, regulate matters amenable to conciliation.

24   Commission of Experts, *supra* note 2, at 71.

25   *Id.*, at 129.

Second, citizens are more likely to consult lawyers who are part of an institution they trust, especially if this service is free or considered inexpensive. Such consultations occur most frequently in connection with family problems and criminal matters. Third, vulnerable population groups living in poverty conditions are more likely to seek help in solving their legal problems if the barriers limiting access and procedures prolonging solutions are reduced. Fourth, the judicial system is not a first option for the poor when resolving conflicts, although the poor will seek assistance if they know it is available. They look for help most frequently in informal and administrative settings. Fifth, negative

Figure 1. Pyramid model for articulating dispute processing options

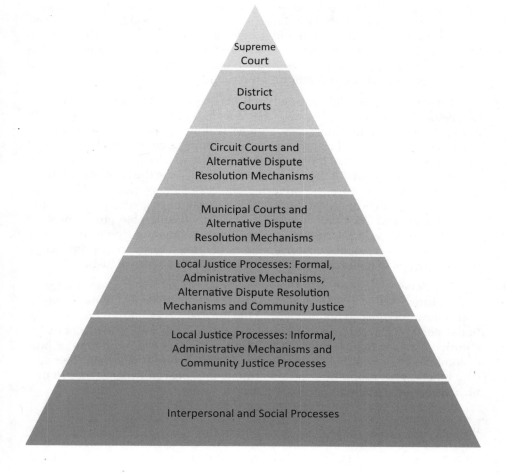

perceptions of the justice system are long-standing, as the first National Justice Survey in 1997 demonstrated and more recent studies confirm. Poor citizens are especially dissuaded by these perceptions and avoid using institutional mechanisms to resolve their conflicts.

Several experts on access to justice advocate a model known as "the pyramid of dispute resolution" (see figure 1).[26] The broad base of the pyramid is made up of an array of interpersonal and social options for dealing with disputes between equals. Entities such as *jueces de paz,* equity conciliators, neighborhood action boards (*juntas de acción comunal*), family counselors, church leaders, and community elders are located at this level. As one ascends the pyramid, levels offer processes that become more formal, more grounded in legal precepts, and more institutionally controlled. *Comisarías de familia,* conciliation centers, university law clinics, *casas de justicia,* local human rights officers (*personerías*), and administrative agencies are located farther upward in the pyramid. The top tier and more formal levels include the judicial structure, entities responsible for investigation and collecting evidence for victim and witness protection, and arbitration centers.

If this pyramid model accurately reflects the desirable distribution of conflict resolution options in a society that does not give priority to litigation in citizens' disputes and differences, a great deal more attention and resources need to be directed by the state toward developing a culture of dialogue and conciliation. The notion of the pyramid and its broad base helps identify many institutional challenges at the informal levels, which are the least consolidated and documented, yet are the preferred choices of many citizens. If the vast majority of conflicts are to be dealt with by community justice processes and equity-based and conciliatory justice services, considerable effort must be made to provide adequate training opportunities, ongoing technical support, basic standards for quality control, and, when necessary, appropriate disciplinary actions to maintain credibility, fairness, and a sense of justice,

The development of an inclusive pyramid model for dispute resolution will require detailed proposals to address the link between ADR mechanisms and community justice options within the judicial system. From an organizational perspective, the model demands a thoughtful and concerted interinstitutional access to justice policy building and calls for a rethinking of how Colombian justice entities currently envision their role concerning their specific functions in promoting social harmony and peaceful coexistence in municipalities and certain territorial regions.

A major challenge for establishing such a model in Colombia is the weak link between ADR, on one side, and municipal and community justice options and the courts, on the other. Because the success of rationalization rests in large part on a system of nonjudicial mechanisms or ADR, it is critical to ask

---

26 R. Uprimny et al., *Justicia para todos? Sistema judicial, derechos sociales y democracia en Colombia* 252 (Grupo Editorial Norma 2006); and B. Sousa Santos & M. Garcia, *El caleidoscopio de las justicias en Colombia* 123–32 (Siglo del Hombre Editores 2001).

basic questions about ADR itself. Are the different ADR mechanisms meeting the conflict resolution needs of citizens? Are they improving access to justice, particularly for the poor and other vulnerable groups? How can these services ensure follow-up of agreements to verify compliance, and what steps should be taken by whom when this is not the case?

Programs such as municipal justice houses provide a venue for integrating legal advice and municipal and community justice services with public prosecutors and public defenders; however, a clear path upward to the courts for cases that cannot be settled or resolved by such entities as justice houses has yet to be traced. Since this program plays a bridging role across alternative and formal justice options, it presents an ideal opportunity to apply the pyramid model and test rationalization approaches. If the Center for Decentralizing Judicial Services, a pilot project under way with support from the Colombian Judicial Superior Council in the Ciudad Bolívar section of Bogotá, achieves its goal of linking lower-level courts directly to the justice houses, a breakthrough may be seen.

A rationalization policy would need to resolve ambiguities along the spectrum of informal-to-formal and better develop the roles and responsibilities across different levels. To accomplish this, the following issues need to be explored: identifying circumstances that warrant greater legal rigor; developing clearer paths for cases that cannot be settled or resolved through primary justice mechanisms to move upward or across to other options; and improving the quality of and coordination between operators and organizations on the bottom tiers while maintaining people's direct participation and the inherent organizational flexibility and simplicity that make community options work;[27] and arranging appropriate forms of institutional support and oversight.

The justice house program would be located midway up the pyramid, integrating lower-level community justice services with municipal administrative options and the first echelons of potential judicial proceedings. Community conciliators, however, are one of the first points of contact for many people, especially in rural and marginalized urban areas. Plotting their positions on the dispute resolution pyramid immediately suggests necessary lines of articulation, both horizontally and vertically, which presently are not clearly established. Rather, duplication and confusion between the roles of equity conciliators and *jueces de paz* are common complaints. Interaction of justice houses and conciliators with municipal judges is presently a largely unmapped territory.

A plethora of legislation, municipal decrees, and national program regulations have assigned functions, responsibilities, and conditions to an

---

27 Community options work when they are appropriated from and have direct effect on the community. When "national institutions" want to exercise control, ways must be found to improve quality and coordination at the community level while still maintaining the inherent local and voluntary characteristics of the community. Too much vertical institutional control can restrict community justice initiatives to the point that they cease to work.

ever-widening range of new justice operators, as if the policy were "the more the better." This situation has given rise to duplication, uncertainty in terms of accountability, and weak controls regarding quality, consistency, and ethics. It also has created obstacles for the coordination of services. Justice-sector leaders are aware of these challenges, some of which may be partly inevitable in light of constitutional developments and other ADR initiatives. However, twenty years after the reform of the constitution, there are no conceptual models or operational protocols that integrate the multitude of formal and informal justice innovations to promote user convenience or institutional efficiency.

What makes these considerations all the more concerning is the fact that the variety of justice services located along the pyramid model are rarely accessible in the majority of Colombian towns. Citizens must find entry wherever they can or travel to larger municipalities to seek other services. New technologies could help to fill the gaps and shorten the distances, since Internet access is definitely more widespread than justice operators.

Beyond such novel strategies, regenerating a law-based culture, accessing legitimate administrative justice institutions, and overcoming the popular perception of costly, time-consuming, incomprehensible legal practices that lead to unpredictable judicial decisions call for focused and strong affirmative action by the state to return justice options to war-stricken or otherwise less-than-lawful Colombian municipalities (see box 5).

Box 5. Local Justice Systems in Municipalities in War-Torn Areas of Colombia

Since 2004, the Colombian national government has strived to regain military control in 11 states seriously affected by the presence, and in some cases dominance, of illegal armed groups. Many of these areas have a history of a very limited state presence, which has been seriously undermined by internal armed conflict. An initial predominantly military intervention in these "consolidation zones" has gradually given way to a wider institutional intervention. In 2013, led by the Presidential Agency for Territorial Consolidation (the Unidad Administrativa de Consolidación Territorial, UACT), 58 municipalities will be involved in the consolidation efforts.

In 2011, the Ministry of Justice and Law funded an analysis of the administration of justice in these regions, which gave rise to a proposal to develop "local justice systems" that recognize formal, informal, and administrative justice operators in meeting the need to strengthen the presence of these entities. Recognized as part of the UACT's actions, this justice-strengthening approach has a territorial vision that reaches beyond the urban center and places more importance on rural settlements and populations. This proposal seeks to reduce justice barriers and improve the efficiency of the administration of justice. Initial implementation has begun in the state of Meta.

Women's Rights and Access to Justice: A Case Study to Illustrate the Challenges of Rationalization

Undoubtedly, mechanisms at the community and municipal levels avoid many of the barriers that often limit access to justice, such as physical and cultural distance, legal formalism, and costs. But such mechanisms are often not suitable for enforcing the rights of vulnerable populations when there is a clear imbalance of power between those involved in the conflict. This is the situation in cases of violence against women and other violations of women's rights.

Specialized family affairs offices (*comisarías de familia*) have been created at the municipal level to provide integrated services for family dispute situations and frequently for victims of domestic and sexual violence.[28] Women's organizations play an integral role in service delivery in main cities, and several networks have been developed in smaller municipalities, some of which cover extensive regions of the country.

Protocols for coordinated attention have been put in place in larger urban cities of Colombia, but capacity to expand integrated service delivery to all municipalities is greatly limited. National entities working on these issues, such as the Ministry of the Interior, Ministry of Justice, Consejería Presidencial para la Equidad de la Mujer (CPEM), and the family justice branch of the Colombian Family Welfare Institute (ICBF), provide directives, formulate policies, and offer assistance. However, the daily responsibility for providing justice services to victims of family violence falls in large part on the shoulders of municipal justice and health and welfare agencies (sometimes combined with nongovernmental actors). At the front line of service delivery, resources, training, coverage, accountability, and institutional capacity are limited and very unevenly spread from one town to the next.

The functions of the *comisarías de familia* have deepened and expanded over time through several reforms in the legal framework and, consequently, they are responsible for "guaranteeing, protecting, reestablishing, and repairing the rights of the members of the family affected by intra-family violence" through the provision of integrated and multidisciplinary services.[29] As stated in current legislation, town councils are responsible for the establishment and operation of *comisarías de familia* in all municipalities. Nevertheless, to date, while the number of municipalities that have *comisarías* has increased, very

---

28   As in other matters, Colombia has moved toward the provision of integrated services rather than relying on judicial remedies alone. An integrated response includes the delivery of social, medical, psychological, legal protection, advocacy, and legal aid/legal defense services.

29   The *comisarías de familia* were created in 1989 as an innovative mechanism to address family violence. These specialized agencies were first recognized formally in the Codigo del Menor of 1989 and later recognized in the domestic violence laws (L. 294, 1996; L. 575, 2000; & L. 1257, 2008) and the criminal procedure code, and in the recently passed Children and Adolescent Code of 2006. In 2011 a study showed the precarious nature of the majority of the 1,217 *comisarías de familia* registered in 1,102 municipalities. *See Comisarías de Familia—Linea de Base Nacional Primera Parte* (Procuraduría General de la Nación (2011).

few have a lawyer specializing in family issues and a multidisciplinary team of psychologists, social workers, doctors, and administrative auxiliaries. For example, in January 2008, only half of the 125 municipalities in the department of Antioquia had *comisarías* that were operating, and many of those did not have the required multidisciplinary team. Smaller municipalities—those located in rural areas, and especially those located in areas affected by the armed conflict—find it difficult to comply with the law and set up integrated services for victims of gender-based violence. Smaller towns frequently assign multiple responsibilities to a single municipal officer.

Family courts, as such, are few and far between;[30] hence coverage limitations are dealt with by transferring certain duties from family courts to *comisarías de familia*, mixed courts, or municipal courts. This is a serious concern for women's rights organizations. The shift has been criticized by many women's rights advocates and is perceived as an orchestrated move by the judicial apparatus to reduce court congestion.[31] Women's organizations argue that shifting responsibility from the judiciary and the court system to the *comisarías de familia* undermines access to the administration of justice for women who are victims of family violence. In addition, they argue that justice operators perceive domestic violence cases as having little legal importance. Other areas of concern include the use of conciliation in cases of domestic violence, given the typical unequal power between male and female parties, and ineffective procedures to monitor the impact of conciliation procedures on women's access to justice and judicial remedies. Studies such as the research undertaken on violence against women in Pereira and Bogotá reveal a critical tension between three objectives: the need to provide easy access for women to institutions that are located close to residential areas; the desire to lighten the burden on the judicial system; and the need to respond to the large volume of cases of intrafamily violence.[32]

Even if coverage is expanded, issues of quality of services and interinstitutional coordination and standards in delivery, resource availability, and sustainability will need to be addressed. Despite 20 years of activity, a number of institutional matters remain unresolved. For example, what agency establishes the standards and characteristics of due process in the *comisarías de familia,* and who provides oversight? What legal and access to justice principles guide the decisions made by the *comisarías*? What is the responsibility of the judicial system or the national family welfare system in terms of training, provision of an adequate work environment, and other technical assistance? As

---

30   The 144 family courts in Colombia are situated in the large cities. For example, there are 23 in Bogotá, 14 in Medellín, and 11 in Cali.

31   *See* M. Hurtado, *Violencias de género y acceso a la justicia* (unpublished paper presented as an officer of the Defensoría Pública para los Derechos de la Niñez, la Juventud y la Mujer, Santa Marta, Colombia, June 2007). Hurtado cites statistics of the Consejo Superior de la Judicatura regarding the tenfold increase in the number of protection orders requested in courts between 1996 and 1998.

32   Corpòración Humanas, *La situación de las mujeres víctimas de violencias de genero en el sistema penal acusatoria, Bogotá* (June 2008).

these issues are sorted out, access to justice for women seeking to resolve the multifaceted problems of family violence remains precarious, especially in municipalities other than the larger cities of Colombia. In very few places beyond the state capitals do a *comisaría de familia* with a multidisciplinary capacity, a family defender, and a family court come together to address violence, protection orders, child custody, parental visits, matrimonial property, and ongoing victims' assistance issues.

While lower levels of the pyramid undoubtedly avoid many of the barriers that inhibit access to justice, they are not suitable for enforcing the rights of vulnerable populations when there is a clear imbalance of power between those involved in the conflict. Be they for dealing with family violence situations, human rights violations, injustices that arise from the armed conflict, or the territorial domination by organized crime, immediate-access channels to higher justice authorities must be open and guaranteed.

Highly Vulnerable Groups Demand Special Access Options

Highly vulnerable groups, such as women forcibly displaced by internal conflict, suffer severe discrimination and violence. The Public Defender's Office conducted a study of 2,200 displaced women who were sexually abused; 8 out of every 10 did not report the abuse because of fear, shame, or lack of services. As of September 2008, of the total alerts issued by the Sistema de Alertas Tempranas (SAT), 69 percent were related to sexual exploitation and assault. As part of a project to address this issue in Magdalena state, the Procuraduría General de la Nación (PGN) concluded that violence against women is used pervasively as a strategy of war.[33] Moreover, local women's organizations were not aware of the services provided by the PGN, the organizations and officials working on the problem did not have the knowledge or the tools to provide appropriate services, and the organizational demand for increased technical assistance to improve the delivery of services to women victims of violence was high. Statistics provided by government entities and NGOs show that between 40 percent and 50 percent of the total displaced population consists of girls and women. Female heads of households represent between 34 percent and 48 percent of all displaced households.[34] In addition, the Social Solidarity Network estimates that in 2002 almost 18 percent of the total number of displaced persons are Afro-Colombians. According to the Human Rights and Displacement Clinic (Spanish abbreviation: COHDES), Afro-Colombians and indigenous groups were the most affected by the armed conflict and displacements. The indigenous population represents 8 percent of the displaced,

---

33 This coincides with the assessments of the IACHR, which found that violence against women is a structural problem in Colombia, where armed actors have used women as pawns.

34 The number of women heads of households increased from 25.8 percent in 1997 to 30.9 percent in 2003, and was higher in some urban areas. The percentage of women heads of low-income households grew from 52 percent to 54 percent between 1992 and 2001 (DANE 2003).

compared to 2 percent of the total population. Afro-Colombians represent 25 percent of the displaced, compared to 9 percent of the total population.[35]

Though important, explaining the myriad of issues affecting the rights of those displaced by Colombia's internal conflict is difficult and beyond the scope of this chapter. The barriers to access to justice for many seem insurmountable. Yet there has been some progress on many fronts. In 2004, for example, some 1,150 families challenged the inefficiency of state programs for displaced people, and the Constitutional Court issued a decision in favor of the rights of displaced people, including the rights of displaced women.[36] The decision instructed the National Council for the Integrated Assistance of Populations Displaced by Violence to comply with the law by March 2004. Due to continued violations of the law and frequent injunction orders, the Constitutional Court instructed the Executive to conduct a complete review of the system (within a six-month period), which had to include a differential analysis of gender, age, ethnicity, and race, among other categories.[37] Government agencies have redoubled efforts to comply, though they are often unable to adequately attend to this ever-growing problem, which seriously and disproportionately affects women and children.

What is even more questionable is that human rights and women's organizations that have provided legal advice and representation for the displaced population have been the object of criminal threats and actions in an endeavor to further isolate these people from the institutions charged with their protection and the responsibility to address their legal rights and needs. Such access to justice issues cannot be approached with the normal barrier and rationalization of services analysis and proposals.

This is also the case for other vulnerable groups that need affirmative action efforts from the highest judicial authorities for establishing groundbreaking legal concepts and legally binding decisions. The mainstream rationalization policy proposed by the commission must address such issues and open fast-track measures for exceptional situations. Rationalization will not be an alternative for protecting particularly vulnerable population groups, such as displaced women. Here the *tutela* and direct access to courts are needed to establish jurisprudence that recognizes rights and explores how they can be implemented.

As the discussion above illustrates, delegating to municipal and nonjudicial actors appears to overcome at least three access barriers by ensuring proximity, access without a lawyer, and specialized family services. But in reality, access to justice for women who are victims of violence is precarious because resources, coverage, and institutional capacity remain uneven and inadequate. If rationalization policies ignore these realities, they face the risk

---

35   Secretariado Nacional de Pastoral Social, Bogotá, Dec. 2001.

36   Const. Ct. Dec. in a *tutela* action, T-025, 2004.

37   Const. Ct. Dec. in a *tutela* action, T-496, May 2008.

of putting in place an approach that reinforces inequities. If rationalization is pursued primarily to satisfy the needs of the court system, it will do so at the expense of the citizen/user. More important, the real tension between efficiency and access to justice for vulnerable groups is a theme that will require further dialogue in the context of a rationalization policy for the delivery of justice services.

Conclusion

The recommendations of the Commission of Experts for Justice Reform should be viewed as a starting point for a national dialogue on access to justice. Rationalization of conflict resolution and justice services will require a thoughtful and concerted interinstitutional policy-building process that includes the participation of civil society organizations. The pyramid model discussed in this chapter offers a systemic view of the different venues for conflict resolution, conflict prevention, and hence peace building in Colombia and might serve as a conceptual tool for thinking through the filtering or rationalization proposal.

If rationalization is to serve the broader goal of access to justice, it must be adapted to deal with the realities of rural areas and small towns and with the needs of the poor and other socially vulnerable population groups. If the variety of justice services contemplated in the pyramid model only exists in large cities, the rationalization proposal is equally limited and will not provide access to justice to many critical areas of the country.

Does the political will exist to overcome the absence of justice services in small towns and outlying rural areas? Can implementing innovative technology and affirmative action help the effort to return to legality in the many regions affected by the armed conflict and other lawless conditions? Small towns and rural areas affected by the conflict need a disproportionate amount of attention to provide legal institutions with the credibility and capacity to offer legitimate conflict resolution and access to justice.

Local governments are positioned at a critical juncture of the pyramid model and play an important role in access to justice. Municipal and community instances provide essential justice services at the grassroots level and are recognized as critical components in long-term peace building efforts; however, they have the least amount of resources and institutional support. This level brings together formal and informal systems of justice, for example, *casas de justicia,* an instance that could prove to be a key component in experiences to develop and test rationalization approaches.

Last, initiatives to improve access have focused on many of the barriers that make the justice system inaccessible for everyone, but particularly for poor and vulnerable groups. Yet, access to justice remains a significant challenge in Colombia, which suggests that an exclusive focus on barriers, while necessary, is not sufficient. This makes a strong argument for seeking a better understanding of the legal and dispute resolution needs of individuals and groups, and of when and how people turn to formal or informal justice options. With the support of the World Bank–financed project, the Ministry of Justice and Law, in conjunction with the Bogotá Chamber of Commerce and an expert justice NGO, Dejusticia, has undertaken a justice-needs study in 14 Colombian cities; the final report should be ready at the end of 2013. A demand-focused analysis should help identify the types of cases in which citizens in general, and more vulnerable groups in particular, would be well served by community, administrative, and municipal justice services. The analysis should also provide visibility for those problems that such services are not positioned to deal with adequately.

Filtering and rationalizing the use of justice services will be an acceptable access to justice initiative only insofar as it recognizes institutional weaknesses that must be addressed at the lower levels of the pyramid model, with special challenges outside the main cities. In the cases of especially vulnerable population groups and problems in pioneering legal areas, where rights are not yet well established and there are insufficient resources to exercise them properly, fast-track access to judicial forums is not negotiable.

To develop effective justice policies for poor and vulnerable populations, future studies must examine demand for conflict resolution in a differentiated manner. Scholarly consideration must be given to differences between men and women; social variables, such as ethnicity, race, income, and age; and differences across geographical regions (urban/rural) and judicial districts. Careful analysis of the demand for justice can enhance access to justice if the analysis is accompanied by the expressed and clear commitment of the justice sector, with attention focused on vulnerable groups.

Transfer of justice responsibilities to municipal governments has not been accompanied by clear implementation policies, adequate funding, or relevant training. Nor is there national oversight to determine how municipal authorities carry out their delegated justice roles. In addition, in some areas where state institutions are present but precariously positioned, the capacity of local government to administer justice is significantly limited due to the presence of illegal armed forces and organized crime groups that exercise control over justice operations.[38] Such a situation can prompt doubts about the credibility of the rule of law and reduce respect and reliance on state institutions for personal safety, which accentuates peoples' extreme social vulnerability.

Rationalizing the use of justice services has the potential to achieve important efficiency gains, improve access to justice, and support long-term peacebuilding efforts, but realizing these goals will require adjustments at all levels of the justice sector and to specific affirmative action policies in small towns and rural areas, and, particularly, for vulnerable population groups.

---

38   M. Villegas et al., *Jueces sin estado: La justicia colombiana en zonas de conflicto armado* (Siglo de Hombres Editores, Dejusticia, Fundación Konrad Adenauer, John Merck Fund 2008).

The Role of Access to Information in Promoting Development

Sean Fraser

During the past quarter century, the right to development has gained significant traction in the field of international human rights law. Despite major legal advances and growing acceptance of the right to development as a legal principle among scholars, and of development more generally as a pressing political objective among states, the practical impact of this trend has been underwhelming in comparison to its enormous potential.

An important precondition to the right to development is the free flow of information that individuals or groups can use to improve the quality of their day-to-day lives. Public authorities often hold this kind of information, and functioning democracies should ensure that their constituents are provided with access to it. The failure to capitalize on the potential benefits of development initiatives is due, to some extent, to the inefficient flow of information regarding the activities of public officials.

This chapter explores the role of access to information in promoting development. In doing so, it discusses which parties bear the responsibility to implement development initiatives and addresses the nature of the obligations incumbent upon them. Following this analysis, the chapter examines how various courts and human rights bodies have used access to information to encourage public participation, promote efficient democratic governance, and protect human rights, all of which contribute to development. This chapter also analyzes the obstacles that inhibit the successful implementation of access to information laws and initiatives and provides recommendations as to how these obstacles may be overcome to increase the flow of information that can improve the lives of individuals and peoples around the world.

Development as a Global Legal Issue

Development is an increasingly important global legal issue. Over the past quarter century, this issue has been framed as a legal right in international law. The United Nations General Assembly has described the right to development as "an inalienable human right by virtue of which every human person and all peoples are entitled to participate in, contribute to, and enjoy economic, social, cultural and political development, in which all human rights and fundamental freedoms can be fully realized."[1]

---

1   Declaration on the Right to Development, A/RES/41/28 (Dec. 4, 1986). This definition gains

States hold the primary responsibility for promoting development.[2] A significant conceptual divide exists between developed and developing states on the issue of which states bear the obligation to promote development in international law. Developing states often rely on the right to development to advocate for support from the international community in their quest for development. Conversely, donor states prefer to rely on the right to development to justify their expectations that recipient governments continually improve their domestic governance by protecting human rights and ensuring the rule of law.[3]

It is obvious that both developed and developing states have a role to play in achieving global development. Although national governments play a role in the progressive development of people within their nation's borders, it would be perilous to ignore the role played by the international community in expediting human progress.[4] Building schools and hospitals, extracting natural resources while respecting environmental obligations, and providing essential services such as housing, water, and electricity come at a cost. The states with the greatest need for these facilities and services often do not have the resources to provide them. Therefore, foreign donors and international economic cooperation are essential in stimulating development. Furthermore, initiatives such as the Millennium Development Goals illustrate how international cooperation can expedite development by setting important political objectives.[5]

---

support through its inclusion in several major international instruments. *See* 1992 Rio Declaration on Environment and Development; the 1993 Vienna Declaration and Programme of Action; the Millennium Declaration; the 2002 Monterrey Consensus; the 2005 World Summit Outcome Document; and the 2007 Declaration on the Rights of Indigenous Peoples. Another major instrument has adopted a separate definition; *see* art. 22, African Charter on Human and Peoples' Rights (hereinafter, African Charter), adopted June 27, 1981, OAU Doc. CAB/LEG/67/3 rev. 521 I.L.M. 58 (1982), entered into force Oct. 21, 1986.

2   Art. 3, Declaration on the Right to Development. The Declaration on the Right to Development provides that "States have the primary responsibility for the creation of national and international conditions favourable to the realization of the right to development."

3   Stephen P. Marks, *Poverty*, in *International Human Rights Law* 618 (Daniel Moeckli et al. eds., Oxford U. Press 2010).

4   *Report of the High-Level Task Force on the Implementation of the Right to Development on Its Sixth Session*, A/HRC/15/WG.2/TF/2/Add.2. The high-level task force on the implementation of the right to development has explained that "the responsibility for the creation of this enabling environment encompasses three main levels: (a) States acting collectively in global and regional partnerships (second preambular paragraph and art. 3); (b) States acting individually as they adopt and implement policies that affect persons not strictly within their jurisdiction (art. 4); and (c) States acting individually as they formulate national development policies and programmes affecting persons within their jurisdiction (art. 2)."

5   Millennium Declaration, A/RES/55/2 (Sep. 8, 2000). *See* also Nico Schrijver, *Many Roads Lead to Rome: How to Arrive at a Legally Binding Instrument on the Right to Development?* in *Implementing the Right to Development: The Role of International Law* 127–129 (Stephen P. Marks ed., Friedrich-Ebert Stiftung and Program on Human Rights in Development of the Harvard School of Public Health 2008).

The Nexus between Access to Information and Development

Access to information is important not merely for its own sake, but for what it can help achieve. As one author has suggested, "In itself, the issue of access to information does not have a natural constituency. What is required is to connect the issue with peoples' daily pressing concerns, and ensure that people see their right to information in the broader context of their right to development."[6] The value of information is derived from its role in facilitating the achievement of other human rights, specifically, those related to development.

An informed populace is the backbone of participatory democracy. Without access to information, this form of governance is not possible. Information creates the opportunity to discuss a range of available options, to vote in accordance with one's best interests and beliefs, and to take part in meaningful public policy discussions and informed political debate. Information also creates awareness among individuals and peoples of what rights they are entitled to and when these rights are being violated. Information provides for the possibility of evidence-based advocacy to draw attention to causes that members of a society feel are important. In the event that the rights of a person or a people are infringed, information provides ammunition to present to an independent judiciary that has the power to provide a remedy for the wrong suffered.

A society that does not allow the public to access information is one that is ripe for corruption. This situation hinders economic growth by deterring international and domestic investment, as well as foreign aid. Corruption in government takes the greatest toll on a nation's most vulnerable population by preventing the poorest members of society from helping themselves climb out of poverty.[7] Information allows the public to hold a government accountable by creating a public awareness of the government's conduct. By providing access to reports, policies, and laws that affect the population, not only is the monitoring of performance made possible, but public trust in the government also grows.[8]

Each of these consequences of the public's right of access to information has a significant impact on development. An informed populace that is aware of its rights and the forms of recourse available in the event that those rights are infringed is better able to hold its government accountable. This reduces incidents of corruption and allows even the most vulnerable members of society to flourish. When freedom of information is protected, an environment

---

6   John Samuel, *Case Studies in Civil Society Advocacy* (paper prepared for the Commonwealth Foundation's seminar on Civil Society and Government—Partners or Protagonists? Oct. 2002).

7   Lala Camerer, *Information and the Quest for Global Accountability*, in *The Right to Know, The Right to Live: Access to Information and Socio-Economic Justice* xi, 139–140 (Richard Calland & Allison Tilley eds., Open Democracy Advice Centre 2002).

8   Samuel, *supra* note 6.

is created that enables the realization of civil, political, economic, social, and cultural rights for all members of society.

How States Have Used Access to Information to Promote Development

With information in hand, individuals and peoples are well equipped to defend, promote, and exercise their rights, a process that leads to tangible human development. Information plays a key role in determining whether a state has fulfilled its obligations to comply with internationally or constitutionally protected human rights norms. This section addresses the actions taken by states that have fostered development by enhancing access to information through the auspices of the United Nations and regional organizations and domestically.

The UN Framework

The UN system of human rights protection can be discerned primarily from the work of the bodies that monitor compliance with human rights treaties, the UN Human Rights Council and the Office of the High Commissioner for Human Rights (OHCHR). Each of these bodies has different tools to promote human rights, including the right of access to information. However, each could do more to liberalize access to information that might assist in promoting development. In addition, treaties that are established under the UN framework that relate to specific subject matter deliver a unique opportunity to provide the general public with access to information that relates to issues addressed by that treaty. This section discusses various aspects of the UN framework that have specifically tackled the right to information. Mechanisms that do not have an ample body of material available that relates to the right to information are beyond the scope of this chapter and are not discussed.

UN Treaty Bodies

Article 19 of the Universal Declaration of Human Rights (UDHR) recognizes the importance of the right to access information when it states, "Everyone has the right to freedom of opinion and expression; this right includes freedom to hold opinions without interference and to seek, receive and impart information and ideas through any media and regardless of frontiers."[9] When the UDHR was adopted in 1948, the expectation was that further treaties would be required to create binding obligations with respect to the human rights contained therein. Since then, nine core instruments have been adopted. The International Covenant on Civil and Political Rights (ICCPR) addresses the right to access public information in Article 19(2), which provides that "everyone shall have the right to freedom of expression; this right shall include freedom to seek, receive and impart information and ideas of all kinds, regardless

---

9   Art. 19, Universal Declaration of Human Rights of the UN General Assembly A/RES/217 A (III) (Dec. 10, 1948).

of frontiers, either orally, in writing or in print, in the form of art, or through any another media of his choice."[10]

This discussion addresses the various mechanisms by which UN treaty bodies use Article 19(2) of the ICCPR and other laws that provide for access to information as a means of promoting development around the globe. These mechanisms include general comments of the various treaty bodies, state reporting obligations, and complaints procedures. Examples of how each of these tools have been used to promote access to information are presented below.

General Comments. Most treaty bodies issue general comments, which are adopted by consensus and provide guidance on the general treaty obligations of state parties to the relevant instrument and outline the scope of the rights contained therein.[11] Although general comments are not legally binding, they are often cited by states and complainants in the context of state reporting obligations, during the applicable complaints process, or even in the judgments of domestic courts.[12]

The Human Rights Committee provided some guidance on the right to information in General Comment No. 34. That document points out that "Article 19, paragraph 2 [of the ICCPR] embraces a right of access to information held by public bodies" and that the right of access to such information applies regardless of how the information is stored and impacts private parties that carry out a public function. General Comment No. 34 also states:

> To give effect to the right of access to information, States parties should proactively put in the public domain Government information of public interest. States parties should make every effort to ensure easy, prompt, effective and practical access to such information. States parties should also enact the necessary procedures, whereby one may gain access to information, such as by means of freedom of information legislation.[13]

General Comment No. 34 also establishes that individuals are entitled to know what personal data are stored by public entities and which individuals or bodies control their files. If those files contain incorrect data or were collected in violation of the law, the right to access personal information includes a right to have personal records rectified. In previous general comments, the Human Rights Committee has shed light on the kinds of information to which persons accused of a criminal offense are entitled,[14] and the entitlement to information about other rights under the ICCPR in general.[15]

---

10   Art. 19(2), International Covenant on Civil and Political Rights, A/RES/2200 (Dec. 16, 1966).

11   Markus Schmidt, *United Nations*, in *International Human Rights Law* 408–409 (Daniel Moeckli et al. eds., Oxford U. Press 2010).

12   *See Secretary of Security v. Sakthevel Prabakar,* 1 Hong Kong L. Rpts. & Dig. (2005) 289.

13   General Comment No. 34, CCPR/C/GC/34 (Sep. 12, 2011), at paras. 18–19.

14   General Comment No. 32, CCPR/C/GC/32 (Aug. 23, 2007).

15   General Comment No. 31, CCPR/C/21/Rev.1/Add. 13 (May 26, 2004).

State Reporting Obligations. Parties to the core human rights instruments are required to submit regular reports to the committee responsible for overseeing the relevant treaty. These reports must outline how the state has implemented the treaty nationally and are subsequently examined by the treaty body, which designates a country rapporteur to prepare a list of issues that is addressed by the state in the form of an updated report.

The examination of state reports takes place in public and in the presence of a delegation from the state party concerned. The public nature of this examination is beneficial in that it represents a proactive approach by the treaty bodies to disseminating information related to human rights and, thus, development. Following the examination, the treaty bodies adopt concluding observations or comments that identify areas of progress for the state as well as problems that persist. Specific recommendations as to how these problems may be resolved are made, and follow-up mechanisms monitor whether progress is in fact being made.[16]

The UN Human Rights Committee expressed unease in relation to Iran's violation of the right to freedom of expression under the ICCPR.[17] The committee was concerned about the government's efforts to stifle the media and in some instances detain them, particularly following the 2009 presidential elections. These efforts represent an infringement of the right to expression of the various media entities and persons in Iran and a violation of the Iranian population's right to seek and receive information. In response to these concerns, the committee recommended:

> The State party should [. . .] ensure that journalists can exercise their profession without fear of being brought before courts. The State party should release, rehabilitate and provide effective judicial redress and compensation for journalists that were imprisoned in contravention of articles 9 and 19 of the Covenant. The State party should also ensure that the monitoring of Internet use does not violate the rights to freedom of expression and privacy as defined in the Covenant.

Interestingly, the concluding observations of other treaty bodies do not refer to Article 19 of the ICCPR because their assessment of a state report is limited to the provisions of the treaty for which they have assumed responsibility. However, various treaty bodies have referred to the need for greater access to information in their concluding observations, which serves as evidence of the relationship between information and other human rights.

---

16 *Report on the Current Working Methods of the Treaty Bodies,* HRI/MC/2009/4 (June 24, 2009), at paras. 75–82. State parties are typically invited to report back to describe what steps have been taken after one year of the examination, and special rapporteurs are routinely appointed for this purpose.

17 *Concluding Observations of the Human Rights Committee: Islamic Republic of Iran,* CCPR/C/IRN/CO/3, available at http://iranhrdc.org/files/pdf_en/UN_Reports/CCPR.C.IRN.CO.3.pdf (accessed May 29, 2013).

For example, the Committee on the Rights of the Child, in its concluding observations in relation to the state report of Timor-Leste, was encouraged by the efforts of Timor-Leste in cooperating with the UN in disseminating information and providing human rights training relating to children's rights to government agencies, civil society, teachers, judicial officers, and other relevant professional groups, and recommended that this practice be continued.[18] The concluding observations also recommended that the state improve children's access to appropriate information from a diversity of sources, especially those aimed at the promotion of a child's social, spiritual, and moral well-being and physical and mental health.[19]

The Committee on the Protection of the Rights of All Migrant Workers and Members of Their Families expressed disappointment in the lack of information provided to migrant workers in Rwanda.[20] The committee recommended that Rwanda intensify its efforts to ensure that migrant workers and members of their families have effective access to information about their rights under the convention and under immigration law, in particular their rights to have access to basic social services, to join trade unions, and to the same treatment as nationals of the state party in respect to conditions of work.[21]

In examining issues relating to women's health in Paraguay, the Committee on the Elimination of Discrimination Against Women drew attention, in its concluding observations, to reproductive rights and the high mortality rate that is a consequence of unsafe abortions in that nation.[22] Among other things, the committee recommended that Paraguay adopt a patient privacy policy to safeguard doctor-patient confidentiality specifically when treating women for abortion complications, and that it "strengthen institutional health-care capacity and the implementation of programmes and policies aimed at providing effective access for women to health-care information and services, in particular regarding reproductive health and affordable contraceptive methods, with the aim of preventing clandestine abortions."

The process of state reporting is robust but inefficient. It can lead to the implementation of expert recommendations, but both the system and participating states are overburdened.[23] If the system is to operate efficiently, it must have the necessary human resources to do so and would benefit from

---

18   *Concluding Observations of the Committee on the Rights of the Child: Timor Leste*, CRC/C/TLS/CO/1 (Feb. 14, 2008), at paras. 22–23.

19   *Id.*, at paras. 37–38.

20   *Concluding Observations of the Committee on the Protection of the Rights of All Migrant Workers and Members of Their Families on the Initial Periodic Report of Rwanda*, CMW/C/RWA/CO/1 (Oct. 10, 2012).

21   *Id.*, at paras. 35–36.

22   *Concluding Observations of the Committee on the Elimination of Discrimination Against Women: Paraguay*, CEDAW/C/PRY/CO/6 (Nov. 8, 2011).

23   Schmidt, *supra* note 11, at 406. Many treaty bodies face backlogs that delay their examination of state reports by up to two years after their submission, and some states are more than a decade behind in their reporting obligations.

implementing a more selective approach toward the information it considers from stakeholders other than the state.[24] A streamlined approach to reporting would also assist in this regard.[25] There has been progress in the form of treaty body harmonization, which has simplified the process somewhat[26] and should be continued to accelerate the process of state reporting that could lead to increased implementation of access to information laws and initiatives on a timely basis.

Complaints Procedures through Treaty Bodies. Various human rights treaty bodies provide a mechanism that is designed to hear complaints that human rights have been violated. For example, the first Optional Protocol to the ICCPR provides a complaints procedure for violations under the ICCPR.[27] This instrument allows both states and individuals to commence claims against parties to the first Optional Protocol before the Human Rights Committee, although to date, the focus has been almost entirely on individual, as opposed to interstate, complaints.

After considering an allegation of the violation of rights, the relevant committee provides "views" or "opinions" that assess the merits of the complaint. These views have shown that the right to information includes a right whereby the media has access to information on public affairs[28] and the right of the general public to receive media output.[29] Other views have demonstrated that prisoners are entitled to access their medical records while incarcerated,[30] and

---

24 *Id.*, at 407–408. Notably, the majority of treaty bodies provide for participation of NGOs in the reporting process, which contributes greatly to the quality of the examination. However, the experience of some committees is that having too many NGOs with differing points of view can slow the process or lead to inconsistencies in the information provided on a particular issue to the point that no meaningful discussion takes place.

25 *Id.*, at note 11. This is particularly evident when one considers that many states are required to submit reports with overlapping issues to a number of different oversight bodies. In dealing with states that have delayed excessively in submitting their reports, the relevant committee may conduct a review of the country on the basis of information it has from existing stakeholders. Provisional concluding observations are then prepared and circulated to the state, but the relevant committee will only publish its provisional concluding observations in the absence of a response from the state.

26 *Id.*, at 415–417. Unfortunately, the recommendation that a single report be submitted made by the UN secretary-general in 2002 was rejected on the basis of the logistical challenges it presented to states. (Secretary-General, *Strengthening the United Nations: An Agenda for Further Change,* A/57/387 [Sep. 9, 2002], at paras. 52–54.) However, the treaty body reporting requirements did lead to harmonized reporting guidelines under each of the core instruments, which are expected to result in better compliance with reporting obligations of states. (Secretary-General, *Effective Implementation of International Instruments on Human Rights, Including Reporting Obligations under International Instruments on Human Rights,* A/63/280 [Aug. 13, 2008] Annex, at para. 42(d)).

27 Optional Protocol to the International Covenant on Civil and Political Rights, adopted by UN General Assembly Resolution 2200A (XXI), 21 UN GAOR Supp. (no. 16) at 59, UN Doc. A/6316 (1966), 999 U.N.T.S. 302, (Mar. 23, 1976).

28 See communication no. 633/95, *Gauthier v. Canada* (May 5, 1999).

29 See communication no. 1334/2004, *Mavlonov and Sa'di v. Uzbekistan* (Mar. 19, 2009).

30 See communication no. 726/1996, *Zheludkov v. Ukraine* (Oct. 29, 2002).

that a state's decisions that may impact the way of life and culture of minorities should be accompanied by a process of information sharing and consultation with affected communities.[31] These cases demonstrate that the complaints process under the rubric of the UN Human Rights Committee has led to useful commentary on the role of access to information in promoting development.

Regrettably, several key weaknesses prevent the treaty bodies' complaints procedures from reaching their full potential. The single greatest problem with treaty bodies' complaints procedures is that the views or opinions they release are not legally binding and cannot be strictly enforced.[32] Although follow-ups conducted by various treaty bodies have been encouraging in some instances, they do not have the effect of a formal judgment that can be enforced against the assets of a perpetrator of human rights violations.[33] Access to legal counsel presents another problem in extending the reach of the complaints process to victims. There is currently no requirement that a complainant retain legal counsel, and the procedural intricacies of the complaints process make the process challenging for an individual who does not have representation or who is illiterate. Accordingly, the process is weakened by the absence of a legal aid system that could serve impecunious complainants.[34]

UN Human Rights Council

The primary duties of the UN Human Rights Council are outlined in General Assembly Resolution 60/251.[35] Among these duties are promoting human rights education and learning, serving as a forum for dialogue on thematic issues, making recommendations to the General Assembly on developing new human rights standards, preventing human rights violations through dialogue and cooperation, and responding promptly to human rights emergencies. Accordingly, the Human Rights Council is positioned to widely circulate information that is useful in promoting development, rather than providing an aggrieved party with a remedy for the violation of its right to information.

---

31 See communication no. 1457/2006, *Poma v. Peru* (Mar. 27, 2009).

32 General Comment No. 33, CCPR/C/GC/33 (Nov. 5, 2008) at para. 11. The Human Rights Committee has stated that, although its views and opinions are not binding, they do "exhibit some important characteristics of a judicial decision." Moreover, "cross-fertilization" of human rights jurisprudence has been characterized by the recognition of treaty body case law before regional human rights bodies and domestic courts, and vice-versa (Schmidt, *supra* note 11, at 415). This development is a positive one in that it avoids legal fragmentation by crafting, albeit slowly, a harmonious body of human rights jurisprudence. (Schmidt, *Vers une jurisprudence international en matière des droits de l'homme: L'expérience du Comité des droits de l'homme de l'ONU*, in *Les juridictions internationales: Complémentarité ou concurrence?* 163–168 (Olivier Delas et al. eds., Bruylant 2005).

33 Schmidt, *supra* note 11, at 413. With the exception of in Colombia, no enabling legislation has been passed that would allow the views or opinions of a UN treaty body to be treated similarly to domestic judicial decisions.

34 *Id.*, at 410–411.

35 UN General Assembly Resolution A/RES/60/251 (Apr. 3, 2006), at para. 5.

The Universal Periodic Review. The Human Rights Council is obligated to undertake a universal periodic review (UPR), a peer review mechanism that addresses each state's fulfillment of its human rights obligations to ensure universal coverage and equal treatment.[36] The UPR has been the source of cautious optimism by human rights experts in that it has shown positive results in terms of implementing change.[37] Since 2008, the UPR has been used by reviewing states to make recommendations to improve access to information on at least 28 occasions. The UPR has led to recommendations that states "introduce and seek prompt passage of access to information legislation";[38] "strictly uphold freedom of the press, including public access to information, and ensure that the complaints made in this regard are properly investigated";[39] and "take measures to guarantee effective access for women and girls to information and services regarding sexual and reproductive health."[40] Twenty-seven of the 28 states in receipt of such recommendations have supported the recommendation provided.[41]

Special Procedures. The Human Rights Council also provides for certain special procedures that are designed to address either "country specific situations or thematic issues that concern all states."[42] Mandate holders, such as special rapporteurs, undertake country visits and fact-finding missions and examine complaints, report to the media, and publish their findings. The special rapporteur on the promotion and protection of the right to freedom of opinion and expression released a report on the "right of individuals to seek, receive and impart information and ideas of all kinds through the Internet."[43]

This report outlines the importance of Internet access in spreading information that promotes human rights, including the right to development, and stated in its recommendations:

> Unlike any other medium, the Internet enables individuals to seek,
> receive and impart information and ideas of all kinds instantaneously
> and inexpensively across national borders. By vastly expanding the

---

36   *Id.,* at para. 5(e).

37   Elvira Dominguez Redondo, *The Universal Periodic Review of the UN Human Rights Council: An Assessment of the First Session,* 7(13) Chinese J. of Intl. L. 721–734 (2008).

38   *Report of the Working Group on the Universal Periodic Review: Vietnam,* A/HRC/12/11 (UPR 2009), at para. 99.

39   *Report of the Working Group on the Universal Periodic Review: Georgia,* A/HRC/17/11 (UPR, 2011), at para. 105.

40   *Report of the Working Group on the Universal Periodic Review: Bosnia and Herzegovina,* A/HRC/14/16 (UPR, 2010), at para. 106.

41   *Report of the Working Group on the Universal Periodic Review: Serbia Addendum,* A/HRC/10/78 Add.1 (UPR, 2009), at para. 9. Only Serbia refused to support such a recommendation, but it did not reject it outright.

42   Schmidt, *supra* note 11, at 398.

43   *Report of the Special Rapporteur on Key Trends and Challenges to the Right of All Individuals to Seek, Receive and Impart Information and Ideas of All Kinds through the Internet,* A/HRC/17/27 (May 16, 2011).

capacity of individuals to enjoy their right to freedom of opinion and expression, which is an "enabler" of other human rights, the Internet boosts economic, social and political development, and contributes to the progress of humankind as a whole.[44]

The report also discusses many of the challenges faced in widely disseminating information online as a result of certain states actively taking steps to restrict information. For example, the special rapporteur found that "China, which has in place one of the most sophisticated and extensive systems for controlling information on the Internet, has adopted extensive filtering systems that block access to websites containing key terms such as 'democracy' and 'human rights.'"[45] The Human Rights Council has created a significant awareness of human rights issues, including access to information, among various stakeholders, which has led to valuable changes in policy, adoption of legislation, and increased protection of human rights.

Office of the High Commissioner for Human Rights

The UN Office of the High Commissioner for Human Rights (OHCHR) has the responsibility of promoting and protecting the effective enjoyment by all of all human rights.[46] This body cooperates with other UN entities and issues recommendations on how to better promote and protect human rights and improve the UN mechanisms relating to human rights. Among the priorities of the OHCHR is the coordination of UN education and public human rights information programs and the promotion of the realization of the right to development.

Knowledge of human rights is an essential precondition to their effective exercise, yet many developing countries have problematic rates of illiteracy, and individuals in all states remain unaware of international human rights standards.[47] These phenomena make the exercise of human rights difficult and necessitate the dissemination of information. It is in this regard that the UN human rights education program seeks to assist. The OHCHR contributes significantly to UN educational activities. It publishes various materials about human rights, including the right to development, and disseminates these publications widely by paper and by electronic means. The OHCHR relies on its many field offices for the production, translation, and distribution of materials and information in furtherance of human rights education initiatives and in training local officials and members of civil society.

Although these educational and training initiatives contribute to a general trend of human rights awareness, measuring their influence is challenging because the initiatives are rarely tied to specific measurable outcomes.

---

44   *Id.*, at para. 67.

45   *Id.*, at para. 29.

46   *General Assembly Resolution on the High Commissioner for the Promotion and Protection of All Human Rights,* A/RES/48/141 (Jan. 7, 1994).

47   Schmidt, *supra* note 11, at 420.

Moreover, their effectiveness is largely dependent on a cooperative local government that is not opposed to the promotion of human rights within its borders. The affiliations that the OHCHR has with domestic human rights bodies around the world are helpful in this respect, although these relationships cannot completely address, for example, access to information in a state where the reigning government does not have the political will to implement meaningful human rights initiatives.

Issue-Specific Conventions

The adoption of international treaties that deal with specific subject matter is another tool that can be used to liberalize access to information laws under the UN framework. The Aarhus Convention is one such example; it creates a linkage between the substantive right to a clean environment and procedural rights, including a right to information.[48] The convention entitles the general public to information regarding the state of the environment, public health, and other factors impacting the environment. The convention codifies the right to request and receive information[49] and imposes a duty on states to collect and disseminate information.[50] The right to information under this convention has been widely implemented by its parties.[51]

The drafting and adoption of treaties on specific topics and issues is bound to continue, and the UN framework provides states with a forum for doing so for the foreseeable future. States should take the opportunity that these instruments provide to bolster the public's right of access to information in relation to issues that impact the public interest. Doing so would allow groups and individuals who are affected by the issues dealt with in a given treaty to protect their own rights or seek help in doing so. This would be a significant step in expediting development initiatives, as the stakeholders on a given topic would be better able to take part in informed debate on matters of public importance.

Regional Organizations

The American Convention on Human Rights (ACHR),[52] the European Convention on Human Rights (ECHR),[53] and the African Charter[54] protect the right to information. These instruments have established human rights bodies

---

48 United Nations Economic Commission for Europe Convention on Access to Information, Public Participation in Decision-Making and Access to Justice in Environmental Matters (June 25, 1998). Approved by Council Decision 2005/370/EC (Feb. 17, 2005).

49 *Id.*, at art. 4.

50 *Id.*, at art. 5.

51 Malgosia Fitzmaurice, *Environmental Degradation*, in *International Human Rights Law* 637 (Daniel Moeckli et al. eds., Oxford U. Press 2010).

52 Art. 13, American Convention on Human Rights (1969).

53 Art. 10, European Convention on Human Rights (1950).

54 Art. 9, African Charter, *supra* note 1.

that issue written decisions involving the role of access to information in protecting human rights and thus promoting development. In addition, regional bodies can assist in the development of access to information legislation by adopting conventions or model laws that increase public participation, improve efficiency in government, and assist in protecting human rights.

Jurisprudence of Regional Human Rights Bodies

The case of *Claude Reyes and Others v. Chile* was the first holding by an international tribunal that the right to freedom of expression includes a right to seek and receive information held by the government.[55] The applicants in this case requested information regarding a deforestation project on the Rio Condor from Chile's Foreign Investment Committee. The Chilean courts provided no acceptable reasons for the committee's refusal to release the information, so the Inter-American Court found that the applicants' right to information under Article 13 of the ACHR was violated. In the wake of this decision, Chile adopted access to information legislation and began training public officials in how to properly administer access to information requests pursuant to the Inter-American Court's direction and supervision.

K.H. and Others v. Slovakia was the first in a series of cases before the European Court of Human Rights that involved the issue of forced sterilization of Roma women from Slovakia.[56] Eight women suspected that they were sterilized without their consent while in Slovakian hospitals to give birth. The women sought copies of their medical records to determine their health status and to protect the integrity of the evidence contained therein for the purpose of potential litigation. The European Court of Human Rights found that Slovakia's refusal to provide access to medical records constituted a violation of the ECHR. The court took the view that Article 8, which deals with the right to respect for one's private and family life, includes informational rights related to health and health status. In addition, the court found that Article 6, which provides a right of access to justice, was violated as a result of the failure to share the information in question.

In *Társaság a Szabadságjogokért (Hungarian Civil Liberties Union) v. Hungary*, the European Court of Human Rights dealt with a request by the Hungarian Civil Liberties Union, a civil rights NGO, to access a copy of a complaint filed with the Constitutional Court by a member of Parliament.[57] The complaint sought a review of amendments to national drug legislation, which was an area of interest for the NGO. The Constitutional Court denied the NGO's request to access the complaint on the basis that it contained personal data and could only be shared with the consent of the author. The court found that the activities of NGOs are essential contributions to an informed public debate

---

55   *Claude Reyes and Others v. Chile,* IACtHR Series C No. 151 (Sep. 19, 2006).

56   *K.H. and Others v. Slovakia,* ECHR 2009/13 (Apr. 28, 2009), no. 32881/04 (4th sec.).

57   *Társaság a Szabadságjogokért (Hungarian Civil Liberties Union) v. Hungary,* App. No. 37374/05, judgment of Apr. 14, 2009.

and warrant similar protection as that afforded to the media. The court ruled that by interfering with the NGO's ability to gather information on matters of public importance, Hungarian authorities violated the applicant's right of access to information.

In *SERAC and Others v. Nigeria*, the African Commission examined a case involving the exploitation of Ogoniland in Nigeria by a subsidiary of Shell Oil Co. and the Nigerian National Petroleum Company.[58] The exploitation was done in a manner that caused significant degradation of the environment, as well as harm to the health of local residents. A group of local and international NGOs launched a complaint to the African Commission, claiming that the Nigerian government was responsible for human rights violations. In rendering a decision, the commission highlighted the importance of information in promoting the right to a healthy environment by finding that the government should have afforded the public an opportunity to participate in decision making through a public consultation process before commencing the project.[59] Among other things, the commission ordered the government to conduct environmental and social impact assessments and to provide information on health and environmental risks to communities that are likely to be affected by oil operations in the future.[60]

Regional Instruments and Model Laws

In addition to the dispute resolution mechanism for international human rights bodies, the political organs of regional organizations can improve the flow of information by adopting conventions that guarantee access to information. The Council of Europe did precisely that when it passed the Convention on Access to Official Documents.[61] This is the first binding international legal instrument that recognizes a general right of access to official documents held by public authorities. In summarizing the treaty, the Council of Europe stated:

> Transparency of public authorities is a key feature of good governance and an indicator of whether or not a society is genuinely democratic and pluralist, opposed to all forms of corruption, capable of criticising those who govern it, and open to enlightened participation of citizens in matters of public interest. The right of access to official documents is also essential to the self-development of people and to the exercise of fundamental human rights. It also strengthens public authorities' legitimacy in the eyes of the public, and its confidence in them.[62]

---

58   *The Social and Economic Rights Action Center and the Center for Economic and Social Rights v. Nigeria,* African Commission on Human and Peoples' Rights, Communication No. 155/96 (2001).

59   *Id.*

60   *Id.*

61   *Council of Europe Convention on Access to Official Documents,* CETS No. 205 (June 18, 2009).

62   Summary available at http://www.conventions.coe.int/Treaty/EN/Summaries/Html/205.htm (accessed May 29, 2013).

The instrument establishes a right of access to official documents and sets out certain permissible limitations on the disclosure of information. It is designed as a set of minimum standards to be applied in the processing of requests for access to official documents and allows for states to build on its contents by passing domestic laws that provide more robust access to official documents.

The African Charter establishes a right of access to information[63] that is elaborated on by the Declaration of Principles on Freedom of Expression in Africa.[64] These instruments guarantee "the right of access to information as a fundamental inalienable human right and as an indispensable component of democracy and development, including socio-economic development."[65] Notwithstanding the recognition by African states that access to information can lead to extensive development, there is a dearth of domestic legislation that provides substance or procedure to the right to information on the continent.[66]

In response to the need for implementation of domestic legislation in Africa, the African Commission adopted the Model Law on Access to Information in Africa.[67] The model law is formulated "as a guide for the development, adoption or review of access to information legislation by African states."[68] The African Commission, as well as civil society organizations that contributed to the effort, should be commended for their work in adopting this model law, which is an important development that other regional human rights bodies should note. Not only African states suffer from an absence of access to information legislation or lack of effective legislation. Other regional organizations should take steps to offer similar guidelines to states that wish to implement or improve legislation on access to information by adopting a model law or convention that is tailored to the needs of member states. These documents should be regularly reviewed and kept up-to-date.

---

63   Art. 9, African Charter, *supra* note 1.

64   Declaration of Principles on Freedom of Expression in Africa, African Commission on Human and Peoples' Rights, 32nd session (Oct. 17–23, 2002).

65   Preamble, Model Law on Access to Information for Africa, African Commission on Human and Peoples' Rights, 53rd session (Apr. 11, 2013) (hereinafter, Model Law).

66   As of 2013, only 11 states had adopted access to information legislation: South Africa (Promotion of Access to Information Act in 2000); Angola (Freedom of Information Law in 2002); Zimbabwe (Access to Information and Protection of Privacy Act in 2002); Uganda (Access to Information Act in 2005); Ethiopia (Freedom of Information and Mass Media Law in 2008); Liberia (Freedom of Information Act in 2010); Guinea (Organic Law on the Right of Access to Public Information in 2010); Nigeria (Freedom of Information Law in 2011); Tunisia (Decree on Access to the Administrative Documents of Public Authorities of Tunisia in 2011); Niger (Charter on Access to Public and Administrative Documents in 2011); and Rwanda (Law Relating to Access to Information in 2013).

67   Model Law, *supra* note 65.

68   *Id.*, at 14.

Domestic Access to Information Legal Regimes

Aside from any obligations that arise in international law, the right to freedom of information is embedded in the constitutions of many states and given content in legislation in at least 95 states around the world.[69] When addressing freedom of information in domestic jurisdictions, the relevant legal regimes are typically characterized by the guarantee of access to data held by the state, and on occasion by private bodies, subject to certain classes of exemptions that justify the government's refusal to disclose information to the requesting party. This form of access to information is important in the context of the right to development because it promotes transparent and accountable governance, which is essential to a functioning democracy.

In discussing the essential components of domestic access to information legislation, the UN Human Rights Committee's General Comment No. 34 provides a description of appropriate legislation on access to information when it states:

> The procedures should provide for the timely processing of requests for information according to clear rules that are compatible with the Covenant. Fees for requests for information should not be such as to constitute an unreasonable impediment to access to information. Authorities should provide reasons for any refusal to provide access to information. Arrangements should be put in place for appeals from refusals to provide access to information as well as in cases of failure to respond to requests.[70]

In some circumstances, where public officials refuse to provide information through the process contemplated by law, a requester can seek recourse through the courts, which determine whether the relevant legislation prohibits the disclosure of information. This section draws on the decisions of various domestic courts to illustrate how a constitution or legislative regime provides a right of access to information that can enhance development within national borders.

Domestic Jurisprudence on Access to Information

CCII Systems Ltd. v. S. A. Fakie NO and Others was the first major case decided by the courts under the South African Promotion of Access to Information Act.[71] It involved the acquisition of a strategic defense package for approximately R 30 billion (approximately US$3 billion). This arms deal has been tarnished by allegations of corruption and secrecy that continue today. A private company that provides defense-related software and computer systems sought access to the draft version of a report that was subsequently altered and accepted by Parliament. The complainant wished to use the report to determine whether

---

69   Art. 19, Freedom of Information, available at http://www.article19.org/pages/en/freedom-of
-information-more.html (accessed May 1, 2013).

70   General Comment No. 34, *supra* note 13, at para. 19.

71   *CCII Systems Ltd. v. S. A. Fakie NO and Others*, High Court of South Africa, Case No.4636/2002.

it had been unfairly excluded from the transaction due to political pressure or impropriety, as opposed to the merits of its bid. The court ordered that a variety of documents relating to the arms deal, including the draft report, must be produced. In this case, access to information legislation was used to promote transparency in government, which is essential to development because of the role transparency plays in preventing corrupt practices.

In *Union for Civil Liberties (PUCL) and Another v. Union of India and Another*, the Supreme Court of India dealt with an attempt by the government to overrule one of its prior decisions by implementing legislation.[72] The prior decision held that Indian citizens are entitled to know certain information about public officials and candidates for public office, including their assets, criminal records, and educational backgrounds, as a result of the constitutional right to freedom of expression.[73] Subsequently, the Indian Parliament amended the Representation of the People Act such that candidates would not be required to make information available that related to their educational qualifications or assets "notwithstanding anything contained in the judgment of any court or directions issued by the Election Commission."[74] The Union for Civil Liberties challenged the constitutionality of the legislation, and the court held that the right to freedom of expression includes voters' "fundamental right to know relevant antecedents of the candidate contesting the elections"[75] and deemed the relevant portions of the legislation to be "illegal, null and void."[76]

In *Greenwatch (U) Ltd v. Attorney General of Uganda and Uganda Electricity Transmission Co. Ltd*, an environmental NGO used Uganda's constitutional right of access to information to prevent the construction of the World Bank–funded Bujagali dam.[77] Greenwatch Ltd. had requested documents relating to the project that both the Ugandan government and the World Bank initially refused to release. The government alleged that the documents being sought did not exist, and later it argued that the disclosure of the requested records would threaten national security. The Uganda High Court did not accept these submissions and concluded that the records being sought were public documents to which Ugandan citizens were entitled access. Although the documents were not released to Greenwatch Ltd. on the basis that it had not adduced evidence as to its status as a citizen, the documents were subsequently made public and were reviewed by the International River Network, which concluded that Ugandans would pay excessive costs if the dam project

---

72   *Union for Civil Liberties (PUCL) and Another v. Union of India and Another*, AIR [2003] SC 2363.

73   *Union of India v. Association for Democratic Reforms and Another* (2002), AIR 2112; 2002 (3) SCR 294.

74   S. 33(b) of Amended Representation of the People Act.

75   *Union for Civil Liberties, supra* note 73, at 9.

76   *Id.*, at p. 41.

77   *Greenwatch (U) Ltd v. Attorney General of Uganda and Uganda Electricity Transmission Co. Ltd* (2002), HCT-00-CV-MC-0139, High Ct. of Uganda.

were to proceed according to the plan at the time.[78] Moreover, it was revealed that a government minister had received a payment from the subsidiary of the project's main contractor.[79] This led the World Bank to suspend its payments for the dam project, which avoided the consequence of excessive payments from Ugandan citizens.

Obstacles to and Recommendations for Promoting Development through Domestic Access to Information Legislation

The Information Abyss: An Absence of a Legal Regime Governing Access to Information. Although many states have implemented legal regimes that govern access to information,[80] the majority have not adopted similar legal frameworks. The absence of a legislative framework that regulates access to information presents obvious problems for the achievement of freedom of information. To begin with, without explicit implementation of legislation or a constitutional provision that confirms the existence of a right of access in a given state, individuals seeking information have little legal authority on which they can rely that would persuade a government that is reluctant to share what is being sought. Additionally, where a right to information is protected in a state's constitution or bill of rights, there may be no procedure for accessing public records to provide the scope of the right's content. Without a legal process that provides for the means to access information, it can be extremely challenging to identify when a violation of the right occurs or to seek recourse if a violation is established.

The obvious solution for states without a legal regime that governs access to information is to adopt one. However, for most states, that is no small task and cannot be achieved without serious political will.[81] As discussed previously, some institutions have produced model laws or binding international covenants that can serve as guidelines when it comes to creating or improving legal regimes on access to information that would be of assistance to states without appropriate legislation. It is essential to recognize that even without freedom of information laws, information can be used to promote development. While a government is taking steps toward the implementation of appropriate legislation, it can disseminate information to the public. For example, a government that does not have access to information legislation may provide public access to libraries, work toward increasing enrollment in schools, protect freedom of expression in the media, expand Internet access to

---

78 *Transparency International Kenya, FOI in Kenya: The Value of the Right to Information*, 58 Adili Newsletter (2004).

79 D. Pallister, *Africa Dam's Passage "Eased by Bribes,"* The Guardian (Nov. 3, 2003), available at http://www.guardian.co.uk/uk/2003/nov/03/davidpallister.

80 Art. 19, Freedom of Information *supra* note 69.

81 *See* http://www.globalintegrity.org/node/512 (accessed May 1, 2013). Global Integrity, an NGO based out of South Africa and the United States, has reported that Ghana's failure to present the access to information bill to parliament, a bill that has been pending since 2002, is due to a lack of political will on the part of the government.

areas that do not have it, or implement any one of a number of other measures that improve the circulation of human knowledge.

Insufficient or Inappropriate Domestic Legal Regimes. Access to information regimes may hamper freedom of information, either by having insufficient provisions that regulate the entitlement of the public to information or through the presence of legislation that is specifically designed to limit the spread of information. Assessing the adequacy of an access to information regime on an ongoing basis is as important as ensuring that the framework is appropriate at the time of adoption. Without continually improving the legal regime governing access to information, even states that were once praised for their progressive legislation will eventually be left with archaic laws.

On some occasions, the problems with existing laws are not limited to the inadequacy of the legislation governing access to information but pertain to instances where the law may have come into existence with the goal of limiting the public's access to information.[82] When seeking to improve access to information legislation, states should look to existing model laws, conduct wide public consultations in good faith, and seek input from other stakeholders or experts, including the media, interested NGOs, and academics. By gathering input from these parties on an ongoing basis, states can ensure that the needs of their population are best served by the laws in place.

Good Law Gone Bad: Insufficient Implementation of Existing Legal Regimes. The failure, or inability, to implement access to information laws that are otherwise commendable is a significant problem that stifles the flow of information and represents a disservice to the population that is subject to the law. One source of this problem is the insufficient number of personnel in government departments who are allocated to work in freedom of information. Solving the dilemma of insufficient human resources requires a rebalancing of the priorities of government departments. It is not enough to say that more funds must be allocated to freedom of information without recognizing that those funds must be taken from another area. Identifying which department's funds must be cut in order to boost the capacity for compliance with freedom of information laws must be the prerogative of the individual government, which is in a position to understand the most pressing priorities of its constituency.

---

82 The Commonwealth Human Rights Initiative, an international NGO that seeks to ensure the protection of human rights within the commonwealth, has been critical of Zimbabwe for this reason. This NGO explained that although Zimbabwe's constitution protects the right to receive and impart ideas and information (Art. 20, Constitution of Zimbabwe, published as a schedule to the Zimbabwe Constitution Order 1979 [S.I. 1979/1600 of the United Kingdom] and as amended to No. 19 of Feb. 13, 2009), the Access to Information and Protection to Privacy Act in that country "provides only very limited provisions on access and privacy, and the main thrust of the Act is to give the government more powers for media censorship and control." See http://www.humanrightsinitiative.org/programs/ai/rti/international/laws_&_papers.htm (accessed May 1, 2013). Furthermore, under the Official Secrets Act, any communication of official information is unauthorized, unless disclosure to the person seeking the information is explicitly authorized.

However, a dedicated portion of a government's budget must be assigned to comply with freedom of information legislation.[83]

An additional problem associated with implementing good law is poor record keeping. Although this may be a consequence of inadequate funding, it also may be due to the absence of an effective system. Establishing effective record-keeping systems is important for every government department and would dramatically reduce the number of mysterious disappearances of government records. It is important to recognize that different government departments deal with different kinds of records. Thus, the system ought to be tailored to the needs of the relevant department. As technology increasingly infiltrates all aspects of human life, it would be preferable, where possible, to include an electronic record-keeping system that complements the use of hard copies. Electronic records would also promote efficiency within the government department by making the search for, and production of, requested documents less complicated.

The lack of adequate training provided to government officials is a major hurdle for the improvement of access to information. Training must be provided to employees who are designated to work in access to information as well as front-line employees. The information provided to government employees in training of this kind, including the up-to-date contact information of the relevant person within departments, should be consolidated in a manual that is made readily available to all employees.

A final consideration that detracts from the successful implementation of an otherwise impressive legislative regime is the lack of a capacity to make requests by groups that could benefit most from information. There are many reasons why this problem may arise. For example, a group may not be aware of its right to access to information. In situations where there is an awareness of a right to information, the group may not understand the connection between holding information and bringing about tangible benefits to personal lives or the community, or there may not be an understanding of the process of filing a request. In some situations, the requester may understand the process completely, but due to other considerations, such as the lack of an Internet connection or financial constraints, the requestor may not be able to file the request in the method contemplated by the legislation.

Civil society organizations have a significant role to play in assisting with these issues. By providing training to community leaders or representatives from other sectors of the population, groups can be educated on their right to know, the process through which they can exercise that right, and the benefits associated with obtaining information. As well, civil society organizations can

---

83   The Open Democracy Advice Centre has recommended that 0.5 percent of an information holder's annual budget be dedicated to implementing South Africa's access to information legislation. *See PAIA Civil Society Network Shadow Report 2011*, available at http://www.saha .org.za/news/2011/September/paia_civil_society_network_releases_shadow_report.htm (accessed May 1, 2013).

assist by providing the capacity to file requests to the appropriate government bodies on behalf of the person or group seeking information.

Conclusion

Development is a major issue on the global political and legal landscape and is being increasingly recognized and implemented by states as they strive to provide citizens with the opportunity to lead meaningful and fulfilling lives. Despite the increasing recognition of development as a legal right and political goal, much of the world remains plagued by poverty, disease, illiteracy, and other indices that suggest that development initiatives have not reached their potential. A major stumbling block in implementing development programs has been the failure to effectively disseminate information that would allow groups and individuals to meaningfully participate in democratic governance.

Information allows individuals and groups a full measure of participation in public life, promotes efficient democratic governance, and protects human rights. Although a significant number of states have taken steps to implement the public right of access to information, many have no law that gives context to the international or constitutional legal right to seek and receive public information. Given that freedom of information is inextricably linked to the promotion of human rights, including the right to development, the failure to implement freedom of information laws at either the international or the domestic level is unacceptable.

The United Nations, regional organizations, and many national governments have taken steps to increase the flow of information, which is a laudable objective, although the results have been mixed. There has been significant progress in raising awareness of the right to information and drawing attention to violations of that right. In addition, dispute resolution mechanisms have been established that provide remedies for the victims of a violation of their right to information. However, the systems that deliver the benefits are often inefficient and their reach is not universal. If states, acting collectively or unilaterally, can muster the political will to continually monitor and improve access to information by global citizens, they can expect to witness expedited progress as a result of investments in development initiatives.

The Search for Opportunity and Inclusion
Insecurity and Migration

EMILIO C. VIANO

In the aftermath of the terrorist attacks that shook the United States on September 11, 2001, and then Spain, the United Kingdom, India, many Middle Eastern countries, and many other places worldwide, extraordinary measures have been taken to control and limit migration. Migration has become strongly "securitized." Among other things, this means that the perspectives, analyses, policies, and legislation related to migration are now mostly framed from the point of view of the security of the state and not so much in terms of the security of the migrants. Indeed, the security of many migrants is endangered from the moment they decide to migrate, and that danger grows more acute as they take a perilous journey that may lead to their victimization, enslavement, and even death. Even prior to migration, the decision to migrate is often related to the insecurity of their environment, racked by conflict, ethnic or religious strife, economic crisis, criminal violence, and fear.[1]

In many developing countries, the violence of development itself is at the root of a score of insecurities that cause people to move away, because they are forced, at times at gunpoint, to leave, or because they are in search of a more just and favorable environment. In a special issue of the journal *Development*, Arturo Escobar[2] underlines the point that violence is essential to development and strongly connected to displacement, an aspect of modernization that has become so common that it is taken for granted and overlooked.[3] One of the many glaring current examples of this dynamic is the construction of the Belo Monte Dam on the river Xingu in the state of Parà in Brazil. This massive project involves the building of water deviation canals, the flooding of thousands of acres of Amazonian forest, and the creation of a lake of some 500 square kilometers (50,000 hectares), making it very difficult and at times impossible for the indigenous populations to use altered fluvial routes for fishing and navigation in a region without roads. The project will uproot and displace indigenous tribes from their tribal lands and have serious negative effects on flora, fauna, and the climate of the region. Violence and the heavy intervention of the Brazilian military police to forcibly remove indigenous tribes accompany

---

1   Ibrahim Sirkeci, *Conflict, the Environment of Human Insecurity and Migration in Iraq in the Aftermath of 2003*, in *Rethinking Global Migration: Practices, Policies and Discourses in the European Neighbourhood* 161–175 (H. Rittersberger-Tilic ed., KORA 2008).

2   Arturo Escobar, *Development, Violence and the New Imperial Order*, 47(1) Dev. 15–21 (2004).

3   Marianne Marchand, *The Violence of Development and the Migration/Insecurity Nexus: Labour Migration in a North American Context*, 29(7) Third World Q. 1375–1388 (2008).

the construction of Belo Monte, along with drug and human trafficking, prostitution, land grabs, and the uprooting of the existing communities.

Similar events are taking place in the Omo River region, one of Africa's—
and the world's—last, great undiscovered places, home to the so-called van-
ishing tribes of Ethiopia. The massive Gilgel Gibe III Dam is scheduled to
begin operations several hundred miles upriver from where the tribes live.
While the controversial project will more than double electrical output in Ethiopia, it will destroy a fragile environment and displace as many as 200,000
indigenous people who rely on the Omo's natural flood cycles to produce
their crops, and whose land may now go dry. Not only were the tribes not
consulted; most locals are reportedly unaware that these changes are coming.
The dam will have catastrophic consequences for the eight different tribes of
the Omo River, who already live a marginal life in this dry and very challenging area. That the end is near in a region once inhabited by some of our earliest
ancestors (*Australopithecus* walked these very river banks) not only is sad but
also points out the violent displacement and life-threatening insecurity that
"development" engenders.

The same is true with farmers forced off their land in various parts of
China; with fishing communities losing their livelihood because of devastating pollution affecting marine life in the Great Barrier Reef area of Australia
due to massive mining and shipping of minerals and the concomitant port
construction and expansion of ship traffic; with other indigenous people losing their land and way of life to powerful and well-connected entrepreneurs
expanding their landholdings to raise cattle or to engage in open-air mining
in the "Triple Frontier" region shared by Brazil, Paraguay, and Argentina, an
area until recently considered impenetrable. Some 20 indigenous groups in
the area, including a totally isolated group in Paraguay believed never to have
had contact with "modern" people, have been abused, forcibly displaced, and
reduced to a life of homelessness, poverty, begging, alcoholism, and resorting to prostitution and petty crime for survival.[4] The Mapuche in southern
Chile and the descendants of the Maya in Chiapas, Mexico, have faced and are
still confronted with similar depredations, displacement, and insecurity, often
with the connivance of the state and the weight of the law.

The insecurity at the root of migration and the violence that accompanies
it are different in nature, intensity, and aftermath, depending on the gender of
the migrant. Although often unrecognized, there are diverse types of insecurity and violence for men and women that stem from their different social and
economic status, their access to power and control, and the equation of power
between them.[5]

---

4   *Sentencia Final,* Tribunal del Juicio Ético a las Transnacionales (Nov. 11, 2011), available at
     http://juicioalastransnacionales.org/2011/11/sentencia-final-del-tribunal-del-juicio-etico-a
     -las-transnacionales/.

5   Marchand, *supra* note 3; and Ibrahim Sirkeci, Jeffrey Cohen, & Pinar Yazgan, *The Turkish Cul-
     ture of Migration: Flows between Turkey and Germany, Socio-economic Development and Conflict,*
     9(1) Migration Letters 33–46 (2012).

Security for the State or for the Migrant?

Since the terrorist attacks in the United States and various other countries, the issues of migration and security have become inextricably linked in current political theory and debate. What "security" means varies largely, of course, depending on who is using the term and why.

A framework for envisioning the relationship between cross-border migration and security, developed by Fiona Adamson,[6] posits three central areas in which migration and the interests of the state may intersect: the sovereignty of the state, the balance of power among the states, and the nature of violent conflict in the international system. One could add other key areas such as the social, cultural, or religious identity of the core inhabitants; the ultimate control over natural, human, and cultural resources, including the language spoken; and the social mores, customs, and legal tenets steeped in a particular tradition and understanding of reality. While migration is generally connected to the security of the state, it is less often linked to individual or human security. Adamson[7] also stresses the fundamental difference in perspective, and therefore in analysis, when one links migration to national security or to human security. While "not necessarily . . . diametrically opposed," the perspectives represent different analytical lenses through which one can assess the security impact of international migration.[8]

Thanks to today's wide and live coverage of world events, there is considerable awareness and appreciation of the hardships and perils of all stages of migration. The migrants themselves recounting their experience; the visual documentation of their suffering made possible by widely available filming technology; the scholarly and action-oriented analysis of what the migrants went through—all these sources support viewing migration as presenting considerable, and at times lethal, challenges to human security. Moreover, the policies and actions taken, mostly by the state, but at times also by individuals, vigilantes, or nonofficial groups, constitute an additional major threat to migrants. Consequently, it seems correct to "[reconceptualize] security in multidimensional and multilevel terms."[9]

In other words, given the plight of many migrants, and the policies and actions of the countries and people they may encounter on their journey or upon reaching their destination, it is justified, indeed necessary, to view the relationship between migration and security above and beyond the dangers that migration may generate for the state, including those stemming from the state's response to it. This change of the lens through which migration is seen

---

6   Fiona Adamson, *Crossing Borders: International Migration and National Security*, 31(1) Intl. Sec. 165–199 (2006).

7   *Id.*

8   *Id.*, at 167.

9   J. Ann Tickner, *Gender in International Relations* 128 (Columbia U. Press 1992).

provides considerable advantages for a realistic understanding of what "migration and security" means "from below," for those directly involved in it and who, most often, are not asked.[10] This applies especially to the dynamics and relations of cultural, linguistic, legal, and financial dominance and control. The resulting chasms and insecurities need to be recognized and stressed. Shining a light on contextually dependent interactions, relationships, and actions is very helpful in analyzing and understanding migration. Recognizing, valuing, and analyzing how marginalized people live and what they experience, especially women and children, is indispensable to gaining a deeper understanding of the connection between apparently common daily events and experiences and the seemingly far-distant issues of international politics and economics.[11] For example, there are strong commonalities between the experiences of Sub-Saharan migrants attempting to get to Europe through North Africa and those trying to get to the United States through Mexico, to Australia through Indonesia and Timor, to Malaysia through Thailand from Myanmar/Burma, and so on, worldwide.

There is no question that migration is a major political, human, and financial challenge facing especially the developed countries today but affecting almost every country, offering a glimpse of hope and a better life to those who live generally in more desperate situations. Poverty, after all, is a relative concept. Even a slight improvement in earnings, obtaining employment, receiving better health and education services, or providing a springboard to a yet better country is enough of a reason for people to face countless hardships to move, at times just "next door."

Technology, the Economy, and the Ebbs and Flows of Migration

The technological advances that make it so much easier and cheaper to travel internationally, communicate with visual contact (e.g., through Skype), send and receive money, move back and forth depending on needs and on the season, and maintain linguistic, religious, cultural, and affective ties have led to an unstoppable surge of migratory movements that characterize much of the international political, labor, and financial sectors of the world today. This surge is most visible where there are land bridges that permit easier contacts, such as between Mexico and Central America and the United States or between western and eastern Europe. The continuous and unabated series of armed conflicts in the world, whether international or domestic, has also generated in many parts of the world massive movements of people seeking to escape mayhem, death, and destruction. From the mass migrations of principally Eastern Europeans after World War II, which led to the creation of the United Nations High Commission for Refugees (UNHCR), to those fleeing

---

10   Gunhild Jorgensen & Kirsti Stuvoy, *Gender, Resistance and Human Security*, 37(2) Sec. Dialogue 207–228 (2006); Jane Freedman, *Analysing the Gendered Insecurities of Migration*, 14(1) Intl. Feminist J. Pol. 36–55 (2012).

11   Jorgensen & Stuvoy, *supra* note 10, at 223; Freedman, *supra* note 10, at 38.

conflict related to the partition of India and other episodes of decolonization in Asia and Africa, to people escaping war, killings, and destruction in South Asia, Central America, East Timor, Darfur and South Sudan, Liberia, Sierra Leone, the Democratic Republic of Congo, Iraq, Afghanistan, Turkey, Burma, and most recently Syria, one can clearly correlate insecurity at home with the quest for security elsewhere.[12]

Even in the case of financial and political turmoil, which does not necessarily involve armed conflict, the ease and low cost of communications awareness of other lifestyles and opportunities abroad through the media, and historical and cultural ties can spur considerable emigration. Thus, many people from South American countries undergoing deep political change and economic uncertainty—such as Argentina, Peru, Bolivia, Ecuador, Venezuela, Nicaragua, Honduras, and El Salvador—migrated during the past 20 years, especially to countries such as Italy or Spain. They have now begun to return to their original countries in response to the economic turmoil and downturn experienced in those European (and other) nations to which they emigrated. Ironically, their countries of origin now offer increased opportunities and attractive possibilities. And even some of the European natives from those same emigrant-destination countries might now migrate abroad. Thus, a country of immigration can become quite rapidly a country of emigration, and vice versa. For example, recent data show that in 2011 the number of Spanish citizens leaving Spain to reside abroad grew 8.2 percent and in 2012 6.3 percent (in 2012, the number was 114,413 persons, 44,000 of them born in Spain). The majority of Spanish citizens living abroad reside in South America, especially Argentina and Brazil, and in Cuba. In relative terms, the countries that in 2012 experienced the most significant increase of Spanish immigrants were Ecuador, Chile, and Peru.[13] Most of the migrants from Spain are naturalized immigrants who are returning to their country of birth.[14]

Ireland, too, can be seen as a country where immigration and emigration fairly often and quickly change direction. Since 1700, and especially because of the Great Famine of 1840, Ireland has been an exporter of millions of emigrants, creating what is called the Irish Diaspora. Presently, it is estimated that 80 million people worldwide could claim some Irish descent, with 50 million of them resident in the United States. Ten percent of British citizens have at least one Irish grandparent.[15] In the 1990s, however, Ireland's economic boom transformed the country into one of "net immigration," with significant numbers of immigrants arriving from outside the European Union. Many Irish

---

12   Sirkeci, *supra* note 1.

13   20minutos.es, *El numero de españoles en el extranjero crece un 6.3% en un año y roza los dos millones* (Mar. 20, 2013).

14   RTVE.es, *El numero de españoles residentes en el extranjero creció en más de 114.000 en 2012* (Mar. 20, 2013).

15   Owen Bowcott, *More Britons Applying for Irish Passports,* Guardian (Manchester, Sept. 13, 2006).

nationals also returned to Ireland from abroad. The enlargement of the European Union to encompass eastern European countries generated a major immigration wave from those countries into Ireland as recently as 2004–2008.[16] Now, with the economic crisis and unemployment hovering around 15 percent, Ireland is once more a country of emigration. Reportedly, between April 2011 and April 2012, 87,000 people left the country looking for a job elsewhere. The data on emigration from Ireland in 2012 show a 240 percent increase from the low number of 2002. The concurrent moving in and out of Ireland by migrants during the past 10 years or so is a dramatic and vivid testament to the unprecedented fluctuations that can take place today at short notice.[17] These drastic changes reflect, and in turn generate, strong feelings and a reality of insecurity and vulnerability.

Additionally, the fact that wealth inequality is falling in most of the world, but rising in the West, foretells new tides of migration, away from the traditional countries of immigration and toward the countries once considered the major source of emigration. Not only is extreme poverty disappearing but also the world as a whole is being transformed into a more equal place, with the developed countries actually going against that trend. This will no doubt profoundly affect current patterns of dominance and of perceived superiority, and alter worldwide migratory currents.

Migration, Terrorism, and Securing the Border

Making migration, and particularly irregular migration, a priority policy issue, especially in the European Union and the United States, is no doubt related to the vast effort to "securitize" it. The expression "irregular migration" mostly covers the cross-border movement of people who enter a country lacking that country's permission to do so. A "regular" or "legal" migrant can become "irregular" as well; for example, the migrant might violate the terms of her visa, overstay his visa, or commit a crime. There is an ample vocabulary referring to this phenomenon. In English, the most common term is "illegal" migrant, while, for example, in French, it is "irregular" migrant or "*sans papiers*." For many reasons, including disagreements on its definition, there are no firm data on irregular migration. Because it is an underground phenomenon, it is not recorded. Consequently, it is not possible to measure it accurately or reliably. It is estimated.

Irregular migration is increasingly seen as primarily a security problem. For this reason, current efforts to reform immigration laws in the United States, for example, are prefaced, first and foremost, by "securing the border"

---

16   Martin Ruhs, *Ireland: From Rapid Immigration to Recession* (country profile, Migration Info., Source, Migration Info. Inst., Sept. 2009).

17   Mary Gilmartin, *The Changing Landscape of Irish Migration, 2000–2012* (Working Paper No. 69, Natl. Inst. for Regl. & Spatial Analysis, Natl. U. of Ireland); Ibrahim Sirkeci, Philip L. Martin, & Eugen Stark, *Editorial: Migration and Development: Comparing Mexico–US and Turkey–Europe*, 9(1) Migration Letters 1–10 (2012).

to make the subject politically palatable. Among the most salient measures taken to demonstrate the government's commitment to security are the construction of a wall hundreds of kilometers long; the use of increased land and air patrols; the deployment of drones to patrol the border nonstop; the use of sensory and night-vision devices to detect movement in remote areas, especially at night; the enlistment of locals to help patrol, spot movement, and report it, and even confront irregular migrants; and making it a crime to provide assistance, food, or water to irregular immigrants crossing the vast desert between Mexico and the United States.[18] In the United States, sealing the border is considered an indispensable prerequisite to regularizing the status of the irregular immigrants who are already in the country, as if this would be a permanent solution and the end of the irregular immigration for years to come.

"Irregular" immigration has been seen and depicted as a threat to the national economy, to the labor market, to decent wages, to gains in compensation and benefits, and to the national heritage, culture, religion, and language. Above all, it has been tied to the menace of international terrorism.[19] Irregular immigration is considered by many to be the major method of entry for foreign terrorists, who can then take advantage of the weaknesses of the system and infiltrate the nation, establishing criminal and terrorist cells in neighborhoods dominated by their ethnic group, and subsequently create havoc and destruction. This perspective has gained a lot of currency, especially after the attacks in Madrid in March 2004 and in London in July 2005; the failed attacks against U.S. airlines by the so-called shoe bomber, Richard Reid, in 2001 and by the so-called underwear bomber, Umar Farouk Abdulmutallab, in 2009; and the continuing perceived threat posed by some immigrant militants in EU countries.[20]

Terrorism, Securitization, and the European Union

In Europe, these terrorist or attempted terrorist events have been used to justify an increased securitization of migration, especially from Africa. The continuing arrival of migrants from Africa has been described as a crisis that must be controlled. This perception was considerably strengthened when thousands of Libyans, Tunisians, and Sub-Saharan Africans arrived on the shores of Italy and Spain in the aftermath of the so-called Arab Spring in 2011. The small Italian island of Pantelleria has been virtually overrun by large groups of migrants faced with a bleak situation upon arrival because of lack of resources

---

18   In France, for example, according to a law approved on December 27, 1994, it is illegal to help or assist an irregular or undocumented immigrant, for example, by providing shelter or food.

19   Derek Lutterbeck, *Policing Migration in the Mediterranean*, 11(1) Mediterranean Pol. 59–82 (2006); Freedman, *supra* note 10, at 39.

20   Hein De Haas, *The Myth of Invasion: Irregular Migration from West Africa to the Maghreb and the European Union* (research report, Intl. Migration Inst., Oxford U. Oct. 2007).

on the island and the distance from the mainland. From August 1, 2012, to August 10, 2013, 24,227 immigrants arrived on this tiny island, which until then had a permanent population of 7,679.

The same happened in the Canary Islands off the coast of the Western Sahara, Morocco, and Mauritania. Greece's porous frontiers have also been used by thousands of migrants from Africa, the Middle East, and points beyond to easily enter the European Union. The lack of a coherent and unified policy and the nonexistence of a federal enforcement agency or group protecting the borders of the European Union have allowed this vast movement of people to continue unabated.

The Cotonou Agreement of 2000 between the European Union and various African countries requires, in its Article 13.5, countries of the ACP (Africa, Caribbean, and Pacific) region to take back their citizens caught residing illegally in the European Union, along with other nationals who crossed those countries on their journey toward the European Union. Since the 1990s, a readmission clause has been routinely included in partnership and cooperation agreements between the European Union and various countries, including Ukraine, Moldova, and Kazakhstan, and in the Euro-Mediterranean association agreements of 2000 with Morocco, Algeria, and Tunisia. In June 2002, the European Union began requiring the readmission clause to be included in any cooperation, association, or equivalent agreement that it signs with any country.

Linking economic and trade policies with developmental assistance and trying to control migration flows through bilateral agreements is practiced not just by the European Union. Member states of the European Union have entered into similar bilateral agreements with Mediterranean countries: France, Italy, and Spain in particular have bilateral agreements to control migration flows. There have been several expulsions also between Mali and Algeria, Mali and Mauritania, Morocco and Algeria, Morocco and the Western Sahara. Moreover, the EU member states closest to North Africa have increased their naval patrols, even beyond territorial waters, and new border control measures have been steadily introduced by the European Union's External Borders Agency. The European Union has also used "the carrot" to motivate African countries to control migration. Considerable amounts of funds for development in the countries of origin of the migrants and for migration-related programs have been made available. Also, a new thematic program on migration and asylum has been funded.[21] However, it is actually estimated that there are about 4 million irregular migrants in the European Union, with the United Kingdom and Italy having the largest number.[22] As a consequence of the turmoil in the Islamic world, especially the wars in Iraq and Afghanistan, and in the aftermath of the Arab Spring, in the first quarter of 2011 there

---

21   European Commission, *Migration and Asylum* (2012), available at http://ec.europa.eu/europe aid/what/migration-asylum/ .

22   Anil Dawar, *Scandal of UK's 863,000 Illegal Immigrants, One in Four of the EU's Total*, Daily & Sunday Express (Dec. 18, 2012), available at http://www.express.co.uk/news/uk/365637 /Scandal-of-UK-s-863-000, citing the 2008 European Union study, *Clandestino*.

was a significant increase in known illegal crossings of the sea frontiers of the European Union, the largest number of any first quarter in recent years.[23] Thus, all these EU approaches and policies have not succeeded in diminishing or stopping irregular migration into the European Union.

Increased State Controls and Increased Journey Insecurity

The most immediate effect of efforts to control and discourage migration is to make it more difficult and dangerous for regular migrants to reach their destinations. Put differently, the insecurity of the migrant journey has increased considerably. More rugged, more isolated, less patrolled routes, or less guarded points of entry must be chosen to reach the desired destination. This increases the cost of the journey, leading to increased indentured servitude on the part of the migrant, who often must pay back those costs with the meager earnings of his or her work abroad. It also increases the possibility of injury or death, given the more inhospitable terrain or longer route; the potential of experiencing violence along the way; and dependency on the guides leading the group, with consequent increased fees, exploitation, and mistreatment.

Ironically, the countermeasures adopted by the European Union, the United States, and other countries have increased the market for, and the importance of, smugglers and traffickers, thus making the migrants more vulnerable and more insecure. These increased power imbalances are often operationalized in the form of financial or sexual exploitation carried out by various actors, ranging from the "coyotes" or "snakeheads" guiding the group, to fellow travelers, to border patrol agents or police, to vigilantes capturing the migrants.[24] Migration increases and strengthens power differentials—often linked to gender, status, national origin, or race—that already existed and functioned before the migration took place. Thus the state's enhanced policies and interventions, meant to discourage and eliminate irregular migration, not only fail to mitigate or discourage it but also often have the negative effect of increasing it, and magnifying the violence and exploitation that accompany it. Amnesty International's report *In Hostile Terrain: Human Rights Violations in Immigration Enforcement in the US Southwest*[25] examines the human rights violations associated with immigration enforcement at the border and in the interior of the United States. Among its findings is that recent immigration policy in certain border areas has pushed undocumented immigrants into using dangerous routes through Mexican and U.S. deserts. Hundreds of people die each year as a result.

---

23 Christal Morehouse & Michael Blomfield, *Irregular Migration in Europe* 6 (Transatlantic Council on Migration 2011).

24 De Haas, *supra* note 20.

25 Published Mar. 28, 2012; available at http://www.amnesty.org/en/library/asset/AMR51/018/2012/en/4905b8cd-8d5b-41b9-a301-3121fca2e1cd/amr510182012en.pdf.

The Feminization of Migration and Insecurity

Migration is becoming increasingly feminized. In the classic model of migration, the migrant was a man, leaving behind his family for his wife to care for, until his return. Traveling in the company of Algerian lawyers in late 1980s from Batna, Algeria, to an oasis in the Sahara, we passed a mountain range with small villages carved out on ledges. The guide pointed them out and mentioned that those villages were full of "white widows," women left behind by emigrating husbands. That pattern has changed considerably in the past 20 years. While the percentage of women among migrants has always been significant, the number of women migrants has increased steadily since 1965 and they presently constitute about half of all international migrants, or an estimated 100 million international migrants.[26] By 2005, with the exception of Asia and Africa, women migrants slightly outnumbered men.[27]

The most dramatic change in female migration has been that women are increasingly emigrating on their own in search of work, instead of moving abroad with their husbands or reuniting with them there.[28] A major reason for the growth of the woman migrant on her own has been the increased prosperity in the world, which has generated a growing demand for services, the field in which the majority of women migrants find employment. For example, the growing wealth of Brazil means that fewer Brazilian women need to work in private homes as maids and caretakers with low pay and long hours. This eventually generates a demand for irregular immigrants from neighboring South American countries to take over those jobs, most often at even lower wages and with no benefits.

Also important has been the aging of the developed countries versus the youthfulness of the developing ones. Increasing employment opportunities and the availability and low cost of transportation and communication (e.g., Internet, cell phones, and Skype) are other important factors behind the seemingly unstoppable flow of migrants.

Eastern European women, especially Romanians, are a good example. Many Romanian women have emigrated on their own, often leaving behind children and husbands, to enter the service sector in Italy, especially caring for the elderly, children, and the sick. In a country like Italy, where the family has traditionally taken primary responsibility for caring for the elderly parent or the infant, *la badante* ("the helper" or "the attendant") has now become a fixture in the socioeconomic life of Italians.

---

26   United Nations Population Division, *Human Development Report, Overcoming Barriers: Human Mobility and Development* (Palgrave McMillan 2009).

27   United Nations Population Fund, *A Passage to Hope: Women and International Migration* 23 (State of World Population series, 2006).

28   Gloria Moreno-Fontes Chammartin, *Female Migrant Workers' Situation in the Labour Market* (paper presented at the Thematic Rev. Seminar of the Mutual Learning Programme of the European Empl. Strategy, Brussels, Apr. 29, 2008); *Reflections on Domestic Work and the Feminization of Migration*, 31(1) Campbell Law Review 67 (Fall 2008).

The feminization of migration is also fueled by two other major recent socioeconomic patterns: the feminization of poverty and of work.[29] Other causes range from economic and social crises in particular regions of the world to employment and career discrimination against women in general but especially against divorced and widowed women, single mothers, and unmarried women past a certain age.[30]

The Woman Migrant and Her Security

Until the end of the 20th century, migration studies by and large overlooked the woman migrant. Women were invisible. The assumption was that all migrants were men and that women were simply "dependents" who, if they left home, followed their husbands or fathers. Thus, if women were discussed, they were included only as wives, daughters, and dependents of the male emigrant. However, this was not always so. Especially during the past 30 years, women have started to be recognized as migrants on their own, as breadwinners, and as the principal providers for the economic needs of their families.

There is no question that men and women relate to migration in very different ways: they exhibit different patterns and behaviors, they react differently to diverse opportunities, they face disparate obstacles and challenges, and they have to deal with different security issues. In human health issues, it has been found that studying only men and extrapolating the findings to include women does not work. That same knowledge should apply to migration and security issues related to women. Like health, diet, exercise, and almost every other issue, migration is not gender neutral. Women face their own, very specific reasons to leave, their own risks, challenges, and vulnerabilities, such as violations of their human rights, discrimination, exploitation, and health-related issues.

The migration-insecurity link can be at work in all stages of migration.[31] From a security standpoint, women very often decide to migrate to escape situations of abuse, denigration, and exploitation. Child abuse, sexual abuse, spouse abuse, forced marriages, servitude, and financial exploitation are often at the root of a woman's decision to leave. In regard to health issues, women choose to leave for various reasons, including being subject to female genital mutilation, child marriage, early sexual activity and pregnancies, overall powerlessness in sexual relations leading to multiple pregnancies, risk of contracting HIV/AIDS and other sexually transmitted diseases, and early aging due to serial pregnancies and backbreaking, incessant work.

---

29 Sally Baden & Kirsti Milward, *Gender Inequality and Poverty: Trends, Linkages, Analysis and Poverty Implications* (unpublished report, BRIDGE 2000); BRIDGE Development—Gender, *Briefing Paper on the "Feminization of Poverty"* (Sussex Inst. Dev. Stud. Apr. 2001); Fiona Adamson & Sally Baden, *Gender, Governance and the "Feminisation of Poverty"* (unpublished report, 2nd version, BRIDGE 1999).

30 Jeffrey Cohen & Ibrahim Sirkeci, *Centuries of Migration: The Global Nature of Contemporary Mobility* (U. of Texas Press 2013).

31 Freedman, *supra* note 10.

These concerns can be exacerbated by patriarchal values and power hierarchies that deny women basic freedoms, important choices, and a minimum
of autonomy. It must not be overlooked that women are also discriminated
against financially: in earnings, in their capacity to support and maintain their
families, and in starting or managing a business. Thus, a woman's decision to
migrate is usually rather complex rather than simple, stemming from a variety
of factors, many of them gender specific. Poverty results not just from limited
or no income but also from lack of or restricted access to opportunity and
choice.[32]

Unfortunately, the values and attitudes mentioned above often accompany women when they finally migrate. The risk of violence is high for all
migrants but more so for women, especially when it comes to sexual violence.
In many cultures, a woman's appearance in a public space is such a departure from accepted norms that it is often considered equivalent to availability
for and even an invitation to a sexual encounter. The men interacting with a
woman traveling by herself see her being there without male protection as an
invitation, a statement of availability, a permission to approach her for sexual
activity or force her into it. These values surfaced recently in March 2013 in
the context of the gang rape of a Swiss woman tourist traveling by bicycle
and camping overnight with her husband in Central India. According to the
BBC, local officials reportedly questioned why the woman, even though with
her husband, would make herself vulnerable to the point of "asking for it"
by camping overnight in a dense forest. Thus, her being there, camping in
the open, was seen as her implicitly giving permission for, even inviting, the
group of men to attack her sexually. The same attitude was apparently at work
when, in March 2013, a British woman tourist in Agra, India, decided to jump
out of the second-floor window of her hotel room to escape an attempted rape
by the hotel owner and another employee who entered her room at 3:45 a.m.
as she was sleeping. A group of Japanese tourists had previously complained
that the same hotel's staff had behaved obscenely toward the women in their
group.[33] Women migrants know only too well that they are often seen as responsible and guilty for men's violent sexual behavior.

Women's dependence on a male guide during some migration journeys
also makes them vulnerable to violent attacks, exploitation, and rape. During
a journey, while crossing a desert or unknown territory, the threat of being
left behind or excluded from the group can be used to force a woman into
unwanted sexual activity with the guide or other men on the journey. Thus,
sexual violence against migrant women becomes "normalized"; it becomes
part of the journey.[34] This reality is frequently experienced by women who
do not have the financial resources to pay the high fees asked by smugglers.

---

32   Sylvia Chant , *Gender, Generation and Poverty: Exploring the "Feminisation of Poverty" in Africa,
Asia and Latin America* (Edgar Elver 2007); Freedman, supra note 10.

33   *British Woman Jumps off Hotel Room to Escape Rape Bid; Hotel Owner Held,* Times of India
(Mar. 20, 2013).

34   Freedman, *supra* note 10, at 46.

Moreover, once the journey is under way, the smuggler may extort more money from everyone because the migrants are now under his control and highly dependent on him for their survival. For some women, agreeing to sexual activity may be the only way to meet aggressive demands for more money.[35] This "sexual-economic" type of transaction is reportedly quite frequent and "normal" in irregular migration. This so-called survival sex on the migrants' route is similar to that of displaced women in refugee camps where sexual favors or agreeing to prostitution may be extorted if a woman wants to obtain food, water, or some measure of protection for herself and her children in chaotic and mob-like situations.[36]

Other Aspects of Insecurity for Women Migrants

It goes without saying that other serious aspects of insecurity are present in these situations when the woman has very little, if any, power to control the situation, negotiate compensation, or control the type and manner of sexual encounter, including whether safe sex will be practiced.[37] Insecurity, especially for women, also arises if a traveling group is attacked by one of the bands that regularly prey on irregular migrants making their way through isolated areas. These violent groups rob migrants of their valuables, at times beat or even kill some of them, steal their food, and often rape women or abduct them and hold them for forced labor, including sexual services.

In the vast, lawless, and isolated no-man's land that some migrants must cross, anything can happen, especially to a woman. It has been reported that at times even a woman's intimate parts may be searched for hidden cash before she is raped. In an attempt to protect themselves from attack, migrant women may be under pressure to find a male as a travel companion and traditional protector. The outcome may unfortunately be for the woman to find herself in an insecure situation at the hands of the male she thought would protect her, but who, instead, is violent and exploitative, taking advantage of the uneven power situation.

Thus, sexual assault and exploitation are frequent ingredients in the dynamics of domination by one gender, most often male, over the other, the

---

35 Joe Doezema, *Forced to Choose: Beyond the Voluntary v. Forced Prostitution Dichotomy*, in *Global Sex Workers: Rights, Resistance and Redefinition* (Kamala Kempadoo & Joe Doezema eds., Routledge 1998).

36 Freedman, *supra* note 10, at 46; U.N. General Assembly, *Investigating into Sexual Exploitation of Refugees by Aid Workers in West Africa, Note by the Secretary General*, A/57/465 (Oct. 11, 2002); and U.N. General Assembly, *A Comprehensive Strategy to Eliminate Future Sexual Exploitation and Abuse in U.N. Peacekeeping Operations, Letter dated 24 March 2003 from the Secretary General to the President of the General Assembly*, A/59/710 (Mar. 24, 2005).

37 Diane Otto, *Making Sense of Zero Tolerance Policies in Peacekeeping Sexual Economies*, in *Sexuality and the Law* (Vanessa Munro & Carl Stychin eds., Routledge Cavendish 2010); Melissa Petro, *Selling Sex: Women's Participation in the Sex Industry*, in *Sex Work Matters: Exploring Money, Power and Intimacy in the Sex Industry* 155–170 (Melissa Ditmore, Antonia Levy, & Alys Willman eds., Zed 2010).

migrant female in a vulnerable situation. Like rape in war, forced or exploitative sex in irregular migration is used to express and reinforce a general culture and pattern of domination to frighten and demean women and to impose male superiority and exercise the so-called man's privilege.

It must be stressed that it is not only men who are involved in irregular migration, especially in the trafficking of women for sexual and labor exploitation abroad. For example, in Nigeria, women manage the process of recruiting Nigerian women for exploitation. They recruit the young victims in Nigeria and also control them once they reach their country of destination. However, men generally supervise and control transporting the "goods" from one country to another and delivering them to their destination.[38]

The State's Use and Abuse of Power: More Insecurity for Migrants

As mentioned previously, the state can make irregular migration much more insecure when it takes more measures to combat, deter, and stifle it. Doing so makes it much more difficult and perilous to migrate, in that migrants must take alternative out-of-the-way routes, often more rugged, arduous, and isolated, with considerable obstacles. The increased "security" measures by the state often also mean more aggressive enforcement, raids, roundups, arrests, incarceration, deportations, human rights abuses, use of excessive force, police abuses, and even death or injury. Thus, one could say that the state and its officials often become more visible and prominent as agents of insecurity for the irregular migrant. Here, too, women bear the brunt of the state's intervention. Women migrants are often treated differently than their male counterparts. Moreover, the failure of the state to recognize and acknowledge the special situation of women in regard to lack of equality and security—treating women in the same manner as men—adds to the difficulties and challenges that women migrants face. It actually exacerbates their precarious situation and exposes them to the danger of continued humiliation, exploitation, and victimization. There are no provisions in place for taking into account the special concerns for their health and the special need that they have to be protected from predatory and exploitative behavior. Children and pregnant women are treated no differently than other irregular migrants; they must endure the same level of brutality and aggression as others. Pregnant women at times even lose their baby due to the rough and uncaring treatment by border protection forces.[39]

The establishment and activities of groups that target undocumented migrants, both during their journeys and afterward, seem to be encouraged and even justified by the enactment of laws that criminalize the daily lives of

---

38   Eugenia Bonetti, *The Strength of Networking between Countries of Origin and Destination* (paper presented at "Consultation against Commercial Sexual Exploitation" conference, Winnipeg, Nov. 3–5, 2006).

39   Mehdi Lahlou, Claire Escoffier, & Najia Hajji, *Evaluation de la situation de la mobilité et du VIH au Maroc* (UNAIDS & Ministère de la Santé Publique 2007).

migrants. Such laws discourage irregular migrants from reporting their victimization and seeking justice. Even worse is the situation of those migrants and trafficked or enslaved persons who go to the police to seek protection and justice and are instead returned to their victimizer and exploiter. Hardened immigration and border control policies do have an impact, increasing the risks that irregular migrants must deal with on their journey and after arrival. They also make it much more difficult and dangerous for community-based networks to provide support and ensure safe journeys.

For example, the criminalization of Latinos and Latino migrants by the state of Arizona through its law SB1070 has had a dramatic effect on the exercise of human and civil rights in that state, especially in the case of communities along the U.S.-Mexico frontier.[40] The expansion of police powers to stop and search people in public places under numerous laws and court decisions is especially connected to the search for irregular migrants and is often driven by racial and socioeconomic stereotyping. The use of these powers is often disproportionate and is a clear expression of unlawful racial and ethnic discrimination, often affecting U.S.-born and naturalized citizens as well, simply because of their appearance. It is clearly a form of institutional racism justified by concerns about irregular migration.[41]

In mid-March 2013, ten lawsuits were filed in the United States alleging unlawful conduct by Customs and Border Protection (CBP) in northern and southern states of the country. The cases filed are meant to demonstrate how CBP agents routinely overstep their statutory mandate by conducting enforcement activities outside border regions, making racially motivated arrests, employing derogatory and coercive interrogation tactics, and imprisoning arrestees under inhumane conditions. The cases include claims of unlawful search and seizure, false imprisonment, intentional infliction of emotional distress, assault, and battery. These cases also highlight the culture of impunity that permeates the behavior of law enforcement officers, vigilantes, and other anti-immigration groups.[42]

Amnesty International's *In Hostile Terrain* report[43] highlights the link between violations of immigrants' rights in the southwestern states of Texas and

---

40   For an archive of articles, commentary, and information related to law SB1070 in Arizona, *see Times Topics* at the *New York Times* website, available at topic.nytimes.com/top/reference/... /Arizona...sb_1070. *See also* Mike Sacks, *On SB 1070: Supreme Court Appears to Favor Arizona on Controversial Immigration Law,* Huffington Post (Apr. 25, 2012), available at http://www .huffingtonpost.com/2012/04/25/sb-1070-supreme-court-arizona-immigration-law_n _1451622.html; Mary Romero & Gabriella Sanchez, *Critical Issues Faced by Latino Defendants,"* in *Hispanics in the U.S. Criminal Justice System: The New American Demography* (Martin Urbina ed., Charles C. Thomas 2012)

41   Anna Souhami, *Institutional Racism and Police Reform: An Empirical Critique,* Policing & Socy. 1–21 (2012).

42   Northwest Immigrant Rights Project, *Widespread Abuse by U.S. Customs and Border Protection Documented in National Wave of Complaints* (Mar. 13, 2013), available at http://www.nwirp .org/news/viewmediarelease/54.

43   *Supra* note 25.

Arizona and the failure of federal, state, and local authorities to enforce immigration laws on the basis of nondiscrimination. The report shows that communities living along the border—particularly Latinos and individuals perceived to be of Latino origin, and indigenous communities—are disproportionately affected by a range of immigration control measures, resulting in a pattern of human rights violations. These unlawful practices are not limited to the United States.

Canada, which is often seen as a global leader with respect to refugee protection, is, like many other countries, creating more barriers for people seeking safety and security. The Protecting Canada's Immigration System Act (Bill C-31) received Royal Assent on June 29, 2012. This new law presents a significant change for people who come to Canada in search of safety. The law includes a policy of long-term detention with inadequate review for designated persons, based solely on the manner in which they arrive in Canada. It allows for the creation of "safe countries of origin" and bars access to the Refugee Appeal Division for some groups of refugees. The law also allows for the detention of children and their families and creates barriers to the timely reunification of families, even for some individuals who are found to be refugees according to the 1954 UN Convention Relating to the Status of Refugees as amended by the 1967 Protocol.[44]

Research shows widespread abuse of police powers in other jurisdictions, such as the United Kingdom,[45] the Netherlands,[46] and Japan,[47] and globally.[48] There is no doubt that immigration enforcement has become an often-used justification for expanding police powers to "stop and search" in the United States and elsewhere.[49] Various countries are trying to apprehend and expel irregular immigrants, often within a framework of racism, discrimination, and stereotyping.

---

44   See *Refugees and Migrants* section of the Canadian Amnesty International website, available at http://www.amnesty.ca/our-work/issues/refugees-and-migrants.

45   · Ben Bowling & Coretta Phillips, *Disproportionate and Discriminatory: Reviewing the Evidence on Police Stop and Search,* 70(6) Modern L. Rev. 936–951 (2007); Rebekah Delson & Michael Shiner, *Regulating Stop and Search: A Challenge for Police and Community Relations in England and Wales,* 14(3) Critical Criminology 241–263 (2006); Jenny Bourne, *The Life and Times of Institutional Racism,* 43(2) Race & Class 7–22 (2001).

46   Joanne P. Van der Leun & Maartje A. H. van der Woude, *Ethnic Profiling in the Netherlands? A Reflection on Expanding Preventive Powers in Arizona,* 21(4) Policing & Socy. 480–488 (2011).

47   Mitsuru Namba, *"War on Illegal Immigrants," National Narratives, and Globalisation: Japanese Policy and Practice of Police Stop and Question in Global Perspective,* 21(4) Policing & Socy. 432–433 (2011).

48   Ben Bowling & Leanne Weber, *Stop and Search in Global Context: Overview,* 21(4) Policing & Socy. 480–488 (2011).

49   A federal judge ruled on August 12, 2013, that the stop-and-frisk tactics of the New York Police Department violated the constitutional rights of minorities in the city. The judge, Shira A. Scheindlin, found that the Police Department resorted to a "policy of indirect racial profiling" as it increased the number of stops in minority communities. That has led to officers' routinely stopping "blacks and Hispanics who would not have been stopped if they were white." *See New York Times,* August 13, 2013, N.Y./Region.

Unlawful and Excessive Force by Law Enforcement

Practices that are unlawful or unconstitutional, or that exceed what is allowed or authorized by law, often stem from a variety of factors. Among these are police practices inimical to immigrants and racial minorities, such as profiling and stereotyping;[50] shrill political discourse and scare tactics; the federal or central government's deportation efforts; and a generalized fear of crime and disorder that leads many people to blame "outsiders" for troubles. These factors make possible and legitimize enforcement policies and practices that "(1) blend techniques of control used on the border with those used in interior enforcement; (2) mix criminal and administrative approaches to apprehension, detention and deportation; (3) invoke national security as a rationale for strict, uncompromising enforcement; and (4) hype the violence aspect of border crossing to support more aggressive interior enforcement."[51] The resulting law enforcement way of operating is thus characterized by ethnic and racial profiling, aggressive surveillance, intrusive stops, excessive searches, unjustified detention of those suspected of being irregular immigrants, and frequent violation of human and civil rights.[52]

These overly aggressive, humiliating practices are incarnated in Arizona in the policies and actions of Sheriff Joe Arpaio, who, since 1992 has been elected and reelected sheriff of Maricopa County, which includes Phoenix, the capital and largest city of Arizona. Maricopa County has almost 4 million inhabitants. Arpaio often conducts sweeping and abusive searches for irregular immigrants on the streets of certain neighborhoods in the county. People arrested are often housed in a controversial jail in the desert where inmates sleep in tents and males are required to wear pink underwear, an obvious attempt to denigrate and humiliate them. Arpaio recently offered to detain in his tent jail irregular immigrants to be released in Arizona by the federal government because of budget problems.[53] The negative effect of Arpaio's pronouncements and practices on the irregular immigrant community is substantial and makes it very difficult, if not impossible, for these immigrants—especially abused, trafficked, and raped women—to seek justice.[54]

---

50   *Id.*

51   Doris Marie Provine & Gabriella Sanchez, *Suspecting Immigrants: Exploring Links between Racialized Anxieties and Expanded Police Powers in Arizona,* 21(4) Policing & Socy. 468–479 (2011). *See* also Doris Marie Provine & Roxanne Lynn Doty, *The Criminalization of Immigrants as a Racial Project,* 27(3) J. Contemporary Crim. Just. 261–277 (2011).

52   Amnesty International's report *Jailed without Justice* exposes the immigrant detention system in the United States as broken and unnecessarily costly. The report focuses on the human rights violations associated with the dramatic increase in the use of detention by the United States as an immigration enforcement mechanism. According to the report, in just over a decade, immigration detention tripled. In 1996, immigration authorities had a daily detention capacity of less than 10,000. Ten years later, more than 30,000 men, women, and children were detained by U.S. immigration authorities each day. The 2009 report is available at http://www.amnestyusa.org/pdfs/JailedWithoutJustice.pdf.

53   Kevin Cirilli, *Sheriff Joe Arpaio Offers to Detain Illegal Immigrants,* Politico (Feb. 28, 2013).

54   For an archive of articles, commentary, and information related to Sheriff Joe Arpaio, see *Times Topics* at the *New York Times* website, available at http://topics.nytimes.com/topics

It is hard to envision exploited and mistreated irregular workers seeking redress from the police and the government when attitudes, pronouncements, and practices similar to Sheriff Arpaio's permeate the official justice system. These practices confirm to the immigrant that the police in their "new" country are no better than the vicious, corrupt, and abusive police they tried to escape from in their country of origin. Also, the exploitation and maltreatment of domestic workers in various forms are not uncommon and often go unreported or ignored, especially when profound socioeconomic, religious, and racial differences play a role in fueling prejudice and lack of caring and basic respect for the immigrant.[55] Reports of women who have escaped from situations of slavery and exploitation and who have sought refuge at police stations only to be returned to their exploiters and tormentors instead of receiving help are sadly not rare in the anecdotal and research literature.[56]

Conclusion

Although the word "security" is frequently mentioned when countries develop policies, laws, administrative rules, and enforcement practices to keep migrants out, the security of the migrants is often overlooked and not even considered an issue.[57] Ironically, stronger and tougher security measures adopted by a country often make the journey of irregular migrants more dangerous, costly, and open to exploitation and victimization. Migrant insecurity continues and even increases after arriving in the destination country. Even in the best of circumstances, when police are trustworthy and not corrupt, the irregular migrant—quite possibly a victim of exploitation or enslavement—finds it very difficult to seek protection and receive justice because of a lack of training for police; language barriers; cross-cultural problems, even with face recognition and identification; poor communication between local law enforcement and victim assistance organizations; and the hidden nature of the crime. The threat of deportation, at times considered a solution to the situation, is an added obstacle to the migrant seeking the security that should be provided by the state.

The ubiquitous discourse on security and the policies enacted to enhance the security of the state need to take into account the security of migrants as well. The best approach to addressing the link between migration and insecurity would be, first, to recognize the existence of the problem, and then to commit to addressing and remedying it. Steps to protect women migrants and to

---

/reference/.../a/Joseph...arpaio/Index/html.

55   Human Rights Watch, *Swept under the Rug: Abuses against Domestic Workers around the World* (2006).

56   Jackie Sheehan, *Human Trafficking between China and the UK* (Discussion Paper No. 54, China Policy Inst., U. of Nottingham 2009); and Robert Moossy, *Sex Trafficking: Identifying Cases and Victims,* 262 (Natl. Inst. of Just. J. 2009).

57   Jef Huysmans, *Security: What Do You Mean? From Concept to Thick Signifier,* 4(2) European J. Intl. Rel. 226–255 (1998).

help them protect themselves are especially important. In a male-dominated world, it is vital to make women aware of their rights, help them strategize how best to assert those rights, and provide an effective network of assistance and support. Human rights and gender-sensitive training for border guards, police, and security personnel should be offered and required. Securing borders and developing effective control approaches while minimizing the migrants' exposure to risk[58] also requires taking into account gender differences in vulnerability and potential for victimization and exploitation. Unless it takes such measures, the state will be unable to safeguard both its own security and the security of migrants.

---

58   Jørgen Carling & María Hernandez-Carretero, *Protecting Europe and Protecting Migrants? Strategies for Managing Unauthorised Migration from Africa*, 13 British J. Pol. & Intl. Rel. 42–58 (2011).

Toward a National Framework Law on Water for India

N. R. Madhava Menon

The existing method of water resource management in India is unsystematic at best. In early 2012, the Ministry of Water Resources of the Government of India published a policy document on water that highlights concerns regarding the management of water resources and seeks the adoption of a comprehensive, coordinated national framework law containing principles binding on central, state, and local governments.[1] At the same time that this report was being prepared, a Working Group appointed by the Planning Commission for preparing the XIIth Five-Year Plan came up with a Draft National Water Framework Bill for water governance in India.[2] In 2010, the Commission on Centre-State Relations[3] had recommended a decentralized, participative legal regime in view of the size of the country, the multiple stakeholders involved, and the constitutional scheme on water use and regulation.[4] This report presents a consensual policy model on water to guide both the central government and the states in legislating water management. It recommends that state acts reflect national policy. Following these initiatives of three different ministries, the Ministry of Water Resources constituted a committee in 2012 to prepare a legislative proposal at the national level incorporating the binding principles and developing institutional mechanisms for management of water resources in the future.[5]

This chapter argues that a national water policy informed by scientific data and measurable outcomes can sustain the availability of water for life, livelihood, and food security in India. Given the division of legislative and administrative powers among the three levels of government in respect to water use and management, the only way to avoid conflicts, costs, and inefficiency is to mandate that all levels of government be obliged to abide by a national framework law. Integrated watershed management is the best strategy to advance such a policy in a cost-effective and efficient federal arrangement. The chapter explores the principles, concerns, and functions of a national framework law on water management in India.

---

1   Ministry of Water Resources, Government of India, Draft National Water Policy (Jan. 2012).

2   Planning Commission, *Draft National Water Framework Act: An Explanatory Note* (2011).

3   Ministry of Home Affairs, Government of India, *Report of the Commission on Centre-State Relations*, vol. 6 (Mar. 2010).

4   *Draft National Water Framework Act, supra* note 2.

5   The committee submitted its report in May 2013. The author is a member of this committee.

Facts and Figures in Perspective

Water is a fundamental element of life on earth. Despite the fact that more than 70 percent of the planet's surface is covered by water, only 3 percent is non-saline—that is, distributed in glaciers, rivers, and lakes and as groundwater. According to an Asian Development Bank study, the quantity of water available per person in South Asia has declined by more than 80 percent between 1951 and 2011.[6] India has access to one-eighth of the average amount of fresh water available per capita globally each year and is thus near the threshold of a chronic water shortage. In other words, India is a water-stressed nation, with per capita availability of water falling from 5,177 cubic meters in 1951 to 1,544 cubic meters in 2011.

According to the *State of the Environment Report—India,* the repository of surface water in India is the 12 major river systems that cross the subcontinent.[7] These form a catchment area of 253 million hectares. Almost half the annual rainfall in India occurs during a period of two to three weeks, and almost 90 percent of river flows (i.e., the total quantity of water flowing through the rivers) occur in four months. More than 70 percent of the water in the rivers drains into the Bay of Bengal, and 20 percent drains into the Arabian Sea. Only 10 percent drains into interior basins and a few natural lakes. The estimated utilizable surface water is 690 billion cubic meters. With the annually replenishable groundwater potential,[8] the total available is 1.122 trillion cubic meters. Indians are unable to conserve water for the off-season because water conservation methods and techniques have not been adequately adopted in India, allowing most of the rainwater to flow into the water basins and the sea.

In terms of water use in India, agriculture receives the largest share—92 percent—most of it in the form of irrigation. Of this, groundwater accounts for 39 percent. Unfortunately, up to 63 percent of the water used in agriculture is lost through evaporation or runoff. The demand for industrial and energy production, which is 63 billion cubic meters, is expected to grow at 4.2 percent per year. Domestic demand, which is 25 billion cubic meters, is also expected to grow with the projected increase in population. It is estimated that by 2025, the total annual water demand of 1.050 trillion cubic meters will be close to the utilizable potential of 1.122 trillion cubic meters. With 70 percent of surface water contaminated by biologic, toxic, organic, and inorganic pollutants, the challenge India faces is how to meet demand in terms of quantity and quality given the constraints of geography and rainfall patterns.[9]

---

6   Tomislav Delinic & Marcel Schepp, *Water for South Asia* 110 (Intl. Reports 28, Konrad-Adenauer-Stiftung, 2012), available at http://www.kas.de/wf/doc/kas_32769-1522-2-30 .pdf?121116134456.

7   Ministry of Environment and Forests, Government of India, *State of Environment Report—India* (2009) (hereinafter *State of Environment Report*).

8   Replenishable groundwater is essentially a dynamic resource that is replenished annually or periodically by precipitation, irrigation return flow, canal seepage, tank seepage, influent seepage, etc.

9   *Report of the Commission on Centre-State Relations, supra* note 3, at 32.

The *State of the Environment Report—India* concludes that "the core challenge of water resources development and management in India is one of governance."[10] The focus of governance, the report proposes, should be integrated water resource management, or the quantitatively and qualitatively sustainable management of interlinked surface waters, aquifers, and coastal waters in a manner that supports social and economic development and strengthens the efficiency of the ecosystem. The core idea of integrated water resource management is that water supply is not an isolated problem but an issue embedded in a larger political, economic, and social context. The main criteria for water use should be the requirements of nature and people as well as the inclusion of affected stakeholders at all levels.

Water and Human Rights Jurisprudence

In 1992, the Dublin International Conference on Water and the Environment stated the core principle on water supply as follows: "The use of water, understood both as a finite resource and an economic asset, inevitably has to be managed by means of a participatory and inclusive approach to ensure a sustainable supply for the entire world population."[11] The idea of the right to water is included in a variety of international agreements, including the Convention on Women's and Children's Rights and the Convention on Economic, Social, and Cultural Rights approved by the UN General Assembly in December 1966, which states: "The human right to water is indispensable for leading a life in human dignity. It is prerequisite for the realization of other human rights."

The Supreme Court of India has interpreted the fundamental right to water as part of the right to life that is enshrined in Article 21 of the Constitution of India.[12] This interpretation puts an obligation on each state to provide unpolluted drinking water to the people. Many states do have legislation regarding water supply to urban areas, and government schemes acknowledge this right in relation to rural areas.[13] In the 2000 judgment on the Sardar Sarovar project, in supporting the construction of the dam, the Supreme Court relied on the fact that the dam would contribute to meeting the water needs of individuals residing in the area.[14] Yet, there is no explicit legislation at the central or state level that gives content and meaning to the right to water. Even policy declarations are vague in this regard.

---

10 *State of Environment Report, supra* note 7, at 112.

11 International Conference on Water and the Environment, *The Dublin Statement and Report of the Conference, Dublin* 4 (World Meteorological Org. 1992).

12 *Subhash Kumar v. State of Bihar,* AIR (1991) SC 420.

13 The Accelerated Rural Water Supply Programme declared 40 liters per capita per day as the basic minimum level of water for an individual.

14 *Narmada Bachao Andolan v. Union of India,* AIR (2000) SC 3751.

The Expert Committee of the Water Resources Ministry revisited the Draft National Water Framework Bill, prepared by the Working Group on the XIIth Five-Year Plan. The Expert Committee has proposed recognizing the right to water in the following words:[15]

(i)   Every individual has a right to a minimum quantity of potable water for essential health and hygiene and within easy reach of the household at an affordable price.

(ii) The minimum quantity of potable water shall be prescribed by the appropriate government after expert examination and public consultation, provided that the minimum quantity of potable water shall not be less than 25 liters per capita per day.

(iii) The right to water for life shall take precedence over water rights, if any, for other uses including agricultural, industrial, and recreational uses.

(iv) The state's responsibility for ensuring people's right to water shall remain despite corporatization or privatization of water services.

(v)   The appropriate government shall specify the quality standards of water supply specified for different uses, such as drinking, other domestic uses, livestock, irrigation, industries etc., and shall ensure that these standards are fully complied with.

Realization of the right to water as a universal entitlement in India will require legislative and administrative measures at all levels of government (federal, state, and local), for which a national framework law binding governments at all three levels is necessary. In a fundamental rights context, the right to water is par with the right to education. This argument is used to resist privatization and corporatization in India and to maintain management of the water supply in the public sector. Because universal entitlement translates into a claim for universal free water, economic reform should not dictate the shape of the right to water.[16]

In a study of how the right to water has developed in India, Philippe Cullet concludes:[17]

> The government is under an obligation to ensure either by itself or through legislation that water laws reflect and conform to the fundamental right. Indeed, one of the important issues that arises in the context of water law is the sectoral manner in which it has developed, thus ensuring that there is not even a common set of principles governing all of water uses and all water bodies. In addition, there is only limited integration of water law with legislation related, for instance, to the environment, food and health. . . . The legislation will

---

15   Unpublished draft proposals under consideration of the Expert Committee.

16   Philippe Cullet, *Rethinking the Right to Water to Ensure Its Realization for All*, 54 J. Indian L. Intl. 38 (2012).

17   *Id.*, at 42.

> also need to address the question of the responsibility of the various actors involved in water supply. . . . The Constitution provides for devolution of water supply to Panchayats and Municipalities at [the] local level.

Water jurisprudence in India has thus changed drastically since the Supreme Court elevated the right to water to a constitutionally guaranteed fundamental right in 1991. Because the right to clean drinking water is part of the right to life and liberty under Article 21 of the Indian Constitution, the state has no choice but to ensure by legislation or executive schemes that water is available to every citizen in the country irrespective of economic or other disabilities. However, at present, clean water is a statutory right only for citizens who live within municipal or corporation bounds and who therefore must pay charges fixed by the municipality for that right. The 1991 interpretation of water as a human right put distinct responsibilities on all levels of governments to take water justice seriously; the Supreme Court can intervene if the government does not ensure the right to water when petitioned by aggrieved citizens. To ensure access to water as a fundamental right, a common legal framework must enunciate principles for central, state, and local governments to follow.

Water Resource Management and Center-State Relations

The Commission on Centre-State Relations examined the issue of the division of legislative powers in relation to water and integrated water resource management. The commission reported:[18]

> The constitution provides a role for the Centre, States and Local Bodies in the management of water. However it is apparent that the primacy in the matter is accorded to the States. Entry 17 in List II— State List of the Seventh Schedule states as follows:
>
> "Water, that is to say, water supplies, irrigation and canals, drainage and embankments, water storage, and water power subject to the provisions of entry 56 of List I."

Entry 56 of List I of the 7th Schedule of the 1950 constitution provides that "regulation and development of inter-State rivers and river valleys to the extent to which such regulation and development under the control of the Union is declared by Parliament by law to be expedient in the public interest."[19] Stemming from this entry, and recognizing that disputes may arise in the use, distribution, or control of waters of an interstate river or river valley, Article 262, provides for parliamentary law in the matter of adjudication of such disputes. Article 262 also states that if Parliament so enacts a law, then neither the

---

18   *Report of the Commission on Centre-State Relations, supra* note 3, at 33–35.

19   The entries are part of the 1950 Constitution of India, which, as of now, has 12 schedules, the seventh of which contains three lists: a Union List, a Concurrent List, and a State List, each containing several entries. The Union has the power to legislate on the entries in the Union and Concurrent Lists; the State has the power to legislate on the State and Concurrent Lists.

Supreme Court nor any other court may exercise jurisdiction in respect to any dispute or complaint.

This central role in water management has evolved over the past century. In preindependence India, the government centralized control over irrigation projects, and the credo was optimum utilization irrespective of political boundaries. The Montague-Chelmsford Reforms of 1919 classified irrigation as a provincial subject, but it was placed in a category "reserved" for central government legislation; hence, there was a measure of control. However, the Government of India Act of 1935 handed control over to the provinces, except in the matter of interstate disputes for which there was a provision to resolve disputes through the aegis of expert investigatory commissions and central executive decisions.

As a consequence of the 73rd and 74th Constitution Amendment Acts and the insertion of the 11th and 12th Schedules, panchayats and municipalities are now empowered with the management of water. Item 3 of the 11th Schedule speaks of a role for panchayats in "minor irrigation, water management and watershed development." Item 11 confers on them responsibilities for "drinking water," Item 13 speaks, inter alia, of "waterways" as a means of communication, and Item 29 mentions the "maintenance of community assets." In the case of municipalities, the 12th Schedule includes under Item 5, "water supply for domestic, industrial, and commercial purposes," and under Item 8, inter alia, the "protection of the environment and promotion of ecological aspects."

The central government exercised its jurisdiction in the matter of interstate rivers by enacting the River Boards Act of 1956, under which central management of any interstate river basin is accomplished either through specific legislation for that basin or by setting up a board to oversee it. In practice, however, the central government has not exercised either route to create a specific river basin organization. (It is interesting to note that the Ganga Basin Authority was set up in 2009 *under the Environment Protection Act*.) The reasons for this have generally been ascribed to the reluctance of states to politically come to agreement in this regard.

In addition to constitutional provisions, central intervention in issues concerning water has been the result of court rulings. In 1977, the Supreme Court directed the central government to set up an authority at the central level to deal with indiscriminate extraction of groundwater.[20] The central government set up the Central Groundwater Authority and prepared draft model groundwater bills in 1970, 1972, 1992, 1996, and 2005. The court upheld this authority's legitimacy under Section 3(2) of the Environment Protection Act of 1986. Similarly, under the Coastal Regulation Zone notification of 1991, harvesting of groundwater within 200 meters of the high-tide line is prohibited. Considering that the Environment Protection Act *was passed by virtue of Article 253,*[21]

---

20   *M. C. Mehta v. Union of India* (1977) 11 SCC 312.

21   Article 253 of the Constitution of India reads: "Legislation for giving effect to international agreements Notwithstanding anything in the foregoing provisions of this Chapter, Parlia-

many scholars question the way that central government jurisdiction has been expanded in what essentially is a state jurisdiction. Similarly, the courts have directed the central government and states about the interlinking of rivers (which in effect means the transfer of water from one basin to another).[22]

Central government initiatives regarding the management of water have resulted in the establishment of a National Water Resources Council in 1983 and a National Water Policy in 2002 and 2012. The council is presided over by the prime minister and includes chief ministers and union ministers as its members. The 2012 National Water Policy Statement calls for the establishment of a National Water Informatics Centre to collect and collate hydrologic data from all over the country to facilitate the development of a database for informed decision making in the management of water. It lays down certain essential principles based on equity and sustainability for water governance employing the public trust doctrine. The National Water Policy Statement prioritizes the uses of water, recognizing the essential needs of all citizens by giving primacy to drinking water. It proposes enhancing the water available for use by promoting watershed development activities, practicing water saving in irrigation use, adopting flood control measures, conserving water, and encouraging stakeholder participation in the management of water resources. The 2012 National Water Policy Statement also proposes institutional arrangements such as a water regulatory authority at the state level, a permanent water dispute tribunal at the central level, and an integrated water resources management system based on river basin–subbasin as the unit for the planning, development, and management of water resources. The 2012 National Water Policy Statement envisaged a national water framework law that establishes general principles on a statutory basis and decentralizes water governance in every state to the lower tiers of government.

Besides the policy on internal waters, the central government must enter into international agreements with neighboring countries regarding international rivers (Ganga, Brahmaputra, Indus) not only in the utilization of such waters but also for exchange of hydrological data of international rivers. To that end, treaties have been entered into with Pakistan, Bangladesh, and Nepal and memorandums of understanding (MOUs) have been signed with China.

---

ment has power to make any law for the whole or any part of the territory of India for implementing any treaty, agreement or convention with any other country or countries or any decision made at any international conference, association or other body." The Environment Protection Act of 1986 was passed in lieu of the decisions made at the UN Conference on Human Environment, held at Stockholm in 1972, to which India was a participant.

22 Networking of Rivers in re (2004) 11 SCC 360.

States and Water Management

States have enacted laws regulating surface water and groundwater, with emphasis on irrigation and other economic activities. The Northern India Canal and Drainage Act of 1873, the Bengal Irrigation Act of 1876, and the Bombay Irrigation Act of 1879 guided the irrigation legislation of most states. Farmers' right to water is not legally recognized under these laws. These acts do not provide for farmer participation in irrigation management or for transfer of funds to water users for undertaking repairs. Farmers remain dependent on state governments and the irrigation bureaucracy for supply and maintenance. The canal officer, an office created under the Indian Irrigation Act, has all the power, and departmental officers are not accountable to water users. There is a lack of transparency and participation in the management of irrigation systems.

The Irrigation Acts continue to regulate the development and use of surface water within state territories. Rules govern cropping patterns, betterment levies, water charges, and schedules when water will be made available. Outside the Irrigation Acts, the Indian Easements Act of 1882 links land ownership and the regulation of groundwater use. Of late, some states have passed legislation to regulate the use of groundwater and thus control overexploitation and misuse.

The jurisdiction of panchayats and municipalities to deal with water-related issues is not enshrined in the 11th and 12th Schedules of the constitution. Panchayats and municipalities are dependent on the enactment of legislation by states on the devolution of functions through executive action. Most preindependence legislation listed water supply as an obligatory function of municipalities. However, today water supply is regarded as a function delegated from state governments to parastatals. In some local body legislation, water supply in municipal area limits is treated as an obligation of the local body. However, legislation permits local bodies to provide this service on payment of reasonable cost, fixed under municipal regulations. Most municipal acts have made it obligatory for the harvesting of rainwater as part of a building plan.

The empowerment of local bodies is envisaged in Article 243-ZD of the constitution, relating to district planning committees, and Article 243-ZE, relating to metropolitan planning committees. In both these articles, it is obligatory for local bodies to prepare draft plans with regard to "sharing of water and other physical and natural resources." However, the only constitutional provision that has the potential of enabling water to be viewed as a common resource in a coordinated manner, albeit at local levels, has not been given due attention.[23]

In 1999, *Integrated Water Resource Development: A Plan of Action* recommended that all state Irrigation Acts be amended to incorporate provision for the formation of farmers' associations to take responsibility for the manage-

---

23   *Report of the Commission on Centre-State Relations, supra* note 3, at 37.

ment of water.[24] As a result, several states amended these Acts to accommodate farmers' participation in water management. Water committees, water users' associations, and beneficiary farmers associations have been included in canal committees and command area development programs.

A people-oriented participatory irrigation management scheme is slowly but steadily evolving in the states. Andhra Pradesh passed a Farmers' Management of Irrigation Act of 1997, providing for a three-tiered system of water management and distribution. The first level is at the primary level (minor canal level). A distributory committee represents the secondary level, and a project committee is the third level. Water user associations are entrusted with preparing a plan of action for maintenance of the system, carrying out the maintenance works in their area of operation, regulating the use of water according to a schedule, monitoring the flow of water, assisting the revenue department in preparing the demand and collection of water rates, and even resolving disputes between members.

At least half the states have either enacted exclusive legislation or amended the Irrigation Acts to provide for participation, though the new regimes vary widely in structure and function. These laws provide for overall control by the state either directly or through regulatory authorities. State authorities determine the command area and can change the jurisdiction of various water user associations (WUAs). In spite of the beneficial effects of such arrangements, criticism has been leveled that WUAs are gender discriminatory and not representative of the entire community. Although women have played a crucial role in household water management and participate in all agricultural activity, they have little say in WUAs, which are male dominated. Membership rules that provide for landholders or heads of households preclude women from becoming members. The relationship between WUAs and panchayati raj institutions (PRIs) is not clear. They exist alongside each other, and their powers overlap. The devolution of power to PRIs is tardy, due to states' reluctance to part with powers to panchayats, and the constitution of WUAs further complicates the issue of local management of water resources. The PRIs are more inclusive (with mandatory inclusion of women, Scheduled Castes and Scheduled Tribes), whereas WUAs represent only landholder interests. These inclusionary differences have raised issues regarding the institutional inability of WUAs to be instruments for equitable use of the water resources of the community.

A marriage of sorts between PRIs and control over water resources occurred with the provisions of the Panchayats (Extension of Scheduled Areas) Act of 1996. This Act gives powers to gram sabhas and panchayats in respect to minor water bodies, especially access to and control over them by tribal communities, as minor water bodies are considered (along with forests) a natural resource base on which people depend for sustenance.

---

24   Ministry of Water Resources, Government of India, *Integrated Water Resource Development: A Plan of Action*, vol. 1 (Sept. 1999).

Thus, the water management scenario in states is a complex institutional arrangement in which the central government, the state, the PRIs, the WUAs, civil society, and the private sector are all involved in the use and management of water resources. Although the Gujarat Infrastructure Act of 1999 provides for private sector participation in water supply and sanitation projects, the Karnataka Municipal Corporation's (Water Supply) Rules give a role to the private sector in urban water delivery systems.

If water is managed in terms of watersheds, then the implication is that the legal regime must facilitate a decentralized and participative arrangement for the management of water. However, considering the size of the country and the presence of multiple stakeholders, the issues in India are so complex that it is not possible for any one tier of government to manage water resources, and a joint effort is the only feasible way forward. "The management of equitable distribution and proper use of this natural resource," the *Report of the Commission on Centre-State Relations* observes,

> by a large population in a country, where rainfall is largely seasonal (with most of the precipitation in a limited number of days), and whose geography is characterized by varied topographical, geological and ecological features is a very complex task. . . . What is ground water at some stage becomes surface water at another and vice versa. . . . In such diverse forms water is not a mere economic resource which can be allocated unidimensionally. It has a societal relevance much beyond the economic, and is a matter of life, livelihood and cultural patterns. Since the stakeholders are so many a legalistic approach to conflict resolution is difficult. . . . It is now acknowledged by most experts that water harvesting and land management become key elements of water management and that these can be most efficiently performed by adopting the watershed approach. If water has to be so managed in terms of watersheds then it follows that the legal regime must facilitate a decentralized and participative regime considering the size of the country and multiple stakeholders.[25]

No one model can satisfy all the demands for this scarce resource in India. Stakeholders need to agree on principles based on equity and inclusion, conservation, and participation. On the basis of these principles, flexibility needs to be given to local administration to manage water use from all available sources. This pattern of decentralized governance is consistent with the federal formula of subsidiarity and efficiency. A template to refer to is the management of forests that has been adopted by Parliament. However, while states without forests can be equal participants in federal governance, states without sufficient water resources cannot survive unless their needs are met from states that have water. This is where the federal government can play a role, using a framework law.

---

25 *Report of the Commission on Centre-State Relations, supra* note 3, at 42–43.

In recent years, there has been a concerted move to a unified and planned approach to conserving all available sources of water and managing the rivers to maximum benefit under the control of the central government. The inter-linking of interstate rivers was recommended by technical committees and the judiciary.[26] However, because of opposition from the states, the initiative was abandoned, and it is unlikely that a constitutional amendment on this topic would get the necessary parliamentary support any time soon.

Expressing its disagreement with the view that water should be shifted from the State List (List-II) to the Concurrent List (List-III) the Commission on Centre-State Relations observed that nothing in the present arrangement prevents the central government or the states from doing what they need to do to promote a participatory approach. The constitution gives a direct responsibility to the states to legislate on the subject of water, and through parts IX and IX(A) enjoins the states to proceed with a further set of devolutions to local bodies. This, the commission concluded, is the appropriate path to a decentralized management of water resources. According to the Commission on Centre-State Relations,

> the Constitutional provisions as they stand are sufficient to address the issues of water use and management. A national consensus must emerge on water policy and this in turn should guide the legislations of the Centre under Entry 56 of List-I and those of the States under Entry 17 of List-II. . . . A hierarchical but co-ordinated set of water-shed agencies need to be set up by joint action of the Centre and States and participation of local bodies with inter-State basins as the focus. The concept of River Basin Organizations has been tried out successfully in several countries including neighbouring China. . . . The European Union has issued the Water Framework Directive which aims at sustainable management of water. It requires all member States to establish water laws conforming to common hydrological principles, which need to be applied on a river basin basis with the active participation of citizens. . . . In India, although no River Board or River Basin Organization has been constituted under the River Boards Act, 1956, a success story is available in the form of planning of the Damodar River system and operation through the Damodar Valley Corporation. Similarly, Bhakra-Beas Management Board, although set up for the limited purpose of power generation, also provides a successful example of integrated management. Similarly, the limited role of maintenance and regulation of the Tungabhadra Reservoir by the Tungabhadra Board for operation and maintenance of Dam and regulation of the flow, establishes the efficiency of integrated management.[27]

---

26   *See* Irrigation Commission, *Report of the Irrigation Commission, 1972* (Ministry of Irrigation and Power 1972); Ministry of Irrigation, *National Perspective for Water Development* (1980).

27   *Report of the Commission on Centre-State Relations, supra* note 3, at 45.

In short, the scheme of integrated water management proposed by the 2010 Centre-State Relations Commission involves the following:

- The development of a national water policy containing principles and directives for all stakeholders to follow in legislative and administrative action and including watershed management.

- Both the central government and state agencies will follow the mutually agreed-to provisions of the national water policy, which includes integrated watershed management.

- All states will establish river basin organizations for the planned development and management of a river basin as a whole or subbasins wherever necessary. The scope and powers of the river basin organizations will be decided by the basin states themselves.

- The central government will create interstate river basin authorities, whose responsibilities will be to oversee major engineering issues and allocations, and not the implementation of schemes or user participation.

- Local bodies, such as of civil society (as in watershed management), users associations (as in irrigation), and joint management groups (as in forestry) will play an active role in all water-related initiatives.

This proposal represents a major shift from an attempt at coordination through a large number of schemes implemented by numerous departments covering large areas (but not necessarily identified watersheds) to a legislatively ordained integration of coordinating authorities responsible for the interstate river basins and identified watersheds, set up by the central, state, and local authorities. The overall responsibility for coordination would be that of the interstate river basin authority set up by the central government under the River Boards Act.

Conclusions

Between 1976–80 and 2001–03, subsidies to agriculture grew from 3 percent of farm output to 7 percent. Over the same periods, government investment in farming was reduced from 4 percent to 2 percent of agriculture GDP. Most of the subsidies are for fertilizers, power, and irrigation water, and these have contributed to the degradation of natural resources.[28]

The costs of the monsoons in India are well-known. The average drop in grain output in a drought year is 11 percent. India's experience with drought is a set of ready policy responses in which the first approach is to draw down grain stocks to feed the poor, lower taxes on food imports, pay more for farm produce, and ensure the availability of power for irrigation. An alternate approach involves rehabilitating water delivery systems; this approach is not popular with the political class or the bureaucracy. Overexploitation of wells

---

28   *Eleventh Five Year Plan (2007–2012), Agriculture, Rural Development, Industry, Services and Physical Infrastructure*, vol. 3, 7 (Plan. Commn., Govt. of India).

and excessive use of groundwater for irrigation supported by a policy of subsidizing power and diesel for farmers' water pumps are leading to distortions in water delivery systems and their sustainability. Nothing short of a national consensus on integrated water management supported by a participatory legal regime can prevent a catastrophe that is waiting to happen.

Targeting Justice Sector Services to Promote Equity and Inclusion for the Poor in Jordan

PAUL PRETTITORE

The justice sector provides a number of direct services to citizens. Those services implemented by governments are frequently focused on court proceedings involving criminal, civil, and family law cases. As with other public sector services, services in the justice sector are often difficult for poor persons to access. Obstacles include a lack of awareness of available services and the procedures to access them, overly complicated procedures for proving eligibility and accessing services, and the relatively high costs of fees. Far too often, services, especially those targeted to the poor, exist on paper but not in practice. Efforts to develop policy to improve services are undermined by a lack of data on demand, as well as on the extent and quality of existing service provision. The lack of a comprehensive policy leads to contradictory approaches to reform; for example, at the same time that enhanced access for the poor is prioritized, fees associated with court procedures are raised and lawyers are required for cases with smaller financial value.

When designed and implemented effectively, justice sector services can play a role in promoting equality and inclusion for poor communities. They can provide mechanisms for individuals to exercise their fundamental rights, thus promoting equality, and for individuals to challenge detrimental government actions or inactions, thus promoting greater inclusion. When targeted properly to the poor, services can provide tools to ensure that the poor are aware of the rules that affect them and are able to enforce these rules in an efficient and effective manner.[1] Such services may include legal aid (information, counseling, and representation), waiver or deferment of court fees, and special procedures to simplify and expedite services that have a significant impact on the poor, such as alimony and child support. Legal aid itself is a "gateway" service, ultimately allowing beneficiaries to access other vital services, for example, court proceedings or entitlements such as social protection benefits.

---

1   The World Bank has advocated for more than a decade for reforms in the justice sector as a means to address poverty. The *World Development Report 2000/2001: Attacking Poverty* (World Bank 2000) associates the rule of law, of which the justice sector is a key component, with creating a predictable and secure environment for economic transactions and leading to better overall economic performance and poverty reduction. The rule of law has been defined as an environment in which the formal rules are publicly known and enforced in a predictable way through transparent mechanisms, such that rules apply to all persons as well as to the state.

Jordan, like other countries in the Middle East, has struggled with the design and implementation of services directed at the poor, namely legal aid services and deferment of court fees. The result is that these services are highly underutilized. The government of Jordan has taken steps to improve service delivery, which could positively impact on equality and inclusion for poor communities. Through a series of legislative amendments, existing services have been improved and new ones have been introduced that, if not aimed directly toward the poor, should benefit them nonetheless. These reforms have focused on key issues such as alimony, child support, and inheritance. The government of Jordan has also provided space for civil society organizations (CSOs) to develop legal aid services in a comprehensive manner. The first widespread survey focusing solely on justice sector issues was conducted by the Department of Statistics in 2011, and the resulting data provide a basis for policy development and reforms that will benefit poor users of court, lawyer, and legal aid services in that country.

Policy Development in the Justice Sector to Promote Equity and Inclusion

Issues of poverty reduction, equity, and inclusion have been addressed in numerous policies and strategies developed by the government of Jordan. However, the justice sector has rarely been linked to efforts in these areas. Past justice sector reform strategies focused on the institutional development of justice sector bodies and the improvement of general service delivery, which, if implemented adequately, would benefit all users of justice sector services but leave many of the unique obstacles faced by the poor in accessing services unaddressed. At present, there is no single entity in Jordan responsible for developing, coordinating, and implementing policy to improve services most impacting the poor. In this vacuum, the development of services will continue in an ad hoc manner, with limited ability to consolidate and build on specific improvements. Policy development needs to be more comprehensively linked to data and analysis concerning the quality and extent of current delivery of services, as well as the demand side from poor communities.

Recent reforms in the justice sector commenced with the establishment of the Royal Committee for Judicial Upgrading, mandated with assessing the justice sector and developing recommendations to build capacity to reflect international good practices. This committee made recommendations on a number of reforms, focused primarily on court administration.[2] The Ministry of Justice subsequently launched the Jordan Judicial Upgrading Strategy (JUST) 2004–2006 as a follow-up to the work of the royal committee. JUST 2004–2006 focused on improving general service delivery and capacity building for

---

2   The recommendations of the Royal Committee for Judicial Upgrading included increasing the number of judges; automating case management procedures; amending legislation to accelerate and simplify court proceedings; and establishing a division within the courts to supervise management of civil cases.

justice sector stakeholders, including the ministry itself, the Jordan Bar Association, and law faculties.[3] Due to the limited monitoring and evaluation of strategy implementation, the impact of these strategies is not well understood.

More recently, strategies have shifted to focus on issues of equality and social justice and have begun to link these issues with justice sector reforms. The We Are All Jordan strategy issued in 2006 promoted enhanced social justice,[4] whereas the National Agenda (2006–2015) promoted the achievement of justice and equality.[5] The concepts of equality and inclusion were linked with the justice sector through the Judicial Upgrading Strategy launched in 2010 (JUST 2010–2012). This strategy included the enhancement of access to justice as a component of the overall plan.[6]

In combination, these strategies have led to a number of achievements in the past decade, including the automation of case management procedures in civil and criminal courts (Mizan); the development of the Ministry of Justice website to provide information to the public on services, procedures for accessing services, and relevant legislation; the automation of functions of the Ministry of Justice (Masaq); the introduction of legislative amendments to streamline procedures (Landlord-Tenant Law, Criminal Procedure Code, Court Formation Law, misdemeanor cases); the introduction of the e-clearance certificate; and the establishment of specialized judicial chambers for the civil and criminal courts to promote the specialization of judges. A number of specialized judicial chambers were also established, including those covering intellectual property, companies, bankruptcy, commercial agencies, contracts, letters of credit, and maritime law.

These achievements should improve the quality of services for the general population, but they are unlikely to translate into enhanced equity and inclusion for poor communities if they are not linked with better-targeted services. For example, although JUST 2010–2012 referenced access to justice, no concrete activities were implemented and no real resources were made available to pursue this policy objective. Although a number of special court chambers were established that will likely benefit the private sector, none were established that cover the types of cases most likely to impact the poor, such as landlord-tenant disputes, consumer complaints, and disputes involving small

---

3   The recommendations of JUST 2004–2006 included improving service delivery, with a focus on efficiency and streamlining procedures; reducing demand for court services; strengthening inspection and monitoring; improving court infrastructure; automating judicial proceedings; improving efficiency of human resource systems; and enhancing service delivery of the public prosecution, notary public, and execution and notification departments.

4   The We Are All Jordan policy initiative promoted the principles of enforcing the rule of law and ensuring social justice.

5   The National Agenda (2006–2015) promotes the aims of enhancing the judicial and legislative systems to improve the rule of law and institutions, achieve justice and equality, and ensure fundamental freedoms, human rights, and democracy.

6   JUST 2010–2012 built on the priorities of JUST 2004–2006, focusing on improving court automation, information technology development, and court infrastructure, and enhancing the services of the execution and notary departments.

financial claims. Most reforms implemented with donor funding, including the case management automation programs, were not extended to cover the sharia courts, which have jurisdiction over family-related cases, which are of prime importance to the poor. And lowering the monetary threshold above which a lawyer must represent the parties in court could result in the exclusion of poorer persons from pursuing such cases, especially because access to legal aid remains a serious problem in civil cases.[7]

Targeting Services Based on Demand

Understanding the demands and priorities of poor communities is vital to effectively targeting services. The government of Jordan took a considerable step in defining needs through a household survey on the justice sector—the first of its kind in Jordan. In 2011, the Department of Statistics conducted the Statistical Survey on the Volume of Demand for Legal Aid (Justice Sector Household Survey), a survey of 10,000 households administered in rural and urban areas throughout the country. The survey covered a number of key issues important to assessing access to justice, including the most common types of legal cases; the costs of accessing courts and lawyers and knowledge of services provided; access to and familiarity with legal aid services; and the economic characteristics of families and individuals with legal disputes. Data based on gender and the monthly expenditure levels of respondents provide valuable information on the types of issues most affecting poor women and the steps they take to address them. In assessing access to services for the poor, it is important to consider the role of gender, given the unique obstacles faced by poor women, as identified in the Justice Sector Household Survey, and the fact poor women seem to need considerable assistance in accessing courts and lawyers, as demonstrated by an analysis of the caseload of the Justice Center for Legal Aid, which shows women account for nearly 70 percent of legal aid beneficiaries.

But data gaps on demand and the extent of service delivery remain. Attempts to better understand demand through analysis of existing service delivery are limited, despite the availability of basic data from key institutions such as the Ministry of Justice, the Ministry of Interior, the Ministry of Labor (Labor Courts), and the Complaints Management Unit of the Ministry of Public Sector Development. These data are not routinely compiled into usable formats or analyzed to shed light on demand and inform service delivery improvement in terms of access to justice for women. Public sector data are not routinely made available to other stakeholders, such as CSOs and academics. Nor are they easily available through the access to information framework currently in place, which suffers from a weak administrative framework.

---

7   In civil cases worth more than JD 1,000, parties are required to be represented by a lawyer; Law of Peace Courts No. 15 (1952) (Qanoun Mahakem al-Solh), art. 9, para 2.

Analysis of the Justice Sector Household Survey

Justice Sector Services and Poverty

The Justice Sector Household Survey provides valuable data on the types of disputes encountered by poor persons and how they address disputes through formal institutions. An analysis of that data (undertaken by the author) reveals several significant features of the ways in which the poor use justice sector services.

Higher Demand, but More Limited Access. The families more likely to report actionable legal issues—68 percent of respondents—fall into the two lowest categories of expenditure levels (less than JD 250 per month and JD 250–499 per month),[8] with only 6 percent falling within the highest expenditure category (more than JD 1,000 per month). Yet, poorer families are more likely to avoid court procedures when they have a dispute, and when they do go to court, they are less likely to have the assistance of a lawyer due to financial restraints (see figure 1). Forty-one percent of families that reported an actionable legal issue and are recipients of the National Aid Fund went to court without a lawyer because they could not afford one.[9] Of those respondents reporting a dispute but not accessing courts because of a lack of financial resources, a large majority reported willingness to file complaints in court if they could receive the following support: lawyer fees, court fees, and associated expenses such as transportation (87 percent); lawyer and court fees (85 percent); and lawyer fees (83 percent).

Figure 1. Use of courts and lawyers, by percentage

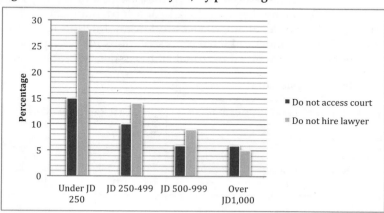

---

8   The categories of expenditure levels per month used in the survey are less than JD 250; JD 250–499; JD 500–999; and more than JD 1,000.

9   National Aid Fund Law of 1986 (Qanoun Sandouk al-Maoune al-Watanie li-sanet). The National Aid Fund, under the authority of the Ministry of Social Development, administers a number of programs to support vulnerable persons. Its largest program, in terms of scope, provides cash support to the poor and others in need. Thus, its beneficiaries represent some of the most vulnerable persons in Jordan.

Different Priorities. The most frequent types of cases reported vary by the expenditure levels of respondents. Poorer persons are more likely to be involved in personal-status disputes than in criminal disputes, while the reverse is true for those with higher expenditure levels. The greatest variation between respondents of different expenditure levels is observed in the category of personal-status cases (see the right-hand column in figure 2).

Figure 2. Frequency of case type by expenditure category

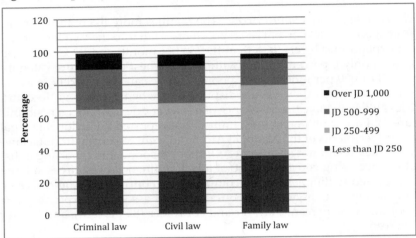

This trend is also reflected in an analysis of the caseload of the legal aid centers of the Justice Center for Legal Aid (JCLA), a Jordanian CSO that is the largest single provider of legal aid services in Jordan. In 2012, JCLA carried out 1,419 consultations and 1,014 legal representations for poor persons. Seventy-one percent of cases involved personal-status issues (see table 1).

Table 1. JCLA caseload analysis, 2012*

Case Type	Legal Consultations		Legal Representations	
Personal status	1,008	71%	719	71%
Civil	254	18%	106	11%
Criminal	111	8%	103	10%
Noncourt procedures (administrative)†	46	3%	86	8%
Total	1,419		1,014	

* Assessment of cases by the six legal aid centers of the Justice Center for Legal Aid in Amman, Madaba, and Zarqa.

† For example, drafting contracts and powers of attorney and filing administrative paperwork.

Within the category of personal-status issues, there is additional variation in terms of the most common types of cases (see figure 3). Alimony and inheritance cases are of more importance to poorer persons, whereas divorce and access to dowries are more important for persons with more resources.

Figure 3. Breakdown of personal-status cases, by expenditure level

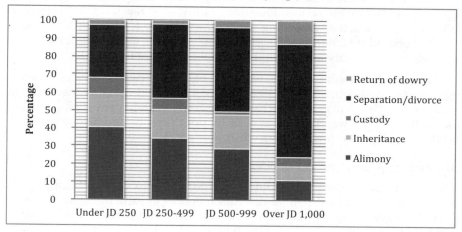

Overall, poorer persons form the bulk of respondents affected by legal disputes involving personal-status cases (see figure 4). There are several possible reasons for this trend. Economic assets falling under personal status—alimony, inheritance, child support, and dowries—may constitute a considerable portion of the overall assets of poor persons, particularly poor women, and are therefore worth fighting for. For those with more financial resources, the obstacles associated with court proceedings may outweigh the financial rewards. They may also have greater access to noncourt procedures such as negotiation through lawyers and mediation.

Figure 4. Frequency of personal-status case categories, by expenditure level

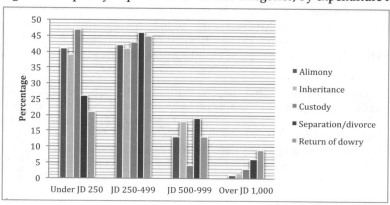

Lack of Knowledge of, and Access to, Special Services. Individuals who did not access courts because of costs expressed willingness to do so if they could receive assistance in covering certain costs, for example, through legal aid services. However, 98 percent of survey respondents were unaware of existing legal aid providers. And of the 2 percent who were aware of services, only 17 percent had tried to access them. The primary reasons for not accessing legal aid services were lack of knowledge of how to reach service providers (35 percent), not actually needing legal aid assistance (33 percent), and complicated procedures for securing services (27 percent). Of those attempting to access legal aid services, 78 percent were able to secure them.

The survey did not measure awareness of, and access to, services covering the deferment of court fees for poor persons involved in court proceedings. But anecdotal evidence suggests these services are rarely provided, primarily due to the lack of awareness of services by poor persons and justice sector officials, as well as complicated procedures for accessing them.

Justice Sector Services and Gender

There are no legislative or regulatory impediments to women bringing disputes to courts or other dispute resolution bodies in Jordan. However, anecdotal evidence suggests that women face societal pressures to avoid pursuing disputes, particularly in relation to personal-status issues and domestic or sexual violence. Social pressure may also steer women away from initiating claims directly with formal institutions—according to the JCLA, more than 70 percent of requests for assistance come from women. The household survey sheds light on the types of disputes women and men report and how they use court and lawyer services to address disputes.

The survey found that men were much more likely to report having had legal disputes. As individuals, men were three times as likely as women (75 percent for men versus 25 percent for women) to report having had a legal dispute in the past five years. Of the households reporting disputes, 92 percent were headed by men and 8 percent were headed by women. The extent to which men, in general, have more legal disputes or are simply more likely to report them is unclear. The reality is likely a combination of both, given the traditional and legal role of men as family guardians, requiring them to undertake more transactions and exposing them to more potential disputes, and the societal pressures on women to avoid raising disputes through formal mechanisms.

Women tend to experience different types of disputes than men do. Personal-status issues are of prime importance. Of respondents claiming to have experienced a legal dispute, women were nearly four times as likely as men to have an issue related to personal-status law—41 percent of women versus 11 percent of men. Women were less likely than men to report legal disputes related to criminal or civil law (see figure 5).

Figure 5. Categories of reported disputes, by gender

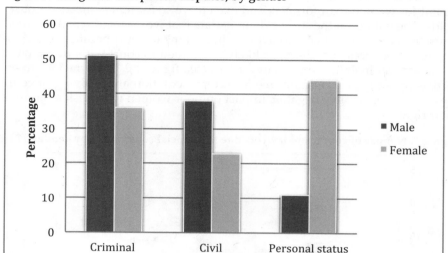

There are variations in the types of disputes men and women will bring to court (see figure 6). Women are more likely than men to avoid going to court for criminal and civil disputes, but not for personal-status cases, which suggests that personal-status issues are viewed by women as more critically impacting their lives. This might be partly explained by the fact that personal-status cases involve access to economic assets that are exclusively available to women (alimony and child support) or primarily available to women (dowries) and represent a considerable source of economic interests for women with limited access to assets (inheritance).

Figure 6. Respondents with actionable disputes who do not bring cases to court, by case type

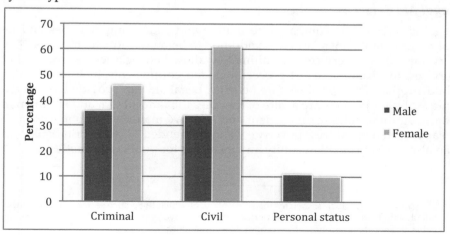

Access to financial resources for addressing disputes is more of a constraint for women than for men, and even more so for female-headed households. The data from the survey demonstrate that women and female-headed households are more likely to avoid filing claims in court because of lack of financial resources and are more likely to proceed to court without a lawyer because of an inability to pay lawyer fees (see figure 7). Thus, the lack of effective systems for providing free legal representation and waiving of court fees has a considerable negative impact on poor women who wish to enforce their rights.

Figure 7. Nonuse of courts and lawyers due to financial constraints, by gender

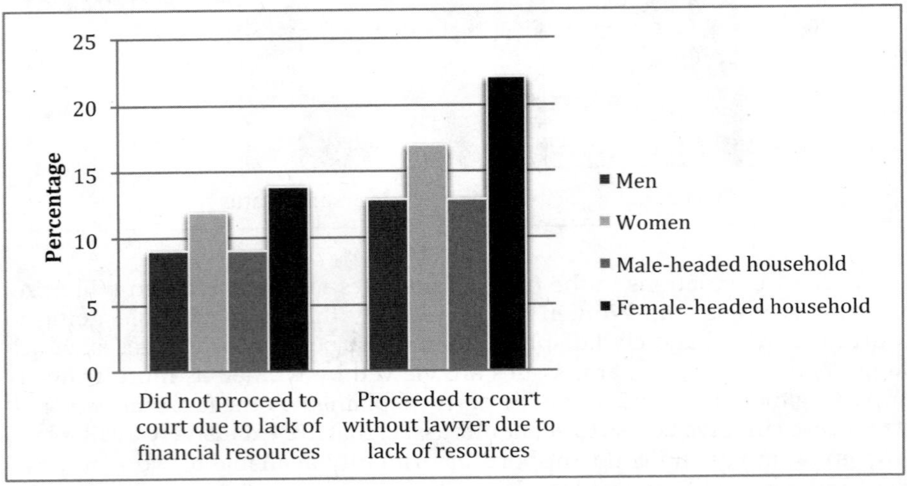

What State-Sponsored Services Are Targeted to the Poor?

Legal Aid Services

Legal aid services encompass information and counseling activities and legal representation by a lawyer. In addition to being services themselves, they serve as gateway services that ultimately allow beneficiaries to access other services, for example, court proceedings and entitlements such as alimony, child support, and social welfare benefits. Legal aid can provide tools to ensure that poor persons are aware of the rules that affect them and aid them in enforcing these rules in an efficient and effective manner. Not only can such an approach help address poverty—as recommended by the World Bank[10]—it can also aid in promoting equity and inclusion for poor communities.

---

10   *See supra* note 1, which associates the rule of law, of which the justice sector is a key component, with better overall economic performance and poverty reduction by creating a predictable and secure environment for economic transactions.

The government of Jordan has focused resources on legal representation, which can be provided through the courts,[11] the Jordan Bar Association,[12] or CSOs. Lawyers are paid to provide legal aid services when appointed through the courts or CSOs, although at a rate lower than they would normally be paid. Legal assistance through the Jordan Bar Association can involve payment from the government or be provided by the lawyer on a pro bono basis.

Deferment of Court Fees

Poor persons involved in court proceedings can request deferment of court fees until the case is resolved. Given the relatively high court fees, including fees for official stamps, this service could provide considerable relief for those unable to afford court proceedings.[13] However, the associated procedures are overly complicated. Applicants must provide numerous documents in a motion to the chief judge of the court for which fees would be deferred.[14] They must also produce witnesses or certification from local officials to attest to their poverty, although there are no set criteria for ascertaining poverty. Collecting numerous documents is burdensome for poor applicants, and review of documents is not the most effective use of the time of senior judges. If the party for whom the fees have been deferred wins the case, fees must be paid at the time the decision is issued, not when it is enforced. Thus, persons are required to pay fees before receiving a financial award.

Specialized Services for Personal-Status Cases

Personal-status cases in Jordan involve family law issues, including marriage, divorce, alimony, child custody and support, inheritance, and dowries. They affect a large segment of the population and, as demonstrated by the Justice Sector Household Survey and the analysis of the JCLA caseload, are of considerable importance to the poor. For example, alimony, child support, and inheritance may be the only considerable economic assets of a poor woman. Personal-status issues are under the jurisdiction of religious courts—sharia courts for Muslims and ecclesiastical courts for Christians—which form part of the formal judicial system but are administered separately from the civil and criminal courts. The National Agenda (2006–2015) includes a recommendation to develop the work of the sharia

---

11   Code of Civil Procedure of 1988 (Qanoun Ousoul Mohakamat Madanie li-sanet).

12   Law of the Regular Attorneys Association of 1972 (Qanoun Nakbaet al-Mohameen al-Nizamieen li-sanet).

13   Based on the indicator "enforcement of contracts" in the World Bank's *Doing Business Report 2012: Doing Business in a More Transparent World* (World Bank 2011). The court costs, as a percentage of the value of the claim, are as follows: Jordan, 8 percent; Syria, 4.5 percent; Lebanon, 3 percent; Iraq, 2.3 percent; West Bank and Gaza, 2.2 percent; and Egypt, 1.3 percent.

14   The required documentation includes certificates from the Department of Land and Survey, stating the applicant does not own land; the Department of Vehicles and Licenses, stating the applicant does not own a vehicle; and the Department of Social Security, stating the applicant has a limited salary or no salary. The chief judge of the relevant court can request additional documentation.

courts, which has led to a strategy on reform developed by the Supreme Judicial Council of the sharia courts. Courts were requested to establish guidelines, including outlining the procedures and documents required for each service, with the guidelines to be posted prominently within court facilities. The sharia courts have also begun work on a strategy to automate procedures of the Supreme Judicial Council and courts.

In 2010, major revisions were made to the Personal Status Code that resulted in the enhancement of existing services and the introduction of new services in the sharia courts.[15] These new services include expedited alimony and child support procedures, direct alimony payments made through an alimony fund, and protections related to the inheritance rights of women (see table 2). They were designed to address current gaps in service delivery. Although not necessarily directly targeted to poor persons, these reforms, if implemented properly, should provide additional tools for the poor to level the playing field in using court services to exercise their rights and access benefits to which they are entitled.

Table 2. Improving services for personal-status issues

Expedited alimony/child support payments	
• Alimony can be requested at the time of filing for divorce, rather than waiting for the finalization of the divorce.	• Addresses the fact that divorce proceedings can take years to finalize, during which time women did not have access to alimony payments, which has a particularly negative impact on poor women.
• Alimony can be paid immediately upon request rather than waiting for a court decision awarding alimony—"expedited alimony."	• Addresses the fact that divorce proceedings can take years to finalize, which has a negative impact on poor women. • Two conditions must be met: a guarantor is provided to guarantee repayment of alimony sums if the subsequent court decision does not provide for alimony; and a witness states that the applicant is able to repay alimony payments if necessary. Similar procedures allow for expedited child custody.
Alimony fund	
• Alimony is paid directly by the sharia courts to women in cases in which husbands fail to pay alimony according to court decisions. • Sharia court personnel are responsible for initiating proceedings against husbands who fail to make alimony payments.	• Enforcement of judicial decisions remains problematic; ensuring payment of alimony from courts directly to women will aid poor women for whom alimony is a considerable economic asset. • Poor women will not incur the added expense of repeatedly requesting courts for enforcement of alimony decisions. • Payments will be made electronically to bank accounts, instead of forcing women to report to court monthly to receive payments.

---

15   Provisional Law No. 36/2010, issued by the Council of Ministers (Sept. 26, 2010).

Access to inheritance	
• Revisions of the process of *takharoj* so that a female heir must wait 12 months after being awarded inheritance rights before such rights can be renounced and transferred to other heirs. • Alternatively, rights to land can be transferred through the Department of Land and Survey after rights have been registered in the name of the female heir, so that a female heir is aware of her rights before renouncing them.	• Address the societal pressure women face in renouncing inheritance rights in favor of male relatives, which has a particularly negative impact on poor women, because inheritance may be the primary means of transferring wealth.

Are State-Sponsored Services Targeted Accurately and Delivered Effectively?

There are a number of gaps in service delivery related to the provision of services targeted to the poor.

Legal Aid Services

There are a number of weaknesses in the targeting of legal aid services. The right to legal aid services exists only for serious criminal cases involving capital punishment or life imprisonment. Yet, data from both the Justice Sector Household Survey and the analysis of the JCLA caseload demonstrate that poor persons have considerable need for assistance related to personal-status and civil cases, a finding consistent with demand globally. Nearly 80 percent of those reporting personal-status disputes fell into the two lowest quartiles of expenditure levels in the Justice Sector Household Survey. And more than 70 percent of cases involving legal consultations and representation by JCLA involved personal-status issues, whereas 18 percent of counseling services and 11 percent of representation services involved civil law issues. Criminal issues accounted for less than 10 percent of services. Extending state-supported legal aid services to personal-status and civil issues would benefit women, who were four times as likely to report personal-status disputes and less likely to have access to a lawyer than men, according to the household survey.

Legal aid services are heavily focused on legal representation by lawyers. However, analysis of the JCLA caseload shows that legal representation is necessary only in about 30 percent of their cases. The vast majority of cases can be addressed through information and counseling. Yet, the government of Jordan has not initiated any comprehensive plan to support public information and awareness, leaving it up to CSOs to attempt to fill the gaps. There is no publicly funded counseling mechanism regarding legal issues.

Providing such services to the poor serves a number of purposes. Both public information and counseling can reach a larger number of beneficiaries than legal representation can because they require less time from service providers per beneficiary and can be targeted to communities or groups as opposed to individuals. They are also cheaper to provide per beneficiary because they require little to no time on the part of lawyers. Establishing public information kiosks or desks or information hotlines could help address needs.

There are numerous gaps in the effective delivery of legal aid. The system for implementing state-sponsored legal aid remains ineffective and underutilized, with very few instances of legal aid granted through either the courts or the bar association. Each mechanism for delivering services faces shortfalls. The process for assigning lawyers by courts is not always clear, and there is no established list of eligible lawyers kept by the court from which assignments can be made. Instead, judges might assign a lawyer present at the courthouse and pay fees that are too low to ensure quality. There are no written procedures for the Jordan Bar Association to follow in assigning lawyers to provide pro bono services, nor is any training or oversight provided to lawyers. Although CSOs have begun to fill the gap in legal aid services, their activities are highly dependent on funding from foreign donors, and the government of Jordan has not yet acted to integrate services.

There is limited use of nonlawyers (local experts, law students, apprentice lawyers) who could provide assistance on legal awareness, information and counseling, or development of pro bono programs for lawyers to provide representation when needed. Monitoring and evaluation of what services are provided are lacking, further negatively impacting the quality of services. For example, an impact evaluation of a legal aid program in Ecuador found positive correlations between the provision of legal aid and access to child support payments and reductions in domestic violence.[16] Experimenting with unbundling services so that lawyers are hired only for the procedures for which they are necessary, and developing pro se representation mechanisms, such as online information and self-help desks, could improve the quality and reach of services. The latter may be particularly beneficial in sharia courts, where parties are not required to have legal representation, and a model may already exist with the informal kiosks established outside court facilities to provide information on forms and procedures for small fees.

Determining eligibility for services is also inefficient, with no clear criteria for determining poverty and cumbersome procedures placed on applicants

---

16   See World Bank, *Impact of Legal Aid: Ecuador* (Rpt. No. 26915, Feb. 2003). For a broader discussion of the economic impact of legal aid services, *see* Bruce M. Owen & Jorge Portillo, *Legal Reform, Externalities and Economic Development: Measuring the Impact of Legal Aid on Poor Women in Ecuador* (Stanford Inst. for Econ. Policy Research Discussion Paper No. 02-32, May 2003).

and officials responsible for reviewing applications. Eligibility guidelines developed by CSOs could serve as a model. Due to institutional weaknesses, there is limited ability to provide services outside Amman, especially to poor, rural areas. And funding for legal aid services is not yet sustainable, with the majority of funding provided by international donors. Development of a legal aid fund, as is under discussion to cover criminal cases, or a sliding scale of payments for services could help address financial sustainability issues. A longer-term strategy for provision of services that balances needs with resources could enhance sustainability.

Deferment of Court Fees

Deferment of court fees is perhaps better targeted to the needs of the poor than state-sponsored legal aid services. Given that court costs in Jordan are relatively high, providing deferment of fees in civil cases will benefit the poor facing cases involving issues such as employment, housing, and consumer affairs, as well as social benefits. If fees are deferred for a party, they are required to be repaid only if the party wins the case. But repayment is supposed to be made at the time the judgment in the case is issued, not upon enforcement. This in particular presents a considerable burden for the poor because they are required to make a payment before receiving their financial award, especially considering the weakness in enforcement of judicial decisions in Jordan and the length of time that might be required for enforcement procedures.

There are no available data on the frequency with which deferment of court fees is requested and awarded, but anecdotal evidence suggests it is provided only rarely. This is due to several factors. There is a general lack of awareness among the public, and even among judges and court staff, that this service exists. Although the Justice Sector Household Survey did not measure the awareness of deferment of court fee services, it did show that roughly 98 percent of respondents were unaware of legal aid services in general; similar findings would likely apply to deferment services. When there is awareness, there is often limited knowledge of the relevant procedures, and potential beneficiaries may be deterred by the overly complicated nature of the procedures. The process for proving eligibility and implementing relevant procedures requires assembling a number of official documents from different government agencies and the production of witnesses, providing a considerable disincentive for intended beneficiaries to apply.

Special Services for Personal-Status Issues

Recent legislative and regulatory amendments have reformed existing services and introduced new services related to several personal-status issues that are of prime importance to the poor, including access to alimony, child support, and inheritance. Based on the findings of the Justice Sector Household Survey and the analysis of the JCLA caseload, these reforms should result in more accurate targeting of services to the poor, especially poor women. These reforms also have the potential for positive impacts on social and economic development by increasing the economic assets of poor women, which can in turn improve women's agency.[17] The results could be better equity and inclusion, particularly for poor women.

A number of policy initiatives are aimed at improving the targeting to poor users of court services and promoting greater equality and inclusion, especially for poor women. Expedited alimony and child support services have been introduced to address the fact that divorce proceedings can drag on for years, during which women may not receive any support. For poor women, given the low rates of female labor force participation, this time lag may mean the elimination of the sole means of financial support.[18] Direct alimony payments by the sharia courts through an alimony fund are designed to compensate for the overall poor enforcement of judicial decisions. Special protections for inheritance rights of women are meant to provide a means for women to counter societal pressure to renounce inheritance rights guaranteed them by law in favor of male relatives.

Traditionally, sharia courts have been more financially accessible to poor persons than criminal and civil courts because court-related costs, such as filing fees and fees for powers of attorney, are lower or nonexistent and parties are not obligated to be represented by a lawyer, thus reducing legal costs. Unfortunately, the same cannot be said for the ecclesiastical courts, where procedures and costs are not clearly framed in legislation and regulations, resulting in ad hoc service delivery.[19] The Justice Sector Household Survey found that average lawyer costs for personal-status issues—roughly JD 542—are considerably lower than for civil (JD 902) and criminal (JD 958) cases.

However, navigation through issues and procedures related to disputes over alimony, child support, and inheritance are complicated, and legal advice may be necessary in order for parties to make informed decisions. For example, division of inheritance is set in law, but the amounts awarded for alimony and child support are negotiable and need to be firmly established through court procedures. Sixty-four percent of household survey respondents found the presence of a lawyer useful for their case.

Mediation services, which for many disputes are obligatory as a first step, are offered free of charge and provide another lower-cost mechanism for the poor. Regulations that support implementation of the alimony fund have been drafted, and once adopted by the Council of Ministers and implemented effectively, the fund could have considerable impact on the social and eco-

---

17   For a more thorough discussion of the agency, access to justice, and development for women in Jordan, *see* World Bank, *Agency, Equality and Access to Justice,* in *Hashemite Kingdom of Jordan, Jordan Country Gender Assessment: Economic Participation, Agency and Access to Justice in Jordan,* ch. 3 (Report No. ACS5158, July 2013) (hereinafter, *Jordan Country Gender Assessment*).

18   For an assessment of women's labor force participation, *see Jordan Country Gender Assessment,* ch. 2, *Women's Economic Participation.*

19   *See* Amal Haddadin, *Good Practices and Lessons Learned in Realizing Women's Rights to Productive Resources: The Case of Jordan* (Jordanian Natl. Commn. for Women, June 2012), available at http://www.unwomen.org/wp-content/uploads/2012/07/EP-Good-practices-and-lessons-learned-in-realizing-womens-right-to-productive-reources-the-case-of-Jordan.pdf.

nomic development of poor women by providing them access to an important economic asset.

Conclusion

Literature on the impact of justice sector services in the promotion of equity and inclusion is minimal. Instead, analytical work has focused primarily on economic impacts without necessarily drawing on links to improved equity and inclusion. Anecdotally, the links seem strong. Equality is a constitutional right in Jordan, and the justice sector plays a role in ensuring that this right can be exercised by vulnerable groups most likely to be faced with inequality, including the poor and women. Improving service delivery to the poor will help level the playing field in the justice sector, which is often tilted in favor of those with more financial resources. If the poor have greater recourse to the justice sector, they will have increased ability to hold public sector entities accountable for nondelivery of services and nonenforcement of rights, which can translate into greater inclusion.

The government of Jordan's approach to improving delivery of justice sector services to the poor has thus far demonstrated mixed results. Justice sector services are underutilized by the intended beneficiaries for a myriad of reasons related to the lack of comprehensive policy, institutional weaknesses, and legislative gaps. Targeting of legal aid services, in particular, is not consistent with the priorities of the poor. Targeting of court deferment services in civil cases is more accurate in terms of addressing an obstacle faced by the poor in accessing courts, but lack of awareness and burdensome procedures to prove eligibility leave the majority of the targeted beneficiaries outside the scope of these services. Special services related to personal status are well targeted to the priority needs of the poor, but because the services have only recently been introduced, it remains to be seen how effective they are in practice.

The Justice Sector Household Survey and the analysis of the JCLA caseload provide three key conclusions in terms of gaps in targeting and implementing services in Jordan:

- Poor persons are more affected by legal disputes, but are less able to access services provided by courts and lawyers, than those with more resources.

- Poor persons are primarily affected by a different set of issues than persons with more resources—poorer persons are disproportionately affected by personal-status cases.

- State-sponsored services that focus on criminal issues and court proceedings are not well aligned with the needs of poorer persons, and awareness of services among targeted beneficiaries remains weak.

Other sources of data can be developed, including the automated case management system of the Ministry of Justice and the Public Sector Complaints Hotline of the Ministry of Public Sector Development, as well as the caseloads of the Ombudsman Bureau, the Anticorruption Commission, and the National Aid Fund. Together, these data could serve as the basis for data-informed reforms to services.

At present, it is difficult to measure the effect of justice sector services on equity and inclusion. Thus, determining the impact of services on the promotion of equity and inclusion of the poor, perhaps complementing a system for measuring impact on poverty, is an important next step for the government of Jordan. Such an assessment will aid in the regular monitoring and evaluation of the quality and reach of existing services, which will guide reforms of existing services to ensure more accurate targeting to poor beneficiaries, in particular in regard to legal aid services. It will also, in combination with data on the demand side of services within poor communities, inform the development of new services aimed at addressing the priorities of the poor within the justice sector. And it can aid in filling a data gap in linking the justice sector with improved equity and inclusion outcomes for the poor.

Serving the Justice Needs of the People

Adopting an Access to Justice Approach in Somalia's Rule of Law Reform

NICHOLAS JOSEPH

Access to justice has gained predominance in rule of law reform efforts in postconflict societies and countries transitioning from authoritarian to democratic rule. Since Western nations began to engage in major rule of law interventions, scholars and practitioners have focused their efforts on understanding and implementing the most appropriate ways to make the law serve the needs of the people, to enable the people to enforce and uphold their human rights, and to ensure that the law advances people's economic and social development.

Since the adoption of the Provisional Constitution on August 1, 2012, Somalia has embarked on its own rule of law reform process. Having learned from the lessons of previous rule of law reform efforts, as well as more nuanced and innovative approaches to justice development and reform, the current Somali government and justice institutions can implement rule of law reforms that contribute directly to the empowerment and economic development of the people of Somalia.

This chapter maps the history of access to justice theory from early interventions in the latter half of the 20th century to current theories and practice aimed at furthering people's access to their legal systems. It then traces the legal, social, and political context of Somalia from the beginnings of postcolonialism to the present. In doing so, it illustrates how justice has interacted with the ordinary citizen in Somalia, presenting evidence that the law has extensively failed to serve Somalis' needs throughout history. Based on this examination of previous rule of law reform in Somalia, the final section of this chapter draws on lessons learned from innovative practices of rule of law reform in recent years and proposes ways in which decision makers can effectively influence the trajectory of Somalia's law reform, to ensure that people are aware that they can avail their rights and know how to do so; and to ensure that there are adequate channels for citizens to seek justice and find remedies for any wrongs they have suffered.

Any statements of fact, opinion, or analysis expressed herein are entirely those of the author and are not attributable to the International Development Law Organization. The author would like to thank Ilary Ranalli for her valuable thoughts and comments on this chapter.

Access to Justice and Rule of Law Reform

It can be asserted that, regardless of the methodology of law reform, all efforts led by international interventions have been for a single purpose: "a commitment to increasing access to legal institutions and the quality of 'justice' delivered by those institutions."[1] Whether through traditional rule of law efforts, which center on the capacity development of lawyers and judges, or the more innovative approaches that emphasize the empowerment of the people to better their lives through the law, all efforts converge on the single aim to enable the "ability of people to seek and obtain a remedy through formal or informal institutions of justice, and in conformity with human rights standards."[2]

The best way to analyze the evolving methods of ensuring access to justice is to understand the context in which individual citizens struggle to gain access to justice in the formal justice systems. Wojkowska[3] and Barendrecht et al.[4] list several problems that limit access to formal justice systems: nonexisting procedures for the protection of specific rights, limited resources available to the claimants to access expensive services, mistrust of the law, intimidation by authorities and resulting fear among claimants, language difficulties, lack of understanding of formal procedures and court atmosphere, unequal power relations, and lengthy periods for handling cases. In addition, formal systems may lack legitimacy if they have previously created conflict and/or been perceived as corrupt. Most people in poor countries do not seek justice from formal courts because of these barriers.[5]

With the above contextual understanding, this section will next look at the evolution of rule of law reform, from the earliest tradition of reform in the 1970s, which focused on institutional strengthening of the state justice infrastructure, to the emergence of legal empowerment theories, which place the impoverished directly at the center of rule of law reform considerations.

Early Rule of Law Reform Projects

In the earliest rule of law reform projects, the emphasis was on improving the quality and competency of the judiciary and the legal profession through training for judges and improved legal education for lawyers. The theory behind supporting this "top-down" approach to rule of law reform was pre-

---

1   Byron M. Sheldrick, *Access to Justice and Legal Empowerment as Vehicles of Poverty Alleviation: Governance Challenges to Linking Legal Structures to Social Change* 2 (Legal Working Paper Series on Leg. Empowerment for Sustainable Dev., Ctr. for Intl. Sustainable Dev. L., 2012).

2   *Programming for Justice: Access for All—A Practitioner's Guide to a Human Rights–Based Approach to Access to Justice* 5 (UNDP, Bangkok 2005).

3   Ewa Wojkowska, *Doing Justice: How Informal Justice Systems Can Contribute* (UNDP, Oslo Governance Ctr. 2006).

4   Maurits Barendrecht, José Mulder, & Ivo Giesen, *How to Measure the Price and Quality of Access to Justice?* (working paper, 2006), available at http://papers.ssrn.com/sol3/papers .cfm?abstract_id=949209.

5   Dan Banik, *Rights, Legal Empowerment and Poverty: An Overview of the Issues*, in *Rights and Legal Empowerment in Eradicating Poverty* 15 (Dan Banik ed., Ashgate 2008).

mised on the belief that with the establishment of a functioning, competent, and independent judiciary and legal profession, individual citizens within the country would have an incentive to use formal channels of justice to avail their rights. In socioeconomic development thinking, the use of the courts and the formal legal system leads to efficient and effective business and thus promotes business within the country and increases the appetite for international investors to invest and operate within the jurisdiction. Rule of law theorists believed that, in turn, a trickle-down effect would bring economic prosperity to others within the country, even though they were not necessarily direct users of the reformed justice system. The problems of this theory, however, were evident after the first wave of large-scale law reform efforts concluded. Building effective, efficient, and uncorrupt legal and judicial systems from the ground up—or worse, trying to challenge the entrenched practices and procedures of a largely inept judicial corps—was a task more difficult than originally fathomed. Although millions of dollars were poured into legal education and training programs, judiciaries are still seen as lacking independence and largely biased.[6]

It could be said that the initial efforts of law reform did benefit some—mainly the elite. However, although measures of GDP or other indicators may have shown a positive correlation in rule of law reform efforts, the multiplier effect originally envisioned, whereby ordinary citizens would see their own economic and social development through reformed judicial infrastructure, was largely unfounded. For many people in these countries, the courts continue to be viewed with distrust and suspicion, and therefore it is fair to conclude that these traditional interventions have not raised the developmental well-being of the many they were intended to serve.[7]

As the global neoliberal agenda grew throughout the 1980s, and with the collapse of the Soviet Union beginning at the end of that decade, rule of law reform efforts moved toward trade liberalization and developing domestic commercial laws capable of bringing a country's economic, and therefore legal, regime into line with the global economic expansion under way in much of the Western world. The successes of such efforts were limited and, again, served the interests of the economic elite. In addition, a global shift to discontent of neoliberal policies meant that elected officials and development agencies were increasingly under attack to change their approaches to the treatment of developing countries in the globalized world.[8]

The Emergence of the Legal Empowerment Paradigm

A new thinking was needed for various governments' approaches to international cooperation in the field of rule of law reform. The Commission on Legal

---

6   Sheldrick, *supra* note 1, at 3.

7   Brian Tamanaha, *The Primacy of Society and the Failures of Law and Development* (Leg. Stud. Research Paper No. 09-0172, St. John's U. School of Law, July 2009).

8   Sheldrick, *supra* note 1, at 3.

Empowerment of the Poor (CLEP) was launched in 2005, comprising members from Denmark, Finland, Iceland, Norway, Sweden, Canada, Egypt, Guatemala, Tanzania, and the United Kingdom.[9] Headed by economist Hernando de Soto and former U.S. secretary of state Madeleine Albright, the commission emphasized the importance of various elements vital to successful law reform for economic development. Property rights, access to justice and the rule of law, and business and labor rights were high on the agenda. More important for the discussion in this chapter, the commission paid due regard to bottom-up and pro-poor approaches. In addition, the commission recognized that the informal and customary justice mechanisms present within countries could act as enablers for access to justice for ordinary citizens.[10] Legal empowerment was aptly defined by the commission as a process of "systemic change through which the poor and excluded become able to use the law, the legal system, and legal services to protect and advance their rights and interests as citizens and economic actors."[11]

An interesting point to note regarding legal empowerment theory is that it focuses on the "legal," that is, the codification and promotion of individual property rights, business rights, and employment rights. However, in addition to the need to ensure the reform of laws adequate to protect the fundamental rights of individuals and their economic interests, the concept of legal empowerment also emphasizes the importance of the "nonlegal." This is in the sense that the nonlegal recognizes "related activities"[12] that complement legal services but that in themselves are not inherently law oriented. These related activities include community organizing, group formation, political mobilization, and use of the media. Legal services can, in and of themselves, constitute and produce legal empowerment, although the greater efficiency of the use of the law is often improved when tied with these related activities.

Historical Perspectives of Justice in Somalia

In proposing solutions to the appropriate rule of law reform program that Somali decision makers and international donors might consider, it is necessary to look at the history of the legal, political, and social context of Somalia. In keeping with the legal empowerment theory, it is necessary to understand how power dynamics affect legal reform efforts and give some insight into the success of any proposed intervention and the obstacles that a rule of law

---

9   *Making the Law Work for Everyone*, vol. 1: *Report of the Commission on Legal Empowerment of the Poor* (Commn. on Leg. Empowerment of the Poor, UNDP 2008) (hereinafter, CLEP Report).

10   *Id.*, at 21.

11   Banik, *supra* note 5, at 12; CLEP Report, *supra* note 9, at 3.

12   Stephen Golub, *Beyond Rule of Law Orthodoxy: The Legal Empowerment Alternative* 26 (Carnegie Endowment Working Paper No. 41, R. of L. Ser., Democracy and R. of L. Project 3, Carnegie Endowment for Intl. Peace 2002).

intervention may face. As Michael Anderson states: "Constitutionalism and the rule of law depend upon sustained political support."[13]

This section highlights how the political, social, and legal context of Somalia has enhanced or hindered people's access to justice. Such a sociopolitical background will provide further insight into how to incorporate various access to justice and legal empowerment approaches into proposed solutions to Somalia's rule of law reform efforts over the coming years. This section addresses three issues that, it can be argued,[14] have hindered access to justice up to the present. The first issue regards how the plurality of legal systems—civil and common statutory law, customary *xeer* law, and sharia law—have brought about a tangle of legal systems offering varying degrees of access while simultaneously creating winners and losers in terms of providing access; among the latter: women, minority groups, and the impoverished. The second issue is Somalia's fallout with colonialism and its struggle to implement effective law reform efforts. The third issue is Somalia's period of dictatorship under the Siad Barre regime, the regime's approach to the rule of law, and the authoritarian and autocratic regime's role in depleting the culture of justice and the rule of law among elites and ordinary citizens in Somalia.

Background of Somalia

Somalia has lacked an effective national government since 1991, when the government collapsed following the ousting of President Mohamed Siad Barre. Over the past two decades, various armed groups have vied for political dominance in South Central Somalia, the most recent of which is Al Shabab, an Al Qaeda–linked armed group that has opposed the federal government and its efforts to put in place a new provisional constitution for Somalia. However, the situation in Somalia has been improving from both a political and a security perspective. A relatively peaceful political transition took place alongside the adoption, on August 1, 2012, of the Provisional Constitution of Somalia, the first official new national constitution in 52 years, which currently awaits a popular referendum. Furthermore, Mogadishu is now under the direct control of the Somali government, with assistance from African Union troops. Major cities in the south of Somalia, including Kismayo, have been recovered from Al Shabab control.

Justice and security are also necessary for Somalia's economic and social development, and vital for the protection of human rights. The current institutions and organizations that make up the security and justice sectors (such as the police, armed forces, and judiciary) are often unable to provide people with adequate services. In the past two decades, donor investment in the area

---

13 Michael R. Anderson, *Access to Justice and Legal Process: Making Legal Institutions Responsive to Poor People in LDCs* 12 (IDS Working Paper No. 178, Inst. of Dev. Stud. 2003).

14 Much of the primary research to find this evidence was undertaken by the Centre for Humanitarian Dialogue in partnership with the UNDP Rule of Law and Security (ROLS) project and is presented in a report: Andre Le Sage, *Stateless Justice in Somalia: Formal and Informal Rule of Law Initiatives* (Ctr. for Humanitarian Dialogue 2005).

of justice has been minimal, which has led to a paucity of qualified justice professionals in the three zones of Somalia: Somaliland, Puntland, and South Central Somalia. The latter zone receives less investment than the other two areas, which currently enjoy relative peace.

The Plurality of Legal Systems

Xeer

Given the total collapse of the state in the early 1990s, it is perhaps not surprising that traditional forms of dispute resolution have flourished and are now the primary form of justice in Somalia. Somali customary law, *xeer*, covers issues ranging from clan relations to personal injuries, including the spectrum from death to minor injuries, penalties for which are paid in livestock. It also covers issues relating broadly to property matters, family law, and territory. The system is not simple or arbitrary. Community elders, charged with adjudicating to reach conclusions over any given case, use procedures and rules of precedent.

Xeer has been highly successful, for example, in settling land disputes and returning property to persons displaced during Somalia's wars. Nonetheless, the system has flaws, including potentially unfair or discriminatory results, in which clans are judged as unequal in standing, and the rejection of clan laws by returning expatriates, among other issues. Perhaps most problematic is the treatment of women under *xeer*. Forced marriage is one of the issues facing women, including the possibility of forcing a rape victim to marry her attacker. Women are also forbidden by *xeer* to inherit certain capital assets.[15]

Sharia

Sharia has historically been applied in Somalia by the civil courts of first instance, particularly regarding issues of family law and inheritance. With the collapse of the state, however, sharia courts began to appear throughout the country and began to focus on both criminal and civil cases, including the apprehension and detention of criminals. These courts also dealt extensively with commercial disputes. The use of sharia law has a number of benefits, most notably the fact that its jurisdiction is unquestioned by all Somalis. However, most of the judges in the sharia courts lack formal training, and religious leaders within clans have tended not to support them.[16]

Statute-Based Justice System

The legislatively mandated structure of the judiciary in Somalia is well defined on paper.[17] At the apex of the formal judiciary is a Judicial Service Coun-

---

15   *Id.*, at 32–38.

16   *Id.*, at 38–47.

17   Two enactments govern the details of the Somali formal judiciary: Law No. 3, June 12, 1962, and Law No. 34, Aug. 11, 1974. Available at http://www.so.undp.org/docs/Somali%20%20Judiciary%20Organization%20Law%20No%203%20of%2012%20June%201962.pdf.

cil, which supervises the entire judiciary. Legislation to date has established a Supreme Court, constituted as the Constitutional Court or High Court of Justice.[18] Beneath the Supreme Court, there is a Court of Appeal,[19] and beneath that, two courts of first instance, the District Court[20] and the Regional Court.[21] The district courts are further divided into criminal (for minor offenses)[22] and civil divisions;[23] and the civil divisions are further divided into family and ordinary sections.[24] The regional courts are also divided into civil and criminal sections, with the civil section further subdivided into ordinary, administrative, and labor sections.[25]

The current statutory justice system, however, lacks qualified legal professionals. Courts are largely based solely in regional capitals, leaving the rural poor little access to these systems due to economic and logistical constraints. Judges and lawyers lack sufficient knowledge of existing laws. The weakness of the legislatures across the regions of Somalia indicates that there are not enough laws enacted to deal with changing social conditions. Physical infrastructure and resources are dilapidated, such that even if there were lawyers and judges sufficiently trained to present and adjudicate on a case, the lack of resources could cause severe delays for the claimants or keep the case from being concluded.[26]

Depleted Culture of Justice

Owing to Somalia's history of colonialism under British and Italian rule and the law reform initiated by Siad Barre in the latter years of his administration, Somalia and Somali people are faced with a number of laws and legal systems that have little resonance with their day-to-day lives, their historical and cultural background, and their entrenched beliefs and values.

At independence in 1960, when British Somaliland and Italian Somalia were united to form the Somali Republic, four distinct legal traditions—British Common Law, Italian (Continental) law, Islamic sharia, and Somali customary law—were in simultaneous operation.[27] To simplify this amalgam of

---

Much of this section is based on Tahlil Haji Ahmed, *Follow-Up Assessment of TFG Judiciary in Mogadishu*, secs. 1.6.1–1.6.4 (UNDP, Somalia 2011).

18   Law No. 3, June 12, 1962, arts. 5–6.

19   *Id.*, at art. 4.

20   *Id.*, at art. 2.

21   *Id.*, at art. 3.

22   *Id.*, at art. 2(4).

23   *Id.*, at art. 2(3).

24   *Id.*, at art. 2(3), which details the District Court's jurisdiction over sharia and customary law.

25   *Id.*, at art. 3(3)(a), which confers jurisdiction to the Regional Court concerning all matters not conferred to district courts.

26   Le Sage, *supra* note 14, at 32, and evidenced in the Somalia Justice Sector Action Plan, 2013–2015, on file with the author.

27   *Id.*, at 18.

laws, the Somali government established a Consultative Committee for Integration of the Legal Systems to recommend how to create a unified justice system. The Law on the Organization of the Judiciary was the outcome of the deliberations, and in 1962 the Somali Parliament enacted the law, with civil and penal codes based on the Italian legal system, and criminal procedure based on the Indian Code.[28] Despite these reforms, or perhaps due to the lack of clarity on jurisdictional issues that this very law was supposed to provide, judges and lawyers continued to apply laws in accordance with their region's legal history.

Shortly after the military coup initiated by General Mohamed Siad Barre, the regime sought swiftly to reform the Somali legal system to reflect the regime's political alignment with the Soviet Union. The regime made a series of changes that largely eliminated the legal provisions or jurisprudence of the sharia and *xeer* legal systems. In addition, the regime significantly modified existing Italian codes to suit the requirements of authoritarian rule. Law No. 1 (October 21, 1969) prescribed authority for all judicial functions, as well as absolute executive and legislative powers, to the regime. In addition to this, Barre operated beyond the rule of law and issued decrees beyond the confines of any legal mandate. The corruption and repressive practices of the dictatorship left negative public perceptions of the formal legal and judicial systems that persist to this day.[29]

Going Forward: Somalia's Rule of Law Reform

Applying contemporary thinking to rule of law reform on the global scale, this section proposes access to justice approaches and innovative legal empowerment processes for Somalia. Noting Stephen Golub's theory of the "nexus"[30] approach that legal empowerment adopts, this section draws on opportunities in which Somalia can look beyond the traditional rule of law approaches to more innovative solutions that put the ordinary citizen—the poor, the disadvantaged, or the minority individual—at the center of such rule of law reform efforts.

As noted in the original definition of access to justice, the "ability of people to seek and obtain a remedy through formal or informal institutions of justice, and in conformity with human rights standards,"[31] the options proposed highlight the use of mechanisms that directly target enhancing the ability of individuals to find a remedy for their grievances. This section first looks at contemporary models used in the formal justice system. The International Development Law Organization (IDLO), under its land-titling initiative, experimented with a number of models to support different communities' ef-

---

28   *Id.*

29   *Id.*, at 20.

30   Golub, *supra* note 12, at 27.

31   UNDP, *supra* note 2.

forts in legally titling their land. Of importance for the discussion here was the effective use of paralegals in reaching this goal. Second, attention will be given to the use of civil society as an agent of change, to be able to build the rule of law among communities and to bring about a culture of justice. Third, the report of a recent IDLO study on the involvement of customary and traditional justice in bringing about improved access to justice for rural communities will be assessed. Law reform is also a vital component of improving individuals' access to justice. This section illustrates how the review of the Somalia Provisional Constitution over the next term of Parliament could provide an opportunity to strengthen the law-making process and to ensure that constitutional and legislative reform and implementation comply with the principles of access to justice, primarily that individuals be adequately equipped and have the incentive to seek remedy for wrongs committed against them.

Paralegals

Paralegals signify the opportunity to provide innovative bottom-up approaches to rule of law reform. Paralegals are not trained lawyers, but one of their strengths is that they are often drawn from the very community they are intended to serve. Following their recruitment, they receive specialized legal training and they are then charged to return to their communities to provide civic awareness and education on various rule of law issues, legal advice, and legal assistance to those in need. The benefits of using this approach, as opposed to the traditional top-down development of lawyers and the traditional legal profession, are severalfold, as illustrated by the work of IDLO and the NGO Namati, discussed below.

In response to the injustices associated with national governments of developing countries granting vast amounts of land to domestic and international investors, recent moves have been made in various countries to enable rural communities to legally title their land and protect it from being sold. In 2009, IDLO and Namati, an organization with its mandate focused specifically on legal empowerment, supported the implementation in these nations of the laws passed to enable rural communities to register their lands as a single legal entity and act as decentralized land administration and management bodies.[32] The Community Land Titling Initiative, which launched a randomized, controlled trial in Liberia, Uganda, and Mozambique to support the communities' efforts, produced a number of lessons learned that can be applied to the current context of Somalia's rule of law reform.

The experimental trials adopted for the initiative tested three models for facilitating community land protection: a full legal services approach, in which communities had direct assistance from lawyers; a pared-down rights-education approach, where information was provided and little else; and a middle-path, community-paralegal approach, in which a community

---

32   *Executive Summary*, in *Protecting Community Lands and Resources: Evidence from Liberia, Mozambique and Uganda* 3 (Rachel Knight et al. eds., Namati & Intl. Dev. L. Org. 2012).

representative was trained and supported in driving the process forward. What proved interesting in the findings of this experiment was that communities receiving full legal services tended to rely on the outside professionals to be able to undertake the land registration process, while communities with paralegals tended to take greater ownership over the process. Additionally, the paralegals' inside knowledge of community issues enabled them to better assist community members in successfully completing the land registration process and securing rights over their communal land. In contrast, state lawyers' lack of understanding of local dynamics largely resulted in their adding little value to the process.[33] The evidence, although directly linked to land registration processes, serves as a valuable tool to scale up and transpose onto other areas of rule of law reform.

Considering the deep distrust of the traditional formal justice system, mentioned earlier in this chapter, the positive effects of using paralegals to serve the justice needs of rural communities, the socially and culturally disadvantaged, and the poor could be put to good use in Somalia. The Somali people have long been at the hands of top-down, or externally driven, legal regimes and have often been at the mostly disadvantaged, receiving end of legal processes. The use of paralegals in law reform efforts in Somalia presents an innovative opportunity to take ownership of legal reform processes. In addition, the fact that paralegals are drawn from the local community—unlike lawyers, who are sent from regional capitals—to provide legal representation indicates that paralegals will be better equipped to navigate through localized political and social obstacles to reach the desired legal outcome.

Civil Society

It has been noted that civil society plays a central role for legal empowerment in rule of law reform processes.[34] In practice, civil society organizations undertake the most detailed research in acute and nuanced areas of law and justice and are thus equipped with the knowledge and capacity to devise a number of innovative reform and development programs. This is in addition to the traditional roles of awareness and advocacy played under past and present rule of law programs, such as the ongoing initiatives under the USAID Governance and Democracy program.[35] Civil society should act as the driving wheel of advocating for appropriate and effective justice reform because it is placed more centrally to those reform processes, being the implementer of justice reform itself.

Although a large-scale civil society community in Somalia is a recent phenomenon, there have been a number of successful projects carried out by the

---

33   *Main Report*, in *Protecting Community Lands and Resources: Evidence from Liberia, Mozambique and Uganda* 10 (Rachel Knight et al. eds., Namati & Intl. Dev. L. Org. 2012).

34   Golub, *supra* note 12, at 28.

35   *See*, generally, http://www.usaid.gov/democracy/index.html.

NGO community in Somalia.[36] If empowered to act as the representative of community interests in advocating for change in government, civil society could become strong enough to lead the agenda in analyzing, researching, and devising rule of law reform projects within Somalia. In Somalia's upcoming justice reform efforts, actors should pay due regard to allocating sufficient time and financial investment to the development of civil society.

Customary and Traditional Justice

As noted previously in this chapter, traditional justice has become the predominant justice mechanism for individuals to address their interests and grievances in Somalia. The *xeer* system is a developed system, is cost-effective, and is the most logistically accessible form of justice for the vast majority of Somalis. Other reform efforts may have placed minimal emphasis on traditional systems of justice, yet these few efforts rarely if ever succeeded in displacing traditional dispute resolution mechanisms for more formal, statutory systems in serving the justice needs of the majority population.[37] As noted in a Department for International Development report, "in many developing countries, traditional or customary legal systems account for 80% of total cases."[38]

There have been some engagements with traditional justice systems in Somalia, most notably by the Danish Refugee Council (DRC) in 2003. The DRC was engaged by elders of a rural community in the Togdheer region in Somaliland seeking support in their attempts to gain insight into how *xeer* might be revised to align more closely with both sharia and human rights standards. A series of dialogues was initiated with 100 elders from five clans of the Togdheer region, in which elders were asked to identify pressing issues and disputes and to come to a unified and workable agreement between the clans. The substantive issues raised in the dialogues included the protection of the accused by community elders; ensuring the statutory prosecution of violent crimes; fair treatment of women, orphans, and minority groups; ensuring that victims of gender-based violence received adequate redress; problems associated with *diya*, or "blood-money," payment and collective punishment; and property rights. The decisions regarding the issues raised were subsequently formulated into an agreement between the elders, or the "National Declaration," as it was called, which was disseminated by the members throughout their communities.

---

36   Such projects are detailed in Le Sage, *supra* note 14, at 51–53.

37   Afghanistan neither incorporated nor prohibited customary law in its 2004 national constitution. For a critique of formal rule of law reform, *see* Kirsti Samuels, *Rule of Law Reform in Post-conflict Countries: Operational Initiatives and Lessons Learnt* (Soc. Dev. Papers: Conflict Prevention & Reconstruction, No. 37, World Bank 2006); and Laurel Miller & Robert Pertito, *Establishing the Rule of Law in Afghanistan* (USIP Special Report, United States Institute of Peace Mar. 2004).

38   Department for International Development, *Safety, Security and Accessible Justice: Putting Policy into Practice* 58 (July 2002).

The outcomes of the initiative undertaken were assessed by IDLO in 2011.[39] It was found that removing the traditional protection of the accused was resolved as the elders' views of the practice were challenged and perceptions of how to deal with the accused were improved. IDLO reported that elders understood that serious criminal offenses should be referred to the statutory courts. However, achieving the fair treatment of women and resolving gender-based violence through statutory court systems were less successful. Another important lesson learned was that the elders and the statutory judiciary began to work together to assist in implementing each other's respective tasks and responding together to the challenges faced by the justice system in responding to the people's needs. Additionally, community elders themselves were placed at the center of any reform or harmonization of customary law with the statutory system and international human rights standards. As the linking point between the formal justice system and the customary system, through which most people gain access to justice, the elders were made agents of change in the process and took ownership of the change rather than opposing another form of top-down imposition of reform of the traditional justice system.

From the evidence gained in IDLO's report on engaging with traditional justice systems in Somalia, it is evident that undertaking bottom-up approaches to reforming justice systems serves the needs of the Somali people in a more effective way. Interveners in the Somali rule of law reform process will be able to see how this approach of engaging with nonstatutory forms of justice is an effective tool in serving the access to justice agenda in Somalia while ensuring that the state has sufficient monitoring and intervention capacity when the traditional justice mechanism may serve as an injustice to select individuals.

Constitutional and Legislative Reform

As the constitutional review process continues over the first term of Parliament, and perhaps in future terms,[40] and as the legislative implementation of a number of provisions in the new constitution takes place, an access to justice approach can be adopted with regard to future decision making by the bodies charged with carrying out these functions. Unlike the constitutions that were built in Europe or the United States, whereby the articles are largely a list of rules and principles for legislators to abide by when enacting new laws, modern constitutions, designed after the fall of authoritarian regimes or after transitions from conflict to peace, tend to provide more detailed prescriptions for the conduct of social affairs under the law.[41] In keeping with this modern approach to constitution making, the Somali constitution, through

---

39   Maria Vargas Simojoki, *Unlikely Allies: Working with Traditional Leaders to Reform Customary Law in Somalia* (IDLO Working Paper Series: Enhancing Leg. Empowerment: Working with Customary Justice Systems: Post-conflict & Fragile States, Intl. Dev. L. Org. 2011).

40   The constitutional review process is detailed in ch. 15 of the Provisional Constitution.

41   For example, the U.S. constitution lists only seven articles, while the South African constitution lists 243 articles.

subsequent iterations over the coming years, could ensure that any legislation implementing its provisions will comply with the theories of access to justice.

At the core of the legislators' thinking should be the consideration of how such a law can serve the needs of the individual seeking justice. Referring back to the original definition of access to justice,[42] the constitution could prescribe checks to ensure that laws provide incentives for individuals to access the justice system. There should be real remedies for claimants addressing the courts. For example, criminal laws that emphasize sanctions for the perpetrator but offer no remedy for the victim will result in apathy on the part of the victim with regard to accessing a court. Legislators must also consider the priority laws required to be put in place. The Somalia Justice Sector Action Plan, presented at the Somalia Conference in London on May 7, 2013, emphasizes the necessity to implement priority laws that will serve the needs of access to justice. The plan looks at the reform of criminal and civil codes, legal aid laws, and police and prison laws, among other instruments. However, it must be emphasized that policy making and legislating do not prioritize haste over comprehensiveness. Reforms of civil codes should be citizen focused and enabled for the poor to use the law to serve their development needs, and should incorporate the specific justice needs of women, socially and culturally marginalized groups, and minority groups.

Conclusion

Somalia's rule of law reform over the coming years will be an ambitious and challenging experience. The country's long-standing history of conflict and its experience of top-down, authoritarian, and abusive legal regimes have fueled a lack of trust in statutory justice systems. Furthermore, individuals lack the awareness or ability to avail their rights or seek remedies for wrongs that they have suffered.

This chapter addresses the newly emerging fields of law reform, which are designed to put the individual citizen—including the poor and marginalized—at the center of rule of law reform efforts, and offers opportunities that Somali reformers can adopt and incorporate into future reform programs. The bottom-up approaches detailed in this chapter, as well as the evidence displayed in several successful rule of law reform efforts within Somalia and abroad, can be adopted to increase individuals' belief, trust, and ability to access formal and informal legal systems to find solutions to their justice needs, uphold their individual rights and freedoms, and better their social and economic situations.

---

42   UNDP, *supra* note 2.

PART III

ENVIRONMENTAL AND NATURAL RESOURCES LAW

The Challenges of Reforming the Urban Legal Framework

A Critical Assessment of Brazil's City Statute Ten Years Later

EDESIO FERNANDES

Legal scholars and urban researchers are increasingly acknowledging that the dominant pattern of combined sociospatial segregation and informality that marks urban development globally has resulted from the exclusionary nature of the urban legal systems prevailing in most developing and transitional countries. Indeed, the legal order has been one of the main factors determining urban informality.[1]

In this context, policy makers, urban managers, and social movements committed to the urban reform agenda have been asking a fundamental question: What does it take to turn national and local urban legal systems into effective factors of sociospatial inclusion? A growing international sociopolitical movement has vigorously argued that the promotion of legal reform is necessary to support any significant attempts at urban reform. As a result, new urban laws governing land rights and management, territorial organization, planning, and housing have been enacted in several countries and cities in recent years, and a serious investment has been made by several nongovernmental and governmental institutions in formulating inclusive legal systems in rapidly urbanizing countries.[2]

But what, exactly, can be expected of these new urban laws? What is required for them to be fully enforced and socially effective? What are the nature, possibilities, and constraints of progressive urban laws vis-à-vis the broader sociopolitical process?

This chapter discusses such general questions through a critical assessment of Brazil's national urban policy law—the 2001 City Statute—which is regarded as a groundbreaking effort to conceive a regulatory framework conducive to providing adequate legal support to governmental and social

---

1   *See,* among other sources, the general analyses and national case studies collected in Edesio Fernandes & Ann Varley eds., *Illegal Cities: Law and Urban Change in Developing Countries* (Zed Books 1998) (hereinafter, *Illegal Cities*).

2   Several of the national laws recently enacted in Latin American countries have been discussed in three special issues of *Revista Fórum de Direito Urbano e Ambiental,* coedited by Edesio Fernandes & Betânia Alfonsin. *See* Revista Fórum de Direito Urbano e Ambiental, 9(54) (2011); 10(57) (2011); and 11(61) (2012) (hereinafter, Revista Fórum).

attempts to promote urban reform. The City Statute was approved following 12 years of intense discussion and fierce disputes within and outside the National Congress. Since its adoption, it has been acclaimed internationally, and in 2006, Brazil won UN-HABITAT's Scroll of Honour for having approved it. Envied by policy makers and public administrators in several countries, the ambitious City Statute has been proposed by the Cities Alliance as a paradigm to be considered internationally.

However, more than 10 years since its approval, there are significant debates about its efficacy. This chapter provides a critical assessment of the conditions of its enforcement as the basis for a more general discussion on the growing expectations around newly approved urban laws in other countries.

A New Urban Land Governance Framework

The 2001 federal law was largely the result of a nationwide process of social mobilization. The City Statute regulated the urban policy introduced by the 1988 federal constitution, which had itself been preceded by an unparalleled process of sociopolitical mobilization, especially through the formulation of the Popular Amendment on Urban Reform, the document produced as a result of a national popular movement that defined the main elements of the debate on urban reform to be considered by the Constituent Assembly.[3]

Both the constitutional chapter and the City Statute are discussed in detail elsewhere;[4] for the purposes of this paper, the main dimensions of the City Statute are as follow:

- It firmly replaced the traditional legal definition of unqualified individual property rights with the notion of the social function of property so as to support the democratization of access to urban land and housing.

- It defined the main articulated principles of land, urban, and housing policy to be observed in Brazil.

- It created several processes, mechanisms, instruments, and resources aimed at rendering urban management viable, with emphasis placed on capturing for the community some of the surplus value generated by state actions that had been traditionally fully appropriated by land and property owners.

- It proposed a largely decentralized and democratized urban governance system in which intergovernmental institutions as well as state partner-

---

3   For an analysis of the law-making process, *see* José Roberto Bassul, *City Statute: Building a Law*, in *The City Statute of Brazil: A Commentary* (Celso Santos Carvalho & Anaclaudia Rossbach eds., Cities Alliance 2010).

4   *See* especially Edesio Fernandes, *Law and Urban Change in Brazil* (Avebury 1995); Edesio Fernandes, *Constructing the "Right to the City" in Brazil*, 16 Soc. & Leg. Stud. (2007); Edesio Fernandes, *Implementing the Urban Reform Agenda in Brazil: Possibilities, Challenges, and Lessons*, 22 Urb. Forum (2011); Revista Fórum, *supra* note 2; and Edesio Fernandes & Raquel Rolnik, *Law and Urban Change in Brazil*, in *Illegal Cities*, *supra* note 1.

ships with the private, community, and voluntary sectors are articulated with several forms of popular participation in the decision- and law-making process.

- It recognized the collective rights of residents in consolidated, informal settlements to legal security of land tenure as well as to the sustainable regularization of their settlements.

These intertwined dimensions of the City Statute constituted a new urban land governance framework in Brazil.

Given the highly decentralized nature of the Brazilian federative system, the materialization of this legal framework was placed in the hands of the municipal administrations through the formulation of Municipal Master Plans (MMPs). Prior to the enactment of the new law, the vast majority of municipalities did not have an adequate regulatory framework in place to govern the processes of land use, development, preservation, construction, and regularization. Most towns and cities also lacked basic information such as maps, photos, and other relevant materials. Of 1,700 municipalities that had a legal obligation to approve such MMPs to apply the City Statute, a remarkable 1,450 had done so by 2013.

However, since the enactment of the City Statute, Brazilian cities have undergone significant changes. Rates of urban growth have decreased, but they are still relatively high, especially in midsize and small cities, which has led to the formation of new metropolitan regions—30 such regions have been officially recognized. Economic development and the emergence of a so-called new middle class, or precarious working class, have aggravated the long-standing urban problems of transportation, mobility, environmental impact, and violence. Infrastructure and energy-provision problems have increased, and the public administration fiscal crisis is widespread, especially at the municipal level.[5]

Above all, the long-existing land and housing crisis has escalated. The housing deficit is still enormous (between six and seven million units), and, despite the impressive number of units already built or contracted, the My House, My Life national housing program has not fully reached the poorest families and has been criticized for reinforcing long-standing processes of sociospatial segregation. Although the levels of land, property, rental appreciation, and, especially, speculation have broken historical records, there is an enormous stock of vacant serviced land, abandoned or underutilized properties (calculated as 5.5 million units), and public land and property without a social function.[6]

---

5   Detailed official data on urban realities and processes in Brazil are regularly provided, organized, and analyzed by IBGE Cidades, available at http://www.ibge.gov.br/cidadesat /topwindow.htm?1, and IPEA, available at http://www.ipea.gov.br/portal/.

6   For official information on the housing program, see http://www.cidades.gov.br/index.php /minha-casa-minha-vida.

Informal development rates are still high, with the densification and verticalization of old settlements and the formation of new settlements, usually in peripheral areas; development also has taken new shapes, in the form of backyarders and informal rental transactions, for example. The proliferation of gated communities in peripheral areas and other metropolitan municipalities means that for the first time rich and poor are competing for the same space. Urban development in new economic frontiers—especially in the Amazon—has largely taken place through informal processes, which have been accompanied by a growing number of land disputes and socioenvironmental conflicts throughout the country.

Over the past two decades, an enormous amount of public resources— land, fiscal incentives, all types of credit, tax exemptions, building, and development rights—has been given to land developers, urban promoters, and builders, usually within the context of urban renewal or revitalization programs; rehabilitation of downtown areas or historic centers; large-scale projects; modernization of harbors, ports, and infrastructure; and global events such as the World Cup and the Olympic Games. The number of resulting forced evictions is staggering, not only in Rio de Janeiro and São Paulo but in municipalities such as Belo Horizonte and Porto Alegre, which had long been committed to the urban reform process. This urban reform process, which was highly visible in the 1980s and 1990s, and was instrumental in the enactment of the 2001 City Statute, seems to have lost momentum; stakeholders have been asking, "Which cities, and for whom?" and have demanded to know who has actually benefited from the enormous transfer of public resources.

What has happened to the City Statute, then? Has it failed, as a growing number of skeptical groups seem to believe? Rather than contributing to the promotion of sociospatial inclusion, has it perversely contributed to the escalating commodification of Brazilian cities—and to the further peripheralization of the urban poor—as some have argued?

More than 10 years since the City Statute was enacted, a comprehensive and critical assessment of the urban land governance framework that it proposed, and especially of the municipal initiatives aimed at implementing it— is urgently needed. This is a moment for reflection, which requires reassessing the main ideas, debates, and experiences around the enactment of the federal law, as well as reaffirming the law's historical principles and objectives. Promoting a critique of the role of all involved stakeholders is fundamental to correcting mistakes, changing courses, and advancing the urban reform agenda.

Some important surveys and comparative studies have already been published.[7] There are also several published case studies, and a "Bank of

---

7   See especially Renato Cymbalista & Paula Freire Santoro eds., *Planos diretores: Processos e aprendizados* (Instituto Polis 2009); Orlando Alves Santos, Jr. & Daniel Todtmann Montandon eds., *Os planos diretores municipais pos-estatuto da cidade: Balanco critico e perspectivas* (Observatorio das Metropoles/Letra Capital 2011); and Sandra I. Momm Schult, Claudia Silbert, &

Experiences" has been created by the Ministry of Cities.[8]

Still, more critical assessment is necessary: to determine if and how the generation of MMPs has effectively translated the general principles of the City Statute into rules and actions, and to identify the main legal and social obstacles to the full implementation of the national law. In addressing these issues, this chapter discusses if and how Brazilian society has made effective use of the many legal possibilities available for recognizing the range of social rights created by the new legal-urban order.

Growing Gaps between the Progressive New Legal Order and the Exclusionary Urban and Institutional Realities

The City Statute—Federal Law 10.257/2001—belongs within the context of a broader legal-urban reform process that has been taking place in Brazil for three decades. Its main direct antecedents were Federal Law 6.766/1979 (urban land subdivision); Federal Law 7.347/1985 (civil public action); the 1988 Federal Constitution (especially Articles 182 and 183, on urban policy); Federal Law 9.790/1999 (civil society organizations of public interest); and Constitutional Amendment 26 (recognizing the social right to housing).

Since the City Statute was enacted, the federal legal order has been complemented by several other important laws: Provisional Measure 2.220/2001 (special concession of use for housing purposes); Federal Law 11.079/2004 (public-private partnerships); Federal Law 10.931/2004 (land and property credit and registration); Federal Law 11.107/2005 (public consortia); Federal Law 11.124/2005 (passed by popular initiative, it created the National Fund for Social Interest Housing); Federal Law 11.445/2007 (sanitation); Federal Law 11.481/2007 (federal land and property); Federal Law 11.888/2008 (technical assistance to communities); Federal Law 11.977/2009 (My House, My Life national housing program and regularization of informal settlements); Federal Law 11.952/2009 ("Legal Amazon"); Federal Law 12.305/2010 (solid-waste control), and Federal Law 12.608/2012 (national policy for civil protection).[9]

All of these federal laws are currently in force, as well as several international conventions and treaties signed and ratified by the National Congress (notably on housing rights) and federal laws on the environment, national heritage, expropriation, and registration. Bills being discussed include one on land subdivision and one known as the "Metropolitan Statute"; white paper topics include the resolution of land conflicts. Also under consideration are countless decrees and resolutions of the National Council of Cities and the National

---

Luiz Alberto Souza eds., *Experiencias em planejamento e gestao urbana: Planos diretores participativos e regularizacao fundiaria* (Edifurb 2010).

8   *See* http://www.cidades.gov.br/index.php/planejamento-urbano/392-banco-de-experiencias.

9   For the texts of the federal laws, *see* http://www2.camara.leg.br/atividade-legislativa /legislacao.

Environmental Council, as well as numerous directives of the public bank Caixa Econômica Federal.

A new legal-urban order—sophisticated, articulated, and comprehensive—has thus been established, bolstered by constitutional recognition of urban law as a field of Brazilian public law, replete with its own paradigmatic principles: the socioenvironmental functions of property and of the city, and the democratic management of the city. The collective right to sustainable cities has been explicitly recognized, reflecting the legal system's clear commitment to the urban reform agenda.

These significant and structural legal changes have been expanded at all government levels—in the federated states and, especially, in the municipalities, particularly through the approval of more than 1,400 MMPs.

This comprehensive new legal-urban order has been supported by the creation of a new institutional order at the federal level. The Ministry of Cities was created in 2003; national conferences have been held every two years since then. The National Council of Cities meets regularly; Caixa Econômica Federal—the world's largest public bank—has promoted several federal plans and projects, especially the Plan to Accelerate Growth (PAC) and the My House, My Life national housing program (the PMCMV), which, combined, amount to the largest social programs in the history of Latin America.[10]

These changes in the legal and institutional orders are fundamentally social conquests, having largely resulted from a historical process of sociopolitical mobilization involving thousands of stakeholders—associations, nongovernmental organizations (NGOs), churches, unions, political parties, and sectors of land and property capital—which, since the late 1970s, have worked for the constitutional recognition of land, urban, and housing issues, as well as for the decentralization and democratization of, and popular participation in, law- and decision-making processes.[11]

At the same time, however, over the past decade, several stakeholders have increasingly denounced the growth of property speculation in Brazil; the elitist utilization of the enormous amount of financial resources generated, especially through the sale of building and development rights in public auctions; the manner in which the so-called unlocking of land values by large projects and events has reinforced sociospatial segregation; the recurrent abuse of legal arguments based on public interest and urgency; and the huge socioenvironmental impact of federal and other programs.[12]

---

10   For detailed official information on PAC, see its website, http://www.pac.gov.br/.

11   For an analysis of the sociopolitical process, see Evaniza Rodrigues & Benedito Roberto Barbosa, *Popular Movements and the City Statute*, in *The City Statute of Brazil: A Commentary* (Celso Santos Carvalho & Anaclaudia Rossbach eds., Cities Alliance 2010).

12   For a critical assessment of the broader context in which the City Statute was enacted, see Erminia Maricato, *The Statute of the Peripheral City*, in *The City Statute of Brazil: A Commentary* (Celso Santos Carvalho & Anaclaudia Rossbach eds., Cities Alliance 2010).

Growing land conflicts, rental prices, urban informality, evictions and re- movals; the worsening of transportation, mobility, and sanitation problems; and especially the increasing commodification of Brazilian cities as they have become at once both the venues and the objects of postindustrial capitalist production, now at the global level given the aggressive penetration of inter- national land and property capital. Such is the new stage of urban develop- ment in Brazil, a stage that has required the strengthening of the individualist and patrimonial legal culture that had long prevailed prior to the enactment of the City Statute: property viewed merely as a commodity; consideration of exchange values but not of use values; the right to use, enjoy, and dispose of property, which often means the right not to use, enjoy, or dispose of—in other words, to freely speculate.

What has happened to the urban reform process? How can the enormous legal and institutional gaps existing in Brazil be explained?

Indeed, there is an enormous gap between the legal-urban order and urban and social realities. The legal-urban order is still largely unknown by jurists and society when not the object of legal and/or sociopolitical disputes. Imple- menting this order, and thereby giving it legal and social efficacy, amounts to a massive challenge.

There is also a huge gap between the institutional order and urban and social realities. The Ministry of Cities has often been emptied of money and power or bypassed by the federal budget or by other ministries; the National Council of Cities has often been emptied or bypassed by the Ministry of Cities or other ministries, having had difficulties renewing levels of social mobiliza- tion. When there is not a lack of projects, duplicity, inefficiency, waste, lack of continuity, and especially bottomless corruption have marked Brazil's frag- mented urban management at all government levels.

It is in this context that skepticism regarding the City Statute has grown among planners, managers, academics, and, most of all, society.[13] The 2001 federal law has been demonized by those who have blamed it for the recent occurrence of sociospatial segregation. In fact, new urban management tools have been appropriated by conservative sectors, and new forms of old pro- cesses of socialization of costs and privatization of benefits have emerged with the reconcentration of public services and equipment.

Is the Critique Legitimate?

Any fair assessment of the City Statute requires rescuing the historical prin- ciples and objectives of the legal-urban order that it consolidated.

---

13   For a discussion on the disputes regarding the City Statute, *see* Raquel Rolnik, *Ten Years of the City Statute in Brazil: From the Struggle for Urban Reform to the World Cup Cities*, 5(1) Intl. J. of Sustainable Dev. (2013).

First, the City Statute fully embraced a new paradigm on the matter of property rights; the fulfillment of a social function was to be a primary condition for the recognition of private property rights. Social functions were to be determined by master plans and other urban and environmental laws—especially those formulated at the local level—with clear definitions not only of individual but also of collective and social rights, as well as of social responsibilities and obligations that result from land and property ownership. While the City Statute affirmed the separation between property and building rights, the legal-urban order it symbolized held that the principle of social functions entailed not only administrative restrictions to property rights but also the legal power of public administrations to oblige individual and collective behaviors, especially through compulsory orders. More than discussing property rights, then, the City Statute addresses the *right to property*, as property has no predetermined content and comprises both exchange and use values.

Second, the City Statute clearly expressed the notion that land and property matters are fundamentally matters of contemporary public law, with the "public order" being larger than the "state order." The legal order has incorporated a set of collective rights to territorial organization, environmental preservation, participation in decentralized processes, and the regularization of informal settlements. It has also recognized the social right to adequate housing. Access to the judicial system, to defend collective rights and diffuse interests, has been opened to individuals, groups, NGOs, and the Ministerio Publico. To date, a solid discussion has not been promoted in Brazil on the legal meaning and implications of the constitutional expression "social functions of the city," and only recently has the debate begun to discuss the need for a fourth dimension, territorial responsibility, to be added to the traditionally accepted forms of legal responsibility—political, administrative, and fiscal —of public administrations.

Third, the City Statute gave a profoundly different meaning to the legal nature of territorial and urban planning, which is no longer merely a discretional policy but an obligation of public authorities, with the failure to act leading to legal liability. Consequently, some Brazilian mayors have already lost their jobs. Together with its traditional regulatory power, urban planning also involves powers to intervene directly in the dynamics of land and property markets, especially to enable vacant land and underutilized properties to serve a social function. It should also recognize all forms of legal tenure and possession, not just of individual property, as well as affirm the social function of public property.

Fourth, as a direct consequence of this socially oriented approach to property rights, the City Statute confronted a long neglected question: who pays the bill and how is it paid for the financing of urban development? Based on the principle of the fair distribution of costs and benefits of urbanization, the City Statute determined the onerous granting of use and building rights; recognized different categories of expropriation; allowed for the capture of surplus value and the social management of land and property value appreciation; and proposed that there should be no acquired rights on urban matters.

Fifth, the nature of urban management was also significantly altered, with the requirement of popular participation as a criterion of legal validity of urban laws and policies, and not merely as a stamp of sociopolitical legitimization. Some MMPs, including São Paulo's, have been annulled due to lack of adequate participation. It should be stressed that all the new tools, mechanisms, and processes should be used within the context of a clearly defined "sociopolitical project for the city," with the city viewed as the sociospatial expression of a sociopolitical pact. For that reason, the Ministry of Cities has launched and promoted a Campaign for Participatory Master Plans.

All in all, law and planning, under the new legal-urban order consolidated by the City Statute, were placed where they had always been: in the heart of the sociopolitical process, especially at the local level. Consequently, it is the very quality of this sociopolitical process that will both determine the meaning of and give concrete meaning to the notion of the social function of property at both the national and municipal levels.

It is unquestionable that, for all its sophistication and successive developments, the legal-urban order still has significant limits: there are several bottlenecks in the judicial system, including the length and cost of judicial procedures; difficulties with the registration system remain challenging; MMPs have not been articulated with an adequate urban management system; municipalism in Brazil is exaggerated and often artificial, and there is not a properly defined metropolitan/regional dimension; the different realities of middle-size and small municipalities, and especially the different realities of north and northeast, have not yet been properly contemplated by the legal order.

Nonetheless, the progress of the legal-urban order is undeniable.

It is in this context that one should ask: Is the federal law the real problem shaping the current urban development processes? Or perhaps, instead, one should ask if there has been an adequate understanding of the new legal-urban order by lawyers, urban planners, public managers, and, of course, society. Have the newly created legal and politico-institutional spaces been occupied? Have the new legal principles been translated into urban policies? Have the new legal rights been claimed by the population? Have the new legal principles been defended by the judicial courts?

Before going any further, it is important to stress that there are many deeply ingrained cultural, sociopolitical, and historical factors influencing the growing skepticism surrounding the federal law that deserve proper attention and in-depth analyses, but for the purposes of this study will only be briefly mentioned:

- There is in Brazil a strong cultural perception of the law—and the legal system—that borders on the messianic, with the law viewed merely as a technical instrument to resolve conflicts and the legal system as objective, neutral, and ahistorical, not as an open-ended sociopolitical process/arena where diverging claims can be disputed, compared, and discussed.

- Critics of the federal law are often moved by a sense of "short-termism," which is understandable when one considers the volume and gravity of the accumulated urban problems in the country but which ignores the long history of neglect of the urban question and the need for more time—and continuity of public actions—to confront such accumulated urban problems.

- There is a traditional perception of the state throughout Brazilian society—resulting from the dominant culture of representative democracy, legal positivism, and excessive formalism—which among other effects has fueled a tradition of patronage, clientelistic sociopolitical dynamics, and excessive dependence on state action, and reduced the "public sphere" to the "state sphere."

- There is a dominant technocratic perception of urban planning as the sole spatial narrative, expressing a technical, apolitical rationality, and as such unrelated to the dynamics of land and property markets.

An Assessment of the MMPs

What has actually happened, then, with the new generation of MMPs?

The existing studies, mentioned earlier in this chapter, have clearly shown that there has been progress on many fronts:

- The general discourse of urban reform has been adopted by most MMPs.
- Specific sectors—the environment and cultural heritage, for example—have been addressed.
- There has been a widespread creation of "special zones of social interest" corresponding to the areas occupied by existing informal settlements.
- Whatever the variations, which naturally express the different political realities in Brazilian municipalities, the participatory nature of the discussion of the MMPs has been remarkable.

Perhaps, though, the main achievement has been the unprecedented production of data and a wide variety of information about Brazilian cities.

Still, there are several problems of legal efficacy undermining the new MMPs:

- Excessive formalism and bureaucracy of municipal laws still exist.
- Further regulation, in the form of subsequent laws, is needed for full enforcement.

- Punctual changes have been promoted without participation.

- Obscure legal language and imprecise technical legal writing (urban laws are rarely written by legal professionals) have widened the scope for legal and sociopolitical disputes.

There are also several problems of social efficacy undermining the new MMPs:

- Most plans remain traditional plans—that is, they are merely technical and regulatory—and often fail to territorialize proposals and intentions, and to intervene in the land structure and land and property markets.

- The emphasis placed on the new tools created by the City Statute lacks a clearly defined project for the city.

- The vast majority of MMPs have failed to recapture any surplus value resulting from state and collective action, and when this *has* happened, there has been limited or no social redistribution of the newly generated financial resources.

Furthermore, most MMPs have placed limited or no emphasis on social housing in central areas, having failed to earmark central, serviced vacant land for social housing. Generally speaking, there are no specific criteria for the expansion of urban zones, public land and property have not been given a social function, and there has been no clearly articulated socioenvironmental approach. Large projects have often bypassed the MMPs, and presumed collective eviction. Most importantly, policies dealing with land, urban issues, housing, environmental conditions, and fiscal and budgetary matters have not been integrated, and the regularization of informal settlements is still largely viewed as an isolated policy, with most MMPs imposing enormous technical difficulties on the legalization of informal settlements. Bureaucratic management and technical complexity have also meant that there has been a widespread lack of administrative capacity to act at the municipal level. Many MMPs are mere copies of models promoted by an "industry" of consultants. Obscure planning language has been as problematic as obscure legal language.

At the other government levels, the precarious institutional systems have experienced several problems. At the federal level, sectoral policies have not been integrated, within or outside the Ministry of Cities; urban policy has not been articulated with environmental policy; and there is no national urban-metropolitan policy or system of cities, and no national territorial policy generally, but especially in regard to the Amazon. The institutional and legal actions of the federated states have been very limited.

Eminently, at all government levels, there is a profound lack of understanding that cities should be concerned about not only social policy and infrastructure for economic development but also the economy itself.

Conclusion

Plus ça change, plus c'est la même chose?

The analysis of the Brazilian case shows that the long-standing disputes leading to the sociopolitical mobilization calling for the approval of the new law have not been automatically abolished by the mere formal enactment of the law. If anything, the disputes have worsened and taken on new dimensions, resulting in a new phase for interested stakeholders, that of disputes over the enforcement of the law.

The rules of the game have been fundamentally altered, but the game is still being played according to the old, elitist, and exclusionary rules. There are many reasons for this development, but only through the promotion of significant changes in the country's legal and planning culture will further progress be possible.

The reaffirmation of old sociospatial segregation processes by all levels of the Brazilian government has occurred despite the legal possibilities for significantly changing the course of things through the formulation of profoundly different and inclusive MMPs. Instead, the events that have unfolded seem to demonstrate that—with the support of lawyers—urban planners and public managers remain, seemingly to a greater extent, hostages to exclusionary land and property markets that they created and developed, and continue to provoke segregation through the public policies that they have implemented.

To break with this perverse logic, and put an end to the renewed legal and political disputes over urban land and property matters, a concentrated effort urgently needs to be promoted to provide more information to planners, legal professionals, and society as a whole on the nature and possibilities of the new legal-urban order symbolized best by the City Statute. The education and training of planners, as well as of legal professionals, judges, prosecutors, and registry officers, is of utmost importance. If judicial courts need to follow public law–urban law principles when interpreting property-related conflicts, rather than embracing obsolete unqualified private law ideas, Brazilian civil society needs to call for more recognition of social and collective rights.

Brazil's legal-urban order has significantly changed, but have the jurists understood that? Has the nature of urban planning been changed accordingly? Have urban managers assimilated the new principles? Has civil society awakened to the new legal realities? To play the game according to the new rules is a fundamental step in the collective construction of sustainable and fairer cities for the present generation and for future ones.

In this context, all things considered, a very cautious optimism can be proposed. Even with due consideration given to its shortcomings and constraints, the law is not the problem. The City Statute has created the most appealing, enabling environment policy makers and managers could dream of in their attempts to promote urban reform.

That said, in the last analysis, to advance urban reform nationally, the future of the City Statute and the new urban-legal order it symbolizes urgently need a thorough renewal of sociopolitical mobilization centered on land, urban, housing, and environmental matters.

It is the task of all progressive stakeholders to defend the City Statute from the proposed (essentially negative) changes being discussed in the National Congress, to overcome the existing obstacles and improve the legal order, and, above all, to fight for the full implementation of the City Statute.

The Brazilian case makes it clear that "bad laws" can make it difficult to obtain collective and social rights and to formulate inclusive public policies. It follows, then, that "good laws" per se do not change urban and social realities, even when they express principles of sociospatial inclusion and socioenvironmental justice, or even, as is the rare case of the City Statute, when the legal recognition of progressive principles and rights is supported by the introduction of the processes, mechanisms, tools, and resources necessary for their materialization.

If decades of sociopolitical disputes were necessary for the reform of the legal-urban order, and for the enactment of the City Statute, a new historical phase has been open since, namely, that of sociopolitical disputes at all government levels, within and outside the state apparatus, for its full implementation.

The fact is that Brazil, and Brazilians, have not yet done justice to the City Statute.

There are many important lessons here for scholars, policy makers, managers, and activists.

Innovative Legal Measures for Climate Change Response in the Green Economy

Integrating Opportunity, Inclusion, and Equity

Marie-Claire Cordonier Segger and Yolanda Saito

There is a pressing need to respond more effectively to the growing impacts of climate change, and to the opportunities of climate finance. This response takes place in the context of a global transition to a new "green economy," a transition that holds great potential to achieve the sustainable development goals of many countries. However, critics have expressed concern that the emerging green economy agenda fails to ensure respect for human rights and social development goals and may undermine the rights of poor and marginalized communities. How to respond to climate change and facilitate access to the benefits of a greener economy—for poverty eradication and sustainable development—in a manner that is truly inclusive and equitable? What is the role of legal and institutional reform in facilitating these important objectives?

As noted in the *Stern Review*, the potential costs of climate-related damage, globally, are likely as high as 20 percent of the world's GDP, while the costs of mitigation and adaptation might be as low as 2 percent.[1] At national and international levels, countries continue to struggle to develop adequate responses to the challenge of climate-compatible development. International efforts are guided by the 1992 United Nations Framework Convention on Climate Change (UNFCCC)[2] with its 1997 Kyoto Protocol[3] and many other related arrangements, some of which are still under negotiation in the Durban Plan for Enhanced Action. Under the UNFCCC, states commit to both environmental protection *and* sustainable development objectives.[4] The treaty regime consistently emphasizes the importance of opening new opportunities for sustainable economic development, especially for the more than

---

Any statements of fact, opinion, or analysis expressed herein are entirely those of the authors and are not attributable to the International Development Law Organization. The authors would like to thank Patrick Reynaud, Caroline Haywood, and Daniela Cuellar for their valuable insights and assistance.

1   Nicholas Stern, *Stern Review on the Economics of Climate Change* (Cambridge U. Press 2007).

2   United Nations Framework Convention on Climate Change (May 9, 1992), 31 I.L.M. 849 (hereinafter, UN Framework Convention on Climate Change).

3   The UNFCCC Kyoto Protocol Status of Ratification can be found at http://unfccc.int/files /essential_background/kyoto_protocol/application/pdf/kpstats.pdf.

4   Marie-Claire Cordonier Segger & Ashfaq Khalfan, *Sustainable Development Law: Principles, Practices and Prospects* (Oxford U. Press 2004).

140 developing countries that are parties to UNFCCC.[5] Under the UNFCCC, a complex matrix of international rules has emerged to guide policies to mitigate climate change in this direction, encouraging the development of sustainable practices in the energy, forestry, transportation, industrial, food and agriculture, housing, and infrastructure sectors; assisting adaptation for coastal, desert, rural agricultural, and other vulnerable people; and supporting new carbon markets and climate finance.[6] However, a great deal remains to be done, especially at the national and local levels.[7]

The Outcome Document of the 2012 Rio+20 United Nations Conference on Sustainable Development (UNCSD), "The Future We Want," calls for bold action toward a transition to a new green economy.[8] Global action toward the green economy is intended to improve resilience to climate change and other threats; secure sources of food, water, and energy; enhance the natural resource base; contribute to poverty eradication; and support better livelihood options. Growth in a green economy must be "sustained, inclusive and equitable," prioritizing the need to be "people-centered and inclusive, providing opportunities and benefits for all citizens and all countries."[9] Essentially, countries have agreed—in global "soft law"—that responses to climate change and the green economy should be an opportunity for all and a threat to none.[10]

In spite of these nuanced and incremental global law and policy developments, concerns remain. The emerging green economy agenda, if it fails to ensure respect for human rights and social justice, for equity and inclusion, may in fact undermine the development process for the poorest and most marginalized communities.[11] In essence, climate change law and policy initiatives, even those taken in the context of building a global green economy, may have important human rights implications. Realizing a just, equitable, and sustainable green economy will require international commitment to the balanced integration of the social, economic, and environmental aspects of sustainable

---

5　Malcolm Dowden, *Climate Change and Sustainable Development: Law, Policy and Practice* 56 (EG Books 2008).

6　David Freestone & Charlotte Streck eds., *Legal Aspects of Implementing the Kyoto Protocol Mechanisms: Making Kyoto Work* (Oxford U. Press 2005) (hereinafter, *Legal Aspects of Kyoto Protocol Mechanisms*); David Freestone & Charlotte Streck eds., *Legal Aspects of Carbon Trading: Kyoto, Copenhagen, and Beyond* (Oxford U. Press 2009) (hereinafter, *Legal Aspects of Carbon Trading*).

7　United Nations Environment Programme (UNEP), *10 Years after Rio: The UNEP Assessment* (UNEP 2002).

8　United Nations Conference on Sustainable Development, *The Future We Want*, UN Doc. A/66/L.56, UNGA 66th Session, July 24, 2012, para. 12 (hereinafter, 2012 UNCSD Declaration), available at http://www.uncsd2012.org/thefuturewewant.html.

9　*Id.*, at para. 25.

10　*Id.*

11　*See*, for example, *Statement of Indigenous Peoples at the UN Conference on Sustainable Development*, May 18, 2010, available at http://www.indigenousportal.com/Economic-Development/1st -UN-Conference-on-Sustainable-Development-A-Green-Economy-in-the-Context-of-Sustainable-Development.html.

development. The post-2015 sustainable development agenda provides an important opportunity to link sustainable development with global justice.[12] Its call for a green economy represents a call for change, however, and this implies risk.[13] Many countries are debating new regulatory measures: to reduce the greenhouse gas emissions that cause climate change; to encourage adaptation, as part of a broader commitment to adopt new laws to promote the green economy; and to foster more sustainable development.[14] Both the 1992 UN-FCCC, through a series of Conferences of the Parties (COPs),[15] and the 2012 UNCSD Declaration[16] encourage countries to ensure inclusiveness and transparency in the design of climate and green economy measures and to enact complementary measures that protect poor and vulnerable groups. However, little concrete guidance is available on how this can actually be done.

This chapter suggests that many developing countries are already leading the way, designing and implementing domestic laws, institutions, and strategies to successfully transition to a green economy that respects human rights for equity and inclusion. Examples of good practice can build confidence and spur innovation, showing that the green economy can be and, in fact, is being built through bold actions by committed nations. Such national policy measures and regulatory and institutional innovations are key to ensuring that, in accessing the benefits of a growing green economy, responses to climate change are both inclusive and equitable, contributing more broadly to just and sustainable development outcomes.

Motivated by the enormity and significance of this global challenge, and by these inspiring national practices, this chapter provides an overview of the legal aspects of the green economy, discusses their human rights implications, and highlights innovative legal practices that respond to climate change while contributing to the sustainable development of a global green economy through equity and inclusion.[17]

---

12   Keynote address by Elizabeth Thompson at the International Development Law Organization (IDLO)–UN Department of Economic and Social Affairs (DESA) high-level event Contributions of Law to the Rio+20 Agenda, held April 19, 2012, at UN Headquarters in New York.

13   *Id.*

14   IDLO/CISDL, *Compendium of Legal Best Practices on Climate Law and Policy* (IDLO 2010). *See* also UNFCCC COP 19, The Doha Climate Gateway, 2012.

15   UNFCCC COP 19, The Doha Climate Gateway, 2012; UNFCCC COP 18, Durban Outcomes, 2011; UNFCCC COP 17, Cancun Agreements.

16   2012 UNCSD Declaration, *supra* note 8, at para. 76.

17   *Id.*, as envisioned in para. 4. This analysis builds on outcomes of the IDLO–UN DESA Legal Experts Panel held at the UN Headquarters in New York, on April 19, 2012 (*see* note 12), and the IDLO Side Event on Legal Preparedness for the Green Economy at the Rio+20 UNCSD in Rio de Janiero on June 18, 2012, as well as subsequent legal research and analysis.

Climate Change, the Green Economy, and Sustainable Development

To date, multilateral efforts to reduce global greenhouse gas emissions and to facilitate a global economy have proceeded largely along separate tracks.[18] The international economic system is defined by the treaties establishing the World Trade Organization (WTO), the treaties' annexes, and other arrangements under negotiation since the 2001 Doha Round was launched, as well as over 3,500 regional and bilateral trade and investment treaties.[19] The global climate regime is shaped by the 1992 UNFCCC, its 1997 Kyoto Protocol, and numerous related arrangements. Although these systems of international rules share a sustainable development objective, the relationship between the two has been fraught with challenges.[20]

In the context of a global green economy, international climate and economic instruments might be mutually supportive instead, if rule of law can assure equity and inclusion. As noted in Article 3(4) of the UNFCCC, each party, when considering which policies would be appropriate for protecting the climate system, should "tak[e] into account that economic development is essential for adopting measures to address climate change."[21] Further, in the UNFCCC, parties commit to "cooperate to promote a supportive and open international economic system," which, it was believed, would "lead to sustainable economic growth and development in all Parties, particularly developing country Parties, thus enabling them better to address the problems of climate change."[22] While climate laws and policies might restrict or constrain certain kinds of economic development, they can also provide incentives for new kinds of development. Indeed, many innovative national climate change measures can be characterized as economic laws themselves. For instance, new policies and regulations are being set in place to establish emissions trading schemes (ETSs), which aim to reduce greenhouse gas emissions by stimulating trade in emission reduction units (ERUs), supporting adoption of and transfer to renewable-energy technologies, and encouraging investment

---

18   Steve Charnovitz, *Trade and Climate: Potential Conflicts and Synergies*, in *Beyond Kyoto: Advancing the International Effort against Climate Change* 141 (Joseph E. Aldy et al. eds, policy report, Pew Ctr. on Global Climate Change, Dec. 2003). *See* also Markus Gehring & Marie-Claire Cordonier Segger, *Trade and Investment Implications of Carbon Trading for Sustainable Development*, in *Legal Aspects of Carbon Trading, supra* note 6.

19   *See* also General Agreement on Tariffs and Trade (adopted Oct. 30, 1947, provisionally entered into force Jan. 1, 1948), 55 U.N.T.S. 194, C.T.S. No. 31 (1948) (GATT); General Agreement on Trade in Services (adopted Apr. 15, 1994, entered into force Jan. 1, 1995) 1869 U.N.T.S. 183; Michael Trebilcock & Robert Howse, *Regulation of International Trade* 336 (3d ed., Routledge 2005); Markus Gehring, Jarrod Hepburn, & Marie-Claire Cordonier Segger, *World Trade Law in Practice* 17 (Globe Law & Business 2006).

20   Christina Voigt, *Sustainable Development as a Principle of International Law: Resolving Conflicts between Climate Measures and WTO Law* (Martinus Nijhoff 2009).

21   UN Framework Convention on Climate Change, 1771 U.N.T.S. 107 (UNFCCC), art. 3(4).

22   *Id.*, at art. 3(5).

in firms adhering to more-sustainable, low-carbon-producing standards.[23] In certain circumstances, an ETS may even provide incentives for the transfer of new sustainable development technologies to developing countries—if an emission rights purchase agreement (ERPA) provides for such transfer—in the context of global carbon markets or climate finance. And in Article 2(3), Annex I (developed country) parties agree to "strive to implement policies and measures . . . in such a way as to minimize adverse effects, including the adverse effects of climate change, effects on international trade, and social, environmental and economic impacts on other Parties, especially developing country Parties."[24] This recognizes that states may need to balance their adoption of new measures to respond to climate change with economic and social imperatives. Indeed, participants in international climate change negotiations have made strong political commitments to the green economy, including financing[25] and programming initiatives.[26]

This global focus on the opportunities inherent in a new green economy, particularly in the context of the response to climate change, is not surprising. Awareness has grown of the link between the environment and development goals, as well as between ecosystem health and the economy.[27] The 2008 global financial crisis triggered reconsideration of traditional growth models, and the G20 in 2009 reaffirmed a commitment to "move toward greener, more sustainable growth."[28] The concept of a green economy has emerged as a means

---

23   *Legal Aspects of Kyoto Protocol Mechanisms, supra* note 6, at sec. 7.

24   Kyoto Protocol to the UNFCCC (adopted Dec. 10, 1997, entered into force Feb. 16, 2005), 37 I.L.M. 22 (Kyoto Protocol), art. 2(2).

25   COP 16 (the 16th session of the Conference of the Parties) proved to be a real culmination of the increasingly robust discussions that began with the Bali Action Plan, which established pillars for the implementation of the UNFCCC, and were scheduled to conclude with the Copenhagen Accord. Most notable was the binding pledge from developed nations of US$30 billion for the period 2010–2012 and of US$100 billion per year by 2020 for climate financing.

26   In addition, the parties came to new agreements, collectively known as the Cancun Agreements, on nationally appropriate mitigation actions (NAMA): the reduction of emissions from deforestation and forest degradation (REDD+); the Clean Development Mechanism (CDM); the Cancun Adaptation Framework (CAF); the Technology Mechanism; and the Green Climate Fund. These initiatives all have hallmarks of green economy initiatives. REDD+, for example, "attempts to create a financial value for the carbon stored in forests, offering incentives for developing countries to reduce emissions from forested lands and invest in low-carbon paths to sustainable development" while also encouraging conservation, sustainable management of forests, and enhancement of forest carbon stocks.

27   The concept was introduced in the book *Blueprint for a Green Economy*, popularly known as "The Pearce Report." One of the key underlying themes in the early years was that the price systems of the day were resulting in an allocation of resources in the economy that was biased against the environment. Environmental assets and services, which were supports for economic and social systems but also inputs in production, were being undervalued. This would result in inefficient consumption of resources and, ultimately, environmental degradation. David William Pearce, Anil Markandya, & Edward Barbier, *Blueprint for a Green Economy* (Earthscan 1989). *See* also David LeBlanc, *Introduction*, 35(3) Natural Resources Forum 151, 151 (2011).

28   Steven Stone, UNEP chief of the Economics and Trade Branch, *The Role of the Green Economy in Sustainable Development* (presentation, Ad Hoc Meeting on the Green Economy: Trade and

to achieve such growth by establishing the environment and social develop-ment as determining factors, rather than externalities, of economic produc-tion, value, stability, and long-term prosperity.[29]

Several leading texts released in recent years have made significant strides in moving the green economy concept from theory into practice. The 2008 Green Jobs Report, released by the International Labour Organization (ILO) and partners, identified strategies for "greening jobs" across several sec-tors, including forestry, food and agriculture, and industry.[30] The 2010 TEEB (The Economics of Ecosystems and Biodiversity) reports focused on build-ing a business case for biodiversity and ecosystem services and defining how such natural assets contribute to national economic bottom lines.[31] The 2011 United Nations Environment Programme (UNEP) report, "Towards a Green Economy,"[32] emphasized the need for strong, enabling frameworks to achieve the integrated human rights, social equity, and environmental objectives of the green economy.[33]

The 2012 UNCSD Declaration states that a green economy should be "people-centered and inclusive, providing opportunities and benefits for all citizens and all countries."[34] A people-centered approach cannot be achieved without proper human rights frameworks in place. A rights-based approach to devel-opment is one that is participatory, empowering, accountable, nondiscrimi-natory, and based on universal, inalienable human rights and freedoms.[35] It must be tailored to the individual situation of each nation to ensure that the unique needs of all people—especially members of oppressed and marginal-ized groups—are taken into account and addressed in a meaningful way.

Sustainable Development Implications, Palais de Nations, Geneva, Oct. 7–8, 2010).

29   See Frequently Asked Questions, at the UNEP Green Economy website, http://www.unep.org /greeneconomy/AboutGEI/ FrequentlyAskedQuestions/.

30   International Labour Organization et al., Green Jobs: Towards Decent Work in a Sustainable, Low-Carbon World (report prepared with the cooperation of UNEP, Intl. Org. Employers, & Intl. Trade Union Confederation, Sept. 2008), available at http://www.unep.org/labour _environment/features/greenjobs.asp.

31   See the TEEB in Business and Enterprise Report and the TEEB Synthesis Report, Mainstreaming the Economics of Nature, available at http://www.teebweb.org.

32   UNEP, Towards a Green Economy: Pathways to Sustainable Development and Poverty Eradica-tion—A Synthesis for Policy Makers (UNEP 2011) (hereinafter, UNEP Green Economy Report), available at http://www.unep.org/greeneconomy.

33   The UNEP Green Economy Report defines the green economy as "one that results in im-proved human well-being and social equity, while significantly reducing environmental risks and ecological scarcities. In its simplest expression, a green economy can be thought of as one which is low carbon, resource efficient and socially inclusive . . . [in which] growth in income and employment is driven by public and private investments that reduce carbon emissions and pollution, enhance energy and resource efficiency, and prevent the loss of biodiversity and ecosystem services." Id., at 2.

34   2012 UNCSD Declaration, supra note 8, at para. 56.

35   United Nations Office of the High Commissioner for Human Rights, Development and Rights: The Undeniable Nexus (speech delivered on June 26, 2000, by Mary Robinson, UN High Com-missioner for Human Rights) (hereinafter, Development and Rights).

Green economy initiatives can not only respect human rights and the environment but also contribute to their strengthening and growth.[36] Unfortunately, however, human rights have not always been at the forefront in dialogues on economic development.[37] And in relation to environmental law and policy, human rights have not always received the attention warranted, often being relegated to vague generalities and conditionalities.[38]

The Cancun Agreements heralded a step forward for the synergy between human rights and development by recognizing, for the first time, that parties should fully respect human rights in all climate change–related actions.[39] Pressure from civil society and forward-looking UNFCCC parties continues to ensure that the momentum from the human rights acknowledgment in the Cancun Agreements is not slowed. Initiatives such as green jobs, sustainable procurement, payment for ecosystem services, internalization of ecological externalities, elimination of perverse subsidies, creation of new carbon taxes, and measures to support trade and investment in green goods and services all trigger important human rights and environmental implications. There is an inherent recognition that the green economy can have an impact on a full range of human rights, including the rights to life, health, food, water, housing, and culture.[40] International debates on climate change are now clearly recognizing certain key human rights in relation to sustainable development and related green economy initiatives.

For example, the *right to consultation for indigenous communities* was clearly recognized in the Cancun Agreements in relation to REDD+.[41] This formal notice is based on ILO Convention 169 and the United Nations Declaration on the Rights of Indigenous Peoples, which seek to protect the culture, property, and land rights of indigenous peoples, including the right not to be forcibly removed from lands or territories.[42] It follows from Principle 22 of the Rio Declaration, which recognizes the vital role indigenous people have in

---

36   See Sébastien Jodoin, *Rights-Based Frameworks for Climate Finance* (Leg. Working Paper, Ctr. Intl. Sustainable Dev. L., 2010), available at http://www.idlo.int/Publications/4_JodoinS %C3%A9bastien%20_RightsBasedFrameworksforClimateFinance.pdf.

37   *Develoment and Rights, supra* note 35.

38   *See*, for example, Sébastien Jodoin, *From Copenhagen to Cancun: A Changing Climate for Human Rights in the UNFCCC?; see* also *Development and Rights, supra* note 35.

39   Cancun Agreements, para. 8. Jodoin notes, however, the stronger "shall" was dropped from the negotiating text and replaced with the lesser "should." *See* Jodoin, *supra* note 38, at 4.

40   Alyssa Johl & Yves Lador, *A Human Rights Based Approach to Climate Finance*, in *Dialogue on Globalization* 2 (Friedrich-Ebert-Stiftung ed., Friedrich-Ebert-Stiftung 2012), available at http://www.ciel.org/Publications/ClimateFinance_Feb2012.pdf.

41   Appendix I. Parties are called to promote and support "respect for the knowledge and rights of indigenous peoples and members of local communities, by taking into account relevant international obligations, national circumstances and laws, and noting that the United Nations General Assembly has adopted the United Nations Declaration on the Rights of Indigenous Peoples," as well as the full and effective participation of relevant stakeholders, in particular indigenous peoples and local communities.

42   Lee Swepston, *New Step in the International Law on Indigenous and Tribal Peoples: ILO Convention No. 169 of 1989*, 15 Okla. City U. L. Rev. 677 (1990).

environmental management and development, and also in the UNFCCC
"companion treaty," the 1992 United Nations Convention on Biological Diversity (UNCBD). This treaty specifically compels parties to

> respect, preserve and maintain knowledge, innovations and prac-
> tices of indigenous and local communities embodying traditional
> lifestyles relevant for the conservation and sustainable use of biolog-
> ical diversity and promote their wider application with the approval
> and involvement of the holders of such knowledge, innovations and
> practices and encourage the equitable sharing of the benefits arising
> from the utilization of such knowledge, innovations and practices.[43]

Similarly, in terms of livelihood and labor rights, there are inherent synergies.
Green economy initiatives necessarily mean "green jobs," which engage livelihood and labor rights not only for new employment opportunities but also
in the context of jobs and methods of livelihood that may be displaced. The
International Covenant on Civil and Political Rights recognizes the right to
self-determination, including the ability for peoples to pursue their economic,
social, and cultural goals, and to manage and dispose of their own resources.
In addition, it recognizes a negative right not to be deprived of means of
subsistence.[44] The International Covenant on Economic, Social and Cultural
Rights also recognizes that negative right, as well as, inter alia, labor rights.[45]

In addition, *rights to participation, access, and benefits sharing* may be directly
relevant for climate change responses in the context of the green economy.
Tangible principles and mechanisms to secure access to information and public participation are perhaps best reflected in the terms of the Aarhus Convention, which guarantees access to information, public participation, and justice
in environmental matters.[46] In climate change debates, the right to information
and equitable participation, as well as access to justice and tangible remedies,
has also been recognized as applicable not only to indigenous groups but
to all affected stakeholders.[47] Equity and inclusion rights are, perhaps, most
clearly noted in the 1992 UNCBD, with its third objective concerning the fair
and equitable sharing of the benefits arising out of the utilization of genetic
resources.[48] Access to genetic resources, where granted, shall be on mutually

---

43   United Nations Convention on Biological Diversity (UNCBD), 1760 U.N.T.S. 79; 31 I.L.M.
     818 (1992), art. 8(j), available at http://www.cbd.int/doc/legal/cbd-un-en.pdf.

44   *Id.,* at art. 1.2.

45   *Id.* at arts. 1.2, 6, 7, 8.

46   Svitlana Kravchenko, *The Aarhus Convention and Innovations in Compliance with Multilateral
     Environmental Agreements,* 18(1) Colo. J. Intl. Env. L. & Policy (2007).

47   Jodoin, *supra* note 38, at 4. *See* also Alyssa Johl & Yves Lado, *A Human Rights–Based Approach
     to Climate Finance,* Friedrich-Ebert-Stiftung, available at http://www.ciel.org/Publications
     /ClimateFinance_ Feb2012.pdf. Also, the Cancun Agreements have recognized this to some
     extent, requiring that REDD+ programs now be implemented in phases, beginning with the
     development of national action plans and capacity building. These action plans must ad-
     dress substantive legal issues such as land tenure, forest governance, gender considerations,
     and the rights of indigenous peoples and ensure full stakeholder input.

48   UNCBD, *supra* note 43, at art 1.

agreed-on terms and shall be subject to prior informed consent of the contracting party providing the resources.[49] For climate change and the green economy more broadly, these concepts have very important implications, especially for any initiatives that involve the use of natural resources, such as forestry, fishing, and mining.

However, explicit recognition of other key human rights remains sparse in international texts related to sustainable development, and little practical guidance is available on ways to respect and protect human rights.[50]

National Legal Frameworks for Green Economy Initiatives

While international instruments provide important guidance, rights-based frameworks need to be implemented effectively on the ground at the national and local levels. A purely top-down approach will not be effective; human rights must be maintained by national and subnational frameworks that address the specific situations of individual states. Well-designed regulatory frameworks can not only protect and foster human rights but also create incentives for individual groups that "drive green economic activity, remove barriers to green investments, and regulate the most harmful forms of unsustainable behavior, either by creating minimum standards or prohibiting certain activities entirely."[51]

The establishment of these frameworks often would require not a complete overhaul but rather a realignment of existing laws, regulations, and standards to better promote and maintain rights within green economy initiatives. Coordination and cooperation across public, private, and government sectors will be necessary to ensure a cohesive approach that does not see the policies and programs of one area contradict or undercut those of another.[52] Innovations can be found in all sectors, and therefore states may also look to nongovernmental organizations and private actors for collaboration in developing innovative legal practices.

The 2012 UNCSD encourages states to develop their own green economy strategies through "a transparent process of multi-stakeholder consultation" and recognizes that "strong governance at local, national, regional and global

---

49   *Id.*, at art. 15.

50   Jodoin, *supra* note 38, at 4.

51   UNEP, *Enabling Conditions Supporting the Transition to a Global Green Economy* 20 (UNEP Green Economy Report 2011).

52   *See*, for example, IDLO-FAO (Sarah Mason-Case), *Legal Preparedness for REDD+ in Zambia: Country Study* (2011), which discusses, inter alia, Zambia's governance framework and existing laws and institutions and highlights the challenges that the country faces in implementing REDD+ initiatives. It also focuses on innovative legal and institutional reforms that will directly and indirectly affect REDD+ in Zambia. Available at http://www.idlo.int/Publications /LegalPreparednessREDDZambiapdf.

levels is critical for advancing sustainable development."[53] In order to build capacity in these areas, states need more guidance about how to promote national and subnational legislative efforts. The challenge lies not in establishing the principles but in implementing them on the ground to ensure that the needs of all groups, particularly the most poor and vulnerable, are taken into account.[54]

Country Innovations: Human Rights Principles in Practice

Several innovative nations are leading the way in implementing green economy initiatives that incorporate the recognition of human rights despite the lack of concrete guidance from international texts. A study of the leading legal best practices can provide a framework from which means and indicators for transitioning to a just, inclusive, and equitable green economy can be discussed and defined in the Rio+20 negotiations.

The government of Vietnam has pioneered the application of free and prior informed consent (FPIC) as a prerequisite for the implementation of its REDD+ climate-finance pilot projects and is the first country to pilot FPIC.[55] The FPIC pilot projects involve a nine-step process that includes awareness raising, recruitment and training of interlocutors, preparing and conducting village meetings, recording decisions on consent, documenting decisions, and independently evaluating and verifying the FPIC process.[56] The process is crucial in safeguarding human rights and prioritizes the rights of participation and inclusion as guiding principles in green economy projects.

Uganda has taken steps in the past five years to transform conventional agriculture production into an organic farming system as a means not only to combat climate change but also to eradicate poverty among the nation's small-scale farmers. In 2009, the government released the Draft Uganda Organic Agriculture Policy. The strategy put in place to implement this policy focuses on nine key areas, including the generation of information, knowledge, and skills through education and training and the participation of special interest groups such as women, youth, and the poor and vulnerable.[57]

The Mexican government has passed the Ley General de Desarrollo Forestal Sustentable (Ley General),[58] which will inform the country's approach

---

53   2012 UNCSD Declaration, *supra* note 8, arts. 38, 44.

54   Jodoin, *supra* note 38.

55   IDLO-FAO, *Legal Preparedness for REDD+ in Vietnam: Country Study* (2011).

56   RECOFTC, Evaluation and Verification of the Free, Prior and Informed Consent Process under the UN-REDD Programme: Lam Dong Province, Vietnam (2010); *see* also IDLO/MONRE, *Legal Preparedness for Climate Change in Vietnam* (MONRE/IDLO 2013)

57   UNEP, *Green Economy: Developing Countries Success Stories* 12–13 (UNEP 2010) (hereinafter, *Green Economy: Success Stories*).

58   General Law on Sustainable Forest Development.

to climate change and, more specifically, to REDD+ initiatives.[59] The Ley General declares that the conservation, protection, and restoration of forest ecosystems, as well as the development of environmental goods and services, are of public benefit and specifically states as an objective the respect and right of use and preferential benefit of forest resources by indigenous communities.[60] This recognition, coupled with awareness and institutional strengthening programs and access to climate finance, holds potential to provide greater equity and inclusion for indigenous peoples in voluntary and government-led climate mitigation activities.[61]

The municipal government in Dhaka, Bangladesh, has established a composting market financed through public-private partnerships and carbon credits through the Clean Development Mechanism.[62] The municipal government granted a concession to a private company—WWR Bio Fertilizer Bangladesh Ltd.—to collect and process organic waste and sell the compost for profit. Community members benefit not only by being able to purchase the cheaper, high-quality compost for their fields but also by having new livelihood options that respect their labor rights. New entrepreneurship opportunities are available for community members to negotiate with fertilizer companies to purchase the bio-fertilizers and market them nationally, opening the potential for inclusion in the green economy.[63]

Community-based resource management (CBRM) laws and policies have been implemented in Botswana to promote sustainable tourism business within local populations.[64] Legally recognized community-based organizations (CBOs) can apply for a permit to engage in commercial activities. This permit grants the CBO control over the natural resources, and the authority to negotiate hunting contracts and other tourism activities. The program offers incentives for communities to implement sustainable-use practices in a communal fashion while providing important locally generated resources to support efforts to adapt to climate change and other vulnerabilities.[65]

---

59   For a more in-depth discussion of Mexico's approach, *see* Frederic Perron-Welch, *Reducing Emissions from Deforestation and Forest Degradation, Forest Biodiversity Conservation and Respect for Human Rights: Mexico's Approach* (Sustainable Dev. L. on Climate Change Working Paper No. 10, IDLO, Mar. 2011).

60   *Ley General de Desarrollo Forestal Sustentable,* at art. 2(V), available at http://www.diputados.gob.mx/LeyesBiblio/pdf/259.pdf.

61   OECD, *OECD Environmental Performance Review: Mexico 2013,* available at http://www.oecd.org/env/country-reviews/mexico2013.htm.

62   IDLO, *Compendium of Legal Best Practices on the Green Economy* (forthcoming).

63   UN-HABITAT, *Solid Waste Management in the World's Cities: Water and Sanitation in the World's Cities 2010,* available at: http://www.unhabitat.org/pmss/listItemDetails.aspx?publicationID=2918.

64   *Id.,* at 60.

65   Bruce Campbell, Eva Wollenberg, & David Edmunds, *Devolution and Community-Based Natural Resource Management: Creating Space for Local People to Participate and Benefit?* (Overseas Dev. Inst. 2002).

The Brazilian National School Feeding Programme was decentralized and localized in an effort to increase food security and improve the nutritional quality of school meals. Underpinning this movement was the promotion of the procurement of local produce, with each municipality obliged to spend 30 percent of its budget for the program on produce grown by family-based farmers. This entire process, made possible because of the belief that good-quality food is a basic right, has encouraged a wider national debate on food security and agrarian development, which is connected to the current promotion of food sovereignty in sustainable agricultural interventions.[66] In terms of adaptation to climate change, food security is one of the most serious concerns for developing countries. Programs addressing this concern, backed by local regulations, can make a significant contribution to human rights and dignity, meeting basic needs of smallholder famers and the urban poor.[67]

The primary goal of India's National Rural Employment Guarantee Act is to supplement wage employment in impoverished areas, but it has the secondary benefit of strengthening resource management by financing rural projects that address causes of drought, deforestation, and soil erosion, "thus restoring the natural capital base on which rural livelihoods depend."[68] The act has aided in increasing the average wage of agricultural laborers by 25 percent over a three-year period, thereby empowering poor and marginalized groups while also promoting the restoration of ecological infrastructure.[69] Such measures hold the potential to assist in improving resilience and adapting to climate change and contribute to a broader green economy in a way that respects equity and inclusion.[70]

Conclusion

The green economy has emerged from theory to become policy and practice. With strong international support, the green economy can be a means to achieve the goals of sustainable development. New climate change response measures, in the context of building a green economy at the local and global levels, must inherently recognize and preserve human rights and social development goals. Making this a reality, however, will require more than a mere recognition of human rights in international texts. Practical policy and guidelines for regulatory and institutional reforms, built on the actual experiences

66   Kei Otsuki, *Sustainable Partnerships for a Green Economy: A Case Study of Public Procurement for Homegrown School Feeding*, 35(3) Natural Resources Forum 213, 220 (2011).

67   Leah M. Ashe & Roberta Sonnino, *At the Crossroads: New Paradigms of Food Security, Public Health Nutrition and School Food*, 1(1) Pub. Health Nutrition 1–8 (2012).

68   *Green Economy: Success Stories, supra* note 57, at 17.

69   *Id.*

70   Pradosh K. Nath & Bhagirath Behera, *A Critical Review of Impact of and Adaptation to Climate Change in Developed and Developing Economies*, 13(1) Env., Dev. & Sustainability 141–162 (2011).

and successes of leading countries, are necessary for countries to accomplish their capacity building goals.

This chapter has outlined how many developing and developed nations are leading the way in defining national and subnational innovations for incorporating human rights principles into climate change policies, laws, and programs for a more inclusive and equitable green economy. The chapter has briefly surveyed leading legal innovations that respond to climate change and build on green economy opportunities that also provide for equity and inclusion.

Beyond examples, tailored legal, regulatory, and institutional assessments; capacity building; and technical assistance are also needed to aid countries as they develop new regulatory frameworks and implement changes in legal practice on the ground. Monitoring and sharing of legal innovations will contribute to the achievement of sustainable development goals. But a start has been made, and it should be encouraged to grow. From national legislation down to programming at the local level, inspiring examples of the synergy between climate change, green economy measures, and meaningful human rights frameworks have begun to emerge. These initial innovative legal practices show country efforts moving away from commonalities and platitudes about human rights and instead undertaking tangible regulatory reforms, inspiring new practices toward an equitable, inclusive, and fundamentally more-just green economy.

The Constitutional Basis of Public Participation in Environmental Governance

Framing Equitable Opportunities at National and County Government Levels in Kenya

ROBERT KIBUGI

The journey to attain effective public participation in Kenyan governance gained traction when democratic space was cut back shortly after the 1982 failed military coup. The public interest and (negative) landmark 1989 judicial decision in *Wangari Maathai v. Kenya Times Media Trust*,[1] a dispute over the illegitimate annexation of a public open space in Nairobi, marked a dark phase, but also the beginning of the end of political repression. The constitutional court then ruled that only the attorney general could represent the public interest in court. This was reversed through Section 3 of the 1999 Environmental Management and Coordination Act (EMCA), which created liberal legal standing (access to justice) for anyone bringing an environmental action. The heterogeneous concept of public participation, however, extends beyond liberal judicial standing to include public representation and consultation during decision making, access to information, and civic education to enhance public awareness on environmental decision making.

The EMCA provides for public consultation as part of its environmental impact assessment (EIA) procedures.[2] Many natural resource–sector laws have followed this lead, internalizing various forms of public participation, especially consultation and representation. The Forests Act permits participatory forestry management, wherein forest communities constitute community forest associations (CFA) and engage in economic and conservation activities

---

This chapter is builds on an earlier (2012) research report by this author entitled "Ensuring Effective Public Participation in Natural Resources Management through Devolved Governments in Kenya." It was a part of a cluster of research themes under a general heading, "Putting People at the Centre: Enhancing Public Participation in Decision Making," commissioned by the Institute for Law and Environmental Governance (ILEG). This chapter has been adapted with the consent of ILEG. The author wishes to thank Kevin Mugenya and Mary Ondiek, who were part of the research team, and Pauline Makutsa, who managed the research. Great thanks also to the peer reviewers and participants in the various review and validation workshops.

1   Kenya Law Reports (Env. & Land) 166–171 (2007).

2   *See* The Environmental (impact assessment and audit) Regulations (2003).

in protected forests.[3] The 2002 Water Act provides for the creation of water resource users associations by residents in river catchments; these associations engage in water resource management, which includes taking a role in the approval of surface water abstraction permits.[4]

These legal mechanisms, although restricted in the scope of public participation, have magnified the equitable role of citizens in environmental decision making. They could set the pace for further innovative legal and practical mechanisms. Such an opportunity for Kenya has been availed by the 2010 Constitution of Kenya. This basic law, promulgated on August 27, 2010, if interpreted innovatively, will expand the space for public participation in environmental decision making for Kenya. This chapter examines this possible outcome.

In undertaking this analysis, the chapter adapts as a normative framework the principles of international environmental law found in Principle 10 of the 1992 Rio Declaration, which identifies the basic concepts for subsidiarity in performance of environmental functions. The conclusion suggests a number of possible legal and/or administrative steps that could further enhance the equitable role of public participation.

Tracing the Constitutional Basis of Public Participation in Kenya

Provisions of the 2010 constitution clearly show that any role citizens may play in governance is based on the sovereign power that citizens hold, both as individuals and as a collective group. This sovereign power may be exercised directly or through elected representatives; in Kenya, it is delegated to the various organs of government at the national and the county levels.[5] The preamble reflects how the sovereign power of the people of Kenya was exercised at the time the constitution was adopted—by emphasizing the firm basis of public participation in governance:

> We, the People of Kenya . . . exercising our sovereign and inalienable right to determine the form of governance of our country and having participated fully in the making of this Constitution . . . adopt, enact and give this Constitution to ourselves and to our future generations.

Article 10 of the Kenyan constitution identifies specific national values and principles of governance that are binding to every state organ, state officer, public officer, and all other persons engaged in applying or interpreting the constitution, in enacting or applying any law, and in making any public policy or decision. These governance values and principles include democracy, public participation, sustainable development, the sharing and devolution of power, transparency, and accountability. Constitutionally, it is apparent that public participation and sustainable development form the backbone of governance

---

3   *Forests Act* 7 (2005). *See* part IV, *Community Participation.*

4   *Water Act,* sec. 15(5) (2002); *see* also *Water Resource Management Rules,* sec. 10 (2007).

5   Kenyan Const. (2010), art. 1 (hereinafter Kenyan Const.).

in Kenya. Constitutional fundamental rights frame further bases of public participation; these include the right to make political choices and to participate in free and fair elections based on universal suffrage.[6] The procedural rights of access to justice, to fair administrative action,[7] and to information[8] complement the realization of environmental, economic, and social rights.

The 2010 constitution introduced a system of devolved government, whereby Kenya has a national government that shares functions with 47 distinctive county governments. Each level of government has functions that are defined in the fourth schedule to the constitution. Public participation is a principal object of devolution, as articulated in Article 174, "(c) to give powers of self-governance to the people and enhance the participation of the people in the exercise of the powers of the State and in making decisions affecting them."

Article 174 further suggests that devolution is intended to realize the principle of subsidiarity, akin to similar provisions in Principle 10 of the Rio Declaration, by recognizing "the right of communities to manage their own affairs and to further their development." These provisions are the basis for the enhanced role of the public; they reinforce the need to innovatively interpret constitutional provisions to ensure that all elements of public participation play an effective role on the threshold of environmental decision making.

International Law and the Normative Content of Public Participation in Environmental Governance

Treaty law and soft law have set the basis for general and specific elements of public participation in environmental decision making, as seen in the soft law principles in various environmental law declarations and publications. The 1972 Stockholm Declaration called for the "acceptance of responsibility by citizens and communities and by enterprises and institutions at every level, all sharing equitably in common efforts"[9] to achieve environmental goals. It stated that individuals and organizations in all walks of life would shape the world environment of the future, both by their values and by the sum of their actions. In 1987, the report of the World Commission on Environment and Development, entitled *Our Common Future*,[10] concurred, arguing in part that the law principally needs community knowledge and support, which entails greater public participation in the decisions that affect the environment.

---

6   *Id.*, at art. 38.

7   *Id.*, at arts. 47–48.

8   *Id.*, at art. 35.

9   Preamble to the 1972 *Stockholm Declaration on the Human Environment*, UN Doc. A/Conf.48/14/ Rev. 1(1973), para. 7.

10   World Commission on Environment and Development, *Our Common Future* (Oxford U. Press 1987) (hereinafter *Our Common Future*).

The ideal object of public participation in environmental decision making would be the attainment of sustainable development. Defined as "development that meets the needs of the present without compromising the ability of future generations to meet their own needs,"[11] sustainable development concerns the welfare of both the people and the environment. An imperative in practical implementation of sustainable development through law and policy is the concept of integration.[12] Integration necessarily implies having a legal basis or process that requires and facilitates consideration of socioeconomic (developmental) and environmental factors to secure a balance of interests.[13] To secure this balance of interests, it is necessary to fulfill the socioeconomic needs of the people and to protect the environment, for both ecological and human benefit. Integration, or the balance of interests, therefore confers a responsibility on people to participate in making decisions in the management of natural resources.

Public participation in environmental governance is a well-articulated general concept in environmental law treaties, conventions, and protocols. Kenya is party to various international treaties that elucidate public participation in environmental governance. These include the United Nations (UN) Convention to Combat Desertification,[14] which stipulates obligations for affected-country parties to "promote awareness and facilitate the participation of local populations, particularly women and youth, with the support of nongovernmental organizations, in efforts to combat desertification and mitigate the effects of drought."[15] The UN Framework Convention on Climate Change, dealing with the very complex challenge of adapting to and mitigating climate change, calls on all parties to "promote and cooperate in education, training and public awareness related to climate change and encourage the widest participation in this process, including that of non-governmental organizations."[16]

Principle 10 of the Rio Declaration, as earlier pointed out, provides useful guidance on a normative content of public participation, stating that "environmental issues are best handled with participation of all concerned citizens, at the relevant level."[17] This principle instructively breaks down elements of

---

11   *Id.*, at 43.

12   *Id.*, at para. 48.

13   See Dire Tladi, *Sustainable Development in International Law: An Analysis of Key Enviro-Economic Instruments* (Pretoria U. L. Press 2007).

14   *See United Nations Convention to Combat Desertification*, 33 *Intl. Leg. Materials* 1328 (1994).

15   *Id.*, at art. 5(d).

16   *See* art. 4, *United Nations Framework Convention on Climate Change*, 31 Intl. Leg. Materials 849 (1992).

17   The normative content set out in Principle 10 of the Rio Declaration amounts to soft international law for lack of binding character on states, as opposed to when the same normative content is crystallized within binding obligations through treaty law, as evident through the Aarhus Convention, in *infra* note 19. The 2006 East African Community Protocol on Environmental and Natural Resource Management, to which Kenya is a state party, similarly

public participation that are key to developing a normative content for practical implementation through national law in Kenya. The four elements of public participation in environmental governance are outlined below.

Public Opportunity to Participate in Decision-Making Processes

This element suggests that the public should participate in all phases of decision making, from designing environmental law, to implementing legal provisions, to ensuring that the intended objectives are fulfilled through the representation, consultation, and actions of all individuals.[18] The nature of this public participation in the environmental decision- and policy-making process is, for instance, exhorted in the Aarhus Convention.[19] This treaty, although not applicable to Kenya, illustrates various platforms through which meaningful participation can be realized. These include public involvement in decision making on specific projects requiring permits, such as public consultations during EIAs; participation in the development of programs and plans affecting the environment; and participation in the development of regulations, policy, or laws.[20] This "participation of the public in decision-making on matters with a potentially significant environmental impact" is also framed as a procedural right by the 2003 African Convention on the Conservation of Nature and Natural Resources.[21]

Access to Information Concerning the Environment

The right of people to access information that is held by public authorities and private entities makes it easier for the public to participate in administrative and judicial processes. It helps promote more rational, informed decision making and it fosters transparent and accountable decision making.[22] Effective access to meaningful information is the first step in empowering citizens to exercise a degree of control over resources and institutions.[23] This right to access information draws its legal foundation from, among other instruments,

---

crystallizes elements of public participation in environmental management into hard law. Both soft and hard international law play significant roles in conceptual justifications and content of municipal laws.

18 Sally Eden, *Public Participation in Environmental Policy: Considering Scientific, Counter-Scientific and Non-scientific Contributions*, 5 Pub. Understanding Sci. 183, 184 (1996).

19 *See Aarhus Convention on Access to Information, Public Participation in Decision Making and Access to Justice in Environmental Matters*, 38 Intl. Leg. Materials 517 (1999) (hereinafter *Aarhus Convention*).

20 *Id.*, at arts. 6–8.

21 *See African Convention on the Conservation of Nature and Natural Resources* (Revised) (July 11, 2003), reprinted in *Compendium of Key Human Rights Documents of the African Union* 95 (Christopher Heyns & Magnus Killander eds., Pretoria U. L. Press 2010).

22 Benjamin Richardson & Jona Razzaque, *Public Participation in Environmental Decision-Making* 181 (Benjamin Richardson & Stepan Wood eds., Hart 2006).

23 *See* Christoph Schwarte, *Access to Environmental Information in Uganda Forestry and Oil Production* (Intl. Inst. Env. & Dev. 2008).

the International Covenant on Civil and Political Rights (ICPR).[24] The ICPR provisions on freedom of expression include the freedom of everyone to seek, receive, and impart information and ideas of all kinds, regardless of frontiers, either orally, in writing, in print, in the form of art, or through any other media of choice.[25] This right to receive information is similarly guaranteed by the African Charter,[26] which is binding on Kenya.

Obligation to Facilitate and Encourage Public Awareness

In 1987, *Our Common Future* expressed its concern with people and changes in human attitudes, noting that these changes depend on an urgent and vast campaign of education, debate, and public participation.[27] This view is reinforced by the 1992 Agenda 21, a nonbinding action plan on sustainable development agreed on by UN member states during the Conference on Environment and Development in Rio de Janeiro, Brazil. In Chapter 36, Agenda 21 makes provisions for education and public awareness, and training with regard to implementation of sustainable development. Education, including formal education, public awareness, and training are highlighted as critical for achieving environmental and ethical awareness; for developing values, attitudes, skills, and behaviors consistent with sustainable development; and for encouraging effective public participation in decision making.[28] Education is therefore a foundational element of public participation, and through training and public awareness it can enhance public sensitivity to environment and development problems. It also can strengthen public involvement in seeking solutions and, particularly, foster a sense of personal environmental responsibility and commitment toward sustainable development.[29]

Formal and nonformal educational systems stand to play a key role. Formal education implies school- or institution-based education, ranging from basic primary education to tertiary institutional or university training. Public awareness of formal education is particularly important because achievement of universal primary education is the second Millennium Development Goal. Enrolling and retaining children in primary schools to receive a basic education was enacted as a special basic right for every child in Kenya by Article 53 of the constitution. Kenya has had a system of universal and free primary school education since 2003. Using formal primary-, secondary-, and tertiary-level education to impart values, knowledge, and awareness of sustainable development is instrumental in realizing intergenerational equity, enabling

---

24 *International Covenant on Civil and Political Rights*, 6 Intl. Leg. Materials 368 (1967).

25 *Id.*, at art. 19.

26 *Id.*, at art. 9.

27 *Our Common Future*, at para. 107.

28 *See Report of the United Nations Conference on Environment and Development, Rio de Janeiro, 3–14 June 1992*, vol. 1: *Resolutions Adopted by the Conference*, res. 1, annexes I and II, para. 36.3 (UN, Sales No. E.93.I.8 and corrigenda) (hereinafter *UN Conference on Environment and Development*).

29 *Id.*, at para 36.8.

younger generations to internalize these values. The concept of education for sustainable development (ESD) provides a ready-to-use mechanism.

With Resolution 59/237, the UN General Assembly adopted the Decade of Education for Sustainable Development (DESD), which extends from 2005 to 2014. The resolution called on national governments to "consider the inclusion . . . of measures to implement the Decade in their respective educational systems and strategies and, where appropriate, national development plans." According to UNESCO, the basic vision of ESD rests on the principle of using education—formal, nonformal, and informal—as an effective vector to bring about change in values, attitudes, and lifestyles to ensure a sustainable future.[30] The objectives of the ESD program are to improve access to quality basic education, reorient existing education programs, develop public understanding and awareness, and provide training.[31] These are reiterated as the key strategic objectives for implementing the ESD strategy for Kenya,[32] which is discussed later in this chapter.

Access to Judicial and Administrative Proceedings, Including Redress and Remedy

Access to justice, according to Connie Ngondi-Houghton,[33] is conceptualized not as an end result but as a continuum that begins with inclusion of rights in the law, awareness of and understanding of the law, easy availability of information pertinent to one's rights, the right to the protection of one's rights by the legal enforcement agencies, easy entry into the judicial justice system, a conducive environment within the judicial system, timely processing of claims, and timely enforcement of judicial decisions. Principle 10 of the Rio Declaration calls on states to provide effective access to judicial and administrative proceedings, including redress and remedy. In this sense, the legal system of any country should ensure that judicial institutions and any administrative mechanisms are effective in order to enhance access to environmental justice for the public.[34] Any proceedings in these mechanisms should be expeditious and inexpensive, and the rules on legal standing should be liberal, with the objective of giving the public concerned wide access to justice.[35] Additionally, the outcomes of the access to justice mechanisms should be binding on public authorities.

---

30   UNESCO, *The UN Decade of Education for Sustainable Development (DESD 2005–2014): The First Two Years* 5 (UNESCO 2007).

31   *Id.*, at 6.

32   *Kenya: Education for Sustainable Development Implementation Strategy* 14 (Natl. Env. Mgt. Auth. 2008) (hereinafter *Kenya: Education*).

33   Connie Ngondi-Houghton, *Access to Justice and the Rule of Law in Kenya* 4–5 (research paper prepared for the Commission for the Empowerment of the Poor, 2006).

34   Robert Kibugi, *Enhanced Access to Environmental Justice in Kenya* 159–160 (Jamie Benidickson & Ben Boer eds., Edward Elgar 2011).

35   *Id.*

Interpreting Constitutional Provisions as Opportunities for Enhanced Public Participation in Environmental Decision Making

It is clear that, through Article 10, the Kenyan constitution boldly pronounces the central role of public participation. The constitution is a framework law, so this chapter reviews the specific provisions that could be molded to reflect a normative content for public participation that is consistent with Principle 10 of the Rio Declaration. The output of this analysis will articulate the opportunities available in Kenyan law for practical implementation of public participation in environmental decision making through law and administrative regulations.

Deriving the Basis of Public Participation from Constitutional Environmental Right and Duty

The constitution, through Article 42 (part of the Bill of Rights), grants a specific right to a clean and healthy environment to every person. The implementation of this right, analyzed below, provides opportunities for public participation.

Foundation of Proactive Public Participation

Article 42 provides that the environmental right shall be realized through legislative and other measures, particularly those contemplated in Article 69, which highlights two sets of obligations. The first set, in Article 69(1), outlines obligations mandatory on the Kenyan state. Four of these obligations are notable, requiring the state to (1) ensure sustainable exploitation, utilization, management, and conservation of the environment and natural resources; (2) work to achieve and maintain a tree cover of at least 10 percent of the land area of Kenya; (3) protect and enhance intellectual property in, and indigenous knowledge of, biodiversity and the genetic resources of the communities; and (4) encourage public participation in the management, protection, and conservation of the environment.

The second set of obligations, in Article 69(2), outlines a duty on every person to cooperate with state organs and other persons "to protect and conserve the environment and ensure ecologically sustainable development and use of natural resources." This environmental duty on citizens of Kenya manifests three arms: (1) a specific obligation on each individual to protect and conserve the environment; (2) a specific obligation on every individual to cooperate with the state organs, and other people, to protect and conserve the environment; and (3) an overall obligation on people, working together and with the state, to conserve the environment, ensure ecologically sustainable development, and use natural resources.

A textual reading reveals that the duty in Article 69(2) casts the mold for proactive public participation, including collaboration with public agencies and officers and other members of the public, in fulfillment of the constitutional duty on citizens. The explicit output of this proactive public-participation obligation is clearly set out as "ensuring ecologically sustainable development, and use of natural resources." Arguably, Article 69(2), through the environmental duty, sets the foundational basis for public participation in environmental decision making, with sustainable development as a clear output.

Equity in Public Participation

The constitutional environmental right, which is implemented through legislative and other measures set out in Article 69, includes an entitlement to have the environment protected for present and future generations. It is an explicit linkage of the right with sustainable development, which concerns both intra- and intergenerational equity. The latter concepts of equity inherently require the ensuring of representation or participation of both genders[36] in a reasonable proportion, and ascertaining that there is adequate representation of younger people for generational succession. Gender equity is a core value of the 2010 Constitution of Kenya, which stipulates that not more than two-thirds of members of elective or appointive bodies shall be of one gender.[37] It is particularly applicable when public representation or consultation is conducted through statutory bodies such as committees created through legislation.

The roles through which the public can take part in environmental decision making could, through legal provisions, take the form of representation in key organs or committees, or being consulted over particular matters, decisions, and projects (such as through EIAs) or proposed laws, policies, and programs. Even when such mechanisms for representation and consultations exist, there are pervading concerns over their effectiveness, or whether they are mere formalities. Arguably, the aim of these mechanisms should be to have public representation and consultations resulting in positive effects on the threshold and direction of decision making. The socioeconomic diversity of society suggests that in order for public representation to accommodate equity, the law should develop criteria for representation to ensure that the concerns of all, from the poorest to the wealthiest, members of the community are articulated. In public participation through representation in decision making forums (such as committees), questions often arise regarding the manner in which representatives are chosen. Are they democratically elected by fellow citizens, or appointed by public officials?

The Right of Access to Information

The Original Constitutional Position on Access to Information in Kenya

Section 79 of the now-repealed constitution[38] did contain provisions akin to guarantees of access to information but those provisions featured a number

---

36 Principle 20 of the Rio Declaration recognizes that women have a vital role in environmental management and development and notes that the full participation of women is essential to achieve sustainable development.

37 Kenyan Const., *supra* note 5, at art. 27.

38 Kenyan Const. (1994) Rev. 2008 (repealed Aug. 27, 2010).

of weak and gray areas. That constitution guaranteed every person in Kenya the freedom to "hold information" as well as to "receive ideas and information without interference,"[39] but the right was not absolute, being restricted on grounds of public health and national security or safety.[40] In addition, while the constitution granted a freedom to receive ideas and information, it did not specify a right to receive the information from the state, due to the Official Secrets Act prohibiting public servants from releasing any confidential information.[41] Nor did the law define the term "confidential," which created the possibility that any government information could be treated as confidential.

The Current Constitutional Position

Article 35 of the 2010 constitution seeks to remedy the past weaknesses and provides for an explicit entitlement to access information as a fundamental right. The article provides that every citizen has the right of access to

> (*a*) information held by the State; and

> (*b*) information held by another person and required for the exercise or protection of any right or fundamental freedom.

This provision raises several pertinent conceptual issues for assessment. Unlike other fundamental rights, it is the only entitlement whose effect is limited to citizens of Kenya. The entitlement includes a right to access information held by the state (public authorities) and by another person (private entities). The provision leaves an open ending to "information held by the State," as opposed to information held by private citizens. Thus, citizens have a right to access pertinent information held by the state without a need to demonstrate that the information is required for exercise of any right or fundamental freedom.

Legislative Attempt to Develop Access to Information Administrative Mechanisms

The Freedom of Information Bill 2012 is proposed as legislation to give effect to Article 35. The bill reiterates that access to information is a legally enforceable right. It proposes a complex administrative procedure governing how public officials should respond to freedom of information requests, notably placing a 15-day limit for processing the requests. It further proposes that requests for information should be rejected only when the information, if released, would be likely to infringe on personal privacy, expose industrial or commercial secrets, or endanger national security.

---

39   *Id.*, section 79(1); *see* also Robert Kibugi, *Development and Balancing of Interests in Kenya* 166–167 (Willemien du Plessis & Michael Faure eds., Pretoria U. L. Press 2011). *See* also the analysis in E. Abuya, *Towards Promoting Access to Information in Kenya* 6 (Apr. 2011), available at http://spaa.newark.rutgers.edu/images/stories/documents/Transparency_Research_Con ference/Papers/Abuya_Edwin.pdf (accessed Aug. 28, 2011).

40   Kenyan Const. (1994), *supra* note 38, at sec. 79(2).

41   *Official Secrets Act*, Cap. 187 *Laws of Kenya*, sec. 3.

Access to environmental information is an administrative process, and thus legislation should endeavor to ease that process to avoid defeating the purpose of the right. The Aarhus Convention underscores the need to ease the administrative burden. Notably, the convention states that requested information ought to be provided "without an interest having to be stated"; most preferably in the form requested; and as soon as possible—within a month, unless the complexity of the information justifies an extension to two months, in which case the applicant should be notified promptly and given reasons for the delay.[42] This provision supports the approach of the 2006 East African Community Protocol on Environment and Natural Resources Management, which, although lacking the detailed content, places an obligation at Article 34 on the states to "ensure that officials and public authorities assist the public to gain access to information." Ideally, therefore, it would be necessary for a law to clarify if any administrative fee was to be levied, and to ensure this was reasonable. Additionally, there should be an administrative or access to justice mechanism through which members of the public can appeal decisions that limit or deny access to information.

Obligation on Public Awareness and Information Dissemination

Public awareness, which is a core element of public participation, is a right that is mutually reinforcing to all other elements facilitating citizen involvement in environmental decision making.

Formal and Informal Education as Avenues for Public Awareness

One constitutional basis of public awareness is freedom of expression, set out in Article 33, particularly the freedom to seek, receive, or impart information or ideas. Another constitutional basis, consistent with the classification by Agenda 21, is found in Article 43, which creates a right to education for every person. The right to education in Article 43 is set out as distinct from Article 53's universal right of all children to free and compulsory basic education. The generic right in Article 43 could be interpreted to include an entitlement to formal and informal education that improves the skills, knowledge, values, and attitudes of people, including for the environmental decision making anticipated in Article 69(2). Applying this constitutional foundation strengthens the argument for developing and undertaking extensive civic education and extension programs and integrating values of sustainability into curricula for basic, secondary, tertiary, and adult education programs.

Adapting Existing Educational Strategies for Public Awareness

The ESD strategy for Kenya[43] focuses on adapting sustainable development to the formal education system and school syllabus, as well as for the training of teachers. Public awareness, one of the strategic objectives of the Kenyan ESD

---

42 *Aarhus Convention, supra* note 19, at art. 4.

43 *Kenya: Education, supra* note 32, at 14.

strategy, is usually undertaken through informal education mechanisms as a key element in inculcating values related to and knowledge about sustainability in natural resources management. The strategy, for instance, acknowledges the role of government in "fostering public awareness, participation and capacity building on ESD at all levels," and of civil society in community involvement at all levels, "through awareness and education programmes and . . . sharing information relating to ESD."[44]

This suggests a key role for generic civic education programs, typically undertaken to disseminate information or educate the public on various matters of governance, such as through the Kenya National Integrated Civic Education (K-NICE) Programme. This is an initiative of the government in collaboration with nonstate actors to develop a nationally owned and sustainable program of civic education.

The strategy for the K-NICE civic education program sets out key result areas: (1) to enhance awareness of the Bill of Rights and national values; (2) to sustain citizens' engagement in constitutional implementation; (3) to improve understanding of land reforms, land use, and land management; (4) to improve understanding and engagement in the implementation of devolved government; and (5) to enhance engagement in the electoral process.[45] The integrated national civic education program has been developed and introduced at a critical juncture in Kenya, and upon implementation it will enhance public participation in general governance and in environmental decision making.

The Role of Extension Education

Another option for undertaking public awareness, which is particularly relevant for environmental decision making, is through extension education. Extension is the function of providing need- and demand-based knowledge and skills to rural populations in a nonformal, participatory manner with the objective of improving their quality of life.[46] Extension is often provided directly to community members, depending on the natural resource activity they are undertaking; it could, for example, be classified as agricultural, forestry, or fisheries extension.

Public awareness and other mechanisms for imparting knowledge, values, and skills for sustainable development will be inadequate unless public authorities have an obligatory role in availing and disseminating pertinent environmental information. As part of the constitutional right of access to information, the government has an obligation to "publish and publicise" any important information affecting the nation. The Freedom of Information Bill

---

44   *Id.*, at 22–23.

45   *Kenya National Integrated Civic Education (K-Nice) Programme: Strategy and Implementation Plan* 11–14 (Ministry of Just., Constitutional Affairs & Natl. Cohesion, 2011).

46   Kalim Qamar, *Modernizing National Agricultural Extension Systems: A Practical Guide for Policy-Makers of Developing Countries* 1 (Food and Agric. Org. 2005).

interprets this as an "obligation on the part of public bodies and officials to disseminate essential information that the public is entitled to know, including their core functions and key activities."[47] Based on Articles 42 and 69 of the constitution, it can be argued that information on the diverse variants of environmental decision making is important to, and has an effect on, the nation.

Access to Justice through Judicial and Administrative Mechanisms

The constitution has incorporated explicit mechanisms that guarantee the right of access to justice, therefore strengthening application of other entitlements that empower citizen or public roles in environmental management. Article 48 obliges the Kenyan state to ensure access to justice for all persons and to ensure that any fee required shall be reasonable and not an impediment to the realization of the right. Access to justice, in practical terms, is realized through judicial and administrative mechanisms for complaints, redress, and remedy. The constitution sets out an extensive judicial structure for the enforcement of fundamental rights, interpretation of the constitution, and resolution of disputes, as well as for upholding provisions of any law.

Liberal Legal Standing to Enforce Environmental Rights

Article 22 entitles any person who claims that a fundamental right has been denied, violated, infringed upon, or threatened to bring a petition for protection or enforcement of that right to the High Court. The provisions on legal standing have been extensively eased relative to the now-repealed constitution, such that a person may file a petition for enforcement of the Bill of Rights on his or her own behalf, on behalf of a group, or in the public interest. In an effort to enhance access to justice, there are powers given the chief justice to create rules of procedure that will facilitate access to justice, including eliminating court fees; minimizing formal procedures, such as possible entertainment of informal documentation for filing petitions; easing procedural technicalities; and permitting persons with particular expertise pertinent to the matter at hand to appear as a friend of the court (amicus curiae). Article 70 of the constitution is similar to Article 22 but specifically provides for actions to enforce constitutional environmental rights without the need to demonstrate standing.

Specialized Environmental Court with Constitutional Enforcement Powers

Pursuant to constitutional authority to create specialized courts with the status of a High Court,[48] Parliament enacted the Environment and Land Court Act, 2011. This specialized Environment and Land Court was established to facilitate the just, expeditious, proportionate, and accessible resolution of environment and land disputes. The court has the power to hear and determine

---

47   Freedom of Information Bill sec. 26(13) (draft, Jan. 5, 2012).

48   Kenyan Const., *supra* note 5, at art. 165. The High Court is created as a court with unlimited original and appellate jurisdiction on civil and criminal matters. Under art. 165(3-b), read with art. 22, it has exclusive jurisdiction to enforce the fundamental rights guaranteed by the Bill of Rights in the 2010 constitution.

disputes relating to environmental planning and protection, trade, climate issues, land use planning, title, tenure, boundaries, rates, rents, valuations, mining, minerals, and other natural resources. Other areas of competence include
compulsory acquisition of land, administration and management of land,
and land contracts and instruments. The law empowers this court, because
it is equivalent to a High Court, with the authority to determine applications
brought under Article 22 of the constitution for enforcement of the fundamental right to a clean environment. This court also enjoys the power to determine
appeals from subordinate courts on matters of land and the environment and
to sit in judicial review of environmental decisions made by public officials
and administrative tribunals.

Innovatively, the court is empowered, on application by parties or on its
own motion, to apply alternative dispute resolution (ADR) mechanisms, including customary law–based approaches that are consistent with the constitution and statute law.[49] Application of ADR provides opportunities for
concerned members of the public to constructively engage with one another
in resolving environmental disputes with plausible impacts on sustainable development.

Independent Ombudsman to Safeguard Administrative Rights

There is a constitutional entitlement to administrative justice through administrative action that is expeditious, efficient, lawful, reasonable, and procedurally fair. If a fundamental right of a person is threatened by administrative
action, the concerned person is entitled to receive written reasons for the decision. This right is a core entitlement that affects the realization of other basic
rights, including access to information and the right to a clean and healthy
environment. Through the Commission on Administrative Justice Act, 2011,
Parliament, under powers set out in Article 59 of the constitution, established
a statutory commission to function as custodian of the right to fair administrative action. The Commission on Administrative Justice (Ombudsman) has
broad powers to protect, uphold, and enforce the right to fair administrative
action.[50] It has the power to institute and undertake investigations into complaints submitted by any person regarding administrative action. The com-

---

49   Environment and Land Court Act, sec. 18 (2012).

50   Sec. 5: The statutory powers of the Commission include (i) investigate any conduct in state
     or public affairs that is alleged to be, or is likely to be prejudicial or improper. (ii) investigate
     complaints of abuse of power, unfair treatment, manifest injustice or unlawful, oppressive,
     unfair or unresponsive official conduct within the public sector. (iii) inquire into allegations
     of maladministration, delay, administrative injustice, discourtesy, incompetence, misbehav-
     iour, inefficiency or ineptitude within the public service; (iv) facilitate the setting up of, and
     build complaint handling capacity in, the sectors of public service, public offices and state
     organs; (v) work with different public institutions to promote alternative dispute resolu-
     tion methods in the resolution of complaints relating to public administration; (vi) provide
     advisory opinions or proposals on improvement of public administration, including review
     of legislation, codes of conduct, processes and procedures; and (vii) promote public aware-
     ness of policies and administrative procedures on matters relating to administrative justice.
     See also Commn. on Admin. Just. Reg., 2013 (Leg. Notice No. 64, April 12, 2013).

mission is empowered to call witnesses and issue summons, and eventually it may be able to recommend prosecution, or advise the complainant on an appropriate form of judicial redress. It may also advise the complainant and the particular public office concerned in the alleged violation on other appropriate methods of settling the complaint or to obtain relief.

The Freedom of Information Bill has proposed a similar administrative mechanism for investigating and adjudicating complaints regarding access to information. Collectively, the structuring and implementation of these administrative mechanisms will impact, negatively or positively, the realization of the right of access to justice and fair administrative action.

The Pursuit of Enhanced Public Participation in Environmental Decision Making through County Governments

Public participation is, through Article 10 of the constitution, binding to county governments. Article 69(1) of the constitution, as previously detailed, sets out mandatory obligations that require both the national and county governments to "encourage public participation in the management, protection and conservation of the environment." A specific responsibility of county governments to ensure public participation in governance is set out in Clause 14, of the fourth schedule to the constitution, as a responsibility to

> ensure and coordinate the participation of communities and locations in governance at the local level and assist communities and locations to develop the administrative capacity for the effective exercise of the functions and powers and participation in governance at the local level.

Although public participation is set out as a function of county governments with respect to general governance, there is no inhibition from adapting it toward enhancing public participation in environmental decision making. This is particularly evident in relation to the functions of county governments in the fourth schedule to the constitution, which include implementing specific national policies and laws on the conservation of agriculture, the environment, soil, and water, as well as on water services and sanitation, among other areas of concern. This public-participation function requires county governments to "assist communities . . . to develop the administrative capacity for the effective exercise of . . . functions . . . and participation in governance at the local level." It is an important legal provision on subsidiarity in governance and, when applied to environmental decision making, synchronizes devolved government in Kenya with the Local Agenda 21 framework.[51] Local Agenda 21 involves cascading Agenda 21 to lower levels of government and places a responsibility on local governments, as the level of governance closest to the people, to play a vital role in educating, mobilizing, and responding to the public to promote sustainable development.

---

51   *UN Conference on Environment and Development, supra* note 28, at ch. 28.

The constitutional provisions on devolution with respect to county governments[52] are given effect through the County Governments Act, 2012.[53] This law came into operation after the first general elections under the 2010 constitution, in March 2013. It contains provisions on public participation that, although generic in nature, could produce innovative constitutional interpretation to enhance citizen roles. These provisions could be modified or expanded through administrative regulations and other practical mechanisms to enhance their utility to environmental decision making. This possibility is examined in the final section of this chapter.

The Village as the Basic Unit of County Administration and Public Participation

The law on devolution mandates that every county government decentralize its functions and services to cities and urban areas, constituencies (as subcounty units), wards, and village units.[54] The village units, as the most basic and local level of government, are closer to the grassroots and will play a key role in facilitating public participation in all aspects of governance, including environmental decision making. Many citizens who live at that level of administration utilize environmental resources such as water and land for livelihood and are therefore at the forefront of making important utilization and management decisions. Statute-mandated accessibility of government at that level is therefore a critical innovation. It will be important to develop regulations on adapting and applying this provision to enhance public participation in environmental management.

The General Framework for Citizen Participation

The law on county governments sets out the framework and principles for citizen participation,[55] including timely access to information and reasonable access to law and policy formulation processes. These principles notably enhance the legal standing of interested or affected persons, organizations, and communities to appeal or review decisions or redress grievances. This is an equitable principle that places particular emphasis on traditionally marginalized communities, women, and youth. If interpreted into regulations or county-level laws, this principle could entrench the equity function of public participation in governance. The utility of this framework is heightened by the principles under which county governments provide reasonable balance in their interactions with nonstate actors in decision-making processes, thus promoting shared responsibility and providing complementary authority and oversight.

---

52   Kenyan Const., *supra* note 5, at ch. 11.

53   County Governments Act, Act No. 17 of 2012.

54   *Id.*, at sec. 48

55   County Governments Act, *supra* note 53, at sec. 87

Within this framework, county governments are obliged to respond to petitions and challenges expeditiously, to limit the resort to court action, and possibly to secure the integrity of public participation. They may also conduct referenda on proposed laws and policies and may be petitioned to do so regarding planning and investment decisions.[56] There is an obligation on county governments to put into place facilitative structures such as town hall meetings, information- and technology-based platforms such as websites, budget-validation forums, or conventional means, such as notice boards, for matters of public interest.[57] Inasmuch as the village is the basic unit of administration, such facilitative structures should be established at the village level, as they are intended to facilitate consultation with citizens and to enhance their contribution to governance. Going forward, with respect to environmental decision making, it will be necessary to persuade county governments to enact framework legislation that will establish the purposes and rationale for convening town hall meetings and budget-validation forums.

The Obligation to Undertake Public Communication

The framework of the law on county governments makes those governments responsible for overseeing public communications and facilitating access to information. Notably, county governments are required to use the media to advocate core development issues such as sustainable environmental management, agriculture, education, health, security, and economics. The law further requires the county governments to develop a framework for mechanisms of public communication, including television stations, information communication technology centers, websites, and community radio stations.[58] These are important mechanisms for furthering the dissemination of general and important information, and for fostering debate and discussion by and among citizens. County-level laws and administrative regulations will be needed.

Citizens' Right of Access to Information

This devolved government law, in furtherance of Article 35 of the constitution, provides that every Kenyan citizen has a right to apply for and to access information held by any county government. The law requires that each county government and its agencies identify and designate an officer to be responsible for access to information requests. County governments may therefore enact regulations to further expeditious access to information, although caution should be taken to prevent conflict with national access to information law. Nonetheless, this provides a useful window for counties to introduce specific administrative regulations of access to environmental information.

---

56   *Id.,* at secs. 88–90.

57   *Id.,* at sec. 91.

58   *Id.,* at sec. 95.

The Obligation to Provide Civic Education

The county government law further provides for civic education, the objectives of which are to empower and enlighten citizens and government, to engage citizens and government on a continuous and systemic basis, to sustain citizens' engagement in the implementation of the constitution, and to heighten citizen demand for service delivery by institutions of governance at the county level. These objectives support the argument that civic education and public awareness form the critical bedrock for all other elements of public participation, because without knowledge it would be difficult to spark interest in governance or to have an impact on people's values and attitudes. In this context, civic education is the starting point for fulfillment of all other elements of public participation, as awareness imparts knowledge on how to be part of governance on matters affecting citizens, such as the management of local natural resources. Importantly, county governments are empowered to develop legislation that puts into place the institutional framework for facilitating and implementing civic education.[59]

Looking Forward to Enhanced Public Participation in Environmental Decision Making

With the constitutional transition in administrative systems and laws, Kenya has undergone a significant transformation that will impact public participation in environmental decision making and sustainable development. Many of the frameworks analyzed in this chapter are generic in nature, designed to enhance public participation in general governance and administration. The normative framework derived from elements in Principle 10 of the Rio Declaration provides a useful guide, against which Kenyan law can be examined to determine the best model for public participation.

From the foregoing analysis, it emerges that the constitutional framework in Kenya is fairly advanced on providing avenues for public participation in governance. The entrenchment of public participation as a binding principle of national governance in the constitution reinforces this view. It is similarly evident that public participation is not merely an entitlement granted to citizens by the state; it is inherently intertwined with the sovereignty reposed on citizens. With this strong foundation, constitutional and other legal provisions provide mechanisms to implement the various elements of public participation, particularly through the Bill of Rights and the system of devolved governments. A reasonably advanced framework can thus be deduced from the national constitution, and even from the law on county governments. While this chapter links these frameworks to environmental decision making, this linkage is not apparent in practice. It is therefore important for the law to take additional steps through legislation and administrative regulations specific to

---

59   *Id.*, at sec. 100.

environmental management. The following seven areas are prime targets for new legislation and regulations.

National Framework on Public Participation in Environmental Decision Making

A legislative or policy framework would determine the thresholds and parameters for public participation in environmental decision making. Such a framework would be particularly relevant as it would provide guidance on how the general provisions on public participation would be adapted for environmental decision making. It would eliminate or limit the misuse of the procedures of public participation by providing clear instruments, mechanisms, or processes that would constitute a comprehensive process of public participation.

Consultative Development of Public Mobilization Regulations, Targets, and Procedures

In order to enhance public participation in environmental decision making, it is important for Kenyan national and county governments to develop regulations that will guide administrative implementation. This would build on the framework law or policy on public participation, proposed above, making the process of development more consultative, to include the general public, members of Parliament, and other stakeholders. The regulations should, for example, aim to set up flexible procedures that could be applied to mobilization (for purposes of consultations), including how to reach people who ordinarily would be unaware or unreachable by conventional approaches such as town hall meetings, media announcements, or Internet postings. The regulations should also include procedures for providing feedback to members of the public, individually or collectively. The absence of feedback is a major cause of apathy to participation in matters of governance, as individuals do not think it worth their time when their complaints or proposals are not acted upon promptly and feedback is not provided. It is thus important for members of the public to have available avenues and mechanisms through which they can receive feedback on complaints and suggestions given to public officers or to representatives to statutory committees.

Preparation of Digests for Dissemination

A potentially important administrative approach for national and county governments and civil society (separately or in collaboration) is to develop dedicated digests of the mechanisms available for public participation. This would involve isolating distinctive legislative and policy provisions and simplifying them, with possible translation into Swahili[60] and/or vernacular languages for dissemination. The dissemination could be facilitated by village government

---

60   Kiswahili is the national language, and one of two official languages in Kenya, as per art. 7 of the 2010 constitution.

offices, either over the Internet or through citizens' forums, including town hall meetings, churches, and market centers.

Integrating Public Participation in Formal Education, Adult Literacy Syllabi, and Civic Education Manuals

In addition to constitutional basis, sustainable development is reiterated as a duty on every Kenyan citizen through Section 23 of the Kenya Citizenship and Immigration Act, 2011. Integration into the education system can provide the means to impart awareness and knowledge on the constitutional and statutory duties that set the basis of public participation through basic education, adult literacy programs, and civic education. The framework that has already been synthesized through the Education for Sustainable Development (ESD) strategy developed by the National Environment Management Authority (NEMA) should, however, be reviewed to incorporate provisions of the 2010 constitution on sustainability duties and devolved governments.

Proactive Disclosure of Information

The proactive disclosure of information that is pertinent to environmental decision making by the government is an instrumental mechanism for dissemination of information. It will also reduce pressure on the formal application process for access to information. Indeed, Article 35 of the constitution obligates the Kenyan national and county government agencies to publish and disseminate any important information affecting the nation.

Public-Interest Environmental Litigation and Alternative Dispute Resolution

Access to justice is an important element of public participation. Although the constitution and statutes make extensive provisions for access to justice mechanisms, the utility of these mechanisms depends on how often they are invoked by the public. They include petitioning the High Court for enforcement of the right to a clean and healthy environment through Articles 22 and 70 of the constitution, bringing civil actions to the Land and Environment Court, and filing complaints for administrative justice with the ombudsman. In addition to preparing digests that simplify the rights, duties, and procedures with respect to these institutions, it is necessary to develop dedicated public and civil society programs that offer legal and paralegal advice on access to justice, including public-interest litigation.

Civic Education

Civic education is an important element of public participation and of the realization of sustainable development because it raises public awareness of the existence of rights, avenues for service delivery, mechanisms for accountability, and paths for actual participation by individual members of the public. Civic education therefore forms a foundation for other forms of public participation. It is important in disseminating information, deepening people's knowledge, availing forums for debate and discussion, and triggering proactive engagement in matters of governance. Civic education is therefore a significant practical approach for implementing public participation. To communicate a consistent message, the content of civic education should be synchronized, since it could be offered by various stakeholders, including the national government, county governments, civil society, and the private sector, among others. The role of the Kenya National Integrated Civic Education (K-NICE) Programme is thus critical, to enhance the level of awareness of rights and encourage participation in governance and to act as a catalyst of constructive and effective citizen engagement in the management of natural resources.

Conclusion

While public participation can be an elusive concept due to its generic nature, the 2010 Constitution of Kenya has opened up new legal and administrative frontiers. It is a basic law focused on the interests of democracy and the well-being of citizens. This is evident in the framing of public participation and sustainable development as binding national values of governance. Nonetheless, with the exception of the basic right to a clean environment and the specific provisions on proactive public participation arising from Article 69 of the constitution, many of the provisions require innovative structuring to enhance the utility to environmental decision making. This could take place through legislation, policy, and administrative mechanisms that ensure a meaningful implementation through the creation of opportunities for equitable citizen participation in environmental decision making. Cascading the constitution through legislation, policy, and other administrative mechanisms proposed in this chapter will set the process in motion.

In order to be adjudged equitable and effective, public participation in environmental decision making must impact the threshold of decision making. If this occurs, those individuals making a contribution in decision making will have been treated equitably, and such legal opportunities could be exploited by more individuals. The design and structuring of such extensive forward-looking mechanisms requires in-depth analysis of constitutional provisions to distill the basic precepts of public participation and to allow for further application with respect to environmental decision making. This chapter has undertaken such an analysis, first identifying a relevant normative content aligned to Principle 10 of the 1992 Rio Declaration, and thereafter succinctly identifying conceptual, legal, and administrative opportunities available to enhance equitable participation of citizens in environmental decision making.

Planning Laws, Development Controls, and Social Equity

Lessons for Developing Countries

RACHELLE ALTERMAN

Implementing or revising planning laws is a booming trend around the globe, especially in developing countries. The tendency in developing countries has been to model planning laws along the lines of those enacted and practiced in advanced-economy countries. Before rushing to emulate the planning laws of advanced economies, however, developing and transition countries should ask some tough questions about the models to be adopted. Perhaps the most important is whether the enactment and implementation of planning laws has enhanced social equity in cities or exacerbated the inequities. When one examines advanced-economy countries, where planning laws and regulatory instruments have been routinely applied and enforced for many decades, the answer to this question is a mixed one.

After an introduction to the relationship between planning laws and urban justice, this chapter delves into the functions played by planning laws and how cities and countries have operated without them, both in the past and more recently. A brief history of the evolution of planning laws around the globe is presented, including their general state in developing countries today. A conceptual framework for thinking about the regulatory layers of development controls leads to an overview of existing research on the effects of planning regulations on social composition of cities and neighborhoods, with a special focus on housing prices. Finally, lessons for developing countries are discussed.

Social Equity, Planning Laws, and Development Controls

Planning laws, planning regulation, and development controls set land use and building characteristics and thus affect the physical environment. Whether intentionally or not, planning regulation may also affect the social composition of regions, cities, neighborhoods, and even city blocks.

Unlike many other types of civic laws, planning laws affect not only one or two distinct spheres, such as governance, business, or child care. Because

I am very grateful to Iris Frankel Cohen—an attorney and urban planner—who has kindly provided me with some of the literature sources and has offered valuable comments.

the entire range of human (and nature-based) activities require the use of space, and because space is often people's major property asset, the procedures, institutions, and rules for controlling urban and rural development affect many spheres of life. Some of these effects can be anticipated, but many are ancillary or unintended. By impacting the use of land and space, planning laws and development control can deeply influence the existing sociocultural and economic order. They may have dramatic implications on personal health and safety, housing prices, employment opportunities, family life, personal time (spent on travel), and accessibility to public services.

Planning regulation can encourage the supply of adequate and affordable housing and thus reinforce social integration, but regulations might also aggravate the separation of social groups, provide greater public amenities to privileged sectors, and raise housing prices, whether intentionally or not. Thus, planning laws may exacerbate social differentiation and social exclusion.

In other words, urban planning in general, and decisions made under planning law in particular, is strongly related to notions of justice. Social justice is an elusive concept. In her book *The Just City*, Fainstein addresses the challenge of evaluating public decision making in urban planning and management. After surveying relevant schools of philosophy, she decides that the concept of equity is preferable to that of equality and better captures the essence of a just city. She defines equity-seeking urban policy as one that "favors the less well off more than the well-to-do. That is, it should be redistributive, not only economically but also, as appropriate, politically, socially, and spatially."[1]

The concept of "distributional equity" is relevant to planning regulations. Because lucrative land in a particular region is limited, legally binding plans or zoning decisions are really a matter of allocating financial gains or losses—what Hagman and Misczynski call "windfalls and wipeouts."[2] The major function of planning regulations is to allocate development rights for different land uses and densities—some lucrative to the landholders (such as designation as market housing or commercial), and some undesirable (such as designation as protected agricultural zone that allows no development). Planning regulations also determine which tracts will have access to effective public services, and which will have little access to services. Planning regulations determine which areas will benefit from positive externalities and which will bear the brunt of negative ones. In other words, planning regulations have major implications for property values and thus for many households.

---

1   Susan Fainstein, *The Just City* 36 (Cornell U. Press 2010).

2   Donald G. Hagman & Dean J. Misczynski eds., *Windfalls for Wipeouts: Land Value Recapture and Compensation* (Am. Plan. Assn. 1978). In a book comparing 13 Organisation for Economic Co-operation and Development (OECD) countries, Alterman analyzes how the law in each country treats the value loss or gain from planning regulations differently. *See* Rachelle Alterman, *Takings International: A Comparative Perspective on Land Use Regulations and Compensation Rights* (ABA Press 2010).

Fainstein defines distributional equity as aiming "at bettering the situation of those who without state intervention would suffer from relative deprivation.[3]" In the context of planning regulation, two baselines for comparison would determine land use distribution if there were no planning controls: market forces and existing sociocultural and political norms. In advanced-economy countries, market forces are the dominant precursors to planning regulations, whereas in developing countries, sociocultural and political norms are also important (sometimes more than market forces).

Although Fainstein does not address planning law directly, her book opens with a debate among planning theorists that is relevant to this chapter. Fainstein asks if planning theory—and urban justice—should center on the way planning decisions are made (procedural) or on their substance and impacts (substantive). The procedural-justice approach focuses on the quality of communication between government and the concerned public, on power relationships or on the instruments of public participation.[4] Fainstein argues that although for the assessment of planning laws and regulations both approaches are relevant, substantive decisions are more relevant in evaluating just planning or a just city.

Every planning law in the world contains both procedural and substantive components that impact the concept of justice. On the procedural side, planning law sets up institutions, ways of communication with the public, access to information, and degrees of legal power granted to stakeholders. On the substantive side, the essence of planning law is the various instruments with which it empowers government bodies to make a difference "on the ground." This chapter adopts Fainstein's perspective in that it examines the instruments of development controls in terms of their impacts, rather than on how they were adopted. However, there is need for more comparative research on the relationship between social equity and planning institutions and procedures.[5]

This chapter uses the term "urban justice" broadly, as suggested by Fainstein,[6] to refer to public policies that promote greater social equity and fairness than the market or preexisting social forces would have engendered without public regulation or intervention.

---

3   Fainstein, *supra* note 1, at 37.

4   John Forester, *The Deliberative Practitioner* (Mass. Inst. Tech. Press 1999); Patsy Healey, *Planning through Debate: The Communicative Turn in Planning Theory*, in *Readings in Planning Theory* 234–258 (Susan S. Fainstein & Scott Campbell eds., Blackwell 2011); Judith E. Innes, *Planning Theory's Emerging Paradigm: Communicative Action and Interactive Practice*, 14 J. Am. Plan. Assn. 183–189 (1995).

5   For an example of such comparative research, *see* Dafna Carmon & Rachelle Alterman, *Planning Theory and the Right for a Fair Hearing in Planning Laws: A Cross-National Perspective* (in preparation).

6   Fainstein, *supra* note 1, at 37.

What and Why Planning Laws?

Different Terms, Shared Elements

Planning laws are called different things in different countries: land use planning, zoning plans, land management, local planning, urbanization, spatial planning, town and country planning, urban and regional planning, city planning, environmental planning, development control. All these terms refer to one or more laws that authorize government bodies to apply a set of instruments to steer or control urban and rural development or conservation. These instruments often include statutory plans (in most countries), zoning bylaws (in the United States and Canada), subdivision or "platting" controls, powers to secure land or financing for public services, and the control of development by means of permits and building and housing codes.

All countries also have laws that empower the state or its organs to take land or buildings for public purposes under a set of conditions.[7] These powers may be included in the planning law or be independent of the planning law. They are known by different terms in different countries: eminent domain, compulsory purchase, compulsory acquisition, expropriation, takings. Although planning laws vary around the world, they usually encompass all or most of these regulatory or interventionist functions.[8] This chapter uses the term "planning law" to include this entire set of instruments, including the control of development through the process of granting (or refusing) building permits.

Urban Development without Planning Laws

The history of planning laws should not be confused with the history of urban planning in general. Urban planning has a long history—in some areas of the world, it can be traced back thousands of years. Even today, urban planning decisions by governments are not necessarily predicated on the existence of planning laws. In some regimes, including those of many developing countries, governments can act directly in making and implementing their own plans for certain aspects of city form.

Before the emergence of regulatory planning laws, public planning tended to focus on only the basic elements that a regime deemed important, such as central roads, water sources, and defense. The standards of use of land and housing by private households and businesses usually did not concern governments unless these actions interfered with the interests of the rulers or other holders of power. Even today, in developing countries—which constitute the majority of urban (and rural) areas in the world—planning laws are either nonexistent or almost irrelevant due to nonimplementation. Instead,

---

7   These differ significantly across countries; the topic is beyond the scope of this chapter.

8   Rachelle Alterman, *National-Level Planning in Democratic Countries: An International Comparison of Urban and Regional Policymaking* (Liverpool U. Press 2001). Compare with the recent large-scale comparative analysis, but on specific aspects only, Alterman, *supra* note 2.

market forces, social norms, or brute power regulates the use of land. Stark social inequities often ensue.

What about when there is total government control over land use? Does that hold the recipe for urban equity? The ideologies that propelled the Communist countries envisioned such a situation in a large-scale experiment of regimes that sought social equity without planning laws. The governments of the Soviet Union and most East European Communist countries did not need the authority of planning laws in order to make their own short- or long-range urban plans. Most developable land was nationalized.[9] State organs or related agencies controlled most land allocation and had the authority to develop it directly or to allow others to develop it. Communist countries were able to plan and implement huge housing projects, intended to create social equality and improve the livelihoods of all.

After the Bolshevik Revolution in 1917–18, Communist planning (without planning law) delivered millions of standardized housing units and upgraded public services. However, in the latter decades of the 20th century, the iniquitous outcomes of Soviet planning became apparent:[10] the title of a paper by Weclzwowicz states the development succinctly: "From Egalitarian Cities in Theory to Non-egalitarian Cities in Practice."[11] Soviet planning turned out thousands of tiny, poorly built housing units in huge blocks. These often looked fine on government plans but turned out to be dismal estates far away from the city center or employment centers, without public transportation or services. In the absence of regulation, environmental degradation became severe. The collapse of the Soviet Union revealed a story of chronic housing shortages, sometimes involving decades-long waiting lists.[12] Yet, those who were close to power were always able to obtain central housing locations.

---

9   B. Renaud & A. Bertaud, *Socialist Cities without Land Markets,* 41 J. Urb. Econ. 137–151 (1997); Kiril Stanilov ed., *The Post-socialist City: Urban Form and Space Transformations in Central and Eastern Europe after Socialism* (Springer 2007); Hopferm Andrezej, *Property Development and Land Use Planning in Poland,* in *Property Development and Land-Use Planning around the Baltic Sea* 55–70 (Kai Böhme, Burkhard Lange, & Malin Hansen eds., Nordregio 2000); Leonid Limonov & Vincent Renard eds., *Russia: Urban Development and Emerging Property Markets* (Association des Etudes Foncières 1995); Stephanie Balme, *Rule of Law as a Watermark: China's Legal and Judicial Challenges,* in *The World Bank Legal Review* vol.4, 179–200 (World Bank 2013).

10   Sonia Hirt & Kiril Stanilov, *The Perils of Post-socialist Transformation: Residential Development in Sofia,* in *The Post-socialist City: Urban Form and Space Transformations in Central and Eastern Europe after Socialism* 215–244 (Kiril Stanilov ed., Springer 2007); Tom Reiner & Ann L. Strong, *Formation of Land and Housing Markers in the Czech Republic,* 61(2) J. Am. Plan. Assn. 200–209 (1995); Vincent Renard & Rodrigo Acosta eds., *Land Tenure and Property Development in Eastern Europe* (Association des Etudes Foncières 1993); Jan K. Brueckner, *Government Land-Use Interventions: An Economic Analysis,* in *Urban Land Markets — Improving Land Management for Successful Urbanization* 3–23 (Somik V. Lall et al. eds., Springer 2009).

11   Grezgorz Weclzwowicz, *From Egalitarian Cities in Theory to Non-egalitarian Cities in Practice: The Changing Social and Spatial Patterns in Polish Cities,* in *Of State and Cities: The Partitioning of Urban Space* 183–199 (Peter Marcuse & Ronald van Kempen eds., Oxford U. Press 2002).

12   The Polish case is an example. *See* Adam Radzimski et al., *Are Cities in Poland Ready for Sustainability? Poznan Case Study* (Real Corp, Proceedings May 18–20, 2010), available at http://www.corp.at.

The lesson from the Communist experiment is that regimes that grant few freedoms to individual initiative do not need, or want, planning laws. Even though the essence of planning laws is to restrain private actions, their very existence is "good news" for personal freedom. The introduction of planning law in China in 1990 can be viewed as a step forward in the democratization of planning and land management.[13]

Planning Laws in Developing Countries

In developing countries, most land area, including urban areas, is not regulated by planning laws, even if laws exist on paper. The key attributes of urban areas in developing countries include widespread poverty; stark socioeconomic disparities; intense rural-to-urban migration; a huge shortage of adequate and affordable housing leading to megaslums with informal tenure; a weak or absent system of land registration and property recording;[14] and governance issues such as transparency and citizen-empowerment deficiencies.[15] In those developing countries that have planning laws on the books, many dating back to colonial times, the laws are absent in practice from the majority of urban areas and enforcement of the laws is haphazard.[16]

The cities of the developing world need planning laws and development controls in order to offer a better quality of life for their residents, greater certainty for their businesses, and more sustainable environmental resources. Cities without planning laws are governed by a combination of an unbridled market, cultural traditions, and brute power. These cities are unable to deal with an insufficient public infrastructure, the absence of public open space, and poor environmental quality. Without planning laws, there is no mechanism that can mitigate "negative externalities" emanating from land use—that is, the many negative impacts on neighbors or the community at large, such as noise, obstruction of sunlight, parking needs, and unaesthetic construction. In the language of economics, private (or even public) land users have no incentive to "internalize" these externalities unless regulations require or incentivize that. An unregulated market will likely produce substandard and dangerous housing of poor environmental quality and great disparities in access to infrastructure, social services, and amenities.[17] In general, an unregulated city

---

13   City Planning Law of the People's Republic of China; available at http://www.china.org.cn/english/environment/34354.htm.

14   UN-Habitat, *Secure Land Rights for All* (Global Land Tool Network 2008).

15   Hassane Cissé, *Legal Empowerment of the Poor: Past, Present, and Future*, in *The World Bank Legal Review* vol. 4, 31–44 (World Bank 2013).

16   C. B. Arimah & D. Adeagbo, *Compliance with Urban Development and Planning Regulations in Ibadan, Nigeria*, 24(3) Habitat Intl. 279–294 (Sept. 2000); Maurice Onyango & Owiti A. K'Akumu, *Land Use Management Challenges for the City of Nairobi*, 18(1) Urban Forum (2007).

17   There is extensive literature on unregulated urban areas in the developing world. *See*, for example, Ayona Datta, *The Illegal City: Space, Law, and Gender in a Delhi Squatter Settlement* (Ashgate 2012).

is host to extreme discrepancies in quality of life.[18] A lack of planning controls is not an option for developing countries.

However, planning laws and their regulatory instruments should be evaluated carefully and adopted only after the assessment of existing knowledge about their performance and (surmised) impacts in developed countries.

Developing countries are at a juncture. Either they lack planning laws altogether, or their existing laws and institutions are functioning only partially. This situation provides an opportunity for a "restart" that advanced economies don't have because planning laws have created a regulatory reality that is difficult to reverse. The time is ripe for developing countries to take a look at their existing planning laws in terms of impacts on social justice, to learn from the experiences of advanced economies, and to be selective in which aspects and instruments of planning laws to adopt and which to reject.

A Brief History of the Emergence of Planning Laws

Building Codes: The Precursors to Planning Laws

In many countries, the precursors to planning laws were building or housing codes. The major thrust in the development of building codes came with the Industrial Revolution in Europe[19] and somewhat later in the United States.[20] The influx of hundreds of thousands of people from rural areas into urban areas forced governments to shed their disinterest in the urban living of the general population. Plagues, fires, and blocked roads were dangers to all social classes. The building or housing codes that emerged called for minimum distances between buildings, a minimum number of windows to enable sunlight penetration, a minimum size for a housing unit, maximum building heights, fire escapes, and plans for sewage-disposal facilities. The need to transport people and goods on a daily basis required passable streets, and thus were born setback rules for buildings on public roads.

Even though building codes dealt with the structural and architectural aspects of buildings, they also created greater social equality in housing

---

18   Nicholas Addai Boamah, *Land Use Controls and Residential Land Values in the Offinso South Municipality, Ghana*, 33 Land Use Policy, 111–117 (2013); Ademola K. Braimoh & Takashi Onishi, *Spatial Determinants of Urban Land Use Change in Lagos, Nigeria*, 24 Land Use Policy 502–515 (2007).

19   Elke Pahl-Weber & Dietrich Henckel eds., *Planning System, and Planning Terms in Germany* (Academy for Spatial Research Aug. 2008); Jeroen van der Heijden, *International Comparative Analysis of Building Regulations: An Analytical Tool*, 1(1) Intl. J. L. in the Built Env. 9–25 (2009); W. A. Fischel, *An Economic History of Zoning and a Cure for Its Exclusionary Effects*, 41(2) Urb. Stud. 317 (2004).

20   Wendy Collins Perdue, Lesley A. Stone, & Lawrence O. Gostin, *The Built Environment and Its Relationship to the Public's Health: The Legal Framework*, 93(9) Am. J. Public Health 1390–1394 (2003). The authors are with the Georgetown University Law Center. *Requests for reprints should be sent to Wendy Collins Perdue, 600 New Jersey Ave, Washington, DC, 20001.*

standards and in access to public services. The legacy of building codes is very much embedded in current urban design and land subdivision.

Pioneering Planning Laws

Yet, building codes did not enable governments to designate different tracts of land for different land use functions, differing densities, or design. As written, these regulations were used as exclusionary instruments (intentionally or not), steering different social groups (income, class, ethnic, religious) to different parts of the city.

Arguably the world's first national planning law was the United Kingdom's 1909 Housing, Town Planning, Etc., Act.[21] The British belief in the merits of planning law was so strong that the government transported this innovation to its colonies. Thus, at a time when even some of the most industrialized countries did not have planning laws, the British empire exported sophisticated (for that time) formats of planning laws around the world.[22] Poor countries became the premature "owners" of planning laws that were born in disparate circumstances. However, the effects of these acts on the colonies were much more limited—and at times dysfunctional and discriminatory[23]—than their effect on the British homeland.

Planning law in the United States emerged without any visible kinship to British law. Instead of resulting from a federal or state legislative initiative, planning law in the United States emerged from the bottom up.[24] Local authorities used their "police power" (an American term similar to regulatory authority) to enact rudimentary zoning ordinances in order to protect the "health, safety, and welfare" of residents.[25] For many years, the legality of the rising wave of local ordinances was in limbo, and many court challenges were submitted. In 1926, the U.S. Supreme Court agreed to hear a zoning challenge.[26] In *Village of Euclid v. Ambler Realty Co.*, the court ruled that zoning was not in violation of any constitutional or other legal right of landowners because

---

21   The official name of the act is indeed Housing, Town Planning, Etc., Bill, HC Deb (Apr. 5, 1909) vol. 3 cc733–98, Hansard. The "etc." reflected the absence at the time of a comprehensive term for what would later become known in the United Kingdom as "town planning." Raymond Unwin, *Town Planning in Practice: An Introduction to the Art of Designing Cities and Suburbs* (Ernest Benn 1909). *See* also Philip Booth & Margo Huxley, *1909 and All That: Reflections on the Housing, Town Planning, Etc. Act 1909*, 27(2) Plan. Persps. 267–283 (Apr. 1, 2012).

22   Robert Home, *Of Planting and Planning: The Making of British Colonial Cities* (E & FN Spon 1997); K. H. Wekwete, *Planning Law in Sub-Saharan Africa—A Focus on the Experiences in Southern and Eastern Africa*, 19(1) Habitat Intl. 13–28 (1995).

23   Vanessa Watson, *The Planned City Sweeps the Poor Away: Urban Planning and 21st Century Urbanisation*, 72(3) Progress in Plan. 151–183 (Oct. 2009).

24   Rachelle Alterman, *A View from the Outside: The Role of Cross-National Learning in Land-Use Law Reform in the USA*, in *Planning Reform in the New Century* 306 (Daniel M. Mandelker ed., Am. Plan. Assn. 2004).

25   J. R. Nolon, *The Importance of Local Environmental Law* 5 (Ctr. Envtl. Leg. Stud. 2001).

26   Unlike supreme courts in many other countries, the U.S. Supreme Court is very selective in what appeals it decides to hear.

the designation in advance of different areas of the town for different land uses is a legally valid extension of nuisance law.[27] The obligatory separation of zones for industry from zones for housing is an advance in prevention of negative externalities. The separation of land uses was—and still is—a major function of zoning.[28]

Thus, the legal road was paved for the use of zoning as a means of creating the physical homogeneity that typifies many American suburbs, and thus relatively homogeneous socioeconomic neighborhoods (see figure 1).[29] As many scholars have noted, zoning can be "credited" as a contributing factor to the stark socioeconomic separations that characterize American land use patterns, especially residential ones.[30]

Planning laws arrived in most West European countries in the 1960s, in the wake of World War II.[31] The rationales for adopting laws varied from nation to nation but often reflected the need not only to physically rebuild destroyed cities but also to create a "welfare state" supplying housing, upgrading schools, and providing public services. These rationales were very different from the thinly concealed exclusionary purposes—or effects—of the American zoning model.

The spread of national planning laws is a complex picture. On the one hand, planning laws, more so than building controls, have a built-in capacity to create social exclusion and inequities through a variety of instruments. No planning laws and regulations are immune from exclusionary effects. There is evidence of exclusionary uses of development control powers not only in the United States, but also in the United Kingdom.[32] On the other hand, the exclusionary use of planning laws is a matter of degree, and there are major differences around the world (although there is no systematic comparative research to document this beyond a few countries). For example, Hirt compares German and Austrian planning regulation with their American zoning counterparts and

---

27   U.S. Supreme Court. *Village of Euclid v. Ambler Realty Co.*, 272 U.S. 365 (1926), available at https://supreme.justia.com/cases/federal/us/272/365/case.html.

28   Among the best-written (and most entertaining) accounts of the evolution of zoning in the United States is Donald L. Elliott, *A Better Way to Zone: Ten Principles to Create More Liveable Cities* 9–18 (Island Press 2008).

29   Rolf Pendall, *Local Land-Use Regulation and the Chain of Exclusion*, 66(2) J. Am. Plan. Assn. 125–142 (2000); Fischel, *supra* note 19.

30   This fact is documented by many U.S. scholars. *See*, for example, Fischel, *supra* note 19; Raphael Fischler, *Linking Planning Theory and History: The Case of Development Control* 19, J. Plan. Educ. Res. 233 (2000); Jonathan Rothwell & Douglas S. Massey, *Density Zoning and Class Segregation in U.S. Metropolitan Areas*, 91(5) Soc. Sci. Q. 1123–1143 (2010); Brueckner, *supra* note 10; Richard H. Chused, *Symposium on the 75th Anniversary of* Village of Euclid v. Amber Realty Co. *Euclid's Historical Imagery*, 51 Case W. Res. 593 (2000–2001).

31   This conclusion can be deduced from European Union, European Commission, *The EU Compendium of Spatial Planning Systems and Policies* (Office for Official Publications of the European Communities 1997) (hereinafter, EU Compendium).

32   S. Davoudi & R. Atkinson, *Social Exclusion and the British Planning System*, 14(2) Plan. Prac. & Res. 225–236 (1999).

Figure 1. A typical U.S. middle-income residential area, homogeneous as a result of a slate of planning regulations

Source: Wikimedia Commons. Photo by Sean O'Flaherty, aka Seano1. Photo from May 24, 2006, cropped from original version from May 9, 2005. Location: San Jose, California.

shows that the former allow for much more mixture of land uses and housing types.[33] In general, European cities and suburbs are often less exclusionary than their American counterparts. So although planning laws and regulations harbor the capacity for exclusionary use, the degree of severity of such use and the measures taken to counteract it are in the hands of policy makers.

Classification of Planning Regulations

There is little systematic comparative knowledge about the components of planning laws, and even less about their performance and impacts.[34] As coun-

---

33   Sonia Hirt, *The Devil Is in the Definitions*, 73(4) J. Am. Plan. Assn. 436–450 (2007); Sonia Hirt, *Mixed Use by Default*, 27 J. Plan. Lit. 375 (2012).

34   Comparative systematic research of more than two or three countries is rare. Some items are outdated. *See* Gerd Schmidt-Eichsteadt, *Land Use Planning and Building Permission in the European Union* (Deutscher Gemeindeverlag Verlag 1995). *See also* EU Compendium, *supra* note 31; Alterman, *supra* note 8. Compare with the recent large-scale comparative analysis, but on specific aspects only, Alterman, *supra* note 2

terintuitive as it may sound, there is no dominant format of planning legislation, nor is there a consensus about best practice. As my prior research shows, beyond some basic shared structures (sometimes with misleading in similarities), there are major differences in the details of planning laws and regulations.[35] This may be true even for adjacent countries with similar cultural traits and geo-demographic attributes.[36]

There is no international depository of planning regulations (or development controls) used in various countries.[37] Regulatory instruments vary not only from country to country but also from city to city. Moreover, there is no internationally agreed-on classification of such regulations. Researchers who have sought to study the relationship between regulations and social factors, especially housing prices, have developed their own classifications.

The majority of research on this topic originates in the United States—perhaps due to the exclusionary history of zoning. The categories that individual researchers have used may reflect their specific normative perspective. For example, Pendall, Puentes, and Martin classify urban growth boundaries as part of the recent "growth management" trend.[38] By contrast, in England and some other West European countries, the use of green belts—a distinctive urban-containment instrument—is well established.[39] Brueckner uses a classification based on free-market ideology and calls growth boundaries "supply restrictions."[40]

Table 1 presents a classification of instruments intended to reflect the evolution of planning regulations. The table reflects the layers of regulations that have accumulated in advanced-economy countries over time. The division into five "generations" is intuitive and may differ from country to country.

---

35 Alterman, *supra* note 2.

36 For example, the planning laws in Sweden and Norway, the Netherlands and Flemish Belgium, France and Wallonian Belgium, England and Ireland, and Germany and Austria differ significantly from each other. See EU Compendium, *supra* note 31; Alterman, *supra* note 2; Schmidt-Eichsteadt, *supra* note 34.

37 The most impressive attempt in this direction is UN-Habitat's Global Land Tools Network (GLTN). It is prescriptive rather than empirical, and it focuses on specific instruments deemed to be lacking in the practice of developing countries. *See* http://www.unhabitat.org /categories.asp?catid=503.

38 Rolf Pendall, Robert Puentes, & Jonathan Martin, *From Traditional to Reformed: A Review of Land Use Regulations in the Nation's 50 Largest Metropolitan Areas* (Research Brief, Brookings Institution, Aug. 2006).

39 Rachelle Alterman, *The Challenge of Farmland Preservation: Lessons from a Six-Country Comparison*, 63(2) J. Am. Plan. Assn. 220–243 (Spring 1997).

40 Brueckner, *supra* note 10. Another type of classification is used by a third large-scale study: Joseph Gyourko, Albert Saiz, & Anita Summers, *A New Measure of the Local Regulatory Environment for Housing Markets: The Wharton Residential Land Use Regulatory Index*, 45 Urb. Stud. 693 (2008).

Table 1. Layers of planning and development control regulations

First generation: Building or housing codes
• Structural soundness
• Durability and safety of construction materials
• Safety from fire damage: architectural and engineering regulations
• Architectural regulations related to health: distances between buildings to allow sunshine, minimum proportion of windows, roof rules
• Minimal size of housing unit and other housing standards
Second generation: Traditional land use and density instruments
• Minimal (or maximum) lot sizes
• Maximum number of housing units per lot
• Maximum building height
• Maximum coverage of lot, setbacks from street and other buildings
• Parking standards
Third generation: Rules about good architecture, urban design
• Rules for architectural quality: style of facades, roofs, color, materials, size of lobby
• Rules about landscaping of private lots: location on plot, types of plants permitted, style
• Rules of historic preservation (what is deemed to be of historic value); restrictions on replacement or extension
• Special design review process (additional procedure and cost)
Fourth generation: Environmental protection
• Requirements to leave part of lots unpaved for groundwater absorption
• Requirements for large lots with set-asides for wetlands or biodiversity
• Rules for energy conservation and passive energy
• Rules for wastewater and waste collection and recycling
• Rules that require investments in renewable energy
• Green belts, urban boundaries
• Agricultural land conservation
• Timing controls for growth management
Fifth generation: Regulatory instruments as public finance substitutes
• Land dedication for public use
• Exactions of other services or amenities in kind
• Impact fees for public services
• Environmental mitigation requirements
• Exactions for affordable housing
• Exactions for "soft" community needs such as employment

At the time it was introduced, each regulatory instrument may have been intended to be socially indifferent or even to further social justice. However, regulations interact with each other, creating cumulatively more restrictions over time rather than the reverse. Restrictions often mean piling on costs or excluding certain sections of the population. Together, the generations of regulations may exacerbate social differences and impair the distribution of urban benefits among social groups.

The first generation, building and housing codes, is the precursor to planning laws. These codes were not implemented with the intention to exclude population groups or to raise housing prices. Some of the building codes refer to engineering, others to architecture or public utilities. Some evolved into the second generation.

The second generation includes traditional instruments for controlling land use and density of development: land use categories, lot sizes, permitted coverage of the lot, setback lines from the road or lot boundaries, floor area ratios relative to plot size, number of housing units, and so on. These types of instruments are the most prevalent among planning regulations internationally. These instruments can be expressed quantitatively and are perceived as helping planners rationalize the calculation of public services needed. Yet, these "objective" measures can also be used in socially unjust ways.

The third generation of regulatory instruments includes design review and historic preservation. Design review established rules, or discretionary decision bodies, to assess architectural design proposals in terms of what is "good architecture." Design rules may control the shape, style, materials, and color of buildings, roof types, and the design of retaining walls. By means of design rules, governments may be able to require that multifamily residential buildings add a large (and expensive) lobby space or recreation facilities. Some design controls restrict the design of private gardens. Design rules may impose restrictions on the shapes, materials, or heights of fences. Many of these requirements cost money and delay the permit approval process and thus may raise housing and other costs (sometimes intentionally).[41]

Historic preservation regulations, part of the third generation, determine what should be protected from new development because of historic value. Historic preservation is tied to specific sociocultural narratives often shared by parts of the population. Preservation regulations have achieved political correctness and are also making inroads in developing countries. But historic regulations can lead to higher property values, loss of affordable housing, and gentrification. Despite a seeming consensus about historic preservation, recent research has shown that historic regulations are often the focus of conflict and legal challenges.[42]

---

41 Nurit Corren & Rachelle Alterman, *Design Control in Israel: Between Freedom of Architectural Practice and Public-Planning Goals* (Ctr. Urb. & Regl. Stud. 1999).

42 Nir Mualam & Rachelle Alterman, *Conflicts over History Preservation: The Role of Tribunals* (in preparation).

The fourth generation includes regulations based on environmental considerations. This is a fast-growing enterprise. In today's era of climate change, national and local governments are adopting an increasing number of environmental restrictions over and above the traditional "amenities" such as open space standards. Table 1 provides examples of requirements, such as a rule that a portion of each plot must remain unpaved to allow for water seepage, or a portion of a plot be set aside for wetlands or urban wildlife. In some countries and municipalities, planning or building regulations have required green construction for energy saving, water conservation, or recycling. But as Frieden noted as far back as 1979, environmental protection may hide socially exclusionary considerations.[43] Environmental protection regulations may have trade-offs with other goals, such as housing prices. Given the status of these regulations, decision makers in developing countries should scrutinize the prospective impacts of environmental regulations on urban justice with extra care.

The fifth generation is different from the others because it deals with planning regulations as levers for financial revenue. The use of planning regulations for financial revenue is both very old and very new. In some countries, requirements of land for public roads embedded in property law or subdivision codes predate planning regulations.[44] Today, the use of finance-substitute instruments such as those listed in table 1 under "Fifth generation" is expanding both geographically and in the range of services being financed (though not without legal stumbling blocks).[45] I have argued elsewhere that such tools have special relevance for developing countries where ample alternative resources do not exist.[46] When adopting planning laws, developing countries should pay special attention to revenue-generating instruments.

The Relationship between Planning Regulations and Social Justice: Research from Advanced-Economy Countries

Because planning laws and development controls have been in operation in advanced-economy countries for many decades, it is reasonable to ask if the practice of development control has contributed to greater or lesser urban social justice and how this contribution has differed across countries.

---

43 Bernard Frieden, *The Environmental Protection Hustle* (MIT Press 1979). The comprehensive empirical study by Gyourko et al., *supra* note 40, shows the incidence of regulations for open-space preservation and their impact on housing prices.

44 Rachelle Alterman ed., *Private Supply of Public Services: Evaluation of Real-Estate Exactions, Linkage, and Alternative Land Policies* (NYU Press 1988).

45 Rachelle Alterman, *Land Use Regulations and Property Values: The "Windfalls Capture" Idea Revisited*, in *The [Oxford] Handbook of Urban Economics and Planning* 755–786 (Geritt Knaap & Nancy Brooks eds., Oxford U. Press 2011); Alterman, *id.*

46 Rachelle Alterman, *Levying the Land: Instruments for Public Revenue and Their Applicability to Developing Countries* (paper presented to the UN-Habitat Governing Council, Apr. 14, 2013).

Methodological Challenges

There are no comparative analyses of the impacts of different types of planning regulations across countries. To attribute impacts to a particular planning regulation, one must argue that there is a causal connection between the regulation and the outcome on the ground (for example, higher housing prices). Yet, there is scarcely any theory from which variables can be deduced. It is difficult to "hold constant" the innumerable variables among countries and local contexts. Comparative research has difficulty linking even one specific topic of planning law to any "explanatory variables."[47]

Most researchers admit that even single-country empirical analysis of the social impacts of planning regulations is difficult from a research perspective.[48] Regulatory instruments interact with each other in different ways in different contexts. Individual impacts are difficult to determine because they may be due not only to planning regulations but to many variables that differ from context to context. Yet, several researchers have undertaken empirical research (especially in the United States) about planning regulations and the relationship (not necessarily causal) with issues such as social composition and housing prices.

The United States as a Laboratory

Due to its legal reality and sociopolitical differences, the United States has proven to be a laboratory for research about the relationship between planning regulations and urban social justice.

Because of the U.S. federal structure and the constitutionally imposed division of powers, different planning laws are enacted from state to state (although there are similarities among some groups of states). In addition, extensive planning and zoning powers are vested in local governments. The United States is home to tens of thousands of empowered local governments. This situation has created unprecedented variety in planning-regulation instruments.[49] In addition, the United States has a history of planning law. Therefore, the United States offers many lessons about the relationship between planning regulations and social justice.

This section considers the rare situations in which advanced economies function without public planning regulations and then proceeds to economies that rely on planning regulations. The chapter then examines building codes, finally addressing the impacts of planning regulations. Throughout, U.S. examples are cited.

---

47   Alterman, *supra* note 2, makes this argument in research on compensation rights for "regulatory takings."

48   Pendall, Puentes, & Martin, *supra* note 38.

49   Alterman, *supra* note 24, at 306.

No Planning Regulations

Among advanced economies, there are few examples of urban areas or housing markets without any planning (or zoning) regulations, and even fewer
without any building codes. However, there is one place where the planning
law clock seems to have stopped: Houston, Texas. Because the United States
has no national-level legislation for planning regulations,[50] Texas has not enacted a state-level planning law that mandates local authorities to enact their
own land use regulations (zoning).

The Texas story has attracted many researchers. Their findings show that
even in Houston, the market is not entirely devoid of planning-like regulations. Instead of zoning, Houston has private-law restrictive covenants self-
imposed by developers or housing associations; these act as facsimiles of public planning regulations.[51] However, private controls can be even less "socially
blind" than public zoning. Siegan was the first to show that private controls
serve the middle and upper segments of the land and housing markets and
are largely absent from poorer areas.[52] But Houston has not taken its hands
entirely off city planning: The city does retain some important powers that
shape city structure, such as siting and providing public roads, utilities, other
public services, and taxation and environmental regulations.

Research shows an ambivalent picture for Houston. On the one hand,
planning regulations have benefitted the better-off groups much more than
other groups and have led to socially exclusive neighborhoods and disparities in the quality of public services. On the other hand, the less controlled
parts of the market retain more affordable housing than may have been available with planning regulations—but with poorer environmental and service
qualities.[53]

Building and Housing Codes

Today, building and housing codes exist in most advanced-economy countries, sometimes based on independent legislation, sometimes integrated into
planning legislation and regulations. Like any regulations, building controls
may place a cost burden on housing and thus affect affordability; the question
for developing countries to consider is, How much?

Unlike with planning regulations, it is relatively easy to define the impact of building codes on housing costs. Not all U.S. states have mandatory
codes, although the majority do. Some local governments impose their own

---

50   Other countries, such as Germany, do have national planning laws. Alterman, *supra* note 8.

51   B. H. Siegan, *No Zoning Is the Best Zoning*, in *A Planner's Guide to Land Use Law* 143–152
(S. Meck & E. M. Netter eds., APA Planners Press 1983); B. H. Siegan, *Land Use without Zoning*
(Lexington 1972); Edwin Buitelaar, *Zoning, More Than Just a Tool: Explaining Houston's Regulatory Practice*, 17(7) European Plan. Stud. 1049–1065 (2009); T. M. Kapur, *Land Use Regulation
in Houston Contradicts the City's Free Market Reputation* 34 Envtl. L. Rep. 10045 (2004).

52   Siegan, *Land Use without Zoning*, *supra* note 51.

53   *Id.*; Buitelaar, *supra* note 51.

codes even without a state mandate. A recent study surveyed the cost burden imposed by codes on housing prices and concluded that these amount to an increment of only a few percentage points.[54] One author cites estimates that building codes may add 15 percent to the cost of construction (without the costs of land, infrastructure levies, etc.). Thus, there is evidence that the cost burden of building codes is lower than that associated with many planning regulations.[55]

The introduction of building codes in developing countries, even without planning regulations, can address basic safety and health needs. However, the establishment of building codes is not a simple matter, because the administrative and enforcement institutions need to be established, with trained professionals available to issue permits and enforce the rules. Thus, these institutions could be viewed as precedents to the introduction of planning laws.

The Generations of Planning Regulations

American researchers have produced a large body of research on the social impacts of planning regulations. This section focuses on two research projects that have provided methods for observing the cumulative layers of planning regulations.[56]

Pendall, Puentes, and Martin surveyed a large sample of U.S. local governments in all regions of the country.[57] Their findings classify municipalities into four groups: low (which they call "wild, wild Texas"), traditional, exclusionary, and reform (growth management). The authors provide a disclaimer that the findings are "not a direct statement of cause and effect" and that more research is needed to discover the precise relationship between "regulator, housing prices, sprawl, and regional opportunity."[58] Yet their findings do portray several clear (though not uniform) relationships between the more stringent layers of regulations and social exclusion (especially in the states in the Northeast and Midwest). The litmus test of exclusionary tendencies that Pendall et al. employ is the likelihood that local governments would approve a small number of two- or three-floor apartment buildings. They found that 30 percent of municipalities within metropolitan areas would not approve even such minimal multifamily housing, preferring single-family (or

---

54   Michael D. Turner, *Paradigms, Pigeonholes, and Precedent: Reflections on Regulatory Control of Residential Construction,* 23 Whittier L. Rev. 3 (2001); other authors have addressed the cost of regulation. *See* also Eric Damian Kelly, *Fair Housing, Good Housing or Expensive Housing? Are Building Codes Part of the Problem or Part of the Solution?,* 29 John Marshall L. Rev. 349 (1996).

55   Richard Clagg, *Comment: Who Remembers the Small Builders? How to Implement Ohio's New Statewide Residential Building Code without Sinking Ohio's Small Builders,* 34 Cap. U. L. Rev. 741 (2006).

56   More American researchers have analyzed planning regulations and their relationship with exclusion or with housing prices—too many to survey here. Brueckner, *supra* note 10, presents a good survey.

57   Pendall, Puentes, & Martin, *supra* note 38.

58   *Id.,* at 32.

double-family) homes. This study and others show what any observer in the United States will note: that zoning law and practice have not shed their exclusionary origins (see figure 1).

Gyourko, Saiz, and Summers developed an index of 11 factors related to the assumed stringency of planning regulations. Among their factors are not only the types of regulations included in table 1 but also some related to decision processes. These researchers created a composite scale of stringency, similar to what this chapter refers to as generations of regulations. Their overall finding is that "community wealth is strongly positively correlated with the degree of local land uses regulations. The higher the median family income, median house value or the share of adults with college degrees, the greater is the community's [score on the index]."[59] This study also confirms the findings of Pendall et al. that the Northeast states are more exclusionary.[60]

The Overregulation Paradox

The recognition of the socially exclusionary effects of U.S. zoning practices gave birth to the term "regulatory barriers." The antidote has been the legal concept of removal of regulatory barriers—a vivid expression of the strained relationship between planning laws and social justice. Here is the paradox: In order to remove the regulatory barriers accumulated over the years, more regulation may be necessary.

One type of regulation that may help correct for the regulatory barriers is inclusionary zoning. This uniquely American concept incorporates recognition that zoning often has an exclusionary effect. Inclusionary zoning is not a uniform instrument but a set of zoning and other planning regulation instruments that vary from place to place. All are intended to combat exclusion by enabling or mandating neighborhoods with some degree or format of mixed housing types, densities, or types of eligible households.[61] The broader set of instruments titled affordable housing includes some regulations intended to mitigate the price hike deemed to be caused by planning regulations (a topic that is beyond the scope of this chapter).[62]

---

59   Gyourko et al., *supra* note 40, at 695.

60   *See* also E. L. Glaeser & B. A. Ward, *The Causes and Consequences of Land Use Regulation: Evidence from Greater Boston*, 65 J. Urb. Econ. 265–278 (2009).

61   Among the body of writing on inclusionary zoning, *see*, for example, Alan Mallach, *Inclusionary Housing Programs: Policies and Practices* (Ctr. Urb. Policy Research, Rutgers U. 1984); B. R. Lerman, *Mandatory Inclusionary Zoning—The Answer to the Affordable Housing System*, 33(2) B.C. Envtl. Aff. L. Rev. 1 (2006); Jerold Kayden, *Inclusionary Zoning and the Constitution*, 2(1) NHC Affordable Housing Policy Rev. 10–13 (2002); D. Porter, *The Promise and Practice of Inclusionary Zoning* (Brookings Symposium on Growth Management and Affordable Housing, May 29, 2003); Fischel, *supra* note 19; Edward Sullivan & Karin Power, *Coming Affordable Housing Challenges for Municipalities after the Great Recession*, 21(3&4) J. Affordable Housing & Community Dev. (2013).

62   There is a huge body of literature on affordable housing in the United States and in other countries. A few key references are T. Iglesias & R. Lento eds., *The Legal Guide to Affordable Housing Development* (ABA and Am. Plan. Assn. 2006); N. Calavita & A. Mallach eds., *Inclu-*

The best-known example of efforts to remove regulations is the New Jersey Supreme Court decisions in the two Mount Laurel cases.[63] The cases were brought to the court because certain local jurisdictions in New Jersey adopted zoning regulations that had minimal lot sizes and no allocation of land for multifamily housing. The developers argued that were it not for these regulations, there would have been a market for their proposed multifamily housing. The court ruled that the state must set up regulatory and quasi-judicial institutions in order to create a "fair share" of affordable housing among municipalities in the state and thus mitigate exclusion. Developers who wish to develop multifamily housing could seek remedy with a special state body.

The Mount Laurel decisions are an example of "audacious judges," as Haar has characterized them at work.[64] What kind of impact have these decisions had? New Jersey's urban poor—regardless of ethnicity or minority status—continue to face many of the same problems in obtaining adequate, affordable housing that characterized the period prior to the rise of the Mount Laurel doctrine. In addition to Gyourko et al., several other researchers have shown that the Mount Laurel decisions have had only limited effects.[65] Some researchers argue that regulations to counteract exclusionary regulations may lead to higher housing prices rather than an increase in affordability.[66]

The Mount Laurel decisions are regarded as the epitome of anti-exclusionary legal measures in the United States. Yet, the empirical findings demonstrate that the exclusionary tendencies of local planning regulations have been more tenacious than the intended effects of the New Jersey court rulings.

The "Piling On" Syndrome

American attempts to remove regulatory barriers hold important lessons. Urban justice would be much better served if planning regulations were carefully scrutinized in advance of their adoption. One may assume that each layer of planning regulation had a laudable public justification when it was adopted: to rationalize urban structure for service provision, to beautify the city, to provide public or private open space, to preserve historically valuable areas, to conserve the natural environment, to mitigate feared hazards. The problem

---

sionary Housing in International Perspective (Lincoln Inst. of Land Policy 2010).

63   *Southern Burlington County NAACP v. Township of Mount Laurel*, 336 A.2d 713 (N.J.) 423 U.S. 808 (1975); *S. Burlington County NAACP v. Township of Mt. Laurel*, 92 N.J. 158, 251, 456 A.2d 390, 438 (1983).

64   C. M. Haar, *Suburbs under Siege—Race, Space and Audacious Judges* (Princeton U. Press 1996).

65   Naomi Bailin Wish & Stephen Eisdorfer, *The Impact of Mount Laurel Initiatives: An Analysis of the Characteristics of Applicants and Occupants*, 27 Seton Hall L. Rev. 1268–1281 (1997); Robin Leone, *Promoting the General Welfare: After Nearly Thirty Years of Influence, Has the Mount Laurel Doctrine Changed the Way New Jersey Citizens Live*, 3 Geo. J.L. & Pub. Policy 295 (2005); Henry A. Span, *How the Courts Should Fight Exclusionary Zoning*, 32 Seton Hall L. Rev. 1 (2001)

66   Jenny Schuetz, Rachel Meltzer, & Vicki Been, *Silver Bullet or Trojan Horse? The Effects of Inclusionary Zoning on Local Housing Markets in the United States*, 48(2) Urb. Stud. 297–329 (Feb. 2011).

is the "piling on" syndrome: Even if each regulation is acceptable on its own, their mutual interactions often lead to compromised social justice.

How does the piling on syndrome occur? Over time, more public objectives emerge, proposed by newly trained professionals who bring more up-to-date notions, by active civic groups, or by elected community leaders. But the previous regulations are already in place and are difficult to roll back due to property values, public finance considerations, and political concerns. The previous layers of regulations often become uncontested norms of "good planning." They are taken for granted by the professionals and the consumers-residents as defining how housing areas ought to look and function, or how public services ought to be located and allocated.

The introduction of each new regulation is rarely accompanied by a requirement to assess the cumulative effects on urban equity issues, such as the cost of housing for different social groups or the equitable access to public services. A good rule might be that a new proposed planning regulation that might impact equity be adopted only after existing regulatory barriers to equity have been reassessed, removed, or relaxed. In a similar spirit, the UK Legislative and Regulatory Reform Act of 2006 grants ministers powers for the purpose of "removing or reducing any burden, or the overall burden, resulting directly or indirectly for any person from any legislation." [67] However, this act focuses on financial and administrative burdens, not on social equity.[68] There are no examples of a similar policy being consistently applied to planning regulations.

Conclusion: Lessons for Developing Countries

The experience of advanced-economy countries with planning regulations depicts a strained relationship with social justice. Urban development can no longer be left to the whims of rulers, social norms, or the marketplace. Planning laws fulfill many important functions in modern societies: they protect the endangered environment and often facilitate the functioning of the market. Countries that have experienced the absence of planning regulations—the former Soviet Union, its allies, and China—are now in the midst of adopting or learning how to implement planning laws.

Advanced-economy countries that have had operational planning regulations for decades have accumulated layers of regulations that are difficult to shake off. Many of these have become "part of the furniture" of urban life, and neither consumers nor decision makers can envision cities without them. Foreign advisers often recommend that developing countries adopt laws and regulations similar to those prevalent in their own countries. Each proposed regulation may sound like a good idea and is likely to be accompanied by

---

67   UK Legislative and Regulatory Reform Act 2006 C51, at art. 1(2); available at http://www .legislation.gov.uk/ukpga/2006/51/contents.

68   *Id.*, at art. 1(3).

eloquently presented examples from beautiful projects in one of the world's rich cities.

However, planners and policy makers in developing countries should take a hard look at each proposed law or regulation.[69] Unlike in advanced-economy countries, the formative stage of planning laws in developing countries leaves enough "degrees of freedom" for decision makers to be selective in what they choose to adopt. They should lead the way in finding ways to evaluate proposed regulations critically in terms of anticipated equity impacts and to be concerned about cumulative effects.

Decision makers in developing countries should take the following advice into account when considering a planning regime:

- Learn from the history of the gradual evolution of planning laws and their rationales. It is not reasonable to introduce planning laws or regulations that exist in advanced-economy countries because these reflect layers of (often forgotten) rationales that have accumulated over time.

- Go back to the basic rationales of planning laws and development control: health, safety, the rationalization of public services, and environmental protection. Choose single regulations that can be assessed individually rather than entire "packages."

- If there are no current planning laws or if existing ones function poorly, consider a graduated strategy: first, adopt a solid administrative-professional basis for introducing building and housing controls, and then, after several years of successful operation, consider gradual introduction of planning laws.

- Create a routine for assessing proposed laws and regulations in terms of their estimated cost effects on housing and other amenities. Discuss the likely trade-offs with other public goals. For example, assess trade-offs of environmental quality, historic preservation, design review, or green building with short- and long-term housing costs. Ask international aid organizations for professional support in this task.

- Assess new planning laws or regulations in regard to their ability to be fairly and systematically enforced across socioeconomic and political groups in society. The costs of long-term enforcement should be factored into the adoption of new land use regulations.

These recommendations will be difficult to carry out, but the adoption and implementation of complete planning laws is much more difficult. A beacon in such recommendations is the recent launching of the Urban Legislation Unit of UN-Habitat,[70] which espouses a "back to basics" approach similar to the one presented in this chapter. If UN-Habitat promotes more policy

---

69 *See* also Carole Rakod, *Forget Planning, Put Politics First? Priorities for Urban Management in Developing Countries,* 3(3) Intl. J. Applied Earth Observation & Geoinformation 209–223 (2001).

70 *See* http://www.unhabitat.org/categories.asp?catid=260.

research along these lines, and organizations such as the World Bank join the momentum, developing countries may be able to adopt planning laws and regulations suited to their own needs. They may be able to harness planning laws to create greater urban justice, rather than to exacerbate urban inequalities. To do this, developing countries and the experts advising them must be willing to heed the lessons that the advanced-economy countries have learned.

Land Use Law and the City

Toward Inclusive Planning

MATTHEW GLASSER

More than half the world's population lives in cities, and cities are expected to account for two-thirds of the urban population by 2030. Cities generate more than 80 percent of gross domestic product today, and this percentage grows every year.[1] Cities provide jobs and account for most global prosperity. As the role of cities becomes ever more vital to the economic stability of developing countries, opportunity, inclusion, and equity in cities have become fundamental concerns. No country has achieved middle-income status without urbanization. At their best, cities are the most efficient mechanism for improving the human condition through economic growth, efficiency, trade, intellectual exchange, and a lightened burden on the global ecosystem.[2] Unfortunately, urban opportunities are not equally available to all, and the contrast between the city of the rich and the city of the poor can be disturbing. This chapter explores some of the ways that the existing legal and regulatory framework for urban planning excludes the poor from opportunity and increases social injustice and vulnerability.

Among the types of laws that are problematic for poor urban dwellers are those that protect legal title to land in formal settlements where the wealthy live, but not in informal settlements that the poor can afford; laws that prohibit (or regulate to the point of prohibition) the informal trading and service economy through which many of the poor earn a living; and planning laws that establish unaffordable land use standards. This chapter focuses on the last of these types and discusses ways in which legal reformers might address the situation to promote opportunity, inclusion, and equity.

An illustration of the problems faced can be found in Katherine Boo's recent book about Mumbai, which opens with a scene of a teenage entrepreneur dodging the police.[3] Abdul earns a living by sorting and packaging recyclables that he buys from rag pickers. Although this is an economically productive and socially useful business, he has no license to engage in this work. His business and his family's informal housing are both illegal, and the family's

---

1   Richard Dobbs et al., *Urban World: Mapping the Economic Power of Cities* (research report prepared for the McKinsey Global Institute, McKinsey & Co. Mar. 2011).

2   One leading urban economist has argued that cities are humanity's greatest invention and our best hope for the future. Edward Glaeser, *Triumph of the City: How Our Greatest Invention Makes Us Richer, Smarter, Greener, Healthier, and Happier* (Penguin 2011).

3   Katherine Boo, *Behind the Beautiful Forevers: Life, Death and Hope in a Mumbai Undercity* (Random House 2012).

precarious existence depends on the arbitrary and variable tolerance of various authorities. Although he and millions like him are at the core of the urban and economic growth that is lifting India and other parts of the developing world out of poverty, they operate outside the protection and sanction of the law and so are vulnerable to extortion, to destruction of their homes and businesses, and to disasters of all kinds.

What Role Does Planning Law Play?

Planning law is largely an urban phenomenon. Farms and villages don't need master plans, zoning, setbacks, or minimum lot sizes. The focus of this chapter is on how urban land use is regulated. Some aspects of land use regulation can exclude and marginalize the poor by prescribing unaffordable standards. This situation is sometimes the result of historical factors, often reflects the interests of elites, and can be the consequence of importing planning and land use regulations from high-income countries into a low-income context. There are at least three dimensions to this problem of exclusion; legal reformers have engaged with each of these:

- The substantive legal framework for land use may be inappropriate[4] to the social and economic context.

- The processes and procedures through which regulations are developed and site-specific decisions are made may not be inclusive.

- Courts that enforce land use regulations and standards may not be as alert to considerations of equity and human rights as reformers would like them to be.

Planning Standards Increase the Cost of Urban Land

Generous minimum lot sizes and restrictive floor area ratios make it illegal for the market to supply, or for the poor to occupy, small living spaces that are affordable. In addition to these standards, land use regulations often prescribe generous setback requirements and street widths, parking and open space requirements, public park and school set-asides, and other standards that have the effect of limiting density. These standards, desirable though they may be from the perspective of those who can afford to live well, limit the intensity of urban development and thus correspondingly increase the scarcity of legally available urban land (or, acknowledging the vertical dimension of cities, of urban living space). Such requirements increase the price of housing and services for all residents.[5] Broad boulevards with generous setbacks and

---

4   "Inappropriate" standards do not take actual conditions on the ground into account. A standard that makes illegal 80 percent of homes, or a like percentage of businesses, is clearly inappropriate. To be appropriate, a land use rule must reflect what most people in a given society would agree is right—a standard with which they are likely to comply without government compulsion.

5   Rachelle Alterman, *Planning Law and Social Justice: A Strained Relationship* (PowerPoint presentation at Law, Justice and Development Week, World Bank 2012).

single-family detached houses may be very pleasant, but they are inherently exclusive and relatively expensive.

Inappropriate Standards Limit Lawful Access to the City

As the unit price of land and housing increases, people naturally consume less. Cramped quarters in New York; Tokyo; and Hong Kong SAR, China are examples of this phenomenon in the developed world.[6] The same phenomenon plays out in the fast-growing cities of low- and middle-income countries. At the bottom of the economic ladder, the poorest live in the most crowded conditions, which they choose intentionally to be close to work and the other opportunities a big city offers. As do their richer neighbors, the poorest trade personal space for proximity to opportunity. But when there is a legal minimum, the choices at the bottom end of the scale become unlawful. Alain Bertaud argues that most minimum land use standards are implicitly aimed at preventing the migration of poor people into cities.[7] He points out that the poor come to live and work in cities no matter what the standards may say. They are looking for jobs and a better life for their children and cannot afford to be fussy. In that context, excessive legal standards have the effect of transforming crowded conditions into violations of the law. This puts individuals at the bottom end of the wage scale at risk: they must be close to work and other opportunities, but they cannot live there legally. They must choose between the risks of eviction and insecurity, on the one hand, and grueling and expensive commuter trips from remote locations, on the other hand.[8] And sometimes they incur additional risks, as when the poor settle in environmentally sensitive or unsafe areas, such as floodplains or unstable hillsides, which may be close to the opportunities of the city but have little or no value to the formal sector because they cannot be legally developed. Such precarious settlements can increase both pollution and vulnerability.[9]

Inappropriate standards can accomplish one of two things: where they are successfully enforced, inefficient patterns of land use are locked in—they become "facts on the ground" and are difficult to change. Low-density cities are expensive to serve with transport and bulk infrastructure, and the unit price of services in low-density developments reflects this. Successful enforcement of generous standards can thus have the effect of permanently excluding the

---

6   *See,* for example, *Overhead Photos of Cramped Apartments in Hong Kong,* Telegraph (June 4, 2013), available at http://www.telegraph.co.uk/property/propertypicturegalleries/9888398 /Overhead-photos-of-cramped-apartments-in-Hong-Kong.html.

7   Alain Bertaud, *Land Use Regulations and Poverty* (PowerPoint presentation at Law, Justice and Development Week, World Bank 2012); similar materials are available at http://alain -bertaud.com.

8   Judy Baker et al., *Urban Poverty and Transport: The Case of Mumbai* (World Bank 2005); Somik Lall et al., *Shelter from the Storm but Disconnected from Jobs: Lessons from Urban South Africa on the Importance of Coordinating Housing and Transport Policies* (working paper, World Bank 2012).

9   Erminia Maricato, *Searching for the Just City: Debates in Urban Theory and Practice* 10 (Routledge 2009).

poor. Alternatively, where inappropriate standards exist but are not routinely enforced, those living in violation of legal standards are at risk of arbitrary and capricious enforcement actions and/or extortion to avoid consequences.

When Land Use Regulation Is Inappropriate, It Divides the City

Where the law prescribes standards or processes that are impractical and inappropriate for a substantial portion of the urban population, it effectively divides the city into a formal sector with rules and standards for the minority who can afford to comply and an informal sector of those who cannot. In the informal sector, standards and requirements are often disregarded, although they may be enforced sporadically and selectively. When people are too poor to comply with standards, they become part of the underclass. And though noncompliance with legal standards is the norm in informal settlements (as with informal trading, where livelihoods are earned), the law plays a critically important role because it defines status: those living outside the law cannot claim its protection. If they are evicted, or their property is confiscated, they are largely without recourse. This socio-legal division can have an intraurban spatial dimension, but even more formidable are boundaries of legal status, with the privileged classes in-bounds and the poor out-of-bounds.[10] "Planning proposals and urban laws apply only to fragments of the city, while the remainder is beyond state control and does not follow the rule of law."[11]

A Divided City Deprives the Poor of Access to Services

For poor families to be able to afford to live in a city, they and those who would sell or rent to them must be able to divide space into small, affordable increments. The poor must live at high densities if they want urban jobs. But the crowded housing the poor can afford often does not meet the standards set by the law. Throughout the developing world, formal land markets with high prices exist alongside informal settlements where people live in crowded, precarious, and often dangerous conditions. These divided cities are a natural consequence of an inappropriate legal framework, and the illegality of informal housing typically has further negative implications for access to basic urban services such as water, sanitation, electricity, and public safety—"public authorities see it as condoning illegality to extend public services, such as policing, to such settlements."[12] The poor, sometimes a majority of a city's population, are condemned to a marginal existence, without entitlement to basic services, without secure tenure, and without the protection of the law.

---

10 South Africa's apartheid planning legislation was perhaps the most egregious and explicit example, but planning laws need not be explicitly exclusionary to have the effect of marginalizing large segments of the population.

11 Maricato, *supra* note 9.

12 Abdul Baasit Abdul Aziz, *What to Do about Slums* (working paper, Joint Center for Housing Studies, Harvard U. 2012).

Some Benefit from a Gray Market for Urban Space

Informality dominates many large cities in the developing world, where much of the population lives in noncompliance with the formal legal system. Such widespread noncompliance can be in the interest of powerful elites who benefit personally and politically from a range of ambiguities: ambiguity about land tenure, permitted land uses, the outcomes of litigation, the enforceability of rights. The private benefits arising in the context of these ambiguities create a strong incentive to maintain ambiguities, and with it the culture of discretionary noncompliance. Rajack et al. speak of an "industry of ambiguity" that benefits private individuals and political campaign finance.[13] Many government planners know they are fighting a losing battle but genuinely want their cities to be world class, and so continue to set unrealistic standards.

> Officials see themselves as a bastion against informality, illegality and anarchy. Their views are often complemented by those of their political principals who see the laws as serving very much the same purposes as their colonial forebears did: to protect the quality of the suburbs or enclaves in which the elite lives and to punish transgressors for failing to comply with the often arcane prescriptions of the law. This leads inexorably to a situation where there is a widespread and generally accurate perception that there are "two laws": one for the well to do and another for the rest.[14]

Planning Laws and Land Use Regulations Are Rarely Inclusive

In much of the developing world, planning law is inherited from a colonial and/or patrimonial past, when it represented the interests and values of a European minority or a local elite.[15] These laws have by and large not been adapted to current local realities, though sometimes they have been amended to limit opportunities for public participation. Berrisford argues that efforts to reform African planning laws fail for two fundamental reasons: first, a failure to identify and involve the key stakeholders; and second, an assumption that technocratic approaches will suffice, as opposed to following basic principles of law making. As a result, he says, "Planning law . . . has tended to have the effect of being no more than an irritant to developers but an oppressive force for the poor, without yielding any significant societal benefits."[16]

---

13   Robin Rajack et al., *The Political Economy of Urban Land Management: Evidence from Mumbai and Nairobi* ((presentation at Annual World Bank Conference on Land and Poverty, Washington DC, Apr. 8–11, 2013).

14   Stephen Berrisford, *Why It Is Difficult to Change Urban Planning Laws in African Countries,* 22 Urban Forum (2011).

15   Marcello Balbo, *Urban Planning and the Fragmented City of Developing Countries,* 15(1) Third World Planning Rev. (1993).

16   Berrisford, *supra* note 14.

Land Use Regulations Can Lead to Forced Eviction

One of the most notorious examples of forced mass eviction based on "improper" use of land is Zimbabwe's Operation Murambatsvina (literally, Operation Drive Out Rubbish, and officially, Operation Restore Order), which destroyed more than 90,000 homes and innumerable small businesses.[17] Similar evictions, sometimes with strong political and/or ethnic overtones, are not unusual in the developing world. In fairness, it should be noted that land use regulations are seldom the only official justification for such destruction— although most slum settlements violate planning regulations, they typically also violate other health and public safety codes, and often the residents lack secure tenure.

New Urban Plans Can Also Lead to Forced Evictions

A slight variation on the theme of evictions due to violations of existing land use regulations occurs when forced evictions are imposed on informal settlements in the name of urban redevelopment, in other words, in order to implement a new urban planning scheme (typically prepared without meaningful participation of those who are to be evicted). UN-Habitat cites examples in Kenya, Zimbabwe, the Dominican Republic, Nigeria, and Brazil.[18] The press regularly reports similar examples from other countries, especially when accompanied by civil unrest or dramatic protests.[19]

How Might Legal Reformers Support Opportunity, Inclusion, and Equity?

Legal Reforms Can Make a Positive Difference

There are at least three avenues to improving development outcomes:

- Planning and land use standards can be established that are affordable and achievable for the majority of urban residents.

- The establishment of planning standards and the development of land use plans can be a genuinely inclusive, pro-poor process.

- Activists and courts can use legal principles of equity and human rights to defend against the most egregious oppression.

---

17   Ben C. Arimah & City Monitoring Branch, *Slums as Expressions of Social Exclusion: Explaining the Prevalence of Slums in African Countries* (mimeograph, UN-Habitat 2001).

18   *Forced Evictions: Global Crisis, Global Solutions* (UN-Habitat 2011).

19   *Hunan Officials "Cover Up" Self-Immolation Protest,* Radio Free Asia (May 28, 2013), available at http://english.rfa.org/english/news/china/coverup-05282013164754.html. At this writing, prolonged urban uprisings in Turkey are testing the government's resolve to proceed with "urban renewal" plans in Istanbul.

The first approach can be thought of as substantive inclusion, the second as procedural inclusion, and the third as equity, in both the legal and the ordinary senses of the word.

Substantively, Legal Frameworks Can Successfully Legitimize Urban Density

In some places, planning laws expressly legitimize the densities that poor urban residents can afford. For example, in Surabaya, Indonesia, *kampong* developments have no minimum street widths and no minimum lot sizes. As a result, a family can buy and occupy a very small piece of land if that is what they can afford. In some *kampongs*, the average density is more than 800 people per hectare.[20] Surabaya's land use planning expressly reserves areas for the development and extension of such dense development near the edge of the city. The government's stable policy of recognizing the legitimacy of dense *kampong*-style development, and of making infrastructure investments within *kampongs*, has created "an invaluable stock of housing affordable to those who . . . are ready to trade off the convenience of a car for the *kampong*'s central location."[21]

Legitimizing Density Helps Avoid Slums and Integrate Cities

Vietnam is a low-income and rapidly urbanizing country. In many parts of the world, this combination has been associated with slum formation. Among the factors that have helped Vietnam avoid this are legitimizing small plot sizes and a permissive attitude toward high floor area ratios.[22] As in Surabaya, the government invests in infrastructure and services in dense settlements—thus, they become integral parts of the urban fabric, rather than marginalized slums. Rather than dividing the city, the approaches taken in Surabaya and Vietnam are inclusive—the legal framework takes account of the need for affordable, well-located urban living space, and includes these dense settlements as legitimate parts of the city, entitled to infrastructure and urban services. These are examples of substantive inclusion, allowing the entire population access to the opportunities offered by urbanization.

Rebalancing of Rights Can Support More Inclusive, Efficient Cities

A substantive rebalancing of rights can provide opportunities for citizens of all income levels to participate in urban life. In any country, there may be tension between the rights of people who want to live and work in the city

---

20   See *Kampung Kebalen Improvement: Aga Khan Award for Architecture*, available at http://www
      .akdn.org/architecture/project.asp?id=443

21   Alain Bertaud, *Note on Surabaya Mobility and Housing Issues* (2012), copy in author's files (part
      of the materials the author received from a World Bank task team working on the Surabaya
      project).

22   *Vietnam Urbanization Review* (Technical Assistance Report, World Bank 2011), https://open
      knowledge.worldbank.org/bitstream/handle/10986/2826/669160ESW0P1130Review000Full0
      report.pdf?sequence=1.

and the rights of people who own property in the city. In a free market, as the American political economist Henry George observed in 1879, the value of land goes up with urbanization. George famously argued that governments should impose significant taxes on the ownership of land so that the owner pays society a rent for the right to use that scarcest urban commodity, well-located land.[23] At least since his time, arguments have raged over the appropriate balance between owners' rights to do as they choose with their land and the community's right to limit private property rights for the public good. The 2001 Brazilian City Statute took the significant step of codifying a "social function of property," a concept that had long existed in Brazilian law, and imposed penalties on owners who hold unoccupied or unused buildings.[24] In other words, the legislation limits the rights of property owners when their properties do not fulfill a social function.[25] In a nod to Henry George, Brazil's City Statute requires graduated taxation of urban real estate and penalizes owners of underutilized property.[26] This encourages densification and more intensive use of prime land.

Good Urban Law Reflects an Evolving Social Consensus about the City

Whatever the issue—density, affordability, access, or sustainability—good urban planning law reflects common values and embodies rules for the city that have general support and by which most people are willing to live. Good law depends on voluntary compliance, rather than on enforcement. At its best, law can protect and balance the rights of property owners and other citizens; it can lend predictability to urban life; and it can provide an environment that supports long-term public and private investments. A sound legal and regulatory framework must be flexible, adaptive, and progressive so that as the social consensus evolves and new challenges arise, the legal framework also evolves. As Roscoe Pound said, "law must be stable, and yet it cannot stand still."[27] The social consensus changes as new issues and technologies emerge. Some urban standards that were accepted in the 20th century seem dangerous and wasteful in a world that is increasingly feeling the effects of climate change. Achieving social consensus starts with genuine participation and transparency in establishing the rules for the city.

The Current Context Is a Useful Point of Departure

As one considers reforming planning law for cities in the 21st century, it is wise to start from to the way cities actually are. Planning law ideally should be

---

23   Henry George, *Progress and Poverty: An Inquiry into the Cause of Industrial Depressions and of Increase of Want with Increase of Wealth* (1879), available at www.henrygeorge.org.

24   O Estatuto da Cidade, Brazilian Federal Law No. 10.257 (July 10, 2001).

25   Maricato, *supra* note 9.

26   Alexandre Dos Santos Cunha, *The Social Function of Property in Brazilian Law* 80 Fordham L. Rev. 1171 (2011).

27   Roscoe Pound, *Interpretations of Legal History* (Cambridge U. Press 1923).

a broadly negotiated outcome of discussion about space and its use, not a tool crafted and enforced by a privileged segment of society with its own perspectives and interests at heart. Planning laws, like other parts of the urban legal framework, must fit their context. Any law that requires 80 percent of people to change the way they live is unlikely to succeed. A law that regularizes the way that 80 percent of the people live, and that pushes the outliers into compliance with community norms and common expectations, has a chance.

Procedural Safeguards Can Promote Inclusive Planning Processes

A United Nations report outlines the key elements of inclusive planning and land use regulation, in the context of a human right to adequate housing:

> [P]lanning and development processes should involve all those likely to be affected and should include the following elements: (a) appropriate notice to all potentially affected persons that eviction is being considered and that there will be public hearings on the proposed plans and alternatives; (b) effective dissemination by the authorities of relevant information in advance, including land records and proposed comprehensive resettlement plans specifically addressing efforts to protect vulnerable groups; (c) a reasonable time period for public review of, comment on, and/or objection to the proposed plan; (d) opportunities and efforts to facilitate the provision of legal, technical and other advice to affected persons about their rights and options; and (e) holding of public hearing(s) that provide(s) affected persons and their advocates with opportunities to challenge the eviction decision and/or to present alternative proposals and to articulate their demands and development priorities.[28]

Many planning laws in developing countries do provide for formal notice and a comment period, but they do not necessarily include all five elements mentioned by the United Nations. And even when these elements are included in the legal framework, they are not always implemented fully or in a way that ensures meaningful participation.

Broader Efforts at Inclusivity Are Called For

Notice and an opportunity to be heard are necessary, of course, but in the context of developing cities, these usually are not sufficient to provide for meaningful participation. Just as the poor often cannot afford the minimum spatial standard that is frequently prescribed in planning legislation, they can seldom afford the kind of civic participation that is envisioned in typical planning legislation. People who must work long hours and care for their families, who must queue for water or stay at home to protect their shacks from demolition

---

28   Miloon Kothari, *Implementation of General Assembly Resolution 60/251 of 15 March 2006, entitled "Human Rights Council": Report of the Special Rapporteur on Adequate Housing as a Component of the Right to an Adequate Standard of Living,* United Nations General Assembly A/HRC/4/18 (2007), available at http://www.sarpn.org/documents/d0002804/index.ph.

and thieves, don't have the time, resources, or experience to participate effectively in public hearings, to file written comments, to pursue objections and appeals, and so on. And many feel little urge to do so, because they have little hope of affecting the outcome—the process is often seen as hopelessly corrupt, with "precooked" outcomes determined by bribes and/or political influence.[29]

Urban Master Plans Are Often Outdated and Were Rarely Developed Inclusively

Almost every city in the world has some form of master plan, and sometimes several generations of master plans. In rapidly urbanizing developing countries, these plans are often out of date and bear little resemblance to the de facto development that has occurred in the years or decades since the plans were updated. In most cases, "expert" planners without meaningful public participation developed these plans. A summary of master plans in Brazil shows that

> [f]or years the authoritarian or technocratic approach by the authorities paid scant attention to the ability of the population to participate in designing urban planning initiatives. The tradition of Master Plans being drawn up by specialists—often consultancy firms with no connective dialogue with the city's inhabitants—permeates official planning practices to this day.[30]

The same could be said of master plans throughout the developing world.

Meaningful Participation Can Be a Requirement for Legal Validity

The 2001 Brazilian City Statute offers a newer model for developing master plans.[31] This approach to land use planning (and other urban issues) provides a land governance framework that is broader than traditional Western or colonial models. This law makes popular participation in land use decisions an essential condition of validity. Under the Brazilian City Statute, the test is not just if there is an opportunity to be heard, but also if there has been effective citizen participation. Although the implementation of the City Statute has proved less dramatic than the law itself, the emphasis on actual participation is remarkable. Fernandes observes that whereas "bad laws" can make inclusive public policies very difficult, "good laws" do not by themselves change urban and social realities.[32] He is cautiously optimistic about Brazil's City Statute and its progeny:

---

29 Berrisford, *supra* note 14.

30 Evaniza Rodrigues & Benedito Roberto Barbosa, *Popular Movements and the City Statute*, in *The City Statute of Brazil: A Commentary* (National Secretariat for Urban Programmes, Brazil Ministry of Cities 2010).

31 O Estatuto da Cidade, *supra* note 24.

32 Edesio Fernandes, *The City Statute of Brazil: A Critical Assessment, 10 Years Later* (presentation at Annual World Bank Conference on Land and Poverty, Apr. 2013).

[A] new legal-urban order has consolidated—sophisticated, articulated and comprehensive—including the constitutional recognition of Urban Law as a field of Brazilian Public Law with its own paradigmatic principles, namely, the socio-environmental functions of property and of the city, and the democratic management of the city. The collective right to sustainable cities was explicitly recognized, and there is a clear commitment in the legal system to the urban reform agenda.[33]

The Brazilian model illustrates one approach to moving away from expert-driven planning and toward planning as a process of community dialogue and agreement.

Equitable and Constitutional Principles Can Support Urban Inclusivity

When slums and those who live in them are by definition outside the law, informal settlements can be bulldozed and squatters can be evicted with the sanction of the law. But common law countries have a tradition of equity principles that can supplement the strict rule of law to avoid harsh results, and many constitutions confer rights that can be asserted to protect the rights of urban dwellers, including the poor. In the context of urban planning and land use legislation and litigation, at least two kinds of constitutional provisions are relevant to issues of urban inclusion and equity. The first is rooted in an assertion of human rights. Kenya's recent constitution provides every person the right "to accessible and adequate housing, and to reasonable standards of sanitation."[34] The second type of constitutional provision puts social limits on the use of private property, as with Brazil's twin sections: one guarantees the right of property, and the immediately following section clarifies that property "shall observe its social function."[35] This latter section is usefully read together with Article 182 of the Constitution, which provides for master plans and then explains that urban property performs its social function when it "meets the fundamental requirements for the ordainment of the city as set forth in the master plan."

Realizing the promise of these equitable and constitutional principles is not automatic or easy. The poor often do not have meaningful access to courts. Judicial procedure can be impenetrable for the poor and asymmetrically advantageous to formal property owners. When local government attempts to encourage affordable urban densities, the wealthy often challenge such schemes and, at a minimum, buy time with lengthy litigation.

---

33   *Id.*

34   Constitution of Kenya, Revised Edition (2010), sec. 43(1)(b).

35   Constitution of the Federative Republic of Brazil (1988), as amended, art. 5, secs. XXII & XXIII.

Some Courts Are Intervening on Behalf of the Poor

In some countries, courts have played important roles in establishing the right of the poor to settle and live in cities, and to participate fully in urban life.[36] Where legislation confers social rights, an active judiciary can intervene to enforce those rights. In South Africa, for example, the constitution expressly provides a right of "access to adequate housing."[37] In the path-breaking *Grootboom* case, families living in a flood-prone settlement, without access to clean water, sewage, or refuse removal services had moved to a hillside that had been identified for eventual low-cost housing. The municipality bulldozed their shacks and destroyed their possessions. Homeless and in desperate circumstances, they brought an action to enforce their constitutional right to housing. The court found that even though the municipality was engaged in a massive housing program to eventually provide shelter and secure title for all, it must provide interim shelter for those "with no access to land, no roof over their heads, and who were living in intolerable conditions or crisis situations."[38] As Justice Albie Sachs has written, "[t]he case showed the extent to which creative lawyers and energetic civil society organizations can help the poor to secure their basic rights."[39]

In a similar case in Nairobi, a high court found that Article 10 of the Kenyan Constitution sets out principles of governance—equity, inclusiveness, nondiscrimination, good governance, and accountability—that bind all state officers and that the forceful eviction of more than 15,000 residents without compensation and resettlement was therefore unconstitutional.[40] Both the South African and the Kenyan cases signal a willingness by some courts to give concrete meaning to the right to housing and urban services.

In this regard, these courts have gone further than a pioneering Indian case, *Tellis v. Bombay*.[41] In that case, state and municipal governments had evicted pavement dwellers and slum dwellers. The plaintiffs argued that they needed a home in the city to earn a living, and that if they were to be evicted from the pavements and informal areas, then they were entitled to resettlement. The Indian court did not agree that all were entitled to resettlement, but it did agree that they had a right to a hearing and that some of them were entitled to resettlement sites if they could prove that they had been counted in the last census. Thus, although *Tellis* did establish a right to live in the city in

---

36 The idea of a "right to the city" was first proposed by Henri Lefebvre in 1968 and has since been widely used by advocates for the urban poor. It encompasses not just the individual right to settle, live, and work in cities but also the right to urban services, and the collective right to shape the city.

37 Constitution of the Republic of South Africa, Act 108 (1996), ch. 2, sec. 26.

38 *Government of the Republic of South Africa and Other v. Grootboom and Others* (2001), (I) SA 46 (CC); (2000), (II) BCLR 1169 (CC).

39 Albie Sachs, *The Strange Alchemy of Life and Law* 164 (Oxford U. Press 2009).

40 *City Slum Dwellers Win Land Suit*, Nairobi Daily Nation (Apr. 11, 2013).

41 *Olga Tellis & Ors v. Bombay Municipal Council* (1985) 2 Supp. SCR 51.

order to earn a living, it did not require the municipality to provide sites for all of those affected. More recently, when Mumbai faced a natural disaster in 2005 due to flash flooding, the high court forced the Maharashtra state government to provide land and infrastructure to relocate thousands of families and facilitated the widening of the banks of the River Mithi, which caused the floods.[42]

The South African, Kenyan, and Indian cases are all rooted in constitutional rights arising under democratically adopted constitutions. These modern constitutions provide the form into which courts can breathe life. These constitutions were only superficially the product of the lawyers that drafted them. At a deeper level, each was the product of serious and sustained social dialogue. In each country, people of all kinds debated vigorously and openly as to the principles and values by which they wanted to be governed. And perhaps this is the important truth: lawyers and judges may be custodians of the law, but the law's value lies in its legitimacy and relevance to the daily lives of citizens.

It is also notable that these courts, all of which have roots in English common law, are acting in the tradition of chancery courts of equity, which intervened to rectify injustice that occurred from the strict application of the law. Although equitable remedies per se no longer exist in some of these countries,[43] the underlying principles of equity, now enshrined in constitutional principles of justice and human rights, shine through. It is an open question whether, in civil law countries, the courts could or would be willing to take a similar path. In any event, the wisest way forward lies in reforming the legal framework for planning and land use to encourage affordable density, including the entire city when investing in infrastructure and services and encompassing all citizens in decisions about land use and planning.

Conclusion

The tremendous growth of cities in the developing world means that most development challenges are now urban challenges. As a result, the legal framework within which cities operate is of urgent importance to development lawyers. The law underpins every aspect of urban life, from land use to service delivery, from infrastructure finance to municipal insolvency.

This chapter highlights one particular challenge: planning law has tended to formally and informally divide cities, providing expensive standards and processes for the privileged few and leaving the majority in an indeterminate status that prevents the poor from accessing urban services that are their right and providing fertile ground for corruption and arbitrary discretion. This exclusion is obviously bad for individuals, but it also diminishes the productive capacity of the poor, of the city, and of the nation.

---

42   Rajack et al., *supra* note 13.

43   *See,* for example, India's Specific Relief Act of 1963, which codified many of the forms of equitable relief.

Law and legal reform can make a profound difference. In the case of land use law, urban land use reform should start with a clear understanding of the actual situation on the ground, rather than abstract ideals. The reform process itself must be democratic and genuinely participatory, reflecting a wide range of inputs from all levels of society. The Brazilian City Statute, and the extensive social dialogue within which it is embedded, shows that there is not a quick fix, and success is not guaranteed, but it does offer a promise of sustainability.

Good urban land use law must consider affordability and the importance of access to the city and must be implemented in a way that allows people to live near jobs and other opportunities by legitimizing the consumption of the amount of space they can afford. The law must also minimize opportunities for the well connected to profit from asymmetrical information access. It must represent a genuine social bargain about how urban land will be used.

PART IV

GOVERNANCE AND ANTICORRUPTION

Fighting Corruption in Education

A Call for Sector Integrity Standards

"What money can't buy, a lot of money can"
— A modern-day Bulgarian proverb

Wang Anshi, a progressive Chinese statesman who lived during the 11th century, believed that the causes of corruption are "bad laws and bad men." His intuition points toward corruption as a function of human behavior and the (permissive) environment in which it takes place. For a while, Wang was quite successful in improving the laws of his time. He failed, however, with the "bad men," who shortly before his death reversed his reforms and ousted him.

The "bad men" of today seem to get around. They also seem to have a certain weakness for schools and universities. According to data in a 2010–2011 survey conducted by Transparency International,[1] 59.4 percent of the population in eastern Europe perceives education as corrupt or extremely corrupt. "Bad men" have also visited African education establishments, corrupting them in the eyes of 56.3 percent of the people living there. The story is the same in the Caucasus (49.2 percent), Southeast Asia (34.4 percent), and Latin America (22.2 percent). Globally, 35 percent of the population in 100 countries has no trust whatsoever in the integrity of their education institutions.[2] Obviously, no sector is immune from malpractice, but education might be more vulnerable than ever before.

For very many people, education carries hope for a better future. The demand for degrees and qualifications is rising rapidly worldwide,[3] and the sector is a priority in most national strategies for economic growth or recovery.

This chapter follows up the session *Strengthening Integrity and Fighting Corruption in Education: Insights and Effective Measures* (available at http://go.worldbank.org/HBZI38VKK0), initiated by the author and moderated by him on behalf of the Organisation for Economic Co-operation and Development (OECD) at Law, Justice and Development Week, held in 2012 at the World Bank in Washington, D.C. The views expressed herein do not necessarily reflect those of individuals and institutions that participated in the session, or of the European Training Foundation.

1   Transparency International, *Global Corruption Barometer Report 2010/2011* (Transparency International 2011), http://www.transparency.org/gcb201011.

2   *Id.*

3   *See*, for example, Cathy Wendler et al., *Pathways through Graduate School and into Careers* (Educational Testing Service 2012) for trends in the United States, but also *Education Indicators in Focus* (OECD Research Brief No. 2012/05, May 2012) for a trend summary for the OECD area, China, and India.

The educational gold rush, then, can stretch the capacity of education systems and professionals to deliver what is expected and can turn academic credentials into a highly desired, sometimes even scarce commodity. Dealing in bogus knowledge and recognition can easily become a norm of behavior, especially in countries with still-limited educational coverage or where high-quality institutions are rare.

The thirst for more and better education also drives a growing demand for more investment in a wide range of items and services related to the expansion of access to education and to quality improvement, such as in school and IT infrastructures, textbooks and learning materials, professional development, school meals, and consultancy services. Between 2000 and 2009, combined public and private spending on education in OECD (Organisation for Economic Co-operation and Development) countries rose by 36 percent, making education one of the three biggest domains of public expenditure in the OECD area.[4] In some reform-oriented countries, the resources allocated for educational improvement can amount to a third of the education budget.[5] The sheer size of the sector and the amount of services and goods that it requires provide abundant opportunities for profit.

The education sector is also vulnerable to corruption because national education systems have a multitude of actors operating in a very complex, often decentralized system that features institutions with considerable autonomy, especially in tertiary education. This can, and frequently does, limit the effectiveness of policy and regulatory interventions and lets malpractice go easily undetected—even more so as dependencies between perpetrators of corruption offenses in education persist beyond those created by the offense itself: students commonly depend on their teachers and parents; teachers and schools depend on education authorities, and sometimes on contributions or approval from parents; and parents depend on teachers for the educational success of their children. To resist a request for a bribe in such a setting can be far more painful than to agree to it.

It is high time to fight corruption in education, for even one corrupt institution and one fake doctor, teacher, or engineer is one too many. In 2001, in their pioneer work on the issue, Jacques Hallak and Muriel Poisson asked an important question: "What can be done?"[6] Since then, governments around the world have become painfully aware of the need to do something and now routinely attach priority to education in their anticorruption strategies and action plans.[7] Is this good enough to stop corruption in education? Hardly, as the fig-

---

4   Educators are also among the largest occupational groups in the workforce. *See Education at a Glance 2012: OECD Indicators* (OECD 2012).

5   *See Review of Secondary Education in Kazakhstan* (OECD 2013).

6   *See* Jacques Hallak & Muriel Poisson, *Corrupt Schools, Corrupt Universities: What Can Be Done?* (International Institute for Educational Planning 2007), which is based on findings from a research project on ethics and corruption in education launched by the UNESCO International Institute for Educational Planning.

7   *See*, for example, the summaries of proceedings of the Steering Group of the OECD Anti-

ures above suggest. More than a decade later and despite some promising efforts to address the problem, the cynical wisdom of the proverb from Bulgaria seems to continue to work well in education institutions worldwide. Is it time to downgrade the optimism of the initial query to: "Can anything be done?"

The moral of the story of Wang Anshi is straightforward: improving laws is good, but when "bad men" are around, it might not be good enough. How can good laws be made and how can they be made to work against corruption in a complex sector such as education? And who are the "bad men," really?

Education policy analysis today is better equipped to tackle complex systemic problems than it was a decade ago and is capable of delivering new answers to some old questions. Large-scale international assessments of educational performance are now fairly common and wide reaching[8] and regularly deliver rich and diversified information on the functioning of national education systems. Data provide new insights into the factors influencing system performance and contribute to a growing pool of evidence on the trajectories of change of education systems and institutions over the past 10 to 20 years, as accumulated by research institutions and international organizations with the capacity and mandate to carry out education policy analysis. These can, and should, be mobilized to deal with the issue at hand.[9]

Cross-border cooperation against corruption in the public sector has also leaped ahead. Around the same time that the OECD was carrying out the first round of its flagship survey of student achievement, the Programme for International Student Assessment (PISA), in 2001, the international community for the first time agreed on a set of anticorruption standards and embodied them in legally binding instruments such as the Council of Europe Criminal Law Convention on Corruption of 1999 and the United Nations Convention against Corruption of 2003 (hereinafter referred to as "the Conventions"), to name only two. Comprehensive monitoring and compliance mechanisms were established to support the signatories of these Conventions with the implementation of standards, but the question of how to "translate" and successfully enforce them at the sector level has been left aside. A review of literature that documents efforts to fight corruption in education would show that education policy makers and researchers rarely if at all refer to them and might in fact not be aware of their existence.

Perhaps it is time to venture into the development of a new, more comprehensive approach in tackling corruption in education—one that will capitalize

---

Corruption Network for Eastern Europe and Central Asia since September 2009 (available at http://www.oecd.org/corruption/acn).

8   Examples include the Programme for International Student Assessment (PISA) of the OECD, which in 2012 covered 64 countries; Trends in International Mathematics and Science Study (TIMSS), which covered 79 countries in 2011; and the Progress in International Reading Literacy Study (PIRLS), which covered 64 countries in 2011, both carried out by the International Association for the Evaluation of Educational Achievement.

9   Mihaylo Milovanovitch, *Understanding Integrity, Fighting Corruption: What Can Be Done?* (Global Corruption Report: Education, Transparency International 2013).

on the positive developments of recent years and be more systematic in analyzing the problem.[10] Sector-specific insights could thereby greatly facilitate
the long-overdue "translation" of international standards into standards of integral institutional and individual behavior on a sectoral level and raise their
effectiveness.

Expectations and Deliverables—Who Are the "Bad Men," Really?

The Conventions establish the offenses for corrupt behavior in the *public sector*.
Public education is implied in the umbrella term "public sector," and shares
with other sectors in the public domain common functional elements such as
public-expenditure management, procurement, rules guiding employment,
and so on. Indispensable as it is in setting cross-border standards, the umbrella term is broad and masks sector-specific elements that might have an impact on the enforcement of anticorruption measures in education, including
legislation based on international anticorruption standards. To "emancipate"
education from the generic notion of a public sector and identify these elements, one would need to take a closer look at education *as a public service* and
determine what this service is about. From the perspective of sector integrity,
there are good reasons for taking this approach.

Education is a social good,[11] and in most countries it is a matter of social
consensus that it should be available to everyone, regardless of income. From
the point of view of participants in education, its availability is measured
by the degree to which their expectations as education stakeholders are addressed by the education system and the services it provides. Instances of dis-
crepancy between deliverables and expectations would be a potential source
of corruption risk (see figure 1), as they would give participants in the system
incentives to revert to malpractice as a "remedy" for shortcomings in educational service provision.

It is reasonable to assume that education systems that would not fail their
stakeholders would experience fewer problems with corruption. In essence,
this assumption should hold for any public service. If issuing a driver's license
in a given country took a year, it is likely that license applicants would wish
for the process to take less time. Some or many of them might be seriously
tempted to shorten the groundless waiting and arrange for a "shortcut," with
help from officials who in turn might be on the lookout for ways to improve
their (low) salaries. An effective preventive solution would target the incentives for malpractice by improving the efficiency of the license-issuing process
and by raising the wages of those who manage it. But what do stakeholders
expect from education?

---

10   The next section features elements of a sector-specific approach to integrity, developed by
     the author in 2011 and piloted under his supervision in Serbia and Tunisia in 2012–13 within
     the framework of the OECD Integrity of Education Systems (INTES) project.

11   Gregory Wurzburg, *Corruption in Education* (unpublished framing paper prepared in the
     course of initial discussions that led to the OECD Integrity of Education Systems project).

Figure 1. Unmet expectations and corruption potential in education

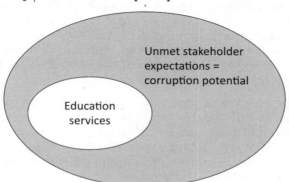

Quality of education is a key education deliverable and probably the most common area of stakeholders' expectations worldwide. Parents and students are usually prepared to go to great lengths to ensure that their expectations in this area are met. Countries where these expectations are not met are exposed to higher risk of malpractice. In the Kyrgyz Republic, for example, the quality of learning in secondary schools is so low that student performance in PISA persistently hurls the country down to the very last place of all economies participating in the survey.[12] Despite a considerable, above-OECD-average share of national wealth invested in education, time for learning at school remains very limited, the curriculum is overloaded, and teaching methods are outdated.[13] Consequently—and despite the cost involved—in 2006 some 64 percent of secondary students in the Kyrgyz Republic regularly resorted to one-on-one, out-of-school private lessons[14] with teachers *from their own schools*! It is not known how much of this practice is in exchange for school grades, but in a country that consistently ranks in the lowest quintile of Transparency International's Corruption Perception Index, the practice nurtures widespread perceptions of corruption in the sector.

Another fundamental set of expectations revolves around *access to education*. This includes fair and equitable provision of education, merit-based transition to higher levels of education, and recognition of academic success. In regions where good schools were rare, or in countries where a certain level of education (usually higher education) was confronted with capacity limitations, parents would be ready to bribe to ensure access to good education for their children. To sort out the capable from the incapable, many countries resort to high-stakes standardized tests, such as the Scholastic Achievement Test, the Graduate Record Examination, or the Law School Admissions Test.

---

12   *PISA 2009 Results: What Students Know and Can Do——Student Performance in Reading, Mathematics and Science* (OECD 2009).

13   *Kyrgyz Republic 2010: Lessons from PISA* (OECD 2010)

14   *PISA 2006 vol. 2: Data* (OECD 2006).

Such tests are decisive for access and are often given more weight in the process of admission. Cheating on them is widespread, throughout the world.[15] In China, for example, exam questions are sold in advance; in South Africa, the entire test is sold in advance; and in the United States and Japan, parents hire exam proxies to take the exam for their children.[16] A study carried out in Russia in 2008–2009 revealed that regional test administrators were involved in falsifying high scores for paying students.[17]

From the perspective of education institutions and the people working in them, another key deliverable would be the *sound management of staff and resources*, including their availability. In fact, staff and resources are the operational backbone of schools and universities,[18] and education systems that fail to operate adequately in these areas are in effect instigating their teachers and administrators to seek "alternative" solutions; for example, to ensure sufficient resources for maintenance of infrastructure, to obtain or keep their jobs, or simply to compensate for below-average wages. In Serbia, a country in which the OECD carried out its first assessment of education-system integrity in 2011, the quality of schools' educational resources as measured by PISA proved to be below the international average, and the perception of resource shortages other than for wages was widespread throughout the secondary education system.[19] In dealing with the combined challenge of limited resources and rising costs, the schools had developed high dependency on private investment[20] and were engaging in thriving economic activities—but without a matching system for oversight and control.[21] Rumors of misappropriation of school funds were widespread, but the number of investigated cases remained low.

In sum, education as a public service is expected to be fair and equitable, of good quality, and provided by institutions with sound management of staff and resources. The existence of identifiable causal links between corruption in the sector and failures in service delivery indicates that malpractice in the education system is determined, at least to a certain extent, by sector-specific policy shortcomings. These supply the mostly "ordinary" people participating in education—parents, students, teachers, and principals—with reasons to turn into Wang's "bad men." The effectiveness of measures against corruption in education therefore depends not only on "good laws" but also on targeted adjustments in education policy.

---

15   Tricia Betrtram Gallant ed., *Creating the Ethical Academy: A Systems Approach to Understanding Misconduct and Empowering Change in Higher Education* (Routledge 2011).

16   *Id.*

17   Anna Nemtsova, *Russia Cracks Down on Fraud in College Entrance Exam*, Chron. of Higher Educ. (Oct. 1, 2009).

18   *Strengthening Integrity and Fighting Corruption in Education: Serbia* (OECD 2012).

19   *Id.*

20   The proportion of private resources that households in Serbia invest in public schools is on average 2.5 times higher than in OECD countries.

21   *Strengthening Integrity and Fighting Corruption in Education: Serbia, supra* note 18.

Bad Laws, or How the Opportunity Makes the Thief

To be sure, failure to deliver on stakeholder expectations does not always lead to corruption. Below-OECD-average performance in PISA, tough university entry, or low salaries do not mean that all potentially disillusioned parents, students, or teachers will resort to malpractice. Some or many of them might be genuinely honest people, with a high level of personal integrity. Others might be inherently "bad," but hindered in their intentions by adequate laws and effective enforcement. This last point deserves further attention.

Corruption depends not only on the presence of motives but also on individual readiness to commit it (this is beyond the scope of this discussion) and opportunity to commit it. Windows of opportunity for corruption in education—or in any other sector—are usually opened by shortcomings in what could be called the prevention and detection framework of a country; that is, the set of such institutions, actors, resources, values, and actions that, taken separately or together, are in place to ensure a range of functions for the prevention and detection of malpractice/corruption on a national and sector level.[22] Examples of preventive deficiencies include failure to criminalize corruption offenses, absence of conflict of interest regulations for staff working in education, inadequate financial control, inefficient school inspections, and lack of administrative transparency, among others.

Box 1. Transparency Against Large-Scale Corruption: The Case of Uganda

Uganda is a good and frequently given example of a country that successfully closed a window of major corruption opportunity in its education system by boosting transparency. A Public Expenditure Tracking Survey (PETS) carried out in 1996 revealed that only 13 percent of the central grant for education actually reached the schools; 87 percent of it was captured by corrupt officials at the district level, leaving 73 percent of all schools in the country with less than 5 percent of the intended funds. As schools had no information on the amount of funding they were entitled to, and the central tier of governance did not verify the use of funds, these actions remained unchallenged.

At the core of policy changes triggered by this dramatic finding was a massive information campaign in which authorities started to publish and broadcast information on intergovernmental transfers of public funds and requested schools to publicly post information on their financial inflows. A follow-up study estimated that the campaign led to as much as a 75 percent improvement: between 1995 and 2001, the leakage of capitation grants to schools fell from 80 percent to 20 percent.

Source: Ritva Reinikka & Nathanael Smith, *Public Expenditure Tracking Surveys in Education* (International Institute for Educational Planning, UNESCO 2004).

---

22   Mihaylo Milovanovitch, Simone Bloem, & Valts Kalnins, *Integrity and Corruption in Education: An Evidence-Based Approach to Malpractice Prevention* (OECD forthcoming).

Like other social phenomena, corruption has causes and consequences. In education, these are linked in a vicious cycle of failure—of cause and effect—in which systemic failure causes corruption, which in turn affects the system and causes it to fail.[23] Breaking this cycle involves the mapping of origins of corruption in the sector in conjunction with the improvement of prevention measures. Even the strongest prevention, detection, and follow-up mechanisms are blind without an understanding of what causes corruption in a sector. The reverse is true as well; opportunities created by weak monitoring and control represent a temptation in even the best of education systems.[24]

Figure 2. Corruption and prevention cycle

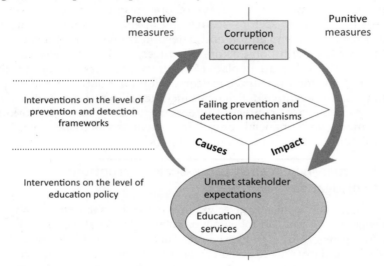

Source: Author, based on Milovanovitch et al. *Integrity and Corruption in Education: An Evidence-Based Approach to Malpractice Prevention* (OECD 2013).

The "What" and "How" of Effective Prevention

Ideally, effective prevention would comprise adjustments in the prevention and detection framework to close windows of opportunity for corruption, but also interventions in the realm of education policy in view of improving sector deliverables and diminishing the reasons for engaging in malpractice. In practice, however, it proves very difficult to coordinate such efforts. The consensus about what constitutes malpractice in education and what and how anticorruption standards would be applicable is patchy, at best. Moreover, education policy makers and institutions tend to lack sector-specific integrity guidance, and anticorruption professionals and bodies have limited understanding of

---

23   *Id.*

24   *Strengthening Integrity and Fighting Corruption in Education: Serbia, supra* note 18.

the sector and its needs while continuing to count on its contribution for the fulfillment of their commendable mandate.

The notion of malpractice becomes very ambiguous when applied to real life in schools and universities. Malpractice is always harmful and damaging to the integrity of a sector, but in education it can easily fall short of qualifying as corruption offense (i.e., an offense entailing criminal liability) by international standards. Private tutoring,[25] for example, constitutes a clear-cut case of corruption in which teachers request their own students to take private lessons as a condition for passing an exam.[26] Things become less clear when teachers purposefully skip parts of the content in regular lessons to stimulate demand for tutoring. This is a good example of a "softer" form of corruption (i.e., malpractice that calls for civil, administrative, or disciplinary punishments) that remains without correspondence in the body of anticorruption standards but one that a diligent prevention/integrity strategy can ill afford to ignore (see figure 3). Other examples of teacher-related, soft forms of malpractice could include teacher absenteeism[27] or "ghost teachers."[28]

Each offense, hard or soft, likely also has a permissible, acceptable equivalent at the lower end of the axis of tolerance represented in figure 3. In the example of private tutoring, this could be cost-free remedial work with low achievers or the giving of presents to teachers at the beginning of an important school year. Figure 3 also applies to manifestations of integrity deficits in any of the three education-service dimensions discussed here.

In order to be effective, prevention measures, which include education policy interventions, must identify and take into consideration relevant practices on both sides of the threshold of tolerance. The complexity of the education system and the cultural and country differences, however, make it difficult to draw a clear line between acceptable practices and softer forms of malpractice, and between soft corruption and criminal offenses. This renders the application of international anticorruption standards to education particularly challenging and suggests a necessity to mobilize the education sector

---

25 For a thorough overview of the private tutoring phenomenon, *see* Mark Bray, *Confronting the Shadow Education System* (UNESCO 2009).

26 *See* Mark Bray, *Shadow Education: The Rise of Private Tutoring and Associated Corruption Risks* (Global Corruption Report: Education, Transparency International 2013).

27 Teacher absenteeism as a soft form of corruption was a theme discussed at the session *Strengthening Integrity and Fighting Corruption in Education* in the Law, Justice and Development Week (LJDW), held in 2012 at the World Bank in Washington, D.C. The topic was introduced by Halsey Rogers (Human Development Network, World Bank), who discussed ways of measuring the prevalence of teacher absenteeism, provided a country example (India), and reported on progress in dealing with the problem.

28 "Ghost teachers" are fictitious teachers whose names are on the payroll although they belong to people who are not in service anymore (because deceased or retired) or who never existed.

Figure 3. Malpractices and threshold of tolerance

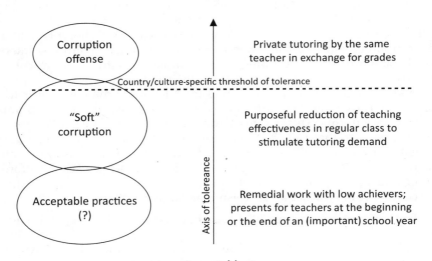

itself to push for an agreement on where to draw the line at what is acceptable practice and, based on that, for definition of complementary, sector-level standards of integral behavior.[29] These standards would target a clearly defined set of soft and hard offenses and be linked to international anticorruption instruments—that is, the Conventions—thus strengthening their effectiveness on a sector level.

National education institutions have an important role to play in this endeavor. They are paramount for the development of awareness and ownership for the integrity effort and are a primary reference point for civil society involvement and for gauging important cultural aspects, such as attitudes toward corruption. A prevention strategy that mobilizes all three layers of prevention responsibility represented in figure 4—national, sector, and institutional—will be able to capture the entire range of sector-specific malpractice, from borderline unethical but tolerated behavior through soft corruption, to corruption offenses as defined by international law.

---

29   The benefits of mobilizing sector expertise for preventing fraud were the focus of the presentation of Alaleh Motamedi (senior procurement specialist, Operations and Policy Group, World Bank), *Procurement in Education,* in the session, *Strengthening Integrity and Fighting Corruption in Education* at the LJDW held in 2012 at the World Bank in Washington, D.C. She argued for a new approach in improving procurement integrity, one that relies on better cooperation between procurement and education specialists to better account for different country contexts and the specificities of market supply and demand in education, and to stimulate stakeholder empowerment and innovative solutions.

Figure 4. Layers of prevention responsibility

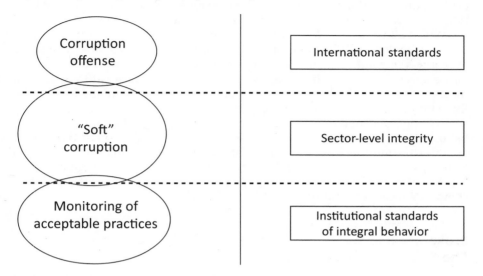

What Next?

The explanatory report to the Criminal Law Convention on Corruption of the Council of Europe notes that even after years of discussions, the international community has failed to agree on a common definition of corruption, and the OECD *Glossary of International Standards in Criminal Law* indicates that "there are as many different definitions of corruption as there are manifestations of the problem itself."[30] International fora, in contrast, have quite successfully focused on agreeing on the definition of certain forms of corruption, such as bribery of foreign public officials (OECD Convention on Combating Bribery of Foreign Public Officials in International Business Transactions), trading in influence (Council of Europe Criminal Law Convention on Corruption), and embezzlement, misappropriation, or other diversion of property by a public official (United Nations Convention Against Corruption).

In education, work in this respect has so far been very limited. Education research over the past 10 to 15 years has concentrated on the production of definitions of corruption, rather than on determining corruption offenses. The definitions produced so far remain too narrow and are applicable only in a limited number of cases, or are too broad and of limited use.[31] It is time to shift the focus to corruption offenses instead.

---

30 *Corruption: A Glossary of International Standards in Criminal Law* (OECD 2008).

31 Nataliya L. Rumyantseva, *Taxonomy of Corruption in Higher Education*, 80 Peabody J. of Educ. 81–92 (2005). Two definitions of corruption are frequently referred to. One is that of Stephen Heyneman, who argues that "education is an important public good [whose] professional standards include more than just material goods." He goes on to define corruption in education

As of this writing (summer 2013), there has been a renaissance of interest by multilateral institutions and their members in discussing a coordination of efforts to combat corruption in education.[32] More than a decade ago, the World Bank[33] and UNESCO[34] drew their attention to the corruption problem in schools and universities, triggering follow-up actions that, with some exceptions (Uganda; see box 1) were neither systematic nor particularly evidence based. The research on the issue at that time was also still young and, most of all, scarce. Today, declarations of good intentions are the least of deliverables to be demanded. The growing political momentum lends itself to supporting a consolidation of available evidence on education into a clear-cut list of actions that constitute offenses involving criminal or other types of liability—the building blocks of a multilateral consensus on integrity standards in the sector. Table 1 illustrates how the differentiated view of education as a public-service deliverable can be used as a starting point in the work on standards-oriented solutions.

Brokerage and Sector Inclusiveness: The Role of International Fora

The standardization of integral behavior in education is not only a conceptual but also a political task that calls for brokerage between states in a suitable international forum. In fact, progress in the political dimension will depend on the "suitability" of the broker. With one notable exception, the UNESCO International Standard Classification of Education, the education sector does not have any international standards or entities that could set them and still relies on best-practice cases or between-country data comparisons without normative value. Other international fora—such as the Council of Europe's Group of States against Corruption (GRECO), the OECD's Anti-Corruption Network

---

as "the abuse of authority for personal as well as material gain" (Steven Heyneman, *Education and Corruption*, 24 Intl. J. Educ. Dev. 6 [2004]). The other frequently used definition is that of Hallak and Poisson, who believe that corruption in education is a "systematic misuse of public office for private benefit whose impact is significant on access, quality or equity in education" (Hallak and Poisson, *Ethics and Corruption in Education: Results from the Expert Workshop Held in Paris on 28–29 November 2001*, http://www.unesco.org/iiep/PDF/Forum15.pdf).

32   *Education Ministers Back Pan-European Anti-corruption Platform and Ethical Code for Teachers,* (press release, Council of Europe, April 27, 2013), available at http://www.coe.int/t/dg4 /education/standingconf/Source/press/Education_Ministers_Conference_press_release2.pdf); *see also* the summary of proceedings from the *Expert Seminar on Prevention of Corruption— Enhancing Practical Implementation and Taking Effective Measures at the Institutional and Sector Levels* (OECD Anti-Corruption Network for Eastern Europe and Central Asia, June 26–27).

33   Through a first round of public expenditure tracking surveys in education and their results.

34   See *Dakar Framework for Action: Education for All; Meeting Our Collective Commitments* (UNESCO 2000). The framework was adopted by the World Education Forum, Dakar, Senegal, April 26–28, 2000.

Table 1. Sample of identity offenses in education

Area of Deliverables/ Expectations	Sample Offenses
Quality of education	• Provision of better learning conditions to individual students whose parents provide financial support to the school, at the expense of "regular" students • Rigged examinations, i.e., through the sale of examination questions • Forced purchase of learning materials authored by the teachers • Purposeful reduction of teaching effectiveness during regular school hours in view of stimulating demand for private tutoring • Private tutoring by the same teacher in exchange for grades
Access to education	• Bribing to ensure access to education, or to allow for transition to higher levels of education • Rigged entrance examinations • Provision by students of intellectual or other services to university teachers in exchange for academic success • Sale of academic credentials
Sound management of staff	• Teacher recruitment based on political or family affiliations, rather than on qualifications and performance • Teacher absenteeism
Sound management of resources	• Manipulation of local data on numbers of students, admission of minorities, or on examination results to obtain more favorable resource or staff allocations • Embezzlement of funds • Use of school infrastructure for generating revenue at the expense of the teaching and learning environment • Use of student labor for generating school revenue under the pretext of providing practical training

Source: Author, based on Katharina L. Ochse, *Preventing Corruption in the Education System: A Practical Guide* (Deutsche Gesellschaft für Technische Zusammenarbeit 2004).

for Eastern Europe and Central Asia, or the Conference of the States Parties to the United Nations Convention Against Corruption—all have a strong mandate to formulate and monitor anticorruption policies, but their legitimacy as brokers of standards on a sector level is limited or yet to be established.

The identification of a suitable broker is a challenge that needs to be addressed before any progress can be made. One way to do this is to invest effort in making international anticorruption fora more sector inclusive. The fact that the Steering Group of the OECD Anti-Corruption Network increasingly includes education in its deliberations shows that this is a feasible option. There are also promising developments in the sector itself. The standing conference of Council of Europe Ministers of Education recently established an anticorruption platform for education that can be mobilized as a brokerage agent. On a more technical level, in the next biennium, the European Training Foundation, the biggest education agency of the European Union, charged with steering knowledge and guiding resource allocations for human capital development in 31 countries neighboring the European Union, is focusing on efficiency and good governance as priority areas.

The times have never been more opportune for putting together resources and coordinating efforts on an issue that deeply concerns all countries, their citizens, and the future of their citizens' education. The success of this endeavor can render the wisdom of the modern-day Bulgarian proverb obsolete, at last.

The Battle between Corruption and Governance in India

Strategies for Tipping the Scale

SRIRAM PANCHU AND AVNI RASTOGI

Over the past few years, India has witnessed an upsurge of public anger at corruption in the upper reaches of the government. With Anna Hazare's movement galvanizing public sentiment in 2011, mass protests against corruption have been held across the country.[1]

Corruption is the abusive use of public power for personal ends and covers everything from the paying of bribes to civil servants in return for favors and the theft of the public purse to a wide range of wrongful economic and political practices in which politicians, bureaucrats, and other vested interests enrich themselves at the expense of the state.[2] There are usually at least two actors involved in a corrupt act. On the one hand are government officials and public functionaries, who hold positions of authority and allocate rights over scarce public resources on behalf of the state; on the other hand are the nonstate actors, private individuals or entities that provide an incentive for corrupt acts and gain an advantage from them. Corruption also involves two distinct acts of redistribution of resources between the bribe payer and the receiver: one is the bribe paid; the other is the allocation of public resources determined by considerations other than public benefit. The latter is why links have been drawn between poverty and corruption.

This chapter begins with a brief introduction to corruption in India and the cost to the country as a result of the large-scale diversion of money from state coffers. It then touches on the prevalent theoretical understanding of the causes of corruption that has informed efforts to tackle corruption, followed by an assessment of anticorruption efforts in India. Although petty corruption is dealt with briefly, the focus is on the kind of reform required to deal with big-ticket political corruption. The chapter concludes by describing a model for an authority that could deal with corruption at the higher levels of government in the Indian context.

---

1   In 2011–12, Anna Hazare, a social activist, led a movement against corruption in India using nonviolent methods of protest such as hunger strikes. The movement garnered a lot of public support before fizzling out by the end of 2012. However, the movement did succeed in bringing the issue of corruption to the fore.

2   Inge Amundsen, *Political Corruption: An Introduction to the Issue* 7 (research report prepared for the Chr. Michelsen Inst., Bergen, Norway 1999), available at http://bora.cmi.no/dspace/bitstream/10202/263/1/WP1999.7%20Inge-07192007_3.pdf (accessed Apr. 3, 2013).

Corruption in India

The "Kissinger Cables" that Wikileaks published in April 2013 spotlight the enduring problem of corruption in India. In 1976, the U.S. Embassy in India made clear to the U.S. State Department that corruption was a cultural, political, and economic fact of life in India.[3] Nepotism and "speed money" were considered acceptable, the embassy reported, and "innovative" ways were found to award contracts to favored bidders. Unfortunately, matters have only worsened since this assessment was made. Whereas at one time the "discerning Indian distinguished between corruption for personal and political purposes" as per the cable, now the corrupt are indiscriminate in their activities.[4]

Corruption in India has two main *avtars*, to borrow the Hindi term for "manifestation." One is the *chai-paani* ("tea water," a reference to daily small expenses) *avtar*, which refers to the all-pervasive greasing of palms that is expected by most public officials as "speed money" to issue documents and licenses and to deliver public services of any kind. The extent of such bribery is evident from the Indian Corruption Study series published by the Centre for Media Studies. The total monetary value of petty corruption nationally in just 11 services covered was estimated at Rs 210.68 billion, or US$3.9 billion,[5] in 2005.[6] The 2010 edition of the study estimated that the amount paid in bribes by rural households in 12 surveyed states for just four public services was Rs 4,718 million, or US$87.37 million, during the preceding year.[7] In 2012, the study focused on urban slum dwellers and found that three of every four slum dwellers had been asked to pay a bribe to the Public Distribution System or for health or municipal services received in the year preceding the survey. The study also found that the incidence of corruption in services had doubled since 2008 in urban India, rising from 34 percent to 67 percent.[8] These statistics are worrisome for a nation grappling with poverty and development.

---

3   P. J. George, *Corruption in India, a "Fact of Life" Say U.S. Diplomats,* The Hindu (Apr. 11, 2013), available at http://www.thehindu.com/news/national/corruption-in-india-a-fact-of -life-say-us-diplomats/article4603544.ece (accessed Apr. 12, 2013).

4   *Id.*

5   The conversions from rupees to U.S. dollars are based on an exchange rate of Rs 54 per US$1.

6   In its 2005 edition, the study covered corruption in the delivery of 11 public services across 20 states. Centre for Media Studies and Transparency International, *India Corruption Study 2005* (June 30, 2005), available at http://iri.org.in/related.../India%20Corruption%20Study %202005.pdf (accessed Mar. 20, 2013).

7   The 2010 study covered four essential services in 12 states in rural areas. The study also found a decline in the general perception of corruption in public services and a reduction in the experience of rural households of paying bribes since 2005, which could be due to the Right to Information Act of 2005 and anticorruption reforms since then. Centre for Media Studies, *India Corruption Study 2010* (Apr. 2011), available at http://www.waterintegrity network.net/index.php?option=com_mtree&task=att_download&link_id=148&cf_id=61 (accessed Mar. 20, 2013).

8   Centre for Media Studies, *India Corruption Study 2012: Expanding Slums & Growing Corruption* (press release, Ctr. for Media Stud., New Delhi, Dec. 7, 2012), available at http://www .cmsindia.org/PressReleaseCMS_ICS_2012.pdf (accessed Mar. 20, 2013).

The second *avtar* of corruption is the big-ticket variety involving huge amounts of money diverted as private gains from public resources. Since 2010, a number of multimillion-dollar scams involving people in high places have been unearthed, including the Commonwealth Games (2010) ,[9] the Adarsh Housing Society scam (2010),[10] the 2G scam (2010),[11] the Tatra scam (2011),[12] the Antrix Devas deal (2011),[13] and "Coalgate"(2012).[14] The Bofors scam (1989),[15] the Harshad Mehta stock market scam (1992),[16] the Jain Hawala case (1997),[17] the fodder scam (1996),[18] and the Telgi stamp paper scam (2003)[19] are slightly older milestones in India's history of corruption. The amount of money involved in these scams and the loss to the exchequer is mind-boggling. The va-

---

9   This refers to a number of corrupt deals involving overstated contracts entered into in preparation for the Commonwealth Games in 2010, leading to a total loss of Rs 23.42 billion, or US$433.7 million, to the exchequer.

10 In 2002, in a transfer okayed by the chief minister and revenue minister of Maharashtra, prime real estate land in Mumbai was allotted for the construction of a cooperative society for the retired personnel of the defense services, primarily Kargil War widows and their families, called the Adarsh Housing Society. Instead, politicians, bureaucrats, and high-ranking military officials were allotted flats in the society at low prices.

11 This scam involves the illegal undercharging by government officials to various telecom companies during the allocation of 2G licenses for cell phone subscriptions. According to the Comptroller and Auditor General of India, the estimated loss to the exchequer amounted to about Rs 1.76 trillion, or US$32.6 billion.

12 Indian Army chief General Vijay Kumar Singh had accused Tatra of supplying substandard military trucks to the army through its Indian partner BEML. The matter came to light when the army chief alleged he was offered a bribe to clear a consignment of substandard trucks. The scam was estimated at Rs 7.5 billion, or US$138.9 million.

13 The deal involved Indian Space Research Organisation leasing the S-band transponders on two satellites to Devas for broadcasting purposes by violating rules and procedures. The total loss was estimated at Rs 2 trillion, or US$37.03 billion.

14 The Comptroller and Auditor General of India has accused the Indian government of giving undue benefits to companies by distributing 155 coal acres in an arbitrary manner instead of auctioning them to the highest bidder during 2004–2009. The scam involves a loss of Rs 1.85 trillion, or US$34.26 billion.

15 Prime Minister Rajiv Gandhi and other politicians and bureaucrats were accused of receiving kickbacks from Bofors AB, a Swedish company, in connection with a contract for the supply of howitzer field guns. A loss of Rs 640 million, or US$11.85 million, was estimated.

16 Harshad Mehta used his position as a stockbroker for banks to illegally use bank-owned money to buy shares at a premium, leading to a boom in the stock market, which came crashing down when the scam was revealed in 1992. The total amount swindled was Rs 30 billion, or US$555.56 million.

17 This scam involved alleged payments to a number of Indian politicians through four *hawala* (an alternative informal money transfer system) brokers amounting to Rs 650 million, or US$12 million. The Jain brothers were found with a list of initials that matched senior politicians with large amounts against their names believed to be indicative of amounts paid to these politicians in bribes.

18 The animal husbandry department in the Bihar state government embezzled funds of around Rs 9.5 billion, or US$175.93 million, meant to purchase cattle fodder, medicines, and animal husbandry equipment, leading to the resignation of Chief Minister Laloo Prasad Yadav and others.

19 Abdul Karim Telgi printed and sold counterfeit stamp papers through 300 agents, leading to a loss of Rs 300 billion, or US$5.56 billion, to the government exchequer.

riety of these scams demonstrates that the problem of the use of public office for private gain is not limited to politicians alone but encompasses the police, the media, public officials and civil servants, education, the armed forces, and the private sector.[20] Corruption has also found its way into the judiciary.

Cost of Corruption

The cost of corruption to India is evident from the findings of a study by Global Financial Integrity, which reports that from 1948 through 2008 India lost US$213 billion in illicit financial flows (or illegal capital flight). That sum was siphoned off by a combination of corruption, bribery, and kickbacks; criminal activities; and efforts to shelter wealth from the country's tax authorities.[21]

If the loss to the exchequer via the scams listed above were to be aggregated, it would amount to more than Rs 4 trillion.[22] At a reinvestment rate of, say, 10 percent per annum, the total annual loss of revenue from this amount would exceed Rs 400 billion. To put the implication of such losses into perspective, consider the following: Rs 22.42 per day or Rs 8,183 a year is the minimum income required to be above the poverty line in rural India.[23] The annual revenue loss calculated above would lift 48 million rural citizens out of poverty.[24]

An equally grave cost of corruption to society and the country can be assessed through the findings of a study conducted on extralegal payments in the provision of driver's licenses in Delhi.[25] This study found that corruption has been institutionalized through middlemen who bribe officers of the government department responsible for testing applicants and issuing driving licenses. Nearly 71 percent of people obtaining licenses did not take the licensing exam, and 62 percent were unqualified to drive (according to the independent test) at the time they obtained a license. Most of these people learned how to drive after obtaining their licenses, and only became proficient to the extent that was useful to them personally, which means that a large number

---

20   Each of these categories earned high scores in the results of the Corruption Perception Index prepared by Transparency International. Transparency International, Consumer Perception Index, available at http://cpi.transparency.org/cpi2012/results/ (accessed Mar. 19, 2013).

21   Dev Kar, *The Drivers and Dynamics of Illicit Financial Flows from India: 1948–2008* (Nov. 2010), available at http://www.gfintegrity.org/storage/gfip/documents/reports/india/gfi_india.pdf (accessed Mar. 20, 2013).

22   The figures mentioned here are based on assessments of the Comptroller and Auditor General of India and news reports.

23   As fixed by the government of India for rural areas at 2011–12 prices.

24   As per government of India data from 2009–10, 29.8 percent of a population of 1.24 billion are below the poverty line.

25   Marianne Bertrand et al., *Obtaining a Driver's License in India: An Experimental Approach to Studying Corruption*, 122(4) Q. J. Economics 1639–1676 (2007). The study shows that corruption not only transfers resources from citizens to bureaucrats but also distorts the allocation of resources by the government in favor of those citizens willing and able to pay higher amounts for services.

of people on Indian roads are unqualified to drive at the socially optimal level (this is evident to even a casual observer of Indian roads). One can imagine how much damage to life and property is caused when so many drivers are insufficiently qualified to be on the road.

Corruption has become a driving force of state action, leading to increased bureaucratic hurdles and red tape and inspiring wasteful, unproductive, and harmful actions. For instance, massive projects and purchases are undertaken not because they are needed or viable but because a good deal of corrupt money can be generated from their associated transactions—a classic case of improper motive leading to misdirected action causing loss to public good. If corruption is a major factor in the making of economically and environmentally critical decisions such as whether a particular company is favored with a contract, whether to build a mega–power plant, or whether small industries should be protected or left exposed to competition from international firms, then the picture of governance that emerges is frightening.

Causes of Corruption

Different motives and different actors are involved in petty corruption and big-ticket corruption. Petty corruption, also referred to as "bureaucratic corruption,"[26] takes place at lower levels of authority. The actors involved are the lower bureaucrats and government officials. Big-ticket corruption, or grand corruption, is political corruption involving political and bureaucratic decision makers at high levels subverting rules of procedure and political institutions to misallocate resources—actions that eventually lead to institutional decay.

Recent research calls for a wide and comprehensive understanding of the causes of corruption. Robert Klitgaard's formulation of corruption as being a function of monopoly, discretion, and accountability[27] offers only a limited understanding of what causes corruption. It fails to take into account factors such as the briber's perspective in influencing public decision making and it does not fully appreciate the underlying incentives and risks.[28] Corruption needs to be recognized as a complex phenomenon, as the consequence of more deep-seated problems of policy distortion, institutional incentives, governance, and ethics.

---

26   Amundsen, *supra* note 2.

27   Corruption = Monopoly + Discretion − Accountability, as developed by Robert Klitgaard, *International Cooperation against Corruption*, 35(1) Fin. & Dev. 3 (1998), available at http://www.imf.org/external/pubs/ft/fandd/1998/03/pdf/klitgaar.pdf.

28   Hiram Chodosh, *Without Identifying the Underlying Causes We Cannot Combat Corruption*, Daily Star (Lebanon) (Nov. 5, 2009), available at http://www.dailystar.com.lb/Law/Nov/05/Without-identifying-the-underlying-causes-we-cannot-combat-corruption.ashx #axzz2QQh286eq (accessed Mar. 24, 2013).

Corruption should also be seen as being influenced by cultural factors such as social norms and values.[29] An underlying cause, for instance, is a marked deterioration of values and the emergence of greed as an accepted social norm.[30] Public interest has become subservient to private interests, and the commitment to working toward Nehru's vision of India has been lost. A breakdown in public institutions, the weakening of the rule of law, and the intertwining of business, politics, and crime are also key factors contributing to the extent of corruption today[31] and must be taken into account when strategies for corruption reform are formulated.

Political explanations of the causes of corruption find a connection between the level of legitimacy of the government and the level of corruption. There is a strong inverse, two-way connection between the strength of institutions and transparency in decision-making processes, on the one hand, and the level of corruption, on the other hand. Democratization provides new incentives for corruption, particularly in election campaigns and when democratically elected leaders are weighing the lucrative possibilities of privatizing state-owned resources.

Economic explanations of corruption focus on the cost and benefit analyses for an individual in committing a corrupt act. Links are also drawn between corruption in developing economies and their systems that permit capitalist exploitation of national resources. An economic perspective also focuses on variables such as salary levels, the mechanisms of control and deterrence, the selection of employees, and the systems of taxation and information. In India, corruption levels have risen noticeably since liberalization of the economy in 1991, attributed to increasing opportunities for errant action by public actors, insufficient salaries of public servants, and the lack of effective deterrent.

Big-ticket corruption in India is the result of a combination of excessive discretion vested in state actors, easy opportunities, a high demand for favors from, inter alia, private and corporate interests, and an abundant supply of black money, accompanied by falling levels of integrity and increasing levels of greed. The existing political system, which obliges political parties to raise considerable sums of money to run their election campaigns, is another perpetrator. Matters are simplified for the corrupt political decision maker by cooperative bureaucratic machinery, which makes it easier to cover one's tracks.

Petty corruption can be attributed to insufficient compensation for government servants and the lack of monitoring of day-to-day official activities. With limited infrastructure and increased workloads, government employees

---

29   Abigail Barr & Danila Serra, *Corruption and Culture: An Experimental Analysis*, 94(11) J. Pub. Economics 862–869 (2010).

30   Ram Manohar Reddy, *How Is India Doing (2012): Revisiting Amartya Sen's 1982 Essay* (Guhan Memorial Lecture, Chennai, India, Dec. 2012), available at http://www.cag.org.in/sites /default/files/Guhan%20Memorial%20Lecture%202012.pdf (accessed May 28, 2013).

31   *Id.*

are simply (illegally) using the means at their disposal to increase their income or finding ways to enrich themselves by distributing the scarce resources they control.

Reform Strategies

Reform strategists seeking to reduce petty corruption have advocated for the increased use of technology and a reduced interface between officials and citizens. The Right to Information Act, which was introduced in 2005, has been used as a tool to spur administrative action. These reforms have met with some success, for example, in Ahmedabad.[32]

Efforts to reform the big-ticket *avtar* have focused on reducing unbridled discretion, increasing transparency and public participation in decision-making processes, and expanding access to information. Attempts have also been made to set up an authority such as the *lokpal*.[33]

The Supreme Court of India has consistently taken a strong stand against corruption, aided by the tool of public interest litigation (PIL).[34] In the Jain Hawala case,[35] for instance, journalist Vineet Narain filed a PIL alleging that, due to the high-profile politicians linked to the case, the Central Bureau of Investigation (CBI) was not conducting a fair and proper investigation and was dragging its feet. To ensure that the CBI functioned in a manner unfettered by political interests, the court devised the doctrine of "continuing mandamus," ordering that the CBI do its lawful duty, with the court reviewing and supervising such discharge of duty to ensure that it was properly and lawfully done. With the use of this doctrine, and requiring the CBI to report to it on progress made, the court kept a watchful eye on the investigation to ensure that it proceeded efficiently. The Supreme Court also made it easier to commence investigations against senior bureaucrats by holding as *ultra vires* a directive that required the prior permission of the head of the department for such investigations.

The Supreme Court's orders in the more recent 2G scam have followed the same lines. The court has held that anticorruption laws must be interpreted to strengthen the fight against corruption and set a limit of three months on

---

32   Centre for Media Studies and Transparency International India, *India Corruption Study 2008,* available at http://www.transparencyindia.org/resource/survey_study/India%20Corruption%20Study%202008.pdf (accessed Mar. 20, 2013); compare with *India Corruption Study 2012, supra* note 8.

33   Roughly translated, *lokpal* means "people's protector" or "caretaker," implying a person or institution that protects public interest. Since 1968, there have been several failed attempts to pass a law in Parliament to establish the institution of a *lokpal* to inquire into allegations of corruption against public functionaries in the central government.

34   Where the court uses its constitutional jurisdiction to take up broad issues of public interests and passes wide-ranging orders for remedial action.

35   *Vineet Narain and Others v. Union of India* A.I.R. 1998 S.C. 889; refer to *supra* note 17.

the government's sanction for prosecution of cases under the Prevention of Corruption Act.[36]

An Assessment

All these strategies and reforms have had some positive impact. However, a critical element in any effective anticorruption regime—but one that is largely absent from current reform measures—is a strong, effective mechanism to detect, prosecute, and enforce the anticorruption laws. India's current legal provisions dealing with corruption and different aspects of it include the Prevention of Corruption Act (1988), the Indian Penal Code (offenses by public servants), the Prevention of Money Laundering Act (2002), the *Benami* Transactions Prevention Act (1988), and the Criminal Law Amendment Ordinance (1944). These laws, however, reflect the scale of the problem rather than the potency of the fight against it. As the U.S. Embassy commented in 1976, "there is a direct and positive relationship between laws against corruption and the extent of corruption itself, i.e., each such law only means that there are more people to bribe."[37]

A related failure in the Indian system is the proliferation of ineffective, overburdened oversight mechanisms such as internal audit, the Comptroller and Auditor General of India, and the Central Vigilance Commission, in addition to law enforcement agencies such as the CBI, the police, and the Anti-Corruption Bureau. The CBI lacks independence and is subject to the control of and interference from political and executive masters who are sometimes themselves suspected of being corrupt.

Dealing with Petty Corruption

While the focus in this chapter is on corruption at the apex of the political and bureaucratic pyramid, one cannot discount the magnitude of orderly, systematic everyday corruption that the ordinary citizen has to contend with. A random checklist, representing no more than a minuscule sample of the ways in which a citizen's quest for a reasonable quality of life is routinely vitiated in India, includes false weight of marketed produce; cheating in ration and fair-price shops; misdirection of benefits in targeting antipoverty programs; bribery to secure routine documents of attestations such as caste certificates; speed money outlays required for the purchase of loan sanctions, licenses, quotas, insurance and social security claims, water supply, electricity connections, and telephone connections; doctored meters in auto-rickshaws, taxis, and other vehicles; capitation fees for admission into schools and other educational institutions; bribes for jobs in the employment market; adulteration of food and drink, which often has fatal consequences (especially in the matter

---

36   *Dr. Subramanian Swamy v. Dr. Manmohan Singh* A.I.R. 2012 S.C. 1185.

37   *Supra* note 3.

of illicit alcohol); and cheating and extortion by professionals, such as medical practitioners. Corruption has become a way of life.

Because of the pervasive nature of petty corruption, a distinct decentralized prevention strategy is needed to deal with it. State initiatives—for example, in Madhya Pradesh, Bihar, Jammu and Kashmir, Delhi, Rajasthan, and Uttar Pradesh—that include legislation on the right to public services and that institutionalize grievance-redress system are steps in the right direction. These Right to Public Services Acts guarantee time-bound delivery of selected services to citizens and are significant because they place the onus of delivery on the service provider. They address the growing demands of citizens to improve public services, reduce corruption by imposing penalties on service providers for defaulting, impose a time frame for delivery of services, and universalize public services. In addition, what was under the citizens' charters[38] an administrative guarantee has been translated into a justiciable legal right under the various Right to Public Services Acts.

Some states have legislated to create the office of a *lokayukta*, an anticorruption ombudsman at the state level, similar to a *lokpal* proposed for the center. The Karnataka *lokayukta*, for example, has seen some success, although other states have experienced problems regarding the autonomy and powers of the *lokayukta*.

The central government has proposed a Citizen's Grievance Redressal Bill. The bill addresses grievances related to public services and corruption in service delivery, that is, petty corruption within a fixed time frame. The Grievance Redress Bill would cover the functioning of the panchayat,[39] government, public sector units, and police. It would look into complaints of violations of the citizens' charter formulated by each government department, identify liabilities of public servants in cases of default, and impose penalties for failure to deliver services or redress grievances in a "time-bound" manner.

Focus of Anticorruption Efforts in the Future

India has seen much attention focused on creating an anticorruption body. The agitation led by Anna Hazare, initially written off by the government, grew to mammoth proportions. Three reasons for this were

- Acceptance of Hazare as a morally upright person with no family stakes in politics, enhanced by his invocation of honesty and probity in public life as well as by his public image—his clothes of white *khadi* (homespun

---

38   Citizen charters are a bid to improve public services by the government. The charters let the public know the mandate of the concerned ministry or department, explain how one can get in touch with its officials, and describe what to expect by way of services and how to seek a remedy if something goes wrong.

39   Panchayats are units of decentralized administration in India at the village, block, and district level, responsible for certain specified matters of rural governance.

cloth) and Gandhi *topi* (cap) were a throwback to the figure of the Mahatma

- Massive support from the middle classes, until then thought to be complacent about corruption and unconcerned with many other public issues
- Vociferous media coverage, with prominent television anchors and newscasters strongly endorsing Hazare's movement, thereby raising its public profile very significantly

Reeling under a series of scams, and scorched by this outpouring of denunciation, the government backpedaled. It entered into negotiations with Hazare's team, agreed to several demands, and improved its own version of a *lokpal* bill. Hazare insisted on widening the scope of the bill and giving it more teeth. It seemed that mutually acceptable and effective legislation was on the horizon. Unfortunately, the all-or-nothing approach of the Hazare negotiating team, as well as doubts raised by other public campaigners on the capacity of a gargantuan *lokpal* to handle corruption from top to bottom, prevented an agreement from being reached. The momentum was lost, and a watereddown version emanated from the official side; once again the country was denied the creation of a strong, efficient, and effective anticorruption body. However, progress was made, and no doubt the fight will resume. Corruption is too widespread and damaging to disappear from the public eye.

The Indian debate has prompted reflection on the structure of an anticorruption body and the strategies needed to make it effective.

In an environment where corruption is widespread, encompassing the entire political and bureaucratic establishment, the question of where to focus reform efforts arises, given the limited resources available to those fighting corruption. The answer should be based on impact—and if the focus were to be on the top rung of the country's leadership, and on creating a more honest class of legislators, bureaucrats, and judges, the impact would be tremendous. An honest senior officer will discipline and control his or her subordinates, as well as set a department-wide example of probity. There is no point in focusing on the bottom rung; and the effort is unsustainable if the top is left untouched.

At present, however, no mechanism controls corruption at the highest levels of the executive, legislature, and judiciary; and if no new mechanism is devised, Indians can bid good-bye to hopes of development and good governance. If the leadership is cleansed, the lower rungs will automatically show more honesty. Cleanliness obeys the law of gravity; it percolates downward. Leadership has its tone and tenor—honest leaders will choose people like themselves for crucial positions and will relegate the others to lesser posts or neuter their ability to abuse power A significant proportion of the bribes demanded at the lower levels—by, say, the registrar of documents, the police inspector; and the petty revenue official—is funneled to the top. Another reason why the focus should be on corruption at the top level is because that is where administrative decisions are made that involve more money, affect more institutions, and impact a greater number of lives.

It is not necessarily true that the more honest officer is the more effective one, yet better governance is more likely to be had from the trustworthy plodder than the clever rascal. Creaming off the corrupt layer would improve personnel, practices, and policies. Efforts must therefore concentrate on the member of Parliament, the minister, the senior civil servant, and the judge. A remarkable feature of the profile of litigation is that cases between individuals involving property, contracts, and the like have been in decline; the vast majority of cases clogging the Indian courts involve relief sought to quash an illegal government order or to direct the government to perform its administrative duty. Many of these cases do not involve a point of law; they are simply instances of wrong administrative action, and the most common cause of such action or inaction is that the demand for a bribe was refused or a bribe was paid by a rival. A direct consequence of more honesty in the administration would be a more responsive and better-functioning government, in turn lowering the need for redress from courts.

Therefore, complaints made by the public at large regarding administrative lapses and individual cases of nonperformance should be redressed by suitable mechanisms, and a corruption-fighting method and strategy should be designed to catch the big fish and not the minnows.

A Model for Tackling Big-Ticket Corruption

A High-Profile Authority

Preferably enjoying constitutional status, the authority for tackling big-ticket corruption should be a permanent, full-time body ("the Authority"), with fixed tenure for members, which cannot be abolished or interfered with by the government. Persons for appointment to the Authority could be sourced from such fields as law, the judiciary, public life, civil service, the media, and academia. The members of the Authority should be limited in number, and anyone tainted with dishonesty or close to those in power should be excluded. One can find even in these days persons with integrity and sturdy independence. The members of this Authority should be selected by a panel drawn chiefly from the ranks of the judiciary and other independent constitutional functionaries such as the Comptroller and Auditor General of India and the Chief Election Commissioner; government officials should be in a minority on the selecting panel. The power to remove someone from office should be reserved to a panel consisting of senior judges.

Target: The Leadership of the Country

The Authority should be a policing mechanism for ministers, legislators, and bureaucrats. It should also oversee others in the pay of the "state," including employees of government agencies and state-owned corporations. However, the focus must be on the top ranks. The Authority must be empowered to train its sight on the leadership of the country—the prime minister, chief ministers, cabinet members and other ministers at national and state levels, civil servants above the rank of joint secretary, heads of statutory bodies and commissions, senior officers of government corporations, and agencies and institutions (including educational and medical institutions). A separate mechanism is suggested below for judges of the Supreme Court and High Courts.

Receipt of Complaints

The Authority should be able to receive complaints from any source, as well as initiate *suo moto* action. Provision should be made to enable the judiciary to refer matters to investigation, especially in cases where it becomes apparent to the Court that there is a corrupt motive behind the action of a public officer.

Protection for whistle-blowers should be part of the complaint-receipt scheme. In recent times, there have been a spate of attacks on those who have used the Right to Information Act to expose wrongdoing. The prospect of coming to harm because of disclosures is a real one. The Authority would have to find a way to receive complaints and material anonymously, as well as to provide witness protection.

Investigative Power

The Authority should have its own investigative body answerable only to it. The Authority should be able to recruit personnel and to select officers from the police and other investigative bodies such as the Central Bureau of Investigation.

There should be no requirement of prior sanction from the government before investigation can be commenced by the Authority.

These two powers—control over the investigative body and the granting of sanction to investigate offenses—are jealously guarded by government. Unless these powers are moved to the Authority, it will be rendered ineffectual. Thorough and impartial investigation should be the foundation of all cases; the investigating officers should have complete independence from all external sources. Their conditions of service and promotional prospects would have to be determined by the Authority. There is a strong case for a separate cadre and higher pay structure for these officers, who must have unblemished reputations for integrity.

Prosecuting Arm

In addition to having an investigative arm, the Authority should have a prosecution wing, answerable only to the Authority, which steps in once the Authority decides on the basis of investigation that the case is fit for prosecution. Choosing and overseeing prosecutors are critical to the success of the Authority—the strongest cases can fail with an inefficient or, worse, corrupt prosecutor. Currently, prosecutors are appointed by the government of the day. Given the anti-incumbency nature of election results, each election tends to bring to power a government eager to prosecute the outgoing government. But given the backlog of cases and the delays in bringing cases to trial, by the time a case can be heard, the accused are likely to be back in power. They will then devise strategies to derail cases against them, including instructions to prosecutors to withdraw cases.

Interim Action: Person and Property

Once a prima facie case is made and the decision to prosecute is made, the accused should be suspended from continuing in office so that he or she cannot use the power of his or her office to influence the proceedings in the case.

Assets suspected to be ill-gotten gains should be frozen, whether they are held in the name of the public officer or his or her ally.

Special Courts

Because the Authority will focus its attention on the candidates for and the holders of high office, the corrupt must be evicted from office speedily and the innocent exonerated with equal alacrity. Magistrates and Sessions judges are overburdened with a mass of criminal cases, and multiple appeals are available against their orders. It is thus necessary for cases to be heard by a higher court. What is needed is a "Special Court" headed by a senior judge. When such a court is to be constituted, the Chief Justice of India would be approached to appoint a sitting or retired High Court or Supreme Court judge. The trial could then be conducted expeditiously. Interim applications could be disposed of quickly and directions given or refused. No appeal would lie against such interim orders. "Expeditiously" would be defined as a period of a few months. Appeals, too, should be disposed of early, but the conviction and bar arising from conviction would hold unless set aside in appeal.

Punishment

Punishment needs to be deterrent in nature—that is to say, it ought to be so heavy that others will think many times before committing such offenses themselves. Those who deprive the state and its citizens of vast amounts of money that could have provided food, shelter, and basic human rights to thousands or even millions of people must receive a punishment equal to the harm caused. The breach of trust by a person holding an office of public trust should bring with it corresponding retribution. If murder of one person can invite a punishment for life, there is no reason why the high-level corrupter whose actions cause grave harm to innumerable people should not receive a similar sentence, with a component of hard labor.

Fines should be commensurate with the gravity of the offense and the extent of private enrichment.

Recovery of Ill-Gotten Gains

Recovery of assets ought to follow automatically after conviction. To Caesar must be rendered what has been pilfered from the state and its people. Where the public servant is proved to be in possession of wealth disproportionate to known sources of income, the excess should vest in the state. The deterrent effect of prosecution and conviction is minimized if one is able to enjoy the gains of one's crime after serving out a sentence, especially when the gains are large enough to be enjoyed by one's children and their children.

Many corrupt officials hold movable and immovable properties not in their own names, but in the names of close relatives or friends. This is referred to as *benami* property (i.e., property held under a false or misleading name; *benami* also refers to the person holding such property). The anticorruption law should ensure that such vicarious holding is no shield, and that where the connection is proved and the *benami* has no other source of income to explain the wealth, these assets are liable to be forfeited to the state.

Apart from creating an Authority for investigation and prosecution, and a Special Court for judicial determination, certain other measures are necessary to check corruption.

The Onus of Proof and the Right to Remain Silent

It is not easy to trace the path of offer and acceptance of the bribe. It is easier to identify assets that could have been acquired from the proceeds of corrupt acts. When the possession of assets, by either oneself or a *benami*, in excess of declared sources of income is established, the onus should shift to the accused to show how he or she acquired such property. If the onus is not discharged, conviction should follow.

Another issue is whether the normal rule against self-incrimination should be applied to such accused when the issue is one of acceptance of illegal gratification for public acts or of misappropriation of public assets. There ought to be a distinction between private transactions and public acts when balancing the individual right to remain silent with the need to obtain information on an offense of state corruption. A public officer must be prepared to give an account of his or her public acts when called upon. As regards the right to remain silent, public servants ought to be treated as a category distinct from the rest. This is because they can wrap the cloak of secrecy around their acts using their office, and the effects of such corruption are gravely deleterious to society. Considering the ramifications of such actions, and the overarching need for probity in public life, there are sufficient reasons to review the doctrine of the right to remain silent to see if an exception should be carved out when dealing with corruption proceedings. This may require a constitutional amendment, which can be justified on the overarching need of curbing corruption, which destroys the rule of law and the fabric of governance.

Stopping the Corrupt from Entering the Legislature

In the parliamentary system of democratic governance, the political executive, the ministers, are drawn from the legislative ranks of the majority party.
A disturbing percentage of members of Parliament and state assemblies have
corruption charges against them.[40] They were not barred from standing for
election or continuing in office. That is because they are presumed to be innocent until proven guilty, a fundamental postulate of fair legal systems. It
is also because it takes a long—a very long—time to reach a conviction in
the courts given the backlogs, technicalities of procedure, and innumerable
objections raised and ingenious obstacles put in place by clever defense lawyers intent on delaying their clients' trials. The case against a prominent chief
minister charged with acquisition of hugely disproportionate assets has been
pending in court for no less than 16 years. The election law in the form of the
Representation of Peoples Act allows persons facing criminal charges to contest elections. This is useful in a scenario in which criminal law is used as a
tool and/or strategy by rivals to paint each other black. It is useless when the
trial is indefinitely postponed.

The anticorruption strategy should respect the presumptive right of innocence while at the same time ensuring that a person guilty of corruption is
denied access to, or tenure in, the portals of legislative power. The main problem is how to exclude from the election process persons who are suspected
of corruption and who have charges filed against them, which indicates that
the investigation has reached a prima facie opinion of guilt. The solution is
an expedited trial. The potential candidate should give notice well ahead of
the election that he or she intends to stand as a candidate and wants the case
to be disposed of early so that he or she may stand without having charges
pending. The case should receive priority for trial. Conviction, unless upset in
appeal, should be a bar to standing for office. In the case of those who face a
corruption charge while holding office, here again a priority trial conducted
within three to six months should determine the issue of culpability. If found
guilty, the person should forfeit office. While an appeal should be permissible,
resumption of office should await success in the appeal.[41]

---

40   Based on studies of the self-declared affidavits filed by candidates before the National Election Commission contesting the national and state assembly elections, the Association for
Democratic Reforms found that 98 candidates with corruption cases under the Prevention of
Corruption Act have been given tickets by various political parties in the 2009 national election
and all state assembly elections held since 2008. Thirty-six of these candidates won the elections. These include 4 sitting MPs in Lok Sabha 2009, 3 sitting MPs in the current Rajya Sabha
and 29 MLAs in various state assemblies. Association for Democratic Reforms, *Report on Law
Makers Facing Corruption Charges under Prevention of Corruption Act: Role of Political Parties* (Jan.
2013), available at http://adrindia.org/sites/default/files/7%20MPs%20and%2029%20MLAs
%20declare%20cases%20under%20Prevention%20of%20Corruption%20Act%20_English
_0%20latest.pdf (accessed Jul. 31, 2013).

41   In a recent judgment, *Lily Thomas v. Union of India,* dated July 10, 2013, the Supreme Court
has in fact accepted the validity of the point made here that a convicted person should not
continue to hold office pending the appeal. The court struck down Section 8(4) of the Representation of People's Act, which provided that a legislator if convicted while holding office
could continue in that office provided that he file an appeal within three months.

This would turn on its head the reliance of the accused on the long delays of the law, and the capacity of corrupt officials and their lawyers to enhance such delay and prolong the trial. If it is provided that the candidate cannot stand for office until the trial is completed, then the interest of the accused is to complete the trial expeditiously. It will then only have to be ensured that the prosecution does not delay, and that meritorious objections of the defense receive quick resolution. This is possible by devising the structure mentioned above. Thus, the oft-repeated "law will take its own course" mantra, which now means a sluggish course much to the comfort of the accused, will become a demand from them that the law take a quick course.

This strategy will keep the dishonest from entering the legislature. It will tend to keep a person honest while in the legislature. If these objectives are achieved, even partially, India will have much cleaner political personnel and practices

Disclosure of Assets

All public servants—judges, ministers, civil servants, legislators—should be required to disclose their assets and those of their family members at the time of entering public office, and to keep the list of disclosed assets updated on a periodical basis. This list would provide the benchmark for the requirement that any additional assets held would have to be explained; failing to provide such an explanation would raise the presumption that they were acquired by corrupt means.

Corrupt Judges

Most legal systems were founded and still operate on the assumption that the judiciary is safe from corruption; those systems have consequently not devised systems to test that assumption. However, times have changed. At one time, the phrase "honest judge" was thought to be a superfluity; all judges were presumed honest, so where was the need for the adjective? Now, in the minds of many, that presumption does not hold good. The situation is serious enough to demand the creation of a system specifically designed to handle corruption in the judicial ranks.

The Authority, as outlined in this chapter, may not be suited to combating corruption within the judiciary, for the simple reason that all cases prosecuted by the Authority would be tried by the judiciary. There is an inherent tension when the judge could potentially be hauled up by the person prosecuting the case (i.e., the Authority). If a particular judge dismisses a slew of cases filed by the Authority, the latter may be a little more eager to investigate a complaint against the former. This possibility may also weigh in the mind of the judge; if so, the scales of justice would not be held evenly. Just as much as the need for probity of the judiciary would warrant a body to check corruption within it, the independence of the judiciary would require that the composition of such a body not detract from the need of the judge to be free from apprehension in the discharge of his or her judicial function. At the same time, such a body should not be composed only of judicial personnel; brethren tend to close ranks and be somewhat kind to themselves. A measure of external presence and transparency will bring the needed sharpness to the endeavor. The prescription would be a body similar to but separate from the Authority. This body would be composed of senior serving and retired judges, with a presence of legislative and executive representation and headed perhaps by a former president or former chief justice. It would have its own investigative and prosecution wing; the judge would not hear cases while the case proceeded at a quick pace; and conviction would entail, among other things, the recovery of assets.

While on the subject of the judiciary, it needs to be said that it has not taken its share of the blame for the tardiness of the justice system in dealing with and deciding the cases of corruption against the high and mighty. Perhaps there is insufficient recognition of the direct connection between disposal of such cases and reducing high-level corruption, while also raising levels of governance. Wonderful lessons would be taught, and remembered, if even a handful of corruption-tainted leaders were to see the inside of jails for long periods, and be deprived of at least some of their assets. It is difficult to understand why a Supreme Court or High Court judge does not get outraged by the languishing of corruption cases for double-digit years, while hearing one more appeal regarding an interlocutory plea that is obviously designed to delay the trial. If the court can bring itself to monitor investigation of cases of scams, surely it ought to monitor the progress of the trial of such cases. Delay in judicial process has become part and parcel of the Indian way of doing things. It is taken so much for granted that, combined with the respect for the judiciary (so well deserved on other counts), citizens live uncomplainingly with the disastrous effects on governance when the course of the law is slow and meandering and often dies on the sands of time.

Conclusion

India can ill afford the losses that are being inflicted on it by corruption. The amount of money lost to the country through the scams that regularly descend on it is mind-boggling. If corruption is substantially curbed, the state will be able to provide far better infrastructure, amenities, and living conditions to its citizens. It will be able to spur development and significantly reduce levels of poverty. India has a population of 1.3 billion people, 65 percent of whom are accepted by the government to be poor.[42] Until some real and effective anticorruption measures are introduced and enforced, every welfare or development scheme introduced by the government will be seen and used only as another opportunity for bureaucrats and their political masters to line their pockets at

---

42   S. Rukmini & M. K. Venu, *Beyond the Debate, Govt. Accepts 65% Indians Are Poor*, The Hindu (Jul. 24, 2013), available at http://www.thehindu.com/news/national/beyond-the-debate-govt -accepts-65-indians-are-poor/article4948698.ece (accessed Jul. 31, 2013).

the expense of the have-nots. No country can prosper with the degradation of administration and governance that corruption brings in its wake.

Corrupt public office holders benefit from the current lackadaisical implementation of inadequate laws. The Supreme Court exerts itself to pursue some high-profile cases, even crossing the border that separates its powers from those of the legislature and the executive. However, there are limits to what even an activist court can do; while it can provide the impetus in a few cases, it cannot handle the problem at large. The public, previously somnolent in the face of corruption, is currently galvanized, but there are limits, too, to what can be achieved by public outrage.

The pervasiveness of corruption could dramatically change, however, if a tough anticorruption body were to be established and the law strengthened to curb corruption. These steps could well tip the scales against corruption. This chapter has argued for the creation of just such a body, one with sharp teeth provided by changes to the law. It is true that transparency, innovative administrative strategies, incentives, and rewards all have their roles to play in the fight against corruption. However, given the extent of corruption and the shamelessness of its practitioners, tough measures will be heeded more than soft approaches. The times demand sticks and stones.

Leveling the Playing Field

A Race to the Top

BART STEVENS AND ROBERT DELONIS

Private sector enterprises in developing countries are key partners in executing the World Bank development mandate, as well as in its efforts to foster integrity in the projects it finances. The private sector drives job creation and the delivery of goods, works, and services needed to end extreme poverty and promote shared prosperity. As the World Bank Development Committee said in its April 2013 vision statement, "the most effective path out of poverty is through access to more and better jobs; this requires rapid and broad-based growth centering on the strong contribution of the private sector."[1]

Opportunity, inclusion, and equity are essential to private sector success. Businesses require a level playing field of economic competition in order to grow and thrive. Fraud and corruption undermine a level playing field: they distort economic incentives, stifle fair competition, and impose a heavy burden on small businesses. All these effects choke economic growth.[2] Moreover, when misconduct occurs in Bank-supported projects, the funds provided by the World Bank are misappropriated—with, in the World Bank's case, the

---

The authors would like to recognize the important contributions from several Integrity Vice Presidency staff members, especially Lisa Bostwick, who provided much of the content for the paper's compliance program discussion, Mamta Kaushal, and Paul Haynes. We would like to give special thanks to Lisa K. Miller, Senior Counsel in LEG, and Steve Zimmermann, INT Director of Operations, for their insightful comments during chapter preparation as well as INT interns, Meng Lu and Tuyet (Amy) Tu. The findings, interpretations, and conclusions expressed herein are those of the authors and do not necessarily reflect the view of the World Bank Group, its Board of Directors, or the governments they represent.

1   Joint Ministerial Committee of the Boards of Governors of the Bank and the Fund on the Transfer of Real Resources to Developing Countries (hereinafter the Development Committee), *A Common Vision for the World Bank Group* (Development Committee paper, Intl. Monetary Fund, World Bank, Apr. 3, 2013).

2   *See,* for example, Cheryl W. Gray & Daniel Kaufmann, *Corruption and Development,* Fin. & Dev. 7–8 (Mar. 1998), arguing that bribery raises transaction costs, increases economic insecurity, leads to inefficient economic outcomes, most adversely impacts small businesses, and undermines state legitimacy; Susan Rose-Ackerman, *"Grand" Corruption and the Ethics of Global Business,* 26 J. Banking & Fin. 1889 (2002), arguing that corruption has significant adverse economic effects, sufficient to oblige multinational companies not to engage in it; Roger P. Alford, *A Broken Windows Theory of International Corruption,* 73 Ohio St. L.J. 1253, 126–169 (2012), arguing that high corruption correlates with reduced economic competitiveness, reduced human development status, and weak civil liberties; and Claes Sandgren, *Combating Corruption: The Misunderstood Role of Law,* 39 Intl. Law 717 (2005), noting corruption's many adverse effects and proposing legal measures to help remedy the problem.

borrowing country's taxpayers bearing the cost—and the development benefits of those projects are undermined.[3]

As Heineman and Heimann observed, "there is a cultural dimension to anti-corruption, which involves transmitting positive values and norms that can strengthen [other] enforcement, prevention, and state-building measures," that needs to be pursued to tackle corruption.[4] Over the past decade, the World Bank has moved to the forefront in developing tools that foster a culture of anticorruption through partnerships with the private sector. This chapter discusses three such tools, which were developed by the World Bank Integrity Vice Presidency (INT): the Voluntary Disclosure Program (VDP),[5] negotiated resolution agreements (NRAs),[6] and the Integrity Compliance Officer (ICO).[7]

The chapter begins by situating INT within the World Bank's governance and anticorruption activities and policies. It briefly introduces the VDP, NRAs, and the ICO, before using a hypothetical case study to demonstrate how these tools are used in INT's work. Following the case study, the chapter returns to each program to discuss it in greater detail. In so doing, the chapter shows how the VDP, NRAs, and the ICO can help replace a "race to the bottom" of bribery with a "race to the top" in which all can access and benefit from inclusive, equitable competition.

The Integrity Context

The World Bank's pursuit of policies and solutions that facilitate private sector growth and competition is fundamental to its mission. The Bank is obliged,

---

3   *See*, for example, UN Development Programme, *Anticorruption Practice Note* 7 (Mar. 2004), which asserts that corruption reduces funds available for social spending; increases costs for health, education, and public services; and disproportionately impacts the poor; Daniel Kaufman, Aart Kraay, & Pablo Zoido-Labaton, *Governance Matters* 1 (World Bank Dev. Res. Group, Macroeconomics and Growth, and World Bank Inst., Governance, Reg. and Fin., Policy Working Paper No. 2196, Oct. 1999), asserting that better governance is causally related to better development outcomes, such as lower infant mortality and higher literacy rates, available at http://info.worldbank.org/governance/wgi/pdf/govmatters1.pdf; and Jong-Sung You & Sanjeev Khagram, *Inequality and Corruption* 5 (Hauser Ctr. for Nonprofit Organizations Working Paper No. 22; Kennedy Sch. Govt. Working Paper No. RWP04-001, Harv. U., Nov. 2004), asserting that there is a significant relationship between high levels of corruption and high levels of income inequality.

4   *See* Ben W. Heineman Jr. & Fritz Heimann, *The Long War against Corruption*, 85 For. Affairs 75, 77 (2006).

5   *See* World Bank Group, *VDP Guidelines for Participants* (undated) (hereinafter *VDP Guidelines*), available at http://www.worldbank.org/vdp; and World Bank Group, *Voluntary Disclosure Program Terms & Conditions* (n.d.) (hereinafter *VDP Terms & Conditions*), available at http://www.worldbank.org/vdp.

6   World Bank Group, *World Bank Sanctions Procedures*, 31–34, art. XI (Apr. 15, 2012) (hereinafter *Sanctions Procedures*).

7   *See* World Bank Group, *Frequently Asked Questions: Integrity Compliance at the World Bank Group* (n.d.) (hereinafter *Integrity Compliance FAQ*), available at http://siteresources.world bank.org/INTDOII/Resources/Q_&_A_for_ICO.pdf.

under its Articles of Agreement, to ensure that its funds are used for their intended purposes.[8] The World Bank fulfills these goals in a number of ways:

- The Bank works with member-country governments to promote national regulatory and macroeconomic environments that encourage investment and innovation,[9] stimulating competition and growth.

- The Bank's procurement policies—reflected in its procurement and consultant guidelines[10]—require open, transparent competition, along with ethical bidder and contractor behavior, in Bank-financed tenders. These requirements help ensure that borrowers receive quality goods, works, nonconsultant services, and consultant services at competitive prices.

- The World Bank prohibits fraud, corruption, collusion, and coercion in its projects, and will sanction firms and individuals found to have engaged in one of these prohibited practices, as well as refer its findings to national authorities.[11] By excluding such actors from its projects, the World Bank helps promote equitable competition.

INT is principally responsible for investigating allegations that parties have engaged in practices that are sanctionable by the World Bank. INT investigations usually involve the collection and analysis of project, tender, and contract documents and information, as well as interviews with involved persons and, in some cases, physical site inspections. Firms that attempt to prevent INT from investigating—for example, by destroying documents,

---

8   International Bank for Reconstruction and Development Articles of Agreement, art. III, sec. 5(B); International Development Association Articles of Agreement, art. V, sec. 1(g); and International Finance Corporation Articles of Agreement.

9   The Development Committee, *Update on the Bank's Business Modernization: Results, Openness, and Accountability* (Apr. 11, 2012), available at http://web.worldbank.org/WBSITE/EXTERNAL /DEVCOMMEXT/0,,pagePK:64000837~piPK:64001152~theSitePK:277473~contentMDK:2316 6515,00.html.

10   *See* World Bank, *Guidelines: Procurement of Goods, Works, and Non-consulting Services under IBRD Loans and IDA Credits and Grants by World Bank Borrowers* (Jan. 2011) (hereinafter *Procurement Guidelines*); and World Bank, *Guidelines: Selection and Employment of Consultants under IBRD Loans & IDA Credits and Grants by World Bank Borrowers* (Jan. 2011) (hereinafter *Consultant Guidelines*).

11   The definitions of these sanctionable practices are found in the Bank's procurement, consultant, and anticorruption guidelines. *See Procurement Guidelines, supra* note 10, at 6–7, para. 1.16; *Consultant Guidelines, supra* note 10, at 9–10, para. 1.23; and World Bank, *Guidelines on Preventing and Combating Fraud and Corruption in Projects Financed by IBRD Loans and IDA Credits and Grants* 3, para. 7 (Oct. 15, 2006) (hereinafter *Anticorruption Guidelines*). The Bank's sanctioning jurisdiction extends only to entities that participate in, or seek to participate in, Bank-financed activities; the Bank cannot sanction the public officials of member-country governments. *See,* for example, World Bank Group, *The World Bank Group's Sanctions Regime: Information Note* 17–23 (undated) (hereinafter *Sanctions Information Note*), available at http://siteresources.worldbank.org/EXTOFFEVASUS/Resources/The_World _Bank_Group_Sanctions_Regime.pdf. The Bank attempts to address misconduct by public officials of member-country governments through referral reports and bilateral engagements with relevant authorities.

threatening witnesses, or preventing INT from inspecting relevant books and records—may be subject to sanctions for engaging in obstructive practices.[12]

If INT obtains sufficient evidence to allow it to conclude that a party engaged in a corrupt, fraudulent, collusive, coercive, or obstructive practice, it can commence a case in the World Bank's administrative sanctions system, through which independent decision makers decide whether and how to sanction the responsible entity.[13] Sanctions apply throughout the World Bank, including private sector work by the International Finance Corporation (IFC) and the Multilateral Investment Guarantee Agency (MIGA) and through the Bank's partial risk guarantee (PRG), project-based partial credit guarantee (PCG), and carbon finance activities.[14] Because the nature and severity of misconduct vary among cases, the World Bank permits the imposition of a variety of sanctions, including letters of reprimand, conditional nondebarment, debarment with conditional release, debarment for a fixed period of time, indefinite debarment, and restitution.[15]

To enhance the deterrent effect of these sanctions, five major multilateral development banks (MDBs)—the African Development Bank, the Asian Development Bank, the European Bank for Reconstruction and Development, the Inter-American Development Bank, and the World Bank—have harmonized their definitions of sanctionable practices and have agreed, subject to an opt-out provision, to cross-debar entities for a period that exceeds one year.[16]

Competition with Integrity: Expanding the Tool Kit

Sanctions help level the playing field by excluding actors that seek to undermine open and fair competition. But no authority can detect and sanction all misconduct. Thus, cooperative tools that promote broad, cultural change within business are necessary for anticorruption success. INT developed the VDP, NRAs, and the ICO to mitigate the impact of fraud and corruption risks

---

12   *Procurement Guidelines, supra* note 10, at 7, para. 1.16(a)(v); *Consultant Guidelines, supra* note 10, at 10, para. 1.23(a)(v); *Anticorruption Guidelines, supra* note 11, at 3, para. 7.

13   For a description of the Bank's sanctions system and its evolution and development, *see* Conrad C. Daly and & Frank A. Fariello Jr., *Transforming through Transparency: Opening Up the World Bank's Sanctions Regime*, in *Legal Innovation and Empowerment for Development*, vol. 4, 101–122 (Hassane Cissé, Sam Muller, Chantal Thomas, & Chenguang Wang eds., 2013).

14   For IFC, MIGA, PRGs, PCGs, and carbon finance activities, the sanctions regime is operationalized "through the inclusion of appropriate provisions in their financing/guarantee documents, technical assistance agreements, and other documentation. Each entity has adopted anticorruption guidelines, which are attached to such entity's respective legal agreements and which further explain the definitions and provide examples relevant to the [World Bank Group's] private sector operations. IFC discloses the sanctions process to prospective partners through its 'mandate letter,' which defines the scope and basic terms of IFC's investment." *Sanctions Information Note, supra* note 11, at 13.

15   See *Sanctions Procedures, supra* note 6, at 23–24, sec. 9.01.

16   Agreement for the Mutual Enforcement of Debarment Decisions (Apr. 9, 2010), available at http://siteresources.worldbank.org/NEWS/ Resources/AgreementForMutualEnforcement ofDebarmentDecisions.pdf.

on World Bank–supported projects and thus enhance development results. The effectiveness and potential impact of these tools depend on the level of sophistication of the national regulatory and governance environments—areas in which the Bank provides capacity-building support to member-country governments.

The Voluntary Disclosure Program

The VDP, launched in 2006, enables INT to obtain information about fraud and corruption in World Bank–supported projects through voluntary and confidential disclosures by firms. Any firm, nongovernmental organization (NGO), or individual is eligible to apply to enter the VDP, save those that are already under investigation by INT.[17]

The VDP incentivizes voluntary corporate governance and integrity reform. VDP participants are not subject to World Bank sanctions for past misconduct, and their identities are kept confidential. In exchange, they must

- agree to not engage in misconduct in the future;

- disclose to INT the results of an internal investigation into past misconduct on Bank-financed contracts signed during or in effect for at least the five years preceding their entry into the VDP; and

- implement an internal compliance program that is monitored by a World Bank–approved compliance monitor for at least three years.[18]

The incentives for corporate reform are backstopped with a significant deterrent. If a participant joins the VDP and then violates a material term or condition, it is automatically debarred for 10 years.[19]

Negotiated Resolution Agreements

NRAs provide an efficient way to resolve ongoing investigations or sanctions cases. They can save considerable resources while providing certainty of outcome for all parties. Although NRAs are generally case specific and leave open the possibility of further sanctions for other misconduct, they often lead to a lesser sanction than would be expected through the full adjudicative process.

Every entity subject to sanction may explore the possibility of an NRA with the World Bank. However, INT retains the discretion to decide whether to settle a particular case. As a minimum, an NRA includes:

- A voluntary admission (or an agreement not to contest) that the entity engaged in sanctionable misconduct

- An agreed-on sanction, usually a period of debarment in excess of one year

---

17 *VDP Guidelines, supra* note 5, at 8–9.

18 *VDP Terms & Conditions, supra* note 5.

19 *Id.,* at 6–7, paras. 43–47.

- The implementation of a corporate compliance program (when appropriate) and cooperation with INT, including on investigations into misconduct by the entity or other parties
- Other case-specific conditions

NRAs are negotiated by INT and cleared by the general counsel, as well as reviewed by the Bank's suspension and debarment officer (SDO)[20] to confirm voluntariness and that the agreed-on sanction falls within the World Bank sanctioning guidelines.[21]

The Integrity Compliance Officer

In cases resulting in a period of debarment with release conditioned on corporate reform, the ICO works with the sanctioned entity to develop good business practices through the creation of robust corporate integrity compliance systems. In many cases, to demonstrate rehabilitation, the sanctioned party must satisfy the ICO that it has in place—and has implemented for an adequate period—an effective integrity compliance program within the context of its operating environment. To help the private sector develop such programs, the World Bank has a set of integrity compliance guidelines that incorporate recognized best practices in good governance and the prevention of fraud and corruption.[22] The integrity compliance guidelines also provide the framework that the ICO uses to determine whether a sanctioned party has implemented an effective compliance program and should be released from sanction. ICO sanction-release decisions may be appealed to the World Bank Sanctions Board.[23]

The decision to use the VDP or NRA options and the ICO's compliance program involves a detailed assessment of case-specific factors. The following hypothetical case study demonstrates how this analysis proceeds.

Hypothetical Case Study: Reform Co.

Reform Co. is a global supplier of goods with several Bank-financed contracts concentrated in one region of the world. It has other contracts financed by other MDBs.

---

20 On March 31, 2013, the Office of Evaluation and Suspension (OES) was renamed the Office of Suspension and Debarment (OSD), and the evaluation and suspension officer (EO) was renamed the suspension and debarment officer (SDO).

21 World Bank Group, *World Bank Sanctioning Guidelines* (Jan. 1, 2011) (hereinafter *Sanctioning Guidelines*), available at http://siteresources.worldbank.org/EXTOFFEVASUS/Resources/WorldBankSanctioningGuidelines.pdf.

22 World Bank Group, *Summary of the World Bank Group Integrity Compliance Guidelines* (n.d.), available at http://siteresources.worldbank.org/INTDOII/Resources/IntegrityComplianceGuidelines_2_1_11web.pdf.

23 *See Sanctions Procedures, supra* note 6, at 27–28, sec. 9.03(e).

Due to the entry into force of new and expanded anticorruption legislation affecting the company's operations, Reform Co. undertook an internal due diligence exercise to review its contracts, subcontractors, and operating methods in a number of developing countries. During this exercise, it discovered that one of its subsidiaries had engaged in misconduct in a number of Bank-financed contracts. Reform Co. engaged external counsel to conduct an in-depth review of the identified misconduct and determine whether such misconduct was limited to the subsidiary or more widespread. External counsel prepared detailed reports with evidentiary exhibits and recorded interviews.

Based on the external counsel's findings, Reform Co. decided to disclose the results of its investigations to local authorities and to seek settlements that included some degree of leniency of sanction. The firm expected these settlements to eventually become public. Reform Co. also began voluntarily refraining from bidding on Bank-financed contracts before it contacted the Bank about the discovered misconduct.

Disclosure to INT

Reform Co. approached INT to voluntarily disclose the misconduct that its internal review had discovered in Bank-financed contracts. Prior to its self-disclosure, the firm was neither investigated by INT nor the subject of a complaint in INT's internal databases.

Reform Co. detailed the findings of its internal review to INT, and its external counsel made a presentation to INT detailing how Reform Co.'s subsidiary colluded with a number of suppliers to divide up MDB-financed contracts. To ensure their success, the firms made corrupt payments to government project implementation officials and submitted fraudulent documents in their bids. When the subsidiary later ceased paying bribes, it found that the project-implementing agency delayed its payments for work completed under several Bank-financed contracts.

Reform Co. provided INT with copies of relevant documents and interview records. These materials were a treasure trove of useful information about corrupt and collusive schemes in several countries, agents involved in those schemes, joint venture partners that engaged in bribery, and competitors who appeared to be using similar schemes to win contracts.

Reform Co. asked INT how it could resolve its subsidiary's engagement in sanctionable practices and sought assistance in determining the illicit profits that it had earned through its misconduct so that it could disgorge these funds to appropriate authorities. The firm told INT that, in response to its investigative findings, it had fired key subsidiary officials, replaced them with a new management team, and introduced a number of changes to its compliance program. It also, as noted earlier, voluntarily ceased bidding on Bank-financed contracts.

INT Considerations and Case Resolution

When evaluating a case like Reform Co's., INT gives significant weight to the firm's response to identified misconduct, including voluntary restraint from bidding, voluntary disclosures of useful information to INT, offers of financial or other remedies, termination of involved staff, and managerial and compliance program reforms.

For Reform Co., most of these factors applied, which favored an amicable resolution—as did the fact that all the available evidence of misconduct came from Reform Co. itself, requiring no INT time or effort. Reform Co.'s response upon discovering its subsidiary's misconduct supported its claim that it would not re-engage in misconduct and that it had a genuine desire to compete on a level playing field. As a result, an NRA was entered into between the Bank and Reform Co. pursuant to which the agreed-on sanction came into effect.

Cooperation and Compliance

From Reform Co.'s detailed disclosures, INT was able to refer specific details of misconduct by public officials to appropriate national authorities. INT used the details of the schemes disclosed by Reform Co. to advise the Bank's operational units on how to prevent similar schemes from succeeding under future Bank-financed projects.

During settlement negotiations, the ICO meets with companies to discuss their compliance program and lay the groundwork for the compliance components of the settlement. Here, Reform Co. informed INT that it already had an existing compliance program and that it had made improvements to that program based on the findings of its internal investigation. Based on these assertions, the ICO met with Reform Co. during settlement negotiations to learn more about the program and assess it against the Bank's integrity compliance guidelines. The program turned out to be comprehensive, and the modifications already made by Reform Co. filled the gaps observed by the ICO. As a result, Reform Co. was given a reduction in its sanction for the program improvements,[24] and once the settlement came into effect, the ICO monitored Reform Co.'s program for a limited period of time before concluding that it was fully implemented and effective.

Details and Lessons of INT's Cooperative Tools

The Voluntary Disclosure Program

The crucial consideration for VDP participation is whether the prospective participant is eligible to enter the program. If the firm is under an active INT

---

24   The World Bank's sanctioning guidelines generally permit up to a 50 percent reduction in a firm's sanction for voluntary corrective action, such as the establishment or improvement, and implementation, of an effective corporate compliance program. *See Sanctioning Guidelines, supra* note 21, at 4–5.

investigation, or maintaining confidentiality is practically impossible (as was the case for Reform Co.), the VDP is generally not an appropriate option.

The VDP is a non-negotiable program. Its terms and conditions are standard and are publicly disclosed on the INT website to ensure the predictability of participant commitments.[25] Participants bear the costs associated with complying with the program (although assistance from the Bank can be sought in exceptional instances),[26] and the mandatory 10-year debarment for noncompliance with the program's terms is a significant penalty.[27] However, companies' disclosure of misconduct under the VDP offers them confidentiality.[28] Under the VDP, INT redacts disclosures made to member countries, Bank management and staff, and other stakeholders.

Although the VDP's confidentiality protections limit how INT can use VDP-provided information, INT substantially benefits from accessing that information. The VDP allows INT wide-ranging access to evidence on the nature and scope of corruption in Bank-financed projects—and it does so more quickly, completely, and inexpensively than is possible with traditional investigative techniques. This information feeds directly into INT's work protecting other Bank-financed projects from fraud and corruption. VDP participant disclosures enable INT to direct its investigative resources toward entities that are more likely to have engaged in misconduct, increasing INT's chances of investigative success and achieving greater impact from its investigative expenditures. Entities reform their own processes, expanding business anticorruption norms.

The VDP is not an appropriate fit for everyone. However, for entities committed to reforming their ways, embracing ethical business practices, and proactively addressing the risks arising from past misconduct, the VDP provides significant benefits to them and to INT—and thus helps level the playing field for all businesses.

The Sanctions System and the Settlement Process

The primary benefits of NRAs are certainty of outcome, saving of time and resources, and the possibility of a lesser sanction in recognition of the firm's cooperation and acceptance of responsibility for its conduct. In contrast, the World Bank's adjudicative process may require significant time; NRA settlements avoid the costs that may be associated with that work.

The World Bank Sanctions System

When INT concludes that a party has engaged in a sanctionable practice, INT submits a Statement of Accusations and Evidence (SAE) that details findings

---

25 *See* http://www.worldbank.org/vdp.

26 *VDP Terms & Conditions, supra* note 5, at 8, para. 52.

27 *Id.,* at 6–7, paras. 43–47.

28 *Id.,* at 6, paras. 38–40.

of sufficient evidence and states the aggravating and mitigating factors that affect the choice of sanction under the Bank's sanctioning guidelines.[29] INT also includes all exculpatory or mitigating evidence in its possession in the SAE.[30] If, while an investigation is ongoing, INT believes that it has found sufficient evidence that a party has engaged in at least one sanctionable practice and continues to investigate other possible sanctionable practices in work it expects to complete within a year, INT can seek an early temporary suspension of a party's eligibility to participate in World Bank–supported projects pending the completion of its remaining investigative work.[31]

The sanctions system has a two-tiered review process. INT first submits its SAE to the suspension and debarment officer (SDO)—for IFC and MIGA, this is the evaluation and suspension officer (EO)—who reviews it to confirm whether INT has presented evidence sufficient to conclude that the party engaged in a sanctionable practice.[32] Because the sanctions system is an administrative proceeding, cases are decided on a preponderance of evidence, or a "more likely than not" standard.[33] INT bears the burden of proving that a party more likely than not engaged in a sanctionable practice.[34] Upon that finding, the burden shifts to the party (called a "respondent") to prove that it did not engage in such a practice.[35]

If the SDO finds sufficient evidence, he or she issues a Notice of Sanctions Proceedings to the respondent, recommends a sanction, and temporarily suspends the respondent's eligibility to receive Bank-financed contracts.[36] The respondent may then file an explanation, due in 30 days, of why the case should be withdrawn or its temporary suspension should be lifted and/or a response, due in 90 days, contesting the case.[37]

If the respondent does not contest the case, the SDO automatically imposes the recommended sanction[38] and, since September 2011, posts a Notice of

---

29 *Sanctions Procedures, supra* note 6, at 10–11, sec. 3.01.

30 *Id.,* at 11, sec. 3.02.

31 *Sanctions Procedures, supra* note 6, at 6–7, sec. 2.01(a). An early temporary suspension has the same effect as a debarment. It prevents a company from being awarded new World Bank–financed contracts for an initial period of six months, subject to possible extension for an additional six months, pending the completion of the INT investigation and the filing of an SAE in the case. *Id.,* at 8–9, secs. 2.02 & 2.04. Because the Bank's sanctions process is confidential, the status of any particular case cannot be disclosed publicly.

32 *Id.,* at 11, sec. 4.01(a).

33 *Id.,* at 22, sec. 8.02(b)(i).

34 *Id.,* at 22, sec. 8.02(b)(ii).

35 *Id.*

36 *Id.,* at 11–14, secs. 4.01–4.02.

37 *Id.,* at 13, sec. 4.02(b), & 15, sec. 5.01(a).

38 *Sanctions Procedures, supra* note 6, at 15, sec. 4.04.

Uncontested Sanctions Proceedings on the Bank's website.[39] If the respondent contests the case, the matter proceeds to the second tier: the World Bank Sanctions Board.[40] The Sanctions Board is a seven-member body comprising four eminent jurists from outside the World Bank and three senior World Bank staff.[41] It is chaired by a nonstaff member.[42] The respondent may contest the case solely on written pleadings, or it may request an oral hearing before the Sanctions Board.[43] INT may file a reply in support of its case, and it may request an oral hearing if the respondent does not do so.[44]

The sanctions process is confidential until a final decision is made.[45] As of May 2011, the SDO had issued Notices of Uncontested Sanctions Proceedings for all uncontested cases, and, as of May 2012, the Sanctions Board had published fully reasoned, written decisions for all contested cases.[46] The first full decisions were posted on May 30, 2012.[47] In December 2011, the Sanctions Board issued a digest of past decisions to provide a public record of prior jurisprudence.[48] The Bank may separately issue a press release when it sanctions a respondent.[49]

Settlements

Settlement can avoid much of this time-consuming process. Although a sanctions case can settle at any time, in practice, settlements are more likely before the sanctions process commences.

Settlement begins with the premise that every subject of an INT investigation, big or small, has the option to discuss entering into an NRA. Thus, prior to launching formal sanctions proceedings, INT will generally advise the subject of the investigation of the availability of the settlement process to resolve the matter. When an entity expresses an interest in pursuing an NRA, INT provides it with a standard term sheet that outlines the key terms that every NRA must contain.

---

39 *See* World Bank, *Evaluation and Suspension Officer Determinations in Uncontested Proceedings* (various dates), available at http://go.worldbank.org/G7EO0UXW90.

40 *Sanctions Procedures, supra* note 6, at 15, sec. 5.01(a).

41 International Bank for Reconstruction and Development, International Development Association, International Finance Corporation, and Multilateral Investment Guarantee Agency, Sanctions Board Statute, p. 2, art. V (Sept. 15, 2010).

42 *Id.,* at 3, art. VI.

43 *Sanctions Procedures, supra* note 6, at 15, sec. 5.01(a), and 18–20, art. VI.

44 *Id.*

45 *Id.,* at 37, sec. 13.06.

46 *Id.,* at 21–22, sec. 8.01.

47 *See* World Bank Group Sanctions Board, *Sanctions Board Decisions* (various dates), available at http://go.worldbank.org/58RC7DVWW0.

48 *See* World Bank Group Sanctions Board, *Law Digest* (Dec. 2011), available at http://go.worldbank.org/S9PFFMD6X0.

49 These press releases are available at http://go.worldbank.org/4UP7MMFCZ0.

Before proceeding with negotiations, INT must be satisfied that the particular case warrants settlement. INT's criteria for determining whether to settle a particular case include:

- Has the respondent admitted culpability (or agreed not to contest evidence of culpability) and expressed remorse?

- Will settlement result in resource savings to the World Bank?

- Has the respondent agreed to cooperate or is it cooperating with the investigation?

- Has the respondent taken corrective measures, or has it shown that it will no longer be a significant fiduciary risk to the World Bank?

INT considers the stage of the case when determining whether to settle. If a case has already progressed to formal sanctions proceedings, INT will be less likely to settle than if the matter is in the investigative stage.

The World Bank takes steps to ensure that all respondents—regardless of size or complexity of or the involvement of legal counsel in the case—enter into settlements voluntarily and with full awareness of what they are doing. Every NRA includes two affidavits, one signed by the respondent and one signed by INT, which certify that the respondent is entering into the NRA fully informed, voluntarily, and without duress.

Once an NRA becomes effective, the agreed-on sanction takes effect, and the respondent (and any sanctioned affiliates) is added to the World Bank's public debarment list. Although the NRA itself is confidential, INT may issue a press release announcing the basic terms of the NRA. Sanctions imposed through settlements are implemented in a fashion identical to that for any sanction imposed through the traditional sanctions process, including the application of cross-debarment.

The respondent works closely with INT to meet its obligations and with the ICO to create or enhance its compliance program.[50] Many NRAs include an obligation to cooperate with INT on inquiries that are both prospective and retrospective. INT's interest in prospective cooperation stems from the desire to learn about new misconduct as it arises. INT is interested in information regarding past misconduct because that misconduct may involve other parties—such as government officials, agents, partners, subcontractors, or competitors—that are still engaged in misconduct under other World Bank–supported projects. Such disclosures provide INT with insight into the types of schemes that affect World Bank–supported projects and facilitate more efficient investigations and more effective preventive advice.

NRAs detail how a firm's cooperation with INT is to proceed. Usually, the respondent conducts an initial review of its past Bank-financed contracts

---

50 Compliance programs are not mandatory in settlements, although some level of compliance review is often included as a condition for release from debarment. ICO activity is discussed in detail later in this chapter.

to identify red flags of possible fraud or corruption. This initial review may be followed by a deeper investigation of a select number of contracts. INT's goal, like the respondent's, is to use this information to promote a level playing field in which all participants conduct themselves according to the highest ethical standards.

Lessons Learned

Unlike for a confidential entrant into the VDP, the publicity of firms' obligations under an NRA may provide them with a degree of protection from future bribe solicitations because they can refer to their NRA commitments as an integrity standard that does not permit the payment of bribes. As such, a settlement offers companies an opportunity to announce conformity with an integrity pact of the sort often identified as an effective tool in curbing corruption.

Respondents exploring the possibility of settlement must, however, be willing to comply with all their obligations, including making complete and thorough disclosures to INT. Firms from jurisdictions where internal investigations and compliance programs are uncommon face a learning curve that can slow their cooperation.

Some settlements involve firms seeking to "turn the page" on past corporate misconduct by undertaking extensive internal investigations, reforming their internal compliance systems, and addressing actual or potential legal actions against them—sometimes in multiple jurisdictions. Such fundamental change in business behavior inevitably helps speed up settlements.

The presence of multiple, ongoing national investigations can create an environment in which a firm believes that seeking a negotiated resolution is in its best interest. But this situation can introduce other complexities. It is important to openly discuss and coordinate these concerns as early in the settlement process as possible.

Confirmation of a firm's operational and legal structures will generally be factored into the basic structure of the settlement. Because these issues are complex and address core questions, such as which entities can be sanctioned and what the appropriate sanction may be, they should be addressed early in negotiations.

A limited number of INT's settlements include restitution or other measures to remedy the harm done by the misconduct.[51] One settled matter involved a firm that had fraudulently claimed reimbursement for approximately US$350,000 from a government ministry. The settlement in this case included the repayment of this amount to the government at issue. Two other settlements involving corruption included payments based on an estimate of the enrichment from the corrupt conduct, and a third case was resolved in part

---

51   "Restitution or other remedy" is one of the sanctions available in the World Bank sanctions system. *See Sanctions Procedures, supra* note 6, at 24, sec. 9.01(e).

through a contribution in kind of medical test kits to the affected country's health authorities.

The flexibility of NRAs makes them a useful tool in fashioning resolutions to World Bank investigations and sanctions cases. Like the VDP, they utilize cooperation and internal reform to build anticorruption cultures in businesses and thus promote open, equitable market competition.

The ICO and the Conditional Release Process

The ICO

The ICO function was established in 2010, in part to implement the World Bank's default sanction of a debarment with conditional release.[52] The World Bank sees the adoption (or improvement) and implementation of effective integrity compliance programs as important ways for the private sector to help prevent, detect, and remedy misconduct. The World Bank made debarment with conditional release the default sanction to incentivize the adoption of such programs and to minimize the chance that the sanctioned party will re-engage in misconduct when it becomes eligible to receive new Bank-financed contracts or otherwise participate in World Bank–supported activities.

The Conditional Release Process

To demonstrate rehabilitation, the sanctioned party must satisfy the ICO that it has in place, and has implemented for an adequate period, an effective integrity compliance program within the context of its operating risk environment.[53] Following the imposition of a conditional sanction, the ICO contacts the sanctioned party to discuss the conditional release process. If the sanctioned entity is a firm, the ICO provides it with a copy of the World Bank's integrity compliance guidelines[54] and requests information regarding its corporate structure, scope of operations, and existing corporate compliance measures. The sanctioned party may also be requested to conduct an integrity risk assessment of its operations. Based on this information, the ICO assesses the sanctioned party's compliance program and identifies suggested improvements.[55]

Once the sanctioned party has its program in place, the ICO monitors its implementation through semiannual written reports. These reports are intended to confirm that the program is fully functioning and effective, not just a "cosmetic" program that exists solely on paper. The ICO may require

---

52   *Integrity Compliance FAQ, supra* note 7, at 1.

53   *Sanctions Procedures, supra* note 6, at 25–29, sec. 9.03.

54   The guidelines are recommended as a resource for businesses by the Criminal Division of the U.S. Department of Justice and the Enforcement Division of the U.S. Securities and Exchange Commission in their joint publication, *A Resource Guide to the U.S. Foreign Corrupt Practices Act* 63 (Nov. 2012), available at http://www.sec.gov/spotlight/fcpa/fcpa-resource-guide.pdf.

55   *See Integrity Compliance FAQ, supra* note 7, at 2–3.

that an independent compliance monitor, external auditor, or other compliance adviser be engaged—at the expense of the sanctioned party—to assist in the evaluation and oversight of the program. An independent compliance monitor usually will be required for firms that are not small and medium-size enterprises (SMEs).[56] These monitors are typically internationally recognized law or accounting firms with experience relating to integrity compliance programs for large companies with international operations; applicable national and local compliance and internal controls regulations; international best practices in integrity compliance; and the conduct of internal investigations on behalf of large companies at the direction of national authorities.

Sanctioned SMEs may be required to engage a compliance expert, typically a local law firm or accounting firm, appropriate civil society organization, or individual expert. For particularly small SMEs, the ICO may suggest resources such as its *Resource Guide for SMEs* (under preparation) and publicly available compliance resources.

Sanctioned individuals are usually required to take appropriate remedial measures to address their sanctionable practices and to complete training and/ or other educational programs that demonstrate a continuing commitment to personal integrity and business ethics in the industry. Sanctioned individuals and the ICO agree on an action plan to be implemented within six months of the imposition of a sanction. In addition to any remedial measures, such action plans typically involve 20 hours of training in each year of sanction on subjects such as ethics, anticorruption, and internal controls. This training must be in excess of any continuing professional education requirements that the individual must meet. The publication of articles, conference presentations, or other individually designed initiatives may fulfill this requirement if the ICO so approves.

Lessons Learned

The ICO has learned valuable lessons during its two years of operation, which are influencing its planned next steps.

Many firms lack familiarity with corporate compliance principles. Many sanctioned parties that have engaged with the ICO have expressed a lack of familiarity with basic corporate compliance principles. These parties usually have limited access to skilled, local compliance advisers or to off-the-shelf resources in their local languages. This absence of a "compliance community" accessible to these firms poses a challenge for them if they seek to develop effective controls systems as their businesses grow.

SMEs face particular compliance challenges. SMEs, which constitute a significant percentage of the firms sanctioned by the Bank, often lack access to local compliance communities. Even if SMEs are able to access information resources,

---

56   The World Bank generally defines SMEs as having at least two of the following characteristics: fewer than 300 employees, total assets of less than US$15 million, or total annual sales of less than US$15 million.

a comprehensive, state-of-the-art, formal compliance program may be unnecessary or prohibitively expensive for them. Indeed, even minor issues, such as the translation of compliance program materials into English (to facilitate their review by nonlocal advisers) may impose significant costs.

To assist SMEs, the ICO is working with other Bank units and civil society counterparts to develop resources specifically designed for SMEs. For example, the ICO is working with the IFC to create an integrity compliance module for the IFC's tool kit for SMEs, which will be available for free through the IFC's website. The ICO also is preparing an SME resource guide, which will provide guidance on applying the World Bank's integrity compliance guidelines to operations and to direct SMEs to other useful public information resources.

Compliance programs can be costly, and this may affect a firm's engagement with the ICO. Compliance program costs vary with a firm's size, industry, operating environments, and risk areas, and costs can be substantial. For example, a large multinational corporation with global operations will likely require a comprehensive program, led by a senior officer and a large team of full-time staff committed to the program. Given these costs, some sanctioned parties may not engage with the ICO if Bank-financed work constitutes a small portion of their operations or if they do not intend to seek Bank-financed contracts in the future.

The ICO is attempting to facilitate participation in the conditional release process by developing informational and diagnostic resources for companies. One tool, presently in development, is an interactive integrity compliance checklist, scalable from SMEs to multinationals, for testing corporate compliance programs. However, there is no shortcut for review time. The ICO has found that it usually requires about six months to assess a program and recommend changes, and at least a year of monitoring (following full program implementation) to confirm that the program is fully implemented and effective. Accordingly, even with a sanctioned party's best efforts, the conditional release process usually requires at least 18 months to complete. The only exception is if a sanctioned party already has a largely effective compliance program in place at the time of sanction, in which case the ICO could complete the conditional release process after the 12-month monitoring and reporting period.

Conclusion

As World Bank president Jim Kim observed in a speech, in the context of the World Bank's development work,

> [c]orruption steals from the poor. It steals the promise of a brighter future. . . . Few issues are more important for development and shared growth than good governance. Public institutions deliver vital services such as health and education, upon which the poor are particularly dependent. Corruption subverts and undermines all these functions and as such serves as a major impediment to devel-

opment. It is in this context that combating corruption both has been and will continue to remain one of the Bank's top priorities.[57]

Tools like the VDP, NRAs, and the ICO are still relatively new, and further research is necessary to quantify their value in promoting open, equitable competition through corporate reform. INT's experience, however, is that these tools can be effective in catalyzing corporate reform and furthering the Bank's integrity goals, particularly when used in tandem with broader good governance and anticorruption efforts. Given their mutual interest in fostering development through opportunity, inclusion, and equity, the World Bank and the private sector are natural partners in furthering the opportunity, inclusion, and equity required to end poverty through sustainable growth and shared prosperity.

---

57   *Anti-corruption Efforts in a Global Environment: A Commitment to Act* (Jan. 30, 2013), available at http://www.worldbank.org/en/news/speech/2013/01/30/world-bank-group-president-jim-yong-kim-speech-anti-corruption-center-for-strategic-and-international-studies.

The World Bank Group Sanctions System and Access to Justice for Small and Medium-Size Enterprises

FRANK FARIELLO AND GIOVANNI BO

Following the adoption of a principle against corruption at the 2004 UN Global Compact Leaders Summit[1] and the entry into force of the United Nations Convention against Corruption in 2005, increased attention has been paid to the detrimental impact of corruption on small-business development. Data show that the smaller the firm, the more likely it is to be negatively affected by corruption;[2] more than 70 percent of small and medium-size enterprises (SMEs) perceive corruption as an impediment to their business, as opposed to approximately 60 percent of larger corporations.[3] International organizations, development agencies, business associations, and nongovernmental organizations have expanded the focus of their research into understanding the negative effects of corruption on small and medium-size business development, given SMEs' prominent role in the business environment worldwide.[4] In particular, the structural differences that exist between small and large corporations have called for the revision and adaptation of anticorruption tools and other measures to prevent corruption in order to account for the specific characteristics of SMEs and to develop tools tailored specifically to fit their needs.[5]

The views expressed in this article are those of the authors and do not necessarily reflect the views of the Board of Executive Directors of the World Bank or the governments they represent.

1   UN Global Compact, *The Ten Principles*, Principle 10 ("Businesses should work against corruption in all its forms, including extortion and bribery"), available at http://www.unglobalcompact.org/AboutTheGC/TheTenPrinciples/index.html.

2   In general, SMEs are more likely to be affected by corruption for a number of reasons, including their limited financial resources, inability to exert a strong influence over public officials, and capital structure. *See* United Nations Industrial Development Organization (UNIDO)/United Nations Office on Drugs and Crime (UNODC), *Fighting Corruption, Corruption Prevention to Foster Small and Medium-Sized Enterprise Development* 7 (2007), available at http://www.unodc.org/unodc/en/corruption/publications.html.

3   UNIDO/UNODC, *Draft Discussion Paper of the Expert Group Meeting on "Small Business Development and Corruption"*, II (Mar. 6–7, 2006), available at http://info.worldbank.org/etools/acportal/docs/T1_3_SmaBizDevAndCrrpt.pdf (quoting World Bank/European Bank for Reconstruction and Development, BEEPS, *Question: How Problematic Is Corruption in the Business Environment?* [2000]).

4   SMEs make up about 90 percent of all established businesses worldwide. *See* UNIDO, *Responsible Trade and Market Access: Opportunities or Obstacles for SMEs in Developing Countries?* 12 (2006), available at http://www.unido.org/fileadmin/media/documents/pdf/Services_Modules/csr_responsible_trade_market_access.pdf.

5   UNIDO/UNODC, *supra* note 2, at 9. Some important tool kits and guidelines have been

Besides with prevention, the battle against corruption is also being fought on the enforcement front. In parallel with, and often as a complement to, a multitude of national systems, the World Bank's sanctions process aims at making sure that firms and individuals found to have engaged in one or more sanctionable practices (known as "respondents") in connection with Bank financing are sanctioned for their illicit practices.

The World Bank's sanctions system originated in 1996 as an internal, administrative process with limited opportunities for respondents to defend themselves.[6] The "rules of the game" were few and largely nonpublic, and decisions were short and conclusive, shared only with the respondent and those within the Bank with a need to know.[7] Since then, the system has evolved significantly toward a quasi-judicial model, with increasing transparency and due process protections, including a double-instance structure, the right to counsel, publicly available rules and procedures, sanctioning guidelines, and other written guidance, as well as published, reasoned sanctions decisions.

This evolution has made the system fairer for respondents that have the capacity to take advantage of the system's features, in particular those that can afford legal counsel. Ironically, however, these changes, and the resulting higher degree of formality, may have had the unintended consequence of making the system less accessible to low-capacity respondents such as individuals and SMEs.

---

developed by international organizations targeting private sector anticorruption compliance. *See,* for example, International Chamber of Commerce, *Rules of Conduct to Combat Extortion and Bribery in International Business Transactions* (1996); Organisation for Economic Co-operation and Development (OECD), *Principles of Corporate Governance* (1999); OECD, *Guidelines for Multinational Enterprises* (updated 2011); Transparency International, *Corruption Fighters' Tool Kit* (2004). In addition to the UNIDO/UNODC joint project, a number of tools have been developed specifically for SMEs. For example, Transparency International published a guide that sets out the process by which smaller businesses can develop an antibribery program relevant to their size and resources. *See* Transparency International, *Business Principles for Countering Bribery—SME Edition* (2008). There are a growing number of initiatives and tools to help SMEs in countering corruption and bribery. The Danish Development Agency, in cooperation with other partners, has developed a website, the Business Anti-corruption Portal (http://www.business-anti-corruption.com), for SMEs operating in developing countries, which provides information on possible corruption risks and ways to avoid and fight corruption. Additional anticorruption tools tailored to SMEs' needs include International Finance Corporation, *SME Toolkit* (2002); Hong Kong Institute of Directors, *SME Corporate Governance Toolkit* (2009); Lebanon Anti-bribery Network, *Code of Ethics and Whistle Blower Procedure for Small and Medium Enterprises* (2009); and Business Unity South Africa, *An Anti-corruption Guide for South-African SMEs* (2009).

6   The process was first formulated in a paper presented to the World Bank executive directors in 1996 and implemented in 1998. The original process included a Sanctions Committee, composed of senior Bank staff, which reviewed allegations of fraud and corruption by bidders, contractors, suppliers, and consultants in IBRD-financed projects and recommended an appropriate sanction to the president of the Bank, who made the final decision on the sanction to be imposed.

7   Dick Thornburgh et al., *Report Concerning the Debarment Process of the World Bank* 10–12 (Aug. 14, 2002), available at http://go.worldbank.org/1O93GTKH40 (hereinafter, Second Thornburgh Report).

The Bank's Legal Vice Presidency (LEG) is about to conclude the first phase of a comprehensive review of the sanctions system.[8] The review found increasingly positive overall performance of the system both in terms of processing times and outputs and in terms of its legal adequacy under due process and global administrative law principles.[9] The Bank's system compares quite favorably with similar systems on these metrics. But a less encouraging development emerged in the course of the review: the majority of respondent SMEs were simply not engaging with the system, either during adjudication or in the rehabilitative process that is intended to follow sanctioning. It became apparent that the system has an "SME issue" that merits further study and concern.[10] Although there are various possible explanations for this pattern of nonengagement, the LEG review hypothesized that, among other things, the system may suffer from an "access to justice" issue.

This chapter examines this hypothesis in some detail. The chapter summarizes the principles underlying the concept of access to justice, including the elimination of unnecessary obstacles to the services of the adjudicative body, such as geographic location as well as language, economic, and procedural barriers. It then examines the possible reasons for SME nonengagement and the possible hurdles that low-capacity respondents may face in accessing the sanctions system. Finally, the chapter explores ways to improve access to justice for low-capacity respondents in the sanctions system and makes the case as to why it is important for the Bank to do so—and not just from a fairness perspective.

Principles of Access to Justice

In recent times, the concept of "access to justice" has been expanded to include a variety of meanings.[11] In general terms, access to justice has been defined as

---

8   More information on the review and consultation process is available at http://www
.worldbank.org/legal/sanctionsreview.

9   *See*, for example, Nico Krisch & Benedict Kingsbury, *Introduction: Global Governance and Global Administrative Law in the International Legal Order*, 17(1) Euro. J. Intl. Law 1–14 (2006); Pascale Dubois & Aileen Nowlan, *Global Administrative Law and the Legitimacy of Sanctions Regimes in International Law*, 36 Yale J. Intl. L. Online (2010), available at http://www.yjil.org /docs/pub/o-36-dubois-nowlan-global-administrative-law-sanctions.pdf.

10   The ideas for improvement that the authors explore in this chapter are based on the analysis of available data. Although there appears to be a fairly clear correlation between the size of a firm and the likelihood it will contest a case, a number of other factors deserve further study and attention, such as typology of cases (e.g., are respondents more likely to engage if there is a claim of corruption or collusion, as opposed to fraud?) and if the firm's main source of business lies in Bank-financed contracts.

11   For a discussion of the evolution of the concept of access to justice, *see* Mauro Cappelletti et al., *Access to Justice*, 94 Harv. L. Rev. 1911 (1981); Lawrence M. Friedman, *Access to Justice: Some Historical Comments*, 37 Ford. Urb. L.J. 3–15 (2009). The term "access to justice" is not commonly used as a legal term and is not expressly used in a number of international human rights instruments, which instead, contain provisions on fair trial and the right to a remedy. *See*, for example, Convention for the Protection of Human Rights and Fundamental Freedoms (ECHR) (Nov. 4, 1950), Europ.T.S. No. 5; 213 U.N.T.S. 221, arts. 6 and 13; Universal

the possibility for an individual to bring a claim before an institution of justice for adjudication.[12] In a more qualified manner, the term is used to express "the right of an individual not only to access a court of law, but to have his or her case heard and adjudicated in accordance with substantive standards of fairness and justice."[13] Finally, in a narrower sense, "access to justice" may be used to refer to the need of the poor to have access to the legal assistance required for the meaningful protection of their rights.[14]

The term "access to justice" is used in this chapter as synonymous with "access to courts" to refer to the broad notion that the structure and machinery of an adjudicative system must be accessible to those who are subject to its jurisdiction and require mechanisms to ensure that participation is effective,

---

Declaration on Human Rights, G.A. Res. 217A (III), at 71, U.N. Doc. A/810 (1948); International Covenant on Civil and Political Rights, 999 U.N.T.S. 171; 6 I.L.M. 368 (1967), arts. 2(3a), 9(4), 14(1), and 14(3c). However, a specific reference to access to justice was introduced in the Treaty on the Functioning of the European Union (TFEU), which stipulates that "the Union shall facilitate access to justice, in particular through the principle of mutual recognition of judicial and extrajudicial decisions in civil matters." Treaty on the Functioning of the European Union (Oct. 26, 2012), 2012 O.J. (C 326), art. 67, para. 4. For other examples of international law instruments referencing access to justice, *see* Convention on Access to Information, Public Participation in Decision-Making and Access to Justice in Environmental Matters, 2161 U.N.T.S. 447; 38 I.L.M. 517 (1999); United Nations Convention on the Rights of Persons with Disabilities, 2515 U.N.T.S. 3 (2008); and Convention on International Access to Justice, 19 I.L.M. 1505 (1980). For an EU-wide comparative analysis of the effectiveness of access to justice as a means of ensuring individuals' rights in the area of nondiscrimination, *see* European Union Agency for Fundamental Rights, *Access to Justice in Europe: An Overview of Challenges and Opportunities* (2010), available at http://fra.europa.eu/sites/default/files /fra_uploads/1520-report-access-to-justice_EN.pdf. For a discussion of the notion of access to justice from a U.S. perspective, *see* Deborah L. Rhode, *Access to Justice* (Oxford U. Press 2004).

12   Francesco Francioni, *The Rights of Access to Justice under Customary International Law*, in *Access to Justice as a Human Right* 1 (Oxford U. Press 2007). A recent overview of the World Bank's existing work in access to justice categorizes access to justice efforts into six groups: court reforms, legal aid, information dissemination and education, alternative dispute resolution, public sector accountability, and research. *See* Vivek Maru, *Access to Justice and Legal Empowerment: A Review of World Bank Practice* (Justice & Development Working Paper Series No. 9, 2009).

13   Francioni, *supra* note 12, at 1. Access to justice intersects with human rights, and it "emerges as an essential component of every system of human rights protection, which, in principle, must be safeguarded also in times of crisis and emergency." (*Id.,* at 56.) *See* also Antônio Augusto Cançado Trindade, *Access to Justice at International Level and the Right to an Effective Domestic Remedy*, in *The Access of Individuals to International Justice* 51–59 (Oxford U. Press 2011); Jeremy McBride, *Access to Justice for Migrants and Asylum Seekers in Europe* (Council of Europe Publishing 2009).

14   Francioni, *supra* note 12, at 1. *See* also Ineke Van De Meene & Benjamin Van Rooij, *Access to Justice and Legal Empowerment: Making the Poor Central in Legal Development Co-operation* (Amsterdam U. Press 2008); Justice Earl Johnson Jr., *Equal Access to Justice: Comparing Access to Justice in the United States and Other Industrial Democracies*, 24 Ford. Intl L.J. S83 (2000); Robert J. Rhudy, *Comparing Legal Services to the Poor in the United States with Other Western Countries: Some Preliminary Lessons*, 5 Md. J. Contemp. Leg. Issues 223 (1994); Mauro Cappelletti et al., *Toward Equal Justice: A Comparative Study of Legal Aid in Modern Societies* (Giuffrè; Oceana Publications 1975); Earl Johnson Jr., *Toward Equal Justice: Where the United States Stands Two Decades Later*, 5 Md. J. Contemp. Leg. Issues 199, 204 (1994).

costs are affordable, and decisions are made in a timely and fair manner by an independent decision-making body.[15]

This section provides an overview of the main general principles of access to justice as applied to the performance of adjudicatory systems.[16] It is important to note that the World Bank's sanctions regime cannot and should not be equated with a civil or criminal judicial system. It is, rather, administrative in nature. Nevertheless, the system's adjudicatory nature makes it suitable for an assessment against these general principles.[17] Moreover, starting at least from its first set of reforms in 2004, the Bank has recognized that it must hold itself to a higher standard of fairness than might otherwise be considered strictly required for a typical administrative process.[18] The sanctions system is part of a larger Bank effort to promote good governance and fight corruption, commonly referred to as its governance and anticorruption (GAC) agenda.[19] In this context, it was the consensus of Bank managers and staff that the Bank has a responsibility to demonstrate, through its own practices, the standards of governance that it hopes will take root in the developing world.[20] In plain terms, the Bank must practice what it preaches.

The basic principles of access to justice can be summarized as follows.

15　*See* European Union Agency for Fundamental Rights, *supra* note 11, at 15 ("According to current usage, then, access to justice is related to a number of terms that at times are used interchangeably or to cover particular elements, such as access to court, effective remedies or fair trial").

16　Bureau of Justice Assistance, U.S. Department of Justice, *Trial Court Performance Standards with Commentary* (1997), available at https://www.ncjrs.gov/pdffiles1/161570.pdf (hereinafter, Trial Court Performance Standards). *See* also American Bar Association, *Access to Justice Assessment Tool: A Guide to Analyzing Access to Justice for Civil Society Organizations* (2012), available at http://www.americanbar.org/content/dam/aba/directories/roli/misc/aba_roli_access_to_justice_assessment_manual_2012.authcheckdam.pdf. Although much literature exists on the general principles underlying the access to justice concept, these standards are particularly useful for the purposes here because they provide concrete benchmarks relevant to an adjudicatory system, against which the Bank's sanctions system may be assessed.

17　More recently, the emerging field of global administrative law (GAL) has called for bringing due process, transparency, and other notions of fundamental fairness to bear on international administrative processes. *See supra* note 9 and Armin von Bogdandy et al., *Developing the Publicness of Public International Law: Towards a Legal Framework for Global Governance Activities*, 9 German L. J. 1375, 1377 (2008) ("The legal framework of governance activities of international institutions should be conceived of as international institutional law, and enriched by a public law perspective, i.e. with constitutional sensibility and openness for comparative insights from administrative legal thinking").

18　*See* Second Thornburgh Report, *supra* note 7, at 7, 21, and 30. Or so it was thought at the time. Since then, a number of developments, particularly in the area of international administrative law and human rights jurisprudence, have raised the bar considerably. *See supra* notes 9 and 17.

19　*See* World Bank, *Strengthening World Bank Group Engagement on Governance and Anticorruption* (Mar. 16, 2007). The GAC strategy was updated in 2012 to respond to the fundamental changes that had swept the world since its adoption in 2007, including the global financial crisis and the rise of civil society movements. *See* World Bank, *Strengthening Governance: Tackling Corruption—The World Bank Group's Updated Strategy and Implementation Plan* (Mar. 6, 2012), available at http://go.worldbank.org/GJU5GEHQ40.

20　*See* Second Thornburgh Report, *supra* note 7, at 7.

First, the broader notion of access to justice requires the elimination of unnecessary obstacles to the services of the adjudicative body, such as geographic location as well as language, economic, and procedural barriers.[21] In this connection, a justice institution must ensure that the parties to the proceedings are able to participate in and understand the hearing as well as read the key documents in the case.[22] The cost of access to proceedings and records should be reasonable, fair, and affordable. Legal aid (i.e., the provision of legal assistance to people otherwise unable to afford legal representation) and the dissemination to the public of as much information as possible about the "rules of the game," both substantive and procedural, are also regarded as crucial in ensuring effective access to justice.[23]

Second, an effective justice system should be able to meet its goals in an expeditious and timely manner. The repercussions for untimely action may have serious consequences for the firms and individuals involved in the proceedings. Expedition and timeliness include the establishment of an effective case management process, compliance with schedules, and prompt implementation of law and procedure.[24]

Third, due process demands equality, fairness, and integrity. Integrity, in turn, requires adherence to duties and obligations imposed on the adjudicative body by the applicable legal and policy framework. In parallel, fairness and equality require that persons similarly situated receive similar treatment

---

21 Trial Court Performance Standards, *supra* note 16, at 7.

22 *See,* for example, Julia Alanen, *Language Access Is an Empowerment Right: Deprivation of Plenary Language Access Engenders an Array of Grave Rights Violations,* 1 Intl. Leg. Stud. Program 93 (2009), available at http://papers.ssrn.com/sol3/papers.cfm?abstract_id=1578607 (arguing that references to the connection between language access and due process/fair trial, now largely limited to defendants in criminal proceedings, should also apply to limited- and non-English-proficient individuals seeking redress in the civil courts); Williamson B. C. Chang & Manuel U. Araujo, *Interpreters for the Defense: Due Process for the Non-English-Speaking Defendant,* 63 Cal. L. Rev. 801–823 (1975). In 2002, the European Union adopted a directive to improve access to justice in cross-border civil and commercial disputes by establishing minimum common rules relating to legal aid. *See* Council Directive 2002/8/EC of January 27, 2003, to improve access to justice in cross-border disputes by establishing minimum common rules relating to legal aid for such disputes, 2003 Official Journal of the European Communities (L26/41).

23 *See* Trial Court Performance Standards, *supra* note 16, at 9 ("Means to achieve this include the use of volunteer lawyers to do *pro bono* work"). In general, the provision of legal assistance to people otherwise unable to afford legal representation is regarded as crucial in ensuring effective access to justice. *See,* for example, Edwin Rekosh et al., *Access to Justice: Legal Aid for the Underrepresented,* in *Access to Justice in Central and Eastern Europe: Source Book* (Public Interest Law Initiative 2003). An explicit connection between access to justice and legal aid is found in the Charter of Fundamental Rights of the European Union, which provides that "[l]egal aid shall be made available to those who lack sufficient resources in so far as such aid is necessary to ensure effective access to justice." Charter of Fundamental Rights of the European Union (Oct. 26, 2012), 2012 O.J. (C 326) 391–407, art. 47.

24 Trial Court Performance Standards, *supra* note 16, at 10. Although the Trial Court Performance Standards and this chapter focus on the adjudicatory phase, expedition and timeliness also call for the prompt investigation of a case.

in proportion to the nature and magnitude of the case and that decisions be reasoned.[25]

Fourth, an adjudicative body must be independent from political influence and other forms of pressure.[26]

Fifth, performance of adjudicative functions should instill public trust and confidence.[27]

These five principles, if properly implemented, also address two of the concerns expressed by SMEs in connection with a recent study on the use of alternative dispute resolution mechanisms for resolving disputes, namely, that the resolution process not take too long and not cost too much.[28]

The World Bank Sanctions System and Access to Justice Principles

Nonengagement by SMEs in the System

The Bank's two-tiered sanctions process, as it presently exists, may be summarized as follows.

Investigation and Preparation of the Statement of Accusations and Evidence

The process starts with the decision of the Bank's Integrity Vice Presidency (INT) to investigate allegations that sanctionable practices have occurred in Bank-financed projects and programs. If, upon concluding an investigation, INT believes that there is sufficient evidence as to the occurrence of a sanctionable practice, it prepares a Statement of Accusations and Evidence (SAE) for submission to the IBRD/IDA suspension and debarment officer (SDO).[29]

Sanctions Proceedings: First-Tier Review

INT initiates a sanctions case by submitting the SAE to the SDO. If the SDO finds that the accusations are supported by sufficient evidence, the SDO issues a Notice of Sanctions Proceedings to the respondent; this notice contains the SDO's recommendation of an appropriate sanction and, where applicable, informs the respondent that it has been temporarily suspended. The respondent

---

25 *Id.*, at 12.

26 *Id.*, at 17.

27 *Id.*, at 20.

28 Rob van der Horst, Renate de Vree, & Paul van der Zeijden, *SME Access to Alternative Dispute Resolution Systems, Final Report* (EIM Business & Policy Research 2006), available at http://ec.europa.eu/enterprise/newsroom/cf/_getdocument.cfm?doc_id=4126.

29 As of March 31, 2013, the title of IBRD/IDA evaluation and suspension officer (EO) was changed to IBRD/IDA suspension and debarment officer (SDO). The titles of the evaluation and suspension officers for IFC, MIGA, and Bank Guarantee operations were maintained. References to SDO in this chapter include the evaluation and suspension officers for IFC, MIGA, and Bank Guarantee operations, as appropriate.

may file an explanation with the SDO seeking either dismissal of the case or a reduction in the recommended sanction. If the respondent chooses not to contest the case before the World Bank Sanctions Board, the noncontested determination becomes final.

Sanctions Proceedings: Second-Tier Review

The respondent may trigger a second tier of review by submitting a written response to the Sanctions Board, an independent body composed of three internal (i.e., Bank staff) and four external (i.e., non-Bank staff) members and chaired by one of its external members. The Sanctions Board considers the case de novo and makes a final, nonappealable decision.

The Integrity Compliance Officer

When the sanction imposed is debarment with conditional release, the Integrity Compliance Officer (ICO) is charged with monitoring compliance by debarred parties with conditions for release from debarment, typically, the establishment and implementation of an integrity compliance program. The ICO is housed within INT, but with functional and administrative reporting lines independent of INT's investigation and litigation units.[30]

Negotiated Resolutions (aka Settlements)

INT may, in appropriate circumstances, enter into negotiations with a respondent at any stage of the sanctions process up to the issuance of a decision by the Sanctions Board or even prior to the initiation of sanctions proceedings. Negotiated resolutions are subject to a number of safeguards to ensure fairness, transparency, and credibility.

In the course of LEG's review of the sanctions system, a pattern of nonengagement by SMEs was discovered. Of the roughly 60 percent of sanctions cases that were resolved at the first tier of proceedings, before the Bank's Office of Suspension and Debarment (OSD), more than 90 percent resulted from what could be termed "defaults" by the respondents, most of them SMEs, because they did not respond in any way to Notices of Sanctions Proceedings, either by submitting an explanation to the SDO or by referring the case to the Sanctions Board. There appears to be a fairly clear correlation between the size of firm and the likelihood it will contest a case.[31]

---

30   The ICO is subject to a code of conduct in order to ensure independence, fairness, and impartiality.

31   As of March 31, 2013, roughly 88 percent of large corporations had contested a case before the Sanctions Board (14 of 16); roughly 57 percent of medium-sized corporations (26 of 46); roughly 27 percent of small corporations (17 of 63); roughly 24 percent of NGOs (5 of 21); and roughly 29 percent of individual respondents (22 of 77). The Bank does not systematically track the profile of respondents according to size. These figures are OSD estimates based on its reading of pleadings presented in sanctions cases and, therefore, remain somewhat conjectural. However, the authors are confident that these figures are sufficiently robust to identify the patterns discussed here.

The pattern continues after sanctions are imposed. The ICO reports that approximately 15–20 percent of the respondents that have been sanctioned with compliance conditions have actively engaged with the ICO.[32] Of these, the majority are large firms that are likely to be able to afford to implement integrity compliance programs (or have already done so for domestic law reasons).

The impact on SMEs has been a point of concern for some external stakeholders, in particular in the context of settlements, where critics have argued that advantage may be taken of SMEs and individuals.[33] These concerns seem to be overstated. The system has various safeguards against abuse and favoritism.[34] Nevertheless, the LEG review did identify occasional signs that these safeguards may need strengthening when dealing with SMEs.[35]

In this connection, it bears pointing out that the standard form of negotiated resolution agreement (NRA) used by the Bank includes a "certificate of voluntariness."[36] In a normal case, OSD relies on this certification without

---

32   As of March 28, 2013, 19 parties were actively engaging in the conditional release process. Of these 19 parties, seven have been classified by the ICO as SMEs. As of that date, four parties had been released (under the post-2010 sanctions procedures) or early released (under the pre-2010 sanctions procedures) after fulfilling compliance conditions, while 11 parties had been released at sanction end dates (under the pre-2010 sanctions procedures).

33   Some critics argue that settlements favor the big players (especially those that are willing to make payments in restitution), who are more likely to get special deals.

34   INT has the discretion to determine, in consultation with the World Bank General Counsel, whether or not it is appropriate to engage in settlement negotiations with a particular respondent and the appropriate terms and conditions for any resulting settlement agreement. *See* Anne-Marie Leroy & Frank Fariello, *The World Bank Group Sanctions Process and Its Recent Reforms* (World Bank 2012), at 21. In addition, agreed-on sanctions must not manifestly violate secs. 9.01 and 9.02 of the World Bank Sanctions Procedures (as adopted Apr. 15, 2012) (hereinafter, Sanctions Procedures) and related guidance, including the World Bank Sanctioning Guidelines (Jan. 1, 2011) (hereinafter, Sanctioning Guidelines), while settlements are subject to limited review by OSD both to ensure that the agreed-on sanction does not manifestly violate the relevant guidance, which should ensure a minimum degree of consistency across respondents, and for voluntariness, that is, that the respondent entered into the settlement agreement freely and fully informed and without any form of duress. *See* Sanctions Procedures, secs. 11.02(a) and (b). Moreover, a study of the actual results of settlements confirms that, after accounting for settlements with cooperation as a mitigating factor, the agreed-on sanctions have been broadly in line with the Sanctioning Guidelines, with larger firms actually incurring heavier penalties (above the baseline of three years) and individuals and smaller firms incurring lesser sanctions.

35   A few SMEs have complained, after the fact, that they did not understand the nature of the sanctions to which they agreed. In one case, an individual respondent complained that it had not been informed that the letter of reprimand would be made public, while in another case a respondent complained that it had not understood the requirements of an integrity compliance program when agreeing to such a condition for release from debarment.

36   The representative of the respondent attests that he/she (i) has full authority to sign the NRA, on behalf of the respondent; (ii) has been given copies of the Sanctions Procedures and the Sanctioning Guidelines; (iii) understands that the negotiated resolution of the case is carried out in place of a determination made by the SDO or the Sanctions Board; (iv) understands that it is not obligated to enter into a negotiated resolution of the cases with INT, but may instead choose to participate in sanctions proceedings; (v) understands that, under the Sanctioning Guidelines, the baseline sanction for engaging in a sanctionable practice is debarment of three years with conditional release, which may be increased or decreased per any

making inquiries of the respondent. Of course, the difficulty is that, in the hypothetical case that a respondent were obligated under duress to sign an NRA, it could also be obligated to sign the certificate. The authors trust that in actuality duress does not occur; a far more likely scenario is that SMEs and other low-capacity respondents simply sign NRAs without asking too many questions.[37]

The ICO also reports that some SME respondents, including those that agreed to implement integrity compliance programs as part of the settlement of a sanctions case, do not understand the requirements involved. And although the ICO provides information on compliance programs, including resources to educate and assist respondents in designing and implementing compliance programs to suit their needs, there has been limited follow-up from respondents.

Possible Reasons for SME Nonengagement

There are various possible explanations for SME nonengagement, some benign, others less so. At its most benign, respondents culpable of misconduct may simply recognize the futility of contesting the SDO's recommended sanction.[38] Some respondents may not care to engage the system, whether culpable or not, either during proceedings before OSD or the Sanctions Board or at the ICO stage, because they do not do enough Bank-related business to make it worth the time and expense of litigating or adopting compliance programs. Less benignly, some bad actors may simply set up operations under another corporate form in hopes of evading the effect of sanctions.

It may also be, however, that the system suffers from an access to justice issue for SMEs and other low-capacity respondents. Since the establishment of the World Bank's sanctions system in 1996, the Bank has periodically made incremental improvements to the sanctions process to increase its efficiency, fairness, and effectiveness.[39] Ironically, as the system has become more sophisticated and provided more robust due process for respondents that have

---

relevant aggravating and mitigating factors; and (vi) has entered into the agreement freely and fully informed of the terms thereof and free from any form of duress.

37   To counter this, INT representatives cosign the certificate of voluntariness to affirm, inter alia, that neither INT nor any other representative of the World Bank has made any statement or engaged in any conduct intended to impose duress on the respondent and that the respondent has entered into the agreement freely and fully informed of the terms thereof and without any form of duress.

38   *See* Second Thornburgh Report, *supra* note 7, at 37 ("Some respondents would recognize that in light of the evidence possessed by the Bank it would be futile to contest the matter further").

39   *See* Leroy & Fariello, *supra* note 34, at 9–11; and Conrad C. Daly & Frank A. Fariello, *Transforming through Transparency—Opening Up the World Bank's Sanctions Regime*, in *The World Bank Legal Review*, vol. 4, 101, 107–110 (2011). *See also* World Bank, *Reform of the World Bank's Sanctions Process* (June 28, 2004); World Bank, *Expansion of Sanction beyond Procurement and Sanctioning of Obstructive Practices* (July 28, 2006); and World Bank, *World Bank Group Sanctions Regime—An Overview* (Oct. 8, 2010).

the means to take advantage of these improvements, it may have become less accessible to respondents without those means.

The SAE and the files of evidence that accompany it are typically voluminous and often contain complex legal arguments. SMEs and other low-capacity respondents may feel overwhelmed when faced with these materials and unable to respond.

The integrity compliance requirements that typically attach to conditions for release from debarment pose a particular challenge for SMEs and other low-capacity respondents. Compliance programs are still in their infancy in many countries, and local experts are hard to find at any price. And these programs are not inexpensive. Although the costs of implementing a compliance program vary depending on size, industry, risk areas, and the legal environment in which the company operates, it has been estimated that an independent compliance monitor for a multinational corporation may charge well in excess of US$1 million in fees over a two-year period.[40] For SMEs, even minor issues such as translation of program materials may pose significant costs.

The Bank's integrity compliance guidelines take into consideration a respondent's size and capacity. The guidelines outline the components of an integrity compliance program whose objective is to prevent, detect, and remediate corruption, collusion, coercion, and fraud within the party and clarify that SMEs may adopt less formal measures in developing a compliance program on account of firm size, business sector, location(s) of operations, and other circumstances particular to the party.

Despite all these barriers to entry, some low-capacity respondents do, in fact, choose to participate, at both the first and second tiers, so the current system cannot be considered entirely inaccessible. Without reaching out to actual respondents, observers can only make educated guesses about the reasons behind the pattern of nonengagement. Yet it is clear that the system, as it is currently constituted, poses some daunting challenges to low-capacity respondents and could be made more accessible—and therefore fairer—to those respondents.

---

40   The annual cost of mandatory ethics and compliance programs under the U.S. Federal Acquisition Regulation have been estimated to run to the tens of millions of dollars for a large corporation. However, the costs to a government contractor of not implementing an ethics and compliance program are deemed to be significantly greater than the costs for carrying out internal investigations, cooperating with external investigators, defending litigation, and settling cases. *See* John T. Jones & Greg Bingham, *Costs of Mandatory Ethics and Compliance Programs* (The Kenrich Group LLC 2009), available at http://www.kenrichgroup.com/news .php. On the broader issue of regulatory compliance, a recent study concluded that the average cost of compliance was US$3.5 million compared to the nearly US$9.4 million for organizations that experience noncompliance-related problems. *See The True Cost of Compliance—A Benchmark Study of Multinational Organizations* (Ponemon Inst. LLC 2011), available at http:// www.tripwire.com/tripwire/assets/File/ponemon/True_Cost_of_Compliance_Report.pdf. For a global snapshot of the state of compliance within firms, *see* Susannah Hammond & Jane Walshe, *Cost of Compliance Survey* (Thomson Reuters 2013), available at http://accelus .thomsonreuters.com/sites/default/files/The-Cost-of-Compliance.pdf.

Analysis of the Sanctions System under Access to Justice Principles

As discussed above, the broader notion of access to justice requires the elimination of unnecessary geographic, language, economic, and procedural obstacles to the services of the adjudicative body.

Geography

The vast majority of SMEs and other low-capacity respondents are located in the developing countries in which Bank-financed projects are implemented. While the first tier of sanctions proceedings before the SDO is entirely paper based and can be conducted by traditional mail, courier, or email,[41] second-tier proceedings before the Sanctions Board typically include hearings.[42] Because the Sanctions Board normally holds its sessions in Washington, D.C., travel costs and other associated costs and hurdles, such as obtaining a visa, likely represent an insurmountable barrier for certain types of respondents, especially SMEs and individuals.

The Sanctions Board's statute allows for sessions to be held elsewhere if the board considers that the efficient conduct of the proceedings so warrants,[43] although the board has never chosen to do so, in part because of cost and in part because, given the Bank's worldwide reach, the cases for any given session may involve misconduct in widely dispersed locations. In addition, hearings may be held via telephone conference or similar communication media, provided that all persons participating in the session can hear one another.[44] When hearings are requested, respondents are given the possibility of selecting their preference for remote participation, thus reducing geographic barriers and their concomitant costs.[45]

---

41   Documents, including explanations and responses, may be delivered or submitted by the respondent by mail or courier or in person. Although, in accordance with sec. 13.05(c) of the Sanctions Procedures, it is in the discretion of the SDO or the secretary to the Sanctions Board to accept submission of materials by electronic means, the practice has been to include in Notices of Sanctions Proceedings an email address for both the SDO and the secretary of the Sanctions Board to which respondents may elect to submit an explanation or a response, respectively.

42   Hearings may be held upon request by the respondent, or by INT, or upon decision by the Sanctions Board chair. See Sanctions Procedures, sec. 6.01.

43   Statute of the Sanctions Board, art. XII, para. 2.

44   Statute of the Sanctions Board, art. XII, para. 3.

45   This has been done in at least five cases. In another instance, a respondent arranged access to a potential witness by teleconference because the witness was unable to secure a visa. For an interesting analysis of the benefits and drawbacks resulting from the use of videoconferencing as an alternative means of providing access to courts under U.S. law, see Developments in the Law—Access to Courts, 122 Harv. L. Rev. 1151–1216 (2009). See also United States v. Lawrence, 248 F.3d 300, 304 (4th Cir. 2001) (holding that "even in an age of advancing technology, watching an event on the screen remains less than the complete equivalent of actually attending it").

Language

Language may be an obstacle for many SMEs and other low-capacity respondents, in particular those from non-Anglophone countries. Although the Bank has no "official" language, English is its working language for reasons of cost and promptness in the conduct of its business.[46] Reflecting general Bank practice, since its inception, the sanctions system has required English-only pleadings and proceedings.[47] This may bar some respondents from effectively defending themselves—non-Anglophone respondents who cannot afford or simply lack access to translation services. (By contrast, the rules governing procurement of goods, works, and services and the selection and employment of consultants under World Bank–financed projects—the context in which the majority of sanctions cases arise—do not require that bidding documents or requests for proposals be prepared in English.[48]) Moreover, the system may prove daunting even for English speakers, as the Sanctions Procedures and other key documents are drafted in legalese.

---

46   Historically, the World Bank Group has approached the issue of languages with flexibility in order to meet its constituent institutions' business needs and purposes. English is the working language of the Bank, the IFC, and MIGA. ICSID, on the other hand, has chosen three official languages in which to carry out its mandate and conduct its business. *See* World Bank, *A Document Translation Framework for the World Bank Group* (Aug. 6, 2003), available at http://documents.worldbank.org/curated/en/m2003/08/2734859/document-translation-framework-world-bank-group. *See* also Edward J. Mason & Robert E. Asher, *The World Bank since Bretton Woods* 66–68 (The Brookings Institution 1973) ("In the early years of the Bank, it was decided that English would be the working language—a decision that saved money and enormously expedited the conduct of business by comparison with the United Nations and most other international agencies").

47   All written submissions in connection with the sanctions proceedings, including the respondent's explanation and/or response, must be in English, except that exhibits shall be in the original language with the pertinent parts translated into English. *See* Sanctions Procedures, sec. 5.02(a).

48   For procurement under international competitive bidding, prequalification and bidding documents may be prepared in English, French, or Spanish. In addition, the borrower has the option to issue translated versions in another language (the "National Language"), which should either be the national language of the borrower or the language used nationwide in the borrower's country for commercial transactions. The contract signed with the winning bidder must be written in the language in which its bid was submitted, which is the one that governs the contractual relations between the borrower and the bidder. If the contract is signed in the National Nanguage, the borrower must provide the Bank with an accurate translation of the contract in English, French, or Spanish. The World Bank's Procurement Guidelines further specify that bidders are neither required nor permitted to sign contracts in more than one language. For procurement under national competitive bidding, there is no requirement that the relevant documents be prepared in English. *See* World Bank, *Guidelines for the Procurement of Goods, Works, and Non-consulting Services under IBRD Loans and IDA Credits & Grants*, secs. 2.15 and 3.4 (Jan. 2011), available at http://go.worldbank.org/XH679K5M60. Substantially similar provisions govern the selection and employment of consultants under World Bank–financed projects. *See* World Bank, *Guidelines for the Selection and Employment of Consultants under IBRD Loans and IDA Credits & Grants by World Bank Borrowers*, secs. 1.22 and 2.5 (Jan. 2011).

Economic Costs

Under access to justice principles, the cost of access to proceedings and records should be reasonable, fair, and affordable. The language and geographical requirements of the Bank's sanctions system can pose considerable costs for respondents, although the system does provide for mechanisms to reduce some of these costs. And although there is no requirement under the Sanctions Procedures that a respondent be represented by an attorney, the complexity of the system makes legal counsel highly desirable, if not an absolute necessity.[49] Legal advice typically does not come cheaply. For reasons of economy, the Bank does not offer legal aid to respondents, and the authors are not aware of significant pro bono work being done by private lawyers in connection with World Bank sanctions, although the Bank itself is beginning to make some efforts in this regard.

Procedural Barriers

One area where the Bank may claim considerable credit is in its procedures, which provide ample opportunity for respondents to mount a meaningful defense. An argument can be made that the 30-day response period that applies to submissions of explanations may be too short for some respondents, in particular those who require translation and/or need to hire legal counsel, but the procedures provide for the extension of this period by application to the SDO.[50] Practice shows that, generally, the SDO has granted extensions of up to 30 days based on reasonable grounds described by the respondent in a written application.[51]

Timeliness

The LEG review found that timeliness is an area in which the system has considerably improved. Processing times have been reduced considerably at every stage, from investigation to adjudication. For example, the time for the ini-

---

49 A respondent may be self-represented or represented by an attorney or any other individual authorized by the respondent, at the respondent's own expense. *See* Sanctions Procedures, sec. 6.02.

50 Upon request by the respondent, a reasonable extension of any time period for the filing of submissions may be granted, as a matter of discretion, by the suspension and evaluation officer, by notice to both parties. *See* Sanctions Procedures, sec. 4.02(b) (extending application of sec. 5.02(b), mutatis mutandis, to the explanation).

51 In one case, the respondent, a Thai medium-size enterprise, argued in its appeal to the Sanctions Board that it was unfair to require the filing of the explanation within 30 days and of the response within 90 days of delivery of the notice, after more than three years had passed from INT's investigation to the initial submission of the SAE, and almost two more years passed before the notice was issued. However, the Sanctions Board noted that the respondent could have, and did not, avail itself of the option to request an extension of time for its written submissions, as provided under secs. 4.02(b) and 5.02(b) of the Sanctions Procedures. Therefore, in the Sanctions Board's view, "the respondent's arguments of prejudice in its submission deadlines lacked foundation." Sanctions Board Decision no. 50 (issued May 30, 2012), at 25, available at http://siteresources.worldbank.org/EXTOFFEVASUS /Resources/WebsiteDecision50.pdf.

tial investigation phase has been cut by more than half if one compares the processing times for the first 25 cases processed under the two-tiered sanctions system against the most recent 25 cases completed as of June 30, 2012. The data also show improvement, albeit less dramatic, in all other phases of the sanctions process, with the periods in the adjudicative phase being much shorter to begin with. Overall, it is fair to say that the system compares favorably with national judicial systems and falls within due process norms. At the same time, there is room for further improvement.

Fairness, Equality, and Transparency

This is an area in which, again, the Bank has made considerable strides over the years, in particular in the area of transparency. While the Sanctions Board Statute and Sanctions Procedures have always been publicly available, the Bank recently enhanced the transparency of the system through publication of uncontested SDO determinations and Sanctions Board decisions in contested cases, the issuance of a *Law Digest*—a compendium of the legal principles underlying Sanctions Board decisions—and the public dissemination of the Sanctioning Guidelines and other guidance materials.[52]

The system provides for fairness and equal treatment through its Sanctioning Guidelines, which, although not binding on decision makers, provide a framework that guides those who have the discretion to impose sanctions as to the considerations that are relevant to any sanctioning decision. The public nature of Sanctions Board decisions, and the fact that they are reasoned, provides further assurance of fairness and equal treatment.[53]

Independence

An adjudicative body must be independent from political influence and other forms of pressure. Here again, the Bank's system has seen a considerable shift in favor of independence, with the transition from an internal Sanctions Committee to a semi-external Sanctions Board, complemented in 2009 by a transition from an internal to an external chair. The code of conduct adopted in 2010 confirms that Sanctions Board members may be removed for misconduct, after due process and decision by the Bank's executive directors.

---

52 World Bank, *The World Bank Group's Sanctions Regime: Information Note*, available at http://siteresources.worldbank.org/EXTOFFEVASUS/Resources/The_World_Bank_Group _Sanctions_Regime.pdf; World Bank, *The World Bank Sanctions Board Law Digest, Upholding the Rule of Law in the Fights against Corruption and Poverty* (World Bank 2011), available at http://siteresources.worldbank.org/INTOFFEVASUS/Resources/3601037-342729035803 /SanctionsBoardLawDigest.pdf; Leroy & Fariello, *supra* note 34; Daly & Fariello, *supra* note 39.

53 Leroy & Fariello, *supra* note 34, at 24–29. The SDO determinations published in uncontested cases also include the SDO's reasoning for the recommended sanction, in terms of the aggravating and mitigating factors considered.

Improving Access to Justice in the Sanctions System

A Few Ideas for Improvement

The issues discussed in this chapter had not gone unnoticed by the actors in the sanctions system even before the review, and the World Bank had already taken a number of steps to make the system more accessible to SMEs and other low-capacity respondents.

For example, INT advises that it takes into account the capacity of a subject of investigation, and whether the subject has legal counsel, in assessing statements in an interview or in response to a show cause letter. OSD has for some time included summaries in its Notices of Sanctions Proceedings that employ plain English and provide an overview of sanctions proceedings and the avenues available to the respondent for contesting the case. In addition to the specific accusations of INT and the SDO determination, the Notice includes a summary of the Sanctions Procedures and instructions to the respondent.

The ICO is taking steps to address the nonengagement of low-capacity respondents after sanction. Although the Bank has had integrity compliance guidelines since it introduced debarment with conditional release as its baseline sanction, the ICO is preparing a reader-friendly guidance note that provides practical and targeted support to SMEs to assist them in developing an effective integrity compliance program. The guidance reflects internationally recognized standards in corporate ethics and compliance and evolving best practices in the field of SME corporate governance. In addition, the ICO has reached out to a network of retired legal counsel with expertise in compliance programs that are willing to provide pro bono advice and support for debarred firms and individuals who wish to receive it.

However, it is the authors' contention that there is more that the Bank Group could and should be doing to make the system more accessible to SMEs and individuals without legal counsel, without incurring undue cost.

Geography and Language

The creation of "know your rights" literature for respondents would help to enhance transparency and create greater equality of arms between low-capacity respondents and INT. The use of plain English throughout sanctions proceedings would help surmount, at least in part, the language barrier that some respondents face. More regular use of videoconferencing or other virtual means to hold hearings would help to reduce or, in some cases, eliminate travel costs.

Costs and Length of Proceedings

A simplified approach to smaller cases would be more manageable for less sophisticated respondents and help make proceedings more expeditious. Other steps to expedite the sanctions process could include more frequent use of panels by the Sanctions Board to consider cases in real time in lieu of periodic plenary sessions.[54]

And although efforts are being made to make integrity compliance more understandable and affordable for SMEs, the Bank may also wish to consider curtailing the use of conditional release in smaller cases involving SMEs in favor of alternative approaches like more severe sanctions for repeat offenses. (This would involve a change to the Sanctioning Guidelines, which currently provide for debarment with conditional release as the default sanction.)

Settlements

In the context of settlements, in cases for which there is a compelling reason to believe that the respondent may lack the capacity to make a fully informed decision or effectively assert its legitimate interests, especially where it lacks legal representation, the SDO could make full use of its power to review the negotiated resolution agreement with heightened scrutiny, including (where appropriate) consultation with the respondent, to verify its understanding of the terms and conditions of the agreement, thus mitigating the risk of low-capacity respondents entering into a negotiated resolution of the case without a full understanding of the implications of doing so.

Independence

In its recent review, LEG called for steps to enhance the independence of the system, most notably through a transition to an all-external Sanctions Board. Although the SDO is a Bank officer, the SDO's independence could be enhanced through increased security of tenure, allowing for a fixed term of office and removal only for cause.

Transparency

The World Bank can rightly claim to have created the most transparent sanctions system among international organizations—and many national agencies as well. Nevertheless, the LEG review calls for even more transparency. Among other things, the Bank will soon make public the *Sanctions Manual*, which sets out Bank management's internal guidance for decision makers in the system on issues including sources of law, hierarchy of norms, treatment of corporate groups, and other topics of relevance to respondents.[55] LEG recently made public its advisory opinions, which set out the General Counsel's

---

54   In a few of the early cases, the first chair of the Sanctions Board chose to form three-person panels to hear sanctions cases, which allowed for "real-time" consideration of referrals. During the term of the second chair, plenary sessions were favored in order to encourage coherence and consistency in approach. As the system matures, there may be opportunities to rely more on panels, in particular for cases that do not present novel or complex issues.

55   Some of the main principles in these areas have already been made public though the Leroy & Fariello article and the Information Note. *See* Leroy & Fariello, *supra* note 34; and *The World Bank Group's Sanctions Regime: Information Note, supra* note 52.

authoritative advice on key substantive legal issues such as mens rea, the concept of recklessness, and theories of collective and derivative liability.

Instilling Trust and Confidence in the System

The LEG review called for more outreach and consultation with external stakeholders in the system, especially when changes in the system are being contemplated. The Bank already does this when making changes to its operational policies, so it should follow suit when dealing with sanctions policy. Stakeholder involvement, in turn, will enable a transparent policy-making process and should increase the level of the overall social and business acceptance of the decisions made in reforming the sanctions regime, resulting in a higher degree of public trust and confidence.

Is Legal Aid for Respondents Viable?

Legal aid is one area in which the Bank may be reluctant to venture, given the potentially prohibitive costs involved. The Bank's Voluntary Disclosure Program (VDP), adopted in 2006,[56] set a precedent for the idea that the Bank should provide low-capacity respondents with legal assistance in order to remove a possible barrier to entry into the program.[57] If the Bank were to provide legal aid, it would need to confront the issue of who would provide such assistance. The ICO, for example, which must assess a respondent's compliance program and decide whether to release the respondent from debarment, would face a conflict of interest if it were to provide direct assistance. One possible way forward, building on the ICO's initiative, would be to encourage the formation of a pro bono bar for respondents among civic-minded lawyers.

A Question of Balance

In considering these ideas and others, the key will be to balance considerations of access and fundamental fairness with the need to keep expenses reasonable. The sanctions system consumes considerable institutional resources, and these resources have increased as the system has grown more sophisticated. It is clear, however, that decisions informed exclusively by considerations of economy for the Bank have the consequence of shifting the economic burden onto respondents, including those whose resources may be limited, such as SMEs and individuals. At the same time, like many governments and other international organizations, the Bank is operating in an increasingly resource-constrained environment. Fairness is important—indeed, it is crucial—but so

---

56   World Bank, *VDP Guidelines for Participants*, sec. 7.2, available at http://siteresources.world
       bank.org/INTVOLDISPRO/Resources/VDP_Guidelines_2011.pdf.

57   To prevent the costs associated with the VDP from deterring small firms from entering the
       program, the Bank allows firms with fewer than 50 employees to petition INT to have INT
       perform some or all of the investigations, report generations, compliance program development,
       and compliance monitoring. As of May 13, 2013, there had been only one instance
       in which a firm petitioned INT to receive, and INT agreed to provide, assistance with the
       compliance monitoring phase.

are the Bank's other activities in favor of the poor. Unfortunately, budgets are a zero-sum game.

The Case for Access to Justice

The question could plausibly be posed: Why should the Bank care if SMEs are disproportionately impacted by the system? The Bank has limited resources for fighting corruption, so why spend those scarce resources to help corrupt actors?

These are not trivial questions. The Bank's sanctions system is founded on the fiduciary duty in its Articles of Agreement that requires that the Bank take appropriate measures to ensure that its financing is used for purposes intended, with due consideration for economy and efficiency.[58] It owes this duty both to the member states that provide the Bank with its financial wherewithal and to its borrowers and their beneficiary populations, who are the principal victims of fraud and corruption. From an economic standpoint, corruption distorts capital flows from their intended and productive purposes. Diverted funds reduce the impact of development assistance and constitute an unproductive burden on the borrower's treasury. The Bank's foremost concern must therefore be the protection of its financing—and the development effectiveness of the projects and programs it finances—by preventing and combating fraud and corruption.

This is not the end of the story, however. From its inception, the Bank has recognized that the manner in which it pursues the fiduciary duty, particularly in the area of sanctions, is crucial to the entire enterprise. In devising the basic blueprint for the Bank's sanctions system, the Thornburgh panel recognized that it was proposing a more formal structure than was common among national or international debarment systems. But the panel noted that there was a consensus among senior Bank managers and professional staff that the Bank was in a unique position, and that the stakes posed by a Bank debarment called for greater process and attention. Notably, the panel recognized that debarment could have a significant adverse effect not only on the debarred entity but also on development effectiveness by reducing the pool of companies available for projects. Given the double-edged sword that sanctions, and particularly debarment, represent, and given the Bank's development mandate, the panel put a premium on considerations of accuracy and fairness.[59]

One should not lose sight of the fact that the system is predicated on a presumption of innocence. That means that until a final determination is made by the SDO or the Sanctions Board, the respondent must not be treated as a corrupt actor. In this light, a firm that is sanctioned by default because it lacks the means to defend itself is a cause for serious concern.

---

58   IBRD Articles of Agreement, art. III, sec. 5(b), and IDA Articles of Agreement, art. V, sec. 6. *See* also Sanctions Procedures, sec. 1.01(a).

59   *See* Second Thornburgh Report, *supra* note 7, at 6.

Even at the ICO stage, after a respondent has been found culpable for misconduct, there are reasons why the Bank should care whether the respondent has engaged or will engage with the system. The Bank's sanctions system is not meant to be punitive in nature; it is protective and—one hopes—rehabilitative in nature. Indeed, that is the stated purpose for imposing conditions for release.[60]

Many SME respondents hail from countries where corruption is endemic. In these environments, small private actors who wish to participate in public procurement often feel they have no choice but to acquiesce to the prevailing corrupt arrangements because public officials or other, more influential private actors impose those arrangements on smaller actors. In these circumstances—although misconduct has occurred—it is overly simplistic to see SME respondents merely as bad actors not worth worrying about.

At its ideal best, engagement with the sanctions system, in particular with the ICO, can be seen as taking the fight against corruption to its highest level, which presupposes some kind of re-education and commitment on the part of the respondent to core integrity values and principles. In turn, this commitment takes shape in the adoption of a compliance program aimed at preventing and avoiding the occurrence of illicit corrupt and fraudulent practices in the future.

The case for access to justice posits that, given all these considerations, the sanctions system cannot be only about "getting the bad guys." The system already provides significant fairness, but it needs to be further improved, particularly to ensure that the significant due process protections it does provide are available to all, not just to those who can afford it, and not just on paper but in fact.

---

60   *See* Leroy & Fariello, *supra* note 34, at 15–16.

Private Civil Actions
A Tool for a Citizen-Led Battle against Corruption

WILLIAM T. LORIS

The fight against corruption relies heavily on the threat of prosecution under criminal laws. To succeed, this approach requires political will and commitment, concerted action by state institutions, and an independent, noncorrupt judiciary. However, the fight against corruption could be expanded and invigorated by providing ordinary citizens and legal entities a clear legal framework for the pursuit of private civil actions against corruption. This chapter proposes a three-point conceptual framework for how civil actions could serve as an additional weapon in the anticorruption arsenal by providing for specific remedial and recovery measures, empowering victims of corruption, and engendering social transformation around cases on which media and civil society can focus. The chapter advocates for the development of regional conventions under which signatory states would expand their obligations under the United Nations Convention Against Corruption by further committing to establishing and implementing a legal framework for private actions against corruption that include features similar to those in the Council of Europe Civil Law Convention on Corruption.

The chapter begins with an outline of the traditional criminal law approach to corruption, which has increasingly paid attention to victims' rights. The chapter then describes the rise of civil actions against corruption, highlighting the objectives of such actions and their advantages when compared to a traditional criminal law approach. The international law basis of private legal civil actions against corruption is explained and difficulties in domestic implementation are discussed. The three-point conceptual framework for using civil actions against corruption is discussed in detail, illustrated by the French *Biens Mal Acquis* cases, and analyzed in terms of access to justice for the poor. The chapter concludes with general thoughts on how civil actions foster development through opportunity, inclusion, and equity.

The author wishes to acknowledge and express appreciation for the substantial support in the preparation of this chapter by Simon N. M. Young, professor of law and director of the Centre for Comparative and Public Law, Faculty of Law, University of Hong Kong. His support included advice on the chapter structure and arguments, editing, and the contribution of the text concerning the *Biens Mal Acquis* cases. The author also wishes to express appreciation for editorial and drafting assistance in the preparation of this chapter by Alison Rende, 2013 Loyola University Chicago PROLAW LL.M candidate, and Bandini Chhichhia, 2012 PROLAW LL.M graduate.

The fight against corruption is normally carried out in the context of a country's criminal justice system. State legislation defines corrupt behavior and assigns penalties for convicted violators. State institutions are the central actors in the detection and investigation of criminal activity, the apprehension of suspected violators, and the prosecution and enforcement of court-ordered penalties and punishment. The general public's role is largely a passive one, even when members of the public have suffered harm from the corrupt acts that are the subject of prosecution.

In recent years, the plight of victims of crime has received greater attention. Several countries have established schemes that provide for the compensation of victims of certain violent crimes, including acts of terrorism.[1] Others have extended the concept of compensating victims to other types of crime. For instance, in the United States, the Mandatory Victim Restitution Act of 1996 authorizes courts to order those convicted of any offense committed by fraud or deceit as a result of which an identifiable victim or victims have suffered physical injury or pecuniary loss to provide restitution to the victims.[2] Enactment of this law was a victory for the victims' rights movement, which succeeded in making the needs and concerns of victims the subject of national concern and focus.[3]

Other examples are Italian and U.S. laws that provide for victim compensation for harm suffered as a result of racketeering and extortion. Italian law allows victims to become parties of interest in relevant criminal proceedings with eventual compensation being made from a dedicated solidarity fund.[4] The U.S. Racketeer Influenced and Corrupt Organizations (RICO) Act allows victims to use civil actions to seek damages for harm suffered from racketeering and corrupt acts.[5] Although the U.S. Foreign Corrupt Practices Act (FCPA) does not provide for a private right of action, U.S. and foreign plaintiffs are using the U.S. courts for private actions based on the same factual settings as those on which FCPA actions are or can be based.[6] These examples are part of the broader trend toward the recognition of the rights and needs of victims

---

1   In particular, in the wake of the terrorist attacks in New York in 2001, in Beslan (Russian Federation) and Madrid in 2004, and in London in 2005, assistance to victims of terrorism has become a priority. *See* Council of Europe, http://www.coe.int/t/dlapil/codexter/victims_en.asp (accessed May 23, 2013).

2   Title II of the Antiterrorism and Effective Death Penalty Act of 1996, Pub. L. No. 104-132, 110 Stat. 1214 (effective Apr. 24, 1996), codified at 18 U.S.C. sec. 3663A.

3   Edna Erez & Julian Roberts, *Victim Participation in the Criminal Justice System*, in *Victims of Crime* 277 (Robert C. Davis et al. eds., 3d ed., Sage 2007).

4   Legge 44 (Feb. 23, 1999); Gazzette Ufficiale 51 (Mar. 3, 1999).

5   *See* Racketeer Influenced and Corrupt Organizations Act, 18 U.S.C. secs. 1961–1968 (1982 & Supp. IV 1986); 18 U.S.C. sec. 1964(c) ("Any person injured in his business or property by reason of a violation of section 1962 of this chapter may sue therefor in any appropriate United States district court and shall recover threefold the damages he sustains and the cost of the suit, including a reasonable attorney's fee").

6   Jason E. Prince, *A Rose by Any Other Name? Foreign Corrupt Practices Act–Inspired Civil Actions*, The Advocate (Mar./Apr. 2009).

of crime as reflected in the UN Declaration of Basic Principles of Justice for Victims of Crime and Abuse of Power.[7]

Each of these schemes is dependent on the initiation and outcome of criminal proceedings. The benefits and protections available to victims hinge on a state's success in detecting, investigating, and prosecuting corrupt activity. If the state fails to act, or where prosecution fails, justice may not be obtained.

The Rise of Private Civil Actions against Corruption

Fortunately, securing justice for the victims of corruption need not begin and end with the vigor of state authorities in fighting corruption or the state's success or failure in prosecuting individual cases of corruption. Victims have an alternative in which they become the moving parties, in which they become the protagonists in the fight against specific instances of corruption. They can do this by undertaking private civil actions against corrupt persons. These civil actions may be closely linked to relevant criminal proceedings, especially with regard to certain procedural issues and the collection of evidence, but they are independent of such criminal proceedings.

The objectives of civil actions are different from those pursued in criminal actions. The latter are aimed at retribution and deterrence. Plaintiffs in civil actions are seeking to secure remedies that will relieve them or compensate them for harm they have suffered as a result of corruption.

Transparency International's 2013 *Global Corruption Report: Education* highlights a number of advantages that civil actions may have in the fight against corruption.[8] The first and most obvious is that having a right to initiate private civil actions against the corrupt makes each person and each legal entity in a given jurisdiction a potential "prosecutor" in her or his own right. This multiplies the points of detection and control of corruption, thus supplementing the scarce resources and reach of official justice institutions. Legal actions by individual victims, be they natural persons or legal entities, send an important warning message to the corrupt and a message of hope and empowerment to the general public.

As a complement to the criminal justice system, private civil actions create a more perilous playing field for those who engage in corrupt practices. The implication for legal reformers is that providing a clear legal framework for private actions of large numbers of well-informed private individuals and legal entities looking after their own interests presents tactical and strategic advantages in the fight against corruption.

---

7   Declaration of Basic Principles of Justice for Victims of Crime and Abuse of Power, A/RES/40/34 (Nov. 29, 1985), available at http://www.un.org/documents/ga/res/40/a40r034.htm (accessed May 23, 2013).

8   *Global Corruption Report: Education* (Transparency International 2013).

In addition, the remedies available in civil proceedings serve victims' interests better than criminal proceedings might. Although a conviction may provide a sense of vindication, unless the particular jurisdiction provides for mandatory compensation for victims, a mere conviction leaves the victims' situation largely unchanged.

It is an advantage when a private party may initiate a civil action even when the state authorities decide not to press criminal charges. The ability of private citizens and legal entities to decide independently whether to initiate private actions limits the circumstances in which a jurisdiction's executive and justice institutions can politically afford to remain inactive.

In jurisdictions where the burden of proof required to succeed in a civil proceeding is lower than that required in a criminal proceeding, civil actions may offer a procedural advantage. Formulations of the standard of proof in civil cases such as "a preponderance of the evidence," "more likely than not," or a "reasonable possibility" are far less burdensome than standards such as "beyond reasonable doubt," which is common in criminal proceedings. But this procedural advantage is not available in all legal systems. Under German law, for example, a "beyond reasonable doubt" standard is applied in civil and criminal proceedings.[9]

Other procedural advantages may be available in civil proceedings in some jurisdictions. Certain jurisdictions' procedural rules provide for a shifting of the burden of proof to the defendant once the claimant has made a prima facie case. A wide range of remedies are normally available to civil claimants, and these can be chosen to fit the circumstances of particular claimants' needs. Procedures may be available to allow the claimant to name defendants in a particular suit who would be considered too remote from a criminal law standpoint to be prosecuted.

Finally, although petty corruption that plagues the poor is likely to be considered too insignificant and too diffuse to be effectively dealt with by criminal prosecutors, the poor would still have access to civil actions to seek redress. In this way, the civil action becomes an inclusive mechanism to realize equality and fairness in society.

These advantages are so clear that one commentator called on the World Bank and other donors to provide support directed at developing the conditions for the pursuit of civil remedies against corrupt officials. That commentator described such remedies as a powerful weapon against corruption and pointed out that for businesses, the prospect of recovery of damages would provide a strong incentive to pursue a civil action.[10] The recent proliferation

---

9   Juliane Kokott, *The Burden of Proof in Comparative and Human Rights Law: Civil and Common Law Approaches with Special Reference to the American and German Legal Systems* 18 (Kluwer L. Intl. 1998).

10   Bryane Michael, *Suing against Corruption*, in *Policy Innovations* (Carnegie Foundation Sept. 2007), available at http://www.policyinnovations.org/ideas/innovations/data/000015/ (accessed May 23, 2013).

of private legal actions by corporate victims of corruption seems to support that assertion.

Other commentators are in agreement. The rise in the use of private legal actions against corruption has been explained by what Simon Young refers to as "the empowering effect of suing, the political significance of these lawsuits."[11] Commenting on her native Nigeria, Abiola Makinwa stated that "the civil law provides a window of opportunity. Creating an environment where the private and public law present a coherent response to the offenders and to the transactions involved in the corruption exchange will push the frontiers of the fight against international corruption."[12]

Expanding the Legal Basis for Private Legal Civil Actions

Although there is new interest in private civil actions against corruption, the legal basis of such actions is well rooted in existing law. Most civil and common law systems provide the basic legal framework for bringing such actions. The starting point is the nearly universal feature in legal systems under which everyone is responsible for harm caused by his or her intentional acts. In civil code jurisdictions, the basic provisions of civil responsibility are relevant. In common law jurisdictions, tort and equity principles can be invoked, and damages and other remedies can be crafted to fit individual cases. Jurisdictions apply these doctrinal frameworks and deal with remedies quite differently, but the basis for initiating private actions is generally available for actions seeking such remedies as restitution, compensation for damages, and court-mandated remedial actions such as injunctions.

Mariani points out that under Italian, French, and German law, the basic civil responsibility provisions of the civil code support such actions seeking such remedies. The right to pursue such suits and seek damages or injunctive or other kinds of relief is also well established.[13]

Political support has deepened and the legal framework for private civil actions has been expanded by the adoption of two international conventions. The first is the 1999 Council of Europe Civil Law Convention on Corruption (the Civil Law Convention).[14] The report accompanying the Civil Law Convention explains that when fighting against corruption,

> civil law is directly linked to criminal law and administrative law. If an offence such as corruption is prohibited under criminal law, a

---

11   Simon Young, *Why Civil Actions against Corruption?* 16(2) J. Fin. Crime 144–159 (2009).

12   Abiola O. Makinwa, *Motivating Civil Remedies for International Corruption: Nigeria as an Illustrative Case Study* 2(2) CALS Rev. Nigerian L. & Prac. 128 (2008).

13   Paola Mariani, *How Damages Recovery Actions Can Improve the Fight against Corruption: The Crisis of Criminal Law Policies and the Role of Private Enforcement in an Italian Case of Judicial Corruption* (Bocconi Legal Stud. Research Paper No. 2007241, Feb. 17, 2012).

14   Civil Law Convention on Corruption, ETS 174 (adopted Nov. 4, 1999), available at http://conventions.coe.int/Treaty/en/Treaties/Html/174.htm (accessed May 23, 2013).

claim for damages can be made which is based on the commission of the criminal act. Victims might find it easier to safeguard their interests under civil law than to use criminal law. Similarly, if an administration does not exercise sufficiently its supervisory responsibilities, a claim for damages may be made.[15]

The Civil Law Convention was the first attempt to define common international rules in the field of civil law and corruption. Article 1 of the Civil Law Convention requires state parties to provide in their domestic law "for effective remedies for persons who have suffered damage as a result of acts of corruption, to enable them to defend their rights and interests, including the possibility of obtaining compensation for damage."[16]

The Civil Law Convention provides for measures to be taken at national levels, provisions promoting international cooperation, and, significantly, monitoring of implementation. The parties are obligated under the Civil Law Convention to undertake to incorporate the convention's principles and rules into their domestic law, taking into account their own particular circumstances.

The Civil Law Convention covers a wide range of issues, including compensation for damage, which may cover material damage, loss of profits, and nonpecuniary loss; liability (including state liability for acts of corruption committed by public officials); contributory negligence (by the plaintiff); reduction or disallowance of compensation, depending on the circumstances; validity of contracts; protection of employees who report corruption; court orders to preserve the assets necessary for the execution of the final judgment and the maintenance of the status quo pending resolution of the points at issue; and international cooperation.

The core provisions of the Civil Law Convention are found in Articles 3 and 5.[17] Article 3 defines the core obligation that the parties ensure that victims of corruption have the right to initiate their own legal proceedings. Article 5 defines the right of victims to claim compensation. The actual language is as follows:

---

15 *Explanatory Report*, Council of Europe Civil Law Convention on Corruption, para. I(a)(12), available at http://conventions.coe.int/Treaty/EN/Reports/Html/174.htm.

16 *See supra* note 14, at art. 1. As of May 20, 2013, the following states were signatories to the convention: Albania, Andorra, Armenia,* Austria, Azerbaijan, Belarus, Belgium, Bosnia and Herzegovina, Bulgaria, Croatia, Cyprus, Czech Republic,* Denmark,* Estonia, Finland, France, Georgia,* Germany,* Greece, Hungary, Iceland,* Ireland,* Italy,* Latvia, Lithuania, Luxembourg, Malta,* Moldova, Montenegro, Netherlands, Norway, Poland, Romania, Serbia, Slovak Republic, Slovenia, Spain, Sweden, FYR Macedonia, Turkey, Ukraine, United Kingdom* (*not ratified). Council of Europe members that had not signed or ratified the convention include Liechtenstein, Monaco, Portugal, Russian Federation, San Marino, and Switzerland. In addition to Belarus, non–Council of Europe member states Canada, the Holy See, Japan, Mexico, and the United States participated in the elaboration of the convention

17 *Supra* note 13, at arts. 3 and 5.

Article 3: Compensation for damage

Each Party shall provide in its internal law for persons who have suffered damage as a result of corruption to have the right to initiate an action in order to obtain full compensation for such damage.

Article 5: State responsibility

Each Party shall provide in its internal law for appropriate procedures for persons who have suffered damage as a result of an act of corruption by its public officials in the exercise of their functions to claim for compensation from the State or, in the case of a non-state Party, from that Party's appropriate authorities.

Another important feature of the Civil Law Convention is that the parties have defined a mechanism for monitoring implementation of the convention. Under the Civil Law Convention, the European Union's Group of States against Corruption (GRECO) is charged with monitoring commitments entered into under the Civil Law Convention by the state parties.[18] Reviews of implementation and related aspects of corruption in the contracting states are undertaken periodically, and the results are made public.

The GRECO system is worth studying in some detail because it may provide a model of how to ensure monitoring and reporting on the implementation of other current or future international conventions or similar arrangements dealing with the control of corruption. For instance, certain GRECO reports highlight the lack of follow-up implementation by specific states, whereas others provide specific information on modifications to the domestic legal framework of others. At present, the Civil Law Convention is limited in application to certain European countries, but it serves as a clear and inspirational example of how far states can go to promote and facilitate civil actions as a tool to fight corruption.

The second and more significant convention that provides for private civil actions against corruption is the UN Convention Against Corruption (UNCAC), to which over 165 states are party.[19] UNCAC is the most comprehensive international convention on corruption and covers a wide range of matters. Using language that closely tracks the Civil Law Convention, UNCAC requires that state parties ensure that measures are taken to facilitate private civil actions. The actual language is as follows:

Article 35: Compensation for damage

Each State Party shall take such measures as may be necessary, in accordance with principles of its domestic law, to ensure that entities or persons who have suffered damage as a result of an act of

---

18 GRECO Statute, Annexed to Council of Europe Committee of Ministers, Resolution (99)5 Establishing the Group of States against Corruption (GRECO, adopted May 1, 1999).

19 United Nations Convention Against Corruption, GA Res. 58/4 (adopted Oct. 31, 2003), available at http://www.unodc.org/unodc/en/treaties/CAC/index.html.

corruption have the right to initiate legal proceedings against those responsible for that damage in order to obtain compensation.[20]

The *travaux préparatoires* that accompanied UNCAC included two interpretative notes relevant to Article 35. The notes explain:

> (a) The expression "entities or persons" is deemed to include States as well as legal and natural persons;

> (b) This article is intended to establish the principle that States parties should ensure that they have mechanisms permitting persons or entities suffering damage to initiate legal proceedings, in appropriate circumstances, against those who commit acts of corruption (for example, where the acts have a legitimate relationship to the State party where the proceedings are to be brought). While article 35 does not restrict the right of each State party to determine the circumstances under which it will make its courts available in such cases, it is also not intended to require or endorse the particular choice made by a State party in doing so.[21]

These notes highlight the relative complexity of implementing the basic Article 35 obligation. Note b refers to the establishment of the principle that state parties should ensure that they have mechanisms permitting persons or entities suffering damage to initiate legal proceedings, in appropriate circumstances, against those who commit acts of corruption. The clear message is that each state party must determine for itself the detailed manner and the detailed legal framework in which it will give substance to this principle in domestic law.

The degree of complexity and the variety of approaches available in implementing the right to private civil action principle in given jurisdictions can be appreciated by comparing the issues involved in this area in different jurisdictions. Olaf Meyer collected a rich set of national commentaries in this regard, which includes jurisdictions as different from one another as Bulgaria and Nigeria.[22] In *Key Issues of Civil Law in Corruption Cases in Bulgaria*, Christian Takoff writes:

> The criminal circumstance of "bribery" cannot be proved in civil law proceedings; they have to be suspended until the criminal law court has rendered its decision. The law does not provide for presumptions helping to prove corruption. It is only the giving and obtaining of the bribe that is proven in criminal law courts.[23]

---

20   Note the distinction between art. 35, which discusses civil actions by entities or natural persons, and art. 53(a), which provides that states can initiate civil actions in connection with asset-recovery proceedings.

21   United Nations Office on Drugs and Crime, Travaux Préparatoires, art. 35, available at http://www.unodc.org/unodc/en/treaties/CAC/travaux-preparatoires.html (accessed May 23, 2013).

22   Olaf Meyer ed., *The Civil Law Consequences of Corruption* (Nomos 2009).

23   *Id.*, at 200.

The removal of bribery from the list of possible corrupt behavior that can be proved in a civil proceeding will affect the way in which the EU Convention or Article 35 of UNCAC can be implemented in Bulgaria. Corrections of this problem need to be dealt with through careful refinement of both criminal and civil law. Dalton's examination of the difficulties in dealing with cultural heterogeneity in making distinctions between bribery and legitimate gift giving hint at the complexities of adjusting national legal systems to the expectations reflected in these international instruments.[24]

Conceptual Framework for Implementation of UNCAC Article 35 and the Civil Law Convention

Given the relatively new interest in private civil actions and the critical importance of the main, criminal, aspects of UNCAC, it is not surprising that implementation of UNCAC Article 35 has not been assigned a higher priority by the state parties in their review and follow-up framework. This does not mean, however, that the basic obligation in Article 35 is any less binding than the convention's other obligations.

The realization of the potential that the civil actions envisioned in Article 35 have in the battle against corruption may require additional work at the regional level aimed at developing the details of reform and building understanding of how to use this new area of law in practice.

One way to organize such an initiative would be for state parties to develop civil action–focused regional conventions. Negotiation of such conventions would provide the needed attention to the detailed changes that Article 35 reforms require, and would provide an opportunity for the involvement of the public at large and the building of a coalition of nonstate actors with an interest in the outcome. Such a coalition could include legal professionals, business leaders, civil society, academics, the media, and members of the public, including the poor. Ideally, each such regional convention would reflect the core purpose by formulating something akin to "The (Region) Convention on the Establishment of Arrangements Favoring Private Civil Actions against Corruption." In the greater European area, where a detailed regional convention already exists, state party interaction in the regional convention's review mechanism would be strengthened by building the kind of formalized coalition of nonstate actors and the direct involvement of that coalition in the review process.

The idea of using regional conventions as a tool to strengthen implementation of a global norm has been applied in the human rights arena, where the Universal Declaration of Human Rights was implemented by various regions in the form of similar and improved instruments: the African (Banjul) Charter

---

24 Marie M. Dalton, *Efficiency v. Morality: The Codification of Cultural Norms in the Foreign Corrupt Practices Act*, 2 N.Y.U. J.L. & Bus. 583–689 (2006).

on Human and Peoples' Rights,[25] the American Convention on Human Rights,[26] and the European Convention on Human Rights,[27] with subsequent revisions in the form of protocols.

Strengthening of regional mechanisms, their attendant processes, and the successful implementation of the reforms that they engender can add value in the fight against corruption by strengthening the remedial/recovery purposes of UNCAC, enhancing the empowerment of victims of corruption by engendering social transformation around real cases on which media and civil society can focus.

Strengthening the Remedial and Recovery Purposes of UNCAC

All civil actions, by their nature, are driven by litigants' hope to secure a right, to recover property, to avoid or minimize ongoing or imminent harm, or to recover full or partial loss occasioned by the actions or inactions of public or private parties. Private civil actions against the corrupt are no different in this respect. They have the same remedial and recovery purposes as other kinds of civil actions.

Extending this observation to the area under discussion, each civil action against corruption in a jurisdiction covered by UNCAC or the Civil Law Convention can be viewed as supporting the remedial and recovery purposes of those conventions. The challenge is to ensure that such actions can be maintained in the courts of the state parties. In many jurisdictions, this will require some legal reform and accommodation.

Given the low priority that implementation of Article 35 has been assigned under the UNCAC review process, a parallel initiative that concentrates solely on Article 35 implementation could hasten the reforms that state parties need to accomplish in this area. If state parties were to follow the suggestion in this chapter that they enter into negotiation of regional conventions that concentrate solely on civil actions against corruption, the regional negotiation processes would provide "faction-forcing events" that bring into focus the details of needed reforms. The Civil Law Convention would provide an excellent starting point for such negotiations because it identifies many of the details that national reforms need to take into account to make civil actions against corruption an effective tool. Involvement of top academic, business, civil society, and legal personalities in the drafting process would provide each country involved with a base of expertise that could be drawn upon for required follow-up.

---

25   OAU Doc. CAB/LEG/67/3 rev. 5, 21 I.L.M. 58 (1982) (adopted June 27, 1981, entered into force Oct. 21, 1986).

26   OAS Treaty Series No. 36; 1144 U.N.T.S. 123; 9 ILM 99 (1969).

27   Council of Europe, European Convention for the Protection of Human Rights and Fundamental Freedoms, as amended by Protocols No. 11 and 14 (Nov. 4, 1950), ETS 5.

Reform for Empowerment

The process described above would provide the impetus for the follow-up work at the national level required to ensure that civil actions against corruption become well supported under the law and well-known in society as a whole. Empowerment of the victims of corruption would come in a variety of forms, as illustrated in the following hypothetical scenarios:

- Private sector businesses and private entrepreneurs would be able to use civil actions to claim compensation for losses suffered as a result of corruption such as bribery in connection with the award of publicly procured contracts, or possibly to have such contracts annulled, whether or not criminal charges in connection with the same acts of corruption have been filed.

- Adjacent landowners would be able to seek court orders to halt works for which building permits have been corruptly procured or where the authorities turn a blind eye to construction without such permits in return for an illegal payment or gratuity.

- Parents whose children have been denied school admission for lack of a private payment to a school official could seek court orders to compel admission.

- The very poor and helpless, who suffer disproportionally from the effects of corruption, would now have a means of seeking redress. Mothers who walk many kilometers to seek care for a child at a public hospital and are forced to pay medical staff as a condition of treatment could file suits to recover those illicit charges or for the damages suffered as a result of being denied admission.

- Small vendors prevented from operating in certain areas by police in the pay of more established shop owners would be able to seek compensation for being denied the opportunity to compete or to compel the police to desist with their evictions.

- Civil society organizations such as legal aid societies and anticorruption groups could direct their efforts nationally by supporting litigation efforts in the form of training and capacity building, funding direct actions, providing assistance to litigants, or filing amicus curae briefs in courts.

Although success in such actions would certainly be important, the sense of empowerment would be experienced to some degree just by bringing such cases to the courts and bearing public witness in the presence of the defendants they plan to prove corrupt. It would also be empowering for observers of such processes to see ordinary people taking a public stand and seeking justice.

The vision of such an awakened and empowered populace is not likely to become a reality unless some of the barriers to success in civil actions against corruption are addressed. These include the cost of civil litigation, jurisdiction over small-value claims, gathering of evidence, proof of the corrupt act, the possibility of retribution against the claimant, acts of the claimant that may have contributed to the corrupt acts complained of, and the measure of damages or design of effective remedial measures. Each country will differ in its approaches, and the obstacles and challenges to access to justice will need to be crafted based on the realities on the ground.

The beginning point for dealing with such issues could be the negotiation of the regional conventions. Creative provisions that fit a region could be crafted for all such issues that will inform the domestic reforms and the practice that grows up in this area. The conventions could include provisions that require or encourage the establishment of domestic provisions needed for the authorization of class action procedures for multiple claimants relating to the corrupt behavior. They could also provide guidance on protection for claimants, speedy procedures to prevent the occurrence of irreparable harm, and the exclusion of contributory causation for payments extorted or paid by a claimant under duress, such as under threat of denial of a public service.

In regions with high percentages of poor people in their populations or where gender equality is an issue, other provisions might be considered for inclusion in the regional conventions. These include the establishment of a duty by the signatories to minimize the cost of litigation such as through the establishment of reduced filing fees for the poor, especially for small matters, and the duty of states to establish and maintain dedicated courts in locations to which poorer litigants have access, including the establishment of mobile courts with simplified procedures, including enforcement procedures, for small-value matters. The inclusion of a requirement that signatory states ensure the availability of legal aid for the poor would send a strong message on access to justice and provide an enabling environment for the poor that would have implications beyond the area of corruption. Provisions requiring that signatory states allow litigants, especially poor litigants, to use local languages and a requirement that signatory states specifically provide for standing to sue for women and public interest groups would further inform and influence the national implementation processes that would follow.

Involvement of women and representatives from poor and rural communities and the NGOs that work in these communities in the preparation of the regional conventions would help the framers develop pro gender and pro poor features in the final texts. This process alone would be an empowering experience.

Civil Actions as a Source of Social Transformation

Irrespective of their outcomes, civil actions against corruption have the potential to serve as powerful motivators for social change. Like a mass protest, a graphic scene of ordinary people lined up to file their writ in the courthouse, all seeking to recover the years of systemic bribes they have had to pay daily in exchange for basic public services, would grip the imagination of the world and generate strong political and moral pressure on those in power to transform their societies. It is the side effects of these suits that matter. They can bring international media attention to a particular case that highlights an injustice. They can galvanize civil society to focus on a common cause. They can generate local debate and demands for action.

In other words, civil actions can have a strong symbolic significance. They can represent a public frustrated with the political process rising up to challenge the status quo, not by anarchy or disorder, but by using law and the courts. They can affirm the value of and strengthen the rule of law and shame those in power.

An instructive example of the symbolic significance that actions of this kind can have is the ongoing French *Biens Mal Acquis* cases involving the alleged corruption-linked assets of the ruling families of several African nations.[28] These cases were initiated not by French authorities but by the persistent efforts of African citizens working together with public interest groups, including Transparency International (TI) France and Sherpa.[29] When the French prosecutors refused to act in 2008, TI France and a citizen from Gabon obtained standing to file a civil party petition to trigger a judicial process, potentially leading to criminal proceedings. Their complaint was ultimately found to be admissible by the Cour de Cassation, noting that the alleged offense of money laundering in France of assets obtained through corrupt practices would be of such a nature as to cause a direct and personal loss to TI France, given the specific nature of its mission.[30] This decision led to the search of mansions; the seizing of assets, including several luxury cars; and the issuing of an international arrest warrant for Teodoro Nguema Obiang, the son of the president of Equatorial Guinea, in 2012. Although the proceedings are pending, the symbolic significance of this action is great because it shows how the civil process in France was used by ordinary individuals and NGOs to generate international attention and concern regarding allegations of kleptocracy.[31] It also distressed African leaders enough that they protested diplomatically and brought a case against France in the International Court of Justice.[32]

A major consideration in such litigation is that although the actual litigants were not poor citizens of the countries from which assets had been

---

28 *See* chronology in Sherpa, *"Biens Mal Acquis" Case: Teodorin Obiang Refuses to Appear before Judicial Authorities* 3 (press statement, July 13, 2012).

29 Gregory Ngbwa Mintsa of Gabon was awarded a Transparency International Integrity Award in 2010 for helping to bring the case against the five African presidents. *See* Transparency International website, http://www.transparency.org/getinvolved/awardwinner /gregory_ngbwa_mintsa.

30 Decision of the Cour de Cassation, Criminal Chamber (Nov. 9, 2010).

31 For reports in international media, *see* Angelique Chrisafis, *France Has Finally Got Tough on Corruption by Seizing a Dictator's Paris Mansion*, The Guardian (Aug. 6, 2012); Lisa Bryant, *Equatorial Guinea in Spotlight with Controversial UNESCO Award*, Voice of America (July 16, 2012).

32 See *Equatorial Guinea Takes France to ICJ over Obiang Corruption Raids*, RFI (Sept. 28, 2012).

stolen, the litigants represented the poor of those countries. The successes of such litigation can be considered as part of the campaign to bring Article 35 to the national level. The victories that such cases represent can be communicated to all citizens of the countries involved, along with the message that their representatives are preparing the ground for all citizens to be able to pursue the corrupt at every level. This is a powerful and transforming message.

Providing individuals the opportunity to pursue the corrupt is in line with the access to justice concepts outlined by the UN special rapporteur on extreme poverty and human rights, Magdalena Sepulveda Carmona, who explained the concept of access to justice as it applies to the judicial protection for economic, social, and cultural (ESC) rights. In the event of a violation of an ESC right,

> each individual has a right to access justice without discrimination of any kind and a right to due process, understood as the right to be treated fairly, efficiently and effectively throughout the justice chain. States have assumed obligations in this regard, by committing to respect, protect and fulfil [these] rights.[33]

Underpinning this right to access to justice is the principle of equality and nondiscrimination.[34] In addition, a number of ancillary rights come into play under access to justice, such as the right to due process, the right to equality before the courts and tribunals, the right to a fair trial, the right to legal assistance, and the right to equality and equal protection of the law. More important, there is a specific right to an effective remedy that is "a key element of human rights protection and serves as a procedural means to ensure that individuals can enforce their rights and obtain redress."[35]

The special rapporteur states that justiciability for ESC rights "entails more than improving access to judicial and adjudicatory mechanisms. It also implies that remedies must be effective, and legal and judicial outcomes must be just and equitable."[36] Depending on the nature of the violation in question, the right to an effective remedy may include reparation, restitution, compensation, rehabilitation, satisfaction, and guarantees of nonrepetition.

---

33   Magdalena Sepulveda Carmona, *Report of the Special Rapporteur on Extreme Poverty and Human Rights* (2012), 27: The right to an effective remedy (e.g., Universal Declaration of Human Rights, art. 8; International Covenant on Civil and Political Rights, art. 2.3; Convention on the Elimination of All Forms of Racial Discrimination, art. 6; Convention against Torture, arts. 13 and 14); the right to equality before the courts and tribunals (e.g., International Covenant on Civil and Political Rights, art. 14.1); the right to a fair trial (e.g., Universal Declaration of Human Rights, art. 10; International Covenant on Civil and Political Rights, arts. 14 and 15); the right to legal assistance (e.g., Universal Declaration of Human Rights, art. 11.1; International Covenant on Civil and Political Rights, art. 14.3(b)–(d)); and the right to equality and equal protection of the law (e.g., Universal Declaration of Human Rights, art. 7; International Covenant on Civil and Political Rights, art. 26).

34   See Carmona, *id.*, at 5.

35   *Id.*, at 4.

36   *Id.*

A similar line of reasoning could be applied to the rights under both UNCAC and the Civil Law Convention. Specifically, the need to ensure access to justice for corruption cases is relevant for a number of reasons:

- First, given the serious nature of the damage suffered, prospective claimants will most likely be persons living in poverty (or in danger of falling into poverty) who have a higher propensity to come into contact with the justice system generally, and so positive benefits reaped in one area can act as preventative measures or deterrents for other areas of the law, such as criminal law.

- Second, development of jurisprudence on social and economic rights can contribute to overcoming deprivation and thus to poverty reduction.

- Third, fair and effective justice systems prevent violent behavior and unfair settlements and reduce violence and conflict within communities.

- Fourth, the inability to pursue justice remedies through existing systems increases vulnerability to poverty and perpetuates violations of rights.[37]

Thus, applying the right to access to justice to corruption cases ensures that a prospective claimant has the economic, social, and legal means to enforce his or her right and to obtain a satisfactory remedy under law.

Conclusion

Despite the increasing will of governments to tackle corruption through the criminal justice system, the will to be free from corruption must come from the people. As illustrated by the *Biens Mal Acquis* cases, private citizens need the support of civil society, the attention of the media, and the efforts of public interest lawyers. But it will be the people themselves, acting within their own cultures and traditions, who will set the course of fundamental shifts in societal values and practices.

The next stage in the fight against corruption can be bottom up and can use the civil action as an instrument for development. In accordance with international and regional conventions, governments should seek to promote and empower citizens with this new opportunity for action. Civil actions can provide public fora for the many battles that it will take for an empowered populace to challenge and overcome the status quo and to show that the people themselves can win the war on corruption. Civil actions serve to promote better governance and accountability in government. They also have the potential to change attitudes and values, and there lies the importance of this powerful new weapon in the fight against corruption.

---

37   *Id.*, at 3–4.

Fostering Opportunity through Development Finance in Africa

Legal Perspectives from the African Development Bank

KALIDOU GADIO

The African Development Bank (AfDB), the premier development finance institution in Africa, possesses an international character and a neutrality from the politics of its member countries, both of which are derived from the prohibition of political activity enshrined in Article 38 of its constitutive agreement.[1] Established in 1964, the AfDB has 53 regional and 24 nonregional member countries.[2] The AfDB has offices in 34 countries across the continent that work together to achieve the bank's mission.[3] Structurally, the AfDB belongs to a family of three separate legal entities: the AfDB, the African Development Fund (AfDF), and the Nigeria Trust Fund (NTF).[4] This chapter focuses on Article 38 of the AfDB Agreement; Article 38 principles are replicated in Article 21 of the AfDF Agreement and implied in Article 4.1 of the NTF Agreement.

The author would like to thank Rowland Atta-Kesson, Legal Consultant of the AfDB, for his in-depth research assistance, analytical legal assessment, and overall assiduous contributions to this chapter. The author is also grateful to Yvonne Fiadjoe, Senior Legal Counsel and Assistant to the General Counsel at the AfDB, and Godfred Penn, Lead Counsel and Adviser to the General Counsel, AfDB, for their comments and analytical review of the chapter.

1   See AfDB, *Agreement Establishing the African Development Bank* (2011), available at http:// www.afdb.org/fileadmin/uploads/afdb/Documents/Legal-Documents/Agreement%20Estab lishing%20the%20ADB%20final%202011.pdf (accessed Apr. 21, 2013).

2   The 24 nonregional member countries are Argentina, Australia, Belgium, Brazil, Canada, China, Denmark, Finland, France, Germany, India, Italy, Japan, Korea, Kuwait, the Netherlands, Norway, Portugal, Saudi Arabia, Spain, Sweden, Switzerland, the United Kingdom, and the United States of America. *See* http://www.afdb.org/en/about-us/ (accessed June 7, 2013). Turkey is just completing the formal process of becoming a nonregional member.

3   These include 29 field offices, 2 regional resource centers (in Nairobi and Pretoria), 3 customized offices (in Guinea Bissau, São Tomé and Príncipe, and Mauritius), and 1 external representation office (in Japan). The opening of the two pilot regional resource centers in January 2012 consolidated regional capacity, enabling more rapid support to clients and field offices through increased technical and specialist skills and facilitating improved dialogue with regional economic communities. For fragile states, the AfDB expanded its presence by opening a fifth office in South Sudan in 2012, in addition to offices opened in Liberia, Burundi, the Central African Republic, and Togo in 2011.

4   Some official communications of the AfDB bundle the three together with the insignia "AfDB group" or "the African Development Bank Group" or "the Bank Group." *See,* for example, African Development Bank Group, *At the Center of Africa's Transformation Strategy for 2013–2022* (AfDB 2013), available at http://www.afdb.org/fileadmin/uploads/afdb/Documents/Policy -Documents/AfDB%20Strategy%20for%202013%E2%80%932022%20-%20At%20the%20

In the foreword to the Ten Year Strategy (TYS) of the AfDB group, the AfDB group's president, Dr. Donald Kaberuka, points out that Africa is the world's second-fastest-growing continent and that "growth must bring jobs and opportunities for all."[5] This chapter addresses the legal implications engendered by the AfDB's ever-increasing role in Africa's development.

This chapter is organized into several sections. It begins with a discussion of how the AfDB group seeks to foster opportunities through the TYS. The central focus of this section is the progressive thrust of the TYS and its implications in the context of Article 38. The chapter then presents a legal analysis that makes a case for a purposive interpretation of Article 38, which allows for "a constructive and creative stretching" of Article 38 without "breaking" it.[6] The next section examines some recent public sector operations of the AfDB group in the context of postconflict recovery and reconstruction interventions, and the special case of premembership interventions in the Republic of South Sudan, to assess how the AfDB group has utilized a presidential directive, best practices, and cooperation with others to foster opportunities.

The AfDB's Ten Year Strategy

The AfDB group charted a vision for the African continent and a path for the AfDB in the 2007 report *Investing in Africa's Future: The African Development Bank in the 21st Century.*[7] This report inspired the work of the AfDB group's

---

Center%20of%20Africa%E2%80%99s%20Transformation.pdf (accessed June 3, 2013). The term "AfDB" is used in this chapter in reference to only the AfDB, and the term "AfDB group" is used in reference to the three entities. The use of those expressions is strictly communication shorthand. As a matter of international treaty law, the constitutive instruments of these entities do not create them as a group. The AfDF is an international financial institution that was "formed as a partnership" between the Bank and mainly non-African donor countries. The purpose of the Fund is to "assist the Bank in making an increasingly effective contribution to the economic and social development of the Bank's members and to the promotion of co-operation (including regional and sub-regional co-operation) and increased international trade, particularly among such members." The NTF, a Special Fund of the bank, provides resources to the low-income regional member countries of the bank. It was established in 1976 with resources provided by the Government of the Federal Republic of Nigeria. The NTF seeks, among other things, to enable Nigeria to make an increasingly effective contribution to the economic development and social progress of Africa.

5　　*See id.,* at iii. This TYS replaces the Medium-Term Strategy (MTS) of the bank, which was in effect from 2008 to 2012.

6　　*See* Hassane Cissé, *Should the Political Prohibition in Charters of International Financial Institutions Be Revisited? The Case of the World Bank* in *The World Bank Legal Review,* vol. 3, 92 (Hassane Cissé, Daniel Bradlow, & Benedict Kingsbury eds., World Bank 2012), borrowing a term coined by World Bank Vice President of Operations Policy and Country Services, Joachim von Amsberg.

7　　AfDB, *Report of the High Level Panel: Investing in Africa's Future: The ADB in the 21st Century* (AfDB 2007), available at http://www.afdb.org/fileadmin/uploads/afdb/Documents Publications/27842402-EN-HLP-REPORT-INVESTING-IN-AFRICAS-FUTURE.PDF (accessed Apr. 23, 2013).

Medium-Term Strategy from 2008 to 2012.[8] The new bank strategy, the TYS covers the years 2013–2022.

Investing in Africa's Future states:

> Africa is on the move. Policy changes and improved governance and management have led to the highest rates of sustained growth since the days of independence. The proportion of the population in extreme poverty is no longer increasing; democratic change is becoming the norm; African-led efforts have reduced conflict. The global context is also favorable, with the large emerging economies creating new opportunities for Africa. More African countries are creditworthy, and investment has increased.[9]

This statement sums up Africa's development drive in the 21st century; the TYS is designed to reposition the AfDB group "at the Center of Africa's Transformation" and to improve the quality of Africa's growth.[10] Of particular interest is how the AfDB group will use the TYS to support Africa's transformation into a continent that is more prosperous, with markedly lower poverty levels and a more equitable distribution of economic and social opportunities, including jobs and income, than the Africa of the 20th century.

Two broad objectives are intended to support this transformation: "inclusive growth" in terms of age, gender, and geography; and "gradual transition to green growth" by building resilience and managing natural resources and sustainable infrastructure. The TYS highlights three areas for special emphasis: utilizing a "continuum" and regional approach in fragile states; supporting value chains in agriculture and food security; and ensuring gender-focused economic empowerment and legal and property rights. These three areas are the basis for five operational priorities: infrastructure development, regional integration, private sector development, governance and accountability, and skills and technology.

The TYS reflects the general views of all stakeholders of the AfDB. It is based on broad-based consultations with all stakeholders, including the governors.[11] A plethora of issue papers on different aspects of the TYS were generated. For example, an issue paper on green growth highlighted a holistic approach to the persistent problems of poverty, social inequality, pollution, environmental degradation, and climate change on the continent.[12] Considering

---

8   *See* AfDB, *African Development Bank Group Medium-Term Strategy (MTS) 2008–2012 of the Bank Group* (2008), available at http://www.afdb.org/fileadmin/uploads/afdb/Documents/Policy -Documents/MTS%20anglais.pdf (accessed June 3, 2013).

9   *See* AfDB, *supra* note 7, at 1.

10   *See* AfDB, *supra* note 4, at 1.

11   *See* AfDB, *Governors' Dialogue Long Term Strategy 2022 Issue Paper* (May 31, 2012**)**, available at http://www.afdb.org/fileadmin/uploads/afdb/Documents/Policy-Documents/LTS%20Issues %20Paper%20for%20Governors%20Dialogue.pdf (accessed Apr. 23, 2013).

12   *See* AfDB, *Briefing Notes for AfDB's Long Term Strategy; Briefing Note 8: Green Growth: Perspectives for Africa and the AfDB in the 21st Century* (Mar. 7, 2012), available at http://www

the extensive consultations that went into the TYS, one can assume that the TYS has the support of AfDB member countries, and this support may be sufficient to refute contrary views such as those held by Jessica Einhorn and Heather Marquette.[13]

A Purposive Interpretation of Article 38

As an international development and financial institution, the AfDB has thrived on results-oriented operations informed by its legal normative order. Article 38 explicitly prohibits political considerations in the AfDB's decision-making process. Little has been written about Article 38,[14] as compared to similar provisions in the constitutive agreements of other multilateral development banks (MDBs). On the interpretation of similar political prohibition clauses in the charters of other MDBs, scholars are divided[15] along the lines of

---

.afdb.org/fileadmin/uploads/afdb/Documents/Policy-Documents/FINAL%20Briefing%20Note%208%20Green%20Growth%20452012.pdf (accessed Apr. 21, 2013).

13   *See* Jessica Einhorn, *The World Bank's Mission Creep,* 80(5) For. Affairs 22 (Sep. 2001), and Heather Marquette, *The Creeping Politicisation of the World: The Case of Corruption,* 52(3) Pol. Stud. 413 (Oct. 2004).

14   What is written often describes in general terms Africa's development experiences and the related policy lessons considered by the bank. *See,* for example, Omar Kabbaj, *The Challenge of African Development* (Oxford U. Press 2003), where the former president of the AfDB group comprehensively describes a number of Africa's key development issues, such as rural transformation, role of the private sector, good governance, regional integration, debt and debt reduction, and the challenge of globalization. *See* also Kwame Donkoh Fordwor, *The African Development Bank: Problems of International Cooperation* xiv (Pergamon 1981), where another former president of the AfDB argues for a balance between politics and diplomacy and the requirements of technical and technocratic management. *See,* further, Karen A. Mingst, *Politics and the African Development Bank* (U. Press of Ky. 1990), for a comprehensive discussion of how politics characterized the formative stages of the AfDB. Similarly, *see* E. Philip English & Harris M. Mule, *Multilateral Development Banks,* vol. 1, *The African Development Bank* (Lynne Rienner 1996). Others have discussed Article 38 by subsuming it under the political prohibition clauses of MDBs generally. *See* John W. Head, *For Richer or for Poorer: Assessing the Criticisms Directed at the Multilateral Development Banks,* 52 U. Kan. L. Rev. 248 (2003–2004), where the author, in providing a general survey and assessment of the criticisms leveled against MDBs, reasons that despite their diversity, MDBs share the same fundamental precepts and structures and all the MDBs have economic development as their motivating aim. *See* also Daniel D. Bradlow, *Should the International Financial Institutions Play a Role in the Implementation and Enforcement of International Humanitarian Law?,* 50 U. Kan. L. Rev. 702 (May 2002), where the author argues that the African, Asian, and inter-American development banks all have mandates similar to those of the IBRD and that their articles of agreement contain political prohibition clauses almost identical to the IBRD's and the IDA's political prohibitions.

15   For example, *see* Cissé, *supra* note 6, at 81–83, where he discusses two schools of thought critiquing the political prohibition clause of the World Bank. One school describes the World Bank's interventions as creeping politicization by virtue of the expansion of its mandate. The other school articulates that the World Bank invokes its political prohibition clause as a constraint.

the so-called mission creep, or creeping politicization,[16] and a narrow economic focus.[17] Of the two views, the former has been faulted as unpersuasive.[18]

In effect, there is no consensus among scholars on this issue. Herbert V.
Morais notes that, although a formal amendment of MDBs' legal mandates and
internal governance structures is desirable to respond to the changing world,
the MDBs' adoption of innovative policies and operational strategies in response to new crises and major developments in international law does not
mean that they have acted outside their legal mandate in spite of their omission to formally amend their respective charters.[19] The suggestion that MDBs
amend their charters is overruled by Robert Hockett, who prefers a simple shift
of focal point of the MDBs, or "a gestalt switch."[20] Even those who question the
incidence of the so-called mission creep admit that there are some useful lessons in it.[21] Hassane Cissé revisits the relevance of political prohibition clauses

---

16   *See* Einhorn, *supra* note 13; the author, a former managing director of the World Bank, argues
      that the World Bank has added new tasks to its mandate. She calls for a redefinition of this
      unwieldy mission of the World Bank by suggesting, among other things, that the World
      Bank should raise the profile of core competencies through its economic lens and narrow its
      focus. *See* also Marquette, *supra* note 13, arguing that there is an increasing politicization of
      the World Bank through its work on corruption.

17   *See* Daniel D. Bradlow & C. Grossman, *Limited Mandates and Intertwined Problems: A New Chal-
      lenge for the World Bank and the IMF*, 17 Hum. Rights Q. 439 (1995), where the authors urge MDBs
      and other international financial institutions to reinterpret their charters to clarify what issues
      are considered "domestic" political issues, and therefore outside the scope of their mandate.

18   *See* Head, *supra* note 14, at 269, 288, 297.

19   *See* Herbert V. Morais, *Testing the Frontiers of Their Mandates: The Experience of the Multilateral
      Development Banks*, 98 Am. Socy. Intl. L. Proc. 64 (Apr. 2004), where the author writes that
      "although the MDBs have not formally amended their charters to redefine their legal man-
      dates, a number of new crises and major developments in international law have propelled
      them to initiate innovative new policies and operational strategies and to devise new instru-
      ments to assist developing and transition countries."

20   Robert Hockett, *From "Mission-Creep" to Gestalt-Switch: Justice, Finance, the IFIs and the Intended
      Beneficiaries of Globalization*, 98 Am. Socy. Intl. L. Proc. 70 (Apr. 2004), where the writer states:

      I would like to suggest ways the IFIs in particular, but also globalization as a whole,
      might be brought to be the blessings they were meant to be, means by which their prom-
      ises might be redeemed. These means will not require changes in the fundamental struc-
      ture of the IFIs or other institutions. Nor will they require radical amendment of their
      mandates—their "missions." Rather, a simple shift of focal point, a gestalt switch so to
      speak, from one to another of the objects that jointly constitute traditional IFI concerns
      will do the trick. Like the well-known image of the duck that can be viewed as a rabbit (or
      is it the rabbit that can be viewed as a duck?) the IFIs and their missions as already con-
      stituted can be viewed in a way that better suggests programs and policies that will make
      friends of all people of goodwill, and that will nourish and sustain such friendships.

21   For example, even after criticizing mission creep as unpersuasive in most respects, Head ob-
      serves that there are some elements of mission creep that make sense and ought to be taken
      seriously. *See* Head, *supra* note 14, at 288. Similarly, Morais, *supra* note 19, at 68, writes,

      One example of the fusion (confusion?) of agendas is the current implementation of the
      Millennium Development Goals promoted by the United Nations, which in themselves
      are laudable and need to be urgently addressed. Yet it is not clear that the World Bank
      and the regional MDBs share a responsibility to implement all these goals. Failure to
      be discerning in taking on new goals imposed from the outside could result in policy
      proliferation or "mission creep."

to modern times.[22] The general thinking seems to be that MDBs should maintain their traditional character of being nonpolitical. The preferred approach is a purposive or teleological interpretation of the political prohibition clauses in the charters of MDBs.[23] This chapter adopts a middle-of-the-road approach of nonpolitical MDBs and a purposive interpretation of the political prohibition clauses. The purposive interpretation is useful in connection with the inter-

---

22   See Cissé, *supra* note 6, at 59–92, where the author examines the relevance of the political prohibition clause of the World Bank's Articles of Agreement. After discussing the arguments for and against the retention of the political prohibition clause, Cissé concludes that the political prohibition clause is as relevant today as it was in 1944, and that in the absence of its amendment, the men and women responsible for providing legal advice on the interpretation of the World Bank's Articles of Agreement should continue the "constructive and creative stretching" of the political prohibition provisions without breaking them.

23   *See* Ibrahim F. I. Shihata, *World Bank Legal Papers* (Kluwer L. Intl. 2000), especially ch. 9, where Shihata concludes his discussion on the prohibition of political activities of the World Bank with the following words:

> The Bank's Articles of Agreement envisage a financial institution of universal membership which takes its decision on the basis of economic consideration and lends after careful technical review of the projects it finances. They prohibit the Bank from interferences in the political affairs of its members and limit its mandate to the development and reconstruction of territories of members by facilitating and promoting investment for productive purposes and promoting the long range growth of international trade and the maintenance of equilibrium in balances of payments. These are indeed broad confines which have been brought, through fifty years of practice, to reach new frontiers, far beyond the originally intended concept, but reasonably accommodated through a continued process of *purposive interpretation.* (emphasis added)

See also Ibrahim F. I. Shihata with Franziska Tschofen & Antonio R. Parra eds., *The World Bank in a Changing World: Selected Essays* 7–13 (Martinus Nijhoff 1991). Similarly, Head, *supra* note 14, at 272, writes "I believe the MDBs have, as Shihata urged us to conclude a dozen years ago with regard to the World Bank, remained largely true to their charter provisions, especially if we are prepared to take a 'purposive' or 'teleological' approach to charter interpretation." *See* also John D. Ciorciari, *The Lawful Scope of Human Rights Criteria in World Bank Credit Decisions: An Interpretive Analysis of the IBRD and IDA Articles of Agreement,* 33 Cornell Intl. L.J. 331, 343–369 (2001). In this work, Ciorciari discusses the ordinary meaning, secondary or intrinsic, and the use of *travaux préparatoires,* or preparatory works, in treaty interpretations. *See* also Morais, *supra* note 19, at 67, where the author addresses the mission creep critics of the World Bank by drawing attention to two factors, one of which he states in the following words:

> The power to interpret their Articles of Agreement has been vested in their Boards of Directors, with a right of appeal or reference also to the Boards of Governors. It is arguable that some of these interpretations, formal or otherwise, may have stretched the meaning of the constitutional provisions to the limit. There is also no provision for independent judicial review of such interpretations. Nevertheless, I believe that, on the whole, the new MDB initiatives have been guided by a purposive interpretation of their charters that has effectively promoted achievement of the goals of development.

pretation of treaties,[24] but it is not without faults when considered in terms of certainty of law.[25]

MDBs have attracted criticism for not being fully democratic[26] and accountable.[27] In essence, MDBs have been urged to be accessible to all their stakeholders, especially those in the private sector.[28] In response, MDBs strive to foster opportunities for their stakeholders through their use of policy-based lending as a tool to encourage borrowing governments to adopt certain economic and financial policies.[29] Interestingly, some of the MDB policies have highlighted noneconomic considerations, which, indirectly have an economic impact, such as good governance, anticorruption measures, and the rule of law. How does Article 38 foster such opportunities? In other words, how should Article 38 be interpreted?

Article 31(1) of the Vienna Convention on the Law of Treaties states: "[A] treaty shall be interpreted in good faith in accordance with the ordinary meaning to be given to the terms of the treaty in their context and in the light of its

---

24   For an example of the use of purposive interpretation of MDBs' charters, *see* Cissé, *supra* note 6, at 84–85, where Cissé responds to the idea that interpretation cannot be used as a tool to ignore or contradict the ordinary meaning of the words used in treaties. Thus, Cissé argues that in rare and unusual instances, interpretation that contradicts the ordinary meaning of the terms of a text may be warranted. He reasons that there may be cases in which interpretation does not function as a means that will "lead to a change in ordinary meaning" of the words used in a text, but merely formalizes or confirms changes in the meaning of a text that have been brought about by obsolescence or incremental interpretations that modify the ordinary meaning of these words.

25   *See,* for example, Bradlow & Grossman, *supra* note 17, at 430–432, who argue that the World Bank uses its creative interpretation of its political prohibition clauses in an ad hoc and arbitrary manner to include some human rights issues, such as female genital mutilation, while at the same time excluding other human rights issues, such as the prevention of torture or the suppression of political dissent on the ground that they are purely "political."

26   *See* Enrique R. Carrasco et al., *Governance and Accountability: The Regional Development Banks,* 27 B.U. Intl. L.J. 1 (2009), alluding to the criticism against the World Bank and the IMF as well as other regional development banks for not being democratic enough.

27   *See* Richard E. Bissell & Suresh Nanwani, *Multilateral Development Bank Accountability Mechanisms: Developments and Challenges,* 6(1) Manchester J. Intl. L. 2–55 (2009), giving an overview of the accountability mechanisms of the World Bank Inspection Panel (WBIP), the Inter-American Development Bank (IDB) Independent Investigation Mechanism (IIM), the Asian Development Bank's (ADB) Accountability Mechanism, the Compliance Adviser/Ombudsman (CAO) of the International Financial Corporation (IFC) and Multilateral Investment Guarantee Agency (MIGA), the European Bank for Reconstruction and Development's (EBRD) Independent Recourse Mechanism (IRM), and the AfDB Independent Review Mechanism (IRM). In comparing the function, structure, and operations of these mechanisms, illustrating their similarities and differences, the authors note that the ADB's accountability mechanism stands out as the only mechanism that provides claimants the opportunity to comment (with management) on the panel's draft investigation report before it is finalized and issued to the board.

28   *See* Daniel D. Bradlow, *Private Complainants and International Organizations: A Comparative Study of the Independent Inspection Mechanisms in International Financial Institutions,* 36 Geo. J. Intl. L. 403 (Winter 2005).

29   *See* Head, *supra* note 14, at 249.

object and purpose."[30] Thus, it is imperative to interpret a treaty in good faith according to the ordinary meaning of its terms in their context and in light of the object and purpose of the treaty. The citation from Article 31(1) of the Vienna Convention is applicable to Article 38 of the AfDB Agreement. What is the ordinary meaning of Article 38?

The Ordinary Meaning of Article 38

At face value, Article 38 seems to be absolute, because it does not allow for any exceptions. The intention of the drafters may be seen as insulating the AfDB from interference from its member states and vice versa.[31] This way, the AfDB is assured of technical competence and neutrality in its dealings with member countries. It is also able to maintain an international legal personality, separate and distinct from its members.

Article 38(1) provides that "The Bank shall not accept loans or assistance that could in any way prejudice, limit, deflect or otherwise alter its purpose or functions." Article 38(2) further provides that

> The Bank, its President, Vice-Presidents, officers and staff shall not interfere in the political affairs of any member; nor shall they be influenced in their decisions by the political character of the member concerned. Only economic considerations shall be relevant to their decisions. Such considerations shall be weighed impartially in order to achieve and carry out the functions of the Bank.

Article 38(3) provides that "The President, Vice-Presidents, officers and staff of the Bank, in discharge of their offices, owe their duty entirely to the Bank and to no other authority. Each member of the Bank shall respect the international character of this duty and shall refrain from all attempts to influence any of them in the discharge of their duties."

These provisions suggest that three purposes can be attributed to Article 38:

- The prohibition against the alteration of the purpose and functions of the AfDB

---

30 *See* Vienna Convention on the Law of Treaties (with annex), 1155 U.N.T.S., (entered into force Jan. 27, 1980) (hereinafter Vienna Convention), available at http://treaties.un.org/doc /publication/UNTS/Volume%201155/v1155.pdf (accessed June 3, 2013).

31 *See* United Nations Economic Commission of Africa (ECA), *The Final Report of the Committee of Nine on the Establishment of an African Development Bank,* E/CN.14/FMAB/1 (Jan. 14–23, 1963), at para. 26:

> Freedom from political influence and the emphasis placed on the maintenance of sound banking principles in all the activities of the Bank—the third leading idea in the case for its establishment—are recognized as indispensable if the Bank is to succeed. They are also essential to mobilizing additional non-African resources for its purposes.

Available at http://repository.uneca.org/bitstream/handle/10855/7761/Bib-47948.pdf?seq uence=1 (accessed June 3, 2013).

- The prohibition against the AfDB's interference in the political affairs of its member countries and the insistence of economic considerations as the only permissible mandate of the AfDB

- The prohibition of member countries' influencing the president, vice presidents, officers, and staff of the AfDB in the performance of their duties

Of the three, the second point is most challenging. It suggests that the AfDB must consider only economic factors and exclude noneconomic factors in its decision making, even when the consideration of an economic factor necessarily involves a noneconomic factor, which does not in any way prejudice, limit, deflect, or alter the AfDB's purpose or functions. For example, the ordinary meaning of Article 38(2) implies that the AfDB must work with any incumbent government—whether de facto or de jure—regardless of political ideology or governance structure; that is, whether a particular regime is democratic or autocratic. Unfortunately, the phrases "political affairs" and "political character" are not defined in the text.

Article 37(3) states that "The President shall be the legal representative of the Bank," replicating Article VIII(5)(a) of the Inter-American Development Bank (IADB) charter.[32] Per Article 36(1) of the AfDB Agreement, the president is a person of the highest competence in matters pertaining to the activities, management, and administration of the AfDB. In Article 37(1), the president is the chairman of the board of directors, and although he or she does not vote, the president does decide in the case of a tie. The president may also participate in meetings of the board of governors, even though the president has no vote. Per Article 37(2), the president is the chief of staff of the AfDB and conducts the current business of the AfDB under the direction of the board of directors. By this, one may infer that the president has lawmaking powers, even though the drafters did not explicitly say so.

A deeper analysis indicates that of the three decision-making organs of the AfDB with lawmaking powers, the president has a legitimate lawmaking power, given that he or she is elected by all the members of the AfDB, whereas the board of governors is appointed and the board of directors is elected through indirect universal suffrage by the countries that compose the constituencies that each represents. Thus, the president's lawmaking powers do not arise merely from his or her competence in matters pertaining to the activities, management, and administration of the AfDB or from the fact that the president is the legal representative of the AfDB.

---

32   *See Agreement Establishing the African Development Bank, Preparatory Work, including Summary Records of the Conference of Finance Ministers*, E/CN.14/ADB/28, 162 (U.N. 1964).

Certain procedural norms[33] of global administrative law[34] are impera-tive for proper lawmaking. The role of the AfDB's general counsel is crucial when it comes to legal interpretation and the drafting of legal documents.[35] For example, following the legal advisory opinions of the general counsel, a presidential directive was drafted in 2010 to allow the continuity of the Af-DB's operations and engagement with de facto governments in some regional member countries.[36] It is contended that this bank practice reflects the attitude envisaged by Article 38(2). Thus, irrespective of the political affairs and politi-cal character of a regional member country (RMC), the AfDB has continued its operations. But does Article 38(2) also mean that the AfDB should continue its

---

33 See Benedict Kingsbury, *Global Administrative Law in the International Practice of Global Regula-tory Governance*, in *The World Bank Legal Review*, vol. 3, 8–9 (Hassane Cissé, Daniel Bradlow, & Benedict Kingsbury eds., World Bank 2012), where Kingsbury explains that global adminis-trative law is based on the insight that much of global regulatory governance can be under-stood as "administration." Intergovernmental organizations engage in such administrative activities beyond the reach of controls imposed by the public law, democratic apparatus, or other review structures of individual states. Therefore, these intergovernmental organizations

    have increasingly sought to shore up their legitimacy, and to enhance the effective-ness of their regulatory activities, by applying to (and between) themselves procedural norms (referred to . . . as "GAL norms") of transparency, participation, reasoned de-cision making, and legality, and by establishing mechanisms of review and account-ability. These procedural norms and mechanisms resemble, at least in their general orientation, administrative law as applied to regulatory agencies and other executive bodies within some national legal systems.

34 For a general discussion of global administrative law, *see* Benedict Kingsbury et al., *The Emergence of Global Administrative Law*, 68 L. & Contemp. Probs. 17 (Summer/Autumn 2005), where the authors explain that global interdependence is far-reaching in such fields as secu-rity, the conditions on development and financial assistance to developing countries, envi-ronmental protection, banking and financial regulation, law enforcement, telecommunica-tions, trade in products and services, intellectual property, labor standards, and cross-border movements of populations, including refugees. The authors note that various transnational systems of regulation and international regulatory cooperation treaties exist. Informal in-tergovernmental networks of cooperation, shifting many regulatory decisions from the na-tional to the global level, also exist. There are transnational administrative bodies—includ-ing international organizations and informal groups of officials who determine the details and implementation of such regulations. Also of increasing importance are regulations by private international standards–setting bodies. A hybrid of public-private organizations, in-cluding representatives of businesses, NGOs, national governments, and intergovernmental organizations, also exists to regulate global administrative law.

35 See Adesegun A. Akin-Olugbade, *Managing Development in a Time of Crisis: The Legal Frame-work for the Temporary Relocation of the African Development Bank*, 38(3) Intl. Lawyer 725, 727 (2004), available at http://www.jstor.org/stable/40708223 (accessed May 10, 2013), where the author and former general counsel writes, "As with the other multilateral development banks, questions of interpretation of the ADB Agreement's provisions are within the pur-view of the powers of the Bank's Board of Directors. Such interpretations may be formal or informal, explicit or implicit, and are usually made on the basis of the General Counsel's advice."

36 See AfDB, *Concerning Continuity of Operations and Engagement with De Facto Government in Regional Member Countries* (African Dev. Bank Pres. Directive No. 3/2010, 2010), available at http://www.afdb.org/fileadmin/uploads/afdb/Documents/Policy-Documents/40-%20EN -%20Concerning%20continuity%20of%20operations%20and%20engagement%20with%20 the%20facto%20governements%20in%20regional%20member%20countries.pdf (accessed May 10, 2013).

operations in a politically unstable regional member country even when the lives and property of the AfDB are endangered?

The answer is obviously no. In some instances, the AfDB has had to relocate its operations, officers, and staff to a temporary agency. The legal opinion issued by a former general counsel, Dr. Akin-Olugbade on the legal conditions for the temporary relocation of the AfDB's activities addresses the conditions under which a decision can be made to transfer or move the AfDB's principal office or headquarters from Abidjan:

> As the crisis in the host country unfolded, with considerable anxiety and concerns about the possible adverse impact on the Bank's business and the security of its staff, certain Executive Directors wanted the Bank to make an expeditious decision and sought the advice of the General Counsel on the appropriate and legally feasible options available to the Bank. Against the backdrop of the provisions of the Bank's Charter prohibiting interference by the Bank in the political affairs of its member countries, and inspired by the fundamental principle that "the client of the Bank's General Counsel is not only the Bank's Management, the Boards, or any particular member country, but the institution as whole, including all its organs," the advice had to carefully balance the many competing interests, in order to avoid any breach of the Bank's obligations under the Headquarters Agreement with the host country.[37]

The Scope of Article 38

What is the scope of a purposive interpretation? In terms of Article 31 of the Vienna Convention, the meaning of Article 38 can be gleaned from the context of the words used therein and in light of the objects and purpose of the overall AfDB Agreement. The context includes the preamble and annexes of the agreement.[38] Other aids to interpretation are subsequent practice of the

---

37 *See* Akin-Olugbade, *supra* note 35, at 728–731, where the author notes that the overarching considerations were, however, adherence to the rule of law and safeguarding the AfDB's interest, that is, ensuring its survival as a viable entity to enable it to continue to deliver on its development mandate.

38 Vienna Convention, *supra* note 30, at art. 31(2), states:

The context for the purpose of the interpretation of a treaty shall comprise, in addition to the text, including its *preamble and annexes*: (a) Any agreement relating to the treaty which was made between all the parties in connexion with the conclusion of the treaty; (b) Any instrument which was made by one or more parties in connexion with the conclusion of the treaty and accepted by the other parties as an instrument related to the treaty. (italics added)

parties[39] and the established meaning of a term.[40] Interestingly, recourse may be possible for supplementary means of interpretation, including the preparatory work[41] of the treaty and the circumstances of its conclusion, to avoid an ambiguous or obscure meaning or manifestly absurd or unreasonable results.[42]

A purposive interpretation is the preferred approach for interpreting the text of a treaty.[43] For example, in relation to the political prohibition clause of the World Bank's Articles of Agreement, Ibrahim F. Shihata has stated that,

> while the Articles stipulated these injunctions as legal obligations, their original drafters realized from the beginning the complexity of this matter and indicated that in the Bank's practice such strict separation between the Bank and the politics of its members would depend on the character of those who would be in charge of the Bank.[44]

This statement suggests a purposive construction of the World Bank's political prohibition clause, which takes into account both the letter of the law and the practices of the World Bank seen in the conduct of those who work for it. In the case of the AfDB, the drafters of Article 38 reasoned that freedom from political influence and sound banking principles are indispensable to

---

39   *Id.*, at art. 31(3), provides:

> There shall be taken into account, together with the context: (a) Any subsequent agreement between the parties regarding the interpretation of the treaty or the application of its provisions; (b) *Any subsequent practice in the application of the treaty which establishes the agreement of the parties regarding its interpretation*; (c) Any relevant rules of international law applicable in the relations between the parties. (italics added)

40   *Id.*, at art. 31(4), provides "A special meaning shall be given to a term if it is established that the parties so intended."

41   The United Nations Economic Commission for Africa (ECA) adopted a resolution in February 1961 by which the ECA executive secretary was tasked to undertake a thorough study of the possibility of the establishment of an African development bank and to report on this matter at the next session of the ECA. The executive secretary in turn appointed a panel of experts. The report of the panel of experts was unanimously adopted by the ECA at its session in February–March 1962. In the ECA resolution adopting the report, the ECA constituted a committee of nine member governments to, among other things, draft a charter for the proposed bank. The ECA resolution also tasked the ECA executive secretary to convene a conference of finance ministers to review the report of the Committee of Nine and to make final decisions. This conference of ministers was held in Khartoum, Sudan, from July 30 to August 4, 1963. The conference of ministers discussed the draft agreement, adopting further amendment, and approved the final text of the Agreement Establishing the African Development Bank. See Agreement Establishing the AfDB, *supra* note 32, at i–ii.

42   Vienna Convention, *supra* note 30, at art. 32, provides:

> Recourse may be had to supplementary means of interpretation, including the preparatory work of the treaty and the circumstances of its conclusion, in order to confirm the meaning resulting from the application of article 31, or to determine the meaning when the interpretation according to article 31: (a) Leaves the meaning ambiguous or obscure; or (b) Leads to a result which is manifestly absurd or unreasonable.

43   *Id.*

44   *See* Shihata, *supra* note 23, at 228.

the success of the AfDB.[45] Meanwhile, the drafters also envisaged a flexible application of the provisions of the AfDB Agreement, including Article 38.[46] Indeed, a close reading of Article 38 mirrors a purposive interpretation. Thus, the AfDB can provide only loans and assistance that do not prejudice, limit, deflect, or otherwise alter its purpose and function. Moreover, those who work in the AfDB owe their allegiance entirely to the bank and to no other authority. With this in mind, it is important to appreciate the meaning of Article 38 in light of the purpose of the AfDB, the drafting history of Article 38, and the relevant rules of international law applicable to the relations between the parties, that is, the AfDB, its members, and all other stakeholders, including other MDBs.

The Purpose and Function of the AfDB

The purpose and function of the AfDB are clearly stated in Articles 1 and 2 of the AfDB Agreement. The AfDB is guided by these two key provisions in all its decisions.[47] However, the functions of the AfDB as explicitly prescribed by the AfDB Agreement are not exhaustive.[48]

The AfDB is authorized to undertake activities and provide services that may advance its purpose, which is the undertaking of any activities that contribute to the sustainable economic development and social progress of its regional member countries.[49] The AfDB's inherent mandate is expansive. For example, some observers have suggested that the AfDB has a leading role as the principal African development finance institution, working with others to promote infrastructure investment, capital market development, and regional integration through different measures.[50] The AfDB is mandated to cooperate

---

45   *See* ECA, *supra* note 31.

46   *Id.,* at para. 27, states "one last consideration which has informed all discussions concerning the Bank is that its approach to its task should be broad and flexible."

47   *See* AfDB, *supra* note 1, at art. 2(3).

48   *Id.,* at art. 2(1), provides that the AfDB must use the resources at its disposal to finance investment projects and programs for the economic and social development of its regional member countries (RMCs), giving special priority to two specific types of projects and programs: (a) projects or programs that by their nature or scope concern several members; and (b) projects or programs designed to make the economies of its members increasingly complementary and to bring about an orderly expansion of their foreign trade. The AfDB is also mandated to undertake, or participate in, the selection, study, and preparation of projects, enterprises, and activities contributing to such development. It also has responsibility for mobilizing and increasing, within and outside Africa, resources to finance such investment projects and programs. Again, it generally has to promote investment in Africa of public and private capital in projects or programs designed to contribute to the economic development or social progress of its regional members. Lastly, the AfDB provides such technical assistance that may be needed in Africa for the study, preparation, financing, and execution of development projects or programs.

49   *Id.,* at art. 1.

50   *See* Cedric Achille Mbeng Mezui & Bim Hundal, *Structured Finance: Conditions for Infrastructure Project Bonds in African Markets* 33 (AfDB 2013), where the authors suggest that the AfDB can meaningfully contribute to the continent's infrastructure needs through political influence. Available at http://www.afdb.org/fileadmin/uploads/afdb/Documents/Project

with national, regional, and subregional development institutions in Africa in carrying out its functions.[51] Such cooperation may also be seen as reflecting the acceptable banking practices or norms among MDBs, and ipso facto, they are permissible functions of the AfDB.[52]

Studies of MDBs tend to be strictly legalistic in nature and articulate that MDBs are nonpolitical bodies. But scholars such as Karen Mingst argue that MDBs, including the AfDB, are political institutions.[53] This view is not convincing in terms of prudent banking practice. To borrow from one writer: "[I]t is one thing to accept the inevitability and usefulness of a political dimension in international decision making, but it is quite another thing to make the political dimension the sole or predominant factor in the deliberative and management process of an institution."[54] Moreover, the goals of the AfDB "call for a combination of relevant technical expertise and managerial skills, aided in appropriate cases by measured political leverage."[55] Similarly, the March 1996

-and-Operations/Structured%20Finance%20-%20Conditions%20for%20Infrastructure%20 Project%20Bonds%20in%20African%20Markets.pdf (accessed May 10, 2013).

51   See AfDB, *supra* note 1, at art. 2(2).

52   This is because the activities of MDBs are sources of international law. *See* José E. Alvarez, *Governing the World: International Organizations as Lawmakers*, 31 Suffolk Transnatl. L. Rev. 591 (2007–2008), where the author challenges the traditional account of modern international lawmaking, given the proliferation of international organizations and their impact on the international plane. He writes that modern treatises acknowledge that international organizations are now considered international legal persons, but scarcely do these treatises examine the consequences of such a proposition. He examines the consequences of such a proposition to argue that the move to international organization has introduced changes in the sources, content, and legally relevant actors of international law, which are changing the compliance and enforcement of international law. Elsewhere, Alvarez suggests that few self-contained regimes exist in international law. He believes that there is no distinction between economic concerns and those of national security, so that there is little or no distinction between international lawmaking and domestic lawmaking; he cites as an example how the World Bank is now taking on goals such as environmental sustainability, anticorruption, tax reform, and privatization. On the role of international organization in international lawmaking, Alvarez writes that international organizations with nearly universal membership have replaced ad hoc conferences of the 19th century as the preferred venue for multilateral treaty making. He divides treaty-making patterns into four categories: international organization (especially UN-sponsored) treaty-making conferences; expert treaty-making bodies; "managerial" forms of treaty making; and institutional mechanisms for "treaty making with strings attached." MDBs are implied in the second category because of their expertise in international economic law. *See* José E. Alvarez, *The New Treaty Makers*, 25 B.C. Intl. & Comp. L. Rev. (2002), available at http://lawdigitalcommons.bc.edu/iclr/vol25/iss2/4 (accessed June 5, 2013). For further discussion on the generation of soft international laws, *see* Dinah Shelton, *Commentary and Conclusions* [to "Human Rights" section], in *Commitment and Compliance: The Role of Non-binding Norms in the International Legal System* (Dinah Shelton ed., Oxford U. Press 2000), who quotes in *International Human Rights: Problems of Law, Policy and Practice*, 4th ed., 137–142 (Richard B. Lillich et al. eds., Aspen Publishers 2000); *see* also M. N. Shaw, *International Law* 92 (4th ed., Cambridge U. Press 1997).

53   *See* Mingst, *supra* note 14. In ch. 1, she argues that international organizations are mushrooming around the globe and they are playing key roles in international politics.

54   *See* Fordwor, *supra* note 14, at xiv.

55   *Id.*

Report of the AfDB's Panel on Governance discounts the view that the AfDB is a political institution.[56] Paragraph 1.14 of the report states:

> Equally as important, the shareholders of the Bank will need to come to an agreement on what the Bank should be, and what role it should assume in the development of the region. Despite its unique origins as a symbol of political cooperation and unity among its founding African member states, the Bank today—if it is to succeed as a development finance institution—has to function as a Bank subject to the requirement of the marketplace. And as a Bank seeking to raise funds in the international market—and make resources available to its regional member countries—it is clear that it cannot function as a political bank.

However, this does not mean that the AfDB, as a creature of international treaty law with legal personality, lives and survives in the confines of society without being affected by the political realities of its environment. In other words, the AfDB's mandate could be described as nonpolitical rather than apolitical.[57] But, one may ask, does this not suggest mission creep?

A Purposive Interpretation and Analysis to Avoid Breaking Article 38

Head[58] and Morais[59] do not agree to the suggestion that MDBs are guilty of mission creep given their expansive functions as nonpolitical international financial intermediaries. Instead they, like Shihata,[60] prescribe a purposive interpretation of the legal mandates of MDBs. There are risks to adopting a purposive interpretative approach to Article 38, including a risk of breach or overstretch,[61] and some people argue that the following three-step analysis is necessary to avoid such risk:

- Is the decision of the bank, or its president, vice presidents, officers, or staff, in pursuit of a legitimate objective, such as being concerned with economic interventions in a member country?

- If it is, does the attainment of that objective demand a consideration of the political situation existing in the member country?

- If so, can the bank or its president, vice presidents, officers, or staff show that the means adopted allows as few political considerations as possible?

---

56   *See* AfDB, *Reforming the Governance Structures of the African Development Bank: Report of the Panel on Governance Established by the Board of Governors of the African Development Bank* (Mar. 1996).

57   *See* Cissé, *supra* note 6, at note 10, where the author distinguishes apolitical from nonpolitical. *Apolitical* means "unconcerned with or detached from politics," and *nonpolitical* means "not involved in politics."

58   *See* Head, *supra* note 14, at 269, 288, 297.

59   Morais, *supra* note 19.

60   *See* Shihata, *supra* note 23.

61   See *supra* notes 24 and 25.

Shihata alludes to the fact that the World Bank could use economic concerns as justification for including political considerations in its work. He reasons that because the World Bank is required to act prudently in its borrowing and its lending operations and to pay due regard to the ability of the borrower to meet its obligations, pure economic consideration without regard for the degree of political instability of a member country is not prudent. But he cautions the World Bank to "limit itself to the necessary analysis needed for the purposes of its work."[62] Such a proportionality test approach would allow for a careful, constructive, and creative stretching of Article 38 without breaching it.

The TYS and Article 38

Without doubt, there is the desire to make the AfDB more agile in responding to the varied needs of its many clients in a rapidly changing world. As the principal shareholders of the AfDB, many African countries are making steady progress toward achieving some of the Millennium Development Goals, notwithstanding persistent challenges. As is typical of developing economies, the economies of most African countries are resource driven and have features of external debt financing.[63] There is also the phenomenon of state failure[64] seen in terms of poor governance[65] in the specific context of corruption.[66] But a study of dysfunctional states that describes some African countries as "anarchic," like Somalia, "phantom or mirage," like the Democratic Republic of Congo, and "aborted," like Angola,[67] is controversial and tenuous. Each African state has unique circumstances and challenges, although nearly a quarter of Africa's population lives in fragile states where there is exceptionally weak institutional capacity, poor governance, political instability, and ongoing or

---

62 See Shihata, *supra* note 23, at 229.

63 See Christiana Ochoa, *From Odious Debt to Odious Finance: Avoiding the Externalities of a Functional Odious Debt Doctrine*, 49 Harv. Intl. L.J. 109 (Winter 2008).

64 For a general discussion of state failures in Africa, see James C. Owens, *Government Failure in Sub-Saharan Africa: The International Community's Options*, 43 Va. J. Intl. L. 1003, 1044–1045 (Summer 2003), identifying dependence on external sources of revenue as a cause of regress in Sub-Saharan Africa.

65 For a discussion of good governance, see Francis N. Botchway, *Good Governance, the Old, the Principle, and the Elements*, 13 Fla. J. Intl. L. 159 (Spring 2001).

66 Hazel M. McFerson, *Democracy and Development in Africa*, 23(3) J. Peace Research 241–248 at 243 (Aug. 1992), available at http://www.jstor.org/stable/424278 (accessed May 10, 2013), where the author writes, "Since independence, a political involution has proceeded in Africa from the adoption of colonial patterns of economic control, through the 'mobilization for development' and central control, to their unintended but inevitable offspring: a predatory and corrupt political system which is often referred to as 'prebendalism.'"

67 See Stephen Ellis, *How to Rebuild Africa*, 84(5) For. Affairs 135, 139 (Sept.–Oct. 2005), borrowing from Jean-Germain Gros, available at http://www.jstor.org/stable/20031711 (accessed May 10, 2013).

past violent conflict.[68] Conflict[69] creates emergencies like displacements, hunger, health hazards, and unemployment that development institutions either try to prevent from happening or must respond to or remedy. Addressing these issues involves eradicating the root causes, some of which are political in nature. This is because a nexus can be found between economic and political considerations when it comes to issues of conflicts. Collier and Hoeffler observe—in relation to the detection of rebellion using both political science and economic theories—that conflict has two essential causal elements: the motive and the opportunity to rebel.[70]

In regard to fostering opportunities, the AfDB group proposes three strategic directions in the TYS:

---

68   *See* AfDB, *Bank Group Support to Conflict-Affected Countries,* ch. 5 in *African Development Report 2008/2009: Conflict Resolution, Peace and Reconstruction in Africa* 60 (Oxford U. Press 2009), available at http://www.afdb.org/fileadmin/uploads/afdb/Documents/Publications/African%20Development%20Report%202008.2009_00_Full_Report.pdf (accessed Apr. 25, 2013).

69   The literature on this subject is expansive and often discussed in relation to natural resources exploitation. For example, *see* Michael T. Klare, *Resource Wars: The New Landscape of Global Conflict* 217–226 (Metropolitan 2001); Michael Ross, *The Natural Resource Curse: How Wealth Can Make You Poor,* in *Natural Resources and Violent Conflict: Options and Actions* 17–19 (Ian Bannon & Paul Collier ed., World Bank 2003); Paul Collier & Anke Hoeffler, *On Economic Causes of Civil War,* 50 Oxford Econ. Papers 563–573 (1998), available at http://oep.oxford journals.org/cgi/reprint/50/4/563 (accessed Apr. 25, 2013); Paul Collier, *Doing Well out of War: An Economic Perspective,* in *Greed and Grievance: Economic Agendas in Civil Wars* 91 (Mats Berdal & David M. Malone eds., Lynne Rienner 2000); Paul Collier, Anke Hoeffler, & Dominic Rohner, *Beyond Greed and Grievance: Feasibility and Civil War,* 61 Oxford Econ. Papers 1–27 (2009), available at http://oep.oxfordjournals.org/cgi/reprint/61/1/1 (accessed Apr. 25, 2013); Ole Magnus Theisen, *Blood and Soil? Resource Scarcity and Internal Armed Conflict Revisited,* 45(6) J. Peace Research 801–818 (2008), available at http://jpr.sagepub.com/cgi/content/abstract /45/6/801 (accessed Apr. 25, 2013); Indra De Soysa & Eric Neumayer, *Resource Wealth and the Risk of Civil War Onset: Results from a New Dataset of Natural Resource Rents, 1970–1999,* 24 Conflict Mgt. & Peace Sci. 201 (2007), available at http://cmp.sagepub.com/cgi/content /abstract/24/3/201 (accessed Apr. 25, 2013); Päivi Lujala et al., *Fighting over Oil: Introducing a New Dataset,* 24 Conflict Mgt. & Peace Sci. 239 (2007), available at http://cmp.sagepub.com /cgi/content/abstract/24/3/239 (accessed Apr. 25, 2013); Thad Dunning, *Resource Dependence, Economic Performance, and Political Stability,* 49 J. Conflict Res. 451 (2005), available at http:// jcr.sagepub.com/cgi/content/abstract/49/4/451 (accessed Apr. 25, 2013); Päivi Lujala et al., *A Diamond Curse? Civil War and a Lootable Resource,* 49 J. Conflict Res. 538 (2005), available at http://jcr.sagepub.com/cgi/content/abstract/49/4/538 (accessed Apr. 25, 2013); Paul Collier & Anke Hoeffler, *Resource Rents, Governance, and Conflict,* 49 J. Conflict Res. 625 (2005), available at http://jcr.sagepub.com/cgi/content/abstract/49/4/625 (accessed Apr. 25, 2013); Paul Collier & Anke Hoeffler, *Greed and Grievance in Civil War,* 56 Oxford Econ. Papers 63 (2004) (hereinafter *Greed and Grievance in Civil War*), available at http://oep.oxfordjournals .org/cgi/reprint/56/4/563 (accessed Apr. 25, 2013); *see* also http://www-wds.worldbank .org/external/default/WDSContentServer/IW3P/IB/2004/03/10/000265513_20040310152555 /Rendered/PDF/28126.pdf (accessed Apr. 25, 2013); James D. Fearon, *Primary Commodity Exports and Civil War,* 49 J. Conflict Res. 483 (2005), available at http://jcr.sagepub.com/cgi /content/abstract/49/4/483 (accessed Apr. 25, 2013).

70   *See* Collier & Hoeffler (2004), *supra* note 69, at 63. The authors use political science and economic theories to posit two essential elements in the cause of conflicts: the motive and the opportunity to rebel. They explain that the political motivation for rebellion is grievance and the economic motivation is greed. One of their proxies for the opportunity to rebel is the extortion of natural resources, and they argue that primary commodity exports influence the risk of conflict significantly.

- Becoming more agile in responding quickly to the varied needs of the AfDB's many clients in a rapidly changing world

- Becoming more selective in promoting Africa's development priorities, including inclusive and sustainable growth, which will require greater attention to collaborating and dividing responsibilities with many development partners

- Becoming more insistent on delivering results

The third direction means going beyond assessing the development results of the work of the AfDB to instilling a results-oriented culture throughout the bank.[71]

The drafting of Article 38 shows the article's resemblance to the political prohibition clauses of other MDBs, such as the World Bank and the Inter-American Development Bank. The history also shows that the original draft of the Committee of Nine had not what is now Article 38(1) but rather what is now Article 38(2) and (3). Being mindful of the African context and the manifest consequences that could be occasioned by a literal interpretation of Article 38, the Conference of Finance Ministers[72] adopted the final draft of Article 38, which includes what is now Article 38(1).[73] The drafters did not intend Article 38 to prejudice, limit, deflect, or otherwise alter the purpose or functions of the AfDB. The TYS guides the AfDB to use the resources at its disposal to finance investment projects and programs relating to the economic and social development of its regional members.[74] When looking specifically at sustainable economic development, one can observe that three of the five operational priorities of the LTS—infrastructure development, private sector development, and skills and technology—are economic in nature.

---

71   See AfDB, *Governors' Dialogue: Long Term Strategy 2022—Issues Paper* (Bank Group Annual Meetings report, Arusha, Tanzania, May 31, 2012), available at http://www.afdb.org/fileadmin/uploads/afdb/Documents/Policy-Documents/LTS%20Issues%20Paper%20for%20Governors%20Dialogue.pdf (accessed Apr. 23, 2013).

72   For a brief introduction to the Committee of Nine and the Conference of Finance Ministers, see ECA, *supra* note 31.

73   *Id.*, at 164. The explanatory notes submitted by the Committee of Nine explain what is now Article 38(2) and (3) in the following words:; "Paragraphs (1) and (2) [i.e., Article 38(2) and (3)] of the Article have, as in the case of the IADB (Art. VIII(5)(d) and (f)), been combined into a single Article (see IBRD Ar. IV(10) and V(5)(c)). A reference to the President of the Bank has been added to para 1. *For the rest, the texts are on traditional lines.*" (italics added)

74   See AfDB, *supra* note 4, at iii, where the president of the AfDB states in the foreword to the TYS:

    The Strategy also addresses the issue of development finance. New global patterns of finance and capital flows, and the discovery of significant oil and gas resources, now make it possible for Africa to mobilize its own savings through, among other things, better management of natural resources. This is an area where the Bank will play a catalytic, leveraging role.

Would Sustainable Development Considerations under the TYS Violate Article 38?

The TYS addresses green growth within the context of sustainable development using a holistic approach that links green growth and green economy as two concepts that can help tackle the challenges of poverty, social inequality, pollution, environmental degradation, and climate change on the continent. Scholars have suggested that MDBs should address sustainable development issues. Günther Handl argues that "MDBs themselves can no longer afford to treat environmental and social concerns as merely incidental to development projects, but have an affirmative duty to incorporate these issues into the mainstream of their development-financing operations."[75] Similarly, Shihata has argued that

> the prohibition of political activities in the MDBs Charters has never been an obstacle to accepting and mainstreaming environmentally and socially sustainable development. He reasoned that this is not political development but economic development which takes full account of environmental and social implications and includes safeguards to assure an outcome that is positive or at least not negative in these respects.[76]

Handl contends that the banks' decisions on lending activities are being legally circumscribed as a function of the emergence of relevant international public policy and law, the internationally mandated criterion for achieving sustainable development.[77] Both Shihata and Handl observe that mainstreaming sustainable development into the mandate of the MDBs is stating the obvious. The issue is whether the AfDB has managed to get this concept right in its TYS.

One can argue that the mandate of the AfDB incorporates sustainable development. Article 1 of the AfDB Agreement explicitly states that "the purpose of the Bank shall be to contribute to the sustainable economic development and social progress of its regional members individually and jointly." When Article 1 is construed literally, one can infer that the controlling theme in the purpose and functions of the AfDB is sustainable economic development. The

---

75 Günther Handl, *The Legal Mandate of Multilateral Development Banks as Agents for Change toward Sustainable Development*, 92 Am. J. Intl. L. 642 (Oct. 1998), available at http://www.jstor .org/discover/10.2307/2998127?uid=3738072&uid=2134&uid=370214251&uid=2&uid=70&uid =3&uid=370214241&uid=60&sid=21102201987457 (accessed Apr. 26, 2013).

76 *See* Co-editors in Chief of the American Journal of International Law, *Correspondence*, 93 Am. J. Intl. L. 625–626 (July 1999).

77 *Id.*, at 626–627. According to Handl, it is not "political," but appropriate for MDBs, like other actors on the international legal plane, to be seen as subject to general international law. As such, MDBs cannot insulate themselves against the reach of evolving international law by invoking a traditional understanding of the principles enshrined in their constituent treaties, especially when the new international norms not only permit but mandate a different view of what constitutes prohibited "political activities."

contours of sustainable development itself are very intricate,[78] and it does not make sense to construe Article 38(2) literally. However, a purposive interpretation of Article 38(2) translates into an examination of the sustainable economic development purpose of the AfDB in Article 1.

In the area of governance and accountability, the AfDB proposes to support institutions that promote inclusion and accountability. This proposal includes strengthening the capacities of parliamentarians, the media, and civil societies.[79] In fragile states, the AfDB notes, fragility is contagious and episodic, and its support must be tailored to diverse needs and a continuum and regional approach built around dialogue, local ownership, and a celebration of success.[80] As evidence of cooperation with other MDBs, the AfDB joined other MDBs to establish an international financial institution anticorruption task force in 2006,[81] and the AfDB signed the Agreement for Mutual Enforcement of Debarment Decisions targeting corruption in 2010.[82] The purposive

---

78   For a general discussion of its historical development and legal framework, *see* Alhaji B. M. Marong, *From Rio to Johannesburg: Reflections on the Role of International Legal Norms in Sustainable Development*, 16 Geo. Intl. Envtl. L. Rev. 21 (2003). In spite of its vagueness, its relevance is shared by both developed and developing countries. *See* Ved P. Nanda, *Sustainable Development, International Trade and the Doha Agenda for Development*, 8 Chap. L. Rev. 53 (2005). By reason of this universal acceptance, this term lends itself to several uses; one writer describes it as "probably suffering from its success as a buzzword." *See* Patricia Nelson, *An African Dimension to the Clean Development Mechanism: Finding a Path to Sustainable Development in the Energy Sector*, 32 Denv. J. Intl. L. & Policy 615 (Fall 2004), discussing the Kyoto Protocol to the United Nations Framework Convention on Climate Change (UNFCCC) and how Africa is neglected in considerations of sustainable development in the energy sector. Of particular significance are efforts at the global level in using the term to address environmental ills associated with global industrialization; *see* Paolo Galizzi, *From Stockholm to New York, via Rio and Johannesburg: Has the Environment Lost Its Way on the Global Agenda?*, 29 Fordham Intl. L.J. 952 (May 2006). In the context of the extractive industry, *see* Andres Liebenthal et al., *Extractive Industries and Sustainable Development: An Evaluation of World Bank Group Experience* (World Bank 2005), available at http://www.ifc.org/ifcext/oeg.nsf/AttachmentsBy Title/ei_report/$FILE/Extractive+Industries+and+Sustainable+Development.pdf   (accessed Apr. 23, 2013).

79   *See* AfDB, *supra* note 4, at 2–3.

80   *Id.*, at 3.

81   *See* AfDB et al., *International Financial Institutions Anti-corruption Task Force* (2006), available at http://www.afdb.org/fileadmin/uploads/afdb/Documents/Generic-Documents/30716700 -EN-UNIFORM-FRAMEWORK-FOR-COMBATTING-FRAUD-V6.PDF(accessedJune5,2013). *See also* Laurence Boisson de Chazournes, *Partnership, Emulation, and Coordination toward the Emergence of a Droit Commun in the Field of Development Finance*, in *The World Bank Legal Review*, vol. 3, 183 (Hassane Cissé, Daniel Bradlow, & Benedict Kingsbury eds., World Bank 2012):

> Another step in terms of cooperative practices among institutions has been the establishment of mechanisms for cooperation and mutual recognition between the World Bank and regional development banks. In the fight against corruption, the actions undertaken and policies adopted by the World Bank and the regional development banks have inspired cooperation. In this respect, in September 2006, the Uniform Framework for Preventing and Combating Fraud and Corruption was put into place by the leaders of the AfDB Group, the ADB, the EBRD, the EIB Group, the IMF, the IDB, and the World Bank Group.

82   *See* International Bar Association, *Global Leaders: Kalidou Gadio*, 66(3) IBA Global Insight 36 (2012). *See* also Stephen S. Zimmermann & Frank A. Fariello Jr., *Coordinating the Fight against*

interpretation and margin of appreciation analysis make the AfDB's involvement in anticorruption efforts consistent with Article 38.

Some Bank Practices and Article 38

Essentially, the AfDB's operations and activities are designed to respond to the development challenges and demands of its RMCs. The AfDB's operations have generated the following issues:

- Are the AfDB's premembership interventions in an RMC compliant with Article 38?

- If AfDB premembership interventions do not compromise the AfDB's role as a neutral arbiter, does such intervention also affect the interests of an existing regional member?

- Is Presidential Directive No. 3 of 2010 compliant with Article 38?

The first two issues are discussed below in the context of premembership operations of the AfDB in the Republic of South Sudan.

AfDB Premembership Interventions and Article 38 Compliance

The Republic of South Sudan was officially admitted into the AfDB as a member on May 31, 2012.[83] Upon the independence of the Republic of South Sudan from the Republic of Sudan, the AfDB signed a Cooperation Agreement with the Republic of South Sudan in September 2011, which provided the legal basis to continue operational assistance and programming activities pending full membership of the new state in the AfDB.[84] The AfDB and its staff assisted in negotiation or mediation exercises involving the two countries, facilitated by the African Union High-Level Implementation Panel (AUHIP). The chair of the AUHIP made a request not only to the AfDB but also to the World Bank and the IMF for technical assistance. The AfDB responded positively to the request.

The assistance included the provision of advisory services to the AUHIP on the economic-related aspects of the negotiations that were intricately linked to other security and political matters. The republics of Sudan and South Sudan and the African Union were comfortable with the AfDB's role.

Fraud and Corruption Agreement on Cross-Debarment among Multilateral Development Banks, in *The World Bank Legal Review,* vol. 3, 189 (Hassane Cissé, Daniel Bradlow, & Benedict Kingsbury eds., World Bank 2012).

83   *See* AfDB, Board of Governors Resolution Authorizing the Accession of the Republic of South Sudan to the African Development Bank Agreement (Resolution B/BG/2012/05, 2012), available at http://www.afdb.org/fileadmin/uploads/afdb/Documents/Boards-Documents/2011%20Annual%20Meetings%20Official%20Records.pdf (accessed May 12, 2013).

84   *See* AfDB, *The First Interim Country Strategy Paper (CSP) for South Sudan Covering the Period 2012–2014* (AfDB 2012).

A critical question is whether or not the AfDB is mandated to provide some form of support to a nonmember country. In line with a purposive interpretation of the AfDB Agreement, this question is answered by examining the conduct of all the parties, including the African Union and the international community. For example, the AfDB provided assistance to the AUHIP because the Republic of Sudan was a member of the AfDB that needed technical assistance, and because that assistance will help a prospective member amicably resolve issues that may aid in its attainment of membership when the time is ripe, especially if Sudan and South Sudan agreed on the "zero option" with respect to the assets and liabilities of the former state of Sudan.[85]

Thus, the AfDB's premembership intervention in South Sudan in the context of the Cooperation Agreement with the Government of South Sudan in September 2011 does not violate Article 38 and it does not compromise the AfDB's neutrality as an arbiter between the Republic of Sudan and the Republic of South Sudan.

The Republic of South Sudan is an interesting case study.[86] For decades, the Republic of Sudan and the now Republic of South Sudan have fought over differences in ideology, politics, resources, land, and oil. These hostilities culminated in the Comprehensive Peace Agreement and the independence of South Sudan on July 9, 2011, and the subsequent recognition of its statehood by the United Nations.[87] The Comprehensive Peace Agreement did not address what is often cited by commentators as the "Abyei issue." The Abyei issue refers to the ownership and control of the oil-rich Abyei area. Thus, at the heart of the dispute is the control of the oil-producing region of Southern Kordofan and the Abyei area. A decision of an international arbitral tribunal, which predated the independence of the Republic of South Sudan, redrew the boundaries of Abyei,[88] but that decision did not end hostilities. The two countries signed a cooperation agreement on September 27, 2012, mediated by the AUHIP, but failed to agree on border areas, including Abyei. Thus, the two countries continue to face security threats posed by the Abyei issue even after

---

85   Under the "zero option," the Republic of Sudan will assume all external debts conditional on (i) a joint outreach to the donor community by both countries; and (ii) Sudan benefiting from debt relief within two years, failing which there will be debt apportionment between the two countries.

86   It presents an interesting case study of the evolving development of the international law principle in relation to the self-determination of peoples in the context of Africa. African countries have retained their respective borders as handed over to them by the colonial administrations. *See* Malcolm N. Shaw, *International Law* 205–206 (6th ed., Cambridge U. Press 2008). Even though there have been instances of border disputes, none has escalated into the declaration of war by one country against another. Instead, the disputes have largely focused on resources and issues of state control. *See* John Campbell, *South Sudan's Challenge to Africa's Colonial Borders* (expert brief, Council on For. Rel., July 7, 2011), available at http://www.cfr.org/sudan/south-sudans-challenge-africas-colonial-borders/p25439 (accessed May 3, 2013).

87   *See* UN Security Council Resolution 1999 (2011) on admission of the Republic of South Sudan to membership in the United Nations, available at http://www.refworld.org/cgi-bin/texis/vtx/rwmain?docid=4e2e54d52 (accessed May 3, 2013).

88   *See* http://www.pca-cpa.org/showpage.asp?pag_id=1306 (accessed May 3, 2013).

the independence of South Sudan, and the African Union is concerned about resolving this issue.[89]

The AfDB has been visible in promoting the development agenda of fragile states in Africa by emphasizing the importance of these states in its long-term strategic plan and medium-term strategic planning.[90] According to the *African Development Report, 2008/2009*, the AfDB plays an active role in a country's postconflict reconstruction and development, and its point of entry is after the cessation of hostilities and the establishment of a transitional government authority with the support of the international community.[91] Bearing this in mind, the AfDB's postconflict reconstruction and development efforts in the Republic of South Sudan are justified considering the support and works of other leading MDBs, like the World Bank and the IMF. In the case of South Sudan, both the World Bank and the IMF were involved in the negotiation processes at some point. Furthermore, there is evidence in the literature to justify the AfDB's involvement in the Republic of South Sudan. For example, Paul Collier has suggested that the right of a postconflict government to dispose of mineral rights should be limited until the society has had the time to properly establish a transparent mineral rights regime. In the African context, he reasons, the exercise of sovereignty over mineral rights by postconflict governments can be restricted by the African Union using the AfDB as its policing implementation agency during the transition period.[92]

AfDB Presidential Directive No. 3 and Article 38

AfDB Presidential Directive No. 3 of 2010 (PD3/2010) sets out the procedures, conditions, and guidelines that govern the AfDB group's engagement with de facto governments in RMCs. PD3/2010 defines de facto governments as governments that have usurped the sovereign authority of lawful governments, or that exist without actual lawful or legal authority, yet openly exercise the powers and functions of the state. Such governments come into power through unconstitutional means, such as by coup d'état, revolution, or abrogation or suspension of the constitution or other relevant laws.

---

89   *See Report of the Chairperson of the Commission on the Status of the Negotiations between the Republic of Sudan and the Republic of South Sudan on the Outstanding Issues in Their Post-secession Arrangements* (Peace and Security Council of the African Union, Feb. 14, 2012); *see* also African Union, Communique on the Report (Peace and Security Council of the African Union, Feb. 14, 2012).

90   *See* AfDB, *Evaluation of African Development Bank Assistance to Fragile States* (approach paper, Jan. 2010), available at http://www.afdb.org/fileadmin/uploads/afdb/Documents/Evaluation -Reports/Evaluation%20of%20Fragile%20States%20Approach%20Paper%20FINAL%20JAN %202010.pdf (accessed Apr. 25, 2013).

91   *See* AfDB, *supra* note 68.

92   *See* Paul Collier, *Post-conflict Recovery: How Should Policies Be Distinctive?* 2 (research paper, Ctr. for the Study of African Economies, Dept. of Economics, Oxford U., May 2007), available at http://users.ox.ac.uk/~econpco/research/pdfs/PostConflict-Recovery.pdf (accessed Apr. 25, 2013).

Paragraph 4 of the directive provides:

> This Directive shall apply to all [AfDB] Bank Group Operations[93] including, but not limited to: (i) public sector operations; (ii) private sector operations; (iii) operations of trust funds such as the Technical Assistance Fund for Middle Income Countries; and (iv) special funds and other [AfDB] Bank Group entities such as the African Water Facility Special Fund and the Fragile States Facility amongst others.

In line with this directive, the AfDB continued its operations in Tunisia, Egypt, and Libya in a strategically cautious manner, being guided by four main principles contained in paragraph 9 of the directive. These are

- Avoiding, to the extent possible, major deterioration of the economic situation of the population of the concerned RMC
- Avoiding major deterioration in the AfDB group's investments or projects
- Taking actions informed by an adequate evaluation of the situation
- Being guided by the views, decisions and best practices of the international community

In a February 14, 2011, press release, the president of the AfDB stated that as "Africa's leading development finance institution, the AfDB would like to be at the forefront of helping Tunisia as it enters this delicate phase of its history, and we call upon other partners to join us in this endeavor."[94] At the time of the January 14, 2011, revolution, Tunisia had the second-largest portfolio of AfDB projects and other commitments. The country strategy paper (CSP) approved by the board of directors of the AfDB in 2007 was replaced by an interim country strategy paper (I-CSP) for a two-year period (2012–2013). In the I-CSP, the AfDB adopted a strategy for the 2012–2013 period that includes revolution-induced priorities and varied factors inherent in the transition process.[95]

Egypt is one of the AfDB's key shareholders and accounts for one of the largest shares of the AfDB's operations portfolio. The January 25, 2011, revolution in Egypt saw the country being governed by the Supreme Council of Armed Forces (SCAF) and supported by ministerial cabinets appointed by the SCAF. The SCAF handed power to the newly elected president, Mohamed Morsi, at the end of June 2011. The AfDB continued to assist Egypt by disbursing funds for ongoing investment projects, notwithstanding the political unrest. As of March 31, 2011, Egypt had 26 operations under implementation.

---

93   As understood in the context of the directive, "operations" include, inter alia, preparatory and appraisal missions, nonobjections, agreement negotiation and signature, disbursements, and presentation to the boards of directors and/or boards of governors.

94   See http://www.afdb.org/fileadmin/uploads/afdb/Documents/Generic-Documents/PRST %20Press%20Statement%20%20Feb%202011%20final%20ENG.pdf (accessed May 5, 2013).

95   See http://www.afdb.org/fileadmin/uploads/afdb/Documents/Project-and-Operations /Catalogue%20Interim%20strategy%20Paper%20Anglais_Mise%20en%20page%201.pdf (accessed May 5, 2013).

The AfDB's postrevolution interventions in Egypt are based, primarily, on pursuing macroeconomic stabilization to support recovery and, secondly, on promoting inclusive growth to reduce poverty.[96]

The political unrest in Libya was inspired by the revolutions in Tunisia and Egypt. By February 27, 2011, the opposition had organized itself around a structured governing body, the National Transitional Council (NTC). The NTC set out detailed plans for the transition process and, in August 2011, issued a temporary constitution according to which Libya is a democratic, independent state with Tripoli as its capital, Islam its religion, sharia law the main source of legislation, and Arabic its official language. Although a founding and relatively large shareholder of the AfDB, Libya has never borrowed from the AfDB group. Hence, the AfDB group's operational engagement with the country has been limited to nonlending activities, mainly knowledge services.

Elsewhere, other regional security threats, including the reemergence of military coups in Guinea Bissau and Mali, have highlighted the political fragility and risks in some African countries. The continuous operation of the AfDB in such RMCs cannot be discounted.

Would Democratic Considerations under Presidential Directive No. 3 Violate Article 38?

Although "democracy" has no universally accepted definition,[97] the simplest explanation of the term is that it is a government that rests on the consent of the governed.[98] Such consent of the governed is given in universally free elections. Democracy provides a mechanism for the governed to change the governors if they are dissatisfied with their performance. In any case, "democracy" is a buzzword often used in tandem with another watchword: "good governance." Francis Botchway, in discussing the theoretical underpinnings of the concept of good governance, extends the definition of that term to cover such elements as democracy, rule of law, effective bureaucracy, discretion, and decentralization. In his view, the correlation between good governance and development is not known; however, democracy is a sustainable means

---

96 *See* AfDB, *Two-Year Interim Country Strategic Plan for Egypt Covering 2012–2013,* available at http://www.afdb.org/fileadmin/uploads/afdb/Documents/Project-and-Operations/2012 -2013%20-%20Egypt%20-%20Interim%20Strategy%20Paper.pdf (accessed May 5, 2013).

97 To one scholar, it is a myth; *see* Ferdinand Lundberg, *The Myth of Democracy* (Carol Publishing Group 1989); another scholar doubts it; *see* Bruce Gilley, *Is Democracy Possible?,* 20(1) J. Democracy 113 (Jan. 2009), available at http://www.journalofdemocracy.org/articles/gratis /Gilley-20-1.pdf (accessed June 5, 2013).

98 *See,* generally, Anthony W. Bradley & Keith D. Ewing, vol. 1, 14 *Constitutional and Administrative Law* (Pearson Longman 2007); *see* also Ibrahim F. I. Shihata, *Democracy and Development,* 46(3) Intl. Comp. & L. Q. 635–643 esp. at 635 (1997):

> By democracy lawyers usually mean that form of government in which the sovereign power resides in and is exercised by the whole body of citizens directly or indirectly through a system of representation. More generally, it is a system where ordinary citizens have a meaningful, even if indirect, role in the affairs of the State, including the formulation of policies and laws and their implementation.

of building a united and cohesive nation.[99] Nancy D. Erbe draws a link between good governance and mediation when she identifies eight interdependent elements of good governance: (1) broad participation in governance that reflects the diversity of the community (ethnic and gender) as well as freedom of association and expression; (2) the rule of law, enforced fairly and impartially; (3) transparency; (4) consensus-based mediation between the diverse stakeholders stressed in the first criterion above, where all discuss and agree to sustainable decisions; (5) egalitarian and inclusive decision making among the myriad societal interests referenced earlier; (6) efficient use of resources; (7) responsiveness to stakeholders' interests; and (8) accountability.[100]

Democracy is mandated by the African Charter on Democracy, Elections, and Governance of 2007.[101] The charter seeks, among other things, to promote adherence, by each state party, to the universal values and principles of democracy. It also seeks to promote and enhance adherence to the principle of the rule of law premised upon the respect for, and the supremacy of, the constitution and constitutional order in the political arrangements of state parties. In Article 4, state parties commit themselves to promote democracy and the principle of the rule of law.

In view of the above, one can argue that, being a creature of law, the AfDB cannot act *ultra vires* its constitutive instrument. However, it is doubtful whether the AfDB, as an international body, can cite its articles of agreement to excuse itself from the performance of its international obligations.[102] Although not a state party to the African Charter on Democracy, Elections, and Governance, the AfDB, as the premier financial institution for Africa, cannot defeat the objects and purpose of the charter. Recently, the AfDB has considered good governance as pivotal to any efficient legal and judicial system. It has therefore highlighted legal and judicial reforms in its Policy on Good Governance and the Governance Strategic Directions and Action Plan.[103]

---

99   *See* Botchway, *supra* note 65.

100 *See* Nancy D. Erbe, *Appreciating Mediation's Global Role in Promoting Good Governance*, 11 Harv. Negot. L. Rev. 355 (Spring 2006).

101 African Charter on Democracy, Elections, and Governance, available at http://au.int/en /sites/default/files/AFRICAN_CHARTER_ON_DEMOCRACY_ELECTIONS_AND_GOVER NANCE.pdf (accessed May 5, 2013). This was adopted on January 30, 2007, and entered into force on February 15, 2012; by July 19, 2012, it had been ratified by 17 and signed by 41 African countries. For a list of countries that signed, ratified, or acceded to the charter, *see* http://au.int/en/sites/default/files/charter%20on%20democracy%20and%20governance_0.pdf (accessed May 5, 2013).

102 *See* Vienna Convention, *supra* note 30, at art. 27.

103 AfDB, *Governance Strategic Directions and Action Plan GAP 2008–2012* (research paper prepared by the Governance, Economic and Financial Management Department, Apr. 17, 2008), available at http://www.afdb.org/fileadmin/uploads/afdb/Documents/Publications /7000017_EN_OSGE%20anglais%20OK.pdf (accessed Apr. 23, 2013).

Conclusion

This chapter has discussed Article 38 of the Agreement Establishing the African Development Bank, which restricts the AfDB and its president, vice presidents, officers, and staff to economic considerations only in their work, without partiality.

Despite this restriction and in response to recent challenges, the AfDB has utilized innovative policy initiatives to foster opportunities and inclusion on the continent, including the provision of premembership assistance to the Republic of South Sudan and the continuity of the bank's operations under Presidential Directive No. 3 of 2010 in postconflict RMCs. The AfDB has adopted a long-term strategy designed to foster opportunities and inclusion through development financing. However, there are legal implications for the bank in terms of its legal mandate in Article 38; this chapter thus suggests a purposive interpretation of Article 38. Furthermore, it argues that the purposive interpretation should be combined with a proportionality test that would allow a careful, constructive, and creative stretching of Article 38 that does not lead to its breach.

PART V

EMPOWERMENT AND EQUITY FOR DIVERSE COMMUNITIES

Nation Building, State Reconstruction, and Inclusiveness

Issues on South Sudan as a New State and Somalia as a Failed but Reemerging State

Vincent O. Nmehielle and John-Mark Iyi

Since time immemorial, humans have sought ways to improve progress and well being through the formation of associations, communities, societies, countries, states, and regional blocs.[1] Deprivations, inequalities, and injustices, however, have often characterized how various segments of these entities related with one another. In a number of cases this has spawned conflicts that have hindered human progress and development. Although our understanding of the cycle of violent conflict caused by deprivation, exclusion, and inequality has deepened, our policy responses have not always been successful in bringing about the institutional transformation necessary to break that cycle.[2] This is particularly the case in conflict-ridden states, postconflict states, and new states emerging from conflict situations that need to be rebuilt to set out on a new and coordinated path of rule of law–driven development. The cases of South Sudan and Somalia fall into the latter category.

Some writers have described nation building as comprising three phases: stabilizing the crisis-ridden country, establishing governance institutions, and enhancing the capacities of those institutions to foster socioeconomic development.[3] Development theorists differentiate between "nation building" and "state building," and between "reconstruction" and "development."[4] "Nation-building is the process of constructing a new political order with a shared identity and a community of shared values.[5] State-building, in contrast, refers to the process of constructing (or reconstructing) state political institutions or

---

1   Rosa Ehrenreich Brooks, *Failed States, or the State as Failure?*, 72(4) U. Chi. L. Rev. 1159, 1169 (2005).

2   Necla Tschirgi, *The Security-Politics-Development-Nexus: The Lessons of State-Building in Sub-Saharan Africa* (Robert Schuman Ctr. for Advanced Stud. European Report on Dev., European U. Inst. Working Paper RASCAS 2010/35, 2010), available at http://www.erd.eu/media/tschirgi.pdf (accessed May 7, 2013).

3   Caio Cesar Paccola Jacon et al., *Nation-Building in South Sudan: Past Struggles and Current Challenges,* available at http://www.sinus.org.br/2012/wp-content/uploads/16-AU.pdf (accessed May 2, 2013) (hereinafter *Nation-Building in South Sudan*).

4   *See* Dan E. Stigal, *Comparative Law and State-Building: The "Organic Minimalist" Approach to Legal Reconstruction,* 29 Loyola L.A. Intl. & Comp. L. Rev. 1, 4 (2007).

5   *Id.,* at 4.

promoting economic development."[6] "Reconstruction refers to the restoration of war-torn or damaged societies to their preconflict situation."[7] "Development, however, refers to the creation of new institutions and the promotion of sustained economic growth, events that transform the society open-endedly into something it has not been previously."[8]

The meaning, scope, content, and measurement of development have changed over the years. In the past, the concept of development focused on economic advancement, but it now includes such variegated dimensions as freedom from fear and want.[9] Similarly, emphasis was on GDP as a reflection of the level of development, but it is now clear that there can be growth without development and, even when development does occur, it may not necessarily reach the majority of the population.[10] Thus was born the concept of human development encompassing all those elements reflective of human progress, such as security, freedom from want and fear, opportunity, and other elements outlined in the Millennium Development Goals and other related documents.[11] The rise of globalization fostered great economic prosperity in the last half of the 20th century.[12] However, it did not necessarily translate into a reduction of poverty, hunger, the number of malnourished children in Africa and other areas of the developing world, or the number of homeless people.[13] Tremendous results have been recorded in the deployment of technology to drive economic development and wealth creation; but inequity in the distribution of this prosperity has also meant that more and more people have been driven into extreme poverty.[14] Thus, despite the remarkable success of this phenomenon, increasingly more people are excluded from participating in global wealth and resources.[15]

---

6   *Id.* Experience shows that it is easier to achieve state building than nation building. "Nation-building can be viewed in terms of its inputs—which, broadly speaking, are manpower, money, and time—and its desired outputs": peace, economic growth, and democratization. Outputs are not directly proportional to inputs but depend to a high degree on the astuteness employed in the deployment and management of resources and the willingness of the particular society to adapt to the changes and reforms being introduced.

7   *Id.*

8   *Id.*, at 4–5.

9   See United Nations, *We the Peoples: The Role of the United Nations in the Twenty-First Century, Report of the Secretary General*, A/54/2000, paras. 66–188 & paras. 189–253 (hereinafter *We the Peoples*). The number of people living on less than $1.25 fell from 47 percent in 1990 to 24 percent in 2008. *See* http://www.undp.org/content/undp/en/home/mdgoverview/mdg_goals /mdgl/ (accessed May 6, 2013).

10   Joseph E. Stiglitz, *Globalization and Its Discontents* 4 (2002); *No Future without Justice: Report of the Civil Society Reflection Group on Global Development Perspectives*, 59 Dev. Dialogue 1, 9, 11 (June 2012) (hereinafter *No Future without Justice*).

11   *See We the Peoples, supra* note 9.

12   Stiglitz, *supra* note 10, at 24.

13   *See No Future without Justice, supra* note 10, at 6.

14   Stiglitz, *supra* note 10, at 24.

15   *Id.* This imbalance was recently echoed thus: "We live in a world where the top 20 percent of the population enjoy more than 80 percent of total income and those in the bottom quintile

The story of the world since the 20th century has been a paradoxical one of want in the midst of plenty. "Persistent poverty, unemployment, social exclusion, and higher levels of inequality and insecurity are threatening care systems, social cohesion and political stability,"[16] as unmitigated globalization continues to increase inequality between and within countries.[17] The spin-offs of these conditions quickly led to a series of "Occupy" movements and protests across the world in 2011–12. However the debate is framed, whether among nations or within countries, the challenge remains the same: how can resources be distributed more inclusively and equitably, affording everyone the opportunity to achieve his or her potential and thereby end the cycle of poverty that has up to now continued unabated? This challenge is greater for a new country such as South Sudan and a reemerging state such as Somalia, especially after decades of brutal conflicts and war.

While the emphasis here is on South Sudan and Somalia, it is safe to say that the cycle of poverty and violent conflicts have been the lot of most postcolonial African states. On several development indexes, African states, particularly those emerging from long periods of conflict and the complete disappearance of any semblance of statehood, occupy the bottom rung of the statistical ladder.[18] At a time when much intellectual capital is being spent on a better understanding of the conflict-development nexus, it is not surprising that the dominant themes of opportunity, inclusion, and equity animate the African discourse.

Upon independence, many African states embraced a strongly state-led development model.[19] However, for several reasons, many of which remain controversial, these efforts were unsuccessful and during the late 1970s and early 1980s these states were forced to abandon their developmental-state model and embraced the neoliberal development prescriptions of international financial institutions (IFIs).[20] Again, by the end of the 1990s, development thinkers in development institutions, donor governments, aid agencies, and academia had to reassess the suitability of this model for Africa given the stark evidence that most African states had become worse off than they were before they embarked on neoliberal policies of liberalization and structural adjustment programs.[21] The causes of the failure of the development

---

get 1 percent of global income." *See No Future without Justice, supra* note 10, at 6.

16   *Id.,* at 7.

17   Stiglitz, *supra* note 10, at 5.

18   *See,* for example, *The World Bank World Development Report 2011: Conflict Security and Development* 344–355 (2012). The new state of South Sudan was not featured in the report for the obvious reason that it only came into existence on July 9, 2011. However, the mother state of Sudan fared no better.

19   *See* John-Mark Iyi, *Democracy and the Development Crisis in Sub-Saharan Africa: Revisiting Some Preconditions for a Developmental State Alternative,* in *International Economic Law: Voices of Africa* 184, 189 (Emmanuel Laryea, Nokuhle Madolo, & Franziska Sucker eds., 2012).

20   *Id.,* at 189.

21   *See* Stiglitz, *supra* note 10, at 5–22, discussing the role of these policies expressed in the Wash-

efforts are still a subject of academic debate. What is settled, however, is that this decline in economic fortunes combined with several other factors to spawn series of violent conflicts across the continent, and where there was already smoldering conflict, it rekindled and exacerbated it.[22] Somalia fits into the former category and the state of Sudan can be placed in the latter. What is important to note in both cases is that, whereas dwindling economic development weakened the ability of the state to perform its functions, it was the interplay of deprivations, injustice, patronage, socioeconomic exclusion, inequalities in governance, and the failure of the state to redress these grievances that ultimately led aggrieved groups to take up arms and challenge the legitimacy of the state. In Somalia, it brought down the Siad Barre government, and in the former united Sudan, it reinforced the claim to self-determination and secession by the South.

Because of the above historical experiences of these countries it is important to ensure that their building and reconstruction should lead to an amelioration of a situation wherein the majority of people live in extreme poverty. Whatever the development program designed for these countries, it must find a way of striking a balance between the need for economic development and the promotion of social justice, equity, and inclusive poverty-reduction strategies.[23] This is crucial particularly because such grievances were partly responsible for the initial conflict; otherwise, the process risks rekindling those grievances and could reignite the conflict and push the groups challenging the legitimacy of the state to taking up arms again and stalling the overall development process.[24] How, then, can states created by postconflict situations, such as South Sudan, and those that are reemerging from failure, such as Somalia, make equity, inclusion, and opportunity for all a component of their development equation?

This chapter attempts to deal with this question. It examines the situation of South Sudan and Somalia as new and reemerging states, respectively, in terms of how to foster opportunity, inclusion, and equity in their quest for development because of their uniquely fragile and difficult circumstances. It explores the possibilities in both countries based on their histories and on current studies and suggests how the challenges of lack of opportunity, exclusion, and inequity in governance could be addressed in the effort to reconstruct the Somali state and to build South Sudan into a viable developing country. To these extents, this study is both analytical and prescriptive. The chapter is divided into four sections, with this introductory background serving as the first. The second section gives a historical context to the issues surrounding

---

ington Consensus in the development malaise of much of the developing world.

22   Suleiman Mohammed, *Civil War in Sudan: The Impact of Ecological Degradation*, 15 Contributions in Black Stud., available at http://www.scholarworks.umass.edu/cibs/vol15/iss1/7 (accessed May 3, 2013).

23   Robin Luckham, *The International Community and State Reconstruction in War-Torn Societies*, 4(3) Confl., Sec. & Dev. 481, 494 (Dec. 2004).

24   *Id.*

Somalia and South Sudan as well as a brief insight into how they arrived at their present situations. In this regard, it is critical to understand the nature of the root causes of the civil war and secession in formerly united Sudan and the state failure in Somalia to better comprehend the state reconstruction efforts in Somalia and nation building in Sudan through a law- and justice-focused development process.

Relying on the issues raised in section two, section three examines how both states can avoid repeating the mistakes that led to the protracted civil war in formerly united Sudan and gave rise to South Sudan, and to the state collapse in Somalia. In doing this, the third section articulates some policy issues and discusses the institutional construction, reform, or reconstruction necessary to establish a governance system that is development oriented and anchored in the rule of law, that emphasizes inclusion and equity while providing opportunity for citizens' participation to realize their potential, and that, in the process, strengthens governance institutions and consolidates the shared values of the peoples while minimizing the dangers of violent conflict and the challenges to state legitimacy. The fourth section offers some concluding remarks.

South Sudan and Somalia in Historical Context

On July 9, 2011, South Sudan came into existence as the world's newest state and the 54th state on the African continent. This was after more than three decades of a bitter civil war between the South, led by the Sudan People's Liberation Army (SPLA), which later transformed into the Sudan People's Liberation Movement (SPLM), and the government of Sudan. Millions of people were killed and hundreds of thousands displaced.[25] Historically, Somalia and greater Sudan share a similar history of plunging into civil strife almost immediately after independence. As with many African countries, the root causes of the conflicts that exploded into full civil wars after independence are traceable to colonial legacies and unresolved postindependence ethnoreligious, economic, and political issues.[26] In the case of Somalia, this was due to the political-survival machinations of Mohamed Siad Barre, who, in a clan-dominated society, played one clan against another to maintain political power.[27] In the

---

25   For a detailed discussion of the subject, *see,* generally, M. W. Daly, *Imperial Sudan: The Anglo-Egyptian Condominium,1934–56* (1991); Mansour Khalid, *The Government They Deserve: The Role of the Elite in Sudan's Political Evolution* (1990); Francis Manding Deng, *War of Visions: Conflict of Identities in the Sudan* (1995); Juliet Flint & Alex de Waal Darfur, *A Short History of a Long War* (2005); Susan E. Cook & Charles K. Mironko, *Darfur: Understanding a Complicated Tragedy,* in *Peace in the Balance: The Crisis in Sudan* 123–138 (Brian Raftopoulos & Karin Alexander eds., 2006); Douglas H. Johnson, *The Root Causes of Sudan's Civil Wars* (2003); Ann Mosely Lesch, *The Sudan: Contested National Identities* (1998); Ruth Iyob & Gilbert Khadiagala, *Sudan: The Elusive Quest for Peace* 133–166 (2006).

26   Daly, *supra* note 25, at 399.

27   Ken Menkhaus, *Governance without Government in Somalia: Spoilers, State-Building and the Politics of Coping,* 31(3) Intl. Sec. 74, 80 (Winter 2006–2007); and Robert I. Rotberg, *The New Nature of Nation-State Failure,* 23(3) Wash. Q. 85, 94 (2002).

case of Sudan, it was the abrogation of political arrangements at independence and the marginalization of a black African population of the South by the Arab North that fueled alienation and helped sustain a bitter civil war.[28]

When the above socioeconomic and political mosaic is situated in the context of the Cold War world of the 1960s, in which most African states, including Sudan and Somalia, attained self-rule, the ramifications and latent peril become palpable. Linking all these pieces in the mosaic are the cultural affinities and identities that shaped the policies of most African states as they struggled to build nations from the conglomeration of peoples within the arbitrarily demarcated colonial borders inherited at independence.[29]

Somalia had been without an effective central government since 1991 and was thus the oldest textbook example of the so-called failed, or collapsed, state in postcolonial Africa.[30] Efforts to reconstruct Somalia failed at various times. The Transitional Federal Government established on the heels of the Nairobi Peace Accords of 2004 struggled but was unable to reestablish effective control. The U.S.-backed Ethiopian intervention to dislodge Al Shabab, the deployment of the African Union Mission in Somalia (AMISOM) since January 19, 2007, and the incursion by Kenya are only some of the most recent efforts to bring peace to Somalia. The collective effort of the African Union (AU), the United Nations, and other partners recently resulted in the establishment of a government following a parliamentary election and the election of a president.[31]

At the heart of the problem of a failed Somalia was the complete disintegration and disappearance of state institutions and various trappings of statehood. Apart from becoming a breeding ground for terrorism, arms smuggling, drug trafficking, piracy, and other manifestations of international criminality, Somalia threatened regional security and stability. Besides the lack of a central government, the fragmentation of the Somali state with the declaration of independence by Somaliland and autonomy (rather than independence) by Puntland further complicates the task of state reconstruction in Somalia. Despite lacking international recognition, Somaliland has functioned effectively for over a decade and has successfully conducted elections. Some commentators now call for international recognition of Somaliland as a strategy for resolving the Somali imbroglio.[32]

---

28   Lesch, *supra* note 25, at 36.

29   Georg Sorensen, *An Analysis of Contemporary Statehood: Consequences for Conflict and Cooperation,* 23 Rev. of Intl. Stud. 253, 261 (1997).

30   Robin Geib, *Armed Violence in Fragile States: Low Intensity Conflicts, Spillover Conflicts, and Sporadic Law Enforcement Operations by Third Parties,* 91 Intl. Rev. of the Red Cross 127, 130 (2009).

31   *Somali MPs Sworn in to Historic Parliament,* BBC News, Aug. 20, 2012, available at http://www bbc.co.uk/news/world-africa-19314308 (accessed Aug. 8, 2012).

32   *See* Alison K. Eggers, *When Is a State a State: The Case for Recognition of Somaliland,* 30 B.C. Intl. & Comp. L. Rev. 211 (2007), who argues that Somaliland met the objective criteria of statehood in international law and so qualified for international recognition.

The Nation-State Concept and State Failure

A state is said to have failed when it can no longer provide social goods to its people and the government loses its legitimacy.[33] State failure passes through phases, state collapse being the final phase.[34] Failed states exhibit several characteristics. According to Robert Rotberg,

> Failed states are tense, deeply conflicted, dangerous, and bitterly contested by warring factions. In most failed states, government troops battle armed revolts led by one or more rivals. Official authorities in a failed state sometimes face two or more insurgencies, varieties of civil unrest, differing degrees of communal discontent, and a plethora of dissent directed at the state and at groups within the state. . . . The absolute intensity of violence does not define a failed state. Rather it is the enduring character of that violence (as in Angola, Burundi, and Sudan), the direction of such violence against the existing government or regime, and the vigorous character of the political or geographical demands for shared power or autonomy that rationalize or justify that violence that identifies the failed state.[35]

In failed states, governance institutions are weak and there is rampant and widespread violence. In the midst of a complete breakdown of law and order, a failed state provides unparalleled opportunities for a few of the citizenry and a breeding ground for criminality. Criminal gangs wield power and substate actors operate different systems of extracting resources. However, a distinction should be drawn between a weak state and a failed state.[36] A state might be weak yet still not "failed" if, while being unable to exercise sovereignty over a small portion of its territory, it can still maintain law and order and provide security and other social goods to the majority.[37] Examples of weak states include Sri Lanka, where the Tamil Tigers controlled about 15 percent of the country until they were defeated, and Colombia, where the FARC rebels controlled about 30 percent of the territory.[38] Somalia, Sierra Leone, Lebanon, and Afghanistan, at their critical stages, were classic examples of failed states.[39]

African States and the Nation-State Conundrum: Demystifying State Failure

At independence, African nationalists, with few exceptions, accepted the Eurocentric modern nation-state as a system of political organization, in complete

---

33   Rotberg, *supra* note 27, at 85.

34   *Id.*

35   *Id.*

36   *Id.,* at 90–91.

37   *Id.,* at 87.

38   *Id.,* at 91.

39   *Id.*

disregard of Africa's precolonial traditional political experiences.[40] This by-
product of a racially induced colonial ideology, which was based on the flawed
assumption that Africans were incapable of any form of political organization,
led to the dismantling of traditional political institutions and systems or, at
best, led to their being reduced to playing a secondary role in the scheme of
organizing governance.[41] Surely, this was bound to have consequences, as the
"modern" postcolonial African state was modeled after the Eurocentric Westphalian tradition despite the accepted historical fact that even in Europe the
nation-state emerged over centuries of political evolution in the presence of
different cultural factors.[42] Thus, African states have struggled to build nations
in the Westphalian sense because of their precolonial makeup and distinct
governance traditions, which, although relegated to the background, still have
implications for the stability of the so-called modern state. At the same time,
modern African states have found it difficult to retrace their footsteps in terms
of organizing themselves along precolonial lines for obvious reasons that are
both political and a result of prevailing international relations and law.[43] In all
of this, the latent fault lines were consecrated by the defunct Organization of
African Unity (OAU), which elected to treat colonial borders as "both artificial
and sacrosanct" through its doctrine of *utipossidetis*, but which continues to
be challenged by self-determination sentiments of various kinds based on the
reality of the political and ethnic makeup of the African continent.[44]

Somalia and State Failure

In July 1960, former British Somaliland (North) and Italian Somaliland (South)
were united to form the state of Somalia, with the South taking dominant
leadership.[45] Even though the political arrangements were based on democratic compromise, inequality between the North and the South, pervasive
corruption, and a divisive clan-based politics soon generated discontent and
led to a coup in October 1969 that brought General Siad Barre to power.[46]
Initially, Barre led a popular government that brought about modernization,
fought corruption, and expanded education, all in an effort at state building.[47]
He aligned with the USSR but soon fell out of favor with the populace, as his
policies became more repressive and dictatorial.[48] Barre began to draw sup-

---

40   Jeffrey Herbst, *Responding to State Failure in Africa,* 21 Intl. Sec.120, 129 (Winter 1996–1997).

41   *Id.,* at 121, 122, 129. *See also* Tonya Langford, *Things Fall Apart: State Failure and the Politics of
      Intervention,* 1(1) Intl. Stud. Rev. 59, 74 (1999).

42   Stephen Krasner, *Abiding Sovereignty,* 22(3) Intl. Pol. Sci. Rev. 229, 240 (2001).

43   Herbst, *supra* note 40, at 132, 134–136.

44   Francis M. Deng, *Africa and the New World Dis-order: Rethinking Colonial Borders,* 11(2) Brook-
      ings Rev. 32 (1993).

45   *See* Redie Bereketeab, *Self-Determination and Secession in Somaliland and South Sudan: Chal-
      lenges to Post-colonial State-Building* 1, 5 (Nordic Africa Inst. Discussion Paper No. 75, 2012).

46   *Id.,* at 5.

47   *Id.*

48   Ved P. Nanda, Thomas F. Muther, Jr. & Amy E. Eckert, *Tragedies in Somalia, Yugoslavia, Haiti,*

port mainly from his own clan group, which, along with his other activities, exacerbated dissatisfaction and alienation in the North.[49] The project of nation building and state construction had to take a backseat when rebels took up arms in resistance to the Barre regime until it collapsed in 1991.[50] The Somali National Movement (SNM) arose as a major rebellious group in the former British Somaliland. Barre used maximum force to quell it.[51] Thus, the SNM became more determined to topple Barre and to revisit the terms of the 1960 union of British and Italian Somaliland.[52] One observation was that "the immense suffering the Isaaq clan [one of the largest in Somaliland] were subjected to by the Barre regime during the war and the domination of the Somali state by southerners finally convinced the Isaaqs to opt for secession, with the idea of independence coming later."[53]

When Somalia collapsed in 1991, the United Somali Congress (USC) controlled Mogadishu, while the SNM controlled Somaliland, which in May 1991 unilaterally declared independence from Somalia.[54] This bold step was motivated by two factors: first, the massive demand by the northern Isaaq clan for independence from southern domination, and, second, the decision of the USC to form a government excluding the SNM.[55] But there was discontent among non-Isaaq minority clans in the North that had earlier supported the Barre regime.[56] Somehow, through negotiations and dialogue, the Isaaq clan was able to reach a compromise and broad-based consensus with the minority clans to support Somaliland independence and statehood.[57] Since then, Somaliland has consolidated the democratic process by successfully conducting four elections and smooth transitions from one government to another, with the most recent elections being held in 2010.[58] In this process, a blend of multiparty politics and traditional clan institutions has supported the process of dialogue, reconciliation, and state reconstruction.[59] Hence Somaliland insists that its self-excision from Somalia was not an act of secession; rather, it was a repossession of a sovereignty that it willingly gave up at independence in the

---

Rwanda and Liberia—Revisiting the Validity of Humanitarian Intervention under International Law, pt. 2, 26 Denv. J. of Intl. L. & Policy 827, 831 (1997–1998).

49   Abdi Ismail Samatar, *Leadership and Ethnicity in the Making of African State Models: Botswana versus Somalia,* 18(4) Third World Q. 687, 689 (1997).

50   Bereketeab, *supra* note 45, at 5.

51   *Id.*

52   *Id.*

53   *Id.,* at 7.

54   Menkhaus, *supra* note 27, at 81.

55   Bereketeab, *supra* note 45, at 7.

56   *Id.*

57   *Id.*

58   *Id.*

59   *Id.*

union with the South.[60] Yet, as of the time of writing, Somaliland has not been recognized by the international community as a state.

South Sudan and Secession

Quite unlike Somalia, South Sudan had never really been an integral part of the state of the old Sudan (The Sudan) even under British colonial rule. The Sudan was administered in a system of "Condominium" and according to Mansour Khalid, it was in this period that "many of the political forces which have since shaped The Sudan's post-independence political scene developed their most important characteristics."[61] A study of the Condominium, by which arrangement Britain and Egypt cooperated in the administration of The Sudan, reveals a pattern of systematic discrimination in all spheres—economic, social, and political, under British colonial rule, South Sudan was treated as a colonial outpost of the North.[62] In the economic, social, and political structure of The Sudan, the British instituted a policy that systematically discriminated against black Africans in the South and favored the Arab North.[63] According to Khalid,

> the colonial pattern of development, though it had destroyed earlier forms of economic exploitation, also installed its own conditions for exploitation, and by favouring certain groups within the country that system had set off the dynamics of marginalization leading to perpetual tension between the different regions.[64]

Fear of domination by the North led the South to convoke a conference in 1954 to articulate the concerns of the South and work out acceptable arrangements that would guarantee some degree of autonomy to the South in an independent Sudan.[65] These issues remained unresolved when Sudan attained independence in 1956.[66] Upon independence, the North adopted the same policy it had seen the British deploy, a policy that regarded the South as a wild frontier where law and order could be imposed only by force, and in implementing it resorted to repression and suppression.[67] These tensions were quickly exacerbated by postindependence developments, resulting in a protracted civil war that lasted over 17 years.[68] This era of the war ended when limited self-rule was granted to the South under the Addis Ababa Accord.[69]

---

60   *Id.*

61   Mansour Khalid, *The Government They Deserve: The Role of the Elite in Sudan's Political Evolution* 45 (Kegan Paul Intl. 1990).

62   *Id.*

63   *Id.,* at 58.

64   Bereketeab, *supra* note 45, at 9.

65   Gerard Prunier, *Darfur: The Ambiguous Genocide* 164 (Cornell U. Press 2005).

66   Khalid, *supra* note 61, at 56, 58–60.

67   Deng, *supra* note 25, at 135.

68   *Id.*

69   Bereketeab, *supra* note 45, at 9.

However, in 1983, the president of Sudan, Ghaffer El Niemeri, unilaterally abrogated this Addis Ababa Accord and imposed sharia law on the whole country, even though the South was predominantly Christian and animist. This triggered another round of civil war, spearheaded by the SPLA under the leadership of John Garang, whose main objective was to lead a popular movement to oust the elites in Khartoum and to usher in an inclusive and plural society throughout Sudan. But this vision, following years of oppression and protracted conflict, diminished and collapsed when the Comprehensive Peace Agreement was signed in 2005, paving the way for a referendum that ultimately resulted in independence for South Sudan on July 9, 2011. It has been observed that "many South Sudanese see the referendum of 2011 as the fulfilment of the process of decolonisation that was denied them in 1956 when Sudan became independent," and that "like the Somalilanders, many South Sudanese invoked separate colonial rule to legitimise their quest for self-determination."[70]

State Reconstruction in Somalia and Nation Building in South Sudan: Challenges of Opportunity, Inclusion, and Equity

State Reconstruction in Somalia

Analysts and practitioners often speak of "state reconstruction" with respect to Somalia.[71] This is because, unlike South Sudan, which was crippled by decades of civil war, Somalia imploded from within, and when state institutions and infrastructure that had existed to support the central government and the state collapsed, they were replaced by rival warlords and conflict entrepreneurs.[72] So, to this end, state reconstruction in Somalia would entail a re-establishment of those government structures and institutions that are necessary for the functioning of a modern state.[73] Among other things, there would be political reform—to achieve good governance through democracy, rule of law, and human rights.[74] There has been ongoing debate on how Somalia can achieve this objective, and series of conferences have been held at different

---

70   *Id.*

71   Ismail I. Ahmed, *The Heritage of War and State Collapse in Somalia and Somaliland: Local-Level Effects, External Interventions and Reconstruction*, 20(1) Third World Q. 113 (1999).

72   At a time when over 50 militia groups were operating in Somalia, the provision of basic services was taken over by traditional rulers, businessmen, and civil society organizations. *See* Lars Ronnås, *Prospects for Peace and Development in the Horn of Africa*, in *Horn of Africa Conference: Good Governance and the Rule of Law as Keys to Peace, Democratization and Sustainable Development* 28 (Ulf Johansson Dahre ed., SIRC Horn of Africa Report No. 4, Lund U., Lund, Sweden, Oct. 2005).

73   See Sharif Hassan Sheikh Aden, *Statement on Somalia*, in *Horn of Africa Conference: Good Governance and the Rule of Law as Keys to Peace, Democratization and Sustainable Development* 40 (Ulf Johansson Dahre ed., SIRC Horn of Africa Report No. 4, Lund U., Lund, Sweden, Oct. 2005).

74   See Ronnås, *supra* note 72, at 15.

world capitals to discuss the matter.[75] Some analysts insist that the clan system is crucial to any process of reconciliation and political reconstruction in Somalia,[76] whereas others maintain that the clan system must be managed carefully as a component of the reconstruction process because it was partially responsible for the state collapse in the first place; what is needed is a total political transformation that will minimize the role of the clans.[77] The major causes of conflicts in many countries in Africa are still linked not only to ethnic or religious differences but also to "control over resources, social justice and marginalisation of groups."[78] Whichever system is adopted, it should be informed by the changing context in Africa, because the causes of conflicts are now shifting from predominantly ethnoreligious factors to questions of control of resources, social inclusion, and economic equity.[79]

Abdi Samatar maintains that the problem was not the existing traditional clan system of political organization but rather the manipulation of this system by the elites for political purposes.[80] The concept of good governance and the rule of law in the reconstruction of Somalia must be localized and should be a blend of contextualized modern state institutions and a reenactment of preexisting traditional structures that Somalis have utilized in conflict resolution and mitigation of a hostile environment with minimum external involvement in the process.[81] "Attempts to promote legal reform as a development project must reflect the strong influence of existing structures"; this is particularly so for Somalia, where interclan rivalry remains a challenge.[82] For political reforms to achieve good governance there must be dedicated leadership, democracy, and the rule of law, none of which is possible in the absence of peace.[83] So the key requirement will be political reform, to achieve good governance and social reforms, to reduce poverty, and to ensure equal oppor-

---

75   *Turkey Hosts Meeting on Somalia*, Al Jazeera, available at http://www.aljazeera.com/video /europe/2012/05/201253162357945454.html (accessed May 7, 2013).

76   Clarissa Ruggieri, *State Reconstruction and Economic Recovery in Somalia: An Alternative Option between Central-State and Clan-Based Systems of Governance*, Middle E. J. of Geopolitics 25, 31–33 (2004).

77   Abdi Ismail Samatar, *Somali Reconstruction and Local Initiatives: Ahmoud University*, 29 World Dev. 641 (2001).

78   *See* Abdilahi Jama, *Introduction*, in *Horn of Africa Conference: Good Governance and the Rule of Law as Keys to Peace, Democratization and Sustainable Development* 18 (Ulf Johansson Dahre ed., SIRC Horn of Africa Report No. 4, Lund U., Lund, Sweden, Oct. 2005).

79   *Id.*, at 18.

80   *See* Samatar, *supra* note 49, at 687–688.

81   *See* Christopher Clapham, *Good Governance and the Rule of Law: What Can They Offer the Horn?*, in *Horn of Africa Conference: Good Governance and the Rule of Law as Keys to Peace, Democratization and Sustainable Development* 51 (Ulf Johansson Dahre ed., SIRC Horn of Africa Report No. 4, Lund U., Lund, Sweden, Oct. 2005).

82   *See* Thomas F. McInerney, *Law and Development as Democratic Practice* 1(1) Voices of Dev. Jurists 17–18 (2004).

83   Ronnås, *supra* note 72, at 15.

tunity and the rule of law.[84] There must also be a deliberate effort to combat corruption and ensure transparency. An independent judiciary is crucial to the rule of law,which is in turn necessary to separate and insulate institutions from the ruling elites and to guarantee equality before the law; otherwise, the state might come under the control of elite groups and the reforms compromised.[85] "So there are three principles to uphold rule of law: the right to equal treatment and fair trials, the separation of state and the legal system and the loyalty of the legal system to the law."[86]

The process of social reform should reflect the increasing economic roles of women through empowerment and inclusion in the development process. Emphasis should be placed on the education of girls, microcredit systems, and access to land and other means of production so they can contribute meaningfully to the process.[87] Though often marginalized and discriminated against, women occupy and play vital roles in the survival equation in conflict and postconflict states' reconstruction because of their unique abilities to adapt different coping mechanisms in extremely challenging circumstances. This capacity can be tapped into and enhanced to help drive the development process from below. This is in addition to their contribution to family stability and the overall social cohesion they bring to society.[88]

When states fail, they produce transborder consequences for the entire region. Regional actors, such as the Inter-Governmental Development Authority (IGAD) and the AU, have rightfully been concerned about and involved in finding a solution to the Somali crisis. At this stage of state reconstruction, they should also play important roles in creating a system that pursues development in an inclusive and equitable way. Regional actors and neighbors can help to provide the enabling environment for these values to thrive. The African Peer Review Mechanism will be particularly useful in this regard, to help the new leaders in Somalia develop new parameters for evaluating the inclusive and equitable policies of governance institutions in the country.

A corollary to the above point is the question of internally displaced persons (IDPs) and the return of refugees. Refugees and IDPs should be factored into the reconstruction and development process. These groups are particularly vulnerable but could contribute meaningfully to the development process if adequately empowered. Therefore, the concepts of opportunity, inclusion, and equity will be of particular significance to these groups, most of which will include people who have lost homes, property, and whatever economic

---

84   *Id.*

85   Morgan Johansson, *State Building, Democracy and the Rule of Law,* in *Horn of Africa Conference: Good Governance and the Rule of Law as Keys to Peace, Democratization and Sustainable Development* 26 (Ulf Johansson Dahre ed., SIRC Horn of Africa Report No. 4, Lund U., Lund, Sweden, Oct. 2005).

86   *Id.*

87   Ronnås, *supra* note 72, at 14–15.

88   *Id.*, at 14.

resources they might have had before displacement. Effective collaboration and policy synergy between domestic institutions and development partners will be key to success in this area. Finally, Somalia has a huge diaspora all over the world, most members of which have acquired useful and critical skills that will be necessary for the development of Somalia. Currently, this diaspora community plays significant roles through remittances, but this can become more institutionalized as part of investment and development funding.[89]

Building a democratic state with strong institutions can be a challenge even for a homogeneous country like Somalia. The major challenge is fashioning an inclusive process of democratization that can in turn establish democratic institutions based on equity and opportunity for all.[90] This is even more challenging because in Somalia there is contention regarding the outlook of the future Somali state and the basis of political authority.[91] For example, Al Shabab, unlike groups that favor a secular state, conceives the relationship between state and religion differently. In this respect, it would be helpful for development programs to strengthen civil society organizations and religious groups in order to build a democratic, inclusive, and equitable Somalia based on the rule of law. Apart from providing a platform for dialogue on national issues, civil society groups need to be able to facilitate consensus building among contending social forces such as religious extremists and moderates for forging an agenda or vision of the future of the Somali state.[92]

The role of international actors in the development process must be handled with care because there is a tendency among development partners and practitioners to foist particular development policy prescriptions on aid recipients. Somalia has proven to be particularly difficult, and development programs should be sensitive to these tendencies. The United Nations, international NGOs, and aid agencies can guide Somalia in capacity building to deliver public administration and provide other social goods, but the process itself must be inclusive and Somalis should be allowed to take ownership and drive the process. As David Anderson rightly points out, "clans and patrilineality have transformed in the modern context, to reflect a broad set of influences prevailing in present-day Somali culture that work upon and through clan structures. Race, class, economic wealth, language, and access to resources mediate and interact through clan relations to organise Somali society."[93] This will enable the process to build on existing and viable preconflict structures or institutions in a way that supports the new state and its development efforts.[94]

---

89   Lisa Magloff, *Investing in Rebel States*, in *Horn of Africa Conference: Good Governance and the Rule of Law as Keys to Peace, Democratization and Sustainable Development* 73, 75, 79 (Ulf Johansson Dahre ed., SIRC Horn of Africa Report No. 4, Lund U., Lund, Sweden, Oct. 2005).

90   Luckham, *supra* note 23, at 500–501.

91   *Id.*, at 499.

92   *Id.*, at 500–501.

93   David M. Anderson, *Clan Identity and Islamic Identity in Somalia* 2 CEADS Papers 1, 14–15 (Mar. 2012).

94   Luckham, *supra* note 23, at 499.

For example, whereas the principle of equity and justice is well established in intraclan relations, it is not the case in interclan associations.[95] It is therefore the Somalian state that can guarantee equality and social justice to all Somali citizens without discrimination.[96] Thus, purposeful leadership will be essential to steer the ship of national rebirth, reconstruction, and development.

Nation Building in South Sudan

Commentators have emphasized development, nation building, and construction with respect to South Sudan, in contrast to the situation in Somalia.[97] This assessment is informed by the fact that although South Sudan faces challenges similar to Somalia's in many respects, its problems also differ from those of Somalia in more ways than one. First, there has never been a true South Sudan state, let alone one to be reconstructed. Second, there never really was "construction" in South Sudan in terms of development and state presence, so it would be anomalous to speak of "reconstruction."[98] Finally, unlike Somalia, which is largely homogeneous, having a common religion, language, and culture, South Sudan is multiethnic and has well over 17 different ethnic groups.[99] Hence the concept of "nation building," as distinct from "state reconstruction," better captures the challenges of South Sudan as a new state: to build a system that is inclusive and equitable among these multiethnic groups. While the civil war lasted, the tendency among writers was to speak of the North-South conflict in the sense that

> the civil war which has plagued southern Sudan over decades has concerned issues of governance, in particular the degree to which the south can act autonomously over its own affairs and benefit from the extraction of the region's rich natural resource base which historically has been dominated by northern political and commercial interests. The war itself has served to reinforce further the economic, social, religious and political divides between the two regions.[100]

The above scenario misses the possibility, or even the existence, of a South-South conflict.[101] As long as the formerly united Sudan state was perceived by

---

95   Abdulkadir Osman Farah, *Somalia: State Reconfiguration and the Role of the Diaspora and Civil Society,* 2 Africa Renaissance 70, 73 (2005).

96   *Id.*

97   Mariam Jooma, *Feeding the Peace: Challenges Facing Human Security in Post-Garang South Sudan* (ISS Situation Report No. 2, Aug. 23, 2005), available at http://www.issafrica.org/publica tions/situation-reports/situation-report-feeding-the-peace-challenges-facing-human-security -in-post-garang-south-sudan-mariam-jooma (accessed May 2, 2013).

98   *Id.*

99   CIA Factbook, available at http://www.cia.gov/library/publications/the-world-factbook .geos/od.html (accessed May 6, 2013).

100 Joanna Macrae et al., *Conflict, the Continuum and Chronic Emergencies: A Critical Analysis of the Scope for Linking Relief, Rehabilitation and Development Planning in Sudan,* 21 Disasters 223, 224 (1997).

101 Naglaa Elhag, *A Tale of Two Wars: The Militarization of Dinka and Nuer Identities in South Sudan,* in *Dilemmas of Development: Conflicts of Interest and Their Resolution in Modernizing Africa* 164,

the South as the oppressive North, the southerners were bound together by the experiences of common suffering and united by the need to defeat a common enemy, thus giving a somewhat false impression of a monolithic South.[102] However, there is fear that interethnic cracks could soon begin to appear; if not carefully managed, such situations could ignite a South-South conflict.[103] This is the reason the concept of nation building, as opposed to mere state construction, or reconstruction, and its component principles of opportunity, equality, and inclusiveness will determine South Sudan's viability and survival as a state. If South Sudan itself is to avoid fragmentation, it must eschew the policies of exclusion, economic inequality, and social injustice that led the South to take up arms against the North-dominated government of Sudan, which resulted in secession in the first place.

In view of the foregoing, the first issue South Sudan will have to deal with will be the question of national identity.[104] What should be the identity of a South Sudan state? As demonstrated above, the policy of Arabization and Islamization pursued by the former Sudan was a major cause of disagreement and conflict between the North and the South. To avoid this pitfall, South Sudan must bring its multiethnic groups together to agree on a vision of the national identity of South Sudan or what that state should look like.[105] This is a tough challenge, but it is not insurmountable. To achieve this, South Sudan leaders must, from the outset, implement policies and build institutions that will entrench the principles of equality, inclusion, and social justice for all ethnic groups. Again, the rule of law and good governance will be crucial to this task. Luckham sums up the challenge thus:

> The central issues tend therefore to concern the future identity of the state more than just its reconstruction. Issues include whether and how to accommodate the demands of separatist groups . . . ; and how to make existing state institutions more inclusive through power-sharing, constitutional reforms, or more equitable distribution of the benefits of development. Even if the state is ultimately partitioned, [as is the case with South Sudan now] the same issues tend to recur, sometimes in an aggravated form, since partition tends to

---

165 (Jon Abbink & Andre Dakkum eds., 2008).

102 Adam Branch & Zachariah Mampilly, *Winning the War but Losing the Peace: The Dilemma of SPLM/A Civil Administration and the Tasks Ahead*, 43(1) J. of Mod. African Stud. 1, 3–4 (2005).

103 *Nation-Building in South Sudan, supra* note 3, at 511.

104 The Sudan had consisted of two sharply contrasting national identities always in conflict: a northern Arab–Islam versus a southern African–Christian/indigenous identity. This has been fueled by ethnic, racial, cultural, and religious differences, which continue to reinforce one another in a vicious circle of violence. *See* Francis M. Deng, *Sudan: A Nation in Turbulent Search of Itself*, 603 Annals of the Am. Acad. of Political and Soc. Sci. 155, 155–156, 157 (Jan. 2006).

105 *Nation-Building in South Sudan, supra* note 3, at 506. This is a tough challenge, though not insurmountable. *See* Stigal, *supra* note 4, at 4.

create new national majorities, . . . many of whom have no more commitment to inclusive politics than their former oppressors.[106]

Though obscured by the North-South war, the fault lines in the question of the identity of a South Sudan state had long been manifested by the intra–SPLM/SPLA squabbles that resulted in splinter groups led by Riek Machar (a Nuer), who accused John Garang (a Dinka) of ethnic domination.[107] Although the Dinka and Nuer are the two largest ethnic groups in South Sudan, the ethnic animosities between them run deep, with the latter accusing the former of pursuing a Dinka domination agenda, and the former accusing the latter of betraying the southern struggle for self-determination and collaborating with the Sudan government.[108]

The leaders of South Sudan must be able to transcend primordial loyalties to mobilize the different ethnic groups around a common South Sudan identity not defined by any particular group but based on the values of equal opportunity, equality before the law, economic inclusion, and social justice. Emphasis should be on tolerance and shared values in order to stimulate nationalist fervor, in which loyalty is given to the South Sudan state first, rather than to individual ethnic groups.[109] The government can draw on the deep sense of traditional practices of dialogue and mediation that pervades most of the southern ethnic groups, who have coexisted for centuries in this regard, to build consensus on national issues.[110] The first concrete evidence of such inclusive policies from the perspective of the ethnic groups would be a developmental approach based on equal opportunity in access to social goods such as education, health, housing, and employment, among others.[111] Human rights and fundamental freedoms will only have meaning for people who perceive themselves to be part of the development process and thus feel a moral obligation to be loyal to the state and to obey the law of the land. This in turn reinforces the leaders' legitimacy and the state's political authority. A lot, therefore, will depend on South Sudan's first postindependence leaders. The government must focus on how

> to reconstitute national citizenship on a more inclusive basis, whilst also recognising and respecting religious, ethnic, gender, and other societal differences. How to do this, and whether to place the emphasis on universal rights or on power sharing and the institutionalisation of cultural differences, is best left to national dialogue and debate.[112]

---

106   *See* Luckham, *supra* note 23, at 499.

107   *Nation-Building in South Sudan, supra* note 3, at 506.

108   Jooma, *supra* note 97, at 14.

109   *Nation-Building in South Sudan, supra* note 3, at 508.

110   *See* Ronnås, *supra* note 72, at 14–15.

111   *Id.,* at 15.

112   Luckham, *supra* note 23, at 498.

Striking a balance between the need for merit and the demands of equal representation will need careful attention at all levels of public life. Because of its own history of discrimination and exclusion, South Sudan must pay close attention to the establishment, location, and distribution of state institutions and resources.[113] This must be done in the most inclusive way possible to give a sense of belonging to all ethnic groups in the country.[114]

Experience shows that under a united Sudan, the racial, ethnic, religious, and cultural differences had been exacerbated by socioeconomic exclusion and inequality between northerners and southerners.[115] Beyond the North-South conflict, which has been largely attributed to socioeconomic exclusion based on religious and racial differences, it is important to realize that such exclusion was also spawned by political patronage and the rent-seeking penchant of political elites that helped in creating and entrenching a system of socioeconomic exclusion that was not only pervasive in the North-South relationship but also in Darfur and the eastern region.[116] Therefore, it is not just the presence of these differences, but the failure to deal with them in a constructive manner and an inclusive process of mediation and dialogue, that led to the conflict.[117] On a political level, South Sudan might be able to surmount this challenge through some sort of federalism, and by allowing the different ethnic groups to participate in decision making to take ownership of and to drive the development and state-building process.[118] Having coexisted for centuries, the different groups have always had traditional means of conflict resolution and community development.[119] Of importance would be to enhance such local initiatives and leverage them in a peace-building process for local cooperation among communities to provide an enabling environment for economic development.

International partners and regional actors such as NGOs, the IGAD, the AU, and the United Nations have important roles to play. Aid donors and development partners would be critical to development takeoff in South Sudan, but there should not be overreliance on foreign aid, which could dry up sooner than envisaged or promised.[120] Furthermore, there may be a disconnect between the policy focus of donors and the local needs of aid recipients. For example, since the U.S. embassy bombings in Kenya and Tanzania, U.S. policy focus in the Horn of Africa has shifted to fighting Al Qaeda–linked terrorist groups and tackling other transnational crimes, such as piracy, in the region. How this squared with local demands came to a head when the Council of

---

113 Magloff, *Investing in Rebel States, supra* note 89, at 78.

114 *Id.*, at 500–501.

115 *Nation-Building in South Sudan, supra* note 3, at 508.

116 Jooma, *supra* note 97, at 4–5.

117 *Id.*, at 18

118 *Id.*

119 Elhag, *supra* note 101, at 169.

120 Derick W. Brinckerhoff & Jennifer M. Brinckerhoff, *Governance Reforms and Failed States: Challenges and Implications,* 68 Intl. Rev. Admin. Sci. 511, 516 (2002).

Islamic Courts established control in Somalia in 2006. Although the council was able to restore stability to Somalia, it did not receive international support because of its fundamentalist postures. Policy makers must therefore balance the needs of external aid with local demands and realities. South Sudan has attracted huge international sympathy and development offers, but its short-term future will depend on how it leverages this assistance. The development model to be pursued by South Sudan should not be foisted on it; it should be one that recognizes existing patterns of economic engagements and must rest on the principles of inclusion and equality while providing opportunity for all to participate. To this end, a democratic developmental state might be a good recommendation, because of its effectiveness in income redistribution and poverty reduction in the process of industrialization and economic development.[121]

Fostering socioeconomic development in South Sudan through opportunity and inclusion would require addressing certain fundamental issues, including the return of refugees and IDPs and enabling their integration into the socioeconomic life of the state.[122] When some of these refugees were forced to flee their homes because of the wars, they abandoned their lands and other means of livelihood. Now, the government's development programs must have as a component the equitable distribution or redistribution of land and other developmental aid.[123] There have been complaints that when the Equatorians (inhabitants of the southern region of present-day South Sudan) fled their villages as a result of the war, the SPLM moved Dinkas into the abandoned lands and villages to give them better access to humanitarian and development aid, thus treating Equatoria as "occupied territory."[124] This is likely to be a source of tension as the Equatorians return to their former villages and lands; the SPLM must find a way of addressing this problem. As one observer commented:

> The mass repatriation of Equatorians represents a political challenge for the SPLM/A, since the returnees and those Equatorians who remained demand rectification of injustices, requiring the government to return Dinka-occupied land to Equatorians and to give them equal access to foreign-provided development and reconstruction resources.[125]

This situation could provide an opportunity for the South Sudan government to enhance its political authority among the different ethnic groups, or it could prompt an explosive interethnic contest over land and access to development resources; much depends on how the government deals with the

---

121 *See,* generally, Iyi, *supra* note 19. Emmanuel Laryea, Nokuhle Madolo & Franziska Sucker eds., *Democratic Developmental State: Revisiting Some Preconditions for a Developmental State Alternative,* in *International Economic Law: Voices of Africa* (2012) argue for this path to economic development for Sub-Saharan African States.

122 *Nation-Building in South Sudan, supra* note 3, at 508.

123 *See* Branch & Mampilly, *supra* note 102, at 5; Jacon et al., *Nation-Building in South Sudan, supra* note 3, at 509.

124 *Nation-Building in South Sudan, supra* note 3, at 510.

125 *See* Branch & Mampilly, *supra* note 102, at 10–11.

situation.[126] The fear of Dinka domination, whether based on reality or misper-ception, will have to be addressed by the SPLM through inclusive policies. The cause of the South had always been championed by the SPLM; even the Comprehensive Peace Agreement that led to the independence of the South was negotiated between the Dinka-led SPLM and the National Congress Party of the North. The dominance of the Dinka in this regard is capable of breed-ing mistrust and fear of postsecession political domination.[127] There is talk of a decentralized government granting some degree of political autonomy to regions in order to foster broad-based participation in the decision-making process by marginalized ethnic groups and to whittle down the influence of the Dinka.[128] The fact that today all the facilities required for oil production and transportation are located in the Sudan even though the actual oil wells are located in the South is in itself evidence of the degree of marginalization exclusion that the South had to endure under a united Sudan, and the exclu-sion and deprivation, or lack of opportunity, that gave fervor to the struggle for independence by the South.[129]

As a country primarily dependent on oil, a nonrenewable resource, South Sudan will have to diversify its revenue base from crude oil, which currently constitutes over 80 percent of its earnings.[130] It can achieve this through major reforms in agricultural policy. Again, the success of this policy will depend on how inclusive it is, because resources such as land will have to be distributed equitably. Other means of production in the agro-allied industries must be al-located in a manner that provides opportunity for participation by all. This is where inclusive policies must be pursued with respect to access to land, both for returning refugees and IDPs, because access to land is crucial to any suc-cessful agricultural development and expansion program as a developmental project across the South.

Conclusion

Somalia and South Sudan share some significant characteristics. Apart from having been conflict zones in decades of civil wars, both states' ethnic groups and clans have a common history of political exclusion, social injustice, and economic inequality. Both have also recently started out on the path of na-tion building and state reconstruction. This chapter highlights the failure of governance on the road to the present condition of both states; situated the en-trenchment of some core values of governance as indispensable drivers of so-cial cohesion, political stability, and socioeconomic development; and argued that nation building and reconstruction efforts in these countries must be an-

---

126 *Id.*

127 *Nation-Building in South Sudan, supra* note 3, at 512.

128 *Id.*

129 *Id.,* at 515.

130 *Id.,* at 516.

chored on these norms. Whatever systems of government and approaches to development that the states choose to adopt, the rule of law, social justice, political inclusion, and equitable participation in the economic life of the state must be the cornerstone of government policies in Somalia and South Sudan. The role of different actors is important, but the reconstruction effort must be driven from the bottom and ownership of the process must be localized in a way that blends existing traditional institutions and coping mechanisms with transformation into a modern, developing nation-state. Somalia and South Sudan must build a national identity by designing policies that emphasize uniting factors and find a way of addressing grievances and other structural issues that heighten group differences.

The secession of South Sudan, on the face of it, has implications for post-colonial Africa, where the doctrine of *utipossidetis* seems to have taken root, but with clear fault lines based on arbitrary colonial demarcations that did not take into account homogeneous identity, culture, and religion. In the same vein, the doctrine continues to be challenged by state practice of egregious human rights violations, lack of good governance, or a form of governance that marginalizes portions of society and the undermining of the rule of law and justice. To a larger degree, the self-determination struggle of South Sudan, like the earlier one of Eritrea and to a lesser extent Somaliland and Puntland, demonstrates these fault lines that point to state fragmentation. It therefore cannot be stressed enough that African states must worry about how various ethnic groups and nationalities are treated in state arrangements, governance, and development. To ensure lasting discouragement of such groups from taking up arms (in the hope that they would receive international sympathy in their struggle for secession), the principles of opportunity, inclusion, and equity must be the watchword and must find resonance in governance and the development process of African states.

Accordingly, the journey ahead for South Sudan and Somalia is indeed a tough one, because of the divisions and tension among the diverse ethnic groups in the case of South Sudan, on the one hand, and the clan mistrust in Somalia, on the other. The challenge of constructing a national identity for South Sudan, as compared with the essentially "state reconstruction" required by Somalia, could make the task of South Sudan even more challenging. All things being equal, the homogeneity of Somalia could be a catalyst for entrenching opportunity, equity, and inclusion and could also serve as a vehicle of national identity around which state reconstruction and national development can revolve. However, South Sudan needs to work harder to truly entrench elements of inclusive government, equal opportunity, and social justice for all its component ethnic groups in order to forge a cohesive nation-building process from the start; otherwise, the deficits of the South Sudan national identity crisis might become acute and give rise to a new round of interethnic South-South conflict. In all, good governance that fosters opportunity, inclusion, and equity will be important for these states not only because they need it for internal survival but also because it has become the best way to measure development.

Enabling Equal Opportunities for Women in the World of Work

The Intersections of Formal and Informal Constraints

JENI KLUGMAN AND MATTHEW MORTON

Morocco is a middle-income country that has seen many legal changes that support women's economic opportunities. Compulsory primary education was introduced in 1963. Since 1995, women have had legal authority to enter into contracts to start businesses without their husband's authorization. International conventions for equal pay, nondiscrimination, and maternity protection have been ratified, and codified in domestic law in 2003. The 2004 Family Code significantly increased women's rights in marriage, upon divorce, and for inheritance and provided for greater protection from sexual harassment; it has been hailed as one of the most progressive legal texts in the Middle East and North Africa region.[1]

Yet, despite this largely supportive legal framework, women's economic opportunities remain limited in Morocco. Women's labor force participation stood at only 27 percent in 2011 (compared to 78 percent for men), unchanged since 1990.[2] Less than 1 percent of women are employers, compared to nearly 3 percent of men,[3] and Morocco ranks 128th out of 135 countries on women's economic opportunity in the World Economic Forum's gender gap ranking.[4] These challenges are not unique to Morocco, and, as in many other countries, men's labor force participation declined over the same time period (from 83 to 78 percent). Nonetheless, the case illustrates that informal constraints can run counter to the potential positive impacts of legal reforms on women's economic empowerment, a recurring theme in this chapter.

As both the *World Development Report 2013: Jobs* and the *World Development Report 2012: Gender Equality and Development* (WDR2012) illustrate, jobs can have intrinsic value for many women, and women's jobs can catalyze

---

Many thanks to Sarah Twigg, Tazeen Hasan, Sarah Iqbal, and the editors for helpful comments and feedback.

1   F. Sadiqi, *Morocco* (Sanja Kelly & Julia Breslin eds., Freedom House 2010).

2   World Bank, Gender Data Portal, available at http://datatopics.worldbank.org/gender/ (accessed Apr. 14, 2013).

3   *Id.*

4   R. Hausmann et al., *Measuring the Global Gender Gap*, in *The Global Gender Gap Report 2012* (Insight Report, World Econ. Forum 2012).

505

development. Yet, major gender gaps remain in labor markets.[5] Globally, women represent about half the world's population, but only 41 percent of the total formal sector workforce. Trends suggest that gains in women's labor force participation worldwide over the past 30 years have been small and slow, still hovering around 51 percent globally but as low as 21 percent in the Middle East and North Africa.[6] And labor force participation rates by themselves mask important differences in how and when women and men participate in the world of work.

Gender gaps persist in terms of the types of jobs that women and men have, how much they are paid, and the extent of their unpaid work, with significant regional variation as well. In South Asia, over 69 percent of women worked in agriculture in 2011, compared to less than 44 percent of men.[7] In a recent analysis of 41 low- and middle-income countries for which gender-disaggregated data were available, 30 countries had higher shares of women than men in nonagricultural informal employment.[8] The majority of employed women in developing countries work in the informal economy, which includes nonagricultural work not regulated or protected by the state. For example, 56 percent of women in Peru were in nonagricultural informal employment in 2009 (compared to 48 percent of men) and 62 percent of women in Uganda (compared to 55 percent of men).[9] Meanwhile, survey data from 13,000 firms in 135 countries indicate that less than one in five firms (18 percent) have a female top manager.[10]

This chapter is grounded in the recognition that women have unequal opportunities in the world of work. Taking a global perspective, it examines legal constraints on women as entrepreneurs as well as constraints on women as employees. While advocacy for legal reforms often focuses on the latter, as will be seen, the legal constraints beyond labor codes, such as those that can limit women's access to assets to use as collateral, can limit the growth of firms.

We begin by outlining a framework for thinking about the role of laws, along with other factors, in enabling or constraining women's economic opportunities. After briefly reviewing the international legal context for women's economic rights, we examine how informal factors, including cultural norms

---

5   *See* World Bank, *World Development Report 2012: Gender Equality and Development* (2011) (hereinafter *World Development Report 2012*); World Bank, *World Development Report 2013: Jobs* (2012), available at http://www.worldbank.org/wdr2012 and http://www.worldbank .org/wdr2013 (accessed Apr. 14, 2013).

6   *See supra* note 2.

7   E. Ekkehard & S. Kapsos, *Global Employment Trends 2012: Preventing a Deeper Jobs Crisis* (Intl. Lab. Office 2012).

8   International Labour Organization *Statistical Update on Employment in the Informal Economy* (2012).

9   International Labour Organization *Key Indicators of Labour Market Database*, available at http://kilm.ilo.org/kilmnet/ (accessed Apr. 14, 2013).

10 World Bank, Enterprise Surveys Database, available at http://www.enterprisesurveys.org/ (accessed Apr. 14, 2013).

and exclusionary practices, can interact with laws to complement or compete with one another to shape women's economic outcomes.

A Framework

Many factors, from low education to high fertility, can limit women's economic opportunities. As will be seen in detail later, laws—as part of formal institutions—can limit or exclude women from economic opportunities by treating them differently simply because of their gender. Some of these laws arise in the realm of labor regulation, such as limits on night work or sector of employment. Importantly, however, legal constraints on women's work often exist beyond discrimination in the workplace.

Women are disproportionately represented in part-time, temporary, non-wage, and domestic work, all of which frequently fall outside the focus of most labor legislation.[11] A recent International Labour Organization (ILO) study estimated that women represent 83 percent of domestic workers worldwide; the study further found that many of these workers are not covered by labor laws, including those guaranteeing maximum weekly working hours, minimum wages, and maternity leave.[12] In some cases, labor laws can be extended to aspects of the labor force in which women are disproportionately represented and unprotected. In Brazil, for example, the constitution explicitly includes domestic workers within its equality provisions that guarantee, among other things, minimum wages, parental leave, retirement pensions, and social security.[13] In other cases, labor laws will have no or little direct impact on many women workers. Some of the most pertinent legal constraints on women in formal or informal work arise upon marriage, including codes that give men control over female spouses' decisions and actions, such as consent requirements for various contracts, papers, and business-related transactions and restrictions on the use of property through titling and inheritance laws.

Laws do not, of course, exist in a vacuum, and adverse social norms and exclusionary practices can have pervasive effects despite progressive legislation. Social norms can constrain women's mobility, fuel intimate-partner violence and sexual harassment, and keep girls out of school and women out of work. Figure 1 identifies social norms as among the informal institutions that affect women's economic opportunities.

---

11   S. Walby, *The European Union and Gender Equality: Emergent Varieties of Gender Regime*, 11 Soc. Pol.: Intl. Stud. in Gender, St. & Society (2004).

12   International Labour Organization *Domestic Workers across the World: Global and Regional Statistics and the Extent of Legal Protection* (Intl. Lab. Office, 2013), available at http://www .ilo.org/wcmsp5/groups/public/---dgreports/---dcomm/---publ/documents/publication/wcms _173363.pdf (accessed Apr. 14, 2013).

13   S. Fredman, *Anti-discrimination Laws and Work in the Developing World: A Thematic Overview* (background paper for the World Dev. Rpt., 2013).

Evidence from Organisation for Economic Co-operation and Development (OECD) countries shows that women's rates of employment fall when larger shares of the population believe men should be given priority on jobs.[14] In some cases, well-intended laws that intersect with norms can even have adverse effects on women's economic opportunities. Such is the case with generous government subsidies to households in Algeria, Egypt, Kuwait, and Yemen, which have tended to discourage female labor force participation.[15]

Figure 1. Legal constraints and women's economic opportunities

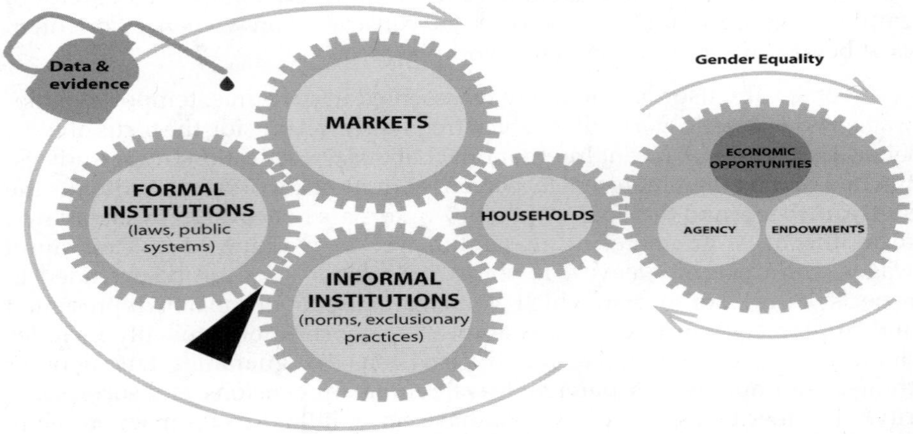

Source: Adapted from World Bank, *World Development Report 2012: Gender Equality and Development* (Washington, D.C.: World Bank, 2012), http://www.worldbank.org/wdr2012.

How markets operate matters as well. Conventional economic theory would suggest that free market economics would eventually eradicate gender discrimination in the workforce.[16] Indeed, many companies are increasingly recognizing the business case to investing in women's economic inclusion.[17] At the same time, some economists have argued more nuanced models.[18] They suggest that discriminating employers can be marginalized in the economy but, more often, market failures can allow inefficiencies, including prejudicial

14   N. M. Fortin, *Gender Role Attitudes and the Labour-Market Outcomes of Women across OECD Countries*, 21 Oxford Rev. Econ. Policy (2005). In Morocco, 65 percent of men and 37 percent of women believe that men should have priority in jobs.

15   Tara Vishwanath, *Opening Doors: Gender Equality in the Middle East and North Africa* (World Bank 2012), available at https://openknowledge.worldbank.org/handle/10986/12552 (accessed Apr. 14, 2013).

16   F. Edgeworth, *Equal Pay to Men and Women for Equal Work*, 32 Econ. J. (1922).

17   IFC Corporate Relations, *Women and Business: Drivers of Development; Telling Our Story*, vol. 5, no. 2 (2011), available at http://www.ifc.org/wps/wcm/connect/e6d87700484e76dda3f5af5f4fc3f18b/TOSwomen_Sep2011.pdf?MOD=AJPERES (accessed Apr. 14, 2013).

18   J. E. Stiglitz, *Approaches to the Economics of Discrimination*, 63 Am. Econ. Rev. (1973).

norms, to persist. Since competition may or may not drive out gender discrimination, there is a need for laws and policy interventions to support women's fair inclusion in the labor market.[19]

Notably, figure 1 highlights the role of data and evidence in greasing the wheels of institutions to promote gender equality. It is essential to improve, regularize, and make publicly available key data to monitor the implementation of legal reforms, institutional conditions, and gender-disaggregated outcomes. The lack of internationally comparable country-level data to monitor outcomes is striking. Gaps include pay and earnings and relative numbers of female and male judges and police officers.[20] Information about the incidence and prevalence of workplace sexual harassment and assault, and experiences with workplace discrimination, is also generally lacking. Sound monitoring and evaluation efforts are vital to track progress over time on both implementation and outcomes and to develop a better understanding of what works.

International Agreements and Conventions: The Human Rights Context

International law provides a remarkably supportive foundation for equal economic opportunities between women and men. This may influence the evolution of international norms, including societal and political norms concerning gender equality, and affect government actions and behaviors.[21] International treaties may also encourage accountability through monitoring and reporting mechanisms.

The Convention on the Elimination of All Forms of Discrimination Against Women (CEDAW), adopted by the United Nations General Assembly in 1979 and ratified by 187 states, is a key foundation for women's human rights globally. It includes, for example, the right to work (Article 11.1a), the right to the same economic opportunities as men (Article 11.1b), equal pay for work of equal value (Article 11.1d), equal benefits (Article 11.1e), and freedom from discrimination on grounds of marriage or maternity (Article 11.2). The United States signed CEDAW under President Carter but has yet to ratify it, along with Iran, Palua, Somalia, South Sudan, Sudan, and Tonga.

Several ILO conventions, the first dating back to 1951, endorse principles of gender equality related to economic opportunities. ILO Convention 100, for example, provides for equal pay for work of equal value; Convention 111 assures equal right to work; and Convention 183 stipulates maternity protection. The Domestic Workers Convention (No. 189) and accompanying

---

19   D. Weichselbaumer & R. Winter-Ebmer, *The Effects of Competition and Equal Treatment Laws on Gender Wage Differentials*, 22 Econ. Policy (2007).

20   Data on a range of social, institutional, health, and economic indicators can be found through the World Bank's Gender Data Portal, available at http://datatopics.worldbank.org/gender/ (accessed Apr. 14, 2013). These indicators are limited, however, by the country data available.

21   H. Koh, *How Is International Human Rights Law Enforced?*, 74 Ind. L.J. (1999).

recommendation (No. 201), both adopted in 2011, extend labor law protection to this group. These global treaties are reinforced by several regional agreements, notably the African Protocol,[22] the Inter-American Declaration,[23] and the European Union Charter.[24]

The extent to which human rights treaties make a difference in practice has long been debated. This is compounded by the difficulty in assessing compliance to, and the effects of, such treaties. The available evidence is mixed. Multicountry analyses of the effects of human rights treaties have found that treaty ratification does not unconditionally predict better human rights practice.[25] In fact, these studies indicate that when regimes are autocratic and civil society is weak, ratification of human rights treaties actually predicts *worse* human rights practice. More encouragingly, a meta-analysis of 263 studies across 62 countries by Weichselbaumer and Winter-Ebmer found positive changes in gender wage gaps to be associated with ratification of the CEDAW and ILO conventions on equal treatment of women and men.[26] The latter study may indicate that the effects of human rights treaties on women's economic empowerment take time to materialize.

The mixed evidence about the impacts of international treaties on state practice and women's economic empowerment reinforces the need to identify and address domestic legal and other constraints that stall and undermine progress.

Key Legal Constraints to Women's Work

As the *Women, Business & the Law* (WBL) study outlines, legal barriers to women's economic opportunities take many forms. They can limit women's economic opportunities, for example, by restricting their ability to access institutions, use property, build credit, or get a job. The WBL study assessed legal gender differentiations based on 26 specific aspects of existing national laws (see box 1).[27] Of the 143 economies studied, 128 had at least one legal differentiation in 2011. In some economies, women face the cumulative effects of multiple legal constraints. The challenge is particularly acute in the Middle

---

22   *Protocol to the African Charter on Human and People's Rights on the Rights of Women in Africa* (July 11, 2003), available at http://www.achpr.org/instruments/women-protocol/.

23   *Declaration on Equal Rights and Opportunity for Women and Men and Gender Equity in Inter-American Legal Instruments* (June 2, 1998), available at http://www.oas.org/juridico/english /ga-res98/eres18.htm (accessed Apr. 14, 2013).

24   *Charter of Fundamental Rights of the European Union* (Dec. 7, 2000), available at http://www .europarl.europa.eu/charter/pdf/text_en.pdf.

25   *See* E. Neumayer, *Do International Human Rights Treaties Improve Respect for Human Rights?*, 49 J. Conflict Res. (2005); O. A. Hathaway, *Do Human Rights Treaties Make a Difference?*, 111 Yale L.J. (2002).

26   Weichselbaumer & Winter-Ebmer, *supra* note 19.

27   World Bank & International Finance Corporation, *Women, Business and the Law 2014* (forthcoming).

East and North Africa region, where women experience at least ten legal differentiations. Yet, it is also notable that legal differentiations persist even in some OECD countries, including France, where women are excluded from some industries, and Germany, where there are restrictions on the hours that pregnant or nursing women may work.

Box 1. Types of legal differentiation that affect women's work

---

Legal differentiations that may be applicable to both married and unmarried women:

1. Applying for a passport
2. Traveling outside the country
3. Traveling outside the home
4. Getting a job or pursuing a trade or profession without permission
5. Signing a contract
6. Registering a business
7. Being "head of household" or "head of family"
8. Conferring citizenship on their children
9. Opening a bank account
10. Choosing where to live
11. Obtaining a national ID card
12. Having ownership rights over property
13. Having inheritance rights over property
14. Absence of gender/sex nondiscrimination clause in the constitution
15. Working the same night hours
16. Doing the same jobs as men
17. Enjoying the same statutory retirement age
18. Enjoying the same tax deductions or credits
19. Having their testimony carry the same evidentiary weight in court
20. Validity of customary law if it violates constitution
21. Validity of personal law if it violates constitution

Legal differentiations that apply only to married women:

22. Being able to convey citizenship to her nonnational husband
23. Being required by law to obey her husband
24. Having inheritance rights to the property of her deceased spouse
25. Administering marital property
26. Absence of legal recognition for contributions to marital property which are not mentioned

---

Source: World Bank & Intl. Fin. Corp., *Women, Business and the Law 2012: Removing Barriers to Economic Inclusion* (2011), http://wbl.worldbank.org.

Removing Legal Constraints to Gender Equality Can Make a Difference

The evidence indicates that legal differentiations are important barriers in practice. In economies with higher numbers of legal gender differentiations, women are less likely to participate in the labor force, own businesses, or serve in management.[28] One recent study found that women comprise 50 percent of the self-employed in Sub-Saharan Africa but only 25 percent of employers; while country GDP appears to have no effect on the share of employers who are female, countries with more gaps in women's economic rights had lower rates of females being employers.[29]

Many governments have made progress on the associated legislative front. Between March 2011 and May 2013, the WBL study recorded 47 legal changes toward more gender parity in 39 economies; no negative changes were recorded. Côte d'Ivoire, for example, reformed its laws to increase women's access to institutions and incentives to work. There is encouraging evidence on the role that gender-smart laws can play in enabling both women's formal and informal work. This section considers examples from laws related to equal treatment, parental leave and flexibility, and access to assets.

Equal Treatment Laws

Many governments have enacted laws against discrimination. Measuring the effectiveness of labor regulations to prevent discrimination is particularly difficult, however, because of the challenge of constructing a plausible counterfactual. Nonetheless, Weichselbaumer and Winter-Ebmer's analysis demonstrated that laws constraining women's working hours or types of employment—which exist today in about 75 countries, including Costa Rica, Nigeria, and the United Arab Emirates[30]—limit women's employment opportunities and significantly increase gender wage gaps. Such evidence suggests that the passage and enforcement of equal treatment laws could make a difference.[31]

Parental Leave and Flexibility Laws

Laws that alleviate some of women's disproportionate caregiving responsibilities can also make a difference. Evidence from high-income countries has shown that paid maternity leave and flexible work policies have positive effects on women's economic opportunities. These kinds of laws can be critical in light of the major "motherhood penalty"[32] on many women's capacity to work. One study of panel data across 97 countries estimated that, on average, a birth reduces a woman's labor supply by almost two years during her

---

28 *Id.*

29 M. Hallward-Driemeier & T. Hasan, *Empowering Women: Legal Rights and Economic Opportunities in Africa* (World Bank 2013), available at http://web.worldbank.org/WBSITE /EXTERNAL/TOPICS/EXTGENDER/0,,contentMDK:23389392~pagePK:210058~piPK:210062 ~theSitePK:336868,00.html (accessed Apr. 14, 2013).

30 World Bank & International Finance Corporation, *supra* note 27.

31 Weichselbaumer & Winter-Ebmer, supra note 19.

32 R. De Silva De Alwis, *Examining Gender Stereotypes in New Work/Family Reconciliation Policies: The Creation of a New Paradigm for Egalitarian Legislation,* 18 Duke J. Gender L. & Policy 305 (2011). Available at http://scholarship.law.duke.edu/cgi/viewcontent.cgi?article=1190&con text=djglp.

reproductive years.[33] The gender differences in the effects of having children on caring responsibilities and work are substantial. In Australia, for example, when men have one child under five, their full-time employment on average *increases* by about 27 percent, whereas when women have one child under five, their full-time employment *drops* by 20 percent.[34]

Research investigating the effects of maternity and parental leave on mothers' labor force participation in OECD countries has found positive effects:

- Analyses of Canadian labor market panel data illustrate that company-extended maternity leave increases the time mothers spend with their children—which could improve children's well-being—and increases the likelihood that new mothers will return to their prebirth employer.[35]

- Legal expansions of maternity leave in Germany have had significant effects on mothers' return-to-work behavior after childbirth, and reduced turnover preserved good job-employee matches and job-specific human capital.[36]

- Expansions of parental leave have also been shown to increase mothers' incomes and career opportunities in Denmark.[37]

Additionally, evidence from the United Kingdom suggests that flexible work options may increase men's caring responsibilities, thus enabling women to participate more in the labor force.[38] While there has been less investigation into the impacts of paid paternity and parental leave policies than into maternity leave, robust parental leave options seem preferable to maternity leave; this allows both men and women equal opportunities to contribute to domestic responsibilities as carers. Workplace accommodation can also be extended beyond children to include caring for the disabled, chronically sick, or elderly;[39] the latter issue is emerging as very important in a number of countries, including, for example, China.[40]

---

33 D. Bloom et al., *Fertility, Female Labor Force Participation, and the Demographic Dividend*, 14 J. Econ. Growth (2009).

34 Australia Human Rights Commission, *Investing in Care: Recognising and Valuing Those Who Care* (vol. 2, Technical Papers, 2013).

35 M. Baker & K. Milligan, *How Does Job-Protected Maternity Leave Affect Mothers' Employment?*, 26 J. Lab. Economics (2008).

36 C. Dustmann et al., *Expansions in Maternity Leave Coverage and Children's Long-Term Outcomes*, 4 Am. Econ. J.: Applied Economics (2012).

37 On Germany, *see* C. K. Spiess & K. Wrohlich, *The Parental Leave Benefit Reform in Germany: Costs and Labour Market Outcomes of Moving towards the Scandinavian Model* (IZA Discussion Paper No. 2372, Oct. 2006); on Denmark, *see* A. W. Rasmussen, *Increasing the Length of Parents' Birth-Related Leave: The Effect on Children's Long-Term Educational Outcomes*, 17 Lab. Economics (2010).

38 A. Hegewisch & J. C. Gornick, *The Impact of Work-Family Policies on Women's Employment: A Review of Research from OECD Countries*, 14 Community, Work & Fam. (2011).

39 De Silva De Alwis, *supra* note 32.

40 Sylvia Ann Hewlett & Ripa Rashid, *Winning the War for Talent in Emerging Markets: Why*

Land and Inheritance Laws

Eliminating legal differentiations that impede women's access to assets is important, including for women who work on family farms, who are self-employed, and who run household enterprises. Often, the most important of such constraints relates to property. There is some evidence that land reforms can reduce gender gaps. An encouraging experience comes from the Hindu Succession Act Amendment (HSAA) in India.

The HSAA provided for explicit inheritance rights of daughters equal to rights of sons and was enacted in four states from 1986 to 1994, which created a natural experiment allowing World Bank economists to assess the impacts of the change on women and children in reform states relative to nonreform states.[41] This study found significant positive effects not only on women's likelihood to inherit land—which was 15 percent higher for women in reform states than for those in nonreform states—but also on their daughters' age of marriage and education attainment. While the reform has not fully erased gender inequalities in inheritance and socioeconomic outcomes, it did demonstrate a positive impact.

Nevertheless, changing laws without also addressing informal constraints can often limit effectiveness. As the Moroccan case in the introduction illustrates, when progressive legal changes confront oppositional social, cultural, and systemic constraints, more diversified and strategic actions are required to translate laws into progress on the ground. The focus now turns to informal constraints that can compound legal constraints or compete with legal reforms to exacerbate gender inequalities in the world of work.

When Laws and Informal Constraints Intersect

This section considers how informal constraints in the forms of inadequate or inaccurate information, social norms, and institutional biases can counteract positive laws to reinforce gender disadvantages in the labor market.

Information

Progressive laws can fail to translate into outcomes in part because men and women are unaware of their rights. A review of 70,000 land records in Sub-Saharan Africa, for example, found that coregistration only increased to 3.4 percent by 2002 (from 1.3 percent at the inception of joint titling in 1980), due to lack of awareness and education, logistical challenges with coregis-

---

Women Are the Solution (Harv. Bus. Rev. Press 2011).

41   K. Deininger et al., *Women's Inheritance Rights and Intergenerational Transmission of Resources in India*, 48 J. Human Resources (2013).

tration, and cultural attitudes.[42] Similar implementation challenges have been documented in other land reform cases around the world.[43]

Research in such countries as Ethiopia and Mozambique has found widespread lack of awareness related to key laws and provisions on land rights, particularly in rural areas.[44] Similarly, data from the multicountry qualitative study *On Norms and Agency* indicate that most men and women, especially those in rural areas, have very limited awareness of laws related to gender equality.[45] Even when respondents had heard of laws—through friends and family, radio, or other media, for example—women often felt that the laws did not apply to them or their community. Given the well-documented restrictions on women's mobility, technologies, and social networks in many cultural contexts, women can be at a particular disadvantage. In India, for example, only 44 percent of women own cell phones (compared to 66 percent of men), and a meager 4 percent of women use the Internet regularly (compared to 9 percent of men).[46]

In Uganda, a study found that key aspects of a major new land law were unknown to the majority of the sample and that awareness was lower among women than men.[47] At the same time, knowledge of the law's provisions predicted significantly more positive land use outcomes. This indicates that, while knowledge of rights can be suboptimal, awareness-raising efforts could yield positive payoffs.

Some initiatives aim to extend awareness through rights-based education.[48] Examples include community-based awareness campaigns, paralegal services, and consultations with local officials, as in Colombia, Cambodia, and the Democratic Republic of Congo, to increase women's and local leaders' awareness of property rights.[49] Outreach efforts in Pakistan helped women

---

42   E. Cooper, *Inheritance and the Intergenerational Transmission of Poverty in Sub-Saharan Africa: Policy Considerations* (Chronic Poverty Research Ctr. Working Paper No. 159, Oxford U., May 2010).

43   J. W. Bruce et al., *Land Law Reform: Achieving Development Policy Objectives* (World Bank 2006), available at https://openknowledge.worldbank.org/handle/10986/7198.

44   *See* UN-HABITAT, *Land Registration in Ethiopia: Early Impacts on Women: Summary Report* (2008); R. Villanuea, *The Big Picture: Land and Gender Issues in Matrilineal Mozambique* (research report, Landesa Ctr. for Women's Land Rights, 2011).

45   A. M. Boudet et al., *On Norms and Agency: Conversations about Gender Equality with Women and Men in 20 Countries* (World Bank 2013).

46   Pew Trust. Data from Spring 2012 Pew Global Attitudes Survey, retrieved from the Pew Trust. Available at http://www.pewglobal.org/2012/04/20/spring-2012-survey-data/.

47   K. Deininger et al., *Legal Knowledge and Economic Development: The Case of Land Rights in Uganda*, 84 Land Economics (2008).

48   Examples of rights-based education initiatives can be found through the UN Women's website, http://www.endvawnow.org/en/articles/943-provide-rights-based-education-and-awareness.html (accessed Apr. 8, 2013).

49   S. Pallas & L. Miggiano, *Women's Legal Empowerment: Lessons Learned from Community-Based Activities* (Intl. Land Coalition briefing note, 2012).

complete marriage forms in ways that strengthened their property rights.[50] Hallward-Driemeier and Hasan suggest that social media, such as radio stations and other technologies, and social networks, such as women's collectives and cooperatives, can be good delivery mechanisms for spreading rights-based education.[51] To date, however, limited evidence is available as to the impacts of such interventions and delivery models on changing knowledge or behaviors related to women's rights.

While there is little evidence on interventions to diffuse rights-based knowledge, there is a growing body of evidence in other areas—notably public health—in which innovative solutions are affecting knowledge and behaviors. Several studies, for instance, have shown positive effects of using short-message service (SMS) texting to spread messages about topics ranging from HIV prevention to smoking cessation.[52] While the appropriate strategies are context dependent, these types of innovations from other disciplines could inform the design, implementation, and evaluation of rights-based education interventions to improve women's equality.

Social Norms

Social norms are beliefs widely held by a society about what people should and should not do.[53] They can be held at multiple levels, including in the home, the community, and the workplace. Oppositional social norms may mean that some progressive laws are never realized. In Mali, for example, a new Family Code was adopted by the legislature, but it was withdrawn before it made it to law due to strong social opposition to provisions such as girls' inheritance rights and women's equality with their husbands in the home. The Family Code that ultimately became the new law in 2012 preserved many of the discriminatory provisions of the original 1962 law.[54] In other cases, despite oppositional social norms, laws with progressive provisions pass with strong advocacy and political leadership, but they fail to translate into practice. The prospects of compliance and effectiveness are particularly vulnerable when laws (formal regulations) conflict with social norms (informal regulations).

Examples of laws failing to translate into practice in the context of competing social norms are many, including from the literature on land and inheritance laws. While the Indian example of the Hindu Succession Act Amendment mentioned above is encouraging for land reform, the evidence more generally is weak and varied. Inheritance reforms were ineffective in Laos, for

---

50   See E. Scalise, *Women's Inheritance Rights to Land and Property in South Asia: A Study of Afghanistan, Bangladesh, India, Nepal, Pakistan, and Sri Lanka* (2009); Pallas & Miggiano, *supra* note 49.

51   Hallward-Driemeier & Hasan, *supra* note 29.

52   B. J. Fjeldsoe et al., *Behavior Change Interventions Delivered by Mobile Telephone Short-Message Service*, 36(2) Am. J. Preventive Med. (2009).

53   L. Bierman & R. Gely, *"Love, Sex and Politics? Sure. Salary? No Way": Workplace Social Norms and the Law*, 25(1) Berkeley J. Empl. & Lab. L. 167 (2004).

54   S. T. Diarra, *Women's Rights in Mali "Set Back 50 Years" by New "Family Code" Law*, Guardian Weekly (May 1, 2012).

example, where gender-neutral inheritance laws enacted in the 1990s failed to account for the fact that inheritance transactions require paperwork and head-of-household status; as such, they still largely favor men, who are more likely to be literate and head of the household.[55]

In Jordan, women legally—both by statutory and sharia religious law— are entitled to own, share, and be jointly titled on land as well as to property inheritance from their husbands. Yet, only 10 percent of Jordanian women own land,[56] and they typically renounce their rights to property in favor of their husbands or other male relatives, thus muting the impacts of their legal rights.[57] When these tensions are identified, policy makers can respond with more gender-informed statutes and actions. The Jordanian government amended the law, mandating that the decedent's property be registered immediately in the name of the female relative and that a three-month waiting period for waiving inheritance rights be enforced, to minimize women's susceptibility to relinquishing land to men who approach them immediately after a death. Other countries, such as Tanzania, have responded to oppositional social norms by passing targeted mandatory joint-titling legislation that ensures spousal co-ownership.

In the financial sector, only 2 countries (the Democratic Republic of Congo and Niger) out of the 141 covered by WBL legally restricts women from opening a bank account in the same way as men,[58] yet only 47 percent of women globally have opened an account at a formal financial institution, compared to 55 percent of men.[59] In many countries, the gap is much wider. In India, for example, 26 percent of women have an account at a formal financial institution, compared to 44 percent of men. In such cases, difficulties related to social norms and access to financial services seem to be more influential than what is written in the law.

Likewise, qualitative research with male participants in sexual harassment information interventions has found that underlying gender norms are a significant obstacle.[60] Even when workplace norms do not endorse harassment

---

55 Andrew D. Mason & Elizabeth M. King, *Engendering Development through Gender Equality in Rights, Resources, and Voice* (policy research report, World Bank 2001), http://documents .worldbank.org/curated/en/2001/01/891686/engendering-development-through-gender -equality-rights-resources-voice (accessed Apr. 14, 2013).

56 UNIFEM, *The Status of Jordanian Women: Demography, Economic Participation, Political Participation and Violence* (2004), available at http://ns.iknowpolitics.org/en/2007/02/status-jordanian -women-demography-economic-participation-political-participation-and (accessed Apr. 14, 2013).

57 A. Hadadin, *Good Practices and Lessons Learned in Realizing Women's Rights to Productive Resources: The Case of Jordan* (UNHROHC 2012), available at http://www.unwomen.org /wp-content/uploads/2012/07/EP-Good-practices-and-lessons-learned-in-realizing-womens -right-to-productive-reources-the-case-of-Jordan.pdf (accessed Apr. 14, 2013).

58 World Bank, Global Financial Inclusion (Global Findex) Database (accessed Apr. 14, 2013).

59 World Bank & International Finance Corporation, *supra* note 27.

60 J. E. Tinkler et al., *Can Legal Interventions Change Beliefs? The Effect of Exposure to Sexual Harassment Policy on Men's Gender Beliefs*, 70 Soc. Psychol. Q. (2007).

or discrimination per se, they may buoy an informal "code of silence" that undermines laws with inaction and underreporting.[61]

The good news is that gender norms can and do change. As the *On Norms and Agency* study shows, younger generations of women are demanding more control over marriage and child bearing than older generations, and they are participating more and more in these decisions.[62] These changes, however, can be slow and fraught with tension. In response to new gender laws, for example, some male respondents in Tanzania expressed perceptions that the laws contributed to women's "big headedness" and that the laws would need to be revised to reinstate women's "respect and discipline."[63]

Some norms that discriminate against women relate to perceptions of what makes an "ideal worker." These norms can privilege men when they intersect with gender norms about the respective roles of men and women in domestic responsibilities. Specifically, workplace norms about what makes an ideal employee typically favor those who work full-time (and, increasingly, more than full-time) and are easily accessible throughout the day.[64] While workplace time norms may appear gender neutral out of context, they can reinforce gender discriminations in the workforce, given the strong social and cultural pressures on women to assume the majority of domestic responsibilities. In these cases, policies that increase workplace flexibility or provide more part-time options may bring more women into the workforce, but they may not overcome the barriers to women's upward mobility unless biased time norms are addressed or men take on a larger share of domestic work.

Interventions to change social norms have grown as an area of focus and evaluation, particularly in the public health community. From nutrition, to substance abuse, to violence, many health-related behaviors and attitudes have strong normative foundations.[65] While many of the trials are small and with short follow-up times, there is also a growing body of evidence from evaluations of gender-transformative interventions that well-designed programs can change men's and boys' attitudes toward gender roles and relationships and produce lasting positive effects.[66] Similar efforts to build the evidence base on changing societal and workplace norms to reduce constraints on women's work are needed.

---

61   Bierman & Gely, *supra* note 53.

62   Boudet et al., *supra* note 45.

63   *Id.*

64   *See* Bierman & Gely, *supra* note 53; B. M. Smith, *Time Norms in the Workplace: Their Exclusionary Effect and Potential for Change*, 11 Colum. J. Gender & L. 271 (2002).

65   *See* E. L. Paluck & L. Ball, *Social Norms Marketing Aimed at Gender Based Violence: A Literature Review and Critical Assessment* (report, Intl. Rescue Comm., 2010); World Health Org., *Changing Cultural and Social Norms That Support Violence* (research brief, 2009).

66   G. Barker et al., *Questioning Gender Norms with Men to Improve Health Outcomes: Evidence of Impact*, 5 Global Pub. Health (2010).

Laws themselves may help foster changes in gender-related norms. For example, 15 years after corporal punishment was banned in Sweden, survey data indicated that the share of parents who reported that they were inclined to hit their children had fallen from approximately 50 to 11 percent.[67] In the United States, Title IX, the 1972 legislation to ensure women and girls equal educational opportunities, including in school athletics, has been largely credited with contributing to changing, though still not leveling, gender norms in the country, particularly in schools and colleges.[68] Again, more analytical work is needed to determine whether laws aimed at increasing women's economic rights—such as equal-pay, work flexibility, land reform, and parental care legislation—correlate similarly with changes in gender norms over time.

In sum, while discriminatory social norms, whether at the level of the workplace, the community, or the nation, can be both powerful and stubborn, they are not immovable. A concerted, multipronged front including smart and consistent laws, policy interventions, and private-sector initiatives can advance women's economic empowerment despite discriminating norms, and it might even change those norms over time. The path to progress, however, demands a stronger evidence base generated through better monitoring systems and rigorous evaluation that helps identify what works, and what does not, in different contexts.

Institutional Biases

Often, institutions responsible for enforcing and interpreting the law embody systematic biases that can reinforce gender discriminations. This section focuses specifically on gender sensitivity in judiciaries, the key institutions responsible for interpreting and applying the law.

Justice systems rarely reflect the diversity of the people they serve, and they often lack appropriate system capacity and design to address gender discrimination.[69] As the WDR2012 demonstrated, this is problematic because, even when relatively few people access the courts directly, the decisions made by courts have broader influence—positive or negative—on the future behavior of institutions and citizens. For example, on the positive side, courts in Nepal have struck down legal provisions that discriminated against women through inheritance laws; in Botswana, they have guaranteed women's equal property rights, thus setting a precedent for unfair customary laws to be challenged; and in India, they have interpreted the constitution and international conventions as making sexual harassment unlawful.[70] Conversely, judges can set discriminatory precedents or thwart the implementation of progressive

---

67 World Health Org., *supra* note 65.

68 L. Kuznick & M. Ryan, *Changing Gender Norms? Title IX and Legal Activism: Comments from the Spring 2007 Harvard Journal of Law and Gender Conference*, Harv. J. L. & Gender (2008).

69 E. Rackley, *Women, Judging and the Judiciary: From Difference to Diversity* (Routledge 2013).

70 *See World Development Report 2012, supra* note 5, at 348; A. Laing, *Women Can Inherit the Earth Rules Botswana Judge*, Telegraph (Oct. 12, 2012).

legal reforms, as was the case in Saudi Arabia, where judges refused to accept women's ID cards, thus forcing them to be represented by male "guardians" in presenting cases.[71]

Some countries have sought to make judiciaries more gender sensitive by creating special courts (e.g., courts on rape and sexual offenses or domestic violence courts) or gender units within the courts to help women navigate judicial processes as well as access broader services. The Democratic Republic of Congo, for example, has implemented mobile gender courts in order to facilitate women's access to justice related to gender-based violence in remote, conflict-affected areas of the country.[72]

Women are underrepresented in the judiciary globally, making up only small minorities of judges, magistrates, and court officers.[73] The United Kingdom, Italy, Egypt, India, and Pakistan are among the many countries with less than 1 in 10 women on their high courts.[74] Views vary as to how much difference this makes. The first woman to serve on the U.S. Supreme Court, Sandra Day O'Connor, once said that a wise female judge will come to the same conclusion as a wise male judge. Yet, her female justice colleagues, Ruth Bader Ginsburg and Sonia Sotomayor, have stated sympathies to the view that one's personal experience, including being female, does matter in the courtroom. In a case involving the strip-searching of a 13-year-old girl, for example, Ginsburg argued that her male counterparts were at a disadvantage in interpreting the sensitivity of being an adolescent girl and subject to intrusive practices.[75]

While gender may not be the primary determinant of how cases are decided, some evidence indicates that the judicial demographic skew does have an influence. An analysis of 556 gender-coded cases related to sexual harassment or sex discrimination in the United States revealed that cases were twice as likely to succeed when a female judge was represented on three-judge appellate panels.[76] In fact, the presence of female judges increased *male* judges' propensity to support the plaintiff in cases of sexual harassment and sex discrimination. In a more recent study in the United States, Boyd et al. found similar results, with female judges having a 10 percent higher probability than their male colleagues of ruling in favor of the plaintiff in sex discrimination cases.[77] Male judges serving alongside female judges were also more likely than other

---

71 E. A. Doumato, *Saudi Arabia*, in *Women's Rights in the Middle East and North Africa: Progress Amid Resistance* (Sanja Kelly & Julia Breslin eds., Freedom House, Rowman & Littlefield 2010).

72 Open Society Justice Initiative, *DRC Mobile Gender Courts* (2011).

73 Hallward-Driemeier & Hasan, *supra* note 29.

74 Rackley, *supra* note 69.

75 N. Lewis, *Debate on Whether Female Judges Decide Differently Arises Anew*, N.Y. Times (June 3, 2009), available at http://www.nytimes.com/2009/06/04/us/politics/04women.html?_r=0.

76 J. L. Peresie, *Female Judges Matter: Gender and Collegial Decisionmaking in the Federal Appellate Courts*, 114 Yale L.J. (2005).

77 C. L. Boyd et al., *Untangling the Causal Effects of Sex on Judging*, 54 Am. J. Pol. Sci. (2010).

male judges to rule in favor of the party alleging discrimination. Interestingly, of the 13 areas of law examined in this study, sex discrimination disputes were the only area of law in which female and male judges ruled differently.

Increasing women's representation on the bench is another way to increase the gender sensitivity of the law in practice, although this has not yet been a common area of focus for development agencies.[78]

Customary and Religious Law

Many countries have plural legal systems that formally recognize religious or customary laws as valid sources of law under the constitution—around 52 countries globally, and most commonly in Sub-Saharan Africa, where 25 countries constitutionally recognize at least one customary or religious legal system.[79] Legal pluralism is generally welcome. It reflects the right of communities to protection of their culture and traditional belief systems. Multiple systems of law, however, can also create a complex web of overlapping systems, which can create barriers to accessing justice and inconsistencies in the laws' treatment of women's rights.

Customary and religious laws can involve both formal and informal institutions, depending on whether and how they are recognized by national constitutions or statutory laws, but, either way, they are often governed by informal norms and practices. Fifty-two economies recognize customary or personal law as a valid source of law under the constitution.[80] In half of those economies, including, for example, Ecuador, Pakistan, and South Africa, the national constitution reigns, and discriminatory traditional laws and practices can be declared illegal under the constitution, which leaves 28 economies in which discriminatory customary or personal laws can undercut women's economic opportunities despite any progressive constitutional provisions.[81]

Such legal pluralism can in some cases diminish the rights afforded by statutory laws.[82] In Africa, customary courts are often biased toward men and can sometimes require women to be represented by men in presenting a case.[83] An analysis of local customary courts in Sierra Leone, for instance, found that many cases brought to the court involved the rights of women (e.g., grievances related to child support or husbands' extramarital affairs) but rarely involved implicated women in the proceedings.[84] Even in cases in which women's rights should be protected by statutory law, customary courts

---

78   J. Doherty, *Women's Representation in Judiciaries Worldwide: Arguments in Favor of Increasing the Gender Diversity on the Bench* (Inst. for Global & Intl. Stud. 2012).

79   World Bank & International Finance Corporation, *supra* note 27.

80   *Id.*

81   Hallward-Driemeier & Hasan, *supra* note 29.

82   *Id.*

83   *Id.*

84   *Id.*

may overstep their jurisdiction. While customary and religious courts can be important mechanisms for preserving culture and values, and in some cases can even protect women's rights better than the statutory laws in place,[85] they also invite more entry points for informal constraints to challenge gender equality. This reality reinforces the need for clear constitutional and statutory provisions for gender equality, as well as strong enforcement systems and complementary interventions to promote women's rights.

Conclusions

The case for eliminating legal constraints to women's economic opportunities is clear. Yet, the scale and complexity of the challenges involved in enabling equal economic opportunities for women and men are formidable. Women often face multiple constraints—both formal and informal and throughout the life cycle that shapes their economic opportunities. The legal framework, and how it functions in practice, is one important part of the puzzle. At the same time, complementary efforts are needed to address informal barriers and overlapping disadvantages. Over time, efforts on several fronts should serve to improve translation of the spirit of progressive laws into measurable gains for gender equality in the world of work.

---

85   For instance, statutory laws that introduced privatization of land during certain period of East African history were viewed as disempowering to women who had greater rights to land usage under customary systems. *See*, for example: A. Tripp, *Women's Movements, Customary Law, and Land Rights in Africa: The Case of Uganda*, 7 African Stud. Q. (2004).

The Role of Law in Promoting the Right to Health for Diverse Communities

DAVID PATTERSON, ELISA SLATTERY, AND NAOMI BURKE-SHYNE

The World Health Organization (WHO) defines *health* expansively: "Health is a state of complete physical, mental and social well-being and not merely the absence of disease or infirmity."[1] This holistic vision of health means that health policies should be integrated into, and should be seen as affected by, all aspects of international development policy. Similarly, reforms in legal frameworks and justice systems should be recognized as having direct and indirect effects on population health, broadly defined.

Increases in gross domestic product are rarely equally distributed. Blanket improvements in national health indicators usually hide pockets of inequality. These pockets often contain women, girls, and diverse populations. The health inequalities are the result of multiple factors, including a lack of access to appropriate health services for disease prevention and treatment.

Health inequalities range across as well as within countries and regions. In the least developed countries of Sub-Saharan Africa, infectious diseases cause most morbidity and mortality. In the rest of the developing world and in Organisation for Economic Cooperation and Development (OECD) countries, noncommunicable diseases (NCDs), such as cancer, cardiovascular and lung diseases, and diabetes, take the largest toll. Concentrated epidemics of human immunodeficiency virus (HIV) infection are found in men who have sex with men and in injecting drug users in societies whose relative affluence usually puts them beyond the reach of other infectious epidemic diseases, such as malaria and typhoid. Anomalies exist—even where NCDs are broadly linked to increased income, such as type 2 diabetes or smoking-related cancers, the very wealthy typically fare better than the middle classes.

An enabling legal environment is essential for effective health policies, access to health services, and delivery of health programs. Without the rule of law, investments in health may be drained through corruption. But even where laws are enforced, poorly designed legal responses to diseases such as HIV can limit access to prevention and treatment programs. An enabling legal environment is more than just legislation. It includes the implementation of laws through regulations, decisions of courts, police practices, prosecutorial discretion, legal literacy and empowerment of diverse

---

Any statements of fact, opinion, or analysis expressed herein are entirely those of the author(s) and are not attributable to the International Development Law Organization.

1   Constitution of the World Health Organization, preamble.

populations, and the availability of affordable, high-quality legal services for these communities.

In the case of HIV, the availability of affordable, skilled lawyers for people living with HIV and those most at risk of HIV infection will partly determine how these communities can address discrimination and other HIV-related legal issues. The Joint United Nations Programme on HIV/AIDS (UNAIDS) has issued specific guidance on the central role of the law in the national response to HIV, including on the importance of legal services in national planning and responses to HIV.[2]

The Commission on Macroeconomics and Health, established in 1999, argued that improved population health is a precondition for economic development, not merely a benefit of economic development.[3] How can the law serve to improve population health both as a human right and as a contribution to economic development? How can the law contribute to the elimination of inequities in population health?[4]

This chapter identifies lessons and trends in public health law affecting diverse communities in developing countries. It commences by reviewing experiences in relation to HIV and explores the lessons for other global challenges to health. HIV is an infectious disease with a relatively long latency period. Antiretroviral treatments mean that many people today live decades with HIV infection—the responses to HIV also provide lessons for how to handle NCDs. The chapter then examines other populations, including people with disabilities, and discusses the additional challenges for women with disabilities. It canvasses the legal obstacles to access to high-quality, affordable medicines in the development context. It then provides examples of the health implications of discrimination for people of different sexual orientations or gender identity, and concludes with recommendations for capacity building of the legal sector on health issues and for the health sector on legal issues.

---

2   *Key Programmes to Reduce Stigma and Discrimination and Increase Access to Justice in National HIV Responses* (Guidance Note, UNAIDS 2012).

3   Jon Liden, *The Grand Decade for Global Health: 1998–2008* (Cntr. Global Health Security Working Group Papers, Working Group on Governance Paper 2, Chatham House, Apr. 2013). *See* also Amartya Sen & Jean Dreze, *India: Economic Development and Social Opportunity* (Oxford U. Press 1995).

4   Since 2009, the health law program of the International Development Law Organization (IDLO) has explored these questions, with initiatives in 23 developing countries in Asia and the Pacific, Latin America, the Middle East, and North and West Africa. The program commenced with a focus on HIV, and in 2011, it included legal aspects of noncommunicable diseases. *See* http://www.idlo.int/healthlaw.

HIV, Law, and Development

The Response to HIV

The enabling legal environment for the response to HIV has been examined, debated, and contested in almost every country. Because the sexual behaviors and drug use that spread HIV infection are often stigmatized or illegal, an appropriate legal environment is crucial to ensuring access to HIV prevention, treatment, and care services and to addressing HIV-related discrimination. Years of experience have shown that HIV-related stigma and discrimination undermine HIV prevention efforts by deterring people from seeking health services and information about how to reduce their risk of exposure to HIV. Fear of stigma and discrimination discourages people living with HIV from disclosing their status and undermines their ability to adhere to HIV treatment, which in turn hampers HIV prevention.

In 1981, when the U.S. Centers for Disease Control reported the first cases of the condition that came to be known as "AIDS," international human rights law, including on the right to health, was already well defined in international human rights treaties. Seven years later, the World Health Assembly adopted the first resolution addressing HIV-related discrimination,[5] and in 1989, the United Nations Centre for Human Rights and WHO convened the first international consultation on HIV/AIDS and human rights.[6] In 1996, the human rights–based response to the global HIV pandemic was adopted as a cross-cutting program theme, along with gender, by the newly created UNAIDS. These principles were expanded at an international expert consultation convened by UNAIDS and the Office of the High Commissioner for Human Rights (OHCHR), and published as the *International Guidelines on HIV/AIDS and Human Rights* in 1998. The guidelines were revised in 2002 to reflect the breakthroughs in treatment for HIV infection and the intellectual property issues arising as donor agencies and developing country governments struggled to deliver new drugs for treating AIDS to the developing world at affordable prices.[7]

In 2001, human rights–based approaches and law reform were anchored in the United Nations General Assembly's Declaration of Commitment on HIV/AIDS. They have been affirmed in subsequent General Assembly resolutions, including the 2011 Political Declaration on HIV/AIDS: Intensifying Our Efforts to Eliminate HIV/AIDS.

---

5   Avoidance of Discrimination in Relation to HIV-Infected People and People with AIDS (World Health Assembly Resolution WHA 41.24, May 13, 1988).

6   World Health Organization (WHO) and Office of the United Nations High Commissioner for Human Rights (OHCHR), *Report of an International Consultation on AIDS and Human Rights, Geneva, 26–28 July 1989* HR/PUB/90/2 (1990).

7   Joint United Nations Programme on HIV/AIDS (UNAIDS) and OHCHR, *International Guidelines on HIV/AIDS and Human Rights: 2006 Consolidated Version* (2006).

UN General Assembly, Political Declaration on HIV/AIDS, 2011

In 2011, UN member states committed

> to intensify national efforts to create enabling legal, social and policy frameworks in each national context in order to eliminate stigma, discrimination and violence related to HIV and promote access to HIV prevention, treatment, care and support and non-discriminatory access to education, health care, employment and social services, provide legal protections for people affected by HIV, including inheritance rights and respect for privacy and confidentiality, and promote and protect all human rights and fundamental freedoms with particular attention to all people vulnerable to and affected by HIV.*

Member states also promised to review laws impeding HIV prevention, treatment, care, and support programs.

* UN General Assembly, Political Declaration on HIV/AIDS: Intensifying Our Efforts to Eliminate HIV/AIDS, A/RES/65/277 (June 10, 2011), para. 77.

The UN monitoring framework for responses to HIV contains the National Commitments and Policies Instrument, which includes explicit indicators on national policies and laws protecting the rights of people living with HIV and key affected populations. State reports are voluntary, and technical assistance is available from UNAIDS to complete the reports. In 2012, 186 out of 193 member states submitted reports on national progress on AIDS.[8] This is an extraordinary record of compliance with a voluntary monitoring mechanism.

Thanks to these reports, improvements in the enabling legal environment in states and across countries and regions can be tracked. These data are compiled by UNAIDS, and the UN secretary-general reports the trends to the UN General Assembly. The rigorous and continuing reporting of national and global policy and legislative responses to HIV is unique and offers valuable lessons for global responses to other health and development challenges, such as NCDs.

The global focus on rights and law brought many constituencies into national debates on HIV: organizations working with children, women's groups, and employers, and organizations of people living with HIV, drug users, and sex workers. Rights language in international and national law framed the discussions. Compulsory HIV testing and quarantine were rejected, and the "AIDS paradox" was asserted as policy: in order to limit the spread of HIV in

---

8   See http://www.unaids.org/en/dataanalysis/knowyourresponse/countryprogressreports/2012countries/.

the general population, the rights of people most vulnerable to HIV infection must be protected.[9]

The most common complaint of discrimination concerns health care settings.[10] People living with HIV are more likely to seek health care, and also to experience discrimination in these settings because of their HIV status. People living with HIV and key affected populations report denial of treatment, substandard treatment, breach of confidentiality, and nonconsensual medical treatment.

The global People Living with HIV Stigma Index initiative includes health care settings as part of its broader study of stigma and discrimination.[11] For example, respondents to an extensive study in Nepal reported discrimination by health personnel.[12] Women living with HIV tend to seek health care services more frequently than men do because of reproductive and maternal health care needs. Rights violations of women with HIV in health care settings, such as coercive sterilization and verbal and physical abuse, are well documented in many parts of the world.[13]

In recent years, legal action has been taken to stop the forced sterilization of women living with HIV.[14] In a first-of-its-kind case in southern Africa, three women living with HIV were told they could have a cesarean section (reducing the chances of passing the HIV virus on to their children) only if they agreed to be sterilized at the same time. The Namibian High Court granted a partial victory for these women, confirming that the human rights of these women were violated when they were coerced into being sterilized while they gave birth. However, the judge dismissed claims that the sterilization amounted to discrimination based on the women's HIV status.[15]

Since the World Health Assembly resolution on discrimination in the context of AIDS in 1988, many countries have adopted legislation to prohibit HIV-related discrimination. For example, in Papua New Guinea, the HIV and AIDS

---

9   Michael Kirby, *Law, Discrimination, and Human Rights: Facing Up To the AIDS Paradox* (speech at the Third International Conference on AIDS in Asia and the Pacific, Nov. 10, 1995), available at http://www.michaelkirby.com.au.

10   David Stephens & Mia Urbano, *HIV and Legal Empowerment*, in *Legal Empowerment: Practitioners' Perspectives* (IDLO 2010).

11   The People Living with HIV Stigma Index is a tool to measure and detect changing trends in relation to stigma and discrimination experienced by people living with HIV. *See* http://www.stigmaindex.org/.

12   The Nepal Stigma Index Study included 1,696 men and 1,614 women living with HIV in Nepal.

13   Open Society Foundations, *Against Her Will: Forced and Coerced Sterilization of Women Worldwide* (2012), available at http://www.opensocietyfoundations.org/sites/default/files/against-her-will-20111003.pdf.

14   Pooja Nair, *Litigating against the Forced Sterilization of HIV-Positive Women: Recent Developments in Chile and Namibia*, 23 Harv. Hum. Rights J. 223 (2010), available at http://harvardhrj.com/wp-content/uploads/2010/10/223-232.pdf.

15   *LM and Others v. Government of the Republic of Namibia*, High Court of Namibia (July 30, 2012).

Management and Prevention Act of 2003 (HAMP Act) is designed to protect people "infected or affected by HIV/AIDS" from discrimination. The HAMP Act states that a

> person infected or affected by HIV/AIDS means a person who (a) is, or is presumed to be, infected by HIV or has, or is presumed to have, AIDS; or (b) has had, is having, is seeking to have or has refused to have an HIV test; or (c) is related to or is associated with a person who is, or is presumed to be, infected by HIV or has, or is presumed to have, AIDS; or (d) is, or is presumed to be, a member of or associated with a group, activity or occupation, or living in an environment, which is commonly associated with, or presumed to be associated with, infection by, transmission of, HIV.[16]

Similar inclusive approaches have been taken in HIV bills in India and Nepal, and, to a lesser extent, Pakistan.[17]

Today, 8 million people have access to antiretroviral treatment (compared to just a few tens of thousands 10 years ago), human rights are entrenched as a key part of the response to HIV, and the number of new HIV infections has decreased worldwide by 25 percent in five years. HIV infection rates and AIDS deaths are falling in all but two regions (Middle East/North Africa and Eastern Europe/Central Asia).[18]

The public health victories over HIV contain lessons for other diseases. They include the contribution of the human rights discourse and its expression through an enabling legal environment, the importance of multisectoral approaches at international and national levels, and the crucial role of communities living with and directly affected by the diseases in law and policy development as well as program delivery.

Lessons Learned from HIV for Other Challenges to Global Health

A Human Rights-Based Approach Is Imperative

First championed in the 1980s by Jonathan Mann at the WHO Global Programme on AIDS, the human rights–based approach was adopted by UNAIDS as a cross-cutting theme in 1996. The UN International Guidelines on HIV/AIDS and Human Rights (1998, revised 2006) linked international human rights law and

---

16 Section 2. Interpretation. *HIV/AIDS Management and Prevention Act* 2003 of Papua New Guinea.

17 IDLO, United Nations Development Programme (UNDP), & South Asian Association for Regional Co-operation in Law (SAARCLAW), *Regional Legal Reference Resource: Protective Laws Relating to HIV, Men Who Have Sex with Men, and Transgender People in South Asia* (2013), available at http://www.snap-undp.org/elibrary/Publications/HIV-2013-Regional-Legal-Reference.pdf.

18 *World AIDS Day Report* (UNAIDS 2012).

national responses. The guidelines were disseminated widely and followed by toolkits for legislators, national dialogues, and monitoring.*

Activism and Social Mobilization Play a Vital Role

Organizations led by people living with HIV were actively supported with funding and technical assistance. Human rights organizations and community groups addressing civil, political, economic, and social rights were engaged, as were women's organizations, child rights, religious, and youth groups, and many others.

Key Populations Must Be Empowered and Legal Professionals Must Be Trained

Capacity building was provided on HIV-related human and legal rights for people living with HIV, key affected populations, and legal professionals. People facing discrimination and other rights violations were linked to legal services, including trained paralegals and community outreach workers.

Engage the Media

Advocacy messages were clear. "Silence = Death"; "Action = Life." Fearful messages were avoided in favor of solutions. Messages were nonjudgmental, targeted to specific communities.

Take a Multisectoral Approach

In many of the hardest-hit countries, responsibility for coordinating the national response to HIV was elevated from ministries of health to a more senior government level with multisectoral responsibilities, such as the office of the president. At the global level, UNAIDS, created in 1996, now comprises 10 UN agencies with a shared division of labor.

Focus on Gender and Key Affected Populations

The social, economic, cultural, and legal factors contributing to the vulnerability of women and key affected populations were rapidly identified and informed programming.

Science, Evidence, and Documentation Are Key

Policymakers were presented with evidence that HIV prevention approaches such as needle and syringe programs, youth sex education, and condom distribution are effective.

Treatment and Prevention Are Linked

Even before it was proven that HIV treatment assists in preventing new cases of HIV infection, the push to offer HIV care, treatment, and support was seen as essential to engaging with key affected populations.

An Enabling Legal Environment Frames National Responses

The legal environment encompasses laws and practices, including the capacity of judges, prosecutors, and police to support public health goals. Access to high-quality, sensitive, and affordable HIV-related legal services for people living with HIV and key affected populations was promoted.

Conduct Global Monitoring and Require Transparency and Accountability

The 2001 UN General Assembly Declaration of Commitment on HIV/AIDS and the monitoring guidelines developed by UNAIDS to track compliance are powerful tools for national and international advocacy and accountability. National monitoring reports submitted to UNAIDS are posted on the UNAIDS website.[†]

* *See* http://hrbaportal.org for more on rights-based approaches.

† The reporting framework includes the National Commitments and Policies Instrument. *See* http://www.unaids.org/en/dataanalysis/knowyourresponse/ncpi/2012countries/

Noncommunicable Diseases (NCDs)

Outside of Sub-Saharan Africa, most ill health is no longer attributable to bacteria, viruses, or parasites. Rather, most avoidable illnesses and premature deaths are caused by unhealthy patterns of consumption of tobacco, animal and certain vegetable fats, sugar, salt, and alcohol. In 2011, the WHO reported that "of the 57 million deaths that occurred globally in 2008, 36 million—almost two-thirds—were due to NCDs, comprising mainly cardiovascular diseases, cancers, diabetes and chronic lung diseases."[19] This figure includes more than 14 million people ages 30–69 in developing countries—more than seven times the estimated number of people who died of AIDS in 2008 (2 million).

Poor families are often heavily burdened by the costs of caring for ill or disabled family members suffering from NCDs, including out-of-pocket payments for health care expenses and the loss of breadwinners. As with HIV, a comprehensive, rights-based, multisectoral response engaging affected communities is required to address the burden of NCDs and their impact. According to the World Bank, NCDs are expected to account for three-quarters of the disease burden in middle-income countries by 2030. In Sub-Saharan Africa, NCDs will account for almost half (46 percent) of all deaths by 2030.[20]

As the global trends in morbidity and mortality shift to NCDs, new legal challenges are arising. Tobacco and alcohol have long been aggressively promoted in many developing countries, which often have weak laws and lim-

---

19　*Global Status Report on Noncommunicable Diseases 2010* (WHO 2011).

20　*The Growing Danger of Non-communicable Diseases: Acting Now to Reverse Course* (World Bank 2011).

ited capacity to enforce the regulation of advertising and sales. Increasingly, dangerous levels of fats, sugar, and salt are found in highly processed foods and beverages. These products are often marketed in developing countries by multinational corporations—the new vectors of preventable disease.

Legal frameworks and the law have the capacity to regulate marketing and require the disclosure of product contents and potential impacts, enabling consumers to make more informed choices. The UN Committee on Economic, Social, and Cultural Rights (CESCR) has emphasized that positive measures are required in order to satisfy the right to health. CESCR stipulates that the right to health, like all human rights, imposes three types or levels of obligations on state parties: the obligations to respect, protect, and fulfill.[21] The obligation to fulfill requires states, inter alia, to take positive measures that enable and help individuals and communities to enjoy the right to health, including by ensuring that the state meets its obligations in the dissemination of appropriate information relating to healthy lifestyles and nutrition and the availability of services; and by supporting people in making informed choices about their health.[22]

The CESCR also stipulates that violations of the obligation to protect the right to health include the failure of a state to "take all necessary measures to safeguard persons within their jurisdiction from infringements of the right to health by third parties." This encompasses omissions such as

> the failure to regulate the activities of individuals, groups or corporations so as to prevent them from violating the right to health of others; the failure to protect consumers and workers from practices detrimental to health, e.g. by . . . the failure to discourage production, marketing and consumption of tobacco . . . and other harmful substances.[23]

Limited liability corporations are legal creations: tobacco, alcohol, food, and beverage corporations are all subject to legal regulation. To be effective, 21st-century national and global health policy must have a firm grip on national and international law.[24] The WHO Framework Convention on Tobacco Control, to which there are 176 parties, is a concrete expression of the opportunities

---

21   The obligation to respect requires states to refrain from interfering directly or indirectly with the enjoyment of the right to health. The obligation to protect requires states to take measures that prevent third parties from interfering with the guarantees espoused in the International Covenant on Economic, Social, and Cultural Rights, art. 12. Committee on Economic, Social, and Cultural Rights, General Comment No. 14, Substantive Issues Arising in the Implementation of the International Covenant on Economic, Social and Cultural Rights, The Right to the Highest Attainable Standard of Health (Article 12 of the International Covenant on Economic, Social and Cultural Rights), E/C.12/2000/4, para. 33.

22   *Id.*, at para. 37.

23   *Id.*, at para. 51.

24   See Roger Magnusson & David Patterson, *Role of Law in Global Response to Non-communicable Diseases*, 378 Lancet 859–860 (Sept. 2011).

offered by anchoring global health policy in international law.[25] Yet there is limited national capacity to implement the convention, and tobacco companies employ the brightest and most highly paid lawyers to challenge governments in the courts on proposals to limit tobacco advertising and sales. Tobacco companies are entrenched in developing country societies via financing for sporting, education, music, and youth events—all areas subject to legal regulation.

The Australian Tobacco Plain Packaging Act 2011 strips all branding from cigarette packaging and requires boxes to be a dull green color with a large health warning and a photo of health damage caused by smoking. In 2012, the High Court of Australia rejected two challenges to this legislation on the grounds of the breach of intellectual property rights: *British American Tobacco Australasia Limited and Ors v. Commonwealth of Australia* and *J T International SA v. Commonwealth of Australia*. Philip Morris Asia then took action in the Permanent Court of Arbitration, alleging that the Tobacco Plain Packaging Act breaches the 1993 Agreement between the Government of Australia and the Government of Hong Kong SAR, China for the Promotion and Protection of Investments.[26]

Litigation to promote tobacco control is not limited to OECD countries. Full-page color tobacco advertisements in magazines placed by Philip Morris Pakistan were found to violate the Prohibition of Smoking in Enclosed Places and Protection of Non-smokers Health Ordinance of 2002. Although the court found against Philip Morris Pakistan, the punishment was minimal: a small fine and a warning that the director of marketing would face up to three months in jail for a second offense.[27]

An example from Bangladesh demonstrates the impact of strong civil society engagement on public health and law. Work for a Better Bangladesh is a civil society organization that holds public awareness activities, mobilizes citizens to report violations of the Smoking and Tobacco Product Usage (Control) Act of 2005, and works with mobile courts to ensure enforcement of this law.[28] Civil society lobbying in Bangladesh was a significant catalyst for the 2013 amendment of the Smoking and Tobacco Product Usage (Control) Act of 2005. The amended law adds tough tobacco control measures, including measures related to smokeless tobacco products. These include a comprehensive ban on tobacco advertisement, promotion, and sponsorship; a ban on sale to and by minors; pictorial health warnings on tobacco packages; and a ban on the use of misleading descriptors (like *light* and *mild*) on tobacco packs. The law

---

25   *See* http://www.who.int/fctc/signatories_parties/en/.

26   Australian Government, Attorney General's Department, *Investor-State Arbitration: Tobacco Plain Packaging*, available at http://www.ag.gov.au/Internationalrelations/InternationalLaw/Pages/Tobaccoplainpackaging.aspx.

27   *The State of Pakistan v. Tarar* (Mar. 20, 2012), available at http://www.tobaccocontrollaws.org/litigation/advancedsearch/?type_litigation=Government%20Enforcement%20Action.

28   *See* http://www.wbbtrust.org/.

applies to products consumed by a majority of Bangladeshis: powdered tobacco (*gul*) and chewing tobacco (*jorda* and *khoinee*).[29]

Many developing country governments still seek to maintain tight control of civil society organizations: freedom of speech and association and access to legal and other information are often limited. A 2013 study of the legal responses to overweight, obesity, and diabetes in four countries in the Middle East and North Africa found some governments unwilling to share even basic information on relevant legal frameworks. The research also revealed concerns about the lack of effective legislative frameworks and their implementation. In Tunisia, for example, a 2008 decree on food product labeling was largely ignored by the food industry: 700 out of 750 processed food products surveyed in 2010 had no or inadequate labeling.[30] The study also noted the lack of legal sector capacity to support public health legal and policy reform in the region.

Other Populations: Persons with Disabilities

The global increase in NCDs has seen a related increase in disabilities. In Mexico, for example, diabetes is the leading cause of blindness and a primary cause of amputations. Disability-related discrimination is of growing concern. The International Diabetes Federation identified addressing discrimination as one of the three objectives of its Global Diabetes Plan 2011–2021.[31]

People with disabilities face discrimination in employment, housing, and access to goods and services. Promoting equality and health requires addressing stigma, discrimination, and abuse in health care settings. Even when there is no outright denial of services, mistreatment or fear of mistreatment by health care professionals undermines public health initiatives by discouraging people from seeking the care that they need.

The Convention on the Rights of Persons with Disabilities provides significant opportunities for developing an enabling legal environment on disability rights.[32] The convention reflects the shift away from a medical model of disability to an interactive social model, enriching understanding of how to promote health and equality.

The interaction between HIV and disability is a compelling example of how social factors, inequity and discrimination, and health status interact. In its discussion of disability and HIV, UNAIDS, WHO, and OHCHR note:

---

29 *See* http://www.fctc.org/index.php/news-blog-list-view-of-all-214/opinion-pieces/1007 -positives-outweigh-negatives-in-bangladeshs-amended-tobacco-control-law.

30 *Report on Law and NCDs in MENA Region: Overweight, Obesity and Diabetes* (IDLO, Ain Shams University, Center for Development Services 2013), available at http://www.idlo.int /healthlaw.

31 *Global Diabetes Plan 2011–2021* (International Diabetes Federation 2011).

32 Convention on the Rights of Persons with Disabilities, GA Res 61/106, UN Doc A/RES/61/106 (Dec. 13, 2006) (hereinafter, CRPD).

The Convention does not explicitly refer to HIV or AIDS in the definition of disability. However, States are required to recognize that where persons living with HIV (asymptomatic or symptomatic) have impairments which, in interaction with the environment, results in stigma, discrimination or other barriers to their participation, they can fall under the protection of the Convention. States parties to the Convention are required to ensure that national legislation complies with this understanding of disability. Some countries have accorded protection to people living with HIV under national disability legislation.[33]

The HIV incidence among people with disabilities has been found to be three times higher than that among people without disabilities in some studies. Factors that increase the risk of HIV infection for people with disabilities include a higher risk of violence and lack of legal protection; lack of sexual health education, including information about HIV prevention and safe sex; and barriers to prevention methods such as condoms, often based on false assumptions that people with disabilities are not sexually active.[34]

Women with disabilities suffer significantly higher rates of violence than men with disabilities and women without disabilities. The Convention on the Rights of Persons with Disabilities recognizes "that women and girls with disabilities are often at greater risk, both within and outside the home, of violence, injury or abuse."[35] The International Network of Women with Disabilities notes that "violence against women and girls with disabilities is not just a subset of gender-based violence: it is an intersectional category dealing with gender-based and disability-based violence."[36] In 2012, the UN special rapporteur on violence against women noted that "social sanctions relating to poverty, race/ethnicity, religion, language and other identity status or life experiences can further increase the risk of group or individual violence against women with disabilities."[37]

In much of the developing world, legal aid services are absent, or scarce and under-resourced. Legal professionals who work on disability rights may not be familiar with the issues that arise for women with disabilities. Women's legal aid organizations may not have a specific background in disability, and services are often not provided in a way that is logistically or structurally ac-

---

33   UNAIDS, WHO, and OHCHR, *Policy Brief: Disability and HIV* 1 (Apr. 2009), available at http://www.who.int/disabilities/jc1632_policy_brief_disability_en.pdf.

34   Human Rights Watch, *Fact Sheet: HIV and Disability* (2011), available at http://www.hrw.org/news/2011/06/08/fact-sheet-hivaids-and-disability.

35   CRPD, *supra* note 32, preamble (q).

36   International Network of Women with Disabilities, *Violence against Women with Disabilities: Barbara Faye Waxman Fiduccia Papers on Women and Girls with Disabilities* 2 (Center for Women Policy Studies, Washington DC 2011) (hereinafter, INWWD paper), available at http://www2.ohchr.org/english/issues/women/docs/VAWHRC20/OtherEntities/INWD.pdf.

37   Rashida Manjoo, *Report of the Special Rapporteur on Violence against Women, Its Causes and Consequences*, A/67/227, para. 20 (2012).

cessible to women with disabilities. Legal professionals may also find that they have to address their own stereotypical and stigmatizing beliefs about the marginalized and stigmatized groups they work with. Of particular importance, legal professionals must understand how intersectional or compounded discrimination affects their clients.

Report of the Special Rapporteur on Torture, 2012

The United Nations special rapporteur on torture has noted that

> some women may experience multiple forms of discrimination on the basis of their sex and other status or identity. Targeting ethnic and racial minorities, women from marginalized communities and women with disabilities for involuntary sterilization because of discriminatory notions that they are "unfit" to bear children is an increasingly global problem. Forced sterilization is an act of violence, a form of social control, and a violation of the right to be free from torture and other cruel, inhuman, or degrading treatment or punishment. . . .

> [There are people with disabilities] either neglected or detained in psychiatric and social care institutions, psychiatric wards, prayer camps, secular and religious-based therapeutic boarding schools, boot camps, private residential treatment centres. . . . Severe abuses, such as neglect, mental and physical abuse and sexual violence, continue to be committed against people with psychosocial disabilities and people with intellectual disabilities in health-care settings.*

* Juan E. Mendez, *Report of the Special Rapporteur on Torture and Other Cruel, Inhuman or Degrading Treatment or Punishment*, A/HRC/22/53 (2013), paras. 48 and 57.

People with disabilities often have limited awareness of the law, the legal system, and their rights. Furthermore, people with disabilities may not know how to claim their rights or whom to report to for the purposes of initiating a complaint process.

Violations of the reproductive rights of women with disabilities—such as involuntary sterilization and coercive family planning practices—in health care settings and other institutional settings are a particularly egregious example of discrimination and abuse in health care settings. The UN special rapporteur on violence against women has stated that "research shows that no group has ever been as severely restricted, or negatively treated, in respect of their reproductive rights, as women with disabilities."[38]

---

38   *Id.*, para. 28. For a more detailed national-level documentation of these violations, *see*, for example, Women with Disabilities Australia, *Dehumanised: The Forced Sterilisation of Women and Girls with Disabilities in Australia* (WWDA Submission to the Senate Inquiry into the In-

Violence against Women with Disabilities

Discrimination and violence against people with disabilities often occur in institutional settings. A 2011 study found that

> researchers and policy makers rarely identify situations, such as physical abandonment or psychological cruelty, as maltreatment. Further, if an intervention is made in a situation where the violence was perpetrated by a personal assistant, a family member or a friend, the incident is often addressed only by the social service system and is rarely considered to be a crime that should be addressed by the police and/or the criminal justice system. There is a lack of credibility accorded to women who require assistive communication or reasonable accommodation in communication and to women who have already been labelled with a psychiatric diagnosis or an intellectual disability.*

* International Network of Women with Disabilities, *Violence against Women with Disabilities: Barbara Faye Waxman Fiduccia Papers on Women and Girls with Disabilities* (Center for Women Policy Studies, Washington, DC 2011), 8.

Access to High-Quality, Affordable Medicines

Multiple legal issues affect the availability of high-quality, affordable medicines in developing countries. These include intellectual property law frameworks that regulate the production, importation, and sale of research-based and generic pharmaceutical products; the growing problem of falsified and substandard medicines; drug theft and illegal diversion of legitimate products; and limited or no access to drugs for pain relief and palliative care.

Challenges involve international legal frameworks, national legislation and regulations, and justice sector capacity to adapt and apply these frameworks. As with other areas of health law, multisectoral approaches are required, involving ministries of health, justice, trade, and finance. The experience in scaling up access to medicines for the treatment of HIV infection has shown that the engagement of civil society organizations and representatives of affected communities in law and policy reform is crucial. Litigation can also be a tool in expanding access to medicines.[39]

---

voluntary or Coerced Sterilisation of People with Disabilities in Australia, Mar. 2013), available at http://www.wwda.org.au/sterilise2011.htm.

39 Hans V. Hogerzeil, Melanie Samson, & Jaume Vidal Casanova, *Ruling for Access: Leading Court Cases in Developing Countries on Access to Essential Medicines as Part of the Fulfilment of the Right to Health* (WHO 2004), available at http://www.who.int/medicines/areas/human _rights/Details_on_20_court_cases.pdf.

Intellectual Property Law

World Trade Organization member states (159 as of March 2013) are required to amend their national intellectual property legislation to comply with the Agreement on Trade–Related Aspects of Intellectual Property Rights (TRIPS). This agreement, although generally protecting the rights of patent holders, provides specific exceptions for pharmaceutical products under certain circumstances. TRIPS permits national legislation to provide for compulsory licenses for the production or importation of generic medicines. These medicines may be available at substantially lower prices than the equivalent product from the patent holder, usually the research-based pharmaceutical company that developed the product. This is a complex and evolving area of international law, and developing countries need support to ensure that their national legislation and procedures take full account of the flexibilities provided by TRIPS to provide high-quality, affordable medicines for the prevention and treatment of diseases of public health significance.[40]

In April 2013, the Indian Supreme Court repudiated "ever-greening," the practice of extending patents for nonessential changes to existing patented drugs. The case involved a patent application for a reformulation of a cancer drug, Gleevec, by the pharmaceutical company Novartis. The Indian Supreme Court acknowledged Novartis's intellectual property rights but limited these rights in reference to the right to health. The court's reference to Article 7 of TRIPS, which links intellectual property to a nation's welfare, set an important national and international precedent.[41]

There has been strong civil society advocacy on intellectual property and access to medicines in both India and Thailand, which has played a considerable role in shaping the debate on access to medicines.

Falsified and Substandard Medicines

Developing countries face a flood of falsified and substandard medicines.[42] Organized crime has permeated the pharmaceutical market, and this illicit trade is transnational, lucrative, and extensive. The results are devastating for patients and their families. Multiple drug-resistant strains of bacteria and parasites resulting from substandard antibiotics and other drugs pose a global public health threat. Ineffective and dangerous products risk undermining public confidence in research-based and generic pharmaceutical industries and even science-based medicine over the longer term. Factors contributing to this assault on public health include a lack of communication between

---

40 See, for example, *Improving Access to Treatment by Utilizing Public Health Flexibilities in the WTO TRIPS Agreement* (UNDP 2010).

41 See Irene Khan, *Putting Intellectual Property to Good Use*, Huffington Post (Apr. 29, 2013).

42 In this chapter, the term *falsified and substandard medicines* is used rather than *spurious/falsely labelled/falsified/counterfeit (SFFC)* to distinguish between medicines that are harmful to the public health—substandard and falsified—and those that infringe on a registered trademark—counterfeit. *See* Lawrence O. Gostin et al., *Stemming the Global Trade in Falsified and Substandard Medicines*, 309(16) JAMA 1693 (2013).

relevant ministries and departments (health, justice, police, customs, and others), weak legal and regulatory frameworks, and a lack of resources and skills to prosecute and convict.

Although these products may involve copyright infringement, it is now generally recognized that criminal law, rather than intellectual property law, is the preferred framework for addressing the problem. The penalties under national law for copyright infringement often do not reflect the grave consequences of these crimes for individual and population health. Where serious injury and loss of life are likely to result, penalties including heavy fines and lengthy terms of imprisonment are appropriate.

In October 2011, the Council of Europe Council of Ministers opened for signature the Convention on the Counterfeiting of Medical Products and Similar Crimes Involving Threats to Public Health (the Medicrime Convention).[43] The convention expressly excludes issues related to intellectual property rights and proposes criminal sanctions for offenses, including manufacturing, supplying, and trafficking in fraudulent and substandard medical products. Where trade is undertaken by criminal organizations, the convention proposes that this be taken into account as an aggravating factor in sentencing, providing for even tougher penalties.

The Commission on Crime Prevention and Criminal Justice has recommended that the United Nations Convention against Transnational Organized Crime (TOC) be invoked to reinforce international cooperation in response to falsified and substandard medicines. Mechanisms may include mutual legal assistance, extradition, and recovery of the proceeds of crime.[44]

Where states impose maximum terms of imprisonment of four years or more for crimes related to falsified and substandard medicines, and where the offenses are transnational in nature and involve organized criminal groups, the TOC provides a framework for regional and international cooperation to address transnational organized crime, which is essential to a comprehensive global response to the problem. It is therefore important that state legislation provide for sufficient and appropriate penalties to allow the TOC to operate in this field.[45]

Drug Theft and Illegal Diversion of Medicines

A related issue is the theft and sale of medicines intended for public sector programs. In April 2011, Africa Fighting Malaria, an NGO in South Africa, reported that antimalaria drugs (specifically artemisinin-based combination therapies), which had originally been obtained for public sector distribution, were increasingly appearing for sale in the private sector.[46] In December 2011,

---

43   See http://www.edqm.eu/en/the-medicrime-convention-1470.html.

44   Commission on Crime Prevention and Criminal Justice, Resolution 20/6 (2011).

45   *Counterfeit Medicines and Organized Crime* (UNICRI 2012).

46   Roger Bate, *Partners in Crime: National Theft of Global Fund Medicines* (briefing paper, Africa

the Global Fund to Fight AIDS, Tuberculosis, and Malaria convened an international consultation on drug theft. The recommendations of that meeting called for strengthened law enforcement, specifically for stakeholders to "[w]ork with law enforcement to promote advocacy and awareness of consequences of theft. Consider partnering with law enforcement to strengthen chain of custody controls. Remove barriers to prosecution, and cooperate on investigations and prosecutions."[47]

Capacity building is needed, including for police, prosecutors, and the judiciary. Given that stolen drugs often appear in neighboring countries or farther afield, the TOC may provide a framework for strengthened international cooperation. Most important, however, is that all parties understand the implications for public health beyond the monetary value of stolen medicines, and hence the importance of appropriate penalties as a deterrent. Just as with falsified drugs, an interrupted supply of essential medicines due to theft will lead to increased morbidity and mortality and increased risk of drug resistance.

Access to Drugs for Pain Relief and Palliative Care

A 2008 study by the International Narcotics Control Board (INCB) found that per capita morphine consumption in Africa was almost 20 times less than the global average (0.33 mg per capita compared with 5.98 mg).[48] Morphine, the main opioid treatment for pain, is relatively affordable and easy to administer. However, because of its status as a controlled medicine, many countries have legal and regulatory barriers to access. Only a handful of African countries have palliative care polices. Factors limiting access also include

- burdensome prescription procedures and limits on the length of opioid prescriptions that result in repeated visits to doctors by patients or family members, draining human and financial resources;

- limitations on the right to prescribe opioids to specialists or to doctors, which undermines access in countries that have a shortage of doctors and rely on midlevel providers, such as clinical officers and nurses, for the majority of health care provision; and

- invasive and stigmatizing surveillance of patients receiving opioids and of health care workers handling controlled substances, which can deter patients from seeking care and health care workers from providing it.

A 2010 study on cancer treatment by the Union for International Cancer Control (UICC) and partners confirmed the observations of the INCB study and highlighted the critical role of the law in facilitating access to health care.

Fighting Malaria, 2011).

47   *High Level Meeting: Theft and Illegal Diversion of Medicines: Meeting Report* (Global Fund to Fight AIDS, Tuberculosis and Malaria 2011).

48   International Narcotics Control Board, *Narcotic Drugs: Estimated World Requirements for 2008 — Statistics for 2006* (United Nations 2008).

The study canvassed 81 countries, representing 87 percent of the global population.[49] Another study by the UICC Global Access to Pain Relief Initiative
(GAPRI) estimated that worldwide, in 2010, at least 2.9 million people died of
HIV or cancer in untreated pain, with 99 percent of these deaths occurring in
developing countries.[50]

The UN special rapporteur on torture and other cruel, inhuman or degrading treatment or punishment has noted that obstacles that unnecessarily
impede access to morphine and adversely affect its availability include overly
restrictive drug control regulations and, more frequently, misinterpretation of
otherwise appropriate regulations.[51]

Innovative approaches are needed to overcome the legal obstacles to pain
relief and palliative care, including capacity building of both medical and legal professionals to understand current legislative frameworks and their limitations, and the sharing of good practices in the prescription and monitoring
of morphine and other drugs for pain relief.

Health and Rights of People of Diverse Sexual Orientation and Gender Identity

In 1994, the United Nations Human Rights Committee, which monitors global
compliance with the International Covenant on Civil and Political Rights, determined that criminal laws prohibiting consensual sex in private between
men were in breach of the covenant.[52] The committee specifically rejected the
suggestion that such laws were needed to prevent the spread of HIV.

In 2009, the Delhi High Court reached a similar conclusion regarding section 377 of the Indian Penal Code (which criminalized same-sex behavior).
The court declared the provision unconstitutional and noted that a human
rights approach protecting the rights of vulnerable populations is critical to
HIV prevention.[53]

In 2011, the United Nations Human Rights Council adopted the first resolution on "human rights, sexual orientation and gender identity" (SOGI).[54]

---

49   See European Society for Medical Oncology, *First International Survey on the Availability of
     Opioids for Cancer Pain Management* (2010), available at http://www.esmo.org/Policy/Interna-
     tional-Access-to-Opioids-Survey.

50   Global Access to Pain Relief Initiative (GAPRI), *Access to Essential Pain Medicines Brief* (2010),
     available at http://www.gapri.org/understand-problem.

51   WHO estimates that in 2012, 5.5 billion people were living in countries with low or no access
     to controlled medicines and had no or insufficient access to treatment for moderate to severe
     pain. Juan E. Mendez, *Report of the Special Rapporteur on Torture and Other Cruel, Inhuman or
     Degrading Treatment or Punishment*, A/HRC/22/53, paras. 51–56 (2013).

52   *Toonen v. Australia*, CCPR/C/50/D/488/1992, UN Human Rights Committee (Apr. 4, 1994).

53   *Naz Foundation and Others v. Government of NCT of Delhi and Others*, High Court of Delhi at
     New Delhi (July 2, 2009).

54   Human Rights Council, *Human Rights, Sexual Orientation and Gender Identity*, A/HRC/

These rights were also highlighted in the 2012 report of the United Nations Global Commission on HIV and the Law. The report recognized that legal frameworks that criminalize consensual same-sex sexual relations do serious harm, perpetuating discrimination and isolating those most vulnerable so that they cannot access the preventive or curative health services they critically need.[55]

Notwithstanding the recognition of SOGI-related rights at an international level, the issue remains a sensitive topic in many countries.[56] Contextual and structural factors entrench the sensitivity of the issue and amplify the vulnerability of people of diverse SOGI. These factors include poverty and inequality; stigma and discrimination; cultural impediments to sex education and sexual discourse; marginalization; violence; and social exclusion.

Most notable is the effect of stigma and discrimination on access to disease prevention and treatment services. People of diverse SOGI may be reluctant to seek medical assistance, fearing stigma, discrimination, and breaches of confidentiality. Accordingly, stigma and discrimination against people of diverse SOGI often results in exclusion from mainstream health programs, which may have significant consequences for a person's long-term health and enhance the person's isolation. Poor health is likely to result in lower social engagement, reduced capacity to work, and reduced ability to contribute to society, as well as increasing isolation. In parallel, exclusion from public health programs has significant public health consequences. Proper treatments for HIV and sexually transmitted infections and the use of condoms can effectively limit transmission. Stigma and discrimination are compounded by punitive and discriminatory legal frameworks, the criminalization of same-sex sexual relations, and law enforcement practices.[57] In this context, these populations are less likely to access health care services.[58]

Effective prevention, treatment, care, and support services for these populations for HIV and other diseases require consideration of their life course and specific vulnerabilities, as well as consideration of the broader environments that affect the delivery of and access to health services. Health care services cannot be effectively delivered to populations hiding from formal or

---

RES/17/19 (July 14, 2011). *See* also Human Rights Council, Discriminatory Laws and Practices and Acts of Violence against Individuals Based on Their Sexual Orientation and Gender Identity, A/HRC/19/41 (2011).

55   *Risks, Rights and Health: Report of the Global Commission on HIV and the Law* 44–48 (UNDP 2012).

56   *See,* for example, Shereen El Feki, *Sex and the Citadel: Intimate Life in a Changing Arab World* (Pantheon 2013).

57   John Godwin, *Legal Environments, Human Rights and HIV Responses among Men Who Have Sex with Men and Transgender People in Asia and the Pacific: An Agenda for Action* (UNDP & Asia Pacific Coalition on Male Sexual Health [ASPCOM] 2010), available at http://regionalcentre bangkok.undp.or.th/practices/hivaids/documents/874_UNDP_final.pdf.

58   *Id.*

state systems because of punitive laws or fear of stigma, discrimination, or prosecution.

The Supreme Court of Nepal addressed the rights of people of diverse SOGI, specifically transgender people, in the 2007 case of *Sunil Babu Pant v. Government of Nepal*. The Supreme Court judgment focuses on the exclusion of transgender people (*metis*). *Metis* were routinely denied citizenship cards, precluding their access to a range of entitlements and public services. The Court emphasized that people of the third gender were entitled to all rights protected by the constitution and international law and ordered that *metis* be given citizenship cards that reflected their gender (as the third gender). The Court further ordered that protections against discrimination on the basis of gender identity and nondiscrimination be enshrined in the new constitution, stating it was the "responsibility of the State to create the appropriate environment and make legal provisions accordingly for the enjoyment of such rights."[59]

In 2012–13, research was undertaken by national human rights institutions (NHRIs) in seven South and Southeast Asian countries to document responses to SOGI rights in the context of HIV.[60] This research noted that NHRIs with the most developed capacity to address SOGI-related rights had a number of common characteristics. These included, but were not limited to, strong and open leadership, the presence of an institutional focal point on SOGI or HIV (or on marginalized or vulnerable groups), and the commitment to communication with civil society, government, and multilateral stakeholders. The study emphasized that a critical factor for catalyzing NHRI engagement on the rights of people of diverse SOGI is the efforts of civil society and the community of people of diverse SOGI. Based on the countries studied, community unity and leadership, combined with diplomatic and persistent advocacy on the rights of people of diverse SOGI, give rise to productive relationships with NHRIs and foster ongoing collaboration and partnership.

In October 2012, at a dialogue of the community of people of diverse SOGI and the National Human Rights Commission (NHRC) of Bangladesh (under the above-mentioned initiative), NHRC Bangladesh announced that, for the first time, it had advocated for the rights of people of diverse SOGI in its submission under the universal periodic review process. The submission of NHRC Bangladesh stated:

> Excluded groups (including Dalits and transgenders) remain some
> of the poorest people in Bangladesh and face marginalization and

---

59   International Community of Jurists, *Casebook on Sexual Orientation and Gender Identity*, ch. 2, available at http://www.icj.org/sogi-casebook-introduction/chapter-two-universality -equality-and-non-discrimination/.

60   IDLO, UNDP, & Asia Pacific Forum of National Human Rights Institutions, *Assessing the Capacity of National Human Rights Institutions to Address Human Rights in Relation to Sexual Orientation, Gender Identity and HIV* (2013) (NRHI SOGI Project). The NHRI SOGI Project aimed to build understanding of the capacity and response of selected Asian national human rights institutions to the human rights issues faced by people of diverse SOGI.

discrimination. In addition the NHRC Bangladesh notes that the Government of Bangladesh did not respect the recommendation with respect to sexual minorities. The NHRC Bangladesh understands the need for the law to be in harmony with the cultural and social mores of the people. Nevertheless, the NHRC Bangladesh believes that it is now time to ensure that all groups, including those who are transgender, intersex or sexual minority, are protected from discrimination.[61]

Research in Asia and the Pacific has also shown that legal environments that are protective and empowering can help combat stigma and discrimination and underpin health promotion efforts that rely on the voluntary cooperation of populations in changing behaviors and accessing health services.[62]

In 2011, Brazil's Supreme Court ruled that same-sex unions were legal and that same-sex couples are entitled to the same rights as heterosexual couples, including health, pension, and inheritance benefits. In addition, under a legal framework developed by Brazil's Federal Medicine Council, the Brazilian public health system provides free sex-change operations.[63] The adaptation of the legal environment to the needs of diverse populations can thus facilitate their access to health care services.

Globally and regionally, lawyers and public health activists are sharing experiences and strategies to advance the health rights of diverse communities. In 2012, at the Asia Pacific Regional Consultation on HIV-Related Legal Services and Rights, lawyers from Vietnam and China described their work to obtain personal identification documents for clients so they could access health services.[64] Although every country is different, there is great value in recognizing the common challenges and in sharing creative solutions to assuring the right to health for diverse populations.

Conclusion: Health, Diverse Communities, and the Law

The right to health is an important avenue through which associated rights, such as the right to equality and nondiscrimination, the right to an adequate standard of living, the right to freedom from torture, the right to privacy, and the freedoms of thought and conscience, speech and expression, can be advanced. Even when other human rights of diverse populations may be

---

61   For all periodic review reports for Bangladesh, *see* http://www.ohchr.org/EN/HRBodies/ UPR/Pages/BDSession16.aspx.

62   Godwin, *supra* note 58.

63   *See* http://www.as-coa.org/articles/explainer-lgbt-rights-latin-america-and-caribbean.

64   IDLO, *Report of the Asia Pacific Consultation on HIV-Related Legal Services and Rights* (2012), available at http://www.idlo.int/Publications/120318AsiaPacificHIV.pdf. Since 2009, IDLO has conducted 11 international and regional consultations on HIV-related legal services and rights. *See* http://www.idlo.int/healthlaw.

rejected, public health goals tend to be accepted and recognized in both the developed and the developing world.[65]

Experience in the context of HIV provides valuable lessons for protecting and promoting the right to health for diverse communities. Not only do all human rights affect the realization of the right to health, but also health can be an entry point for addressing other rights of diverse communities. Multisectoral approaches are essential—not only at the national level, for example, in government and academia, but at regional and international levels among intergovernmental organizations and donor agencies. Regional and international collaboration is also essential to address the threats to global health posed by transnational organized crime. The legal issues are increasingly complex. There are growing limitations on national sovereignty to legislate on health matters due to increasingly stringent international legal frameworks to promote trade and investment.

The experience in multiple regions and contexts has led to the conclusion that an enabling legal environment is essential to protect and promote the right to health for diverse communities. There are also broader public health and economic benefits of preventing and treating infectious and noncommunicable diseases.

There is an urgent need for capacity building in public health law based on human rights. This should include collaboration in research and teaching among university faculties of law, medicine, and other health sciences and the active involvement of civil society organizations representing people living with health conditions and those most vulnerable. Above all, civil society organizations representing communities most affected must be engaged in policy development and program implementation.

---

65 See David Patterson, Shereen El Feki, & Khadija Moalla, *Rights-Based Approaches to HIV in the Middle East and North Africa Region*, in *Current Legal Issues* vol. 16 (Oxford U. Press forthcoming).

The Right to Health and Development

The Case of Uganda

SIOBHÁN MCINERNEY-LANKFORD AND MOSES MULUMBA

Improved health is both a factor and an outcome of sustainable development.[1] This chapter explores the right to health as a development priority and the role of the law in advancing it, particularly for the poorest and most vulnerable in developing countries. It draws on approaches that argue for a human rights paradigm as a means of linking health with laws, policies, and practices that underpin sustainable development and foster accountability.[2] It analyzes the interface of human rights law[3] and development and presents the right to health as an example of the convergence between human rights and development and the ways in which the respect, protection, and fulfillment of human rights can help secure the conditions for people to live in dignity. Notwithstanding the still-contested parameters of the right to health,[4] this chapter builds on the growing body of literature that asserts the centrality of the right to health in shaping health policy and the delivery of health services around the world.[5] The chapter draws on the legal content of the right to health to suggest ways in which human rights can add value to development policies and programs.[6]

The authors thank Nathan Lankford and Alicia Yamin, for comments on earlier drafts of this chapter, and Christian Jimenez Tomas and James Samuel Zeere for research assistance. Responsibility for errors or omissions remains with the authors. The views expressed in this article are those of the authors and do not necessarily reflect the views of the Board of Executive Directors of the World Bank or the governments they represent.

1   This chapter emanates from a panel on the Health Law and Rights Access to Justice and Inclusion for Society's Most Marginalized Populations, during the 2012 World Bank Law, Justice and Development Week; Opportunity, Inclusion, and Equity, in which the authors participated as chair and panelist, respectively.

2   UN System Task Team on the Post-2015 UN Development Agenda, *Health in the Post 2015 UN Development Agenda—Thematic Think Piece UNAIDS, UNICEF, UNFPA and WHO* (May 2012), 8: "Health as a contributor to the achievement of sustainability goals; health as a potential beneficiary of sustainable development; and health as a way of measuring progress across all three pillars of sustainable development policy." *See* A. Yamin, *The Right to Health under International Law and Its Relevance to the United States,* 95(7) Am. J. Pub. Health 1156–1161 (2005).

3   This chapter does not seek to engage in the moral and political philosophy discussions that have burgeoned around the right to health and retains a focus on international law and its potential value added to development and health policy.

4   *See* J. Ruger, *Towards a Theory of a Right to Health: Capability and Incomplete Theorized Agreements,* 18 Yale J.L. & Hum. Rights 273; B. Toebes, *The Right to Health as a Human Right in International Law* (Intersentia 1998).

5   J. Harrington & M. Stuttaford eds., *Global Health and Human Rights* (Routledge 2010).

6   Anand Grover, *Report of the Special Rapporteur on the Right of Everyone to the Enjoyment of the Highest Attainable Standard of Physical and Mental Health,* A/HRC/17/25 (Apr. 12, 2011).

This chapter charts the contours of the right to health under international law, examining the meaning of this right as a normative goal as well as its potential instrumental role for other goals, particularly poverty reduction and the attainment of the Millennium Development Goals (MDGs), half of which relate to health. The chapter explores in preliminary terms what such a legal norm could offer to the pursuit of health goals in development policy and programming at the international level and the domestic levels, using Uganda as an example. The chapter examines how the legal provision of the right to health affects the protection of poor people's access to health services, including through constitutional health rights litigation. Using the example of Uganda, the analysis considers how a substantive constitutional provision enshrining the right to health defines the role of the state in guaranteeing health rights and empowers the public and civil society to enforce those rights. It looks specifically at the litigation of maternal health rights in a developing country, which lacks a substantive constitutional provision on the right to health, to assess the value of formal and enforceable legal protection for a human right.

Right to Health under International Law

In this chapter, "right to health"[7] is employed as shorthand for the right of everyone to the enjoyment of the highest attainable standard of physical and mental health,[8] as enshrined in the World Health Organization (WHO) Constitution,[9] Article 25 of the Universal Declaration of Human Rights (UDHR), Article 12 of the International Covenant on Economic, Social, and Cultural Rights (ICESCR),[10] and a range of other international human rights treaties, such as, the International Convention on the Elimination of All

---

7   *See,* generally, J. Wolff, *The Human Right to Health* (Norton 2012).

8   *See,* generally, J. Tobin, *The Right to Health in International Law* (Oxford U. Press 2011).

9   Preamble, Constitution of the World Health Organization (1948). The constitution was adopted by the International Health Conference held in New York June 19 to July 22, 1946, signed on July 22, 1946, by the representatives of sixty-one states (Off. Rec. World Health Org., 2, 100), and entered into force on April 7, 1948.

10   Art. 12:

     1. The States Parties to the present Covenant recognize the right of everyone to the enjoyment of the highest attainable standard of physical and mental health.

     2. The steps to be taken by the States Parties to the present Covenant to achieve the full realization of this right shall include those necessary for:

          (a) The provision for the reduction of the stillbirth-rate and of infant mortality and for the healthy development of the child;

          (b) The improvement of all aspects of environmental and industrial hygiene;

          (c) The prevention, treatment and control of epidemic, endemic, occupational and other diseases;

          (d) The creation of conditions which would assure to all medical service and medical attention in the event of sickness.

     Adopted December 16, 1966; entry into force January 3, 1976, in accordance with art. 27, U.N.T.S.; I.L.M.

Forms of Racial Discrimination,[11] the Convention to Eliminate All Forms of Discrimination Against Women (CEDAW),[12] the Convention on the Rights of the Child (CRC),[13] the International Convention on the Protection of the Rights of All Migrant Workers and Members of Their Families (MWC),[14] and the Convention on the Rights of Persons with Disabilities (CRPD), as well as regional instruments such as the African Charter on Human and Peoples' Rights,[15] the Protocol of San Salvador,[16] and the European Social Charter.[17] In

---

11 Art. 5(e)(iv) of the International Convention on the Elimination of All Forms of Racial Discrimination of 1965.

12 CEDAW makes several provisions for the protection of a woman's right to health, in particular arts. 11(1)f, 12, and 14(2)b.

13 CRC contains extensive and elaborate provisions on the child's right to health, including art. 24, which is fully dedicated to the right to health of the child, and arts. 3(3), 17, 23, 25, 32, and 28, which contain protections for especially vulnerable groups of children.

14 Art. 25(1): "Migrant workers shall enjoy treatment not less favourable than that which applies to nationals of the State of employment in respect of remuneration and: (a) Other conditions of work, that is to say, overtime, hours of work, weekly rest, holidays with pay, safety, health, termination of the employment relationship and any other conditions of work which, according to national law and practice, are covered by these terms."

Art. 28: "Migrant workers and members of their families shall have the right to receive any medical care that is urgently required for the preservation of their life or the avoidance of irreparable harm to their health on the basis of equality of treatment with nationals of the State concerned. Such emergency medical care shall not be refused them by reason of any irregularity with regard to stay or employment."

15 Art. 16 of the African Charter: "1. Every individual shall have the right to enjoy the best attainable state of physical and mental health. 2. States Parties to the present Charter shall take the necessary measures to protect the health of their people and to ensure that they receive medical attention when they are sick."

16 Additional Protocol to the Interamerican Convention of Human Rights (Protocol of San Salvador).

Art. 10: Right to Health:

1. Everyone shall have the right to health, understood to mean the enjoyment of the highest level of physical, mental and social well-being.

2. In order to ensure the exercise of the right to health, the States Parties agree to recognize health as a public good and, particularly, to adopt the following measures to ensure that right:

    a. Primary health care, that is, essential health care made available to all individuals and families in the community;

    b. Extension of the benefits of health services to all individuals subject to the State's jurisdiction;

    c. Universal immunization against the principal infectious diseases;

    d. Prevention and treatment of endemic, occupational and other diseases;

    e. Education of the population on the prevention and treatment of health problems; and

    f. Satisfaction of the health needs of the highest risk groups and of those whose poverty makes them the most vulnerable.

17 Art. 11: The right to protection of health

With a view to ensuring the effective exercise of the right to protection of health, the Contracting Parties undertake, either directly or in co-operation with public or private organisations, to take appropriate measures designed inter alia:

addition to these treaties, a range of soft law measures such as the Rio Declaration[18] protect particular aspects of the right to health or elaborate on the right in greater detail.[19] For the purposes of this chapter, however, Article 12 of the ICESCR and the processes connected with the covenant are the framework for analysis, providing legally binding provisions that apply to all individuals in the 146 ratifying states.

As the Committee on Economic, Social, and Cultural Rights (CESCR) confirmed in its general comment on the right to health,

> Health is a fundamental human right indispensable for the exercise of other human rights. Every human being is entitled to the enjoyment of the highest attainable standard of health conducive to living a life in dignity. The realization of the right to health may be pursued through numerous, complementary approaches, such as the formulation of health policies, or the implementation of health programmes developed by the World Health Organization (WHO), or the adoption of specific legal instruments. Moreover, the right to health includes certain components which are legally enforceable.[20]

Thus, the right to health is both a freestanding right, and instrumental to, or constitutive of, other rights in that its realization is a prerequisite to the enjoyment or definition of such rights. Without the right to health, the realization of rights to education, work, and a host of civil and political rights as well as other economic, social, and cultural rights is not possible. Conversely, the right to health is closely related to and dependent on a range of other human

---

1. to remove as far as possible the causes of ill health;

2. to provide advisory and educational facilities for the promotion of health and the encouragement of individual responsibility in matters of health;

3. to prevent as far as possible epidemic, endemic and other diseases.

18   Principle 1 of the Rio Declaration: "Human beings are at the centre of concerns for sustainable development. They are entitled to a healthy and productive life in harmony with nature." Health pervades the outcome document of the Rio+20; UNCSD, *The Future We Want,* A/Res/66/288 (Sept. 11, 2012), *see* esp. paras. 138–146.

19   For example, the 1993 Vienna Declaration and Program of Action Principles for the Protection of Persons with Mental Illness and the Improvement of Mental Healthcare and the Declaration on the Elimination of Violence against Women. Resolutions of the commission, including on access to medication (2002/32) and disabilities (2002/61), articulate the right to health, reaffirming its status as a human right. The Programme of Action of the International Conference on Population and Development held in Cairo in 1994, as well as the Declaration and Programme for Action of the Fourth World Conference on Women held in Beijing in 1995, contain definitions of reproductive health and women's health, as well as HR Council and Commission resolutions. For a detailed list of international instruments relevant to the right to health, *see* Paul Hunt, *Report of the Special Rapporteur on the Right to Health to the Commission on Human Rights,* UN Doc. E/CN.4/2003/58 (Feb. 13, 2003), Annex 1.

20   Committee on Economic, Social, and Cultural Rights, General Comment No. 14, Substantive Issues Arising in the Implementation of the International Covenant on Economic, Social, and Cultural Rights, The Right to the Highest Attainable Standard of Health (art. 12 of the International Covenant on Economic, Social, and Cultural Rights), E/C.12/2000/4 (Aug. 11, 2000). For example, the principle of nondiscrimination in relation to health facilities, goods, and services is legally enforceable in numerous national jurisdictions.

rights[21] that are determinants of the right to health, such as access to food, water, sanitation, housing, work, and education; privacy; freedoms of association, assembly, and movement; and nondiscrimination. As such, the right to health under Article 12 of the ICESCR protects health in a strict sense, as well as the underlying determinants of health.

Content of the Right to Health

As with many human rights, defining the normative content of the right to health with precision can be challenging. Nevertheless, the guidance and interpretations of the committee and the special rapporteur are resources that can help provide a definition and extrapolate its content.[22]

> The right to health is not to be understood as a right to be healthy. The right to health contains both freedoms and entitlements. The freedoms include the right to control one's health and body, including sexual and reproductive freedom, and the right to be free from interference, such as the right to be free from torture, non-consensual medical treatment and experimentation. By contrast, the entitlements include the right to a system of health protection which provides equality of opportunity for people to enjoy the highest attainable level of health.[23]

In this way, the right to health implies freedom from interference in the health and well-being of individuals, as well as entitlement to a certain minimum standard of treatment and the provision of essential elements that are underlying determinants of the right to health, such as water and sanitation, food, and housing.

In terms of a practical definition of the content of the right to health, the CESCR has identified four qualitative vectors:[24] availability, accessibility, acceptability, and quality.[25]

---

21 Committee on Economic, Social, and Cultural Rights, General Comment No. 15, Substantive Issues Arising in the Implementation of the International Covenant on Economic, Social, and Cultural Rights, The Right to Water (arts. 11 and 12 of the International Covenant on Economic, Social, and Cultural Rights), E/C.12/2002/11 (Jan. 20, 2003), para. 3.

22 As John Tobin astutely observes, "the act of interpretation is not simply the process of attributing a meaning to the right to health but ultimately an act of persuasion, an attempt to persuade the relevant interpretive community that a particular interpretation of the right to health is the most appropriate meaning to adopt." J. Tobin, *Introduction* 16 (Melbourne Leg. Stud. Research Paper No. 562, 2011).

23 General Comment No. 15, *supra* note 21, at para. 8.

24 General Comment No. 14, *supra* note 20, at para. 12.

25 Note that the WHO, successive Special Rapporteurs on the Right to Health, and others subscribe to this formula.

Availability

Functioning public health and health care facilities, goods, and services, as well as programs, must be available in sufficient quantity within a state. This includes safe and potable drinking water and adequate sanitation facilities; hospitals, clinics, and other health-related buildings; trained medical and professional personnel receiving domestically competitive salaries; and essential drugs, as defined by the WHO Action Programme on Essential Drugs.

Accessibility

Health facilities, goods, and services must be accessible to everyone without discrimination within the jurisdiction of the state. Accessibility has four overlapping dimensions, a number of which have direct relevance for development and health interventions for the poorest and most marginalized: nondiscrimination; physical accessibility; economic accessibility (affordability) such that health facilities, goods, and services are affordable for all; and information accessibility.[26]

Acceptability

All health facilities, goods, and services must be respectful of medical ethics and culturally appropriate. In this, they must be respectful of the culture of individuals, minorities, peoples, and communities and sensitive to gender and life-cycle requirements, as well as being designed to respect confidentiality and improve the health status of those concerned.

Quality

Health facilities, goods, and services must be scientifically and medically appropriate and of good quality. This requires, inter alia, skilled medical personnel, scientifically approved and unexpired drugs and hospital equipment, safe and potable water, and adequate sanitation.

Obligations Arising from Article 12 of the ICESCR

As with all rights enshrined in international human rights treaties, the right to health generates obligations to respect, protect, and fulfill for parties to the covenant.[27] As with other rights in the covenant, the interpretation of the right

---

26   Committee on Economic, Social, and Cultural Rights, General Comment No. 12, Substantive Issues Arising in the Implementation of the International Covenant on Economic, Social, and Cultural Rights, The Right to Adequate Food (art. 11 of the International Covenant on Economic, Social, and Cultural Rights), E/C.12/1999/5 (May 12, 1999), para. 12. In respect to affordability, the general comment emphasizes equity, stating that payment for health care services, as well as services related to the underlying determinants of health, must be based on the principle of equity, ensuring that these services, whether privately or publicly provided, are affordable for all, including socially disadvantaged groups. Equity demands that poorer households not be disproportionately burdened with health expenses as compared to richer households.

27   According to General Comment Nos. 12 and 13, the obligation to fulfill incorporates an obligation to *facilitate* and an obligation to *provide*. The obligation to fulfill also incorporates an

to health remains contested, and, as John Tobin observes, "an adequate normative account of a human right requires that it have a well specified counterpart
obligation."[28] Tobin argues that despite the apparently amorphous nature of
the counterpart obligation(s) pertaining to the right to health, "it remains possible to articulate a persuasive account of how states can implement this obligation in a way that is principled, practical, coherent, and context sensitive."[29]
This section traces the contours of the counterpart obligation(s) arising from
the right to health.

The obligation to *respect* requires states to refrain from interfering directly
or indirectly with the enjoyment of the right to health. This obligation requires
that states refrain from denying or limiting equal access for all persons to preventive, curative, and palliative health services; avoid enforcing discriminatory practices as a state policy; and abstain from imposing discriminatory practices relating to women's health status and needs. The obligation also requires
states to refrain from limiting access to contraceptives and other means of
maintaining sexual and reproductive health, and refrain from unlawfully pol-
luting air, water, and soil, for example, through industrial waste from state-
owned facilities.[30]

The committee has interpreted the obligation to *protect* as requiring states
to take measures that prevent third parties from interfering with Article 12
entitlements. This may imply an obligation to adopt legislation or to take other
measures ensuring equal access to health care and health-related services provided by third parties to ensure that privatization of the health sector does not
constitute a threat to the availability, accessibility, acceptability, and quality of
health facilities, goods, and services.[31] This obligation is particularly relevant
to development interventions given its emphasis on measures to protect all
vulnerable or marginalized groups of society, such as women, children, adolescents, and older persons.

Finally, the obligation to *fulfill* has been understood by the committee to
require states to adopt appropriate legislative, administrative, budgetary, judicial, promotional, and other measures toward the full realization of the right
to health. This obligation requires state parties, inter alia, to give sufficient recognition to the right to health in the national political and legal systems, preferably by way of legislative implementation, and to adopt a national health
policy with a detailed plan for realizing the right to health. States must ensure
the provision of health care, including immunization programs against the
major infectious diseases, and ensure equal access for all to the underlying

---

obligation to *promote* because of the critical importance of health promotion in the work of
WHO and elsewhere.

28   Tobin, *supra* note 22, at 18.

29   *Id.*, at 19.

30   General Comment No. 14, *supra* note 20, at para. 34.

31   *Id.*, at para. 35.

determinants of health, such as nutritiously safe food and potable drinking water, basic sanitation, and adequate housing and living conditions.[32]

Consistent with the international obligations identified in General Comment No. 3,[33] the committee has also identified international obligations under Article 12 requiring state parties to respect the enjoyment of the right to health in other countries, including preventing third-party violations. Consistent with its interpretations in other contexts, this obligation may require states to provide financing to facilitate access to essential health facilities, goods, and services in other countries.[34]

Progressive Realization

The covenant provides for progressive realization[35] in order to accommodate the incremental process of realizing economic and social rights and resource constraints.[36] As Alston and Quinn observe, it is the "lynchpin of the entire Covenant [. . .] upon its meaning turns the nature of state obligations. Most of the rights granted depend in varying degrees on the availability of resources and this fact is recognized and reflected in the concept of 'progressive achievement.'"[37] The committee has insisted that the "progressive realization" of the covenant rights requires the taking of "deliberate, concrete and targeted" steps and the notion of a "minimum core" provides an understanding of the direction that those steps should follow and an indication as to when their direction

---

32   General Comment No. 14, *supra* note 20, at para. 36. In addition, the general comment obligation to fulfill (facilitate) requires states inter alia to take positive measures that enable and assist individuals and communities to enjoy the right to health. State parties are also obliged to fulfill (provide) a specific right contained in the covenant when individuals or a group are unable, for reasons beyond their control, to realize that right themselves by the means at their disposal. The obligation to fulfill (promote) the right to health requires states to undertake actions that create, maintain, and restore the health of the population (para. 37).

33   Committee on Economic, Social, and Cultural Rights, General Comment No. 3, Substantive Issues Arising in the Implementation of the International Covenant on Economic, Social, and Cultural Rights, The Nature of States Parties Obligations (Art. 11 of the International Covenant on Economic, Social, and Cultural Rights), E/1991/23 (Dec. 14, 1990). This is based on the covenant's obligation of all state parties to take steps, individually and through international assistance and cooperation, especially economic and technical, toward the full realization of the rights recognized in the covenant.

34   General Comment No. 14, *supra* note 20, at para. 39.

35   The literature treats "progressive realization" as either an obligation or a concept. It is perhaps best understood as an overarching concept that defines the nature of all substantive obligations in the covenant.

36   Despite this obligation, the committee has refused to rule that deliberately retrogressive measures are a prima facie violation. This has been criticized by Matthew Craven, *The International Covenant on Economic, Social and Cultural Rights: A Perspective on Its Development* 131–132 (Oxford U. Press 1995).

37   P. Alston & G. Quinn, *The Nature and Scope of States Parties' Obligations under the International Covenant on Economic, Social and Cultural Rights,* 9(2) Hum. Rights Q. 156–229, 172 (1987).

becomes retrogressive.[38] In addition, the covenant imposes obligations of immediate effect, requiring that state parties take steps to realize the right to health and that the right be realized and exercised without discrimination of any kind. "Such steps must be deliberate, concrete, and targeted towards the full realization of the right to health."[39]

A corollary to progressive realization is the presumption against retrogressive measures. If any deliberately retrogressive measures are taken, the state has the burden of proving that the measures were introduced after the most careful consideration of all alternatives and that they are duly justified by reference to the totality of the rights provided for in the covenant in the context of the full use of the state party's maximum available resources.[40] The concepts of both progressive realization and maximum available resources are open-ended and continue to be discussed at a high level of generality, and concrete tools have yet to be developed to enable an effective assessment of their meaning in practice.[41] More recent analyses and tools have emerged to guide states in the resolution of resource allocation dilemmas arising from such obligations.[42] A number of these center on the nature of the process of decision making and the need for it to be shown to be principled, evidence based, consultative, transparent, and evaluative.

Thus, far from allowing the notion of progressive realization to provide a means to delay or avoid obligations under the ICESCR, the CESCR has bolstered it through its interpretations of other component parts of Article 2(1) ICESCR. As a result, the obligation appears to require "a continuous improvement of conditions over time without backward movement of any kind—in what may be described as a form of 'ratchet effect.'"[43]

Minimum Core

The concept of a "minimum core" of ICESCR rights derives from General Comment No. 3, in which the committee confirmed its view that "a minimum core obligation to ensure the satisfaction of, at the very least, minimum essential

---

38 Katharine G. Young, *The Minimum Core of Economic and Social Rights: A Concept in Search of Content,* 33 Yale J. Intl. L. 113, 121 (2008), available at http://www.yale.edu/yjil/PDFs/vol_33/Young%20Final.pdf.

39 General Comment No. 14, *supra* note 20, at para. 30.

40 *Id.,* at para. 32. *See also* the more recent *Interim Report of the Special Rapporteur on the Right of Everyone to the Enjoyment of the Highest Attainable Standard of Physical and Mental Health Related to Health Financing Since the Full Realization of the Right to Health Is Contingent upon the Availability of Adequate, Equitable and Sustainable Financing for Health at Both the Domestic and International Levels,* A/67/302 (Aug. 13, 2012).

41 R. Robertson, *Measuring State Compliance with the Obligation to Devote the "Maximum Available Resources" to Realizing Economic, Social, and Cultural Rights,* 16(4) Hum. Rights Q. 693–714, 703 (1994).

42 E. Felner, *Closing the "Escape Hatch": A Toolkit to Monitor the Progressive Realization of Economic, Social, and Cultural Rights,* 1(3) J. Hum. Rights Prac. 402 (2008); Tobin, *supra* note 8, at ch. 2.

43 Craven, *supra* note 36, at 131.

levels of each of the rights is incumbent upon every State party."[44] The committee aimed to establish a common, minimum legal standard[45] in the face of "the inherent relativism of the programmatic standard of 'progressive realization'" and to provide "an understanding of the direction that the steps should follow and an indication as to when their direction becomes retrogressive."[46]

The concept of a minimum core is not a clear or fixed one, and commentators have struggled to establish its genesis, justification, and organizing principles. Even as defined in relation to minimum core obligations, the concept has not been interpreted consistently by the committee.[47] According to Young, three basic approaches can be identified:[48] a minimum legal content for the notoriously indeterminate claims of economic and social rights; a baseline of socioeconomic protection across countries and across varied economic policies and vastly different levels of available resources; and a manageable and moderate legal measure in the context of global redistributive debates.[49]

In respect to the right to health, the committee has elaborated on the core obligations that ensure the satisfaction of minimum essential levels of the right to health; many of these have potential relevance to development interventions through their emphasis on poor, vulnerable, or marginalized groups:[50]

- To ensure the right of access to health facilities, goods, and services on a nondiscriminatory basis, especially for vulnerable or marginalized groups.

- To ensure access to the minimum essential food that is nutritionally adequate and safe, to ensure freedom from hunger to everyone.

- To ensure access to basic shelter, housing, and sanitation and an adequate supply of safe and potable water.

- To provide essential drugs, as from time to time defined under the WHO Action Programme on Essential Drugs.

- To ensure equitable distribution of all health facilities, goods, and services.

- To adopt and implement a national public health strategy and plan of action, on the basis of epidemiological evidence, addressing the health concerns of the whole population. The strategy and plan of action shall be devised, and periodically reviewed, on the basis of a participatory and

---

44   General Comment No. 3, *supra* note 33, at para. 10.

45   Even in this respect, Young notes that the committee has variously equated minimum core with a presumptive legal entitlement, a nonderogable obligation, and an obligation of strict liability; Young, *supra* note 38.

46   *Id.,* at 121.

47   *Id.,* at 154.

48   Normative essence (a moral standard for prescribing the formulation of rights); minimum consensus; or minimum core obligation or set of obligations. These three basic approaches are summarized at *id.,* 116–117.

49   Id., at 113.

50   *See* also Paul Hunt, *The Right of Everyone to Enjoy the Highest Attainable Standard of Physical and Mental Health,* A/58/427 (Oct. 10, 2003), para. 53.

transparent process. The strategy and plan shall include methods, such as the right to health indicators and benchmarks, by which progress can be closely monitored. The process by which the strategy and plan of action are devised, as well as their content, shall give particular attention to all vulnerable or marginalized groups.[51]

However, as Young points out,

> It is difficult to determine whether the Committee designated these obligations as core because of their immediate practicability or their greater moral salience; on both grounds, the core obligations are subject to criticism. The Committee's response to the practicability of the core obligations (and by implication, their affordability) is to posit a duty of assistance and cooperation on both state parties and non-state actors who are "in a position to assist."[52]

Monitoring the Right to Health

Although limited progress has been made in developing monitoring tools to assess compliance with economic and social rights,[53] a growing range of tools exists to monitor the progressive realization of such rights, including the right to health. In Uganda, for example, with the support of the United Nations Development Programme (UNDP), the Uganda Human Rights Commission developed the Toolkit for Data Collection and Monitoring the Enjoyment of the Right to Health.[54] The principal mechanism for monitoring the right to health under the covenant is the periodic reporting process, although a complaints mechanism now exists with the entry into force of the Optional Protocol to the ICESCR.[55] Key components in the effective monitoring of the right to health are human rights indicators and benchmarks, as well as analysis of budget expenditure allocation by sector.[56] As the special rapporteur noted, the reliance on indicators is especially important because of progressive realization and the fact that what is expected of a state will vary over time.[57] States must select appropriate indicators to help them monitor different dimensions of the right to health, and each indictor requires disaggregation of data on the various prohibited grounds of discrimination.

Distinguishing features of right to health indicators[58] include their derivation from the specific right to health norms and the purpose to which the

---

51 General Comment No. 14, *supra* note 20, at para. 43.

52 Young, *supra* note 38, at 156.

53 Felner, *supra* note 42, at 408.

54 Uganda Human Rights Commission, *Toolkit for Data Collection and Monitoring the Enjoyment of the Right to Health* (2010).

55 The protocol entered into force on May 5, 2012, three months after being ratified by 10 parties. It currently has 10 state parties and 32 signatories.

56 *See* Felner, *supra* note 42, at 411–414.

57 Hunt, *supra* note 50, at para. 5.

58 *See* also Gunilla Backman et al., *Health Systems and the Right to Health: An Assessment of 194*

indicator is put—that is, the right to health monitoring with a view to holding duty bearers to account.[59] Such right to health indicators fall into three categories: structural indicators, process indicators, and outcome indicators. The categories are not immutable and may overlap, and some indicators may qualify for more than one category:[60]

- Structural indicators address whether or not key structures, systems, and mechanisms that are necessary for or conducive to the realization of the right to health are in place.[61] These might include whether a state constitutionalizes the right to health; whether it has a national human rights institution with a mandate that includes health, a national strategy, and a plan of action to reduce maternal mortality; and an essential medicines list.[62]

- Process indicators can be designed to help a state monitor the variable dimension of the right to health that arises from the concept of progressive realization.[63] These indicators monitor effort rather than outcome and could include indicators such as the percentage of births attended by skilled health personnel or the percentage of people with advanced HIV infection receiving antiretroviral combination therapy.[64]

- Outcome indicators measure the results achieved by health-related policies, such as MDG indicators.[65] These might include indicators such as the number of maternal deaths per 100,000 live births, HIV prevalence among the population aged 15–24 years, and incidence and death rates associated with malaria.

Right to Health and Its Potential Relevance to Development

Health as a Development Priority

In 2006, the *World Development Report* recognized that health has both intrinsic and instrumental importance:

Countries, 372 Lancet 2047–2085 (2008), which includes 72 indicators of the right to health. This list comprises structural, process, and outcome indicators.

59   Hunt, *supra* note 50, at para. 10.

60   *See* more generally the work of the Office of the High Commissioner for Human Rights (OHCHR) on human rights indicators, including *Human Rights Indicators: A Guide to Measurement and Implementation* (2012). *See* also OHCHR, *Report on Indicators for Monitoring Compliance with International Human Rights Instruments*, HRI/MC/ 2006/7 (May 11, 2006), and *Report of the UN High Commissioner for Human Rights Focused on the Use of Indicators in Realizing Economic, Social, and Cultural Rights*, E/20011/90 (Apr. 26, 2011).

61   Hunt, *supra* note 50, at para. 18.

62   *Id.*, at para. 19.

63   *Id.*, at para. 22.

64   *Id.*, at para. 27.

65   For the official list of the indicators, *see* http://mdgs.un.org/unsd/mdg/Host.aspx ?Content=Indicators/OfficialList.htm.

Alongside the intrinsic importance of health as a dimension of welfare, poor health can directly include an individual's opportunities—his or her earnings capacity, performance at school, ability to care for children, participation in community activities and so on. This important instrumental function of health implies that inequalities in health often translate into inequalities in other dimensions of welfare.[66]

Health is central to development.[67] The specific links between promoting health and sustainable development have long been acknowledged. It is generally recognized that securing a certain level of health-related development is a prerequisite for the overall economic development of a country,[68] and that diseases such as HIV/AIDS and malaria can have long-term negative impacts on economic growth.[69]

Thus, assessing development and poverty reduction in terms of capabilities,[70] one can see that the right to health may have both constitutive and instrumental relevance. As Anand Grover, the special rapporteur on the right to health, notes:

> The right is constitutive insofar as ill health and adequate protection of the right to health are symptoms and constituent parts of inadequate human development and poverty, and instrumental in that the enjoyment of the right to health is instrumental in securing other human rights, such as the right to education and work, which are essential to the achievement of human development.[71]

Paul Hunt, the former special rapporteur, put it in the following way: "Good health is central to creating and sustaining the capabilities that poor people need to escape from poverty. . . . Good health is not just an outcome of development: it is a way of achieving development."[72]

---

66   World Development Report, *Equity and Development* 29 (Oxford U. Press 2006).

67   UN System Task Team, *supra* note 2.

68   Jocelyn E. Finlay, *The Role of Health in Economic Development* (PGDA Working Papers 2107, Program on the Global Demography of Aging 2007), states: "Accounting for the simultaneous determination of the key variables—growth, education, fertility—the results show that the indirect effect of health is positive and significant."

69   J. Gallup & J. Sachs, *The Economic Burden of Malaria* 7 (CID Working Paper No. 52, July 2000); J. Sachs & P. Malaney, *The Economic and Social Burden of Malaria*, 415(7) Nature 780–785 (Feb. 2002); S. Dixon, S. McDonald, & J. Roberts, *AIDS and Economic Growth in Africa: A Panel Data Analysis*, 13 J. Intl. Dev. 411–426 (2001); United Nations Department of Economic and Social Affairs/Population Division, *The Impact of AIDS* (United Nations 2004), especially ch. 8, 81–89.

70   Amartya Sen, *Human Rights and Capabilities*, 6(2) J. Hum. Dev. (July 2005); Martha Nussbaum, *Creating Capabilities: The Human Development Approach* (Harv. U. Press 2011).

71   Grover, *supra* note 6, at paras. 12–13.

72   Paul Hunt, *The Right of Everyone to the Enjoyment of the Highest Attainable Standard of Physical and Mental Health*, 2002/31 E/CN.4/2003/58 (Feb. 13, 2003), para. 46.

It is unsurprising then that health has become an increasingly important focus of development work. Health is a prominent theme in both the Millennium Declaration (2000) and the Millennium Development Goals (MDGs): 3 of the 8 MDGs address health directly and others address underlying determinants of health.[73] Moreover, at least 8 of the 16 MDG targets, and 17 of the 48 related indicators, are health related. The 2010 High-Level Plenary Meeting of the General Assembly confirmed states' commitment to promoting global public health to achieve the MDGs and to ensure respect for human rights, to "promote gender equality and the empowerment of women as essential means of addressing the health of women and girls, and to address the stigmatization of people living with and affected by HIV and AIDS." According to the *MDG Report for Uganda,* several of the health targets, including those related to child and maternal mortality, access to reproductive health, and the incidence of malaria and other diseases, have progressed slowly.[74] The report notes that every day in Uganda, an estimated 16 women die in childbirth, averaging one death every 90 minutes and nearly 6,000 every year. Indeed, MDG Goal 5 (improve maternal health) is one of the goals toward which progress has been observed to be too slow, and the report devotes a special section to it.

Links between Poverty and Health

The multilayered connections between poverty and health are also widely recognized.[75]

As Paul Hunt, the former special rapporteur on the right to health, observed,

> Ill-health causes poverty by destroying livelihoods, reducing worker productivity, lowering educational achievement and limiting opportunities. Because poverty may lead to diminished access to medical care, increased exposure to environmental risk, the worst forms of child labour and malnutrition, ill health is also often a consequence of poverty. In other words, ill health is both a cause and a consequence of poverty: sick people are more likely to become poor and the poor are more vulnerable to disease and disability.[76]

---

73   UN Enable, The Millennium Development Goals: Goal 4: Reduce child mortality; Goal 5: Improve maternal health; Goal 6: Combat HIV/AIDS, malaria, and other diseases. Available at http://www.un.org/millenniumgoals/.

74   Government of Uganda, *Millennium Development Goals Report for Uganda: Special Theme: Accelerating Progress towards Improving Maternal Health* (Ministry of Finance, Planning and Economic Development, Kampala 2010).

75   *See,* generally, Chris Beyrer & H. F. Pizer eds., *Public Health and Human Rights: Evidence-Based Approaches* (Johns Hopkins U. Press 2007).

76   Hunt, *supra* note 72, at para. 45.

Similarly,

> Securing the sexual and reproductive health of populations has an integral role in eliminating poverty and promoting economic growth, alongside its direct effects on individuals' health. Ensuring access to reproductive services, including family planning, is a vital step in disrupting the "repetitive cycle" of poverty, inequality and slow economic growth that is perpetuated by limited reproductive choices.[77]

In sum, a number of observations are apposite: first the deep and multi-tiered relevance of health for development; second, the interdependence of health (and the right to health) and other elements of welfare (and other human rights);[78] and third, the importance of recognizing that both health and the right to heath are important for instrumental and intrinsic reasons.

What has arguably been missing, however, is greater recognition of the potential role of the normative and legal framework in attaining health outcomes[79] and, more particularly, the role of the right to health itself in achieving the MDGs.[80] Recognition of these roles is addressed in the next section.

Potential Contribution of the Right to Health

What Is Distinct about an Approach Predicated on the Right to Health?

The realization of the right to health depends on an effective and integrated health system that encompasses medical care and addresses the underlying determinants of health.[81] However, not all approaches to improving health and strengthening health systems necessarily advance the right to health. For instance, the WHO identifies six essential building blocks that make up health systems: health services (medical and public health); a health workforce; a health information system; medical products, vaccines, and technologies;

---

77 Grover, *supra* note 6, at para. 5, citing the United Nations Population Fund (UNFPA), *The ICPD and MDGs: Close Linkages*, XV–3, available at http://www.un.org/esa/population/publications/PopAspectsMDG/14_UNFPA.pdf.

78 On health and human rights, *see* P. Farmer, *Rethinking Health and Human Rights: Time for a Paradigm Shift*, in *Pathologies of Power: Health, Human Rights and the New War on the Poor* 213–246 (U. Calif. Press 2003); *see*, generally, Beyrer & Pizer, *supra* note 75.

79 *Report of the Special Rapporteur on the Right to Health* (main focus: health-related Millenium Development Goals), para. 15.

80 For a general discussion of the role of international human rights in advancing achievement of the MDGs, *see* S. McInerney-Lankford, *Legal Accountability: From Human Rights Obligations to Development Policy and the MDGs*, ch. 7 in Malcolm Langford, Andy Sumner, & Alicia Ely Yamin eds., *MDGs and Human Rights: Past, Present and Future* (Cambridge U. Press 2013).

81 P. Hunt & G. Backmann, *Health Systems and the Right to the Highest Attainable Standard of Health,* 1(1) Health & Hum. Rights (2008).

health financing; and leadership, governance, and stewardship. However, as some experts have noted, although these can be thought of as building blocks for the realization of the right to health, "a health system might have all these building blocks but still not serve human rights. For example, the system might include both medical care and public health but not secure fair access, or there might be a health information system but key data might not be suitably disaggregated."[82]

In order to fully realize the right to health and fully serve human rights, health system needs to reflect the following features:

- *Legal recognition:* The right to health must be recognized in national law and by ratifying relevant human rights treaties.

- *Standards:* Health systems must include detailed standards, which strengthen general legal provisions.

- *Participation:* Health systems must include institutional arrangements for active and informed participation in strategy development, policy making, implementation, and accountability by all relevant stakeholders, including disadvantaged individuals, communities, and populations.

- *Transparency:* Information on the quality, availability, and pricing of essential medicines must be accessible by those in the public, private, and nonprofit sectors.

- *Equity, equality, and nondiscrimination:* Health systems must be accessible to all, including those living in poverty, minority groups, indigenous people, women, children, people living in slums and rural areas, people with disabilities, and other disadvantaged individuals, communities, and populations. Additionally, health systems must be responsive to the particular health needs of women, children, adolescents, and elderly people. Outreach programs should ensure that disadvantaged people have the same access as more privileged people.

- *Respect for cultural differences:* Health systems must be respectful of medical ethics and culturally appropriate, that is, respectful of the culture of individuals, minorities, peoples, and communities and sensitive to gender and life-cycle requirements.

- *Quality:* All health-related services and facilities must be of good quality.

- *Planning:* States must have comprehensive national health plans, encompassing both the public and private sectors, for the development of health systems.

- *Referral systems:* Health systems should have a mix of primary (community-based), secondary (district-based), and tertiary (specialized) facilities and services, providing a continuum of prevention and care.

---

82   Backman et al., *supra* note 58.

- *Coordination:* Health systems and the right to health depend on effective coordination across a range of public and private stakeholders (including nongovernmental organizations) at the national and international levels.

- *International cooperation:* Health systems have international dimensions, which are also reflected in countries' human rights responsibilities of international assistance and cooperation.

- *Legal obligation:* Crucially, the right to the highest attainable standard of health gives rise to legally binding obligations.

- *Monitoring and accountability:* Individuals and communities should have the opportunity to understand how those with responsibilities have discharged their duties and provide those with responsibilities the opportunity to explain what they have done and why. Where mistakes have been made, accountability requires redress. Accountability is not a matter of blame and punishment but a fair and reasonable process to identify what works, so it can be repeated and revised as necessary.

Similarly, in an effort to unpack the right to health, the special rapporteur on the right to health identified ten key elements that underpin the right to health framework:[83]

- Identification of relevant national and international human rights laws, norms, and standards

- Recognition that the right to health is subject to resource constraints and progressive realization, requiring the identification of indicators and benchmarks to measure progress over time

- Recognition that the right to health imposes some obligations that are of immediate effect, and are not subject to progressive realization

- Recognition that the right to health includes freedoms and entitlements

- The objective of ensuring that all health services, goods, and facilities shall be available, accessible, acceptable, and of good quality

- That states have duties to respect, protect, and fulfill the right to the highest attainable standard of health

- That special attention should be given to issues of nondiscrimination, equality, and vulnerability

- Opportunities are required for the active and informed participation of individuals and communities in decision making that has a bearing on their health

- Developing countries have a responsibility to seek international assistance and cooperation, whereas developed states have some responsibilities toward the realization of the right to health in developing countries

---

83   Grover, *supra* note 6.

- That effective, transparent, and accessible monitoring and accountability mechanisms must be available at the national and international levels

What Can the Right to Health and Its Normative Framework Offer Health-Related Development Interventions?

A fundamental premise of this discussion is that the right to health is important for both instrumental and intrinsic reasons, and, in relation to the latter, that it may advance a range of other goals, including some related to development.[84] According to the special rapporteur on the right to health, "the right to health framework complements current development approaches by underlining the importance of aspects such as participation, community empowerment, and the need to focus on vulnerable populations."[85] In the context of defining the post-2015 agenda for the MDGs,[86] the UN System Task Team has proposed that "a human rights based approach to health is essential" to address health issues more effectively.[87]

This section builds on the distinct contribution that the right to health may make to development. The discussion centers on two themes: first, the requirement that special attention be given to issues of nondiscrimination, equality, and vulnerability; and second, the importance of identifying relevant national and international human rights laws, norms, and standards. The latter implicitly recognizes that the right to health imposes obligations and requires effective, transparent, and accessible monitoring and accountability mechanisms at the national and international levels.

Focus on the Poor, Vulnerable, and Marginalized

According to Paul Hunt, former special rapporteur on the right to health, "The right to health—and other human rights—has a significant and constructive role to play in poverty reduction. Policies that are based on national and international human rights are more likely to be effective, sustainable, inclusive, equitable, and meaningful to those living in poverty."[88]

The contribution of the right to health perspective to development must be understood in the broader context of the general contribution that human rights may make to development through a focus on nondiscrimination and inequality; the participation of the poor, rendering policy choices that have a

---

84   A useful background resource to this chapter, and to this section in particular, is Stephen P. Marks ed., *Health and Human Rights: Basic International Documents* (3d ed., Harv. Series on Health and Hum. Rights, Harv. U. Press 2012).

85   Paul Hunt, *The Right of Everyone to the Enjoyment of the Highest Attainable Standard of Physical and Mental Health*, A/59/422 (Oct. 4, 2004), para. 15.

86   *See* also WHO, *Positioning Health in the Post-2015 Development Agenda* (WHO discussion paper, Oct. 2012).

87   UN System Task Team, *supra* note 2, at 6. On rights-based approaches to health, *see* Elvira Beracochea, Corey Weinstein, & Dabney Evans, eds., *Rights-Based Approaches to Public Health* (Springer 2010).

88   Hunt, *supra* note 85, at para. 44.

disproportionately harmful impact on the poor impermissible; and the role of international assistance and cooperation.[89] This element is particularly important in the context of the MDGs, whose the focus on aggregate measures of achievement has been a frequent criticism.[90] Participation of poor people is essential to rights-based approaches to development, including the right to health.[91]

In the context of health, Hunt suggests that a poverty reduction strategy based on the right to health would emphasize improving poor people's access to health services, for example, by identifying diseases that have a particular impact on the poor and introducing immunization and other programs specifically designed to reach the poor; improving the effectiveness of public health interventions to the poor, for example, by implementing basic environmental controls, especially regarding waste disposal in areas populated by the poor; reducing the financial burden of health protection on the poor, for example, by reducing or eliminating user fees for the poor; and promoting policies in other sectors that bear positively on the underlying determinants of health, for example, supporting agricultural policies that have positive health outcomes for the poor.[92]

From a different perspective, development interventions in the area of health which respect human rights are also likely to be more effective. For example,

> "naming and shaming" people who test positive to HIV, in violation of their right to privacy and confidentiality, creates stigma and deters others from seeking out testing and counseling; a development intervention designed to combat the spread of HIV that respects the human rights of those directly affected by and those most at risk of HIV will ultimately be more effective in achieving its stated goals.[93]

As the Alma-Ata Declaration confirmed, an effective health system relies on core elements of right to health and human rights principles such as equity, community participation,[94] health promotional activities, and international cooperation. In respect of essential health interventions, the declaration underscored key determinants of the right to health that are consistent with the more holistic views of health contained in interpretations of both the CESCR and the

---

89   *Id.*, at para. 56.

90   M. Langford, *A Poverty of Rights: Six Ways to Fix the MDGs,* 41(1) IDS Bull. 83 (2010).

91   A. Yamin, *Suffering and Powerlessness: The Significance of Participation in Rights-Based Approaches to Health,* 11 Health & Hum. Rights 5 (2011).

92   Hunt, *supra* note 85, at para. 57.

93   Grover, *supra* note 6, at paras. 41 & 42, at footnote 1. *See* also UN System Task Team, *supra* note 2, at 8.

94   "The people have the right and duty to participate individually and collectively in the planning and implementation of their health care." Adopted at the International Conference on Primary Health Care (Sept. 6–12, 1978).

special rapporteur on the right to health.[95] These include education, food supply and nutrition, and the adequate supply of safe water and basic sanitation.

Enhanced Accountability of Duty Bearers

Notwithstanding claims about the indeterminacy of the right to health, including in relation to the definition of its minimum content;[96] inconsistencies in its interpretation by the CESCR; and the difficulty of determining whether the minimum content is the same in developing countries as it is in developed countries, the right to health possesses a distinct quality in being grounded in a legal obligation under international law[97] and in enforceable legal norms within domestic legal frameworks across the world.[98] "Perhaps the most important source of added value in the human rights approach is the emphasis it places on the accountability of policy-makers and other actors whose actions have an impact on the rights of people. Rights imply duties, and duties demand accountability."[99] Through the leverage provided by the law,[100] the right to health may help increase accountability for health interventions by offering a legal standard against which to assess health interventions through the norms enshrined in law, as well as the indicators and benchmarks developed based on those norms.[101] This facilitates monitoring and evaluation, as well as more formal compliance with the right to health, and in some cases provides recourse mechanisms and remedies for aggrieved individuals and groups. As noted by Paul Hunt, the former special rapporteur on the right to health, the legal genesis of the right to health implies "the notion of obligation and thus the requirement of effective, transparent, and accessible mechanisms of accountability."[102] Put differently, an approach predicated on the right to health considers that "the 'how' of health and development is as important as the 'what'"[103]—in this way, it emphasizes process and means as much as outcomes.

---

95 *See* also UN System Task Team, *supra* note 2, at 7.

96 *See*, for example, Young, *supra* note 38.

97 *See* also J. Brunnée, *International Legal Accountability through the Lens of the Law of State Responsibility*, 36 Netherlands Y.B. Intl. L. 21–56 (2005).

98 See M. Langford, ed., *Social Rights Jurisprudence: Emerging Trends in International and Comparative Law* (Cambridge U. Press 2008).

99 P. Hunt, S. Osmani, & M. Nowak, *Summary of the Draft Guidelines for a Human Rights Approach to Poverty Reduction* (OHCHR 2004).

100 *Id.*, at 737.

101 This may include monitoring and evaluation. Realizing that accountability as it is understood within the human rights framework relies on transparency, access to information and active popular participation are necessary in order for accountability to be realized. *See* A. Ely Yamin, *The Central Role of Accountability in Applying a Human Rights Framework to Health*, 10(2) Health and Hum. Rights 1, 2 (2008).

102 Hunt, *supra* note 85, at para. 56.

103 UN System Task Team, *supra* note 2, at 8.

The legal accountability underpinning human rights norms is enshrined in international rule of law and is reflected in the complaints procedures under human rights treaties[104] (and, to a less formal extent, in the work of treaty monitoring bodies), which are strengthened by assessment methodology and the development of human rights indicators.[105] These international norms add value by operating at different levels, whether international, domestic, or local. Some experts opine that despite variances in countries' constitutional approaches to international law obligations, once ratified, human rights treaties are typically transposed into domestic legal frameworks, which can in turn generate rights-based policy that gives meaning to international treaty obligations and provides for individual causes of action, ensuring human rights accountability for local health advancement.[106] As a result of health rights litigation aimed at the enforcement of human rights,[107] human rights now provide the structure of legal accountability for national policy in a number of developing countries.[108] The remainder of this chapter considers these elements and the influence of the right to health on accountability for health policy and outcomes in the context of Uganda.

Domestic Enforceability: The Case of Uganda

Brief Description of Uganda

Uganda is a landlocked country located in and part of the East African Community, whose other members are Kenya, Tanzania, Rwanda, and Burundi. Uganda has demonstrated an intention to recognize the right to health and is a signatory to a number of international covenants that recognize the right. Uganda ratified the Covenant on Economic, Social, and Cultural Rights in 1966, the Convention on Elimination of All Forms of Discrimination Against Women in 1981, the Convention on Rights of the Child in 1986, the Covenant

---

104 *See,* for example, ICCPR Optional Protocol of December 16, 1966 (entered into force Mar. 23, 1976) 999 U.N.T.S. 302; CRC Optional Protocol and ICESCR Optional Protocol of December 10, 2008 (not yet in force).

105 *See* http://www.ohchr.org/EN/Issues/Indicators/Pages/HRIndicatorsIndex.aspx.

106 B. Mason Meier et al., *Bridging International Law and Rights-Based Litigation: Mapping Health-Related Rights through the Development of the Global Health and Human Rights Database,* 14 Health & Hum. Rights 1 (2012).

107 *See,* for example, M. Langford, ed., *Social Rights Jurisprudence: Emerging Trends in International and Comparative Law* (Cambridge U. Press 2008); V. Gauri & D. Brinks, *Courting Social Justice: Judicial Enforcement of Social and Economic Rights in the Developing World* (Cambridge U. Press 2008); A. Yamin & S. Gloppen, *Litigating Health Rights: Can Courts Bring More Justice to Health?* (Harv. U. Press 2011).

108 Meier et al., *supra* note 106, at 2.

on Civil and Political Rights in 1995,[109] and the African Charter on Human and Peoples' Rights in 1986.[110]

With a total population estimated at 33 million people, Uganda has a life expectancy of 54 and 57 years for males and females, respectively, with a child mortality rate of 90 per 1,000 births.[111] Malaria is responsible for the largest proportion of deaths arising from medical conditions, with 5,958 of the 231,873 malaria cases being fatal in 2012.[112] The country's progress in the fight against HIV/AIDS has slowed down; UNAIDS estimates the number of people living with HIV/AIDS in Uganda to be 1,400,000,[113] or 7.2 percent of the adult population, up from 5 percent in 2000.[114] Only 54 percent of the people living with HIV/AIDS have access to antiretroviral treatment,[115] and of these, only 50 percent of the women living with HIV/AIDS have access to antiretroviral therapy for the prevention of mother-to-child transmission; yet the maternal mortality rate stands at 310 deaths per 100,000 live births,[116] which exceeds the MDG target of 131 deaths per 100,000 live births.[117] The implication of these statistics is that although some progress has been made in providing basic health services to the public, a significant percentage of people still lack access to basic health services.

To discharge its obligation to provide a minimum standard of health care, the Ugandan government has deployed a comprehensive multitier system of health service delivery primarily involving hospitals spread across the country supported by health centers established at each of the local levels of political administration. At the top of the pyramid are general hospitals, national referral hospitals, and regional referral hospitals. General hospitals provide preventive, promotive, curative, maternity, in-patient, surgery, blood transfusion, laboratory, and medical imaging services. National referral hospitals provide comprehensive specialist services and conduct health research and teaching in addition to providing the services offered by general hospitals. Regional

---

109 *See* http://treaties.un.org/pages/ViewDetails.aspx?src=TREATY&mtdsg_no=IV-4&chapter=4 &lang=en.

110 *See* http://www.achpr.org/instruments/achpr/ratification/, Ratification Table: African Charter on Human and Peoples' Rights.

111 WHO, *Country Statistics, Uganda,* available at http://www.who.int/countries/uga/en/.

112 Global Health Observatory Data Repository, *Uganda Statistics Summary (2002–Present),* available at http://apps.who.int/gho/data/node.country.country-UGA?lang=en/.

113 Uganda Aids Commission, *Global AIDS Response Progress Report* 2 (Country Progress Report Uganda, Apr. 2011), available at http://www.unaids.org/en/dataanalysis/knowyourresponse /countryprogressreports/2012countries/ce_UG_Narrative_Report%5B1%5D.pdf.

114 UNAIDS Country Profile, *Uganda Statistics,* http://www.unaids.org/en/regionscountries /countries/uganda/.

115 Global Health Observatory Data Repository, *supra* note 112.

116 WHO, *Countdown to 2015 Launches the 2012 Report,* available at http://www.who.int/pmnch /topics/part_publications/countdown_2012_report/en/index1.html.

117 Uganda Maternal and Child Health Data, available at http://www.countdown2015mnch .org/country-profiles/uganda.

referral hospitals, which are spread across the country, provide specialist clinical services such as psychiatry; ear, nose, and throat services; ophthalmology; higher-level surgical and medical services; and clinical support services (laboratory, medical imaging, pathology), in addition to teaching and research.[118]

Down the pyramid are health centers I, II, and III.[119] Health center (HC) IIIs provide basic preventive, promotive, and curative care; support supervision of the community and HC IIs under their jurisdiction; and provide laboratory services for diagnosis, maternity care, and first referral cover for the subcounty. HC IIs provide the first level of interaction between the formal health sector and the communities and provide out-patient care and community outreach services. An enrolled comprehensive nurse is essential to the provision of comprehensive services and linkages with the village health teams, which play a supervisory role in maintaining and promoting basic health care in their respective villages. In 1997, administration of health services was transferred from the central government to the local government units of administration under the Local Government Act.[120] These structures are meant to demonstrate the government's undertaking of its obligation to provide health services in accordance with its international obligations; however, the fact that the structures exist does not necessarily mean that the state is satisfying its obligations.

These structures play an important role in increasing access to basic health care facilities for Ugandans across the country, and although it is debatable whether the right to highest attainable standard of health is being realized, the statistics available on health service provision across the country demonstrate some progress in the realization of the right.

Health as a Development Issue in Uganda

Health is a key contributing factor to poverty for the majority of communities in Uganda.[121] To implement health programs in line with the national Poverty Reduction Strategy Paper (PRSP), Uganda developed the Health Sector Strategic Plan (HSSP), which has been revised as HSSPI, HSSP II, and the Health Sector Strategic and Investment Plan.[122] The current HSSP clearly articulates that it was partly developed to operationalize the health sector component of the national PRSP, now referred to as the National Development Plan (NDP).[123]

---

118   Health Sector Strategic Plan III, cl. 2.1.2.

119   *Id.*, at cl. 2.1.5.

120   The Local Government Act, 1997.

121   Moses Mulumba, *Mainstreaming Disability into the Poverty Reduction Processes in Uganda: The Role of the Human Rights–Based Approach to Development* (thesis in fulfillment of the requirement for the MPhil degree in rehabilitation, U. of Stellenbosch, 2010).

122   *Id.*

123   Ministry of Health, *Health Sector Strategic and Investment Plan: Promoting People's Health to Enhance Socio-economic Development, 2010/11–2014/15* (Ministry of Health, Uganda, July 2010).

The NDP is Uganda's PRSP, formerly known as the Poverty Eradication Action Plan (PEAP), developed and launched in 1997 as a framework for addressing the key poverty challenges.[124] Since then, poverty levels have reduced from 56 percent to 31 percent.[125] The PEAP provided an overarching framework to guide public action in a bid to eradicate poverty.[126] The NDP extends until 2040 and is intended to build on the achievements registered during the PEAP period, while recognizing the need to improve planning and utilize resource approaches. With the focus on poverty reduction, the NDP process is targeting resource utilization for better economic growth, thus transforming the country from peasantry into modernization.[127]

The NDP cohesively assesses the progress the government has made in realizing national objectives and proposes strategies by which the government intends, through each of its sectors, to realize some of the objectives. The NDP, while recognizing the progress made by the health sector in the provision of health services, acknowledges the shortcomings of the sector inter alia in the reduction of the maternal mortality rate;[128] the resurgent HIV/AIDS rate;[129] inadequate human resources at the health centers across the country[130] despite an effort by the government to widen health service provision by constructing more health centers around the country;[131] and inadequate funding, which has jeopardized the realization of the Uganda National Minimum Health Care Package (UNMHCP).[132]

To address these shortcomings, the NDP proposes various measures, such as strengthening the organization and management of the national health system, mobilizing sufficient resources to finance health sector programs, ensuring universal access to the UNMHCP, emphasizing vulnerable populations, and building and utilizing partnerships between the private and public stakeholders in the provision of health services.[133] To implement these strategies and policies, the government launched Uganda Vision 2040, which proposes to reduce the infant mortality rate to 4 deaths per 1,000 live births and reduce the maternal mortality rate to 15 deaths per 100,000 live births before the year 2040.

---

124 MFPED, Poverty Eradication Action Plan (PEAP).

125 Id.

126 Moses Mulumba, Facilitating Disability Inclusion in the National Development Agenda in Uganda: What Role Can the Human Rights–Based Approach Play?, J. Hum. Rights & Peace Ctr. (2012).

127 National Development Plan, 2010/11–2014/15, Growth, Employment, and Prosperity for Socioeconomic Transformation (Republic of Uganda, Apr. 2010), available at http://www.npa.ug /docs/NDP2.pdf.

128 Id., at para. 601.

129 Id., at para. 598.

130 Id., at para. 608.

131 Id., at para. 610.

132 Id., at cl. 7.5.2, para. iv.

133 Id., at cl. 7.5.3.

The national plan's strategies and objectives as set forth in Uganda Vision 2040 provide benchmarks against which the government's commitment to protect, provide, and fulfill the right to health is evaluated and portray the efforts to be taken by the state to that effect. Although these strategies and objectives are ambitious and laudable, they have remained largely aspirational and have not been implemented. Recent budgetary allocations for government financing of the health service were significantly reduced despite the government's stated intention to increase health sector financing and curb corruption in the sector. These developments have led human rights activists to call for greater government accountability for health. These advocates rely on the right to health as a framework for accountability and as a mechanism to assess the progress of implementation of health policies and strategies.

Policy Framework for the Realization of the Right to Health in Uganda

As part of its obligation to fulfill—by giving sufficient recognition to the right to health in the national political and legal systems—Uganda has taken a number of steps, including the adoption of a national health policy with a detailed plan for realizing the right to health. These steps are aimed at providing guidance and streamlining the provision of health services across the country. The National Health Sector Strategic Plan defines the UNMHCP, which obliges the government to provide component services and entitlements as expeditiously as possible. The UNMHCP bears similarities to the concept of "minimum core" as elaborated by the Committee on Economic, Social, and Cultural Rights in General Comment No. 3. The package itself comprises the same elements as those identified as "obligations of comparable priority" in General Comment No. 14.[134]

National Health Sector Strategic Plan III (2011-2015)

The National Health Sector Strategic Plan (HSSP) sets forth in clear terms the government's intention to provide health services to the public. It explicitly recognizes the right to the highest attainable standard of health as a fundamental right and undertakes to implement its objectives in the national context. The HSSP protects the right to health by recognizing the right to access information about health, including diagnosis, treatment, costs, and prognosis as avenues through which informed consent to medical treatment can be made. It further acknowledges that the right to health entails not only the

---

134 General Comment No. 14, *supra* note 20, para. 44: "The Committee also confirms that the following are obligations of comparable priority: (a) To ensure reproductive, maternal (pre-natal as well as post-natal) and child health care; (b) To provide immunization against the major infectious diseases occurring in the community; (c) To take measures to prevent, treat and control epidemic and endemic diseases; (d) To provide education and access to information concerning the main health problems in the community, including methods of preventing and controlling them; (e) To provide appropriate training for health personnel, including education on health and human rights."

right to access basic health services but also to access safe and adequate water supplies, sanitation, education, and a safe environment, among others.[135]

In its own provision of core obligations, as envisaged by General Comment No. 14, the government proposes the UNMHCP, which is a set of basic health care services that should be accessible to everyone.[136] The package is composed of clusters, including health promotion, disease prevention, and community health initiatives, encompassing epidemic and disaster preparedness and response, maternal and child health, nutrition, prevention, management and control of communicable diseases, and prevention, management and control of noncommunicable diseases.[137]

Although the HSSP III lays out strategies and objectives of the government in extending basic health services to the public, it falls short of specifying the basic, minimum services that every Ugandan should be able to access and it does not specify the obligations of the government in respect to these so that the government might be held accountable for them. An obligations-based approach to the minimum core could help ensure the full realization of the right to health in two ways.[138] First, a focus on the state's obligations would demand a full analysis of the particular actions incumbent on the government in order to implement the right to health. This could facilitate the analysis of realistic, institutionally informed strategies for rights protections. Second, an analysis of state obligations would include an inventory of activities that the state must refrain from undertaking because they interfere with the realization of the right to health.[139] By not prescribing the specific services to be provided in the UNMHCP and not explicitly enumerating the obligations of the state in realizing the UNMHCP, mechanisms for holding the government accountable for health outcomes are severely inhibited. The government thereby fails to realize the minimum core of health services that should be accessible to everyone in Uganda, and it cannot be held accountable for this failure due to the absence of clear standards against which its actions or omissions can be measured. The realization of the right to the highest attainable standard of health depends, therefore, on the specific articulation of the services to be provided in the UNMHCP as well as a clear articulation of the obligations implied in its provision.

Uganda National Health Policy II (2010)

The Uganda National Health Policy is informed by the National Development Plan and was created to provide for the development of service provision in the health sector: its principal focus is the UNMHCP as the primary vehicle through which the highest attainable standard of health care should be pro-

---

135   National Health Sector Strategic Plan III (2011–15), cl. 5.4.1.

136   *Id.*, at cl. 6.3.

137   *Id.*

138   Young, *supra* note 38.

139   *Id.*, at 152.

vided in Uganda. As a policy objective, the government undertakes to ensure universal access to quality promotive, preventive, curative, rehabilitative, and palliative services for all prioritized diseases and conditions to all people in Uganda, with emphasis on vulnerable populations.[140] To realize this, the government commits to provide an optimal level of all necessary health resources, including human resources, medicines and other health supplies, health infrastructure, and financing.[141]

Primary health care remains the principal means for providing health services through the district health systems supported by the hospitals in the national health systems.[142] As with HSSP III, the main shortcoming of this policy is its failure to outline with clarity the obligations of the government in its provision of health services to the public. Although the Uganda National Health Policy is explicit in its aim to provide basic services, the core content of the health services which the government undertakes to provide, as well as the government's obligations in their regard, remain indefinite. These policies are supplemented by strategic plans and guidelines for the provision of health services and the administration of specific sectors, including the Uganda Hospital Policy (2006), the National Reproductive Health Policy (2012), and the National Adolescent Health Policy (2004).

An assessment of the policies put forward by the government makes it clear that the right to the highest attainable standard of health is recognized in Uganda. However, weaknesses and shortcomings arise in terms of implementation because of the inadequate commitment of human and financial resources. Another complicating factor is that the health sector in Uganda remains largely funded by donor sources, with the government committing comparitively little; when donor funding becomes unpredictable or is withdrawn, the entire health sector is negatively affected.

Legal Framework for the Provision of Health Services in Uganda

Central to the realization of health rights is the incorporation of the right to health into national legal and regulatory frameworks in terms that articulate the obligations to respect, protect, promote, and fulfill in its regard.[143] In Uganda, the national constitution is the supreme law of the country, and any law that is inconsistent with the constitution's provisions has no force or effect, to the extent of the inconsistency.[144] This means that enshrining a right as a constitutional right offers it a heightened standing and renders it a benchmark to assess the government obligations to respect, protect, promote, and fulfill that right.

---

140 Government of Uganda, Uganda National Health Policy II (2010), cl. 6.5.1.

141 *Id.*, at cl. 6.6.

142 *Id.*, at cl. 2.4.

143 Moses Mulumba et al., *Constitutional Provisions for the Right to Health in East and Southern Africa* (EQUINET Discussion Paper 81, 2010).

144 *See* art. 2 of the constitution.

The Constitution of the Republic of Uganda of 1995 is divided into two parts: the National Objectives and Principles of State Policy and the Articles of the Constitution. The former is designed to guide the organs of the state in interpreting the constitution and implementing state policies, whereas the latter are binding substantive provisions. The constitution lacks a substantive provision on the right to the highest attainable standard of health, but it does make mention of the right under the Directive Principles of State Policy. This means that the right to the highest attainable standard of health is a socioeconomic objective to guide the government's actions, rather than a binding constitutional right.

Under the National Objectives and Principles of State Policy, the state undertakes to provide basic medical services to the population,[145] to take steps to provide a basic water management system at all levels,[146] and to provide adequate resources for organs of the government for their effective functioning at all levels.[147] The national objectives are important to the realization of the right to health because they stipulate the primary responsibilities of the government with respect to the right. Their influence was reinforced by a constitutional amendment of 2005, which clarified that the government ought to govern on the basis of the National Objectives and Principles of State Policy.[148] This amendment rendered the National Objectives and Principles enforceable in a manner analogous to the Articles of the Constitution. Although this amendment also rendered the National Objectives and Principles justiciable, the import of Article 8A has not yet been tested in the Ugandan courts of law. The closest case was the 2011 petition *Center for Health Human Rights and Development & 3 Ors v. AG*, on maternal health. The case was thrown out of court on preliminary grounds and was not considered on substance.[149]

Chapter 4 of the Articles of the Constitution contains Uganda's Bill of Rights, and although it does not expressly include the right to health, the right is included by reference through Article 45, which incorporates all other rights and freedoms of international covenants and treaties to which Uganda is party, including the Covenant on Economic, Social, and Cultural Rights. Furthermore, other rights essential to the realization of the right to the highest standard of health are incorporated by the constitution, including the right to a clean and healthy environment,[150] the right to access to information,[151] the

---

145 Objective 20.

146 Objective 21.

147 Objective 8.

148 The Constitution of the Republic of Uganda as Amended by Constitution (Amendment) Act No. 11 of 2005.

149 *Center for Health Human Rights and Development & 3 Ors v. AG*, Constitutional Petition No. 16 of 2011 (unreported).

150 Art. 39.

151 Art. 41.

protection of freedom and the right to life,[152] the protection of human dignity and from inhumane treatment,[153] the rights of women,[154] and the rights of children.[155]

Although Uganda has ratified most of the international covenants and treaties providing for the right to health and these have been reflected in its health policy instruments, very little progress has been made in implementing the same provisions in the health regulatory framework. Processes have been initiated to reform the laws providing for the regulation of the health sector to bring the old laws into conformity with Uganda's international obligations. Examples include the Public Health Act (October 15, 1935, last reviewed in 1970), the Mental Treatment Act (August, 31, 1938, last reviewed in 1970), the Pharmacy and Drugs Act (June 15, 1971, last reviewed in 1993), and the Venereal Diseases Act (September 30, 1977).

Although the efforts to update Uganda's regulatory framework are laudable, some of the laws proposed by the parliament contain provisions that would significantly inhibit the realization of the right to health. In respect to HIV/AIDS, although the criminalization of the transmission of HIV/AIDS might in some instances be argued to have the effect of curbing the transmission of HIV/AIDS, the stigmatization and discriminatory effect would be significant. Such initiatives could result in the denial of the right by encouraging people to conceal their HIV status, thereby jeopardizing efforts to promote HIV testing and offer access to antiretroviral therapy. The proposed 2009 Anti-homosexuality Bill carried serious implications for the right to health because it sought to stigmatize people based on their sexual orientation and could compel such people to shun centers where they could access health care for the fear of being unfairly treated based on their sexual orientation or subjected to criminal proceedings. The amendment of the intellectual property laws through the Industrial Property Bill has largely updated the current laws,[156] which did not exploit the flexibilities afforded developing countries in the TRIPS Agreement[157] to promote access to medicines.[158] Agreements like the August 30 decision,[159] which permits the government to issue compulsory licenses for

---

152 Art. 22.

153 Art. 24.

154 Art. 33.

155 Art. 34.

156 The Patent Act, ch. 216, Laws of Uganda.

157 Agreement on Trade-Related Aspects of Intellectual Property Rights, Annex to the WTO Marakesh Agreement (1994), available at http://www.wto.org/english/docs_e/legal_e /27-trips.pdf.

158 For example, the WTO Doha Declaration on the TRIPS Agreement and Public Health, Ministerial Conference, Fourth Session, Doha (Nov. 9–14, 2001).

159 Implementation of Para. 6 of the Doha Declaration on the TRIPS Agreement and Public Health, Decision of the General Council of Aug. 30, 2003, Ministerial Conference, Fourth Session, Doha (Nov. 9–14, 2001), available at http://www.wto.org/english/tratop_e/trips_e /implem_para6_e.htm.

essential medicines in emergency circumstances, have not been relied on or utilized despite the limited ability of people to access proper medication.

Thus, although some progress has been made in updating the national regulatory framework governing the health sector, the absence of a substantive provision defining the obligations of the various stakeholders in the health sector remains a significant gap in the protection of the right to health in Uganda.

Enforcement of the Right to Health in Uganda

A cornerstone of implementing the right to health is its enforcement by the Courts of Judicature established under the constitution that have the mandate to exercise judicial power.[160] The Court of Appeal, sitting as the Constitutional Court, is mandated to entertain all matters involving interpreting the provisions of the constitution.[161] The constitution is the supreme law of Uganda, and therefore all authority, power, and acts must be exercised in conformity with the constitution.[162] It is from this supremacy that the Constitutional Court derives its jurisdiction to entertain all matters involving the violation of human rights, which are provided for in Chapter 4 of the constitution. The court's remedial powers include the power to declare certain acts unconstitutional and to order redress as appropriate in the circumstances. Because the right to health is primarily provided for in the constitution (through the constitutional amendment that incorporated the National Objectives and Principles of State Policy), the Constitutional Court is central to the enforcement of the right to health through litigation used to assess whether acts of the government violate the right to health. In *Joyce Nakacwa v. AG and 2 Ors,* where a preliminary objection was raised regarding the jurisdiction of the court to determine the constitutionality of a matter involving health rights, the Constitutional Court ruled that it had the jurisdiction to entertain any matter that involved interpretation of the constitution.[163]

Although the Constitutional Court's powers are limited to the interpretation of provisions of the constitution, the High Court of Uganda is empowered to adjudicate cases of human rights violations and provide adequate redress.[164] The powers of the High Court are mainly remedial and can be invoked only when health rights have actually been violated or threatened, whereas the Constitutional Court's powers are mainly declaratory in determining whether

---

160 Constitution of the Republic of Uganda (1995), art. 126(1).

161 *Id.,* at art. 137(3).

162 *Id.,* at art. 2(2).

163 *Joyce Nakacwa v. The Attorney General of Uganda, Kampala City Council, Mrs Miwanda as the LC1 Chairperson, Nakawa Trading Centre,* Constitutional Petition No. 2 of 2001, available at http://www.globalhealthrights.org/wp-content/uploads/2013/02/CC-2002-Joyce-Nakacwa-v.-Attorney-General-and-Ors..pdf (accessed Apr. 11, 2013).

164 Constitution of the Republic of Uganda, art. 50.

an act is a violation of the constitution or not. The powers of the Constitutional Court are therefore more appropriate for upholding the right to health when the government—through an act of Parliament or through any other exercise of public power—violates or threatens to violate the right to health. The powers of the High Court, on the other hand, are most appropriate for providing redress when an individual's right to health has been violated. Both courts play a key role in promoting health rights advocacy by raising awareness on the justiciability of the right to health and clarifying the rights and responsibilities of the stakeholders in the provision of health services. In an effort to promote accessibility and counter the significant financial burdens of litigation, the constitution enables any person to pursue a constitutional claim when the rights of another person have been violated.[165] This has enabled civil society organizations to pursue judicial remedies on behalf of the poor and indigent whose rights have been violated.

Quasi-judicial bodies have been established to supplement the role of the courts in adjudicating claims of health rights violations. The Equal Opportunities Commission (EOC) was established by the Equal Opportunities Commission Act of 2007 to monitor, evaluate, and ensure that policies, laws, plans, programs, activities, traditions, cultures, usages, and customs of state organs are compliant with equal opportunities and affirmative action in favor of marginalized groups.[166] The commission can investigate on its own initiative, or on a complaint by any person, any act or omission that seems to constitute discrimination or marginalization or to otherwise undermine equal opportunities; and examine any law, proposed law, or policy likely to impair equal opportunities to persons in employment or enjoyment of human rights.[167] The EOC's judicial powers include the power to require the attendance of any person before it to give evidence and to receive evidence and draw such conclusions from the evidence as it deems fit.[168] The commission also has the power to refer any matter to any institution that can better handle the matter in its opinion and to recommend or order any institution or person to perform any action necessary to promote equal opportunities. The EOC therefore plays a key role in addressing discriminatory practices that impair the realization of the right to health.

The Uganda Human Rights Commission[169] can investigate on its own initiative or upon a complaint made by any person any violation of the right to health and also monitors the government's compliance with international

---

165 *Id.*, at art. 50

166 Equal Opportunities Commission Act of 2007, sec. 14(1).

167 *Id.*, at sec. 14(2).

168 *Id.*, at sec. 15.

169 *Id.*, at art. 51 of the Constitution of the Republic of Uganda. The Uganda Human Rights Commission is chaired by a judge of the High Court of Uganda or a person qualified to be a judge of the High Court of Uganda.

treaty and convention obligations on, for example, the right to health.[170] The commission has a wide range of administrative powers, including the power to issue sermons or other orders requiring any person to attend the commission and the production of any document or record relevant to an investigation, question any person on any matter under investigation, require any person to disclose any information within his or her knowledge relevant to any investigation by the commission, and commit persons for contempt of its orders.[171] The commission can, if it is satisfied that there is an infringement of a human right or freedom, order appropriate remedies, such as the release of the detained person, the payment of compensation, or other legal remedy or redress.[172]

Although progress has been made in litigation on rights such as the right to a clean and healthy environment, which is provided under the Ugandan constitution, very little litigation has been brought on the right to health. This may be attributable to the absence of a substantive constitutional provision on the right to health, limited awareness of legal provisions protecting health, and a widely held perception among sizable proportions of the population that essential services in Uganda remain a privilege provided by the government. Some observers argue that an insufficiently progressive judiciary and human rights commission have hampered the few attempts to litigate the right to health.

Litigation of the Right to Health in Uganda: The Maternal Health Case

Maternal mortality and morbidity are well-established benchmarks used to measure the quality of health care available to mothers.[173] Most maternal deaths are caused by five major complications of pregnancy: hemorrhage (the risk of which is increased if a woman is anemic), sepsis, hypertensive disorders of pregnancy, obstructed labor, and unsafe abortion; nearly all these deaths can be prevented by good-quality health care.[174]

In Uganda, the situation remains grave even with a 50 percent reduction in the maternal mortality rate between 1990 and 2010, with the number of deaths per 100,000 live births in 2010 at 310.[175] This is far above the MDG target of 131 deaths per 100,000 live births, and if the projections of the Countdown

---

170 Constitution of the Republic of Uganda (1995), as amended in 2005, art. 52(1).

171 *Id.*, at art. 53(1).

172 *Id.*, at art. 53(3).

173 *Id.*

174 *Joint UN Expert Technical Opinion on Maternal Health and the Right to Health, in the Matter of Constitutional Petition No. 16 of 2011* 6 (Jun. 20, 2011), available at: http://www.cehurd.org /wp-content/uploads/downloads/2012/02/JOINT-UN-EXPERT-OPINION-ON-MM-20th-of-June-2011-FINAL.pdf (accessed Sept. 14, 2012).

175 WHO, *Countdown to 2015 Launches the 2012 Report*, available at http://www.who.int/pmnch /topics/part_publications/countdown_2012_report/en/index1.html.

to 2015 Report are accurate, Uganda will not make that target by 2015.[176] Maternal health care is central to the realization of the right to the highest attainable standard of health for women given their natural reproductive and maternal functions. It is therefore a violation of a woman's right to health if she is unable to access the basic health care necessary for her condition, including both prenatal and postnatal care. The minimum core content of the right to health in this regard requires that mothers before, during, and after labor be able to access the basic health care necessary for their condition, and it is the obligation of the state to ensure that every mother has access to such services.

Women's right to health is supported in the Ugandan Constitution by gender rights, including those providing for affirmative action for women. Article 33 obliges the state to provide facilities and opportunities necessary to enhance the welfare of women to enable them to realize their potential and advancement, and to protect women and their rights, taking into account their unique status and natural maternal functions. The failure to provide basic health services to mothers goes beyond a violation of the right to health as envisaged in international instruments and amounts to a violation of the equality provisions of the Ugandan Constitution.

Other jurisdictions have made significant progress in litigating maternal health as a central component of the right to health for mothers where the state has failed in its obligation to provide basic maternal health care to mothers. In Brazil, for instance, the state was held to be in violation of the right to health and the right to life for failure to secure safety during pregnancy and childbirth that led to the death of a petitioner's daughter. The mother was medically induced to deliver a dead fetus, having waited in a coma for more than eight hours for an ambulance to transport her to a referral hospital. She, too, died.[177] In South Africa, the constitutional court condemned a government program that inhibited the provision of Neviripine, which was necessary to prevent the transmission of HIV from mother to child.[178]

In 2011, following several cases in which mothers lost their lives due to failure to access maternal health care when they needed it, the Center for Health Human Rights and Development, a civil society organization, brought a case before the Constitutional Court of Uganda to challenge the failure by the government to provide adequate maternal health care services to mothers around the country despite its reiteration of a commitment to do so.[179] Inspired

---

176 Uganda Maternal and Child Health Data, available at http://www.countdown2015mnch.org/country-profiles/uganda.

177 *Maria de Lourdes da Silva v. Brazil, Committee on the Elimination of Discrimination Against Women* (CEDAW), 49th Session, (July 11–29, 2011).

178 *Minister of Health and Others v. Treatment Action Campaign and Others* (No. 2) (CCT8/02) (2002) ZACC 15; 2002 (5) SA 721; 2002 (10) BCLR 1033 (July 5, 2002), available at http://www.saflii.org/za/cases/ZACC/2002/15.html.

179 *Center for Health Human Rights and Development, Professor Ben Twinomugisha, Rhoda Kukiriza and Inziku Valente v. Attorney General, Constitutional Court,* Petition No. 16 of 2011, available at http://www.cehurd.org/wp-content/plugins/download-monitor/download.php?id=26.

by the plight of mothers trying to access quality health care to no avail,[180] the case, known as *Petition 16*, was based on two women who lost their lives because they could not access medical assistance during childbirth when they needed it.

Sylvia Nalubowa bled to death at Mityana Hospital, a government facility, having failed to secure an emergency operation to remove the baby from her womb. She delivered a baby at a Health Center III facility only to find out that she was carrying twins and needed an emergency operation to remove the second baby, which the Health Center III was not equipped to conduct. When she was transferred to Mityana Hospital, she spent the final moments of her life in excruciating pain while bleeding and begging for an emergency operation to remove the baby, who lived.

Jennifer Anguko went to Arua Hospital, a government facility, when her labor pains started, hoping to be assisted in delivering her baby. Ten hours later, she had not been attended to by any health practitioners, who neglected her despite being asked repeatedly for help. By the time the hospital staff did tend to her, Jennifer had died, as had the baby she was carrying.

These two cases exemplify extreme failings in the protection of maternal health rights and maternal health service delivery in Uganda. They formed the basis of a constitutional challenge, the petition of which had initially been based upon eleven grounds. After the scheduling conference, seven grounds were agreed on to be submitted for the court's determination.

A preliminary objection by the government resulted in the case being dismissed, and the petition did not proceed for consideration on the merits. The government argued that the petition would require the court to make a determination on political matters, thereby involving the court in what is the exclusive preserve of the executive and the legislature under the constitution. The petitioners in response argued that the preliminary objection was misconceived because the petition required the court to make a determination on the constitutionality of various acts and the omissions of the government as assessed against the standards prescribed by the constitution, and that such a determination is fully within the constitutional mandate of judicial review reserved for the judiciary.

The court ruled in favor of the government, basing its decision on the precedents of *Marbury v. Madison*, *Coleman v. Miller*, *Baker et al. v. Carr et al.*, and *Major David Tinyefuza v. Attorney General*, relying on the political question doctrine.[181] The court's decision hinged on whether the acts and omissions of the government in implementing the right to health can be litigated in courts of law, and the court held that they could not. The court reasoned that some

---

180 Martin Okudi, *Seven Pregnant Mothers Die in Labour*, Daily Monitor, available at http://www.monitor.co.ug/News/National/Seven+pregnant+mothers+die+in+labour+++councillor/-/688334/1498320/-/7crwua/-/index.html.

181 *Marbury v. Madison*, 5 U.S. 137, *Coleman v. Miller*, 307 U.S. 433, *Baker et al. v. Carr et al.*, 369 U.S. 186 (1962), *Major David Tinyefuza v. Attorney General*, Constitutional Petition No. 1 of 1997.

powers are placed exclusively within the jurisdiction of the executive or legislative branch, such that courts of law cannot make judicial determination on them because to do so would lead to an encroachment of the constitutional discretion conferred on the executive and the legislature, thus violating the doctrine of separation of powers.[182] The preliminary objection was accordingly upheld, and the petition was dismissed; the petitioners brought an appeal to the Supreme Court, where it is pending.

The Way Forward for the Right to Health in Uganda

Although the petition is still pending, it is, in some significant respect, already a success story for the right to the highest attainable standard of health in Uganda. For the first time in Uganda, the right to health was made the subject of litigation and gained significant recognition outside the courts.

The petition brought together civil society and academia in support of the right to health by generating dialogue on justiciability. It ignited a social movement around health rights and helped raise people's awareness of their entitlement to access health services as a matter of government obligation, not privilege. This is especially important in Uganda, where quality affordable health services should primarily be funded and provided for by the government and where the services provided by the private sector are neither affordable nor accessible to the average Ugandan. Uganda has made positive progress in developing policy frameworks to conform to international obligations, although the problem of enforcement and implementation of these objectives to ensure that people can in fact access health care services remains. Another challenge in Uganda relates to accountability mechanisms where such access is not afforded and where the right to health is not upheld. Other challenges that define the context for health in Uganda are widespread poverty, low production capacity of pharmaceutical products, and understaffing of health centers.

A key dimension of enshrining health as a legally binding and enforceable right would be to add the right to health as a fundamental right and freedom in the Ugandan Constitution's Bill of Rights. This would constitute a key step toward enumerating a comprehensive act providing for the government and other stakeholders' obligations, as well as enforcement provisions to protect the right to health. This would also bolster the implementation of existing legal and regulatory provisions by giving force to the overarching right to health as a substantive constitutional right. Such a change would allow for an enhanced role of civil society in helping the government identify priorities in the health sector and in generating advocacy and dialogue on the obligations of the government in relation to the right to health.

In sum, it is submitted that it is enhanced accountability mechanisms—particularly in respect to justiciability, implied by the right to health—which can effectively secure improved health outcomes in Uganda.

---

182 *Id.*

Conclusion

Through its analysis of the right to health, this chapter has illustrated how development can help create the conditions for the realization of human rights and how law and rights can help advance development goals. Nevertheless, significant challenges remain, and enshrining the right to health in law is a necessary but not sufficient condition for the realization of better health outcomes and sustainable development in the health sector. International commitments must be effectively translated into domestic legal provisions. Those domestic laws must adequately and appropriately reflect the right to health and offer the right the requisite constitutional standing and comprehensive protection. The law must be fully implemented and supported by the appropriate regulatory provisions that include sufficiently detailed guidance for public bodies on the nature and content of their obligations. Moreover, the law remains one element and tool among many to advance those broader goals; other elements include a range of public policies, advocacy, public dialogue, awareness raising, development research, and economic analysis, as well as grassroots political mobilization. Moreover, the law itself is beset with limitations, including elite capture, insufficient access to justice; the limited impact of legal strategies in certain circumstances, and the confined power of international human rights tribunals. It is clear that realizing the right to health in developing countries demands a long-term, multitiered, and interdisciplinary approach in which the law fulfills just one among several key functions.

Mainstreaming the Marginalized in Development

Conceptualizing the Challenges in India

Pulapre Balakrishnan

There is a movement within democracies across the globe arguing for public policy to be judged by its inclusiveness. It is most evident in Brazil, India, and South Africa, but it is also evident in the older democracies of the United States and the United Kingdom. Thus, there is the slogan "No Child Left Behind" in the United States, while the theme underlying India's Twelfth Five-Year Plan, launched in 2012, is "Inclusive Growth." This chapter analyzes the challenge of mainstreaming the marginalized in India within the overarching theme "Fostering Development through Opportunity, Inclusion, and Equity."

Apart from the fact that the author's professional knowledge is mostly confined to India, there are two reasons why the choice of the context makes good sense. First, the challenge of inclusion, though formidable, is not insurmountable in India presently. This renders a study of the Indian case highly relevant. Second, long before the pursuit of inclusion as a criterion by which to judge public policy attained the prestige that it has today, the idea that the deprived should somehow be central to policy making figured in the political discourse of the country. This is most evident in the lines from Jawaharlal Nehru's speech to the Constituent Assembly over August 14–15, 1947, in which he saw Indian independence as the moment "[t]o bring freedom and opportunity to the common man, to the peasants and workers of India; to fight and end poverty and ignorance and disease; and to create social, economic and political institutions which will ensure justice and fairness to every man and woman."[1] That this project has yet to succeed does not render the Indian case study irrelevant. On the contrary, it brings a certain urgency to a study of continuing marginalization there, one that can serve to show how to structure public policy to achieve inclusion—a lesson that may be of interest to governments in many parts of the world.

This chapter commences with an exploration of the relationship between freedom, opportunity, and development. Drawing on the work of Amartya Sen, it argues that at the core of this nexus is the notion of *capability*. It is now

---

I thank K. P. Sankaran, Amrit Tandon, and Biju Paul Abraham for discussions and comments; R. Govinda and Madhumita Bandyopadhyay for assistance with the data; and N. R. Madhava Menon for advice on what should go into the article. Errors, if any, are mine alone.

1   Jawaharlal Nehru, *Speech to the Constituent Assembly on 14–15 August, 1947*, in *Selected Works of Jawaharlal Nehru*, 2d ser., vol. 3, 135 (Jawaharlal Nehru Memorial Fund 1985).

only a step away to propose that the marginalized be seen as those who lack the basic capabilities enjoyed by the mainstream. Although India's constitution is in many ways impressive, its provisions are, on their own, inadequate to the task of mainstreaming the marginalized. After pointing out what is needed to build the necessary capabilities, the chapter concludes, by reference to some specific instances of governance failure, that the future of development in India, now the world's third-largest economy in terms of purchasing power parity, lies squarely in the space of politics.

Liberty and Capability

As may be expected, given the vision of the republic held out by its founders, the Indian constitution adopted in 1950 had in it provisions to address the marginalized. That over six decades later India is still concerned with the issue suggests that these provisions, discussed below, have not been universally enabling. India remains seriously challenged in terms of the low income of a substantial section of its population, the inadequate supply of public goods, and the low level of social indicators generally.

In approaching the issue of mainstreaming the marginalized, it is vital to start with a generic description of marginalization. This task is guided by the concept of "capabilities" proposed by Sen.[2] Capabilities are embodied endowments that enable "functionings," which are themselves in the nature of actions that individuals consider valuable. Borrowing from mathematics, functioning, then, can be seen as the mapping from capabilities to freedom. For Sen, "freedom" was the freedom to do or act, and this conception took him straight to the idea of development as the expansion of freedoms.[3] This view of development constitutes a standpoint from which to understand marginalization.

The marginalized can now be seen as the unfree within a society, in that they are not free to undertake the actions that they value. And working backward from the conception of development as freedom, marginalization can be located in the absence of what Sen referred to as "basic" capabilities. Now, marginalization reflects "basic capability (in) equality."[4] That is, the marginal in a society are those who, unlike the mainstream, do not possess the capabilities that enable them to achieve the set of functionings considered valuable. Further, and significantly from a practical point of view, so long as these capabilities are not genetic, society, provided that it can muster the resources, can endow all its members with the same set of capabilities deemed basic.[5] It is

---

2   *See* Amartya Sen, *Equality of What?*, in *Tanner Lectures on Human Values*, vol. 1 (S. McMurrin ed., Cambridge U. Press 1980).

3   Amartya Sen, *Development as Freedom* (Oxford U. Press 1999).

4   *See* Sen, *Equality of What?*, *supra* note 2, at 219. Text in parentheses has been inserted by the author.

5   The idea of capabilities, and their place in a theory of justice, has been contested. *See* the essays in Harry Brighouse & Ingrid Robeyns eds., *Measuring Justice: Primary Goods and Capabilities* (Cambridge U. Press 2010).

important when trying to understand marginalization that the numerical factor is irrelevant. The marginalized can well be the majority in a society, and it is not necessary to go to the apartheid era in South Africa to encounter such a situation. Some may argue that this is the case in India today, at least in certain dimensions. While more work would be required to describe to the last detail the capabilities that lead to the expansion of individual freedom, it is argued here that is education that contributes most to the building of these capabilities. Beyond its clear economic potentiality, education also has the capacity to neutralize what has been recognized as *cultural* capital by Pierre Bourdieu.[6] Those familiar with the Indian reality would recognize the role of cultural capital in reproducing marginality in its society.

By adopting the premise of "development as freedom," one can see that the distribution of freedom in a society is closely tied to the distribution of capabilities, because it is the range of an individual's functionings that defines the extent of his or her freedom. And these functionings are closely tied to capabilities.

Although developed by Sen, this view of freedom derives from the work of the political philosopher Isaiah Berlin. Clarifying that he used the terms "liberty" and "freedom" interchangeably, Berlin imagined two concepts of liberty: freedom from restraint and freedom to do. The first he termed "negative" freedom, and the latter "positive" freedom. This compact formulation calls for some clarification. For Berlin, the notion of negative freedom was best understood as follows: "I am normally said to be free to the degree to which no man or body of men interferes with my activity. Political liberty in this sense is simply the area within which a man can act unobstructed by others."[7] On the notion of positive freedom, Berlin said: "The 'positive' sense of the word 'liberty' derives from the wish on the part of the individual to be his own master. I wish to be somebody, not nobody; a doer . . . conceiving goals and policies of my own and realizing them."[8]

Berlin's work proved to be a minefield because he drew a distinction between notions of freedom that became central to the discourse on rights, justice, and welfare in at least one intellectual tradition. We are now able to see that as there cannot be freedom to act so long as there are restraints, for Sen's idea of development to be actualized, both concepts of liberty are essential. Negative and positive freedoms are, as it were, the "necessary" and "sufficient" conditions, respectively, in the space of development. Each of the two notions of freedom comes with its own implicit role for the state. For negative freedom to prevail in a society, the state must act as a "night watchman" or "traffic policeman" to ensure that the liberty of an individual is not encroached on. Yet, Berlin left the answer to the question of the role of the state

---

6   Pierre Bourdieu, *The Forms of Capital*, in *Handbook of Theory and Research for the Sociology of Education* 241–58 (J. Richardson ed., Greenwood 1986).

7   Isaiah Berlin, *Two Concepts of Liberty* 3 (Clarendon Press 1958).

8   *Id.* at 8.

in the case of positive freedom open-ended, pointing out only that the notion of positive freedom has been used to rationalize authoritarian regimes in history. It is clear, however, that to endow individuals with capabilities, the state would have to be more than a mere night watchman. Agreement on the role of the state in development is, of course, unlikely to be attained easily.

As has been stated, if "development" means "the expansion of freedoms," and freedom itself derives from capabilities, a definition of the essential or basic capabilities is necessary. Sen himself desisted from drawing up such a list, arguing that it ought to be left to a democratic process to arrive at the functionings a society considers valuable enough for its members to achieve. He thought of the notion of basic capability as quite a general one and imagined that its application would have to be culture dependent, especially in the weighting of different capabilities. Other philosophers, such as Martha Nussbaum, while fully immersed in Sen's capability-based approach to development, have taken the view that a list is indispensable. Nussbaum actually drew up such a list.[9]

However, Sen, while refusing to be tied down to any particular set of capabilities, nevertheless provided an important insight into the question of how to deal with marginalization. As individuals do not come into the world rigged with capabilities, and resources are needed to equip them accordingly, extending the basic capabilities across the population would require a collective commitment to the expansion of individual freedom. Despite its philosophical ring, this is actually a practical suggestion. And despite its idealistic tone, it is downright economistic in inspiration. Collective or public action is needed to equip individuals with capabilities; if individuals could endow themselves, they would not remain marginal.

This implies that empowering individuals requires what Sen has referred to as "public action," or a collective effort in a democracy. As for the inspiration from economic theory that was previously referred to, a parallel may be seen between the need for public action in the present context and that of the appropriate response to market failure in an unfettered economy. Recall that market failure is the failure of an economy of private agents to attain the desired optimum, thus validating some form of public intervention.[10]

It is necessary here to flag a red herring in the discourse on marginalization in India, namely, that a focus on quality detracts from the main concern. If the development of capabilities is one of the goals of education, the efficacy of education must be the focus of our attention. For example, once the impor-

---

9   See Martha Nussbaum, *Human Rights and Human Capabilities*, 20 Harv. Hum. Rights J. 21–24 (2007). However, Sen and Nussbaum converge toward the position that it is education that is central to capabilities. For further reference, *see* Melanie Walker & Elaine Unterhalter, *The Capability Approach: Its Potential for Work in Education*, in *Amartya Sen's Capability Approach and Social Justice in Education* (Melanie Walker & Elaine Unterhalter eds., Palgrave Macmillan 2010).

10   See Francis M. Bator, *The Anatomy of Market Failure*, 72 Q. J. of Economics 351–379 (1958).

tance of "capabilities" is embraced, the outcome of an educational arrangement cannot be ignored. It is difficult to be satisfied with a halfway house for the marginalized en route to the mainstream via the provision of education. For example, those who have completed their schooling can either implement differential calculus or they cannot; either they are able to read the classics of their culture in their mother tongue or they cannot; either they can distinguish between a cell and a tissue or they cannot. Moreover, they need to realize the salience of citizenship, the core of which is to be able to balance rights with responsibilities under self-government. Education is meant to develop cognitive skills, to train individuals to recognize patterns, to distinguish between the whole and the parts, and, above all, when faced with a rapidly changing technology environment, to learn to learn continuously. Where these capabilities have not been developed, the original educational initiative must be deemed to have failed, whatever may be the rhetoric accompanying its provision.

The recognition of capabilities as the foundation of freedom implies that the quality of education defines its efficacy. There is a tendency in India to denounce as "the pursuit of elitism" any initiative intended to make India's public education system more effective by raising quality. Such denunciations are a form of avoidable sentimentality. Even as the marginalized have revealed their own preference by voting with their feet,[11] as far as public education is concerned, sticking with the demonstrably indifferent quality of public education in the country would be self-defeating[12] within a project of mainstreaming the marginalized. In fact, it is such sentimentality that has turned many Indian initiatives aimed at the marginalized over the past half century into a form of provisioning for poverty through income support, rather than an enabling of individuals to lead productive and fulfilling lives. This is in stark contrast with the global experience in democracies.

It may have something to do with the legacy of the caste system in India, whereby hierarchy is glossed over when not actually justified by reference to the benevolence of the ruler, a practice that has a residual presence even among elected governments in its democracy. Whatever the provenance of India's public policy toward the marginalized, its consequence is that goods are distributed but power is not. Be that as it may, income support to the poor does not constitute a program of building capabilities, which is the strategy that should be central to the project of mainstreaming the marginalized.

To sum up, while capabilities ultimately reside in individuals, when barriers exist to attaining them, a social commitment to equipping individuals with the basic capabilities is needed. The next section proposes what should be the core of such an approach, but not before examining what has been attempted in India.

---

11   Data point to the growing share of private schools in catering to India's growing population.

12   The reader is cautioned against interpreting this observation as making a case for privatization. The author's view on the matter will become apparent in the next section of the chapter.

Formal Rights and Substantive Opportunity

The founders of the Indian republic were high-minded men,[13] and this is reflected in its idealistic constitution. These well-meant constitutional provisions, however, have failed to usher in development as freedom as envisaged by Sen. In light of the framework expounded here, the founders failed, because, even though they were alert to the importance of negative freedoms, those freedoms were insufficient to fill the foundational role of capabilities in a credible project to expand positive freedoms. For example, of what use is the "right to property" when one does not have the opportunity to earn a livelihood, or earns so low a wage as not to be able to save? Similarly, of what use is the constitutional provision "freedom of expression" when one is illiterate or poorly educated?

India's founding fathers did not completely overlook these possibilities; they conceived of the Directive Principles of State Policy.[14] These principles were meant to serve as a guideline to the state in the making of policy. They include the goals of social justice and economic welfare and explicitly refer to the provision of education. The principles, however, are not justiciable and are of little use when citizens are faced with career politicians devoted more to maximizing their own "private" utility functions as opposed to some mythical "social" welfare function.

It is now possible to see how India's constitutional provisions, whether in the form of the directive principles or of fundamental rights, may have proved to be inadequate. By placing them in the context of the discourse on development initiated by Sen, while the latter are justiciable, in that the violation of the rights may be challenged in courts of law, they remain within the realm of "negative" freedom. The directive principles can be invoked to build capabilities, but they are not justiciable. Thus, if the Indian state represented by its political class cannot be reined in to act decisively in the desired direction, the directive principles are not of much use to the marginalized. Economists recognize this as the "principal-agent problem." The clearest instance may be in the context of corporate governance, but it bears applicability in the social sphere. The principal-agent problem can readily emerge in the governance of so vast and diverse a society as India. However, the origins of the idea and its implications are most easily understood in the context of corporate governance.

Under contemporary capitalism, shareholding is widespread and firms are run by the managers. This feature, Robin Marris has observed, effectively separates ownership from control.[15] He identified the form as *managerial* capi-

---

13 The members of the Constituent Assembly that deliberated on the constitution were overwhelmingly male.

14 The distinction between "fundamental rights" and "directive principles," and the tension that can arise when they are invoked at the same time, is central to understanding India's constitutional provisions. For a concise contemporary introduction, *see* Madhav Khosla, *The Indian Constitution* (Oxford U. Press 2012).

15 *See* Robin Marris, *The Economic Theory of Managerial Capitalism* (Basic Books 1964).

talism, as opposed to the *entrepreneurial* capitalism of the 19th century. The implication of managerial capitalism is that there is now no guarantee that the managers, who are the agents, will manage the firm in the interest of the principals, who are the shareholders.[16] Under actually existing democracy, as opposed to some idealized form, the principal-agent problem is an ever-present threat. In a parliamentary democracy, citizens own democracy, so to speak, but it is the legislature that governs the country via a permanent bureaucracy that in theory is accountable to parliament but in reality is under no one's control. The conundrum *Quis custodiet ipsos custodes?* "Who will guard the guards themselves?" best captures the implication of such an arrangement. Coined before the beginning of the Christian era to capture the challenge of enforcing marital fidelity, it has a direct bearing on the issue of governance.

As seen in the previous section, Sen asserted that there is no universally accepted measure of capabilities; he refused even to list any on the grounds that agreement should be arrived at by a democratic process. However, poverty remains very high in India; that at least a third of its population is considered to be poor, according to a low poverty line, indicates that a substantial proportion of the population is marginalized. This after 60 years of independence, during which unending pronouncements have been made about the rationale of economic policy being the eradication of poverty.

It is now 40 years since Indira Gandhi coined the slogan "*Garibi Hatao,*" or "Eradicate Poverty," meant to communicate the intent of the policies her government was adopting. While the economics of this failed experiment needs to be understood, the framework outlined heretofore would have served to predict the outcome. The means adopted by Indira Gandhi were mainly draconian controls on the private corporate sector combined with an extortionate tax rate rationalized as "socialism." This by itself could do little to lift the poor out of poverty; in fact, the economy promptly contracted as private investment declined, as could have been predicted. In terms of the useful distinction drawn by Berlin, controls effectively restricted the area of liberty of the capitalists; that is, the controls constricted the negative freedom of capitalists but could do little to expand the positive freedom of the workers.

This experience of dealing with marginalization should hardly be surprising. In a market economy, individuals have two livelihood options: to work for others or to work for themselves. While peasants are seen as working for themselves, this option is available only to those who own land. In a country with a low land-man ratio, non-landowning peasants must seek employment or become entrepreneurs. Capabilities endowed through education and training are crucial to whether they will be able to earn their livelihoods as successful entrepreneurs or as productive laborers for hire in the market. The persistence of poverty reflects the underinvestment in building capabilities that has plagued

---

16   Marris' insight was to be vindicated some four decades later when managers of the financial sector came close to wrecking the global economy by taking excessive risks in the pursuit of personal reward. *See* Paul Krugman, *The Return of Depression Economics and the Crisis of 2008* (Norton 2009).

public policy in India for over half a century. The final section of this chapter is devoted to this issue. But first, the rest of this section offers a critical appraisal of India's approach toward marginalization during the past half century.

Historically, there have been two approaches to dealing with poverty or marginalization in India. The first was prevalent in the 1950s, when policy makers believed that a growing economy would lift the poor out of poverty. While the idea that growth was a necessary condition for poverty alleviation made good sense, the strategy could not succeed fully without the expansion of education and the upgrading of skills. More recently, the approach appears to have altered. Now the keyword is "inclusion," chosen to reflect the intent of public policy to mainstream the marginalized. What is meant by "inclusive growth" is revealed in the government's increasing resort to transfer payments of various kinds that have come to represent public policy. There has also been a proliferation of so-called rights promulgated through acts of parliament such as the right to work or even the right to food. Apart from the fact that it is not yet clear whether these rights are justiciable, if marginalization is understood as unequal capabilities, these proclamations do not even address the problem, as they leave the capabilities of the population untouched.[17] In fact, this approach is not really different from *annadanam*, or the ritual feeding of the poor in India's temples. It not only smacks of paternalism but, more significantly, implies that the poor may never be enabled to go about on their own, being permanently on state-sponsored drip.

A particular version of the approach may be found in a speech in 2008 by the finance minister, Palaniappan Chidambaram: "India must touch a 10 per cent growth and sustain it for 10, 20 and 30 years"[18] to make poverty part of history. The minister went on to say that growth was not an end in itself but part of a strategy to "raise resources and acquire the capacity to spend more money on the provision of goods and services that will mitigate the hardship of millions of poor people and bring some cheer into their lives." This is perhaps the clearest articulation of the rationale of the Indian state in the early 21st century. This approach does not square with one of mainstreaming the marginalized through the building of capabilities, and it appears self-defeating: as the government spends an increasing share of its revenues on subsidizing consumption, there is little left for public capital formation. The growth of the economy must then slow down, and with it the growth of revenues necessary to feed the government's welfare schemes. Given their more or less similar starting points in the early 1950s, the experience of China in this dimension is relevant to India. China spent public funds on health and education but made sure to maintain the high rate of public investment, necessary for growth.

---

17   For an assessment of whether these rights have worked for the poor, *see* S. K. Das, *India's Rights Revolution: Has It Worked for the Poor?* (Oxford U. Press 2013). Of course, it must also be acknowledged that not much time has elapsed since their promulgation.

18   Speech outlining the policies of his government delivered in Singapore. *See* C. Rajamohan, *If Poverty Has to Go, Growth Must Touch 10 Percent and Continue,* Indian Express (Mar. 27, 2013).

What Does It Take to Build Capabilities?

Education may be identified as the single most important input into the building of capabilities of a human being. To education may be added health, as there is clinical evidence that learning can be thwarted by malnutrition.[19] Research in the field of education points to three features. First, there are increasing returns to learning. By this is meant that learning is a function of the stock of knowledge already embedded in the individual; the initial educational inputs influence the productivity of later ones. Second, early child development is crucial, as the development of neural circuits and the behavior that they mediate are most plastic at this stage and therefore most receptive to environmental influences. Third, a part of mental development is believed to be prenatal and therefore related to the health of expecting mothers. All of this adds up to the implication that some parts of an individual's capabilities are developed at a very early stage in the life cycle. This, in turn, has implications for educational policy, particularly for how public spending should be distributed across educational levels. Somewhat surprisingly, studies from the United States show the rate of return to public spending being highest at the preschool level.[20]

Education has long been identified as the medium for the development of human cognitive skills. However, while cognitive skills may be paramount, there are also noncognitive skills—such as tenacity and perseverance, not to mention attributes such as motivation—that should be included in the list of capabilities that may be counted as "basic." These, too, can be inculcated. Randomized control trials conducted in the United States have shown that special school programs can make a difference in these areas. But there is a third dimension to be considered. Education, including play school, takes place during the period in a child's life when values, such as empathy, develop. Skills, both cognitive and noncognitive, through spillovers, and values such as empathy, by contributing to social cohesion, generate externalities that are not captured by the market. Social cohesion may be thought of as a public good. It has been demonstrated in economic theory that in the presence of externalities, and vis-à-vis public goods, private provision may be expected to be suboptimal. This in turn suggests that there are sound reasons for the government to take the lead in such instances. Very likely, it is because education is believed to generate externalities that education has been largely privately provided in Western Europe and the United States since at least the 19th century.

Acemoglu and Robinson argue that one characteristic of successful nations is the fairly equal distribution of power. Surely this is not unrelated to publicly provided, uniform compulsory education. This arrangement ensures

19   *See* Mathew Jukes, *The Long-Term Impact of Pre-school Health and Nutrition on Education*, 26 Food and Nutrition Bull. S193–S201 (2006).

20   *See* James Heckman, *Skill Formation and the Economics of Investing in Disadvantaged Children*, 312 Sci. 1900–1902 (2006).

a degree of equality of opportunity and brings about a sense of social cohesion, thus widening the cohort of stakeholders in the progress of the country. There is a potential virtuous cycle here. Of course, the movement toward a more egalitarian provision of education, without sacrificing quality, requires a certain social transformation. This can be seen in the fact that the United States, France, and Russia, each in a widely differing region of the world but sharing a fairly egalitarian school system, are united by a history of revolutionary change, though of differing forms. In the United States, the transformation began even before 1776, the settlers having rejected some of the values of the mother country[21] in the very act of migration to an alien land.

The importance of social transformation in context can be seen by returning to India. Though unadorned by the language of academic philosophy, education as an equalizing force was not only imagined by Gandhi but also central to his vision of society in an independent India.[22] He emphasized "basic" and "meaningful" education for all; however, because the social transformation necessary for his vision to become a reality did not gain ground in the country, a credible project of mainstreaming the marginalized did not take off.

Table 1. Adult literacy rates worldwide, 2000–2004

World	2000–2004
Arab States	82
Central and Eastern Europe	70
Central Asia	97
East Asia and the Pacific	99
Latin America and the Caribbean	92
North America and Western Europe	90
South and West Asia	99
Sub-Saharan Africa	59
India	61

Source: "Comparing Education Statistics across the World," *Global Education Digest* (Paris: UNESCO, 2006), p. 174.

Note: An adult is defined as being 15 years old or older.

Given the argument that education has to be central to mainstreaming the marginalized, the case of India proves instructive. Table 1 provides comparative figures on adult literacy rates in India and countries broadly grouped throughout the world. India figures poorly in a global comparison, managing to stay even only with Sub-Saharan Africa.

---

21 *See* Daron Acemoglu & James Robinson, *Why Nations Fail: The Economic Origins of Power, Prosperity and Poverty* (MIT Press 2012).

22 *See* M. K. Gandhi, *Constructive Programme: Its Meaning and Place* (Navajivan Mudranalaya 1941), for a discussion of his "Constructive Programme."

Table 2 looks at the distribution of the population by educational attainment in India around 2010.

Table 2. Distribution of educational attainment (persons per 1,000 by completed level of education)

	Illiterate	Literate without formal schooling	Primary	Middle	Higher secondary	Diploma	Graduate	Post-graduate
Rural:								
Male	316	9	381	141	123	5	20	5
Female	489	7	329	93	69	2	9	2
All	400	8	355	118	96	4	14	4
Urban:								
Male	178	8	301	150	211	17	96	28
Female	284	8	293	131	187	6	68	22
All	229	8	298	141	205	12	83	25

Source: Education in India: 2007–08 Participation and Expenditure (National Sample Survey Report No. 532; New Delhi: Government of India, 2010), pp. A16–A21.

Even in the urban areas less than a quarter of the population has been educated up to the secondary level. For the rural areas, the figure is less than 10 percent. These are disturbingly low figures. Given the distribution of the Indian population between urban and rural segments, one would expect the aggregate figure for those with a secondary education or higher to be around 16 percent. A comparative study would be useful. Taking the same indicator of educational attainment for the year 2000, the figures for China and Malaysia were 48 percent and 41 percent, respectively. Viewed historically, the fraction of the population that had completed secondary education in India in 2005 was less than half of that in China in 1975.[23] While China's advantage over India in the field of education should come as no surprise, that this advantage is shared even by Malaysia may be seen as an eye-opening statistic to many. There is also the gender dimension to be noted. Table 2 shows that at every level, and in both the rural and urban areas, Indian women fare worse than men in educational attainment.

---

23   For comparative data on these three countries, *see* Michelle Riboud & Hong Tan, *Improving Skills for Competitiveness*, in *Accelerating Growth and Job Creation in South Asia* (Ejaz Ghani and Sadiq Ahmed eds., Oxford U. Press 2009). While recognizing China's superior performance vis-à-vis India as regards educational provision, it should be borne in mind that this was achieved in an environment without political liberty and severe restrictions of various kinds on the population. The India-China comparison should thus be seen as pointing to one of the failings of India's democracy rather than as a validation of the path adopted by China's dictatorship.

Turning to the related issue of public provision for education, table 3 provides comparative data on public expenditure as a share of GDP over five decades. Again, that public expenditure on education in India has generally been less than that of East Asian nations is overshadowed by the finding that it is also lower than in the East African economies included in the table.[24]

Table 3. Public expenditure on education as a percentage of national income

	1970	1980	1990	2000	2010
Ethiopia	1.8	3.3	4.9	4.8	4.7
Kenya	5.0	6.8	6.7	6.4	6.7
Bangladesh	1.4	1.5	2.0	2.5	2.2
India	2.8	2.8	4.0	4.1	3.2
Pakistan	1.7	2.0	2.6	1.8	2.4
Thailand	3.5	3.4	3.6	5.0	3.8
Republic of Korea	3.6	3.7	4.2	3.8	5.0
Peru	3.8	3.1	3.8	3.3	2.7
Brazil	2.7	3.6	4.6	3.8	5.7
Argentina	3.3	2.7	1.1	4.6	6.0
United Kingdom	5.3	5.6	5.4	5.3	5.4
France	4.9	5.0	5.8	5.8	5.9
United States	6.6	6.7	5.3	4.8	5.6
Japan	3.9	5.8	4.7	3.5	3.8

Sources: Statistical Yearbook (New York, United Nations) and *Global Education Digest* (Paris: UNESCO, 2011, 2012).

Note: In (the minority of) cases where data were unavailable for the first year of a decade, data for the closest year have been entered.

To adjust for population and income, table 4 measures expenditure per student as a percentage of GDP per capita. This serves as an index of public expenditure in relation to a country's capacity to pay for it. The data show that spending for primary education in India is lower than in all the other countries in the panel except Bangladesh and Peru. Kenya, the only representative from Sub-Saharan Africa in the table, spends substantially more than India per student in primary education in relation to its per capita income.

---

24   The countries were chosen on the basis of data availability and with an eye on regional representation.

Table 4. Public expenditure per student across
level of education as a percentage of GDP per
capita (2009–2010)

	Primary	Secondary	Tertiary
Kenya	22.3	22.0	
Bangladesh	8.8	12.0	27.7
India	8.9	16.2	55.0
Thailand	24.4	9.3	22.7
Republic of Korea	23.1	23.6	13.0
Peru	8.3	10.1	9.0
Brazil	20.5	20.9	28.9
Argentina	16.8	27.1	19.1
United Kingdom	24.3	31.1	20.6
France	18.4	29.3	39.8
United States	22.4	25.2	19.4
Japan	23.7	24.3	25.3

Source: "Comparing Education Statistics across the World,"
Global Education Digest (Paris: UNESCO, 2011), pp. 232–234.

However, for tertiary education, the figure for India is the highest among all the economies represented. Even for those aware of the top-heavy nature of public spending on education in India, the factor by which spending per student at the tertiary level exceeds that at the primary level must be unexpected, especially in a global comparison. In this context, note that in the United States and the United Kingdom, for example, public expenditure is higher for primary education than it is for tertiary education. The ranking is exactly the opposite in India. India has privileged the highest levels of education. The data presented so far, then, show that in a country where the adult literacy rate in 2010 was around 65 percent, the pattern of public spending on education contributed little toward mainstreaming the marginalized.

Table 5. Public versus private expenditure on education (as a percentage of GDP, 2001–2002)

	Public sector			Private sector		
	Primary	Secondary	Tertiary	Primary	Secondary	Tertiary
France	1.7	2.7	0.9	negligible	0.2	0.2
United Kingdom	1.8	2.5	0.8	0.1	0.4	0.3
United States	2.3	2.0	1.2	0.3	0.2	1.5
India	1.5	1.7	0.8	0.1	0.1	negligible

Source: "Comparing Education Statistics across the World," *Global Education Digest* (Paris: UNESCO, 2004), pp. 134–141.

Table 5 looks at expenditure on education by the public and private sectors. What is interesting is that spending on "schooling"—defined here as primary and secondary education—in the advanced Western economies is undertaken overwhelmingly by the public sector. In France, there is negligible spending on schooling by the private sector. In India, the public sector spends more on primary education than the private sector, but public spending on schooling is substantially less than that of the richest countries of the world.

The far greater levels of literacy and the stock of education measured by the number of years of primary and secondary education in the advanced economies are surely related to public spending on education, especially schooling. The data presented above may be interpreted to suggest that in a comparison with India, the rich economies of the world have invested more in developing the basic capabilities of their citizens via publicly funded education. Observing this, we would want to understand why the process of building capabilities is being held back in India? Is it solely a matter of the inadequate funding of education?

The rest of this chapter argues that the mainstreaming of the marginalized by the enhancement of their capabilities is being held back because Indian democracy is facing a crisis of governance. What does it mean to be "governance challenged"? There are no simple answers, but there must be a beginning if there is to be an end to the drought of public action in the sphere of equalizing capabilities. And a good beginning would be to recognize one of the symptoms of this crisis. Thus it is that India is unable to ensure that outcomes of public intervention match intent. While there are many spheres in which this is the case, the focus here is on public expenditure on education, health, and infrastructure.

Since 2002, public expenditure on primary education has been on the increase in India. But outcomes, as shown by one of the few independent audits of learning—undertaken by the NGO Pratham—are very poor and getting worse. Pratham's most recent report[25] for rural India has stated the follow-ing: "Reading levels [show] decline in many states. Nationally, reading levels have declined in many states across North India. The All India figure for the proportion of children in Std V able to read a Std II level text has dropped from 53.7% in 2010 to 48.2% in 2011." Further, "Arithmetic levels also show a decline across most states. . . . Nationally, the proportion of Std III children able to solve a 2-digit subtraction problem with borrowing has dropped from 36.3% in 2010 to 29.9% in 2011." All this at a time when, as is documented in the report, "private school enrollment is rising in most states." Clearly the global debate on the relative importance of resources versus restructuring[26] of the system in raising educational attainment is of great relevance to India, but it is not reflected in the mainstream discourse, despite evidence of teacher absenteeism alongside a worsening teacher-pupil ratio. Greater importance appears to be given to spending rather than governance, of which restructur-ing would be a part. The poor learning outcomes reported are not surprising in light of one account of the governance of the flagship program of the gov-ernment of India aimed at early school students in Kashmir: "The Sarv Shik-sha Abhiyan (SSA) had been launched with much fanfare with an objective to benefit lakhs[27] of students, particularly those who live in rural areas and do not have easy access to education. But due to its poor implementation, lack of monitoring and allegations of irregularities, the scheme seems to be direction-less in the state." The author also warns of an inability of the state bureaucracy to absorb such large fund infusions from the central government.[28]

Next, a look at the health sector. Studies on the effectiveness of the government-sponsored Integrated Child Development Scheme (ICDS), col-lected and discussed in *Lifting the Curse* by Lawrence Haddad and Sushila Zeitlyn, speak of the indicators of child nutrition in India worsening. The authors explicitly identify "better governance," rather than resources, as the input crucial to improving nutrition indicators for India's children.[29]

---

25 *Annual Status of Education Report 2011: Rural* (Pratham 2012).

26 *See* E. A. Hanushek & L. Woesmann, *Education Quality and Economic Growth* (World Bank 2007). The global debate has a strong bearing on India, as seen in the substantial rise in both public and private spending on education in the country.

27 A *lakh* is an Indian number equivalent to one hundred thousand.

28 Shujaat Bukhari, *Education in the Country's Heaven—The Hell We Care!*, Governance Now (Oct. 1–15, 2012).

29 *See* Lawrence Haddad & Sushila Zeitlyn, *Lifting the Curse: Overcoming Persistent Undernutri-tion in India*, 40 Inst. of Dev. Stud. Bull. (2009). Some four years later, the authors' conclusion on the working of the ICDS over the five-year period 2006–10 has been validated by a report of the comptroller and auditor general, India's constitutional watchdog on the use of public funds. The report identified poor infrastructure and the absence of hygiene in the *anganwa-dis*, or public kindergartens. In the light of the argument being developed in this chapter, this speaks of lapses such as medicine kits being unavailable due to "the failure of State Govern-ments in spending funds released to them by the Centre." *CAG Audit Reveals Lapses in ICDS Implementation*, Hindu (Mar. 7, 2011). Resources do not seem to be the problem in India any longer.

The final instance of governance failure is taken from the agricultural sector, in particular the case of irrigation. It has been known for some time now that while public expenditure on irrigation has soared, the expansion of area under irrigation has moved at a glacial pace.[30] While the records for irrigation give all-India figures, a recent application made under the Right to Information Act in the state of Maharashtra has brought into the public domain pathologies such as projects not having come onstream in over four decades.[31] The figures quoted with respect to the estimated loss to the public exchequer are disturbingly large.

These examples from different areas of the economy reflect the challenge faced by India's democracy in ensuring that the intention is not carried through in government programs. They also indicate that it is governance alone that by now stands in the way of "mainstreaming the marginalized" in the country, as *effective* public policy is central to the task. The history of economic development has shown that very few countries have been successful in this dimension without expanding education, health, and infrastructure via the public sector. At the same time, there are few countries that have so little to show for their public spending over decades as India.

It is possible to conceive of two ways of neglecting a problem. The problem may be neglected by not giving it sufficient attention. Or it may be neglected by starving its solution of the necessary resources. It could be said that for about half a century after 1947, there was neglect of the problem of marginalization on both counts; that is, there were neither sufficient resources nor attention. For about a decade now, with faster growth and, in the case of education, more external funding, there has been a substantial increase in public spending on the social sector but no visible improvement, possibly due to worsening governance.

To return to the original concerns, if marginalization is what is wished to be addressed, staying focused on the building of capabilities via schooling is a must. Two considerations may be flagged. First, the world is far more complex today than it was in the 1950s, when modern India started out on its journey. Early education now has to go well beyond the Three Rs. In the context of the challenges posed by globalization, rapidly changing technology, emerging ecological constraints, and making democracy work, learning to learn continuously must be part of the capability set of citizens. Second, inasmuch as marginalization is related to inequality, the move toward a certain degree of uniformity, at least at the level of primary and secondary education, has to be contemplated. The diversity of school boards, and their divergent levels of prestige, is marked in India today. As stated, uniformity can also contribute to social cohesion.

---

30   *See* Pulapre Balakrishnan, *Economic Growth in India: History and Prospect* (Oxford U. Press 2010), for data on expenditure and the recorded outcome.

31   Http://ibnlive.in.com/newstopics/maharashtra-irrigation-scam.html (accessed Apr. 13, 2013).

Conclusion

India is no longer a poor economy. In 2011 it overtook Japan as the third-largest economy of the world when output is measured in purchasing power parity terms. Possessing the resources needed to mainstream its marginalized citizens is no longer a constraint. Then what is?

It is hoped that this article has, first, demonstrated that India is now governance challenged, and, second, proposed one way of seeing this, namely, in terms of the ability to match outcome with intent in the public sphere. More generally, India is unable to generate the public goods essential for mainstreaming the marginalized. From an economic point of view, it is salient to view democracy as individuals combining to solve the coordination problem that results in the absence of public goods in a society. Or, to put it positively, citizens give themselves a democratic form of government mainly to ensure that they have the public goods that they value. The Westminster model and the political parties that populate it were meant as a mere instrumentality here. In India, an acute case of the principal-agent problem has come to mean that democracy first benefits the political parties, whose main objective, it seems, is to capture the state apparatus to enrich their constituents. The extraordinary increases recorded in the assets of politicians while they are in power reflects precisely this. Interestingly, all parties govern in the name of the marginalized. The present state of affairs may be expected to continue in India so long as a substantial section of the population is poor and ill educated, leaving them unable to govern the actions of their elected representatives.

This chapter has refrained from speaking about the program of economic reforms initiated in India in 1991, mainly liberalization of the policy regime, which has been received positively in the West. This is not accidental. It should have become clear by now that mainstreaming the marginalized cannot be achieved by a program of increasing integration of India with the rest of the world via trade and industrial policy reforms. The economic reforms were aimed mainly at achieving such integration. While this project has merits, it cannot be a substitute for a development policy. Mainstreaming the marginalized requires that this objective be brought into the center of the public policy agenda of the country. It requires that focus be trained on the interventions that will benefit the marginalized. A section of India will remain marginalized as long as the development of their capabilities remains marginal.

The Right to Information as a Tool for Community Empowerment

ANUPAMA DOKENIYA

The right of people to have access to information about the functioning of post–World War II governments was incorporated into international human rights conventions as a complement to the freedom of expression. Driven by concerns about the erosion of accountability in the face of growth in the public sector, a few countries also adopted legislation guaranteeing the right to public information to their citizens (and in some cases, noncitizens) over the subsequent decades.[1]

More recently, the right to information (RTI) has ascended to greater prominence in the international human rights pantheon. It has been incorporated into the constitutions and legislative systems of a host of countries, including several developing countries. The first big wave was in Eastern Europe, where countries adopted RTI laws[2] as part of the post-Soviet democratic transition process, followed by other countries also going through a democratic transition, such as South Africa, in the wake of the end of apartheid, and Mexico, with the victory of Vicente Fox and the Partido Acción Nacional (PAN) in 2000. By 2013, 94 countries had enacted RTI laws, and several other countries had active movements supporting the passage of such legislation.[3]

An RTI law gives citizens[4] the right to access government records without being obliged to demonstrate a legal interest or standing—a fundamental shift in the principle guiding access to public information from "need to know" to "right to know." Further, global standards on RTI have converged on the principle of *maximum disclosure*—meaning that the right of access extends to a

---

1   Alasdair S. Roberts, *Blacked Out: Government Secrecy in the Information Age* (Cambridge U. Press 2006); John M. Ackerman & Irma E. Sandoval-Ballestero, *The Global Explosion of Freedom of Information Laws,* 58(1) Admin. L. Rev. 85–130 (2006).

2   These laws are labeled in different countries as right to information (RTI), freedom of information (FOI), or access to information (ATI) laws. The idea of freedom is tied to the concept of liberties, or *freedom from* restraints, for example, from censorship. The idea of a right, on the other hand, connotes a positive *right to* something. Access to information is often characterized as a positive right because it denotes a right to something—in this case, public information. Several laws are also labeled ATI laws without denoting the principle of a legal entitlement. This chapter uses the term *right to information* when referring to these laws, even though some of them might be titled FOI or ATI.

3   *93 Countries Have FOI Regimes, Most Tallies Agree* (Oct. 19, 2012), available at http://www.freedominfo.org/2012/10/93-countries-have-foi-regimes-most-tallies-agree/; *Rwanda Publishes New Law on Right to Information* (Mar. 13, 2013), available at http://www.freedominfo.org/2013/03/rwanda-publishes-new-law-on-right-to-information/.

4   In some instances, the right extends to all interested parties, including noncitizens.

broad range of government documents, unless explicitly forbidden by a limited regime of exceptions to protect overriding public and private interests.[5] Under an RTI law, therefore, a "presumption of disclosure" and transparency supersedes the "presumption of secrecy" that has traditionally characterized the functioning of government.[6] These principles embody a fundamental reconfiguration of state-society relations if the law is adequately implemented.

This chapter discusses the fundamental paradigm shift in the way that RTI is conceptualized and used. For much of the 20th century, RTI was seen as a complement to, or even a component of, freedom of expression and media rights. Over the past two decades, the potential of RTI as an instrument for furthering the realization of economic and social rights has become clear. Although most of the earlier laws were championed by political elites, civil society groups—primarily domestic, supported by international nongovernmental organizations (NGOs)[7]—have been the driving force for the adoption of newer laws. These groups highlight the potential of RTI as a tool to expose high-level corruption, and one that can be used by even the poorest communities to hold government accountable for the expenditure of public resources and the delivery of services, entitlements, and livelihood opportunities. The second section of this chapter sketches this evolution and highlights cases in which communities in some of the poorest and least-developed regions have succeeded in using RTI in this way. These cases belie the perspective that access to government information is reserved for educated and technically savvy citizens and is beyond the reach of poor, illiterate communities.[8]

The chapter also presents lessons learned about what factors enable communities to leverage the potential of RTI and what hinders them. Although the cases discussed are compelling, inspirational, and indicative of the potential of RTI, they are relatively few. Most of the cases in this chapter are from India and Mexico, two of the highest-profile implementers of RTI over the past decade, and a few are from other countries: South Africa, Argentina, and

---

5   The inclusion of a negative list that enumerates the categories of information exempted from disclosure expands the scope of the law to all other categories of information. Exceptions are subject to time limits; a harms test assessing if disclosure would cause harm to the protected interest; and a public interest override, meaning that information should still be released if the overall benefit of disclosure outweighs the harm to a protected interest. Hard overrides apply absolutely, for example, for information about human rights, corruption, or crimes against humanity. RTI applies to public agencies, but the definition of what constitutes a public agency has become challenging, given the increasing privatization of government and the increasingly prominent role private bodies play in the delivery of public services. Furthermore, measures for proactive disclosure; procedures for facilitating access, protecting whistle-blowers, and providing adequate grievance redress mechanisms; and sanctions for failure to disclose are all considered essential elements of good-practice laws.

6   Max Weber, *Economy & Society* (UC Press 1979).

7   Among them, the Carter Center, the Open Society Initiative, the Commonwealth Human Rights Initiative, and Article 19.

8   Rob Jenkins & Anne Marie Goetz, *Accounts and Accountability: Theoretical Implications of the Right-to-Information Movement in India*, 20(3) Third World Q. 603–622 (1999), available at http://www.archonfung.net/docs/pal218/JenkinsGoetz.AccountsAccount.pdf.

Brazil. There are a number of countries where the laws that have been passed have had little meaning for communities or for development outcomes. The third section of the chapter highlights factors that might explain why RTI has empowered communities in some contexts and why it has had little relevance in others. For instance, in all the cases examined, civil society groups—both grassroots and more organized formal groups—played a role in mobilizing communities, raising awareness, putting pressure on local officials, and advocating for sanctions or reforms when RTI exposed corruption or nonperformance. But in areas where grassroots civil society groups have little capacity to fulfill this intermediary role, or where the state is less responsive to civil society pressures, change has been difficult.

RTI as an Enabler of Other Rights

A brief discussion of the international human rights framework—and especially the principle of interdependence—is helpful as a background to understanding the evolution of RTI as an enabler of other rights. The 1948 Universal Declaration of Human Rights (UDHR) provides the foundation for the international human rights framework and enumerates key universal human rights in its 30 articles. Subsequently, a number of international covenants[9] created "soft" international law for the enforcement of these rights. These rights have been characterized as three generations of rights:[10]

- First-generation human rights refer to civil and political rights such as freedom of speech, the right to a fair trial, freedom of religion, and voting rights.[11]

- Second-generation human rights are economic, social, and cultural, such as the rights to food, housing, education, health care, social security, employment, unemployment benefits, and an adequate standard of living.[12]

- Third-generation human rights refer to the collective rights of groups and communities to self-determination, economic and social development, a healthy environment, and intergenerational equity and sustainability.[13]

---

9   http://www.ohchr.org/EN/HRBodies/Pages/TreatyBodies.aspx.

10   Karel Vasak, *Human Rights: A Thirty-Year Struggle: The Sustained Efforts to Give Force of Law to the Universal Declaration of Human Rights,* 30 UNESCO Courier 11 (Nov. 1977). Although the UDHR and international covenants based on it do specifically refer to three generations of rights, the rights enumerated in these covenants easily fit into one of the three categories.

11   Arts. 3–21 of UDHR and the International Covenant on Civil and Political Rights (ICCPR), United Nations High Commissioner for Human Rights (1966), available at http://www2.ohchr.org/english/law/ccpr.htm#art19.

12   Arts. 22–27 of the Universal Declaration, and the International Covenant on Economic, Social, and Cultural Rights (ICESCR) (1966), available at http://www.ohchr.org/Documents/ProfessionalInterest/cescr.pdf, and the International Covenant on Economic, Social and Cultural Rights, adopted by the General Assembly of the United Nations (Dec. 16, 1966), available at http://www.ohchr.org/EN/ProfessionalInterest/Pages/CESCR.aspx.

13   Although the UDHR does not deal extensively with third-generation rights, it underlines the importance of the commons for the realization of other rights: "Everyone is entitled to a

Most countries are signatories to these covenants and are required to undertake measures to ensure the realization of these rights. The state's obligations vis-à-vis first-generation rights are primarily to refrain from imposing restraints, for instance, by enacting laws that ensure freedom from restrictions or control such as censorship. The second-generation social and economic rights, on the other hand, are positive rights in that they impose on the state a complementary duty to undertake measures to enable the realization of these rights. Second-generation rights have been controversial because they can be seen as sanctioning a more activist role by the state and because states may not be able to ensure their full realization, at least in the short term, due to resource limitations. Human rights are purported to be absolute, while economic policy making inevitably entails trade-offs, making enforceability of these rights challenging.

Despite critiques, social and economic rights have established a firm place in the international human rights discourse and policy arena, with the implicit understanding that political and civil rights mean little if people are not able to access basic services, protections, and livelihood opportunities, and an implicit recognition that the realization of human rights is likely to be progressive rather than immediate.[14] International development aid is premised on the need to ensure basic social and economic welfare to all. Multilateral institutions such as the World Bank have implicitly integrated attention to these rights in their work, moving beyond the traditional focus on large infrastructure, economic management, finance, and trade issues to furthering access to health services, education, and social protection, as well as launching initiatives for gender inclusiveness and community development. These institutions build stringent social and environmental safeguards into projects to ensure that development efforts do not hurt the fundamental rights of existence and livelihoods of communities affected by these projects.[15] Countries have also launched developmental projects and poverty-reduction strategies to provide citizens with access to services and livelihood opportunities, an implicit adherence to the aspiration to ensuring social, economic, and community rights for everyone.

The inherent synergy among these rights is highlighted by the principle of interdependence, that is, the fulfillment of any right depends, wholly or in part, upon the fulfillment of others.[16] So, for example, the achievement of social

---

social and international order in which the rights and freedoms set forth in this Declaration can be fully realized."

14   ICESCR qualifies states' obligations with a progressive realization clause, requiring that every state party "undertake . . . to take steps . . . to the maximum of [its] available resources, with a view to achieving progressively the full realization of the right recognized in the . . . Covenant."

15   http://www.worldbank.org/.

16   The Vienna Declaration and Program of Action (VDPA), adopted at the World Conference on Human Rights (June 25, 1993), declares that all human rights are "universal, indivisible and interdependent and interrelated"; available at http://www.unhchr.ch/huridocda /huridoca.nsf/(symbol)/a.conf.157.23.en.

and economic welfare is necessary before citizens can exercise their political and civil rights. The exercise of civil and political rights might itself aid in furthering social and economic welfare goals. In other words, although each right is itself of intrinsic importance—critical to ensure the dignity and equality of all people—each right is also instrumental to the realization of other rights.

Sen's seminal work on "development as freedom" provides perhaps the most eloquent exposition of the inextricable links between rights (used in this article synonymously with freedoms):

> [T]here is strong evidence that economic and political freedoms help to reinforce one another, rather than being hostile to one another (as they are sometimes taken to be) . . . social opportunities of education and health care, which may require public action, complement individual opportunities of economic and political participation and also help to foster our own initiatives in overcoming our respective deprivations.[17]

In empirical work, Sen has pointed to the importance of freedom of expression of the media:

> India has not had a famine since independence, and given the nature of Indian politics and society, it is not likely that India can have a famine even in years of great food problems. The government cannot afford to fail to take prompt action when large-scale starvation threatens. Newspapers play an important part in this, in making the facts known and forcing the challenge to be faced.[18]

Other research has demonstrated the importance of a free media in ensuring greater accountability by the state, leading to better social and economic outcomes.[19]

Throughout much of the 20th century, RTI was cast in distinctly political terms and seen as a complement to freedom of expression and media rights. Although Resolution 59(1), adopted in the UN General Assembly's first session in 1946, declared, "Freedom of information is a fundamental human right and is the touchstone of all the freedoms to which the United Nations is consecrated," it also defined the right as "the right to gather, transmit and publish *news* [italics added] anywhere and everywhere without fetters" and one necessary "in any serious effort to promote the peace and progress of the world."[20] The political underpinning, especially when viewed in the postwar

---

17 Amartya Sen, *Development as Freedom,* Preface (Oxford U. Press 1999).

18 Amartya Sen, *Food Battles: Conflicts in the Access to Food,* 10(1) Food & Nutrition 81–89 (1984).

19 State governments are more responsive to decreases in food production and crop flood damage via public food distribution and calamity relief expenditure where newspaper circulation is higher and electoral accountability is greater; *see* Timothy Besley & Robin Burgess, *The Political Economy of Government Responsiveness: Theory and Evidence from India,* 117(4), Q. J. Econ. 1415–1451 (Nov. 2002).

20 *Resolutions Adopted by the General Assembly During Its First Session* (1946), available at http://www.un.org/documents/ga/res/1/ares1.htm.

context, was clear. Article 19 of the UDHR, adopted two years later, closely ties together the rights of free expression and access to information: "Everyone has the right to freedom of opinion and expression; this right includes freedom to hold opinions without interference and to seek, receive and impart information and ideas through any media and regardless of frontiers."[21] The 1966 International Covenant on Civil and Political Rights (ICCPR) adopted the same language.[22]

In several countries, media have used RTI laws to access information on high-profile cases exposing corruption. A prominent recent example is the parliamentary expenses scandal in 2010 in the United Kingdom, where a series of freedom of information (FOI) requests lodged by NGOs and investigative journalists revealed unethical and illegal claims under the parliamentary expenses system; the responsible members of Parliament were subsequently convicted, reprimanded, or suspended.[23] In India, Mexico, Romania, and Peru, as well as in other countries, high-level corruption scandals have been uncovered using RTI laws.[24]

In the past couple of decades, however, in the spirit of the first sentence in the UN General Assembly's Resolution 59(1), RTI has begun to be viewed as an enabler of the realization of social, economic, and community rights. The environmental movement was a pioneer in underlining the importance of information to safeguard the rights of the commons and enable communities to have a voice in concerns about their environment.[25] This trend is reflected in the 1998 Convention on Access to Information, Public Participation in Decision-Making and Access to Justice in Environmental Matters (the Aarhus Convention).[26] Although the Aarhus Convention is primarily a European instrument, sponsored by the United Nations Economic Commission for Europe, it has been important in solidifying the principle of access to information as an essential part of sustainable environmental governance.

Aid agencies have underscored the importance of RTI laws in furthering social and economic welfare by enabling citizens to participate in decision making; to monitor officials on the delivery of obligations, including by

---

21 Universal Declaration of Human Rights (1948), available at http://www.un.org/en/documents /udhr/.

22 International Covenant on Civil and Political Rights, adopted by the General Assembly of the United Nations (Dec. 19, 1966), available at http://treaties.un.org/doc/Publication/UNTS /Volume%20999/volume-999-I-14668-English.pdf.

23 Robert Hazell, Ben Worthy, & Mark Glover, *Does FOI Work? The Impact of the Freedom of Information Act 2000 on British Central Government* (Palgrave Macmillan 2010).

24 H. Mander & A. S. Joshi, *The Movement for Right to Information in India: People's Power for the Control of Corruption* (Paper presented at the Commonwealth Human Rights Initiative Conference on Pan-Commonwealth Advocacy for Human Rights, Peace and Good Governance in Africa, Jan. 21–24, 1999).

25 Vivek Ramkumar & Elena Petkova, *Transparency and Environmental Governance*, in *The Right to Know: Transparency for an Open World* (Ann Florini ed., Columbia U. Press 2007).

26 http://ec.europa.eu/environment/aarhus/.

exposing corruption or nonperformance; and to access justice and grievance redress mechanisms when their rights are violated. The World Bank's 2004 *World Development Report* suggests that information enables citizens to exercise direct influence over service providers (the short route of accountability) and hold policy makers accountable, who in turn hold providers accountable (the long route of accountability).[27] For instance, publicly available and easy-to-understand information on the standards of public service provision enables citizens to put pressure on service providers through tools such as score cards, report cards, and social audits, and to express their dissatisfaction to politicians (for instance, through voting), who in turn hold service providers accountable for adhering to these standards. The potential of access to information to expose corruption is particularly important because corruption is a major impediment to the realization of fundamental rights—for instance, corruption in a public distribution system affects the right to food, corruption in a supply of pharmaceuticals hinders the right to health, and corruption and teacher absenteeism hamper the right to education.

Research studies have also demonstrated the usefulness of access to information broadly, and RTI specifically, for community-level development outcomes.[28] A recent field experiment on access to ration cards among New Delhi's slum dwellers found that slum dwellers who submitted information requests under India's RTI law received their ration cards almost as fast as those paying "speed money" to the administration, while most of those who either presented a letter of support from a local NGO or applied for the card through the standard process did not receive the card during the one-year period in which the research was conducted.[29]

The role of civil society groups—both professional NGOs working on behalf of citizens and grassroots NGOs working directly with communities, helping them make information requests—in several developing countries, and the success of these groups in using RTI to extract information salient to poor citizens and communities, has been remarkable. In Mexico, rural, social, and civic movements have claimed the right to information as a tool for their social, economic, and civic struggles.[30] In India, starting with Mazdoor Kisan Shakti Sangathan's equation of the "right to know" with the "right to

---

27 World Bank, *World Development Report 2004: Making Services Work for Poor People* (World Bank 2004).

28 Martina Bjorkman & Jakob Svensson, *Power to the People: Evidence of a Randomized Field Experiment on Community-Based Monitoring in Uganda,* 124(2) Q. J. Econ. 735–769 (2012); Claudio Ferraz & Frederico Finan, *Exposing Corrupt Politicians: The Effects of Brazil's Publicly Released Audits on Electoral Outcomes,* 123(2) Q. J. Econ. 703–746 (2008); S. Khemani, *Does Community Monitoring Improve Public Services? Diverging Evidence from Uganda and India* (World Bank Research Brief, Sept. 16, 2008); P. Pandey, S. Goyal, & V. Sundararaman, *Community Participation in Public Schools: Impact of Information Campaigns in Three Indian States,* 17 Ed. Econ. 3 (2009).

29 Leonid V. Peisakhin & Paul Pinto, *Is Transparency an Effective Anti-corruption Strategy? Evidence from a Field Experiment in India,* 4(3) Reg. & Gov. 261–280 (2010).

30 Jonathan Fox, Carlos García Jiménez, & Libby Haight, *Rural Democratization in Mexico's Deep South: Grassroots Right-to-Know Campaigns in Guerrero,* 36(2) J. Peasant Stud. (2009).

live," grassroots movements have mobilized around RTI across the country. In South Africa, the prominent NGO Open Democracy Access Center (ODAC) has assisted communities in using RTI law to make information requests related to health care, development, and access to resources, as well as to obtain information about how local government funds are being spent.[31] In Bangladesh, several examples are emerging of communities using the country's RTI law to access information on entitlements under specific government programs, including food, agriculture and land distribution, health, and rural employment, on land records, and on labor and environmental regulations, as well as general information about government programs.[32] Some of these cases are highlighted below.

Mazdoor Kisan Shakti Sangathan, India

The most celebrated example of grassroots community mobilization around information access rights is that of the Mazdoor Kisan Shakti Sangathan (MKSS), or the labor and farmers' movement in the northwestern Indian state of Rajasthan.[33] Aided by prominent activists, MKSS launched a successful mass mobilization movement in the 1990s to access documents related to the payment of wages under the government's drought-relief schemes. These disclosures showed that workers were being paid considerably below their stated incomes and that allocations from the government were being pilfered by local officials, who were billing the central and state governments for the full amount. The disclosures were followed by a series of *jan sunwais*, or public hearings, at which detailed accounts, derived from official expenditure records and other supporting documentation were read out loud to the villagers.

Although access to public information had been recognized as a right with a Supreme Court ruling in the 1970s, MKSS tied the movement firmly to the Indian constitution's framework of basic social and economic rights, particularly provisions guaranteeing the right to life and livelihood, exemplified in slogans such as "the right to know is the right to live."[34] It also launched a concerted campaign for RTI. Its sustained advocacy efforts, along with the formation, in 1996, of the National Campaign for People's Right to Information (NCPRI)—a coalition of grassroots organizations and other NGOs from

---

31   Richard Calland, *Annex 3: Freedom of Information*, in *Review of Impact and Effectiveness of Transparency and Accountability Initiatives* (Transparency and Accountability Initiative 2010).

32   *The Power of Using the Right to Information Act in Bangladesh: Experiences from the Ground* (Commonwealth Human Rights Initiative, Affiliated Network for Social Accountability South Asia, and World Bank Institute), available at http://wbi.worldbank.org/wbi/Data/wbi/wbicms/files/drupal-acquia/wbi/Final%20version%20-%20The%20Benefits%20of%20Using%20the%20RTI%20Act%20in%20Bangladesh.pdf.

33   Aruna Roy & Nikhil Dey, *The Right to Information: Facilitating People's Participation and State Accountability* (10th International Anti-corruption Conference, Oct. 7–11, 2004); Aruna Roy & Nachiket Udupa, *Mass Job Guarantee*, Himal South Asian (Oct. 2004), available at http://www.himalmag.com/The-mass-jobguarantee_nw4749.html.

34   Jenkins & Goetz, *supra* note 8.

across the country—accelerated the national momentum for the passage of an RTI law, on the agenda since the 1970s, in 2005.[35]

Women's Network for the Common Good, Mexico

In Guerrero, a peasant women's health rights campaign, the Women's Network for the Common Good, mobilized hundreds of women in demanding information on the federal government's flagship conditional cash-transfer program, Oportunidades, on health-related laws, ministry regulations, and program operating procedures that clearly define the basic health services to which rural communities are entitled.[36] Information requested included rules governing basic public health services in rural communities, services, fees, lists of medicines and supplies that health centers were supposed to have in stock, the number of doctors and nurses allocated to health centers, and expenditures of health centers. The requests led to the release of substantial information, although the federal government could not provide information on the administration of resources in specific health centers, which are managed by state governments. Yet, despite the remarkable mass mobilization, improvement in the quality of public health services has been challenging.

Parivartan, India

In India, a Delhi-based NGO, Parivartan,[37] mobilized urban communities to demand information on corruption in the public distribution system that supplies basic provisions at subsidized prices (or rations) to households below the poverty line. Aided by Parivartan, these communities demanded information about ration supplies from the food and civil supplies department, comparing those records with the records of the ration shops, which frequently divert supplies to the open market to sell them at higher prices. In the tradition of MKSS, Parivartan organized *jan sunwais*, where comparison of government records with the records of the shops revealed massive fraud. As a result, licenses for several shops were taken away and the local public distribution system improved.

Open Democracy Advice Centre, South Africa

Villagers in Emkhandlwini used South Africa's FOI law, with the help of the Open Democracy Advice Centre (ODAC), to request the minutes of council meetings on the provision of water, the municipality's integrated development plan, and its budget. When the documents revealed that the village was supposed to receive access to clean water, villagers solicited the help of the media to publicize the issue. The municipality installed fixed water tanks and delivered mobile water tanks to the community. When the supply became erratic, villagers used the law again to request a service-level agreement

---

35   *Id.*

36   Fox, Jiménez, & Haight, *supra* note 30.

37   http://www.parivartan.com.

between the municipality and the company delivering water. Because such a contract had not been created, constituting a breach of South Africa's public finance legislation, the municipality was reported to the auditor general for investigation.[38]

Maderas del Pueblo del Sureste, Mexico

In 2006, Maderas del Pueblo del Sureste, an environmental NGO supporting indigenous people and rural communities in Chiapas, Mexico, filed access-to-information requests using the federal Transparency Law, seeking information about a sewage project that was negatively affecting a village, which was receiving waste from a neighboring town and had no access to clean water. Information released through these requests showed that the water-treatment system was not properly designed and needed a filter system that had not been installed. The Cintalapa sewage project was halted, and authorities publicly acknowledged that changes had to be made to ensure that water was properly treated.[39]

FUNDAR, Mexico

In Mexico, prominent NGO FUNDAR pressed for the disclosure of information related to subsidies for poor farmers and the supply of drugs for AIDS victims. In 2007, FUNDAR requested information from the Ministry of Agriculture on the list of beneficiaries of PROCAMPO, the largest federal farm subsidy program in the country, designed to support the poorest farmers and reduce inequality in the rural sector. Although the Ministry of Agriculture responded to this information request, the information was issued in unreadable formats and was incomplete. When more complete and legible information was made available at the direction of the information commission IFAI, it showed that the bulk of farm subsidies were being allocated not to the country's poorest and smallest farmers but to the richest and most productive farmers, and the corruption included nepotism and patronage. FUNDAR and other NGOs created an online repository of this information to keep the pressure on the ministry.[40] Although the Minister of Agriculture was removed from his post, no changes to the list of beneficiaries or the program's rules of operation were made. When subsequent investigations revealed continuing evidence of corruption and nepotism, resignations followed, and the government imposed ceilings on eligibility for subsidies. But abuses have continued.[41] The information obtained through the federal Transparency Law was crucial in uncovering corruption and misallocation of subsidies.

---

38 M. Dimba, *Access to Information as a Tool for Socio-Economic Justice* (International Conference on Right to Public Information, Feb. 26–29, 2008).

39 Emilene Martinez-Moralez, *Documents in Action: FOI Success Stories in Mexico* (Mar. 20, 2009), available at http://www.freedominfo.org/2009/03/mexico-success-stories/ (accessed Nov. 30, 2011).

40 http://www.subsidiosalcampo.org.mx.

41 Fox & Haight 2010, 140.

Center for Environmental Law, Mexico

The Center for Environmental Law (CEMDA) used the federal Transparency Law to generate information to bolster a court case against the proposed La Parota dam. This legal strategy won many victories—including a 2007 injunction that suspended construction. CEMDA gained access to the environmental impact assessment, which revealed the illegality of the authorization to proceed with construction without environmental clearance. In 2009, the Federal Electricity Commission's response to an information request explicitly recognized that the commission lacked valid legal permits and that it had not been able to request the necessary change of land use approvals (because negotiations for community approval remained suspended).

Center for Legal and Social Studies, Argentina

In Argentina, the Center for Legal and Social Studies (CELS), a human rights NGO, engaged in strategic litigation using international legal instruments and local access to information laws[42] to uncover information about child malnutrition and child mortality in the wake of the economic crisis that hit the country in the early 2000s. CELS and other social organizations demanded malnutrition statistics from several local government offices, such as the local Ministry of Health, municipal hospitals, and other health-related establishments. In most cases, the requests were denied or only partial documentation on malnutrition cases was provided, compelling CELS to take legal action against a local Ministry of Health. Subsequently, the ministry admitted that its studies had found increased prevalence of low weight among children and that its data were outdated and incomplete.

Lessons for Scaling up RTI

These cases illustrate the potential of RTI in helping communities realize social, economic, and community rights. But this potential has been far from fully tapped. A recent study found that in many countries that have passed RTI laws, there is little evidence of awareness about, and use of, RTI laws by ordinary citizens in rural or urban areas. And even in countries where RTI is better used, the largest user base continues to be urban professionals in the media, private, public, and academic sectors.[43] The cases discussed above, as well as the complementary literature cited, provide some lessons about conditions that enable or hinder the exercise of RTI. Many of these conditions reflect fundamental political economy dynamics that are difficult to address, particularly for outside agencies. But attention to these issues by both local civil society groups and RTI implementers is critical if RTI is to be an effective tool for developmental gains.

---

42 Argentina has a presidential decree that guarantees access to information that applies only to the national executive government and is not upheld in many instances.

43 Anupama Dokeniya, *Implementing Right to Information: Experiences from Case Studies* (World Bank 2013).

Link Information Rights with Issues of Particular Relevance for and Concern to Local Communities

Poor communities, whether in rural or urban areas, living at the edge of survival, are concerned with fulfilling their basic needs—health, water, and sanitation, access to subsidized food, and livelihood opportunities. Access to information is relevant to them if it is clearly linked to these goals. In Mexico, for example, Citizen Attention, a social welfare program, each year receives more information requests than are directed to the entire executive branch, clearly signaling that there is an appetite for information when the information is relevant to social and economic priorities.

In many contexts, RTI is seen as a political rather than a developmental tool, one championed by large NGOs focused on political accountability and corruption issues, rather than by smaller grassroots NGOs working in poor communities and service delivery sectors. In Uganda, while governance-focused NGOs in the capital, Kampala, are engaged on this issue, interviews with a number of small NGOs working in service delivery sectors, conducted as part of an RTI implementation study, showed that they were not aware of the RTI law or did not see it as relevant to their needs. But RTI can indeed be used as a tool by grassroots NGOs. In India and Mexico, grassroots organizations working on community development and in the service delivery sectors have actively used RTI. In India, MKSS, which was critical to the struggle for access to information, was formed in the early 1990s to fight against failures in the enforcement of minimum-wage laws and corruption in the public distribution system for subsidized food and other essential commodities. The focus on access to information emerged out of the need to hold officials accountable for delivering on the entitlements of communities in these areas. In Mexico, communities in the Guerrero and Acapulco-Coyuca regions used RTI to expose pilfering of education funds by local officials and the existence of ghost teachers on the payroll.[44]

Harness the Power of Collective Action and Build Coalitions

Civil society coalitions focused on RTI have emerged both within and across countries. In India, the Indian National Coalition for People's Right to Information (NCPRI) brought together urban professionals and rural activists in a powerful national movement.[45] More recent anticorruption movements that have caught the popular imagination and led to unprecedented social mobilization sprang directly from the RTI movement, with many of the same leaders and groups championing the causes, most notable among them, veteran activist Anna Hazare. In Mexico, the right-to-know movement bridged resistance-oriented and negotiation-oriented social and civic movements to take ad-

---

44   Fox & Haight, *supra* note 41.

45   Amita Baviskar, *Is Knowledge Power? The Right to Information Campaign in India* (Sept. 2007), available at http://www.ids.ac.uk/ids/Part/proj/pnp.html.

vantage of the state's 2006 RTI law.[46] The Self-Managed Social Development Promoters (PADS) helped a diverse range of rural civil society groups from pragmatic, nonideological groups that focus mainly on community-based economic development for those engaged in contestation on issues such as large infrastructure projects and human rights. Where grassroots organizations do not have effective mobilizing capacity, the impact of RTI is limited.

Focus Advocacy Efforts on Strong, State-Level Laws

Some of the most salient issues of immediate and pressing concern to communities are the responsibility of the state governments. When national RTI laws do not apply at the state level and state-level laws on RTI either do not exist or are weak, communities may have little recourse. For instance, in Mexico, the national law applies only to federal public bodies, and the federal government has no power to regulate openness at the subnational level. Concern has been expressed that the RTI laws that have now been adopted by 32 subnational entities do not meet minimum transparency standards.[47] In India, although most states have separate RTI laws and state-specific implementation institutions, such as the state information commissions, the central law overrides state-level laws. How this issue is addressed depends on the political tradition and constitutional norms in each individual country, but the discrepancies point to the need to direct advocacy efforts toward state-level laws.

Ensure Capacity in Local-Level Institutions

Official resistance and capacity constraints are significant challenges to RTI implementation in public administration. Control over information translates into money for public officials—for instance, when bribes must be paid to get information, or when corruption continues unchecked in the absence of transparency. Relinquishing control over information reduces opportunities for bribery, patronage, and kickbacks. Furthermore, RTI laws entail additional responsibilities without necessarily providing additional resources or rebalancing other responsibilities. In India, more than 30 percent of rural information officers polled in one survey admitted that they did not want RTI to be part of their responsibilities, and more than 10 percent of public information officers cited a lack of financial and other incentives as the reason for their reluctance.[48] Thus, public officials and state actors have deployed a variety of strategies to resist the implementation of RTI laws, from attempting to create

---

46   Fox, Jiménez, & Haight, *supra* note 30, at 200.

47   For a comprehensive analysis of access to information and transparency laws, *see* Diego Ernesto Díaz, *Métrica de la Transparencia* (CIDE 2007).

48   RTI Assessment & Analysis Group (RaaG) & National Campaign for People's Right to Information (NCPRI), *Executive Summary, Safeguarding the Right to Information: Report of the People's RTI Assessment 2008* (Oct. 2009), available at http://rti-assessment.org/exe_summ _report.pdf.

restrictive amendments to harassment of requesters to mute refusals or releasing incomplete or incomprehensible information.[49]

Training and awareness-raising initiatives, signaling and modeling behavior by both political and individual agency leaders, and appropriate incentives and rewards are some strategies that could address these challenges. But RTI implementation efforts tend to stay focused on central-level institutions without adequate attention to state and local institutions, even though implementation challenges might be more pronounced at this level. In Mexico, for instance, in the Oportunitades case, although rural women were able to access federal documents, state documents that provided details on how money was actually spent were much harder to access. State health officials were reluctant to provide information and attempted to intimidate requesters by visiting their homes to question them on why they wanted the information. In India, respondents to a survey pointed out that when they filed requests, particularly in rural areas, officials often harassed them.[50] Robust plans for local-level institutions, therefore, need to be an integral part of RTI implementation plans.

Information commissions and courts are important allies in enabling communities to realize the right to information, as several of the cases above highlight. But information commissions sit in the national or state-level capitals, and poor, rural communities might not be able to afford sustained litigation for the release of information. Collective action and support from civil society organizations can be vital to help raise the profile of demands, as in the case of MKSS. But collective action needs to be matched with appropriate grievance redress mechanisms at the local level, including an internal appeals system within local government agencies.

Tailor Solutions to Local Context

Local governments might find it challenging to put in place information management systems and may have little capacity or resources to do so. Taking an incremental approach, organizing and cataloging the most urgent and frequently sought documents, and educating the public about the availability of these documents through the publication of registers of documents, notice boards, and community outreach are feasible steps in these contexts. Although technology-mediated solutions for information access might be effective for urban, well-educated, technically savvy professionals,[51] in poorer communities, the role of the information officer as an intermediary is crucial to help users frame and direct their requests. Provision of information without fees and the admission of oral requests when requesters cannot read and write are other critical measures to take.

---

49   Dokeniya, *supra* note 43.

50   RaaG & NCPRI, *supra* note 48.

51   Mexico's Sistema Informatizado de Solicitudes de Informacion (SISI) is among the most successful; in fact, most requests at the central level in Mexico are lodged through this platform.

Conclusion: From Access to Accountability

As the cases indicate, although the use of RTI has enabled access to information, the record on translating this information into better social and economic outcomes is mixed. For example, mass mobilization around health rights under Oportunitades resulted in important disclosures but did not immediately translate into better health outcomes. The exposés of patronage in PROCAMPO led to resignations, but abuses continued. In India, the recent cases of corruption demonstrate how intransigent this challenge is.

The results chain from the provision of information to changes in the actions and choices of communities, and consequently the incentives and behavior of officials, is relatively under-researched and inadequately understood. If exposure of corruption or inefficiency, media outrage, or popular discontent does not affect the incentive structures of politicians or officials, attempts at change are unlikely to be effective. Strengthening understanding of how incentives are affected by the disclosure of information—through the threat of reputational or financial sanctions or loss of elections or employment—is crucial to strengthening the complex relationships of access to information, accountability, and development outcomes. For instance, studies have shown that the disclosure of corruption in local government might reduce the likelihood of incumbent re-election,[52] and specific and informed policy proposals have had a positive effect on turnout and electoral support for the candidates, more so than targeted or clientelist electoral promises.[53] Building a robust evidence base on these dynamics, through experimental research, anecdotal data, and detailed case studies is critical to illuminating how the right to know can actually translate to the right to live.

---

52   Ferraz & Finan, *supra* note 28.

53   Leonard Wantchekon, *Can Informed Public Deliberation Overcome Clientelism? Experimental Evidence from Benin* (working paper, Princeton U. 2009).

Conclusion

A Challenging New Era for Law, Justice, and Development

HASSANE CISSÉ AND MARIE-CLAIRE CORDONIER SEGGER

In this book, diverse concepts of development guide both theoretical analyses and discussions of practical lessons learned from recent examples of development. Development as a concept has had a rich and interesting history since it came to prominence after World War II. In the initial years, countries viewed development with an aloofness that matched their suspicion of whether this was yet another ploy by the West to dominate "underdeveloped" countries or whether it was indeed a vehicle that could drive change.[1] Later, countries considered the question of how development should be defined and what its scope should be; for decades, scholars busied themselves with propounding an all-encompassing definition of the concept of development. Elliott Burg, in a brilliant definitional exposition, presented various theories of development advanced by scholars and theorists. The economic growth approach defined development as a raise in per capita output, as a means of building strong market economies, and, by extension, as the freedom to have a say in decisions that shape one's life or, at least, to have an opportunity to do so. Social theory linked development to the distributional aspects of economic life and, while conceding that growth is necessary, argued that such growth must be matched with equitable distribution of both tangible and intangible resources. From a legal and political perspective, theorists like Justice William Douglas linked development to democratic institutions and a free society.[2]

The authors thank Elizabeth Hassan and Daniela Cuellar for their insights and invaluable assistance in the preparation of this chapter. Opinions and submissions contained herein are the authors' and do not necessarily represent the views of their institutions. Responsibility for errors and omissions remains with the authors.

1   *See,* generally, the introductory discussion in Arturo Escobar, *Encountering Development: The Making and Unmaking of the Third World* ch. 1, particularly 3–11 (Princeton U. Press 2011).

2   For extensive discussion on theories of development, *see* Elliott M. Burg, *Law and Development: A Review of the Literature and a Critique of Scholars in Self-Estrangement,* 25 Am. J. Comp. L. 492 (1977). *See* also, Daniel Nyhart, *The Role of Law in Economic Development,* 1 Sudan L.J. & Rpts. 394, 398 (1962); David Trubek & Marc Galanter, *Scholars in Self-Estrangement: Some Reflections on the Crisis in Law and Development Studies in the United States,* Wis. L. Rev. 1062 (1974); Amartya Sen, *Development as Freedom* (Oxford U. Press 2011); Robert Seidman, *Law and Development: A General Model,* 6 Law & Socy. (1972); and David Trubek, *Toward a Social Theory of Law: An Essay on the Study of Law and Development,* 82 Yale L.J. 1 (1972).

Prominently, the economic growth theory linked growth to prosperity.[3] Multidimensional in some respects but limited in others, the theory gained recognition among world leaders and still grounds much of present-day discourse. President Harry Truman, articulating what would later become part of the Truman Doctrine, declared greater production to be the key to prosperity and peace.[4] Decades ago, this may have been a compelling submission; however, as Joseph Stiglitz notes, this perspective is too narrow and insufficient in today's context. He argues that "it may be possible to raise productivity and even change mindsets within an enclave of the economy without achieving a true development transformation of the society as a whole."[5] Thus, Stiglitz emphasizes that efforts should include broadly participatory processes—such as voice, openness, and transparency—that promote truly successful long-term development, noting that although these processes may not guarantee success and may carry inherent risks, an understanding of these principles and values nonetheless helps practitioners design strategies and processes that are more likely to lead to successful and sustainable growth and development.[6]

There are many different definitions of development, but none is necessarily wrong. Development is broad and covers all the areas mentioned: development is a body of interrelated concepts that work together. As the chapters in this volume demonstrate, rule of law and justice are crucial elements of the development process. Thus, one could easily agree with Arturo Escobar's submission that "one could criticize a given approach and propose modifications or improvements accordingly, but the fact of development itself, and the need for it, could not be doubted . . . development [has] achieved the status of a certainty in the social imaginary."[7] As has been suggested, for sustainable development to become a reality on the ground in developed and developing countries, an interactional corpus of embedded and effective international and regional treaties, national and local laws, rules, and governance systems is needed, one that integrates social, economic, and environmental priorities

---

3   For detailed discussion on the theories of growth and development, *see* Barbara Ingham, *The Meaning of Development: Interactions between "New" and "Old" Ideas*, 21(11) World Development, 1803–1821 (1993).

4   *See* Harry Truman's inaugural speech of January 20, 1949, as cited by Escobar, *supra* note 1, at 3.

5   Joseph Stiglitz, *Participation and Development: Perspectives from the Comprehensive Development Paradigm*, 6(2) Rev. of Dev. Econ. 163–182 (2002).

6   Similarly, Cissé, Biebesheimer, & Nash argue that today, "development equated solely with 'growth,' at all costs is no longer viewed by many around the world as the optimal means for a country's path towards prosperity. Indeed, all these terms—development, growth, and prosperity—have over the years expanded to become broader and generally more inclusive. . . . [M]ore and more indications seem to point towards a more vocal and powerful demand from various quarters for more equitable and inclusive growth at the macro, meso and micro levels." *See* Hassane Cissé, Christina Biebesheimer, & Richard Nash, *Toward Greater Justice in Development*, in *The Law of the Future and the Future of Law* vol. 2, 87 (Sam Muller et al. eds., Torkel Opsahl Academic Epublisher 2012); Gerald M. Meier & Joseph E. Stiglitz eds., *Frontiers of Development Economics: The Future in Perspective* (World Bank 2002).

7   Escobar, *supra* note 1, at 5.

in a balanced way.[8] In the face of this reality, the indispensability of development has become apparent, and attention has shifted to the elements and scope of development, what approach should be adopted, what priorities or values ought to be pursued, and what methodologies or strategies need to be employed to achieve them. Just as development is constantly evolving and expanding to accommodate new or persistent challenges, so must the thinking and approach move with the times.

Current Development Landscape and Challenges

Traditionally, a great deal of emphasis was placed on tangible deliverables of development or public goods, such as infrastructure and educational and health care facilities. By all means, these are critical. However, in the current development landscape, these are not the only deliverables that people expect. Traditional thinking has expanded to include intangible deliverables, and there is a growing demand for values such as rule of law and justice, participation and inclusion, equity, good governance, and sustainability over the long term. The current development landscape requires more attention to law and justice, such that efforts must now include or be hinged on these values.

In the last several years, the world has experienced a number of events that have had far-reaching economic, political, and financial impact on states, from the 2007–8 global economic meltdown to the Arab Spring, as well as ongoing conflicts in some countries. These events have highlighted the interconnectedness among legal, sociopolitical, and economic systems. They have also exposed gaps in laws and policies and emphasized how the perception that systems and institutions are unjust and exclusionary can lead to significant social and political unrest. Indeed, in spite of new international treaties and laws on trade and investment that cover most countries of the world, there are significant challenges to integrating social and environmental concerns into the economic policy and related rules for trade and investment regimes that can deliver more sustainable development to citizens.[9] Interestingly, the need for more inclusion and equity is evident even in high-growth countries. For example, although China has carried out significant institutional and economic reforms—especially in the areas of trade and commerce—that boosted economic activities, studies show increasing inequalities and disproportionate poverty reduction.[10] The growth in GDP has not necessarily translated into better standards of living for the poor, at least not to the expected degree.

---

8   M.-C. Cordonier Segger & A. Khalfan, *Sustainable Development Law: Principles, Practices and Prospects* (Oxford U. Press 2004).

9   *Sustainable Development in World Trade Law* (M.-C. Cordonier Segger & M. Gehring eds., Kluwer L. Intl. 2005); and *Sustainable Development in World Investment Law* (M. Gehring, M.-C. Cordonier Segger, & A. Newcombe eds., Kluwer L. Intl. 2010).

10   Jayati Ghosh, *Poverty Reduction in China and India: Policy Implications of Recent Trends*, DESA Working Paper No. 92st/Esa/2010/Dwp/92 5 (Jan. 2010), available at http://sa.india environmentportal.org.in/files/wp92_2010.pdf; *see*, generally, Augustin Kwasi Fosu, *Growth, Inequality, and Poverty Reduction in Developing Countries: Recent Global Evidence* (background

The *World Development Report 2011* (WDR 2011) emphasizes that fragility and conflict have become critical and urgent development challenges.[11] It is true that the world is experiencing a diminishing number of interstate and civil wars. This is encouraging in the present and for the future. Yet, violence is not always associated only with war. Local violence involving militias or between ethnic groups, gang violence, local resource-related violence, and violence linked to trafficking or associated with global ideological struggles can have a serious impact on governance and the development of states. These vicious circles have left states such as South Sudan, the Democratic Republic of Congo, and East Timor fragile and vulnerable.[12] Apart from being causes of fragility and conflict, these forms of violence also weaken and diminish or destroy the institutions that would otherwise contain conflicts and resolve injustice peacefully. Unsurprisingly, most countries facing fragile and conflict situations rank below average on the rule of law index for 2012–13.[13]

But the detrimental impact of fragility and conflict is not confined to law and justice systems. The entire development process is affected. For example, countries in fragile and conflict situations are lagging behind in achieving the Millennium Development Goals (MDGs); at the present pace, they will not be able to achieve a majority of the goals by the 2015 deadline. The WDR 2011 further points out that on average, a country that experienced major violence during the period from 1981 to 2005 has a poverty rate 21 percentage points higher than a country that saw no violence in that time frame, and the average cost of civil war is equivalent to more than 30 years of GDP growth for a medium-size developing country. Fragility and conflict can lead to the loss of progress for the span of an entire generation. This impact extends to human development; more often than not, vulnerable groups are most affected.[14] In this regard, the 2006 Geneva Declaration on Armed Violence and Development, endorsed by more than 100 states, affirmed that "living free from the threat of armed violence is a basic human need."[15]

---

paper for the Global Dev. Outlook—Shifting Wealth: Implications for Dev., OECD Dev. Ctr. 2010), available at http://www.oecd.org/dev/pgd/44773119.pdf.

11   *World Development Report 2011: Conflict, Security, and Development* 53–55 (World Bank 2011).

12   See Harmonized List of Fragile Situations FY 14, available at http://siteresources.worldbank .org/EXTLICUS/Resources/511777-1269623894864/HarmonizedlistoffragilestatesFY14.pdf.

13   M. Agrast et al., *WJP Rule of Law Index 2012–2013*, particularly 158–181 (World Justice Project 2012–13), available at http://worldjusticeproject.org/sites/default/files/WJP_Index_Report _2012.pdf (accessed July 15, 2013).

14   Countries in fragile and conflict situations account for one-third of the deaths from HIV/ AIDS in poor countries, one-third of the people who lack access to clean water, one-third of children who do not complete primary school, and one-half of all child deaths. *See* World Bank, *Fragility, Conflict, and Violence: Working Differently in Fragile and Conflict Affected Situations*, available at http://web.worldbank.org/WBSITE/EXTERNAL/PROJECTS/STRATEGIES /EXTLICUS/0,,contentMDK:22979282~menuPK:8150332~pagePK:64171531~piPK:64171507 ~theSitePK:511778,00.html (accessed July 15, 2013).

15   *See* Geneva Declaration on Armed Violence and Development (2006), available at http:// www.genevadeclaration.org/fileadmin/docs/GD-Declaration-091020-EN.pdf.

Sadly, these are not the only challenges to grapple with. States continue to struggle with the challenges of globalization and the economic, social, and political changes prompted by financial crises, environmental degradation and climate change, food shocks, health crises, and natural disasters. As the Commission on Growth and Development pointed out, developing countries today must overcome some global trends their predecessors did not face, including climate change; food security; a youth bulge in poor countries that is not matched with adequate opportunities for growth; fragmentation of the international development space; and weakly coordinated international responses to global challenges.[16] How can states respond to these challenges? How can they capitalize on recent experiences and use lessons learned as building blocks for the future? With their focus on opportunity, inclusion, and equity, the authors of the chapters in this volume explore the potentially transformative role of effective law and justice tools in addressing these challenges and achieving better development outcomes.

The Increasingly Important Role of Law and Justice in Development

As is apparent in this volume, law is one tool that the international community is placing on the front burner of development efforts, and it is doing so for a very good reason: law is an instrument of change. This instrumentalist approach can be traced back to the law and development movement of the 1960s, which advanced law as a tool that can shape human behavior and achieve development with emphasis on rules and the role of the state.[17] Although the movement was heavily criticized and declined in the following decade,[18] it set the pace for a deeper appreciation of the role of law in development—starting with the rule of law revival of the 1990s[19]—and inspired more proactive efforts to include law in development.

In exploring this development thinking, one cannot overlook the need for justice. Law and justice are inextricably linked—and, like two sides of the same coin, complement each other.[20] Whereas law concerns the rules, policies, institutions, and systems that govern a society and facilitate the realization of its goals, justice is a thread that runs through the entire fabric of society and introduces a "people-conscious" dimension that ensures that development actually serves and impacts people in a fair, positive, and empowering manner. In this regard, as Amartya Sen argues,

---

16 Commission on Growth and Development, *The Growth Report: Strategies for Sustained and Inclusive Development* 9 (World Bank 2008), available at http://siteresources.worldbank.org /EXTPREMNET/Resources/489960-1338997241035/Growth_Commission_Final_Report.pdf (accessed July 22, 2013).

17 *See* Trubek & Galanter, *supra* note 2.

18 *See* Burg, *supra* note 2.

19 *See* Thomas Carothers, *The Rule of Law Revival*, 77(2) Foreign Affairs 95–106 (1998).

20 Rudolf Machacek, *Law and Justice: Two Sides of the Same Coin* 1(5) Facta universitatis: L. & Politics 571–580 (2001).

> justice cannot be indifferent to the lives that people can actually live
> ... institutions and rules are, of course, very important in influencing
> what happens, and they are part and parcel of the actual world as
> well, but the realized actuality goes well beyond the organizational
> picture, and includes the lives that people manage—or do not man-
> age—to live.[21]

An overwhelming body of literature expounds on the importance of law and justice in development.[22] But beyond theory, practical evidence spotlights the role of law and justice in tackling the natural and the manmade crises highlighted above. Interestingly, these events have introduced new dynamics to development thinking: they have brought to the fore people's demand for improvements in their access to, the reach of, and the quality of public goods; and they have increased pressure on states for systems that more adequately respond to these needs and level societal imbalances and inequities. This justifies more attention on norms and values that can help states meet these demands.

Assessing Law and Justice in Development: Are We There Yet?

Having noted the importance of law and justice in development, a useful question to ask is, How far have we come in mainstreaming law and justice into development and how has this contributed to achieving development outcomes? It is difficult to assess the impact of law and justice, but one can draw from experiences that support the instrumentality of law and justice. For instance, as Anupama Dokeniya notes in her chapter in this volume, "The Right to Information as a Tool for Community Empowerment," some communities in rural and extremely poor regions of India and Mexico have been able to use the right to information as a tool to expose pilfering of resources meant

---

21   Amartya Sen, *The Idea of Justice* 18 (Harvard U. Press 2009).

22   For an informative theoretical discussion of the role law plays in development, *see* David Trubek, *Toward a Social Theory of Law: An Essay on the Study of Law and Development*, 82 Yale L.J. 1 (1972). *See* also Robert B. Seidman, *The State, Law, and Development* (Croom Helm 1978); David Trubek & Marc Galanter, *Scholars in Self-Estrangement: Some Reflections on the Crisis in Law and Development Studies in the United States*, Wis. L. Rev. 1062 (1974); Daniel Nyhart, *The Role of Law in Economic Development*, 1 Sudan L.J. & Rpts. 394, 398 (1962); John H. Merryman, *Comparative Law and Social Change: On the Origins, Style, Decline and Revival of the Law and Development Movement*, 25 Am. J. Comp. L. 457 (1977); Brian Tamanaha, *Review of "The Lessons of Law-and-Development Studies,"* 89(2) Am. J. Intl. L. 470–486 (Apr. 1995). For more recent literature, *see* Sen, *supra* note 21; Stephen Golub, *The Commission on Legal Empowerment of the Poor: One Big Step Forward and a Few Steps Back for Development Policy and Practice*, 1 Hague J. on Rule of L. 101–116 (2009); Pilar Domingo, *Why Rule of Law Matters for Development* (Overseas Dev. Inst. 2009); Michael Sandel, *Justice: What's the Right Thing to Do?*, 91 B.U. L. Rev. 1303 (2011); Hassane Cissé, *Legal Empowerment for the Poor: Past, Present, Future*, in *The World Bank Legal Review* vol. 4, 31 (2012); Stephen Golub, *Make Justice the Organizing Principle of the Rule of Law Field*, 1 Hague J. on Rule of L. 61–66 (2009). Recent reports on the post-2015 development agenda are also informative. *See*, particularly, *Delivering Justice: Programme of Action to Strengthen the Rule of Law at the National and International Levels*, Report of the Secretary-General, U.N. Doc. A/66/749 (hereinafter *Delivering Justice*), and *The Report of the High-Level Panel of Eminent Persons on the Post–2015 Development Agenda*, in *A New Global Partnership: Eradicate Poverty and Transform Economies through Sustainable Development* (United Nations 2013), available at http://www.un.org/sg/management/pdf/HLP_P2015_Report.pdf (accessed Aug. 7, 2013).

for basic services and entitlements by local officials. She found that in several instances, the exposure of these infractions helped mobilize communities to demand corrective actions, resulting in policy changes that ultimately enabled better access to services, entitlements, and livelihood opportunities.

In Indonesia, a recent law and justice initiative led to new laws requiring courts to provide legal services to the poor and increased budgetary and policy changes that enable women—who head almost 10 million Indonesian households[23]—to access government services such as health insurance, rice subsidies, and cash transfer payments.[24] Justice sector reform was included in Afghanistan's reconstruction process and, as a result, more judicial institutions were built and judges and judicial officers were trained to enhance access to justice and dispute resolution mechanisms.[25] In Sierra Leone, where delivery of health care services was impeded by corruption and mismanagement, a justice reform scheme designed to increase access to justice for the poor and social accountability has been able to train paralegals to provide people with an understanding of what the state is supposed to provide and to whom, as well as where pressure can be applied when the state fails. This has empowered people by giving them the ability to demand and receive better health care services.[26]

As one reminisces on successes achieved and juxtaposes these with prevailing challenges, three questions come to mind: Are we there yet? Are we almost there? Or are we at least on the right track? Looking at the numerous cutting-edge technological advancements; at increased infrastructural facilities covering various sectors, including health, education, energy, and agriculture; and at the growth in GDPs and increased economic activities in many countries, one might believe that we are there or almost there. But smart development looks beyond the apparent, to see how growth in tangibles translates into better lives for people by providing intangibles. Thus, as Escobar has noted, early development efforts can be critiqued for not looking deeper to determine whether or not people lived better lives or were better off than before.[27]

There is still no method to ensure that development efforts have optimum impact on primary beneficiaries—the people—and this is in part a result of practices that hinder opportunity, inclusion, and equity. For example, as the *World Development Report 2012* shows, laws in many countries discriminate against women, blocking opportunities for them to better enjoy the benefits of

---

23   Indonesian Bureau of Statistics (Badan Pusat Statistik), *Statistik Gender 2009* 18 (Bureau of Statistics 2010).

24   *See* World Bank, *Justice for the Poor*, available at http://web.worldbank.org/WBSITE/EXTER NAL/TOPICS/EXTLAWJUSTICE/EXTJUSFORPOOR/0,,contentMDK:22906721~menuPK:79 14193~pagePK:148956~piPK:216618~theSitePK:3282787~isCURL:Y,00.html.

25   World Bank, *Initiatives in Justice Reform 1992–2012* 114–115 (World Bank 2012).

26   *Justice for the Poor*, *supra* note 24.

27   *See* Escobar, *supra* note 1.

development.[28] Women enjoy fewer legal protections and property rights than men and are far more likely to work in low-paying, low-status occupations and remain underrepresented in senior-level politics and management.[29] The rule of law index shows that many countries, especially low-income countries, rank below average in terms of the strength of rule of law systems.[30] In the Arab Spring, most of the protests were dominated by cries for more inclusion and opportunities for more equitable growth, jobs, and participation in governance.

Based on this evidence, when one asks, Are we there yet, or are we almost there? the answer is no. Development transcends institutions and systems; it must include determining how institutions and systems improve people's lives in the form of tangible or intangible benefits that only strong law and justice institutions can help secure. This point is supported by Sen's submission that "development requires the removal of major sources of unfreedom: poverty as well as tyranny, poor economic opportunities as well as systematic social deprivation, neglect of public facilities as well as intolerance or overactivity of repressive states."[31]

But are we at least on the right track? The answer is possibly yes, as indicated by successes achieved thus far. More compellingly, the international community is beginning to take overt actions to mainstream law and justice into development. This is evident from the recent resolution of the UN High-Level Meeting on the Rule of Law.[32] The UN General Assembly declared that rule of law and development are strongly interrelated and mutually reinforcing. It emphasized that rule of law at the national and international levels is essential for sustained and inclusive economic growth, sustainable development, the eradication of poverty and hunger, and the full realization of all human rights and fundamental freedoms, including the right to development. Following this, as the UN Secretary-General's report on delivering justice emphasizes, justice is key to economic, social, and political stability.[33]

The role of law and justice was further reaffirmed by the report of the High-Level Panel of Eminent Persons on the Post–2015 Development Agenda. The panel faulted initial MDG efforts for not paying enough attention to the poorest and most excluded people as well as to the devastating effects of conflict and violence on development, stressing that the importance to development of good governance and institutions that guarantee the rule of law, free speech, and open and accountable government was not included, nor was the

---

28 *World Development Report 2012: Gender Equality and Development* (World Bank 2012).

29 *Id.*

30 World Justice Project, *supra* note 13, at 32.

31 Sen, *supra* note 2, at 3.

32 UN General Assembly, *Rule of Law at National and International Levels,* United Nations, A/RES/67/97 (adopted Dec. 14, 2012).

33 *Delivering Justice, supra* note 22.

need for inclusive growth to provide jobs.[34] The report proposed 12 universal goals and national targets for the post-2015 agenda, highlighting the need for strong institutions that increase participation, accountability, and access to justice while stemming conflict and violence.[35] In the report, the 27-member panel calls for the new post-2015 goals to drive five major transformational shifts:

- Move from "reducing" to ending extreme poverty, leaving no one behind.
- Put sustainable development at the core of the development agenda.
- Transform economies to drive inclusive growth.
- Build accountable institutions, open to all, that will ensure good governance and peaceful societies.
- Forge a new global partnership based on cooperation, equity, and human rights.[36]

These developments evidence an increased willingness of the international community to engage in and more actively pursue justice as a value, while more firmly entrenching rule of law at the national and international levels. Building on this trend, various chapters in this book explore the different components of law and justice and advance tools and recommendations on how they can be more effectively used to foster development.

Contributions of Law and Justice to Fair and Sustainable Development

The chapters in this volume demonstrate lessons that legal scholarship and practice can refer to, discoveries about how law and justice can contribute to a truly sustainable development that opens opportunities in a way that is both inclusive and equitable. In particular, three important lessons can be distilled from the diverse themes and chapters included in this volume. First, access to justice and rule of law can serve as a pathway for social inclusion, taking into account progress in securing justice and rule of law reform, and in improving governance through anticorruption. Second, regulatory innovation might serve as a useful instrument to help people secure more sustainable economic development opportunities, so that law supports economic development that is sustainable and provides a framework for citizen engagement in environmental protection and sustainable resources governance. Third, legal empowerment can help secure greater equity for diverse communities while ensuring through better governance that the benefits of social reforms are accessed equitably.

---

34 *A New Global Partnership: Eradicate Poverty and Transform Economies through Sustainable Development*, Report of the High-Level Panel of Eminent Persons on the Post–2015 Development Agenda 8 (United Nations 2013).

35 *Id.*, at 30–31, 50–53.

36 *Id.*, at 29.

Access to Justice and Rule of Law as a Pathway for Social Inclusion

The first lesson from this volume is that access to justice and rule of law can serve as a pathway for social inclusion, taking into account progress in securing justice and rule of law reform and in improving governance through anticorruption. This lesson is woven through several chapters, in terms of both global and regional experiences, from countries as diverse as Jordan, Somalia, Colombia, and India.

In Jordan, as Paul Prettitore makes clear, poor people currently face a number of challenges in accessing justice services. "Targeting Justice Sector Services to Promote Equity and Inclusion for the Poor in Jordan" examines the impact on the poor of factors such as a lack of awareness of available services, overly complicated procedures, relatively high court fees and legal costs, and inadequate data on and analysis of the problem. Improving service delivery to the poor will help level the playing field in the justice sector, which is often tilted in favor of those with more financial resources. If the poor have greater recourse to the justice sector, Prettitore concludes, they will be better able to hold public sector entities accountable for nondelivery of services and nonenforcement of rights, which will put the poor on a pathway to greater inclusion.

The potential for law to serve as such a pathway is particularly important when development, security, and migration are intertwined, as Emilio C. Viano demonstrates in "The Search for Opportunity and Inclusion: Insecurity and Migration." He argues that a fragile state, a failed state, a state where insecurity is rampant and the rule of law is absent, can become the epicenter of centrifugal forces that propel migration movements. He also notes that worldwide concern about terrorism and the export of instability generate centripetal forces that lead to and justify "securitizing" borders, limiting immigration, rejecting immigrants, and scrutinizing anyone of foreign origins. Focusing on the security and the welfare of migrants, especially women, the chapter explores measures and policies to avoid trafficking, exploitation, enslavement, and servitude, emphasizing the importance of respecting the rule of law, especially international refugee law, in the countries of destination. It suggests that law and justice, particularly improved law enforcement, can prevent victimization of migrants on the part of the system, opening opportunities. In this way, the chapter provides evidence that law can be a pathway for social inclusion.

Such pathways to inclusion and equity are equally important for delivering rule of law in postconflict societies, as two chapters about Somalia and South Sudan conclude. In "Serving the Justice Needs of the People: Adopting an Access to Justice Approach in Somalia's Rule of Law Reform," Nicholas Joseph notes that access to justice is becoming increasingly important in rule of law reform. He argues the need to direct efforts to grassroots, bottom-up, and pro-poor approaches to justice development rather than adopting a strictly top-down approach of strengthening the state's judicial and legal infrastructure. Learning from practice to date; analyzing Somalia's legal, social, and political context; and assessing innovative approaches to justice reform in recent years, Joseph discusses how the Somali government as well as interveners in the country can focus on equity, inclusion, and opportunity in developing rule of law cultures, rather than strengthening and often solidifying the elite status of justice and legal institutions. These issues are further explored in an insightful contribution from Vincent O. Nmehielle and John-Mark Iyi, "Nation Building, State Reconstruction, and Inclusiveness: Issues on South Sudan as a New State and Somalia as a Failed but Reemerging State." As these authors note, South Sudan and Somalia are both conflict zones that have experienced decades of civil wars; the ethnic groups and clans of both states share histories of political exclusion, social injustice, and economic inequality; and both recently started out on the path of nation building and state reconstruction. The chapter calls for the entrenchment of certain core values of governance as indispensable drivers of social cohesion, political stability, and socioeconomic development, arguing that nation-building and reconstruction efforts in these countries must be anchored on these norms. Both states must design policies that emphasize uniting factors and find a way to address grievances and other structural issues that heighten group differences for any meaningful development to take place. Taken together, these three chapters show that the law can serve as a pathway for social inclusion in countries facing fragile and conflict situations.

Equally intricate pathways can be identified for emerging economies, although not all rule of law reforms are effective for inclusion in all situations. As David F. Varela and Annette Pearson explain in "Institutional Responses to Social Demands: Enhancing Access to Justice in Colombia," since the 1991 Colombian Constitution created a variety of new access to justice measures, the country has witnessed groundbreaking jurisprudence and institutional development in many branches of the justice sector. However, a policy of rationalization for these new access options is needed, especially for vulnerable social groups. In Colombia, changes in the way access to justice was defined led to the creation of wide-ranging programs to combat a number of barriers that reduced access, especially for poor and vulnerable groups. Focusing on smaller towns, especially small war-torn municipalities, where justice options are very limited and articulation among justice services is weak, the chapter finds that although mechanisms at the community and municipal levels avoid many of the barriers that often limit access to justice (for example, physical and cultural distance, legal formalism, and costs), such mechanisms are often not suitable for enforcing the rights of vulnerable populations when there is a clear imbalance of power among those involved in the conflict, particularly in cases of violence against women and other violations of women's rights. This examination offers an important caution as countries seek new ways to secure social inclusion by improving rule of law and access to justice.

Indeed, as is clear in various chapters, such pathways for social inclusion can be hijacked by governance challenges, especially corruption. For instance, in "The Battle between Corruption and Governance in India: Strategies for Tipping the Scale," Sriram Panchu and Avni Rastogi examine corruption in

India against the backdrop of the myriad graft scandals that have erupted over the past few decades and the Anna Hazare movement's demand for the institution of a strong anticorruption body—the *lokpal*. The chapter argues for a focus on fighting big-ticket corruption and proposes a strategy for tackling such corruption, including the establishment of a high-profile permanent authority that would concentrate on the leadership of the governance structure. Powers and procedures designed for the success of such a body are spelled out, alongside a proposal for a separate mechanism for holding the judiciary accountable. In both these chapters, it is clear that although law can open pathways for social inclusion, societies must tailor their strategies, focusing simultaneously on different—yet embedded—levels of jurisdiction for institutional and individual transformation.

Recent experiences in addressing social inclusion through law are examined from a multilateral perspective in two other chapters. "Leveling the Playing Field: A Race to the Top," by Bart Stevens and Robert Delonis, starts from the premise that the World Bank Group (WBG) and the private sector are natural partners in anticorruption efforts, given their mutual interest in fostering development through opportunity, inclusion, and equity. The authors argue that the WBG seeks to end exteme poverty through sustainable growth and shared prosperity, and this can be achieved only with a thriving private sector that operates in an environment of equal treatment under the rule of law and fair competition when bidding for contracts. The chapter highlights three tools, developed by the WBG's Integrity Vice Presidency (INT), that fight corruption through partnership with private firms: the Voluntary Disclosure Program (VDP), Negotiated Resolution Agreements (NRAs), and the Integrity Compliance Officer (ICO). By highlighting lessons learned from the VDP, NRAs, and ICO through a case study of how they are used in INT's work, the chapter concludes that such programs can help replace a "race to the bottom" of bribery with a "race to the top" in which all parties can access and benefit from inclusive, equitable competition. The utility of such multilateral mechanisms for law and social inclusion is also highlighted by Kalidou Gadio in "Fostering Opportunity through Development Finance in Africa: Legal Perspectives from the African Development Bank." With Article 38 of its constitutive instrument expressly prohibiting consideration of noneconomic matters such as "the political affairs" or "the political character" of its members, the African Development Bank is mandated to consider only economic factors in intervention. Examining how such interventions comply with the absolute prohibition of Article 38 in the absence of an exception, the chapter argues that a purposive rather than a literal construction of Article 38 may contribute to sustainable development. It suggests that a margin of appreciation could allow the bank, its president, vice presidents, officers, and staff to make innovative economic interventions in regional member countries with minimal political considerations. In such ways, rule of law programming at the international level can reinforce and support the efforts of countries to use law as a pathway for social inclusion.

These chapters provide an important lesson for the rule of law, justice, and development sector. One can conclude that justice reforms can serve as a pathway for social inclusion, although a great deal depends on ensuring access to justice for the most marginalized actors while also improving transparency and governance through anticorruption measures and careful reinterpretation of institutional mandates. Especially for those in the most desperate situations, such as migrants and women who have been victims of violence, the key is to build people's confidence in justice systems at local, national, and global levels so that all people are able to engage actively in securing rule of law in their countries.

Regulatory Innovation as an Instrument for Sustainable Economic Development Opportunities

A second lesson from this volume is that regulatory innovation might serve as a useful instrument to help people secure more economic development opportunities, whereby law supports sustainable economic development and provides a framework for citizen engagement in environmental protection and resources governance. Certain chapters take a global or regional approach to such innovations, while others specifically examine how innovative regulations are being activated to secure sustainable development in countries such as South Africa, Kenya, India, Brazil, and Ethiopia.

As the chapters in this volume make clear, in many developing countries, regulatory regimes can serve to foster or frustrate economic opportunity and sustainable development for people. Indeed, as Patricia O. Sulser and Cyril Chern argue in "Keeping Public-Private Partnership Infrastructure Projects on Track: The Power of Multistakeholder Partnering Committees and Dispute Boards in Emerging-Market Infrastructure Projects," expanding and improving traditional and social infrastructure and public services (such as water and sanitation; electricity generation, transmission, and distribution; roads, railways, ports, and airports; hospitals and clinics; schools; and prisons) are intrinsic to sustainable economic growth and poverty alleviation. However, the authors note, in public-private partnership (PPP) and private sector infrastructure development projects, disputes inevitably arise during the course of these projects, and PPP projects to date have not specified the use of contemporary dispute resolution methods such as facilitative mediation, dispute boards, or conciliation, leading to high unplanned costs and delays when disputes arise, as well as unnecessary damage to reputations and relationships. The chapter proposes that stakeholders in complex multistakeholder infrastructure projects structured as PPPs or fully private sector projects in emerging markets adopt a culture and routine mechanism to anticipate, evaluate, and resolve disputes on a real-time basis through mechanisms such as multistakeholder committees and standing dispute boards. By incorporating the necessary processes into the project structure, selecting and empowering boards, justifying cost, and maximizing effectiveness, stakeholders can anticipate better results. Such regulatory innovations hold the potential to improve economic opportunities in development.

Reforms in the rules of insolvency can also make a contribution to economic opportunity, as three chapters calling for innovative reforms demonstrate. First, in "The Treatment of Insolvency of Natural Persons in South African Law: An Appeal for a Balanced and Integrated Approach," André Boraine and Melanie Roestoff point out that, although the South African system provides for both liquidation and repayment plans for overindebted consumer debtors (that is, natural persons), there is no principled view and approach regarding the treatment of the insolvency of consumer debtors in South African law. The authors appeal to South African lawmakers to address this weakness, providing suggestions for future insolvency law reform. Second, as Hdeel Abdelhady argues in "Specialized Insolvency Regimes for Islamic Banks: Regulatory Prerogative and Process Design," there may be a need to adopt specialized, administratively managed resolution regimes for Islamic banks, and as Islamic banks grow in size and number, enabling legal and regulatory environments will be required for sustainable growth. Abdelhady argues that sharia insolvency rules must be interpreted in accordance with, and furthering the objectives of, Islamic legal and historical views of market regulation, which require that regulators be empowered to advance lawful market conduct, market discipline, transparency, and consumer protection. It is not sufficient to examine conventional insolvency regimes applicable only to banks, because Islamic banking encompasses banking and capital market activities. Taking into account the orderly liquidation framework adopted in the United States, the chapter suggests that harmonized resolution frameworks are required for Islamic banks, proposing a new model to address current deficits in relevant legal and regulatory environments, advance the sharia policy of effective market regulation, incorporate banking and capital market provisions befitting the cross-market nature of Islamic banking, and advance convergence of Islamic and conventional insolvency regimes. Third and more broadly, in "The Role of Personal Insolvency Law in Economic Development: An Introduction to the World Bank *Report on the Treatment of the Insolvency of Natural Persons*," José M. Garrido focuses on the Working Group of the World Bank's Insolvency Task Force, which completed its report on the treatment of the insolvency of natural persons in 2013. The chapter describes the approach taken by the report, explaining the main issues that a personal insolvency regime needs to address in order to contribute to development and to counteract the negative side effects of increased access to finance. It argues that the concept of discharge occupies a central role because it provides the possibility for insolvent debtors to return to a productive life for their own benefit and for the benefit of society as a whole. It is clear, from these three chapters, that innovative approaches to insolvency can secure greater economic opportunity in development.

Chapters also explore recent experiences with regulatory innovations for sustainable economic development, with three chapters on trade-related law and policy innovations. In "Protecting Traditional Practices and Country of Origin in Developing Countries through Fair Trade and Intellectual Property Rights," Beth Anne Hoffman and Charles Boudry consider legal and institutional challenges and the potential for branding and trademarking products on the international market. Examining experiences in Ethiopia, the authors find that the creation of coffee growers' cooperatives, the production of specialty coffees, and accessing high-valued markets through specific labeling are some ways that local producers in less developed countries have leveraged the price of their products on the international market, particularly through Fair Trade certification. They demonstrate that Ethiopia's legal and policy responses, particularly through branding and trademarking coffees on the international market, were able to bolster coffee exports, explaining the challenges and the potential of these innovations to open economic opportunities for more sustainable development. In "Tools for More Sustainable Trade Treaties with Developing Countries," Markus W. Gehring proposes that the application of impact assessments to development policies and plans such as trade agreements be expanded to take into account not just physical environmental issues but also questions of equity, inclusion, and opportunity. With a focus on the European Union's sustainability impact assessment (SIAs), he argues that such processes might identify and encourage more sustainable trade treaties with developing countries. He highlights the connections among law, policy, and development, demonstrating that, to serve as a useful tool for fostering development opportunities through inclusion, SIAs could be expanded from nation-states and trading blocs to multilateral approaches, for example in the trade policy review mechanism of the World Trade Organization. Such trade law innovations provide challenges and opportunities for sustainable development, as is clear in "The Role of Law in the Green Economy: Challenges and Opportunities for the Liberalization of Environmental Goods and Services," by Fabiano de Andrade Correa. The chapter shows that trade can be a driver in the transition to a green economy by helping to create and strengthen markets for environmental goods and services (EGS). In the global context of the frozen WTO Doha Round, the chapter draws attention to the Asia-Pacific Economic Cooperation and to recent trade agreements concluded by the European Union and argues that although the inclusion of EGS liberalization in a regional context can provide a building block for this issue to move forward and incentive for the transition to a green economy, there may still be a need to design a multilateral framework regulating this issue. As the three chapters explain, although regulatory innovations may help transform economic growth into sustainable development, international processes must take such innovations into account for trade law and build on them.

The need for legal innovations to ensure that the green economy is inclusive and equitable is analyzed by Marie-Claire Cordonier Segger and Yolanda Saito in "Innovative Legal Measures for Climate Change Response in the Green Economy: Integrating Opportunity, Inclusion, and Equity." As the authors eloquently explain, while "the future we want" that was envisioned by the 2012 United Nations Conference on Sustainable Development calls for a new green economy that responds to pressing priorities of poverty eradication and climate-compatible sustainable development, at national and local levels, in different countries and legal systems, existing regulatory frameworks favor the old ways of doing business in spite of growing evidence of their unsustainable character. The authors recommend that for a greener economy to take root, participatory legal and institutional reforms are needed, opening new economic opportunities for all. Indeed, innovative legal instruments are being pioneered in many countries. To be just and implementable, however, these reforms must address questions of inclusion and equity, ensuring that the most poor and vulnerable can access the benefits of the new global green economy.

A regulatory innovation for achieving environmental protection for more sustainable development is discussed in several chapters, including "The Constitutional Basis of Public Participation in Environmental Governance: Framing Equitable Opportunities at National and County Government Levels in Kenya," by Robert Kibugi. Recognizing that the 2010 Constitution of Kenya frames public participation and sustainable development as binding values of governance, and that various provisions of this law, if innovatively interpreted, present viable legal and administrative opportunities to expand space for equitable public participation in environmental decision making, the chapter distills pathways that enhance public participation, including through devolved county government legislative and administrative authority. It also looks forward, proposing several legal and administrative measures to enhance existing laws or to adapt them specifically to environmental decision making. The utility of public participation, as a legal norm, depends on the potential for practical implementation. Such structural challenges, and the ability of regulatory innovation to enable more effective responses to emerging global and national challenges, are also evident in the insightful contribution by N. R. Madhava Menon, "Toward a National Framework Law on Water for India." The chapter explains that, for 1.3 billion people in India who are dependent on seasonal rains and on interstate rivers, management of water resources has been a contentious issue in federal relations. Menon points to a series of Indian Supreme Court judgments that recognize a right to water and that read it into the guaranteed right to life and liberty, thereby placing an obligation on the state to provide unpolluted drinking water to the people. Menon notes that the Constitution of India gives the states (provinces constituting the Union of India) the authority to legislate on water and assigns to local bodies the power to implement schemes to provide water; the only power that resides with the central (federal) government is the regulation of interstate rivers and river valleys. The scheme of distribution of powers of water management to the three levels of government has not been able to secure sustainable use and management of water in accordance with a new national water policy. Highlighting current attempts to legislate a framework law that establishes principles and procedures in water use and management binding on all three levels of governments, the chapter underscores how, in an emerging crisis in water availability and governance, such a law might be adopted and effectively implemented. Both chapters demonstrate how national-level legal innovations can transform development toward sustainability in emerging economies and highlight the need for a tailored and country-specific approach.

Some chapters in this volume examine advances and innovations in urban planning laws and institutions. In "Planning Laws, Development Controls, and Social Equity: Lessons for Developing Countries," Rachelle Alterman considers mandatory planning laws. She argues that planning regulations and development controls enacted in developing countries are often modeled on equivalents in advanced-economy countries, and considers whether planning regulations contribute to social justice or exacerbate social disparities. She concludes that decision makers in developing countries—or representatives of aid organizations—should assess proposed planning laws and instruments carefully before suggesting transplantation from an advanced economy to a developing one. Developing countries might consider a "back to basics" approach, adopting graduated strategies for introducing planning laws and regulations and being cautious with layers of planning regulations. In "The Challenges of Reforming the Urban Legal Framework: A Critical Assessment of Brazil's City Statute 10 Years Later," Edesio Fernandes provides a critical assessment of the enforcement of Brazil's 2001 City Statute. The chapter distills the real, as well as false, expectations around newly approved urban laws in other countries. Considering the design of new urban laws governing land rights and management, territorial organization, planning, and housing, Fernandes explains what can be expected of these new urban laws in rapidly urbanizing countries and what is required for them to be fully enforced for social effectiveness. Calling attention to the broader sociopolitical process, the chapter provides an innovative and critical analysis of the nature, possibilities, and constraints of progressive urban laws. In "Land Use Law and the City: Toward Inclusive Planning," Matthew Glasser introduces the instruments by which the law affects development outcomes in cities. He explains that when the law prescribes standards or processes that are impractical and inappropriate for a substantial portion of the population, it divides the city into a formal sector for those who can comply and an informal sector for those who cannot. Those living outside the law cannot claim its protection; they are vulnerable to eviction, confiscation of their property, and destruction of their homes and investments and are largely without recourse. However, in some places, laws expressly legitimize density that provides the poor with affordable access to the city, jobs, and other opportunities. The chapter highlights key court decisions from developing countries that have protected the rights of those living in informal settlements, concluding by noting that good urban law must consider affordability and the importance of access to the city.

In all three chapters, it is clear that by avoiding unnecessary complexity in urban planning laws and taking an approach that focuses on securing inclusion through accountability and voice, regulatory innovations can help secure development that is more sustainable and more equitable. The message that ties these chapters together, across sectors and across regions of the world, is that regulatory innovation has a role to play in enabling people to secure more sustainable economic development opportunities. At national and global levels, innovative legal measures, including carefully designed mechanisms for transparency and citizen participation, can support more sustainable economic growth, whether through new forms of public-private partnerships, culturally appropriate finance and insolvency regimes, fair trade and intellectual property protections, sustainability assessment of trade negotiations, liberalization of environmental goods and services, public participation, environmental governance techniques, legal preparedness for climate change and the green economy, interjurisdictional water governance, or pro-poor urban planning. The difference between success and failure often depends on transparency and inclusion and whether interventions are appropriate; tailored specifically for the needs of stakeholders and to the national environmental, social, and economic context; and locally owned by those who implement them.

Legal Empowerment as a Means to Secure Greater Equity

The third lesson from this volume is that legal empowerment can provide a means to secure greater equity when citizen ownership of and engagement with the law, policy, and institutions play a role in securing empowerment and equity for diverse communities, while ensuring through better governance that benefits of social reforms are accessed equitably. Several chapters highlight this message.

Legal empowerment can help secure greater equity for those struggling with law and policy frameworks. In "Enabling Equal Opportunities for Women in the World of Work: The Intersections of Formal and Informal Constraints," Jeni Klugman and Matthew Morton highlight how multiple constraints in markets, institutions, culture, and households reinforce gender inequalities, including in the world of work. Legal discrimination presents one important barrier, although legislative reforms can also be thwarted by implementation challenges, notably poor information, adverse social norms, and institutional biases. The chapter reviews key legal constraints that reinforce gender disparities in jobs, as well as the ways in which informal constraints can inhibit well-intended legal reforms from increasing women's economic opportunities and advancement. It concludes that various types of legal reforms and complementary policy efforts are needed to redress gender gaps in the world of work. By engaging with women to take down legal and informal constraints, thereby improving governance, reformers could secure greater equity.

The need for political as well legal empowerment to bring about greater equity is highlighted in "Mainstreaming the Marginalized in Development: Conceptualizing the Challenges in India," by Pulapre Balakrishnan. The chapter argues that capability is at the core of the nexus between freedom, opportunity, and development, and hence the marginalized in a society are those who lack the capabilities enjoyed by the mainstream. Although India's constitution is in many ways impressive, Balakrishnan points out that its provisions are, on their own, inadequate to the task of mainstreaming the marginalized.

In two chapters linking law, health, and development, policy change, legal empowerment, and institutional strengthening are highlighted as crucial for inclusion and equity, alongside the need for enabling legislation and its enforcement. In "The Role of Law in Promoting the Right to Health for Diverse

Communities," David Patterson, Elisa Slattery, and Naomi Burke-Shyne note that health is a human right under international law and many national constitutions. However, as the authors explain, discrimination and stigma, as well as weak legal and regulatory frameworks, are major impediments to realizing the right to health. The law can be used to secure the right to health in the context of infectious diseases such as HIV, as well as noncommunicable diseases such as cancer and diabetes, for diverse communities, including people with disabilities, women, and sexual minorities. Examples include ensuring that intellectual property laws allow access to affordable medicines and reducing health threats from counterfeit drugs and drug theft. The chapter concludes that an enabling legal environment is essential to the protection and promotion of the right to health for diverse communities. Focused on a specific developing country example in "The Right to Health and Development: The Case of Uganda," Siobhán McInerney-Lankford and Moses Mulumba argue that improved health is both a factor and an outcome of sustainable development. They explore the right to health as a development priority and the role of the law in advancing it, particularly for the poorest and most vulnerable in developing countries. The right to health is an example of the convergence between human rights and development, and the authors consider the ways in which the respect, protection, and fulfillment of human rights can help secure conditions for people to live in dignity. This chapter builds on the growing body of literature asserting the centrality of the right to health in shaping health policy and the delivery of health services around the world. It draws on the legal content of the right to health to suggest ways in which human rights can add value to development policies and programs.

Education, as well as health, is raised as a key field in which legal empowerment is needed to secure equity and inclusion in "Fighting Corruption in Education: A Call for Sector Integrity Standards," by Mihaylo Milovanovitch. As a high-stakes sector, education is increasingly vulnerable to corruption, and there is a need to "translate" international anticorruption standards into sector standards of integral behavior in education. The chapter urges the adoption of a more sector-specific prevention approach that targets not only criminal offenses but also softer, yet equally harmful, forms of corruption, calling for a cross-border agreement on what constitutes malpractice in education. In essence, the chapter proposes both ways to improve regulatory frameworks for education in order to achieve greater equity and means to increase citizen accountability through law and governance reforms.

Similarly, in encouraging small business's access to information, justice and empowerment can play a role. In "The World Bank Group Sanctions System and Access to Justice for Small and Medium-Size Enterprises," Frank Fariello and Giovanni Bo examine the challenges of inclusion for small and medium-size enterprises (SMEs) in the context of a recently concluded preliminary review of the World Bank sanctions system that found that the majority of respondent SMEs are simply not engaging with the system, during adjudication or in the rehabilitative process that is meant to follow sanctioning. This chapter also finds that the World Bank's sanctions system might be facing challenges in access to justice and suggests ways to make the system more accessible to low-capacity respondents.

Three inspiring pieces discuss new legal empowerment tools for inclusion and equity. As noted by Sean Fraser in "The Role of Access to Information in Promoting Development," although the right to development has gained acceptance among states and scholars, its practical implementation has been underwhelming in comparison to its vast potential. The failure to maximize the benefits of the right to development is due, at least in part, to the inaccessibility of information that groups and individuals can use to promote and protect their human rights. In exploring the status of the right to development in international law, the chapter discusses the obligations associated with the right to development and the parties who bear duties of implementation and demonstrates how access to information can promote the realization of the right to development, drawing on decisions of various domestic courts and international human rights bodies. By addressing the obstacles that face the successful implementation of access to information laws, the chapter concludes that it is possible to maximize the free flow of information, which will improve the day-to-day lives of individuals and peoples around the globe.

In "The Right to Information as a Tool for Community Empowerment," by Anupama Dokeniya, right to information laws are proposed as potential tools for community empowerment. Dokeniya highlights cases from India and Mexico in which communities in rural and extremely poor regions were able to use right to information as a tool to expose pilfering of resources meant for basic services and entitlements by local officials. In several instances, the exposure of these infractions mobilized communities to demand corrective actions, resulting in changes in policies. However, in other countries, the existence of a right to information law has been of little use because of low awareness, weak civil society groups that play an essential role as intermediaries and mobilizers in accessing information, and low capacity and high unwillingness in local government officials to release information. Incentives are affected by the disclosure of information—through the threat of reputational or financial sanctions or the loss of elections or employment—and the relationship between access to information, accountability, and development outcomes is complex.

In "Private Civil Actions: A Tool for a Citizen-Led Battle against Corruption," William T. Loris argues that the fight against corruption can be expanded and invigorated by providing ordinary citizens and legal entities a clear legal framework for the pursuit of private civil actions against corruption. He proposes a three-point conceptual framework of how civil actions may serve as an additional weapon in the anticorruption arsenal by providing for specific remedial and recovery measures, empowering victims of corruption, and engendering social transformation around real cases on which media and civil society can focus. To support the three points, Loris advocates the development of regional conventions under which signatory states would expand their obligations under the UN Convention Against Corruption by committing to establish and implement a legal framework for private actions against corruption and including features similar to those in the Council of Europe Civil Law Convention on Corruption.

As demonstrated by these chapters on the right to information and the potential for civil action, legal empowerment techniques are not just helpful in ensuring the right to development and greater equity for women and disadvantaged groups in different sectors of social policy, such as labor, education, and health. They can also improve the quality of governance itself, opening space for small enterprise, ensuring access to information about development, fighting corruption, and securing community engagement in the development process.

Designing a Smarter Law and Justice Framework for Development

Despite the unprecedented efforts that have been made in achieving development goals in the past two decades, the majority of people are not yet able to enjoy the benefits of development. Weak or broken laws and justice systems disempower the poor or otherwise prevent them from exercising those basic rights and benefits so far achieved. The Commission on Legal Empowerment of the Poor reported in 2008 that about 4 billion people are impoverished as a result of their exclusion from the protection of the law.[37] As various chapters in this book demonstrate, weak governance, conflict and violence, inequity, and exclusionary policies or implementation of such policies all hinder meaningful and optimum impact. The vulnerable in a society bear the brunt of these hardships.[38] The value of whatever progress is made is therefore limited to the extent that these vices and challenges remain. There is a great deal more to be done in this regard, and much depends on the approach used.

What, then, is a better, smarter, and wiser approach to development than the one we have tried in the past? As noted, this volume offers three important lessons. First, access to justice and rule of law can become a pathway for social inclusion, although a great deal depends on progress in securing justice and rule of law reform and on improving governance through anticorruption. Second, regulatory innovation that is tailored to specific conditions can help countries secure more sustainable economic development opportunities so that law supports sustainable economic development and provides a framework for citizen engagement in environmental protection and sustainable

---

37 *See Making the Law Work for Everyone:* vol. 1, *Report of the Commission on Legal Empowerment of the Poor* 3 (Commn. on Leg. Empowerment of the Poor 2008).

38 Assessing the early impact of development efforts, Escobar found that "wherever one looked, one found the repetitive and omnipresent reality of development: governments designing and implementing ambitious development plans; institutions carrying out development programs in the city and countryside alike, experts of all kinds studying underdevelopment and producing theories ad nauseam. The fact that people's conditions not only did not improve but deteriorated with the passing of time did not seem to bother most experts." See Escobar, *supra* note 1, at 5. This observation is only partially true today—especially because development has appreciably impacted and improved the lives of many—but it reflects some of the lapses or gaps in contemporary efforts because a vulnerable part of society remains either excluded or unable to adequately benefit from progress made.

resources governance, although a great deal depends on enabling local and international contexts. Third, legal empowerment can provide a means to secure greater equity when barriers are taken down and diverse communities gain empowerment and equity, while ensuring through better governance that benefits of social reforms are accessed equitably.

In considering the question of what is a better, smarter, and wiser approach, three things should guide us: the values we must pursue to secure the outcomes we desire; taking stock of past efforts in order to learn what works and what does not and in what context; and the application of tools that can help achieve better outcomes and turn ideals and aspirations into reality. To get to this point, law and justice must play an enhanced role.

This book could not have come at a more critical or appropriate juncture. At this writing, the international community is in the process of designing a post-2015 development agenda that will guide and inform future directions in achieving the MDGs.[39] In relation to this, Jeffrey Sachs, the special adviser to the UN Secretary-General on the MDGs, has proposed four pillars for the post-2015 goals: an end to poverty in all its forms; an environmental agenda including climate change; improved governance; and social inclusion and equity. The post-2015 agenda will also involve aligning the MDGs and Sustainable Development Goals (SDGs), as per the 2012 United Nations Conference on Sustainable Development Rio+20 outcome document, *The Future We Want*.[40]

Future Directions: The Justice Lens of Development

The world has reached a redefining period in history. Borrowing the words of former UN Secretary-General Kofi Annan, we are in the process of "rebuilding the fabric of modern life."[41] Thus, as Marie-Claire Cordonier Segger and C. G. Weeramantry have argued:

> a very important aspect of this fabric of modern life is found in our evolving laws and justice systems. These systems are intricately woven upon the shared values, morals and ethics of [an] increasingly interconnected and interdependent world. Among the shared values, there is found a growing sense of respect for the common interest of all, a sense of responsibility for our common future. This

---

39   In July 2012, the UN Secretary-General appointed a 27-person High-Level Panel of Eminent Persons on the Post–2015 Development Agenda to hold consultations and provide independent analysis and recommendations on the process. Post-2015 thematic consultations have covered inequalities, health, education, growth and employment, environmental sustainability, governance, conflict and fragility, population dynamics, hunger, food and nutrition security, energy, and water in more than 55 countries that involve youth, women, children, labor groups, and civil society and aim to broaden participation in the post-2015 discussions. An overview of the post-2015 agenda can be found at http://www.un.org/millennium goals/beyond2015-overview.shtml.

40   Rio+20 Outcome document, *The Future We Want*, available at http://www.un.org/en/sustain ablefuture.

41   Kofi Annan, speech delivered at the World Summit on Sustainable Development (2002).

responsibility, in certain instances recognized as a duty, engenders special attention to the needs of the most vulnerable and voiceless, especially the world's poor.[42]

A justice dimension should illuminate and guide future efforts because, as potent as the law is, it will take us only partway.[43] Hence, it is also necessary to approach development using a justice lens. By its very nature, justice emphasizes both "fair treatment and fair results,"[44] ensuring a people-centered approach that transcends institutional setups.[45] It is a strand that cuts through every fabric of society, and when matched with law, justice can unlock endless possibilities for sustainable development outcomes and meaningful impact.

This justice lens triggers a new set of questions to be asked in the design and implementation of every development project. First, will the outcomes be both just and equitable, and will they be perceived as such by intended beneficiaries? Second, will the development processes, strategies, or tools help lead to such outcomes, and can they be sustained over the long term? And third, are voice, social contract, and accountability mechanisms systematically woven into the process in a manner that gives people an opportunity to participate in such a process and enjoy accruing benefits? Voice ensures that all stakeholders are heard and that there is the right scope of participation and degree of meaningful consultation. Social contract ensures the full and fair definition of the rights and obligations of parties and provides for the equitable sharing of economic benefits and social protections. Accountability mechanisms allow intended beneficiaries to provide feedback, hold relevant actors up to their responsibilities, and enforce their rights with adequate remedies when their expectations are not met or when there is a failure to deliver. Ultimately, a justice lens will inspire a more people-oriented approach that, if it is designed and implemented appropriately, can make a difference in the quality and effectiveness of sustainable development outcomes.

---

42   *Introduction to Sustainable Justice: Implementing International Sustainable Development Law*, in *Sustainable Justice: Reconciling Economic, Social and Environmental Law* 1–2 (Marie-Claire Cordonier Segger & C. G. Weeramantry eds., Martinus Nijhoff 2005).

43   *See* also Golub's submission on the limitations of rule of law as an organizing principle in *Make Justice the Organizing Principle of the Rule of Law Field*, *supra* note 22.

44   *Id.*

45   Sen, *supra* note 21, at 18.

Afterword

IRENE KHAN
DIRECTOR-GENERAL
INTERNATIONAL DEVELOPMENT LAW ORGANIZATION

The rule of law is an essential pillar for fostering development, whether in countries emerging from conflict, striving towards economic recovery, or seeking to enhance economic growth. Yet, around the world we see a deep disconnect between the formal mechanisms of the rule of law and people's lived experience of justice and equity, and we hear a rallying cry for human rights and human dignity for all.

The message is clear: sustainable development and economic growth must be based upon principles of equity, empowerment, inclusion, and full participation.

This volume of *The World Bank Legal Review* comes at a timely moment. The themes explored in the *Review* highlight the urgency and complexity of some of the more pressing development challenges facing our world today: climate change, energy and food insecurity, great disparities among people in getting fair access to natural resources, unfair trade rules and regulations, seemingly intractable conflict and political instability, chronic job insecurity, and population displacement. The contributors to this volume point to interesting and innovative ways in which states, civil society, and businesses can use the rule of law to bring about sustainable, inclusive, and equitable economic growth and development outcomes.

As many contributors emphasize, if state institutions, laws, policies, and practices are to be effective and sustainable drivers of economic development, they must be based on solid principles of justice, equality, and nondiscrimination. Poverty eradication and the reduction of social and economic inequality require profound, human-centered, and sustainable social and economic transformation based on rule of law frameworks that ensure inclusion, equity, empowerment, and participation.

Traditionally, the focus of justice sector development has tended to be almost exclusively on state actors and institutions, but increasingly the world has come to realize that citizens, civil society, and private actors play a key role in supporting, promoting, and—most importantly—demanding transparency, accountability, equity, and human rights, which are the bedrock of good governance and the rule of law. More and more, successful and sustainable development initiatives are combining measures to strengthen institutions and legal systems with initiatives to promote equitable participation and empowerment of individuals, groups, and communities.

The World Bank Legal Review presents some encouraging and interesting examples of innovative legal practices, from tackling corruption to leveling the playing field for business, to protecting traditional practices through fair trade and intellectual property rights, to empowering women, minorities, and people with disabilities, to designing locally owned legal solutions to tackle climate change and promote the green economy.

This volume is more than a summary of practical experiences and academic analyses. It is a reminder that fostering development through opportunity, inclusion, and equity is not only about effective policies and institutions; it is also about promoting a culture of justice based on the rule of law. As we move forward, that need to ensure justice for all must guide the international community's endeavors to set the post-2015 development agenda.

Index